Deviance: the interactionist perspective

Earl Rubington
NORTHEASTERN UNIVERSITY

Martin S. Weinberg
INDIANA UNIVERSITY

text and readings in the sociology of deviance

HM
291
.R75
1978

Deviance the interactionist perspective

• **THIRD EDITION**

Macmillan Publishing Co., Inc.
NEW YORK

Earlier editions copyright © 1968 and 1973
by Macmillan Publishing Co., Inc.

Macmillan Publishing Co., Inc.
866 Third Avenue, New York, New York 10022

Collier Macmillan Canada, Ltd.

Library of Congress Cataloging in Publication Data

Rubington, Earl, comp.
  Deviance, the interactionist perspective.

  Includes bibliographical references.
  1. Deviant behavior. 2. Social interaction.
I. Weinberg, Martin S., joint comp. II. Title.
HM291.R75 1978   301.6'2   77–3880
ISBN 0–02–404400–8

Printing: 1 2 3 4 5 6 7 8   Year: 8 9 0 1 2 3 4

The purpose of this book has been to present students with recent and important work in the sociology of deviance. We have, however, limited ourselves to one particular approach to this study. We call this approach the interactionist perspective.

The interactionist approach to the study of deviance is by no means new. But until the appearance of the first edition of *Deviance: The Interactionist Perspective,* students had to search for statements of the approach as well as for studies that exemplified it. The purpose of the first edition, then, was to present the interactionist approach to the study of deviance and to make readily available the excellent studies that set forth or illustrate it. In the succeeding editions, we have updated the readings, and in the third edition we have made special efforts to make our own text more readable.

We see this book as having two major uses. As a statement on the interactionist perspective on deviance and a collection of readings employing that approach, the book can be used in deviance courses that are taught from the interactionist point of view. The second use is that of adjunct to deviance courses that are organized around other points of view. Most of the papers presented in this book can very easily stand on their own merits, and even if the book does nothing more than familiarize readers with these works, it will have served its purpose.

Finally, we would like to extend our appreciation to Barbara Henn, Linda DuPlantis, Elizabeth Sullivan, Stuart Hadden, Odis Bigus, and John O'Connor for their suggestions and criticisms. A special note of thanks is due Sue Kiefer Hammersmith for her first-rate editing of our text.

-E. R.

M. S. W.

preface to the third edition

table of contents

Part Two
the formal regulation of deviance   159

Part Three
deviant subcultures 271

Part Four
deviant identity

Deviance: the interactionist perspective

general introduction

This book examines deviance as a social phenomenon. Central to this approach is the notion that deviance is, above all, a matter of social definition. That is, an alleged behavior or condition is "deviant" if people say it is. The social aspect of deviance becomes clear when someone perceives another person as departing from accepted norms, interprets the person to be some kind of deviant, and influences others also to regard the person as deviant and to act on the basis of that interpretation. As a *social* phenomenon, then, deviance consists of a set of interpretations and social reactions.

When people are interpreted as being deviant, they are usually regarded as being a particular *type* of deviant. These types may be general (e.g., ex-convict, mentally ill, sexually "loose," retarded), or they may be more specific (e.g., car thief, paranoid schizophrenic, call girl, Mongoloid). Whether these labels are general or specific, they usually suggest what one can expect of the so-called deviant and how one should act toward the deviant (e.g., with suspicion, avoidance, vigilance, vengeance). And in coming to terms with such labeling the "deviants" may revise their self-concepts and their actions in accordance with the way they have been labeled. For example, a child who has been typed by school authorities as having a speech problem may become self-conscious and shy, with a concomitant loss of self-esteem, because s/he has been told s/he doesn't talk properly.

At the same time, social typing does allow people to relate to one another in an organized manner. Imagine how much more complicated it would be for policemen, for example, to do their jobs if they did not have a set of categories in which to place people ("she's a hooker"; "he's a junkie"; "he looks like he might be casing that store"; "she's a teenaged runaway"; "he's a derelict with no place to go").

The interactionist perspective focuses on just such issues as these—how people typify one another; how they relate to one another on the basis of these typifications; and the consequences of these social processes. As such, the interactionist perspective helps immensely in our understanding not only of the sociology of deviance but also of social process in general.

THE PLAN OF THE BOOK

The selections that follow spell out the interactionist perspective in greater detail. The first half of the book, which consists of Parts

One and Two, deals with how people define some persons as deviant and act on the basis of these definitions. Part One shows how deviance is dealt with in primary groups and informal relations and how a person is singled out and assigned a deviant status by intimates such as family members. Part Two deals with these processes in the formal regulation of deviance. For example, it considers how agents of social control, such as the police, define persons as deviants, how they act on these definitions, and what some of the consequences of formal sanctions are.

The second half of the book (Parts Three and Four) discusses the deviants themselves: how they respond to being typed by others, how they type themselves, and how they form deviant groups. Part Three examines how deviants develop and sustain their own subcultures and how people become involved in them. Part Four shows how persons may take on deviant identities through self-typing, how they manage deviant identities, and how they may eventually regain "respectability."

This book, then, focuses not on people's motivations for doing things that are regarded as deviant but rather on the *sociology* of deviance—the processes that divide society into different types of people and the social effects of these processes.

the social deviant

Sociology is the study of social relations. Sociologists study how people arrive at common definitions of their situation; how they form groups based on such definitions; how they go on to set down rules of conduct, assign social roles to each other, and enforce their rules. Sociologists examine these questions as part of the larger question: How is social order produced and sustained?

Deviance refers to an alleged breach of social order. By looking at deviance we can come to a better understanding of the dominant social order. At the same time, the study of deviance also sheds light on the way "deviant" patterns and life-styles are themselves organized.

There are at least two ways of studying deviance as a social phenomenon. The first is to approach deviance as objectively given; the second, as subjectively problematic.

Deviance as objectively given. Sociologists who treat deviance as objectively given delineate the norms and values of the society under study and regard any deviation from these norms and values as "deviant." These sociologists generally make three assumptions. First, they assume that there is widespread consensus in the society in the realm of norms and values; this widespread agreement, they believe, makes it relatively easy to identify deviance. Second, they assume that deviance typically evokes negative sanctions such as gossip or legal action. Third, they assume that the punishment meted out to the deviant reaffirms for the group that it is bound by a set of common values and norms. The major questions raised by this approach are the following: what sociocultural conditions are most likely to produce deviance? why do people continue to deviate despite the negative sanctions that are brought to bear on them? and how can deviance best be minimized or controlled?

From these assumptions and questions, certain procedures have evolved for studying deviants. First list the "do's" and "don'ts" of the society or group. Then study the official records kept on persons who violate these rules. Interview persons appearing in these records and consult agents of social control such as police and judges. Try to discover the ways in which deviants differ from nondeviants (e.g., are deviants more likely than nondeviants to come from broken homes?) in order to discern the kinds of social and cultural conditions that seem to make deviant behavior more likely. Try to derive a theory to "explain" deviance, and then apply the theory for the correction and prevention of deviance.

Part One

The strength of this approach is the sharpness and simplicity with which it phrases questions. The weak points of this approach follow from its key assumptions. In the United States there are so many different groups and ways of thinking that people often do not agree on values and norms. Because of this lack of agreement, and also because of the fact that some people get caught whereas others avoid discovery, it is often very difficult and complex to identify who is deviant and who is not. Also, most social control agencies operate with selective enforcement, so that certain categories of people are more likely than others to be punished for their deviance. Thus the nature, causes, and consequences of deviance are neither simple nor uniform.

Deviance as subjectively problematic. Sociologists who focus on the social differentiation of deviants generally make another set of assumptions. First, they assume that when people and groups interact they communicate with one another by means of shared symbols (verbal and body language, style of dress, etc.). Through such symbolic communication, it is assumed, people are able to type one another and formulate their actions accordingly. Second, they assume that deviance can best be understood in terms of this process, that deviant labels are symbols that differentiate and stigmatize the people to whom they are applied. Finally, sociologists using this approach assume that people act on the basis of such definitions. Thus people treat the alleged deviant differently from other people. The alleged deviant, in turn, may also react to this definition. On the basis of these assumptions, sociologists using this perspective focus on social definitions and perspectives and on how these influence social interaction. On the one hand, they focus on the perspective and actions of those who define a person as being deviant. They look at the circumstances under which a person is most likely to get set apart as deviant, how a person is cast into a deviant role, what actions others take on the basis of that definition of a person, and the consequences of these actions. On the other hand, these sociologists also focus on the perspective and reactions of the person adjudged to be a deviant. They consider how a person reacts to being so adjudged, how a person adopts a deviant role, what changes in group memberships result, and what changes occur in the alleged deviant's self-concept.

Whereas the objectively given approach focuses primarily on the social characteristics of the deviant or the conditions that give rise to deviant acts, the subjectively problematic approach focuses on the definitions and actions both of the deviants themselves and of the people who label them deviant, and on the social interaction between the two. Thus we call the latter approach the interactionist perspective.

This book adopts the interactionist perspective, approaching deviance as subjectively problematic rather than as objectively given. In this book, then, deviants are considered simply as people who are socially typed in a certain way. Such typing usually involves an attempt to make sense of seemingly aberrant acts. As people seek to make sense of such acts, they generally employ stereotypical interpretations that define the actor as a particular kind of person (a kook, a drunk, a psychopath, etc.), that include a judgment about the moral quality of the deviant or his or her motives, and that suggest how a person should act toward the deviant. The social definitions of deviance, then, consist of a *description,* an *evaluation,* and a *prescription.* For example, a "kook" is a person who is mildly eccentric (description). The term connotes that "kooks" are odd but not particularly evil or dangerous (evaluation). Thus one may display dislike or friendly disrespect toward them (prescription). A person who comes to be defined as a "psychopath," on the other hand, is considered to be both odd and severely unpredictable (description). The psychopath is often regarded as self-centered, evil, and dangerous (evaluation). And the psychopath is to be taken seriously at all times; a person who shows dislike or disrespect toward a "psychopath" does so at great personal risk (prescription). Thus the definition of a person as a particular type of deviant organizes people's responses to that person. And the more people who share the definition that a person is a particular type of deviant, the greater the consequences.

Taking the subjective approach to deviance, Part One of this book examines such phenomena more specifically. The topics treated in this part of the book include how people type, or label, others as deviants; the accommodations people make to the so-called deviance; the cultural context of typing; and how people may collaborate to exclude deviants from their midst.

THE PROCESS OF SOCIAL TYPING

Sociologically, deviance is approached here in terms of social differentiation. This differentiation arises from the perception that something is amiss. If a potential typer, or labeler, ignores or excuses the alleged aberrant quality of a person or event, it goes unlabeled as deviant. For instance, a person who works hard is expected sometimes to be tired and cranky, and in such situations people may not attach any particular importance to this behavior. Once an act or a person is typed as "deviant," however, a variety of social phenomena may come into play. These phenomena include who types whom, on what grounds, in what ways, before or after what acts (real or imputed), in front of what audience, and with what effects.

Let us for a moment consider the conditions that seem to make typing more effective. First, typing generally has the most effect when the typer, the person typed as deviant, and other people all share and understand the deviant definition in their social relationships. The typer and others act toward the "deviant" in accord with their shared understanding of the situation. Aware of having been so typed, the deviant, in turn, takes that shared understanding into account in relating to people. Thus, willingly or otherwise, all parties may subscribe to the definition. When this happens, the definition of the person as a particular type of deviant is most socially effective, or confirmed. As an example, consider a hypothetical woman who is casual about sexual contacts. If at some time one of her sexual partners gives her some money shortly after the sex act, or if she herself suggests that she might receive some money for her sexual favors, then her status may be subsequently redefined. Thereafter she may no longer be considered merely "loose" but a prostitute instead. Her sexual partners may begin to think of her in this way, and she may also come to think of herself in these terms. In time she may adopt the occupation (prostitution) that is consistent with this typing.

Second, social types are generally more apt to be accepted by other people if a high-ranking person does the typing. Effective social typing usually flows down rather than up the social structure. For example, an honor bestowed by the President of the United States is more likely to be consequential than an honor bestowed by a low-ranking official. Conversely, a denouncement by a very high-ranking person such as the president of a company will usually carry more weight, and be confirmed by more people, than a denouncement by a low-ranking person such as one of the company's janitors.

Third, deviant typing is also more apt to be effective if there is a sense that the alleged deviant is violating important rules or expectations and that the violations are extreme. For instance, if factory workers are tacitly expected to turn out only a limited amount of work, a worker who produces much more than the norm may be singled out and ostracized as a "rate-buster." On the other hand, a person who wears short-sleeved shirts in the winter is unlikely to be typed and treated as a deviant.

Fourth, it also seems that negative social typing is more readily accepted than positive typing. For one thing, "misery loves company"; people find comfort in learning about the frailties of others. In addition, norms seem to be highlighted more by infraction than by conformity. Also, negative typing is seen as a valuable safeguard if the type indicates an aberrant pattern that will probably continue and that has major consequences. Some police officers, for instance, expect upper-class adolescents to misbehave in their youth but later to become influential and respected citizens, while they expect slum adolescents who are vandals, troublemakers, or delinquents to become hardened criminals in adulthood; thus such police officers are more likely to negatively type slum youths than upper-class youths who break the same laws.

Fifth, typing will be accepted more readily if the audience stands to gain from the labeling. Endorsing attention to another person's deviant behavior, for example, may divert attention from one's own. It may also sustain a status difference between oneself and the so-called deviant.

When social typing is effective, there are three kinds of consequences that most often follow: self-fulfilling prophecy, typecasting, and recasting. In the self-fulfilling prophecy, typing is based on false beliefs about the alleged deviant, but the actions other people take on the basis of these false beliefs eventually make them become a reality. For example, both black and white police officers believe that it is more difficult to arrest blacks than whites. As a result, they tend to use more force in arresting blacks, and in turn they experience more resistance from blacks. In typecasting, the deviant stereotype is so widely accepted that confirmation of the typing proceeds rapidly, and typer, audience, and the person typed relate to each other in an automatic manner. For instance, if one person types another as a thief, any audience can generally predict and understand the typer's attitudes and actions. In recasting, the most complex of the three consequences, the deviant is expected to behave conventionally and is encouraged to disprove the deviant typing (e.g., to reform). Probation officers, for example, may encourage conventionality by restricting the opportunities of their probationers to continue their deviant ways. In the first two consequences of typing, the typer and audience restrict the deviant's opportunities to disprove the deviant typing. In recasting, the typer and the audience restrict the deviant's opportunities to confirm the deviant typing.

ACCOMMODATION TO DEVIANCE

As noted above, sociologically, deviants are persons who have been effectively labeled as deviant, and *effectively* means simply that the label does in fact affect social relations. The person who has been typed as a deviant, for example, acquires a special status that carries a set of new rights and duties or changes in old ones, and a new set of expectations about future conduct. Thus when people type a certain person as deviant, they imply, "We now expect you to engage in deviant actions." In some cases, this expectation amounts to a license to deviate, as when a group may not only tolerate but actually shelter a deviant in its midst. More often, however, the expectation of deviant conduct gives other people license to treat the deviant in a demeaning way.

The pace of events in the labeling process is one of the critical factors in this entire process. If aberrant conduct occurs only gradually and irregularly within a small, intimate group, deviant typing may not take place at all. Even if the events place some immediate strain on relationships, members of the group may adjust to the strain without perceiving the person any differently. Eventually, though, some critical point may be reached at which the group becomes aware that things are not what they used to be. Sometimes the members of the group have long entertained suspicions of deviance, and their accommodation represents an acknowledgment that the deviation is here to stay. In other instances, though, even as they type the person as deviant, group members may be optimistic that the deviance is only temporary. In any case, the group's accommodation to the so-called deviance has usually been going on for some time before labeling actually occurs.

THE CULTURAL CONTEXT

The process of social typing occurs within a cultural context. Each culture, for example, has its own assortment and corresponding vocabulary of types. Thus in our own culture we no longer talk about "witches"; consequently, no one is so typed. Similarly, if we had no word for or concept of "psychopath," no one would be so typed. The culture's repertoire of deviant types and stereotypes is ordinarily defined, sustained, and controlled by highly valued realms of the culture (e.g., psychiatry, law, religion). In addition, it should also be noted, different categories are used in different subcultures. "Heretics," for example, are typed only in the religious sector.

Because different groups and cultures have different ideas about deviance, however, typing often has an ethnocentric bias. People in one culture or subculture may be quick to type an outsider as deviant, for instance, simply because the outsider's life style is so different from their own. Among persons within the same culture or subculture, on the other hand, the risks of being typed deviant are usually smaller.

Once a person has been labeled, the question of how to relate to the deviant is more easily resolved when cultural prescriptions exist. These include the prescriptions, for example, that sick people should be treated and evil people punished. In sum, typing is easier to act on when cultural guidelines exist.

THE ROLE OF THIRD PARTIES

As already noted, in intimate, primary groups, people are usually slower to type one of their members as deviant than are outsiders. Such in-group labeling does happen at times, however, particularly if the deviant's aberrant behavior has begun to cause considerable strain for the rest of the group. When this happens, the typing of the person as deviant is often facilitated or precipitated by some outsider or outside agency—in short, by some third party.

In some cases the third party may act without solicitation. A wife, for example, may fail to recognize that her husband is involved with another woman until the community gossip (the third party) so informs her; she may then type her husband as a philanderer and may, through separation or divorce, exclude him from the family.

In other cases a member of the primary group may seek out the third party in order to validate such typing or to exclude the deviant from the group. If a man's wife is emotionally disturbed, for example, he may turn to third parties outside the family (a psychiatrist, the courts, the sheriff, etc.) in order to remove his wife from the home, officially labeling her as mentally disturbed, and seeking treatment for her.

Thus we have seen some of the ways in which the social definition of deviants proceeds. A violation of rules, real or imputed, can activate the process of social typing, and a variety of social factors affect its success. The nature and likelihood of this typing are influenced by the cultural context. People may at first attempt to accommodate these alleged violations. Over the course of time, however, the deviant may no longer be protected. Third parties may intervene, and at that point exclusion of the deviant may take place.

1 | *the process of social typing*

Alleged deviance implies that some rule or expectation has been violated. Yet not all such violations are noticed and labeled as deviant. Also, different groups are quicker to label certain types of violations as deviant, and the same group may be quicker to label at one time than another.

In the first reading Becker describes a number of conditions that are involved when a person is labeled deviant; he also discusses the consequences of such labeling. In the next selection Kitsuse uses homosexuality to illustrate how people type a person as deviant, and how they then act on this social definition. Erikson discusses the basis on which communities single out certain types of conduct to be defined as deviant. In the final selection Lofland views the labeling of deviance in the context of social conflict.

Outsiders

HOWARD S. BECKER

DEVIANCE AND THE RESPONSES OF OTHERS

[One sociological view] . . . defines deviance as the infraction of some agreed-upon rule. It then goes on to ask who breaks rules, and to search for the factors in their personalities and life situations that might account for the infractions. This assumes that those who have broken a rule constitute a homogeneous category, because they have committed the same deviant act.

Such an assumption seems to me to ignore the central fact about deviance: it is created by society. I do not mean this in the way it is ordinarily understood, in which the causes of deviance are located in the social situation of the deviant or in "social factors" which prompt his action. I mean, rather, that *social groups create deviance by making the rules whose infraction constitutes deviance,* and by applying those rules to particular people and labeling them as outsiders. From this point of view, deviance is *not* a quality of the act the person commits, but rather a consequence of the application by others of rules and sanctions to an "offender." The deviant is one to whom that label has successfully been applied; deviant behavior is behavior that people so label.[1]

Since deviance is, among other things, a consequence of the responses of others to a person's act, students of deviance cannot assume that they are dealing with a homogeneous category when they study people who have been labeled deviant. That is, they cannot assume that those people have actually committed a deviant act or broken some rule, because the process of labeling may not be infallible; some people may be labeled deviant who in fact have not broken a rule. Furthermore, they cannot assume that the category of those labeled deviant will contain all those who actually have broken a rule, for many offenders may escape apprehension and thus fail to be included in the population of "deviants" they study. Insofar as the category lacks homogeneity and fails to include all the cases that belong in it, one cannot reasonably expect to find common factors of personality or life situation that will account for the supposed deviance.

What, then, do people who have been labeled deviant have in common? At the least, they share the label and the experience of being labeled as outsiders. I will begin my analysis with this basic similarity and view deviance as the product of a transaction that takes place between some social group and one who is viewed by that group as a rule-breaker. I will be less concerned with the personal

[1] The most important earlier statements of this view can be found in Frank Tannenbaum, *Crime and the Community* (New York: McGraw-Hill Book Co., Inc., 1951), and E. M. Lemert, *Social Pathology* (New York: McGraw-Hill Book Co., Inc., 1951). A recent article stating a position very similar to mine is John Kitsuse, "Societal Reaction to Deviance: Problems of Theory and Method," *Social Problems, 9* (Winter, 1962), 247–256.

and social characteristics of deviants than with the process by which they come to be thought of as outsiders and their reactions to that judgment. . . .

The point is that the response of other people has to be regarded as problematic. Just because one has committed an infraction of a rule does not mean that others will respond as though this had happened. (Conversely, just because one has not violated a rule does not mean that he may not be treated, in some circumstances, as though he had.)

The degree to which other people will respond to a given act as deviant varies greatly. Several kinds of variation seem worth noting. First of all, there is variation over time. A person believed to have committed a given "deviant" act may at one time be responded to much more leniently than he would be at some other time. The occurrence of "drives" against various kinds of deviance illustrates this clearly. At various times, enforcement officials may decide to make an all-out attack on some particular kind of deviance, such as gambling, drug addiction, or homosexuality. It is obviously much more dangerous to engage in one of these activities when a drive is on than at any other time. (In a very interesting study of crime news in Colorado newspapers, Davis found that the amount of crime reported in Colorado newspapers showed very little association with actual changes in the amount of crime taking place in Colorado. And, further, that people's estimate of how much increase there had been in crime in Colorado was associated with the increase in the amount of crime news but not with any increase in the amount of crime.)[2]

The degree to which an act will be treated as deviant depends also on who commits the act and who feels he has been harmed by it. Rules tend to be applied more to some persons than others. Studies of juvenile delinquency make the point clearly. Boys from middle-class areas do not get as far in the legal process when they are apprehended as do boys from slum areas. The middle-class boy is less likely, when picked up by the police, to be taken to the station; less likely when taken to the station to be booked; and it is extremely unlikely that he will be convicted and sentenced.[3] This variation occurs even though the original infraction of the rule is the same in the two cases. Similarly, the law is differentially applied to Negroes and whites. It is well known that a Negro believed to have attacked a white woman is much more likely to be punished than a white man who commits the same offense; it is only slightly less well known that a Negro who murders another Negro is much less likely to be punished than a white man who commits murder.[4] This, of course, is one of the main points of Sutherland's analysis of white-collar crime: crimes committed by corporations are almost always prosecuted as civil cases, but the same crime committed by an individual is ordinarily treated as a criminal offense.[5]

Some rules are enforced only when they result in certain consequences. The

[2] F. James Davis, "Crime News in Colorado Newspapers," *American Journal of Sociology*, LVII (January, 1952), 325–330.

[3] See Albert K. Cohen and James F. Short, Jr., "Juvenile Delinquency," in Robert K. Merton and Robert A. Nisbet, eds., *Contemporary Social Problems* (New York: Harcourt, Brace, and World, 1961), p. 87.

[4] See Harold Garfinkel, "Research Notes on Inter- and Intra-Racial Homicides," *Social Forces*, 27 (May, 1949), 369–381.

[5] Edwin H. Sutherland, "White Collar Criminality," *American Sociological Review*, V (February, 1940), 1–12.

unmarried mother furnishes a clear example. Vincent[6] points out that illicit sexual relations seldom result in severe punishment or social censure for the offenders. If, however, a girl becomes pregnant as a result of such activities the reaction of others is likely to be severe. (The illicit pregnancy is also an interesting example of the differential enforcement of rules on different categories of people. Vincent notes that unmarried fathers escape the severe censure visited on the mother.)

Why repeat these commonplace observations? Because, taken together, they support the proposition that deviance is not a simple quality, present in some kinds of behavior and absent in others. Rather, it is the product of a process which involves responses of other people to the behavior. The same behavior may be an infraction of the rules at one time and not at another; may be an infraction when committed by one person, but not when committed by another; some rules are broken with impunity, others are not. In short, whether a given act is deviant or not depends in part on the nature of the act (that is, whether or not it violates some rule) and in part on what other people do about it.

Some people may object that this is merely a terminological quibble, that one can, after all, define terms any way he wants to and that if some people want to speak of rule-breaking behavior as deviant without reference to the reactions of others they are free to do so. This, of course, is true. Yet it might be worthwhile to refer to such behavior as *rule-breaking behavior* and reserve the term *deviant* for those labeled as deviant by some segment of society. I do not insist that this usage be followed. But it should be clear that insofar as a scientist uses "deviant" to refer to any rule-breaking behavior and takes as his subject of study only those who have been *labeled* deviant, he will be hampered by the disparities between the two categories.

If we take as the object of our attention behavior which comes to be labeled as deviant, we must recognize that we cannot know whether a given act will be categorized as deviant until the response of others has occurred. Deviance is not a quality that lies in behavior itself, but in the interaction between the person who commits an act and those who respond to it. . . .

In any case, being branded as deviant has important consequences for one's further social participation and self-image. The most important consequence is a drastic change in the individual's public identity. Committing the improper act and being publicly caught at it place him in a new status. He has been revealed as a different kind of person from the kind he was supposed to be. He is labeled a "fairy," "dope fiend," "nut" or "lunatic," and treated accordingly.

In analyzing the consequences of assuming a deviant identity let us make use of Hughes' distinction between master and auxiliary status traits.[7] Hughes notes that most statuses have one key trait which serves to distinguish those who belong from those who do not. Thus the doctor, whatever else he may be, is a person who has a certificate stating that he has fulfilled certain requirements and is licensed to practice medicine; this is the master trait. As Hughes points out, in our society a doctor is also informally expected to have a number of auxiliary traits: most people expect him to be upper middle class, white, male, and

[6] Clark Vincent, *Unmarried Mothers* (New York: The Free Press of Glencoe, 1961), pp. 3–5.

[7] Everett C. Hughes, "Dilemmas and Contradictions of Status," *American Journal of Sociology*, L (March, 1945), 353–359.

Protestant. When he is not there is a sense that he has in some way failed to fill the bill. Similarly, though skin color is the master status trait determining who is Negro and who is white, Negroes are informally expected to have certain status traits and not to have others; people are surprised and find it anomalous if a Negro turns out to be a doctor or a college professor. People often have the master status trait but lack some of the auxiliary, informally expected characteristics; for example, one may be a doctor but be female or Negro.

Hughes deals with this phenomenon in regard to statuses that are well thought of, desired and desirable (noting that one may have the formal qualifications for entry into a status but be denied full entry because of lack of the proper auxiliary traits), but the same process occurs in the case of deviant statuses. Possession of one deviant trait may have a generalized symbolic value, so that people automatically assume that its bearer possesses other undesirable traits allegedly associated with it.

To be labeled a criminal one need only commit a single criminal offense, and this is all the term formally refers to. Yet the word carries a number of connotations specifying auxiliary traits characteristic of anyone bearing the label. A man who has been convicted of house-breaking and thereby labeled criminal is presumed to be a person likely to break into other houses; the police, in rounding up known offenders for investigation after a crime has been committed, operate on this premise. Further, he is considered likely to commit other kinds of crimes as well, because he has shown himself to be a person without "respect for the law." Thus, apprehension for one deviant act exposes a person to the likelihood that he will be regarded as deviant or undesirable in other respects.

There is one other element in Hughes' analysis we can borrow with profit: the distinction between master and subordinate statuses.[8] Some statuses, in our society as in others, override all other statuses and have a certain priority. Race is one of these. Membership in the Negro race, as socially defined, will override most other status considerations in most other situations; the fact that one is a physician or middle-class or female will not protect one from being treated as a Negro first and any of these other things second. The status of deviant (depending on the kind of deviance) is this kind of master status. One receives the status as a result of breaking a rule, and the identification proves to be more important than most others. One will be identified as a deviant first, before other identifications are made. . . .

[8] *Ibid.*

Societal Reaction to Deviant Behavior

JOHN I. KITSUSE

Sociological theory and research in the area traditionally known as "social pathology" have been concerned primarily with the classification and analysis of *deviant forms of behavior* and relatively little attention has been given to societal reactions to deviance.[1] In a recent paper, Merton has noted this lack of a "systematic *classification* of the responses of the conventional or conforming members of a group to deviant behavior."[2] Similarly, Cohen has observed that "a sociology of deviant behavior-conformity will have to devise ways of conceptualizing responses to deviant behavior from the standpoint of their relevance to the production or extinction of deviant behavior."[3] In this paper, I shall discuss some of the theoretical and methodological issues posed by the problem of societal reactions to deviant behavior and report on a preliminary attempt to formulate a research design which specifically takes them into account.

I propose to shift the focus of theory and research from the forms of deviant behavior to the *processes by which persons come to be defined as deviant by others.* Such a shift requires that the sociologist view as problematic what he generally assumes as given—namely, that certain forms of behavior are *per se* deviant and are so defined by the "conventional or conforming members of a group." This assumption is frequently called into question on empirical grounds when the societal reaction to behaviors defined as deviant by the sociologist is non-existent, indifferent, or at most mildly disapproving. For example, in his discussion of "ritualism" as a form of deviant behavior, Merton states that it is not that such behavior is treated by others as deviant which identifies it as deviant "since the overt behavior is institutionally permitted, though not culturally prescribed."[4] Rather, the behavior is deviant because it "clearly represents a departure from the cultural model in which men are obliged to move onward

Reprinted from *Social Problems,* Vol. 9, No. 3 (Winter 1962), pp. 247–256.

[1] A notable exception is the work of Edwin M. Lemert who systematically incorporates the concept of societal reaction in his theory of sociopathic behavior. See *Social Pathology,* McGraw-Hill: New York, 1951.

[2] Robert K. Merton, "Social Conformity, Deviation, and Opportunity-Structures: A Comment on the Contributions of Dubin and Cloward," *American Sociological Review,* 24 (1959), pp. 177–189.

[3] Albert K. Cohen, "The Study of Social Disorganization and Deviant Behavior," in *Sociology Today,* R. Merton, L. Broom, and L. Cottrell, eds., Basic Books: New York, 1959, pp. 465–466.

[4] Robert K. Merton, *Social Theory and Social Structure,* revised, Free Press: New York, 1957, p. 150.

and upward in the social hierarchy."[5] The discrepancy between the theoretically hypothesized and empirically observable societal reaction is also noted by Lemert: "It is fairly easy to think of situations in which serious offenses against laws commanding public respect have only mild penalty or have gone entirely unpunished. Conversely, cases are easily discovered in which a somewhat minor violation of legal rules has provoked surprisingly stringent penalties."[6]

Clearly, the forms of behavior *per se* do not activate the processes of societal reaction which sociologically differentiate deviants from non-deviants. Thus, a central problem for theory and research in the sociology of deviance may be stated as follows: What are the behaviors which are defined by members of the group, community, or society as deviant, and how do those definitions organize and activate the societal reactions by which persons come to be differentiated and treated as deviants? In formulating the problem in this way, the point of view of those who interpret and define behavior as deviant must explicitly be incorporated into a sociological definition of deviance. Accordingly, deviance may be conceived as a process by which the members of a group, community, or society (1) interpret behavior as deviant, (2) define persons who so behave as a certain kind of deviant, and (3) accord them the treatment considered appropriate to such deviants. In the following pages, this conception of deviance and societal reaction will be applied to the processes by which

persons come to be defined and treated as homosexuals.

SOCIETAL REACTIONS TO "HOMOSEXUAL BEHAVIOR"

As a form of deviant behavior, homosexuality presents a strategically important theoretical and empirical problem for the study of deviance. In the sociological and anthropological literature[7] homosexual behavior and the societal reactions to it are conceptualized within the framework of ascribed sex statuses and the socialization of individuals to those statuses. The ascription of sex statuses is presumed to provide a complex of culturally prescribed roles and behaviors which individuals are expected to learn and perform. Homosexual roles and behaviors are conceived to be "inappropriate" to the individual's ascribed sex status, and thus theoretically they are defined as deviant.

With reference to American society, Allison Davis states: "Sex-typing of behavior and privileges is even more rigid and lasting in our society than is agetyping. Indeed, sexual status and colorcaste status are the only life-long forms of rank. In our society, one can escape them in approved fashion only by death. Whereas sexual mobility is somewhat less rare today than formerly, sex-inappropriate behavior, social or physical, is still one of the most severely punished infractions of our social code."[8] In Lemert's terminology, norms concerning sex-

---

[5] *Ibid.*, p. 150.

[6] *Op. cit.*, p. 55.

[7] For examples, see Talcott Parsons and Robert F. Bales, *Family Socialization and Interaction Process,* Free Press: New York, 1955, pp. 103–105; Ruth Benedict, "Continuities and Discontinuities in Cultural Conditioning," *Psychiatry,* 1 (1938), pp. 161–167; Abram Kardiner and Associates, *Psychological Frontiers of Society,* Columbia University Press: New York, 1945, pp. 57, 88, etc.; Clifford Kirkpatrick, *The Family,* Ronald Press: New York, 1955, pp. 57–58; Margaret Mead, *Sex and Temperament,* William Morrow: New York, 1955.

[8] Allison Davis, "American Status Systems and the Socialization of the Child," *American Sociological Review,* 6 (1941), p. 350.

appropriate behavior have a high degree of "compulsiveness" and social disapproval of violations is stringent and effective.[9] Homosexuals themselves appear to share this conception of the societal reaction to their behavior, activities, and subculture.[10]

Such a view of homosexuality would lead one to hypothesize that "sex-appropriate" (and conversely "sex-inappropriate") behaviors are unambiguously prescribed, deviations from those prescriptions are invariably interpreted as immoral, and the reactions of the conventional and conforming members of the society to such deviations are uniformly severe and effective. The evidence which apparently supports this hypothesis is not difficult to find, particularly with reference to the definition and treatment of male homosexuals. Individuals who are publicly identified as homosexuals are frequently denied the social, economic, and legal rights of "normal" males. Socially they may be treated as objects of amusement, ridicule, scorn, and often fear; economically they may be summarily dismissed from employment; legally they are frequently subject to interrogation and harassment by police.

In citing such evidence, however, it is important to note that the societal reaction to and the differentiation of homosexuals from the "normal" population is a consequence of the fact that the former are "known" to be homosexuals by some individuals, groups or agencies. Thus, within the framework of the present formulation of homosexuality as a form of deviant behavior, the processes by which individuals come to be "known" and treated as sexually deviant will be viewed as problematic and a problem for empirical investigation. I shall not be concerned here with the so-called "latent homosexual" unless he is so defined by others and differentially treated as a consequence of that definition. Nor will I be concerned with the variety of "internal" conflicts which may form the "clinical" picture of the homosexual except insofar as such conflicts are manifested in behavior leading others to conceive of him as a homosexual. In short, I shall proceed on the principle that it is only when individuals are defined and identified by others as homosexuals and accorded the treatment considered "appropriate" for individuals so defined that a homosexual "population" is produced for sociological investigation.[11] With reference to homosexuality, then, the empirical questions are: What forms of behavior do persons in the social system consider to be "sex-inappropriate," how do they interpret such behaviors, and what are the consequences of those interpretations for their reactions to individuals who are perceived to manifest such behaviors?

In a preliminary attempt to investigate these questions, an interview schedule was constructed[12] and administered to approximately seven hundred individuals, most of whom were college undergraduates. The sample was neither random nor representative of any specified population, and the generalizability of the interview materials is limited except insofar as they are relevant to the previously noted hypothesis that homosexual behavior is uniformly defined, in-

---

[9] *Op. cit.,* Chapter 4.

[10] Evelyn Hooker, "Sequences in Homosexual Identification," read at the meetings of the American Sociological Association, 1960; Donald Webster Cory, *The Homosexual in America,* Greenburg: New York, 1951, esp. Part I.

[11] This principle has been suggested by Harold Garfinkel. See "Some Sociological Concepts and Methods for Psychiatrists," *Psychiatric Research Reports,* 6 (1956), pp. 181–195.

[12] The interview schedule and methods were conceived and constructed in consultation with Aaron V. Cicourel.

terpreted, and negatively sanctioned. The interview materials will therefore be used for the purpose of illustrating the theory and method of the present conception of deviance and societal reaction.

The objectives of the interview were threefold: It attempted to document (1) the behavior forms which are interpreted as deviant, (2) the processes by which persons who manifest such behaviors are defined and (3) treated as deviant. Thus, in the construction of the interview schedule, what the interviewees considered to be "deviant" behavior, the interpretations of such behavior, and the actions of subjects toward those perceived as deviant were addressed as empirical questions. Labels such as alcoholic, illiterate, illegitimate child, and ex-convict were assumed to be categories employed by persons in everyday life to classify deviants, but the behavior forms by which they identify individuals as deviants were treated as problematic. "Sexual deviant" was one of ten categories of deviants about which subjects were questioned in the interview. Among the more than seven hundred subjects interviewed, seventy-five stated they had "known" a homosexual and responded to questions concerning their experiences with such individuals. The data presented below are drawn from the protocols of interviews with this group of subjects.

The interview proceeded as follows:

The subject was asked "Have you ever known anyone who was a sexual deviant?" If he questioned the meaning of "deviant," the subject was asked to consider the question using his own meaning of "sexual deviant."

When the subject stated he had known a sexual deviant—a homosexual in this case—as he defined the term, he was asked to think about the most recent incident involving him in an encounter with such a person. He was then asked "When was the first time you noticed (found out) that this person was a homosexual?" followed by "What was the situation? What did you notice about him? How did he behave?" This line of questioning was focused on the interaction between the subject and the alleged deviant to obtain a detailed description of the situation which led the subject to define the person as homosexual. The subject's description of the person's behavior was systematically probed to clarify the terms of his description, particularly those which were interpretive rather than descriptive.

EVIDENCE OF HOMOSEXUALITY

Responses to the question "When was the first time you noticed (found out) that this person was homosexual?" and the related probes suggest that an individual's sexual "normality" may be called into question with reference to two broad categories of evidence. (*a*) *Indirect evidence* in the form of a rumor, an acquaintance's experience with the individual in question subsequently communicated to the subject, or general reputational information concerning the individual's behavior, associates, and sexual predilections may be the occasion for suspecting him to be "different." Many subjects reported that they first "found out" or "knew" that the individuals in question were homosexuals through the reports of others or by "reputation." Such information was generally accepted by the subjects without independent verification. Indeed, the information provided a new perspective for their retrospective as well as prospective observations and interpretations of the individuals' behaviors. An example of how hearsay organizes observation and interpretation is the following statement by a 35-year-old male (a draftsman):

I: Then this lieutenant was a homosexual?
S: Yes.
I: How did you find out about it?
S: The guy he approached told me. After

that, I watched him. Our company was small and we had a bar for both enlisted men and officers. He would come in and try to be friendly with one or two of the guys.

I: Weren't the other officers friendly?

S: Sure, they would come in for an occasional drink; some of them had been with the company for three years and they would sometimes slap you on the back, but he tried to get over friendly.

I: What do you mean "over friendly"?

S: He had only been there a week. He would try to push himself on a couple of guys—he spent more time with the enlisted personnel than is expected from an officer.

(b) *Direct observation* by the subject of the individual's behavior may be the basis for calling the latter's sexual "normality" into question. The descriptions of behavior which subjects took to be indicative of homosexuality varied widely and were often vague. Most frequently the behaviors cited were those *"which everyone knows"* are indications of homosexuality. For example, a 20-year-old male subject reports an encounter with a stranger at a bar:

I: What happened during your conversation?

S: He asked me if I went to college and I said I did. Then he asked me what I was studying. When I told him psychology he appeared very interested.

I: What do you mean "interested"?

S: Well, you know queers really go for this psychology stuff.

I: Then what happened?

S: Ah, let's see. I'm not exactly sure, but somehow we got into an argument about psychology and to prove my point I told him to pick an area of study. Well, he appeared to be very pensive and after a great thought he said, "Okay, let's take homosexuality."

I: What did you make of that?

S: Well, by now I figured the guy was queer so I got the hell outta there.

The responses of other subjects suggest that an individual is particularly

suspect when he is observed to behave in a manner which deviates from the *behaviors-held-in-common* among members of the group to which he belongs. For example, a behavior which is presumed to be held-in-common among sailors in the U.S. Navy is intense and active sexual activity. When a sailor does not affirm, at least verbally, his interest in such activity, his competence as a "male" may be called into question. A 22-year-old engineer, recently discharged from the Navy, responds to the "how did you first know" question as follows:

All of a sudden you just get suspicious of something. I began to wonder about him. He didn't go in for leave activities that most sailors go for. You know, girls and high times. He just never was interested and when you have been out at sea for a month or two you're interested. That just wasn't Navy, and he was a career man.

Although the responses of our subjects indicate there are many behavioral gestures which "everyone knows" are indicators of homosexuality in males, there are relatively few such gestures that lead persons to suspect females of homosexuality. Following is an excerpt from a 21-year-old college co-ed whose remarks illustrate this lack of definite indicators *prior* to her labeling of an acquaintance as a homosexual:

I: When was the first time you noticed she was a deviant?

S: I didn't notice it. I thought she had a masculine appearance when I first saw her anyway.

I: What do you mean?

S: Oh, her haircut, her heavy eyebrows. She had a rather husky build.

I: Exactly when did you think she had a masculine appearance?

S: It was long after [the first meeting] that I found out that she was "one."

I: How do you define it?

S: Well, a lesbian. I don't know too much about them. It was _____ who told me about her.

I: Did you notice anything else about her [at the first meeting]?
S: No, because you really don't know unless you're looking for those things.

Unlike "effeminate" appearance and gestures in males, "masculine" appearance in females is apparently less likely to be immediately linked to the suspicion or imputation of homosexuality. The statements of the subject quoted above indicate that although "masculine appearance" is an important element in her conception of a lesbian, its significance did not become apparent to her until a third person told her the girl was a homosexual. The remarks of other subjects in our sample who state they have "known" female homosexuals reveal a similar ambiguity in their interpretations of what they describe as indicators of sexual deviance.

A third form of evidence by direct observation is behaviors which the subjects interpreted to be *overt sexual propositions*. Descriptions of such propositions ranged from what the subjects considered to be unmistakable evidence of the person's sexual deviance to ambiguous gestures which they did not attempt to question in the situation. The following is an excerpt from an interview with a 24-year-old male school teacher who recounts an experience in a Korean Army barrack:

I: What questions did he [the alleged homosexual] ask?
S: "How long have you been in Korea?" I told him. "What do you think of these Korean girls?" which I answered, "Not too much because they are dirty." I thought he was probably homesick and wanted someone to talk to. I do not remember what he said then until he said, "How much do you have?" I answered him by saying, "I don't know, about average I guess." Then he said, "Can I feel it just once?" To this I responded with, "Get the hell out of here," and I gave him a shove when he reached for me as he asked the question.

In a number of interviews, the subjects' statements indicate that they interpreted the sequence of the alleged deviants' behavior as progressively inappropriate or peculiar in the course of their interaction with them. The link between such behavior and their judgment that a sexual proposition was being made was frequently established by the subjects' growing realization of its deviant character. A 21-year-old male subject recalls the following experience involving his high school tennis coach who had invited him to dinner:

S: Anyway, when I get there he served dinner, and as I think back on it—I didn't notice it at the time—but I remember that he did act sort of effeminate. Finally he got up to change a record and picked up some of my English themes. Then he brought them over and sat down beside me. He began to explain some of my mistakes in my themes, and in the meantime he slipped his arms around me.
I: Would you say that this was done in a friendly manner or with an intent of hugging you or something?
S: Well, no, it was just a friendly gesture of putting his arm around my shoulder. At that time, I didn't think anything of it, but as he continued to explain my mistakes, he started to rub my back. Then he asked me if I wanted a back rub. So I said, "No! I don't need one." At this time, I began thinking something was funny anyway. So I said that I had to go. . . .

THE IMPUTATION OF HOMOSEXUALITY

When a detailed description of the subject's evidence concerning the alleged homosexual was obtained, he was asked, "What did you make of that?" to elicit information about how he interpreted the persons observed or reported behavior. This line of questioning yielded data on the inferential process by which the subject linked his information about the individual to the deviant category "homosexual."

A general pattern revealed by the subjects' responses to this section of the interview schedule is that when an individual's sexual "normality" is called into question, by whatever form of evidence, the imputation of homosexuality is documented by *retrospective interpretations* of the deviant's behavior, a process by which the subject re-interprets the individual's past behavior in the light of the new information concerning his sexual deviance. This process is particularly evident in cases where the prior relationship between the subject and the alleged homosexual was more than a chance encounter or casual acquaintanceship. The subjects indicate that they reviewed their past interactions with the individuals in question, searching for subtle cues and nuances of behavior which might give further evidence of the alleged deviance. This retrospective reading generally provided the subjects with just such evidence to support the conclusion that "this is what was going on all the time."

Some of the subjects who were interviewed were themselves aware of their retrospective interpretations in defining individuals as sexually deviant. For example, a 23-year-old female graduate student states:

I: Will you tell me more about the situation?

S: Well, their relationship was a continuous one, although I think that it is a friendship now as I don't see them together as I used to; I don't think it is still homosexual. When I see them together, they don't seem to be displaying the affection openly as they did when I first realized the situation.

I: How do you mean "openly"?

S: Well, they would hold each other's hand in public places.

I: And what did you make of this?

S: Well, I really don't know, because I like to hold people's hands, too! I guess I actually didn't see this as directly connected with the situation. What I mean is that, if I hadn't seen the other incident [she had observed the two girls in bed together] I probably wouldn't have thought of it [i.e., hand-holding] very much. . . . Well, actually, there were a few things that I questioned later on that I hadn't thought really very much about. . . . I can remember her being quite affectionate towards me several times when we were in our room together, like putting her arm around my shoulder. Or I remember one time specifically when she asked me for a kiss. I was shocked at the time, but I laughed it off jokingly.

THE INTERACTIONAL CONTEXTS OF SOCIETAL REACTIONS

When the description of the alleged deviant's behavior and the subject's interpretations of that behavior were recorded, the subject was asked "What did you do then?" This question was directed toward documenting societal reactions to deviant behavior. Forms of behavior *per se* do not differentiate deviants from non-deviants; it is the responses of the conventional and conforming members of the society who identify and interpret behavior as deviant which sociologically transform persons into deviants. Thus, in the formulation of deviance proposed here, if the subject observes an individual's behavior and defines it as deviant but does not accord him differential treatment as a consequence of that definition, the individual is not sociologically deviant.

The reactions of the subjects to individuals they defined as homosexuals ranged from immediate withdrawal from the scene of interaction and avoidance of further encounters with the alleged deviants to the maintenance of the prior relationship virtually unaltered by the imputation of deviance. The following responses to the question "What did you do then?" illustrate the variation in sanctions directed toward persons defined as homosexuals.

Explicit disapproval and immediate withdrawal: The most negatively toned and clearly articulated reaction reported by our subjects is that of the previously quoted Korean War veteran. It is interesting to note that extreme physical punishment as a reaction to persons defined as homosexuals, a reaction which is commonly verbalized by "normal" males as proper treatment of "queers," is not reported by any of the subjects. When physical force is used, it is invariably in response to the deviant's direct physical overtures, and even then it is relatively mild, e.g., "I gave him a shove when he reached for me."

Explicit disapproval and subsequent withdrawal: In the following excerpt, a 20-year-old male college student describes an encounter with a man whom he met in a coffee shop. In the course of their conversation, the man admitted his homosexuality to the subject. The two left the coffee shop and walked together to the subway station.

I: What happened then?
S: We got to the subway whereupon he suggested that he hail a cab and take me up to Times Square—a distance of almost 40 blocks.
I: Did you agree, and what did you think?
S: Yes, I thought he was just being very nice and I had no qualms about getting in a cab with a homosexual since I was quite sure I could protect myself against any advances in a cab.
I: What happened then?
S: When we had ridden a little distance, he put his hand on my knee, and I promptly removed it saying that it just wasn't right and that I wanted nothing of it. However, after a while, he put his hand back. This time I didn't take it away for a while because I was interested in what he would do. It was the funniest thing—he rubbed and caressed my knee the same

way in which I would have done this to a girl. This time I took his hand and hit him across the chest with it, telling him to "cut it out." Finally, we got to Times Square, and I got out.

This example and that provided by the Korean War veteran's reaction to behavior interpreted as overt sexual propositions suggest the possibility that responses to persons suspected of homosexuality or defined as homosexuals on the basis of more indirect evidence of appearance, "confessions," hearsay, reputation, or association will vary within an even wider range of applied sanctions. Indeed, the statements of subjects concerning their responses to persons alleged to be deviant on such evidence indicate that the modal reaction is disapproval, implicitly rather than explicitly communicated, and a restriction of interaction through partial withdrawal and avoidance. It should be noted further that although the subject's silent withdrawal from an established relationship with an alleged deviant may represent a stronger disapproval than an explicitly communicated, physically enforced sanction against a stranger, moral indignation or revulsion is not necessarily communicated to the deviant. The subject's prior relationship with the alleged deviant and the demands of propriety in subsequent interactions with him qualify the form and intensity of the sanctions which are applied. Thus, when the organization of the subject's day-to-day activities "forces" him into interaction with the deviant, expressions of disapproval are frequently constrained and diffused by the rules of deference and demeanor.[13] The following excerpts provide illustrations:

Implicit disapproval and partial withdrawal: A 20-year-old co-ed's reaction to a girl she concluded was a homosexual was expressed as follows:

[13] Erving Goffman, "The Nature of Deference and Demeanor," *American Anthropologist,* 58 (1956), pp. 473–502.

Well, I didn't want to be alone with X [the homosexual] because the four of us had two connecting rooms and I was in the room with X. As much as I liked the girl and felt sorry for her, I knew she could really wring me through the wringer. So the rest decided that I should tell her that if she and Y wanted to be homos, to do it somewhere else and not in the room.

No disapproval and relationship sustained: The "live and let live" response to homosexuals, which is implied in the preceding reaction, was not uncommon among the subjects. Some subjects not only affirmed the right of the homosexual to "live his own life" but also reported that their knowledge of the deviance has had little or no effect upon their subsequent relationships with the deviants. In this regard, the mildest reaction, so mild that it might be considered no reaction at all, was that of a 19-year-old male college student:

I: What was your reaction to him?
S: My reactions to him have always been friendly because he seems like a very friendly person. Uh, and he has a very nice sense of humor and I've never been repelled by anything he's said. For one thing, I think he's tremendously interesting because he seems to have such a wide range for background. . . .
I: When was the last time you saw this person?
S: Last night. . . . I was sitting in a restaurant and he walked in with some friends. . . . he just stopped in and said hello, and was his usual friendly self.
I: What in particular happened after that?
S: Actually, nothing. He sat down with his friends, and we exchanged a few words about the records that were playing on the juke box. But nothing, actually. . . .

The theoretical significance of these data for the conception of deviance and societal reaction presented here is not that the subjects' information is of dubious accuracy or questionable relevance as evidence of homosexuality. Nor

is it that the subjects' interpretations of them are unreasonable, unjustifiable, or spurious. They suggest rather that the conceptions of persons in everyday life concerning "sex-appropriate" or "sex-inappropriate" behavior may lead them to interpret a variety of behavioral forms as indications of the same deviation, and the "same" behavioral forms as indications of a variety of deviant as well as "normal" behavior. An individual's sexual "normality" may be made problematic by his interpretations and re-interpretations of his behavior by others, and the interpretive process may be activated by a wide range of situational behaviors which lend new significance to the individual's past and present behavior. His behavior with respect to speech, interests, dress, dating, or relations with other males are not *per se* significant in the deviant-defining process. The data suggest that the critical feature of the deviant-defining process is not the behavior of individuals who are defined as deviant, but rather the interpretations others make of their behaviors, whatever those behaviors may be.

With specific reference to homosexuality as a form of deviant behavior, the interview materials suggest that while reactions toward persons defined as homosexuals tend to be negatively toned, they are far from homogeneous as to the forms or intensity of the sanctions invoked and applied. Indeed, reactions which may appear to the sociological observer or to the deviant himself as negative sanctions, such as withdrawal or avoidance, may be expressions of embarrassment, a reluctance to share the burden of the deviant's problems, fear of the deviant, etc., as well as moral indignation or revulsion. In none of the interviews does the subject react with extreme violence, explicitly define or directly accuse the deviant of being a "queer," "fairy," or other terms of opprobrium, nor did any of them initiate legal actions against the deviant. In view of the extreme negative sanctions against homosexuality which are posited on theoretical grounds, the generally mild reactions of our subjects are striking.

The relative absence of extreme and overtly expressed negative sanctions against homosexuals among our subjects may, of course, reflect the higher than average educational level of the sample. A sample of subjects less biased toward the highly educated, middle-class segment of the population than was interviewed in this preliminary study may be expected to reflect a more definite pattern with reference to such negative reactions. We must, therefore, be cautious in generalizing the range of reactions among our subjects to the general population. It is equally important to note, however, that these data do indicate that reactions to homosexuals in American society are not *societal* in the sense of being uniform within a narrow range; rather, they are significantly conditioned by sub-cultural as well as situational factors. Thus, not only are the processes by which persons come to be defined as homosexuals contingent upon the interpretations of their behavior by others, but also the sanctions imposed and the treatment they are accorded as a consequence of that definition vary widely among conventional members of various sub-cultural groups.

The larger implications of these data are that a sociological theory of deviance must explicitly take into account the variety and range of conceptions held by persons, groups, and agencies within the society concerning any form of behavior. The increasing differentiation of groups, institutions, and sub-cultures in modern society generates a continually changing range of alternatives and tolerance for the expression of sexual as well as other forms of behavior. Consequently, it is difficult if not impossible to theoretically derive a set of *specific behavioral prescriptions* which will in fact be normatively supported, uniformly practiced, and socially enforced by more than a segment of the total population. Under such conditions, it is not the fact that individuals engage in behaviors which diverge from some theoretically posited "institutionalized expectations" or even that such behaviors are defined as deviant by the conventional and conforming members of the society which is of primary significance for the study of deviance. A sociological theory of deviance must focus specifically upon the interactions which not only define behaviors as deviant but also organize and activate the application of sanctions by individuals, groups, or agencies. For in modern society, the socially significant differentiation of deviants from the nondeviant population is increasingly contingent upon circumstances of situation, place, social and personal biography, and the bureaucratically organized activities of agencies of control.[14]

[14] For a discussion of such contingencies, see Edwin M. Lemert, *op. cit.*, Chapter 4, and Erving Goffman, "The Moral Career of the Mental Patient," *Psychiatry,* 22 (1959), pp. 123–142.

Notes on the Sociology of Deviance

KAI T. ERIKSON

It is a common practice in sociology to picture deviant behavior as an alien element in society. Deviance is considered a vagrant form of human activity which has somehow broken away from the more orderly currents of social life and needs to be controlled. And since it is generally understood that this sort of aberration could only occur if something were wrong within the organization of society itself, deviant behavior is described almost as if it were leakage from machinery in poor condition: it is an incidental result of disorder and anomie, a symptom of internal breakdown.

The purpose of the following remarks will be to review this conventional outlook and to argue that it provides too narrow a framework for many kinds of sociological research. Deviation, we will suggest, recalling Durkheim's classic statement on the subject, can often be understood as a normal product of stable institutions, an important resource which is guarded and preserved by forces found in all human organizations.[1]

I

According to current theory, deviant behavior is most likely to occur when the sanctions governing conduct in any given social setting seem to be contradictory[2]—as would be the case, for example, if the work rules posted by a company required one course of action from its employees and the longer-range policies of the company required quite another. Any situation marked by this kind of ambiguity, of course, can pose a serious dilemma for the individual: if he is careful to observe one set of demands imposed upon him, he runs the immediate risk of violating some other, and thus may find himself caught in a deviant stance no matter how earnestly he tries to avoid it. In this limited sense, deviance can be viewed as a "normal" social response to "abnormal" social circumstances, and we are therefore invited to assume that every act of deviation results from some imbalance within the social order—a condition of strain, anomie, or alienation.

This is a slightly revised version of a paper that appeared in *Social Problems*, 9 (1962), pp. 307–314.

[1] Emile Durkheim, *The Rules of Sociological Method* (translated by S. A. Solovay and J. H. Mueller), New York: The Free Press of Glencoe, 1958.

[2] The best-known statements of this general position, of course, are by Robert K. Merton and Talcott Parsons. Merton, *Social Theory and Social Structure*, Revised Edition, New York: The Free Press of Glencoe, 1957; and Parsons, *The Social System*, New York: The Free Press of Glencoe, 1951.

This approach to the study of deviant behavior has generated a good deal of useful research, but it has at least one serious drawback for investigators who share an interest in what is known as "social problems." The "anomie" theory (if we may use that convenient label for a moment) is designed to account for all behavior which varies in some technical way from the norms of the community, whether or not that behavior is considered a problem by anyone else. For example, the bank teller who becomes a slave to routine and the armed bandit who relieves him of the day's receipts both register as deviants according to the logic of this scheme, since each is deviating in his own way from the ideal standards of the culture. Yet the most important difference between these men is one that the "anomie" theory cannot easily take into account: the bank teller, no matter how desperate his private needs, does not ordinarily create any concern in the rest of the community, while the bandit triggers the whole machinery of social control into vigorous action. In short, the "anomie" theory may help us appreciate the various ways in which people respond to conditions of strain, but it does not help us differentiate between those people who infringe the letter of the norm without attracting any notice and those who excite so much alarm that they earn a deviant reputation in society and are committed to special institutions like prisons and hospitals.

II

From a sociological standpoint, deviance can be defined as conduct which is generally thought to require the attention of social control agencies—that is, conduct about which "something should be done." Deviance is not a property *inherent in* certain forms of behavior; it is a property *conferred upon* these forms by the audiences which directly or in-directly witness them. The critical variable in the study of deviance, then, is the social audience rather than the individual actor, since it is the audience which eventually determines whether or not any episode of behavior or any class of episodes is labeled deviant.

This definition may seem a little indirect, but it has the advantage of bringing a neglected sociological issue into proper focus. When a community acts to control the behavior of one of its members, it is engaged in a very intricate process of selection. After all, even the worst miscreant in society conforms most of the time, if only in the sense that he uses the correct spoon at mealtime, takes good care of his mother, or in a thousand other ways respects the ordinary conventions of his group; and if the community elects to bring sanctions against him for the occasions when he does misbehave, it is responding to a few deviant details set within a vast array of entirely acceptable conduct. Thus it happens that a moment of deviation may become the measure of a person's position in society. He may be jailed or hospitalized, certified as a full-time deviant, despite the fact that only a fraction of his behavior was in any way unusual or dangerous. The community has taken note of a few scattered particles of behavior and has decided that they reflect what kind of person he "really" is.

The screening device which sifts these telling details out of the person's over-all performance, then, is a very important instrument of social control. We know very little about the properties of this screen, but we do know that it takes many factors into account which are not directly related to the deviant act itself: it is sensitive to the suspect's social class, his past record as an offender, the amount of remorse he manages to convey, and many similar concerns which take hold in the shifting moods of the community. This may not be so obvious when the screen is dealing with extreme forms of deviance like serious crimes, but in the day-by-day filtering processes which take place through the community this feature is easily observable. Some men who drink too much are called alcoholics and others are not, some men who act oddly are committed to hospitals and others are not, some men who have no visible means of support are hauled into court and others are not—and the difference between those who earn a deviant label and those who go their own way in peace depends almost entirely on the way in which the community sifts out and codes the many details of behavior to which it is a witness. In this respect, the community screen may be a more relevant subject for sociological research than the actual behavior which is filtered through it.

Once the problem is phrased in this way we can ask: How does a community decide what forms of conduct should be singled out for this kind of attention? The conventional answer to this question, of course, is that society sets up the machinery of control in order to protect itself against the "harmful" effects of deviation, in much the same way that an organism mobilizes its resources to combat an invasion of germs. Yet this simple view of the matter has not always proven to be a very productive one. In the first place, as Durkheim and Mead pointed out some years ago, it is by no means clear that all acts considered deviant in a culture are in fact (or even in principle) harmful to group life.[3] In the second place, it is gradually becoming more evident to sociologists engaged in this area of research that deviant behavior can play an important part in keeping the social order intact.

This raises a number of interesting questions for sociology.

III

In recent years, sociological theory has become more and more concerned with the concept "social system"—an organization of society's component parts into a form which sustains internal equilibrium, resists change, and is boundary maintaining. In its most abstract form, the "system" concept describes a highly complex network of relations, but the scheme is generally used by sociologists to draw attention to those forces in the social order which promote a high level of uniformity among human actors and a high degree of symmetry within human institutions. The main organizational drift of a system, then, is seen as centripetal: it acts to draw the behavior of actors toward those centers in social space where the core values of the group are figuratively located, bringing them within range of basic norms. Any conduct which is neither attracted toward this nerve center by the rewards of conformity nor compelled toward it by other social pressures is considered "out of control," which is to say, deviant.

This basic model has provided the theme for most contemporary thinking about deviation, and as a result little attention has been given to the notion that systems operate to maintain boundaries. To say that a system maintains boundaries is to say that it controls the fluctuation of its constituent parts so that the whole retains a defined range of activity, a unique pattern of constancy and stability, within the larger environment.[4] Because the range of human behavior is potentially so wide, social groups maintain boundaries in the sense that they try to limit the flow of behavior within their domain so that it circulates within a defined cultural territory.

[3] Emile Durkheim, *The Division of Labor in Society* (translated by George Simpson), New York: The Free Press of Glencoe, 1952; and George Herbert Mead, "The Psychology of Punitive Justice," *American Journal of Sociology*, 23 (1918), 577–602.

[4] Cf. Talcott Parsons, *The Social System, op. cit.*

Boundaries, then, are an important point of reference for persons participating in any system. A people may define its boundaries by referring to a geographical location, a set of honored traditions, a particular religious or political viewpoint, an occupational specialty, a common language, or just some local way of doing things; but in any case, members of the group have some idea about the contours of the niche they occupy in social space. They know where the group begins and ends as a special entity; they know what kinds of experience "belong" within these precincts and what kinds do not.

For all its apparent abstractness, a social system is organized around the movements of persons joined together in regular social relations. The only material found in a system for marking boundaries, then, is the behavior of its participants; and the kinds of behavior which best perform this function are often deviant, since they represent the most extreme variety of conduct to be found within the experience of the group. In this sense, transactions taking place between deviant persons on the one side and agencies of control on the other are boundary maintaining mechanisms. They mark the outside limits of the area within which the norm has jurisdiction, and in this way assert how much diversity and variability can be contained within the system before it begins to lose its distinct structure, its cultural integrity.

A social norm is rarely expressed as a firm rule or official code. It is an abstract synthesis of the many separate times a community has stated its sentiments on a given kind of issue. Thus the norm has a history much like that of an article of common law: it is an accumulation of decisions made by the community over a long period of time which gradually gathers enough moral eminence to serve as a precedent for future decisions. And like an article of common law, the norm retains its validity only if it is regularly used as a basis for judgment. Each time

the group censures some act of deviation, then, it sharpens the authority of the violated norm and declares again where the boundaries of the group are located.

It is important to notice that these transactions between deviant persons and agents of control have always attracted a good deal of attention in this and other cultures. In our own past, both the trial and punishment of deviant offenders took place in the public market and gave the crowd a chance to participate in a direct, active way. Today we no longer parade deviants in the town square or expose them to the carnival atmosphere of Tyburn, but it is interesting to note that the "reform" which brought about this change in penal policy coincided almost precisely with the development of newspapers as media of public information. Perhaps this is no more than an accident of history, but it is nevertheless true that newspapers (and now radio and television) offer their readers the same kind of entertainment once supplied by public hangings or the use of stocks and pillories. An enormous amount of modern "news" is devoted to reports about deviant behavior and its punishment: indeed the largest circulation newspaper in the United States prints very little else. Yet how do we explain what makes these items "newsworthy" or why they command the great attention they do? Perhaps they satisfy a number of psychological perversities among the mass audience, as commentators sometimes point out, but at the same time they constitute our main source of information about the normative contours of society. In a figurative sense, at least, morality and immorality meet at the public scaffold, and it is during this meeting that the community declares where the line between them should be drawn.

People who gather together into communities need to be able to describe and anticipate those areas of experience which lie outside the immediate compass of the group—the unseen dangers which in any culture and in any age seem to threaten its security. Traditional folklore depicting demons, devils, witches and evil spirits, may be one way to give form to these otherwise formless dangers, but the visible deviant is another kind of reminder. As a trespasser against the group norms, he represents those forces which lie outside the group's boundaries: he informs us, as it were, what evil looks like, what shapes the devil can assume. And in doing so, he shows us the difference between the inside of the group and the outside. It may well be that without this ongoing drama at the outer edges of group space, the community would have no inner sense of identity and cohesion, no sense of the contrasts which set it off as a special place in the larger world.

Thus deviance cannot be dismissed simply as behavior which *disrupts* stability in society, but may itself be, in controlled quantities, an important condition for *preserving* stability. . . .

Deviance As Social Conflict

JOHN LOFLAND

As used by sociologists, the concept of deviance and its variants are merely somewhat more abstract versions of common-sense, everyday designations. Such popular designations include "crime," "criminal," "deviate," "pervert," "nut," "kook," "lunatic," "oddball," "weirdo," and the like. The deviance vocabulary represents sociologists' attempt to encompass these more colorful words of the layman. Sociologists and laymen alike bracket together certain acts and categories of persons as deserving a kind of attention that is different from that accorded all other acts and categories of persons. One way, then, to approach a definition of deviance is in terms of the basis upon which sociologists and laymen accomplish this broad bracketing.

PARTIES IN CONFLICT

The basis of this bracketing can best be pursued, not through a search for distinctive features of deviance per se, but rather in terms of general and generic dimensions of social organization and social response. Within such dimensions, the defining of persons and acts as deviant can be seen as a particular instance of generalized ways in which social organization and social definition can differ. At the level of a single and *total society,* such a basis is found in the dynamics of what proportion of a society, how well organized and how powerful, are *fearful* of, and feel *threatened* by, some other portion of the society. Organized social life can be viewed as a game in which actors and collectivities defend themselves against distrusted and suspected others. Suspicion, distrust, fear and threat are central themes in all large-scale and differentiated societies. A political constitution like that of the United States even builds in a division of powers to take account of such feelings and to institutionalize their expression.

The parties playing the game around these basic themes can, of course, differ considerably along a variety of dimensions. Taking first *who is feared* or felt to be threatening, some basic distinctions reside in the *population size* of the feared party, the degree of its *organization* and the amount of its *power* relative to the size, organization and power of those who fear it. Taking only size and degree of organization together, some typically identified feared parties are: (1) individuals or small groups who have a limited degree of organization; (2) relatively small but thoroughly organized groups with leaders; and (3) large, well-organized groups within a total society.

On the other side, that of *who is fearful* or is perceiving a threat, parties may vary along the dimensions of: (1) the proportion of the society which feels threatened (e.g., a small minority, a sizable minority or a majority); (2) how strongly the party feels threatened (ranging from mere amusement to a "basic threat to our way of life"); (3) the extent to which the party is organized; and

(4) how much power, relative to the feared party, is possessed by those threatened. The amount of power of who is threatened refers in particular to their ability to bring the resources of the state to bear upon the party felt to be threatening. Those fearful parties who can voice their fears at the public level, who receive at least some public legitimation, and who have the legal structure act in compliance with their wishes (namely, to incarcerate or banish the feared party) are parties with the greatest amount of power.

These variations in size, organization, degree of fear and amount of power among factions of a society provide a basis upon which we can roughly define deviance and see its relation to some other kinds of power games. What is called deviance is but one of a series of generically related situations, some of the more popular forms of which are identified in Chart . . . [1].[1] Deviance is the name of the conflict game in which individuals or loosely organized small groups with little power are strongly feared by a well-organized, sizable minority or majority who have a large amount of power.

Under different levels of fear, size, organization and power between parties in

CHART 1. Conflict Situations
Dimensions of the Character and Relations of Parties in Conflict

Resulting Popular Definition of the Conflict Situation	Size and Organization of Party Feared	Economic and Political Power of Party Feared Relative to Party Fearing	Degree to Which the Well-Organized Opposing Large Minority or Majority Feels Fearful or Threatened
Deviance ("Crime," etc.)	Individual or small, loosely organized groups	Almost none	Very high
Civil Uprising or Disorder	Small loosely organized minority	Relatively low	Very high
Social Movement	Sizable organized minority	Relatively low	Mild
Civil War	Large, well-organized minority	Relatively high or almost equal	Very high
Mainstream Party Politics in the United States	Large, organized minority	About equal	Mild

[1] It is testimony to the rich diversity of human life that [the] Chart . . . represents only a few of several hundred possible conflict situations. For example, if one combines the three dimensions of party feared (size, organization and power) and the four dimensions of party fearing (size, organization, power and degree of fear), and if each dimension is merely dichotomized (a massive oversimplification), the result is 128 different conflict situations.

conflict, there are corresponding changes in public definitions of the situation. Persons and acts in a small, powerless minority that are at one time regarded as merely deviant may, at another time, be felt to constitute a civil uprising, social movement or civil war. Theft, arson, assault, torture and murder perpetrated by individuals is simply deviance; when perpetrated by a loosely organized minority acting in concert such acts might be imputed to have a political meaning, and, when performed in the context of a civil or revolutionary war—that is, by a well-organized minority—they are acts of war or of liberation or legitimate defense. (When undertaken in conflicts between nations, such acts can be among the highest forms of patriotic display. When Audie Murphy killed German soldiers, he was a hero. When Charles Whitman shot Texas civilians, he was a mad killer.)

The imputation of even greatly feared acts and persons as deviant seems to depend less upon particular behavior per se than upon the respective size, degree of power and degree of organization of parties to an issue.

Beyond the excluded conflict situations indicated in Chart 1, there are two other items which some investigators have defined as deviant or as a basis for defining deviance. First, acts that are only *mildly* feared, even if so feared by a large and powerful majority in relation to single powerless individuals or small groups, seem more cogently considered simply as *inappropriate* behavior. Social life is replete with occurrences of tardiness, rudeness, impoliteness, overfamiliarity, embarrassments, *faux pas,* etc.[2] These continuing but mild vexations are better analyzed as features of the sociology of everyday life.[3] Second, strong

fears of some act or class of actors that emanate from a relatively small and not very powerful minority involves *special pleading* and, *at the level of the total society,* the objects of these fears are not rendered deviant. The Prohibition Party's fear of alcoholic consumption and the people who consume it defines a class of deviance for the Prohibitionists, but they are largely bereft of following and social power. Militants of the left and right of both races, who see wisdom in stockpiling firearms to defend against oppressors, apparently have very strong fears of "leftists," "whites," "blacks," or those felt to be ubiquitous Communists in disguise. As long as such groups remain small minorities and lack much power, the objects they define as fearful are merely matters of some slight controversy. Any such group can, of course, come into a position of some power, perhaps to the extent of forcing the game of civil war, or, with sufficient power, of creating a new game of who is defined as deviant about what. Consider, for example, what former Alabama Governor George Wallace and his followers define as deviant:

Bearded professors on some of our college campuses . . . are sympathizing with the enemy, they are encouraging youths to burn draft cards, and some are saying openly, the Viet Cong should win and furnishin' food, blood and clothes to the enemy.

If I were President I would hale 'em before a grand jury and prosecute 'em for treason for that is what it is and traitors is what they are . . . never mind the thin line that we haven't declared war. (Vestal, 1967.)

Given the wide range of groups and perspectives in American civilization, it is probably the case that almost any act or person is strongly feared by *some* so-

[2] Definitions of the field like "behavior which violates institutionalized expectations" (Cohen, 1959:462) thus seem much too broad and group together items of too many varieties.

[3] Within perspectives such as presented by Goffman, 1959, 1961 and 1967.

cial category or organized group. If it is to be possible to isolate a *category of deviance* rather than simply a multitude of conflicts, it is essential that there be involved at least a powerful minority—even if not a majority—who feel a strong sense of threat and fear. . . .

REFERENCES

Cohen, A. K. "The Study of Social Disorganization and Deviant Behavior," in R. K. Merton, L. Broom, and L. S. Cottrell, editors, *Sociology Today.* New York: Basic Books, Inc., 1959, pp. 461–84.

Goffman, E. *The Presentation of Self in Everyday Life.* New York: Doubleday Anchor, Inc., 1959.

———— *Encounters: Two Studies in the Sociology of Interaction.* Indianapolis, Ind.: The Bobbs-Merrill Co., Inc., 1961.

———— *Interaction Ritual.* Garden City, N.Y.: Doubleday & Co., Inc., 1967.

Vestal, B. "How Wallace Carries Out His 'Spoiler' Campaign." *Ann Arbor News,* June 22, 1967.

2

accommodation to deviance

When an alleged violation of rules or expectations has occurred, people may respond in a variety of ways. At first they may fail to notice the alleged deviation. When they do notice it, they may respond in several different ways; they may optimize, neutralize, normalize, or pessimize. To optimize is simply to see the assumed deviance as only temporary. To neutralize is to disregard it as not really significant. To normalize is to regard it as but a variation of normal behavior. To pessimize is to regard the deviance as permanent. These can be considered accommodations when they enable people to live with the deviance.

In the first reading in this chapter Yarrow, Schwartz, Murphy, and Deasy describe the ways in which wives manage, for a time, to normalize their husbands' mental illness. Sampson, Messinger, and Towne then discuss the way in which mental illness can be neutralized within a family. In the final selection Jackson portrays the array of responses and accommodations that wives make in trying to deal with their husbands' alcoholism.

The Psychological Meaning of Mental Illness in the Family

MARIAN RADKE YARROW
CHARLOTTE GREEN SCHWARTZ
HARRIET S. MURPHY
LEILA CALHOUN DEASY

The manifestations of mental illness are almost as varied as the spectrum of human behavior. Moreover, they are expressed not only in disturbance and functional impairment for the sick person but also in disruptive interactions with others. The mentally ill person is often, in his illness, a markedly deviant person, though certainly less so than the popular stereotype of the "insane." One wonders what were the initial phases of the impact of mental illness upon those within the ill person's social environment. How were the disorders of illness interpreted and tolerated? What did the patients, prior to hospitalization, communicate of their needs, and how did others—those closest to the ill persons—attempt, psychologically and behaviorally, to cope with the behavior? How did these persons come to be recognized by other family members as needing psychiatric help?

This paper presents an analysis of cognitive and emotional problems encountered by the wife in coping with the mental illness of the husband. It is concerned with the factors which lead to the reorganization of the wife's perceptions of her husband from a *well* man to a man who is mentally sick or in need of hospitalization in a mental hospital. The process whereby the wife attempts to understand and interpret her husband's manifestations of mental illness is best communicated by considering first the concrete details of a single wife's experiences. The findings and interpretations based on the total sample are presented following the case analysis.

ILLUSTRATIVE CASE

Robert F., a 35-year-old cab driver, was admitted to Saint Elizabeth's Hospital with a diagnosis of schizophrenia. How did Mr. F. get to the mental hospital? Here is a very condensed version of what his wife told an interviewer a few weeks later.

Mrs. F. related certain events, swift and dramatic, which led directly to the hospitalization. The day before admission, Mr. F. went shopping with his wife, which he had never done before, and expressed worry lest he lose her. This was in her words, "rather strange." (*His behavior is not in keeping with her expectations for him.*) Later that day, Mr. F. thought a TV program was about him and that the set was "after him." "Then I was getting worried." (*She recognizes the bizarre nature of his reactions. She becomes concerned.*)

Reprinted from the *Journal of Social Issues*, Vol. 11, No. 4 (1955), pp. 12–24.

That night, Mr. F. kept talking. He reproached himself for not working enough to give his wife surprises. Suddenly, he exclaimed he did have a surprise for her—he was going to kill her. "I was petrified and said to him, 'What do you mean?' Then, he began to cry and told me not to let him hurt me and to do for him what I would want him to do for me. I asked him what was wrong. He said he had cancer. . . . He began talking about his grandfather's mustache and said there was a worm growing out of it." She remembered his watching little worms in the fish bowl and thought his idea came from that. Mr. F. said he had killed his grandfather. He asked Mrs. F. to forgive him and wondered if she were his mother or God. She denied this. He vowed he was being punished for killing people during the war. "I thought maybe . . . worrying about the war so much . . . had gotten the best of him. (*She tries to understand his behavior. She stretches the range of normality to include it.*) I thought he should see a psychiatrist . . . I don't know how to explain it. He was shaking. I knew it was beyond what I could do . . . I was afraid of him . . . I thought he was losing his normal mental attitude and mentality, but I wouldn't say that he was insane or crazy, because he had always bossed me around before . . ." (*She shifts back and forth in thinking his problem is psychiatric and in feeling it is normal behavior that could be accounted for in terms of their own experience.*) Mr. F. talked on through the night. Sometime in the morning, he "seemed to straighten out" and drove his wife to work. (*This behavior tends to balance out the preceding disturbed activities. She quickly returns to a normal referent.*)

At noon, Mr. F. walked into a store where his wife worked as a clerk. "I couldn't make any sense of what he was saying. He kept getting angry because I wouldn't talk to him. . . . Finally, the boss's wife told me to go home." En route, Mr. F. said his male organs were blown up and little seeds covered him. Mrs. F. denied seeing them and announced she planned to call his mother. "He began crying and I had to promise not to. I said, . . . 'Don't you think you should go to a psychiatrist?' and he said, 'No, there is nothing wrong with me.' . . . Then we came home, and I went to pay a bill . . ." (*Again she considers, but is not fully committed to, the idea that psychiatric help is needed.*)

Back at their apartment, Mr. F. talked of repairing his cab while Mrs. F. thought of returning to work and getting someone to call a doctor. Suddenly, he started chasing her around the apartment and growling like a lion. Mrs. F. screamed, Mr. F. ran out of the apartment, and Mrs. F. slammed and locked the door. "When he started roaring and growling, then I thought he was crazy. That wasn't a human sound. You couldn't say a thing to him . . ." Later, Mrs. F. learned that her husband went to a nearby church, created a scene, and was taken to the hospital by the police. (*Thoroughly threatened, she defines problem as psychiatric.*)

What occurred before these events which precipitated the hospitalization? Going back to their early married life, approximately three years before hospitalization, Mrs. F. told of her husband's irregular work habits and long-standing complaints of severe headaches. "When we were first married, he didn't work much and I didn't worry as long as we could pay the bills." Mrs. F. figured they were just married and wanted to be together a lot. (*Personal norms and expectations are built up.*)

At Thanksgiving, six months after marriage, Mr. F. "got sick and stopped working." During the war he contracted malaria, he explained, which always recurred at that time of year. "He wouldn't get out of bed or eat. . . . He thought he was constipated and he had nightmares. . . . What I noticed most was his perspiring so much. He was crabby. You couldn't get him to go to a doctor. . . . I noticed he was nervous. He's always been a nervous person. . . . Any little thing that would go wrong would upset him—if I didn't get a drawer closed right. . . . His friends are nervous, too. . . . I came to the conclusion that maybe I was happy-go-lucky and everyone else was a bundle of nerves. . . . For a cab driver, he worked hard—most cab drivers loaf. When he felt good, he worked hard. He didn't work so hard when he didn't." (*She adapts to his behavior. The atypical is normalized as his type of personality and appropriate to his subculture.*)

As the months and years went by, Mrs. F. changed jobs frequently, but she worked more regularly than did her husband. He continued to work sporadically, get sick intermittently, appear "nervous and tense" and refrain from seeking medical care. Mrs. F. "couldn't say what was wrong." She had first one idea, then another, about his behavior. "I knew it wasn't right for him to be acting sick like he did." Then, "I was beginning to think he was getting lazy because there wasn't anything I could see." During one period, Mrs. F. surmised he was carrying on with another woman. "I was right on the verge of going, until he explained it wasn't anyone else." (*There is a building up of deviant behavior to a point near her tolerance limits. Her interpretations shift repeatedly.*)

About two and a half years before admission, Mrs. F. began talking to friends about her husband's actions and her lack of success in getting him to a doctor. "I got disgusted and said if he didn't go to a doctor, I would leave him. I got Bill (the owner of Mr. F.'s cab) to talk to him. . . . I begged, threatened, fussed . . ." After that, Mr. F. went to a VA doctor for one visit, overslept for his second appointment and never returned. He said the doctor told him nothing was wrong.

When Mr. F. was well and working, Mrs. F. "never stopped to think about it." "You live from day to day . . . When something isn't nice, I don't think about it. If you stop to think about things, you can worry yourself sick . . . He said he wished he could live in my world. He'd never seem to be able to put his thinking off the way I do . . ." (*Her mode of operating permits her to tolerate his behavior.*)

Concurrently, other situations confronted Mrs. F. Off and on, Mr. F. talked of a coming revolution as a result of which Negroes and Jews would take over the world. If Mrs. F. argued that she didn't believe it, Mr. F. called her "dumb" and "stupid." "The best thing to do was to change the subject." Eighteen months before admission, Mr. F. began awakening his wife to tell of nightmares about wartime experiences, but she "didn't think about it." Three months later, he decided he wanted to do something besides drive a cab. He worked on an invention but discovered it was patented. Then, he began to write a book about his wartime experiences and science. "If you saw what he wrote, you couldn't see anything wrong with it. . . . He just wasn't making any money." Mrs. F. did think it was "silly" when Mr. F. went to talk to Einstein about his ideas and couldn't understand why he didn't talk to someone in town. Nevertheless, she accompanied him on the trip. (*With the further accumulation of deviant behavior, she becomes less and less able to tolerate it. The perceived seriousness of his condition is attenuated so long as she is able to find something acceptable or understandable in his behavior.*)

Three days before admission, Mr. F. stopped taking baths and changing clothes. Two nights before admission, he awakened his wife to tell her he had just figured out that the book he was writing had nothing to do with science or the world, only with himself. "He said he had been worrying about things for ten years and that writing a book solved what had been worrying him for ten years." Mrs. F. told him to burn his writings if they had nothing to do with science. It was the following morning that Mrs. F. first noticed her husband's behavior as "rather strange."

In the long prelude to Mr. F.'s hospitalization, one can see many of the difficulties which arise for the wife as the husband's behavior no longer conforms and as it strains the limits of the wife's expectations for him. At some stage the wife defines the situation as one requiring help, eventually psychiatric help. Our analysis is concerned primarily with the process of the wife's getting to this stage in interpreting and responding to the husband's behavior. In the preceding case are many reactions which appear as general trends in the data group. These trands can be systematized in terms of the following focal aspects of the process:

1. The wife's threshold for initially discerning a problem depends on the accumulation of various kinds of behavior which are not readily understandable or acceptable to her.

2. This accumulation forces upon the wife the necessity for examining and adjusting expectations for herself and her husband which permit her to account for his behavior.

3. The wife is in an "overlapping" situation, of problem—not problem or of normal—not normal. Her interpretations shift back and forth.

4. Adaptations to the atypical behavior of the husband occur. There is testing and waiting for additional cues in coming to any given interpretation, as in most problem solving. The wife mobilizes strong defenses against the huband's deviant behavior. These defenses take form in such reactions as denying, attenuating, balancing and normalizing the husband's problems.

5. Eventually there is a threshold point at which the perception breaks, when the wife comes to the relatively stable conclusion that the problem is a psychiatric one and/or that she cannot alone cope with the husband's behavior.

These processes are elaborated in the following analysis of the wives' responses.

METHOD OF DATA COLLECTION

Ideally, to study this problem one might like to interview the wives as they struggled with the developing illness. This is precluded, however, by the fact that the problem is not "visible" until psychiatric help is sought. The data, therefore, are the wives' reconstructions of their earlier experiences and accounts of their current reactions during the husband's hospitalization.

It is recognized that recollections of the prehospital period may well include systematic biases, such as distortions, omissions and increased organization and clarity. As a reliability check, a number of wives, just before the husband's discharge from the hospital, were asked again to describe the events and feelings of the prehospital period. In general, the two reports are markedly similar; often details are added and others are elaborated, but events tend to be substantially the same. While this check attests to the consistency of the wives' reporting, it has, of course, the contamination of overlearning which comes from many retellings of these events.

THE BEGINNINGS OF THE WIFE'S CONCERN

In the early interviews, the wife was asked to describe the beginnings of the problem which led to her husband's

TABLE 1 Reported Problem Behavior at Time of the Wife's Initial Concern and at Time of the Husband's Admission to Hospital

Problem Behavior	Initially		At Hospital Admission	
	Psychotics N	Psycho-neurotics N	Psychotics N	Psycho-neurotics N
Physical problems, complaints, worries	12	5	7	5
Deviations from routines of behavior	17	9	13	9
Expression of inadequacy or hopelessness	4	1	5	2
Nervous, irritable, worried	19	10	18	9
Withdrawal (verbal, physical)	5	1	6	1
Changes or accentuations in personality "traits" (slovenly, deceptive, forgetful)	5	6	7	6
Aggressive or assaultive and suicidal behavior	6	3	10	6
Strange or bizzare thoughts, delusions, hallucinations and strange behavior	11	1	15	2
Excessive drinking	4	7	3	4
Violation of codes of "decency"	3	1	3	2
Number of Respondents	23	10	23	10

hospitalization. ("Could you tell me when you first noticed that your husband was different?") This question was intended to provide an orientation for the wife to reconstruct the sequence and details of events and feelings which characterized the period preceding hospitalization. The interviewer provided a minimum of structuring in order that the wife's emphases and organization could be obtained.

In retrospect, the wives usually cannot pinpoint the time the husband's problem emerged. Neither can they clearly carve it out from the contexts of the husband's personality and family expectations. The subjective beginnings are seldom localized in a single strange or disturbing reaction on the husband's part but rather in the piling up of behavior and feelings.

We have seen this process for Mrs. F. There is a similar accumulation for the majority of wives, although the time periods and kinds of reported behavior vary. Thus, Mrs. Q. verbalizes the impact of a concentration of changes which occur within a period of a few weeks. Her explicit recognition of a problem comes when she adds up this array: her husband stays out late, doesn't eat or sleep, has obscene thoughts, argues with her, hits her, talks continuously, "cannot appreciate the beautiful scene" and "cannot appreciate me or the baby."

The problem behaviors reported by the wives are given in Table 1. They are ordered roughly; the behaviors listed first occurred primarily, but not exclusively, within the family; those later occurred in the more public domain. Whether the behavior is public or private does not seem to be a very significant factor in determining the wife's threshold for perceiving a problem.

There are many indications that these behaviors, now organized as a problem, have occurred many times before. This is especially true where alcoholism, physical complaints or personality "weaknesses" enter the picture. The wives indicate how, earlier, they had assimilated these characteristics into their own expectations in a variety of ways: the characteristics were congruent with their image of their husbands, they fitted their differential standards for men and women (men being less able to stand up to troubles), they had social or environmental justifications, etc.

When and how behavior becomes defined as problematic appears to be a highly individual matter. In some instances, it is when the wife can no longer manage her husband (he will no longer respond to her usual prods); in others, when his behavior destroys the status quo (when her goals and living routines are disorganized); and, in still others, when she cannot explain his behavior. One can speculate that her level of tolerance for

his behavior is a function of her specific personality needs and vulnerabilities, her personal and family value systems and the social supports and prohibitions regarding the husbands' symptomatic behavior.

INITIAL INTERPRETATIONS OF HUSBAND'S PROBLEM

Once the behavior is organized as a problem, it tends also to be interpreted as some particular kind of problem. More often than not, however, the husband's difficulties are not seen initially as manifestations of mental illness or even as emotional problems (Table 2).

Early interpretations often tend to be organized around physical difficulties (18% of cases) or "character" problems (27%). To a very marked degree, these orientations grow out of the wives' long-standing appraisals of their husbands as weak and ineffective or physically sick men. These wives describe their husbands as spoiled, lacking will-power, exaggerating little complaints and acting like babies. This is especially marked where

TABLE 2 Initial Interpretations of the Husband's Behavior

Interpretation	Psychotics N	Psychoneurotics N
Nothing really wrong	3	0
"Character" weakness and "controllable" behavior (lazy, mean, etc.)	6	3
Physical problem	6	0
Normal response to crisis	3	1
Mildly emotionally disturbed	1	2
"Something" seriously wrong	2	2
Serious emotional or mental problem	2	2
Number of Respondents	23	10

alcoholism complicates the husband's symptomatology. For example, Mrs. Y., whose husband was chronically alcoholic, aggressive and threatening to her, "raving," and who "chewed his nails until they almost bled," interprets his difficulty thus: "He was just spoiled rotten. He never outgrew it. He told me when he was a child he could get his own way if he insisted, and he is still that way." This quotation is the prototype of many of its kind.

Some wives, on the other hand, locate the problem in the environment. They expect the husband to change as the environmental crisis subsides. Several wives, while enumerating difficulties and concluding that there is a problem, in the same breath say it is really nothing to be concerned about.

Where the wives interpret the husband's difficulty as emotional in nature, they tend to be inconsistently "judgmental" and "understanding." The psychoneurotics are more often perceived initially by their wives as having emotional problems or as being mentally ill than are the psychotics. This is true even though many more clinical signs (bizarre, confused, delusional, aggressive and disoriented behavior) are reported by the wives of the psychotics than of the psychoneurotics.

Initial interpretations, whatever their content, are seldom held with great confidence by the wives. Many recall their early reactions to their husbands' behaviors as full of puzzling confusion and uncertainty. Something is wrong, they know, but, in general, they stop short of a firm explanation. Thus, Mrs. M. reports, "He was kind of worried. He was kind of worried before, not exactly worried . . ." She thought of his many physical complaints; she "racked" her "brain" and told her husband, "Of course, he didn't feel good." Finally, he stayed home from work with "no special complaints, just blah," and she "began to realize it was more deeply seated."

CHANGING PERCEPTIONS OF THE HUSBAND'S PROBLEM

The fog and uneasiness in the wife's early attempts to understand and cope with the husband's difficulties are followed, typically, by painful psychological struggles to resolve the uncertainties and to change the current situation. Usually, the wife's perceptions of the husband's problems undergo a series of changes before hospitalization is sought or effected, irrespective of the length of time elapsing between the beginnings of concern and hospitalization.

Viewing these changes macroscopically, three relatively distinct patterns of successive redefinitions of the husband's problems are apparent. One sequence (slightly less than half the cases) is characterized by a progressive intensification; interpretations are altered in a definite direction—toward seeing the problem as mental illness. Mrs. O. illustrates this progression. Initially, she thought her husband was "unsure of himself." "He was worried, too, about getting old." These ideas moved to: "He'd drink to forget. . . . He just didn't have the confidence. . . . He'd forget little things. . . . He'd wear a suit weeks on end if I didn't take it away from him. . . . He'd say nasty things." Then, when Mr. O. seemed "so confused," "to forget all kinds of things . . . where he'd come from . . . to go to work," and made "nasty, cutting remarks all the time," she began to think in terms of a serious personality disturbance. "I did think he knew that something was wrong . . . that he was sick. He was never any different this last while and I couldn't stand it any more. . . . You don't know what a relief it was . . ." (when he was hospitalized). The husband's drinking, his failure to be tidy, his nastiness, etc., lose significance in their own right. They move from emphasis to relief and are recast as signs of "something deeper," something that brought "it" on.

Some wives whose interpretations move in the direction of seeing their husbands as mentally ill hold conceptions of mental illness and of personality that do not permit assigning the husband all aspects of the sick role. Frequently, they use the interpretation of mental illness as an angry epithet or as a threatening prediction for the husband. This is exemplified in such references as: "I told him he should have his head examined," "I called him a half-wit," "I told him if he's not careful, he'll be a mental case." To many of these wives, the hospital is regarded as the "end of the road."

Other wives showing this pattern of change hold conceptions of emotional disturbance which more easily permit them to assign to their husbands the role of patient as the signs of illness become more apparent. They do not as often regard hospitalization in a mental hospital as the "last step." Nevertheless, their feelings toward their husbands may contain components equally as angry and rejecting as those of the wives with the less sophisticated ideas regarding mental illness.

A somewhat different pattern of sequential changes in interpreting the husband's difficulties (about one-fifth of the cases) is to be found among wives who appear to cast around for situationally and momentarily adequate explanations. As the situation changes or as the husband's behavior changes, these wives find reasons or excuses but lack an underlying or synthesizing theory. Successive interpretations tend to bear little relation to one another. Situational factors tend to lead them to seeing their husbands as mentally ill. Immediate, serious and direct physical threats or the influence of others may be the deciding factor. For example, a friend or employer may insist that the husband see a psychiatrist, and the wife goes along with the decision.

A third pattern of successive redefinitions (slightly less than one-third of the cases) revolves around an orientation outside the framework of emotional problems or mental illness. In these cases, the wife's specific explanations change but pivot around a denial that the husband is mentally ill.

A few wives seem not to change their interpretations about their husband's difficulties. They maintain the same explanation throughout the development of his illness, some within the psychiatric framework, others rigidly outside that framework.

Despite the characteristic shiftings in interpretations, in the group as a whole, there tend to be persisting underlying themes in the individual wife's perceptions that remain essentially unaltered. These themes are a function of her systems of thinking about normality and abnormality and about valued and devalued behavior.

THE PROCESS OF RECOGNIZING THE HUSBAND'S PROBLEM AS MENTAL ILLNESS

In the total situation confronting the wife, there are a number of factors, apparent in our data, which make it difficult for the wife to recognize and accept the husband's behavior in a mental-emotional-psychiatric framework. Many cross-currents seem to influence the process.

The husband's behavior itself is a fluctuating stimulus. He is not worried and complaining all of the time. His delusions and hallucinations may not persist. His hostility toward the wife may be followed by warm attentiveness. She has, then, the problem of deciding whether his "strange" behavior is significant. The greater saliency of one or the other of his responses at any moment of time depends in some degree upon the behavior sequence which has occurred most recently.

The relationship between husband and

wife also supplies a variety of images and contexts which can justify varied conclusions about the husband's current behavior. The wife is likely to adapt to behavior which occurs in their day to day relationships. Therefore, symptomatic reactions which are intensifications of long-standing response patterns become part of the fabric of life and are not easily disentangled as "symptomatic."

Communications between husband and wife regarding the husband's difficulties act sometimes to impede and sometimes to further the process of seeing the difficulties within a psychiatric framework. We have seen both kinds of influences in our data. Mr. and Mrs. F. were quite unable to communicate effectively about Mr. F.'s problems. On the one hand, he counters his wife's urging that he see a doctor with denials that anything is wrong. On the other hand, in his own way through his symptoms, he tries to communicate his problems, but she responds only to his verbalized statements, taking them at face value.

Mr. and Mrs. K. participate together quite differently, examining Mr. K.'s fears that he is being followed by the F.B.I., that their house has been wired and that he is going to be fired. His wife tentatively shares his suspicions. At the same time, they discuss the possibility of paranoid reactions.

The larger social context contributes, too, in the wife's perceptual tug of war. Others with whom she can compare her husband provide contrasts to his deviance, but others (Mr. F.'s nervous friends) also provide parallels to his problems. The "outsiders," seeing less of her husband, often discount the wife's alarm when she presses them for opinions. In other instances, the friend or employer, less adapted to or defended against the husband's symptoms, helps her to define his problem as psychiatric.

This task before the wife, of defining her husband's difficulties, can be conceptualized as an "overlapping" situation (in Lewin's terms), in which the relative potencies of the several effective influences fluctuate. The wife is responding to the various sets of forces simultaneously. Thus, several conclusions or interpretations of the problem are simultaneously "suspended in balance," and they shift back and forth in emphasis and relief. Seldom, however, does she seem to be balancing off clear-cut alternatives, such as physical versus mental. Her complex perceptions (even those of Mrs. F. who is extreme in misperceiving cues) are more "sophisticated" than the casual questioner might be led to conclude.

Thus far, we have ignored the personally threatening aspects of recognizing mental illness in one's spouse, and the defenses which are mobilized to meet this threat. It is assumed that it is threatening to the wife not only to realize that the husband is mentally ill but further to consider her own possible role in the development of the disorder, to give up modes of relating to her husband that may have had satisfactions for her and to see a future as the wife of a mental patient. Our data provide systematic information only on the first aspect of this problem, on the forms of defense against the recognition of the illness. One or more of the following defenses are manifested in three-fourths of our cases.

The most obvious form of defense in the wife's response is the tendency to *normalize* the husband's neurotic and psychotic symptoms. His behavior is explained, justified or made acceptable by seeing it also in herself or by assuring herself that the particular behavior occurs again and again among persons who are not ill. Illustrative of this reaction is the wife who reports her husband's hallucinations and assures herself that this is normal because she herself heard voices when she was in the menopause. Another wife responds to her husband's physical complaints, fears, worries, nightmares, and delusions with "A lot of normal people think there's something wrong when there isn't. I think men are that way; his father is that way."

When behavior cannot be normalized, it can be made to seem less severe or less important in a total picture than an outsider might see it. By finding some grounds for the behavior or something explainable about it, the wife achieves at least momentary *attenuation* of the seriousness of it. Thus, Mrs. F. is able to discount partly the strangeness of her husband's descriptions of the worms growing out of his grandfather's mustache when she recalls his watching the worms in the fish bowl. There may be attenuation, too, by seeing the behavior as "momentary." ("You could talk him out of his ideas.") or by rethinking the problem and seeing it in a different light.

By *balancing* acceptable with unacceptable behavior or "strange" with "normal" behavior, some wives can conclude that the husband is not seriously disturbed. Thus, it is very important to Mrs. R. that her husband kissed her goodbye before he left for the hospital. This response cancels out his hostile feelings toward her and the possibility that he is mentally ill. Similarly, Mrs. V. reasons that her husband cannot be "out of his mind" for he had reminded her of things she must not forget to do when he went to the hospital.

Defense sometimes amounts to a thorough-going *denial*. This takes the form of denying that the behavior perceived can be interpreted in an emotional or psychiatric framework. In some instances, the wife reports vividly on such behavior as repeated thoughts of suicide, efforts to harm her and the like and sums it up with "I thought it was just a whim." Other wives bend their efforts toward proving the implausibility of mental illness.

After the husband is hospitalized, it might be expected that these denials would decrease to a negligible level. This is not wholly the case, however. A breakdown of the wives' interpretations just following the husband's admission to the hospital shows that roughly a fifth still interpret their husband's behavior in another framework than that of a serious emotional problem or mental illness. Another fifth ambivalently and sporadically interpret the behavior as an emotional or mental problem. The remainder hold relatively stable interpretations within this framework.

After the husband has been hospitalized for some time, many wives reflect on their earlier tendencies to avoid a definition of mental illness. Such reactions are almost identically described by these wives: "I put it out of my mind—I didn't want to face it—anything but a mental illness." "Maybe I was aware of it. But you know you push things away from you and keep hoping." "Now you think maybe you should have known about it. Maybe you should have done more than you did and that worries me."

DISCUSSION

The findings on the perceptions of mental illness by the wives of patients are in line with general findings in studies of perception. Behavior which is unfamiliar and incongruent and unlikely in terms of current expectations and needs will not be readily recognized, and stressful or threatening stimuli will tend to be misperceived or perceived with difficulty or delay.

We have attempted to describe the factors which help the wife maintain a picture of her husband as normal and those which push her in the direction of accepting a psychiatric definition of his problem. The kind and intensity of the symptomatic behavior, its persistence over time, the husband's interpretation of his problem, interpretations and defining actions of others, including professionals, all play a role. In addition, the wives come to this experience with different concepts of psychological processes and of the nature of emotional illness, itself, as well as with different tolerances for emotional disturbance. As we have seen, there are also many supports in society for maintaining a picture of normality concerning the husband's behavior. Social pressures and expectations not only keep *behavior* in line but to a great extent *perceptions* of behavior as well. . . .

Family Processes and Becoming a Mental Patient

HAROLD SAMPSON
SHELDON L. MESSINGER
ROBERT D. TOWNE

Becoming a mental patient is not a simple and direct outcome of "mental illness"; nor is hospitalization in a mental institution, when and if it comes, the automatic result of a professional opinion. Persons who are, by clinical standards, grossly disturbed, severely impaired in their functioning, and even overtly psychotic may remain in the community for long periods without being "recognized" as "mentally ill" and without benefit of psychiatric or other professional attention. It is clear that becoming a mental patient is a socially structured event.[1] The research reported here is directed to increasing our understanding of the nature and significance of this structuring as it mediates the relations between individuals and the more formal means of social control. The re-

search explores (*a*) the relationship between patterns of family means for coping with the deviant behavior of a member who later becomes a mental patient and (*b*) efforts of the future patient or members of his family to secure professional help.

The broad nature of this latter relationship may be inferred from a number of published findings. Yarrow and her colleagues have documented the monumental capacity of family members, before hospitalization, to overlook, minimize and explain away evidence of profound disturbance in an intimate.[2]

The post-hospital studies of the Simmons group have suggested that high "tolerance for deviance" in certain types of families is a critical determinant of the likelihood of poorly functioning and

Reprinted from *The American Journal of Sociology*, Vol. 68 (July 1962), 88–96, by permission of The University of Chicago Press and the authors. Copyright 1962 by The University of Chicago Press.

This report is based on a study carried out by the California Department of Mental Hygiene and partially supported by Grant No. 3M-9124 from the National Institute of Mental Health.

[1] Erving Goffman, in "The Moral Career of the Mental Patient," *Psychiatry*, XXII (May, 1959), 123–42, discusses a variety of "career contingencies" that may intervene between deviant behavior and hospitalization for mental illness. Also see the articles in *Journal of Social Issues*, XI (1955), ed. John A. Clausen and Marian Radke Yarrow, under the general title of "The Impact of Mental Illness on the Family." August B. Hollingshead and Frederick C. Redlich (*Social Class and Mental Illness: A Community Study* [New York: John Wiley & Sons, Inc., 1958], chap. vi, "Paths to the Psychiatrist") also emphasize this point.

[2] Marian Radke Yarrow, Charlotte Green Schwartz, Harriet S. Murphy, and Leila Calhoun Deasy, "The Psychological Meaning of Mental Illness in the Family," *Journal of Social Issues*, XI (1955), 12–24. Also see Charlotte Green Schwartz, "Perspectives on

sometimes frankly psychotic former patients avoiding rehospitalization.[3] Myers and Roberts found that few mental patients or their families sought or used professional assistance before hospitalization until the problems they encountered became unmanageable.[4] Whitmer and Conover reported that the occasion for hospitalization was ordinarily not recognition of "mental illness" by the patient or his family but inability to cope with disturbed behavior within the family.[5]

These observations and our own permit two inferences. First, both before and after hospitalization some type of accommodative pattern ordinarily evolves between a disturbed person and his family which permits or forces him to remain in the community in spite of severe difficulties. Second, it is the disruption of this pattern which eventually brings a disturbed person to psychiatric attention.[6] An investigation of typical family accommodations to the deviant behavior of future patients, and how these accommodations collapse, should therefore contribute to our understanding of the ways in which individuals and the intimate social networks of which they are members are rendered less and more accessible to institutionalized devices of social control. Specifically, it should provide us with a glimpse of those dynamic family processes which determine a future mental patient's accessibility to community, particularly psychiatric intervention; these same processes determine the accessibility of the family. It should also contribute to our understanding of the meaning of such intervention to the future patient and his family. Such family accommodations pose strategic problems for the persons who constitute and man community remedial facilities. These are problems seldom taken into explicit or systematic account by such persons problems beyond but related to the pathology of the patient.

We shall be concerned here with two phases in the relationship between the future patient and his family and with the connections between these phases and the course of events leading to hospitalization. The first phase consists of the

---

Deviance—Wives' Definitions of Their Husbands' Mental Illness," *Psychiatry*, XX (August, 1957), 275–91; Hollingshead and Redlich, *op. cit.*, esp. pp. 172–79; and Elaine Cumming and John Cumming, *Closed Ranks* (Cambridge, Mass.: Harvard University Press, 1957), esp. pp. 91–108.

[3] See Ozzie G. Simmons, *After Hospitalization: The Mental Patient and His Family* (Hogg Foundation for Mental Health, n.d.) and the several studies by the Simmons group cited there.

[4] Jerome K. Myers and Bertram H. Roberts, *Family and Class Dynamics* (New York: John Wiley & Sons, Inc., 1959), pp. 213–20. These findings also suggest that lower-class families are better able to contain an extremely disturbed person for long periods of time than are middle-class families; the latter call on outside help more rapidly when "major psychotic decompensation" occurs. This would follow from the argument presented by Talcott Parsons and Renée Fox in "Illness, Therapy, and the Modern Urban American Family," *Journal of Social Issues*, VIII (1953), 31–44.

[5] Carroll A. Whitmer and Glenn C. Conover, "A Study of Critical Incidents in the Hospitalization of the Mentally Ill," *Journal of the National Association of Social Work*, IV (January, 1959), 89–94 (see also Edwin C. Wood, John M. Rakusin, and Emanuel Morse, "Interpersonal Aspects of Psychiatric Hospitalization," *Archives of General Psychiatry*, III [December, 1960], 632–41).

[6] Another inference we have made, and which we discuss elsewhere, is that an important set of effects of community devices of social control pertain to family patterns of accommodation. In important ways, it is through these that individuals are controlled, rather than by direct action (Harold Sampson, Sheldon L. Messinger, and Robert D. Towne, "The Mental Hospital and Family Accommodations" [unpublished manuscript, 1962]).

evolution of a pattern of accommodation within the family to behavioral deviance on the part of the future patient.[7] The second phase consists in the disruption of this pattern of accommodation. Our observations are derived from a study of seventeen families in which the wife-mother was hospitalized for the first time in a large state mental institution and therein diagnosed as schizophrenic.[8] We established a research relationship with both patient and spouse at the time of admission and continued to see them regularly and frequently throughout hospitalization, and for varying periods extending to more than two years following first release. We conducted about fifty interviews with the members of each marital pair, including typically one or more joint interviews. Other relatives, psychiatrists, physicians, hospital personnel, and other remedial agents who had become involved with the patient or family over the years were also interviewed. Interview materials were supplemented by direct observation at home and in the hospital, and by such medical and social records as we could locate and gain permission to abstract.

These methods, which are described more fully elsewhere,[9] enabled us to reconstruct the vicissitudes of these marital families from courtship through marriage, child-bearing and child-rearing, eventual hospitalization of the wife, and well into the period following the patient's first release. We shall focus here on a longitudinal analysis of two patterns of accommodation which evolved between these women and their families prior to hospitalization and the disruption of these patterns. The patterns are examplified by eleven and four cases, respectively; two of the seventeen families do not appear to be adequately characterized by either pattern. In order to present the patterns in some detail, our analysis will be developed in terms of selected families exhibiting each type of accommodation. This does not exhaust the empirical variety to be found even in the limited number of cases studied here. In the concluding section, however, emphasis will be placed on common patterns of relationship between future mental patients and their immediate interpersonal communities, as well as on the conditions under which these patterns deteriorate and collapse.

THE UNINVOLVED HUSBAND AND SEPARATE WORLDS

In the first situation, exemplified by eleven families, the marital partners and their children lived together as a rela-

[7] This phase emphasizes one side of a complicated reciprocity between family relations and the deviance of family members. We have focused on the other side of this reciprocity —family relations as they sustain and promote deviant behavior—elsewhere (see Robert D. Towne, Sheldon L. Messinger, and Harold Sampson, "Schizophrenia and the Marital Family: Accommodations to Symbiosis," *Family Process* (forthcoming), and Robert D. Towne, Harold Sampson, and Sheldon L. Messinger, "Schizophrenia and the Marital Family: Identification Crises," *Journal of Nervous and Mental Diseases*, CXXXIII [November, 1961], 423–29). There is a large and growing literature on this topic, particularly as it concerns schizophrenia, much of which is referred to in the various citations to be found in *The Etiology of Schizophrenia*, ed. by Don D. Jackson (New York: Basic Books, Inc., 1960).

[8] Detailed characteristics of the families studied may be found in Harold Sampson, Sheldon L. Messinger, and Robert D. Towne, "The Mental Hospital and Marital Family Ties," *Social Problems*, IX (Fall, 1961), 141–55. In two of seventeen cases, a brief psychiatric hospitalization in a county hospital had occurred earlier; in a third case, the woman had been hospitalized in a private sanitarium for one month earlier in the same year she entered the state institution.

[9] *Ibid.*

tively independent, self-contained nuclear family, but the marital relationship was characterized by mutual withdrawal and the construction of separate worlds of compensatory involvement. At some point during the marriage, usually quite early, one or both of the partners had experienced extreme dissatisfaction with the marriage. This was ordinarily accompanied by a period of violent, open discord, although in other cases, the dissatisfaction was expressed only indirectly, through reduced communication with the marital partner. Whatever the means of managing the dissatisfaction when it occurred, in each of these families the partners withdrew and each gradually instituted a separate world. The husband became increasingly involved in his work or in other interests outside the marital relationship. The wife became absorbed in private concerns about herself and her children. The partners would rarely go out together, rarely participate together in dealing with personal or family problems, and seldom communicate to each other about their more pressing interests, wishes, and concerns. The marriage would continue in this way for some time without divorce, without separation, and without movement toward greater closeness. The partners had achieved a type of marital accommodation based on interpersonal isolation, emotional distance, and lack of explicit demands upon each other. This accommodation represented an alternative to both divorce and a greater degree of marital integration.

It is a particularly important characteristic of this type of family organization that pathological developments in the wives were for a time self-sustaining. The wife's distress, withdrawal, or deviant behavior did not lead to immediate changes of family life but rather to an intensification of mutual withdrawal. In this setting, the wives became acutely disturbed or even psychotic, without, for a time, very much affecting the pre-existing pattern of family life. This is exemplified in the following cases:

In the evenings, Mr. Urey worked on his car in the basement while his wife remained upstairs, alone with her sleeping children, engaged in conversations and arguments with imaginary others. This situation continued for at least two years before Mrs. Urey saw a psychiatrist on the recommendation of her family physician. Another two years elapsed before Mrs. Urey was hospitalized. During this period, Mr. Urey became ever less concerned with his wife's behavior, accepting it as a matter of course, and concerned himself with "getting ahead" in his job.

For two years prior to hospitalization, Mrs. Rand was troubled by various somatic complaints, persistent tension, difficulty in sleeping, a vague but disturbing conviction that she was a sinner, and intermittent states of acute panic. Mr. Rand was minimally aware of her distress. He worked up to fourteen hours a day, including weekends, in his store, and eventually a second job took him out of the home three evenings a week. On those infrequent occasions when his wife's worries forced themselves on his attention, he dismissed them curtly as absurd, and turned once again to his own affairs.

In these families the patterned response to distress, withdrawal, or illness in the wife was further withdrawal, by the husband, resulting in increasing distance between, and disengagement of, the marital partners. These developments were neither abrupt nor entirely consistent, but the trend of interaction in these families was toward mutual alienation and inaccessibility of each partner to the other. In this situation, early involvement of the wife in a professional treatment situation was limited by her own withdrawal and difficulty in taking the initiative for any sustained course of action in the real world, as well as by the husband's detachment.

This pattern of mutual withdrawal eventually became intolerable to one or the other partner, pressure for a change was brought to bear, and the family suffered an acute crisis. In some cases, pressure for change was initiated by the husband. In other cases, such pressure was initiated by the wife in the form of increasing agitation, somatic and psychic complaints, and repeated verbal and behavioral communications that she was unable to go on. However the pre-hospital crisis was initiated, and whether it signaled a desire for increased or reduced involvement by the initiating partner, the change indicated an incipient collapse of the former pattern of accommodation.

In four of the eleven cases considered here, the pre-hospital crisis was primarily precipitated by a shift in the husband's "tolerance for deviance." In two of these cases, the wives had been chronically and pervasively withdrawn from role performances and at least periodically psychotic. One husband, in the midst of job insecurities and a desire to move to another state to make a new start, pressed his wife to assume more responsibility. Another husband, approaching forty years of age, reassessed his life and decided that the time had come to rid himself of a wife whom he had long considered "a millstone around my neck." These husbands sought medical or psychiatric assistance specifically to exclude their wives from the family; the two wives were passively resistant to hospitalization. The explicit attitude of the husbands was that they wished the hospital to take their wives off their hands.

In the other two cases, the disruption of the earlier accommodation was associated with the establishment, by the husband, of a serious extra-marital liaison. Here, as in the two cases referred to above, there appeared to be no marked change in the wife's conduct prior to this indication of a desire by the husband for total withdrawal.

Virtually identical family processes were apparent in those cases where the manifest illness of the wife was itself the source of pressure for change, the harbinger of the collapse of the prior marital accommodation. The wife's illness intruded itself into family life, at first with limited impact, but then more insistently, like a claim which has not been paid or a message that must be repeated until it is acknowledged. The wife's "complaints" came to be experienced by the husband as, literally, complaints to him, as demands upon him for interest, concern, and involvement. These husbands, however, uniformly initially struggled to preserve the earlier pattern, that is, to maintain uninvolvement in the face of demands which implicitly pressed for their active concern. Thus, as the pre-hospital crisis unfolded, the wife's manifest illness assumed the interpersonal significance of a demand for involvement, and the husband's difficulty in recognizing her as seriously disturbed had the interpersonal significance of a resistance to that demand. The excerpt cited earlier from the Rand case illustrates this process if we add to it the observation that during these two years Mrs. Rand's difficulties recurrently came to the husband's attention in the form of momentary crises which compelled at least the response of curt dismissal.

In this situation, the husband initially assumed a passive or indifferent attitude toward his wife's obtaining professional help. But if she became involved with a psychiatrist, physician, minister, or social worker who took some interest in her life situation, the husband became concerned with the treatment in a negative way. The treatment "wasn't necessary," it "wasn't helping," it "cost too much money." In addition to these deprecations was a hint of alarm that the treatment would challenge the husband's pattern of uninvolvement.[10] For example, Mr. Rand, whose working schedule was mentioned earlier, worried that his wife's psychiatrist might support her complaint that he did not spend enough time at home. Thus the involvement of the wife with a psychiatrically oriented helper was experienced by the husband, at least initially, as a claim upon himself—for money, for concern, and most centrally, for reinvolvement. We have reported elsewhere[11] that there is some basis for this feeling. The treatment process, especially during hospitalization, does tend to induct the husband into the role of the responsible relative, and thereby presses for the reestablishment of reciprocal expectations which had been eroded in the earlier family accommodation.

In most of these cases, these processes led to more extreme deviance on the part of the wife which eventually came to the attention of the larger community, thereby resulting in hospitalization. For example, Mrs. Urey, who had been actively psychotic for some time, was hospitalized only after she set fire to her home. In brief, the wife's distress is at first experienced by the husband as an unwarranted demand for his reinvolvement in the marital relationship, he withdraws further, and her behavior becomes more deviant.

We may conclude this section with a few more general remarks. The pre-hospital crisis, in each of these cases, marked, and was part of, the disruption of a pattern of accommodation which had been established between the marital partners. The disruption was in effect initiated by one of the partners and resisted by the other.[12] The former accommodation and the way in which it came to be disrupted were important determinants of the processes of "recognizing" the wife as mentally ill, of seeking and using professional help, and of moving the wife from the status of a distressed and behaviorally deviant person within the community to that of a mental patient. These processes, in fact, can only be understood within the context of these family patterns. The problems of early intervention in cases of serious mental illness and of effective intervention in the later crises which ordinarily do come to psychiatric attention cannot even be formulated meaningfully without consideration of these interpersonal processes which determine when, why, and how sick persons become psychiatric patients.

THE OVERINVOLVED MOTHER AND THE MARITAL FAMILY TRIAD

In a contrasting situation found in four cases, the marital partners and their children did not establish a relatively self-contained nuclear family. Rather, family life was organized chronically or periodically around the presence of a maternal figure who took over the wife's domestic and child-rearing functions.[13]

This organization of family life was a

---

[10] In one case, the psychiatrist urged the husband to seek treatment for himself.

[11] Sampson *et al.*, "The Mental Hospital and Marital Family Ties," *op. cit.*

[12] Wood, Rakusin, and Morse, *op. cit.*, have arrived at a related conclusion on the basis of an analysis of the circumstances of admission of forty-eight patients to a Veterans Administration hospital. "There is also evidence to suggest that hospitalization can for some patients be a way of demanding that those close to them change their behavior, just as it can be an expression by relatives that they are dissatisfied with the patient's behavior."

[13] This person was the wife's mother in three cases, her mother-in-law in the fourth. This distinction is not critical in the present context, and we shall refer to "the wife's mother," etc.

conjoint solution to interlocking conflicts of the wife, husband, and mother. In brief, these mothers were possessive and intrusive, motivated to perpetuate their daughters' dependency, and characteristically disposed to assume the "helpful" role in a symbiotic integration with her. The daughters ambivalently pressed for the establishment or maintenance of a dependent relationship with their mothers and struggled to break the inner and outer claims of the maternal attachment. The husbands responded to anxieties of their own about the demands of heterosexual intimacy and marital responsibility, as well as their own ambivalent strivings toward maternal figures, by alternately supporting and protesting the wives' dependence on the maternal figure. The resulting family organization, in which the mother was intermittently or continuously called upon for major assistance, represented an alternative to both a relatively self-contained, independent nuclear family and to marital disruption with the wife returning to live within the parental family.

In direct contrast to the family accommodation described in the preceding section, the wives in "triadic" families did not quietly drift into increasing isolation and autism. Here, sickness or withdrawal by the wife were occasions for intense maternal concern and involvement. This development was ordinarily abetted by the husband. The resulting situation, however, would come to be experienced as threatening by the wife. She would come to view her mother as interfering with her marriage and her fulfilment of her own maternal responsibilities, as restricting her freedom, and as preventing her from growing up. At this point a small but often violent rebellion would ensue, and the husband would now participate with his wife to exclude the mother from family life. Such cycles of reliance on the mother followed by repudiation of her recurred over the years with only minor variations.

This accommodation complicated seeking and using professional help, but in a distinctively different way than in the family setting depicted earlier. Here, the family accommodation included this patterned response to withdrawal, illness, or distress in the wife: the mother replaced the wife in her domestic and child-care functions, and established with the wife a characteristic integration involving a helpless one who needs care and a helpful one who administers it; the husband withdrew to the periphery of the family system, leaving the wife and mother bound in a symbiotic interdependency.

In this patterned response, outside help was not simply superfluous but constituted an actual threat to the existing interdependency of mother and daughter (by implying that it was inadequate, unnecessary, or even harmful), whereas in the type of family accommodation previously described, treatment was experienced as a threat to the husband's uninvolvement; here, treatment was a threat to the mother's involvement.

It was the failure of this family accommodation which led to the wife's contact with the physician or psychiatrist. This failure occurred when, simultaneously, the wife rebelled against the maternal attachment but could not establish with her husband the previously effective alternative of temporary repudiation of that attachment. The following example demonstrates these processes:

Mrs. Yale became anxious, confused, and unable to cope with the demands of daily life in the context of increasing withdrawal by her husband combined with increasing inner and outer pressure for reinvolvement with her mother. Her mother, Mrs. Brown, was living with the marital family, and remaining by the side of her troubled daughter night and day. Mr. Yale had become increasingly involved in shared interests with a circle of male friends, and felt disaffected from family life.

Mrs. Brown later characterized this period to the research interviewer: "I think Mary resented me because I tried to help and do things for her. She didn't want me to help with her work. She didn't seem to want me around—sort of resented me. She kept saying she wanted to be on her own and that she didn't have confidence because I was always doing things for her. She even resented me doing the dishes. I just wanted to help out." At this point, Mrs. Brown considered her daughter to be seriously emotionally disturbed, and thought psychiatric help would be advisable.

In such cases, the behavior which led family members to doubt the young woman's sanity consisted of hostility, resentment, and accusatory outbursts directed toward the mother. In these violent outbursts toward the maternal figure, the daughter was indeed "not herself." It was at just this point that the daughter's behavior constituted a disruption of the former family pattern of accommodation and led toward involvement with outside helpers. The mother might now view outside helpers as potential allies in re-establishing the earlier interdependency. The psychiatrist, however, was unlikely to fulfil the mother's expectations in this regard, and then he became an heir to the husband in the triadic situation, a potential rival to the mother-daughter symbiosis.

Shortly after outpatient treatment began, Mrs. Brown took her daughter on an extended vacation which effectively interrupted the treatment, detached the daughter from her incipient attachment to the psychiatrist, and re-established the pattern of mother-daughter interdependency with the husband at the periphery of involvement.

We may summarize, then, certain connections between this type of family accommodation and the use of professional help prior to hospitalization. The initial response of the family to the wife's distress was to attempt to reinstate a familiar pattern: a drawing together of mother and daughter in symbiotic interdependency, and a withdrawal of the husband to the periphery of the family. This accommodation was disrupted by the eruption of the daughter's formerly ego-alien resentment toward her mother, and at this point the latter was likely to view physicians or psychiatrists as potential allies in restoring the former equilibrium. The psychiatrist, however, was unlikely to play this part and became, for the mother, a rival to the interdependency. For the daughter, also, this meaning of treatment invested it with the dangerous promise of a possible separation from the maternal figure. In this drama, the husband was likely to play a relatively passive if not a discouraging role, affording the wife little if any support in what she experienced as a threatening and disloyal involvement outside the family.

The way in which the hospitalization of the wife came about, in the collapse of this family accommodation, also provided contrasts to the processes depicted in the preceding section. As the prehospital crises developed, the wife sought to withdraw from continuing intolerable conflict in the triadic situation. At first, the wife felt impelled to choose between regressive dependency on a maternal figure and the claims of her marital family, but was unable to either relinquish the former or achieve inner and outer support for the latter. Both alternatives were transiently affirmed and repudiated in the period preceding hospitalization, but in time she came to feel alienated from *both* mother and husband, and driven toward increasing *psychic* withdrawal. This process did not resolve her conflicts or remove her from the triadic field, and in time she herself pushed for physical removal.

Thus, in two of the four triadic cases, the wife herself, with a feeling of desperation, explicitly requested hospitalization. In a third case, the disturbed wife was brought to a psychiatrist in the company of both mother and husband, refused to return home with them after the appointment, and was thereupon hospitalized. In the fourth case, the wife was initially co-operative to a hospitalization plan, but equivocation by the husband and psychiatrist delayed action, and the wife gave herself and her daughter an overdose of drugs, thereby precipitating the hospitalization. This last case resembles the most common pattern described in the preceding section, in which the wife is driven to extreme deviance which comes to the attention of the larger community and compels hospitalization. But the secondary pattern, in which a husband takes primary initiative for hospitalizing a reluctant wife because she has become a "millstone around my neck," was entirely absent.

DISCUSSION

The career of the mental patient and his family ordinarily comes to the attention of treatment personnel during the course of an "unmanageable" emergency and fades from view when that emergency is in some way resolved. Prior to this public phase of the crisis, and often again after it, the disturbance of the patient is contained within a community setting. It is the collapse of accommodative patterns *between* the future patient and his interpersonal community which renders the situation unmanageable and ushers in the public phase of the pre-hospital (or rehospitalization) crisis.

Our analysis has been addressed to ways in which two particular organizations of family life have contained pathological processes, to the ways in which these organizations were disrupted, and to the links between family dynamics and

recognition of illness, seeking and using professional help, and the circumstances of mental hospitalization. The analysis carries us beyond the observations that families often "tolerate" deviant behavior, may resist "recognition" that the future patient is seriously disturbed, and may be reluctant to use help, toward a systematic view of "typical" accommodations around deviance and typical patterns of crisis.

It is, of course, by no means evident how typical the patterns we have described may be. Although the analysis is confined to certain marital family organizations and does not entirely exhaust our own empirical materials, we suggest that the presentation does touch upon two common situations encountered in work with the mentally ill and their families. In the first situation, the future patient and his immediate interpersonal community move from each other, effect patterns of uninvolvement, and reciprocate withdrawal by withdrawal. The future patient moves, and is moved, toward exclusion from interpersonal ties and from any meaningful links to a position in communal reality. This situation, as we have seen, is compatible with very high "tolerance for deviant behavior," which may permit an actively psychotic patient to remain *in* the community while not psychosocially *of* it.

The accommodation may be disrupted by a shift in the "tolerance" of the interpersonal community, however determined,[14] or from the side of the future patient by increasing agitation which signals an attempt to break out of inner and outer isolation. Here, hospitalization is a possible route toward further disengagement of the patient from his interpersonal community, or conversely, toward re-establishment of reciprocal expectations compatible with re-engage-

---

[14] The determinants may be extraneous to inherent family processes. Thus, in a case not included in the present sample, the movement of a family from farm to city altered the family's capacity to retain a psychotic young man and precipitated his hospitalization.

ment. Whatever the outcome, a strategic therapeutic problem is posed by the chronic pattern of mutual disinvolvement and withdrawal.

In the second situation, the future patient and a member of his immediate interpersonal community become locked in mutual involvement, effect patterns of intense interdependency, and reciprocate withdrawal by concern. The future patient moves and is moved toward a bond in which interlocking needs tie the participants together rather than isolate them. This situation is also compatible with high tolerance for deviant behavior, but here because the deviance has become a necessary component of the family integration. It is this type of family process, rather than the first type, which has attracted most psychiatric interest,[15] although there is no reason from our data to suppose that it is the more common.

In the cases observed the disruption of this accommodation took the form of an ego-alien movement by the future patient against the claims of the overwhelming attachment. Here, hospitalization is at once a route of escape from intolerable conflict in the interpersonal community, and a potential pathway toward re-establishing the earlier pattern of accommodation. The strategic therapeutic problem posed is the contrasting one of modification of a chronic pattern of intense involvement.

The observations reported do not yield precise knowledge as to how psychiatric intervention might routinely be brought about early in the development of a serious mental illness, whether or when this is advisable, and how intervention might be more effective later on. The observations indicate, rather, that we must confront these questions in their real complexity, and investigate more closely and persistently than heretofore the characteristic ways in which families cope with severe psychiatric disturbances, the ways in which these intra-family mechanisms are disrupted, and the significance of the family dynamics which form the crucial background of the eventual encounter between patient and clinician.

[15] See Jackson (ed.), *op. cit.*

The Adjustment of the Family to the Crisis of Alcoholism

JOAN K. JACKSON

. . . Over a 3-year period, the present investigator has been an active participant in the Alcoholics Anonymous Auxiliary in Seattle. This group is composed partly of women whose husbands are or were members of Alcoholics Anonymous, and partly of women whose husbands are excessive drinkers but have never contacted Alcoholics Anonymous. At a typical meeting one fifth would be the wives of Alcoholics Anonymous members who have been sober for some time; the husbands of another fifth would have recently joined the fellowship; the remainder would be equally divided between those whose husbands were "on and off" the Alcoholics Anonymous program and those whose husbands had as yet not had any contact with Alcoholics Anonymous.

At least an hour and a half of each formal meeting of this group is taken up with a frank discussion of the current family problems of the members. As in other meetings of Alcoholics Anonymous the questions are posed by describing the situation which gives rise to the problem and the answers are a narration of the personal experiences of other wives who have had a similar problem, rather than direct advice. Verbatim shorthand notes have been taken of all discussions, at the request of the group, who also make use of the notes for the group's purposes. Informal contact has been maintained with past and present members. In the past 3 years 50 women have been members of this group.

The families represented by these women are at present in many different stages of adjustment and have passed through several stages during the past few years. The continuous contact over a prolonged period permits generalizations about processes and changes in family adjustments.

In addition, in connection with research on hospitalized alcoholics, many of their wives have been interviewed. The interviews with the hospitalized alcoholics, as with male members of Alcoholics Anonymous, have also provided information on family interactions. Further information has been derived from another group of wives, not connected with Alcoholics Anonymous, and from probation officers, social workers and court officials.

The following presentation is limited insofar as it deals only with families

Reprinted from *Quarterly Journal of Studies on Alcohol*, Vol. 15 (December 1954), pp. 564–586.

From the Department of Psychiatry, University of Washington School of Medicine, Seattle, Washington. This report is part of an alcoholism project at the University of Washington which has been supported by the State of Washington Research Fund under Initiative 171.

seeking help for the alcoholism of the husband. Other families are known to have solved the problem through divorce, often without having attempted to help the alcoholic member first. Others never seek help and never separate. There were no marked differences between the two groups seeking help, one through the hospital and one through the A.A. Auxiliary. The wives of hospitalized alcoholics gave a history of the family crisis similar to that given by women in the Auxiliary.

A second limitation is that only the families of male alcoholics are dealt with. It is recognized that the findings cannot be generalized to the families of alcoholic women without further research. Due to differences between men and women in their roles in the family as well as in the pattern of drinking, it would be expected that male and female alcoholics would in some ways have a different effect on family structure and function.

A third limitation is imposed for the sake of clarity and brevity: only the accounts of the wives of their attempts to stabilize their family adjustments will be dealt with. For any complete picture, the view of the alcoholic husband would also have to be included.

It must be emphasized that this paper deals with the definitions of the family situations by the wives, rather than with the actual situation. It has been noted that frequently wife and husband do not agree on what has occurred. The degree to which the definition of the situation by the wife or husband correlates with actual behavior is a question which must be left for further research.

The families represented in this study are from the middle and lower classes. The occupations of the husbands prior to excessive drinking include small business owners, salesmen, business executives, skilled and semiskilled workers. Prior to marriage the wives have been nurses, secretaries, teachers, saleswomen, cooks

or waitresses. The economic status of the childhood families of these husbands and wives ranged from very wealthy to very poor.

METHOD

From the records of discussions of the Alcoholics Anonymous Auxiliary, the statements of each wife were extracted and arranged in a time sequence. Notes on informal contacts were added at the point in the sequence where they occurred. The interviews with the wives of hospitalized alcoholics were similarly treated. These working records on individual families were then examined for uniformities of behavior and for regularities in changes over time.

The similarities in the process of adjustment to an alcoholic family member are presented here as stages of variable duration. It should be stressed that only the similarities are dealt with. Although the wives have shared the patterns dealt with here, there have been marked differences in the length of time between stages, in the number of stages passed through up to the present time, and in the relative importance to the family constellation of any one type of behavior. For example, all admitted nagging but the amount of nagging was variable.

When the report of this analysis was completed it was read before a meeting of the Auxiliary with a request for correction of any errors in fact or interpretation. Corrections could be presented either anonymously or publicly from the floor. Only one correction was suggested and has been incorporated. The investigator is convinced that her relationship with the group is such that there would be no reticence about offering corrections. Throughout her contact with this group her role has been that of one who is being taught, very similar to the role of the new member. The over-all response of the group to the presentation indicated that the members individually felt that they had been portrayed accurately.

The sense of having similar problems and similar experiences is indicated also in the reactions of new members to the Auxiliary's summarization of the notes of their discussions. Copies of these summaries are given to new members, who commonly state that they find it a relief to see that their problems are far from unique and that there are methods which successfully overcome them.

STATEMENT OF THE PROBLEM

For purposes of this presentation, the family is seen as involved in a cumulative crisis. All family members behave in a manner which they hope will resolve the crisis and permit a return to stability. Each member's action is influenced by his previous personality structure, by his previous role and status in the family group, and by the history of the crisis and its effects on his personality, roles and status up to that point. Action is also influenced by the past effectiveness of that particular action as a means of social control before and during the crisis. The behavior of family members in each phase of the crisis contributes to the form which the crisis takes in the following stages and sets limits on possible behavior in subsequent stages.

Family members are influenced, in addition, by the cultural definitions of alcoholism as evidence of weakness, inadequacy or sinfulness; by the cultural prescriptions for the roles of family members; and by the cultural values of family solidarity, sanctity and self-sufficiency. Alcoholism in the family poses a situation defined by the culture as shameful but for the handling of which there are no prescriptions which are effective or which permit direct action not in con-

flict with other cultural prescriptions. While in crises such as illness or death the family members can draw on cultural definitions of appropriate behavior for procedures which will terminate the crisis, this is not the case with alcoholism in the family. The cultural view has been that alcoholism is shameful and should not occur. Only recently has any information been offered to guide families in their behavior toward their alcoholic member and, as yet, this information resides more in technical journals than in the media of mass communication. Thus, in facing alcoholism, the family is in an unstructured situation and must find the techniques for handling it through trial and error.

STAGES IN FAMILY ADJUSTMENT TO AN ALCOHOLIC MEMBER

The Beginning of the Marriage. At the time marriage was considered, the drinking of most of the men was within socially acceptable limits. In a few cases the men were already alcoholics but managed to hide this from their fiancées. They drank only moderately or not at all when on dates and often avoided friends and relatives who might expose their excessive drinking. The relatives and friends who were introduced to the fiancée were those who had hopes that "marriage would straighten him out" and thus said nothing about the drinking. In a small number of cases the men spoke with their fiancées of their alcoholism. The women had no conception of what alcoholism meant, other than that it involved more than the usual frequency of drinking, and they entered the marriage with little more preparation than if they had known nothing about it.

Stage 1. Incidents of excessive drinking begin and, although they are sporadic, place strains on the husband wife interaction. In attempts to minimize drinking, problems in marital adjustment not related to the drinking are avoided.

Stage 2. Social isolation of the family begins as incidents of excessive drinking multiply. The increasing isolation magnifies the importance of family interactions and events. Behavior and thought become drinking-centered. Husband–wife adjustment deteriorates and tension rises. The wife begins to feel self-pity and to lose her self-confidence as her behavior fails to stabilize her husband's drinking. There is an attempt still to maintain the original family structure, which is disrupted anew with each episode of drinking, and as a result the children begin to show emotional disturbance.

Stage 3. The family gives up attempts to control the drinking and begins to behave in a manner geared to relieve tension rather than achieve long-term ends. The disturbance of the children becomes more marked. There is no longer an attempt to support the alcoholic in his roles as husband and father. The wife begins to worry about her own sanity and about her inability to make decisions or act to change the situation.

Stage 4. The wife takes over control of the family and the husband is seen as a recalcitrant child. Pity and strong protective feelings largely replace the earlier resentment and hostility. The family becomes more stable and organized in a manner to minimize the disruptive behavior of the husband. The self-confidence of the wife begins to be rebuilt.

Stage 5. The wife separates from her husband if she can resolve the problems and conflicts surrounding this action.

Stage 6. The wife and children reorganize as a family without the husband.

Stage 7. The husband achieves sobriety and the family, which had become organized around an alcoholic husband, reorganizes to include a sober father and experiences problems in reinstating him in his former roles.

Stage 1. Attempts to Deny the Problem

Usually the first experience with drinking as a problem arises in a social situation. The husband drinks in a manner which is inappropriate to the social setting and the expectations of others present. The wife feels embarrassed on the first occasion and humiliated as it occurs more frequently. After several such incidents she and her husband talk over his behavior. The husband either formulates an explanation for the episode and assures her that such behavior will not occur again; or he refuses to discuss it at all. For a time afterward he drinks appropriately and drinking seems to be a problem no longer. The wife looks back on the incidents and feels that she has exaggerated them, feels ashamed of herself for her disloyalty and for her behavior. The husband, in evaluating the incident, feels shame also and vows such episodes will not recur. As a result, both husband and wife attempt to make it up to the other and, for a time, try to play their conceptions of the ideal husband and wife roles, minimizing or avoiding other difficulties which arise in the marriage. They thus create the illusion of a "perfect" marriage.

Eventually another inappropriate drinking episode occurs and the pattern is repeated. The wife worries but takes action only in the situations in which inappropriate drinking occurs, as each long intervening period of acceptable drinking behavior convinces her that a recurrence is unlikely. As time goes on, in attempting to cope with individual episodes, she runs the gamut of possible trial and error behaviors, learning that none is permanently effective.

If she speaks to other people about her husband's drinking, she is usually assured that there is no need for concern, that her husband can control his drinking and that her fears are exaggerated. Some friends possibly admit that his drinking is too heavy and give advice on how they handled similar situations with their husbands. These friends convince her that her problem will be solved as soon as she hits upon the right formula for dealing with her husband's drinking.

During this stage the husband–wife interaction is in no way "abnormal." In a society in which a large proportion of the men drink, most wives have at some time had occasion to be concerned, even though only briefly, with an episode of drinking which they considered inappropriate (7). In a society in which the status of the family depends on that of the husband, the wife feels threatened by any behavior on his part which might lower it. Inappropriate drinking is regarded by her as a threat to the family's reputation and standing in the community. The wife attempts to exert control and often finds herself blocked by the sacredness of drinking behavior to men in America. Drinking is a private matter and not any business of the wife's. On the whole, a man reacts to his wife's suggestion that he has not adequately controlled his drinking with resentment, rebelliousness and a display of emotion which makes rational discussion difficult. The type of husband-wife interaction outlined in this stage has occurred in many American families in which the husband never became an excessive drinker.

Stage 2. Attempts to Eliminate the Problem

Stage 2 begins when the family experiences social isolation because of the husband's drinking. Invitations to the homes of friends become less frequent. When the couple does visit friends, drinks are not served or are limited, thus emphasizing the reason for exclusion from other social activities of the friendship group. Discussions of drinking begin to be sidestepped awkwardly by friends, the wife and the husband.

By this time the periods of socially acceptable drinking are becoming shorter.

The wife, fearing that the full extent of her husband's drinking will become known, begins to withdraw from social participation, hoping to reduce the visibility of his behavior, and thus the threat to family status.

Isolation is further intensified because the family usually acts in accordance with the cultural dictate that it should be self-sufficient and manage to resolve its own problems without recourse to outside aid. Any experiences which they have had with well-meaning outsiders, usually relatives, have tended to strengthen this conviction. The husband has defined such relatives as interfering and the situation has deteriorated rather than improved.

With increasing isolation, the family members begin to lose perspective on their interaction and on their problems. Thrown into closer contact with one another as outside contacts diminish, the behavior of each member assumes exaggerated importance. The drinking behavior becomes the focus of anxiety. Gradually all family difficulties become attributed to it. (For example, the mother who is cross with her children will feel that, if her husband had not been drinking, she would not have been so tense and would not have been angry.) The fear that the full extent of drinking may be discovered mounts steadily; the conceptualization of the consequences of such a discovery becomes increasingly vague and, as a result, more anxiety-provoking. The family feels different from others and alone with its shameful secret.

Attempts to cover up increase. The employer who calls to inquire about the husband's absence from work is given excuses. The wife is afraid to face the consequences of loss of the husband's pay check in addition to her other concerns. Questions from the children are evaded or they are told that their father is ill. The wife lives in terror of the day when the children will be told by others of the nature of the "illness." She is also afraid that the children may describe their father's symptoms to teachers or neighbors. Still feeling that the family must solve its own problems, she keeps her troubles to herself and hesitates to seek outside help. If her husband beats her, she will bear it rather than call in the police. (Indeed, often she has no idea that this is even a possibility.) Her increased isolation has left her without the advice of others as to sources of help in the community. If she knows of them, an agency contact means to her an admission of the complete failure of her family as an independent unit. For the middle-class woman particularly, recourse to social agencies and law-enforcement agencies means a terrifying admission of loss of status.

During this stage, husband and wife are drawing further apart. Each feels resentful of the behavior of the other. When this resentment is expressed, further drinking occurs. When it is not, tension mounts and the next drinking episode is that much more destructive of family relationships. The reasons for drinking are explored frantically. Both husband and wife feel that if only they could discover the reason, all members of the family could gear their behavior to making drinking unnecessary. The discussions become increasingly unproductive, as it is the husband's growing conviction that his wife does not and cannot understand him.

On her part, the wife begins to feel that she is a failure, that she has been unable to fulfill the major cultural obligations of a wife to meet her husband's needs. With her increasing isolation, her sense of worth derives almost entirely from her roles as wife and mother. Each failure to help her husband gnaws away at her sense of adequacy as a person.

Periods of sobriety or socially acceptable drinking still occur. These periods keep the wife from making a permanent or stable adjustment. During them her husband, in his guilt, treats her like a queen. His behavior renews her hope and rekindles positive feelings toward him. Her sense of worth is bolstered temporarily and she grasps desperately at her husband's reassurance that she is really a fine person and not a failure and an unlovable shrew. The periods of sobriety also keep her family from facing the inability of the husband to control his drinking. The inaccuracies of the cultural stereotype of the alcoholic—particularly that he is in a constant state of inebriation—also contribute to the family's rejection of the idea of alcoholism, as the husband seems to demonstrate from time to time that he can control his drinking.

Family efforts to control the husband become desperate. There are no culturally prescribed behavior patterns for handling such a situation and the family is forced to evolve its own techniques. Many different types of behavior are tried but none brings consistent results; there seems to be no way of predicting the consequences of any action that may be taken. All attempts to stabilize or structure the situation to permit consistent behavior fail. Threats of leaving, hiding his liquor away, emptying the bottles down the drain, curtailing his money, are tried in rapid succession, but none is effective. Less punitive methods, as discussing the situation when he is sober, babying him during hangovers, and trying to drink with him to keep him in the home, are attempted and fail. All behavior becomes oriented around the drinking, and the thought of family members becomes obsessive on this subject. As no action seems to be successful in achieving its goal, the wife persists in trial-and-error behavior with mounting frustration. Long-term goals recede into the background and become secondary to just keeping the husband from drinking today.

There is still an attempt to maintain the illusion of husband–wife–children roles. When father is sober, the children are expected to give him respect and obedience. The wife also defers to him in his role as head of the household. Each drinking event thus disrupts family functioning anew. The children begin to show emotional disturbances as a result of the inconsistencies of parental behavior. During periods when the husband is drinking the wife tries to shield them from the knowledge and effects of his behavior, at the same time drawing them closer to herself and deriving emotional support from them. In sober periods, the father tries to regain their favor. Due to experiencing directly only pleasant interactions with their father, considerable affection is often felt for him by the children. This affection becomes increasingly difficult for the isolated wife to tolerate, and an additional source of conflict. She feels that she needs and deserves the love and support of her children and, at the same time, she feels it important to maintain the children's picture of their father. She counts on the husband's affection for the children to motivate a cessation of drinking as he comes to realize the effects of his behavior on them.

In this stage, self-pity begins to be felt by the wife, if it has not entered previously. It continues in various degrees throughout the succeeding stages. In an attempt to handle her deepening sense of inadequacy, the wife often tries to convince herself that she is right and her husband wrong, and this also continues through the following stages. At this point the wife often resembles what Whalen (5) describes as "The Sufferer."

Stage 3. Disorganization

The wife begins to adopt a "What's the use?" attitude and to accept her husband's drinking as a problem likely to be permanent. Attempts to understand one another become less frequent. Sober periods still engender hope, but hope qualified by skepticism; they bring about a lessening of anxiety and this is defined as happiness.

By this time some customary patterns of husband–wife–children interaction have evolved. Techniques which have had some effectiveness in controlling the husband in the past or in relieving pent-up frustration are used by the wife. She nags, berates or retreats into silence. Husband and wife are both on the alert, the wife watching for increasing irritability and restlessness which mean a recurrence of drinking, and the husband for veiled aspersions on his behavior or character.

The children are increasingly torn in their loyalties as they become tools in the struggle between mother and father. If the children are at an age of comprehension, they have usually learned the true nature of their family situation, either from outsiders or from their mother, who has given up attempts to bolster her husband's position as father. The children are often bewildered, but questioning their parents brings no satisfactory answers as the parents themselves do not understand what is happening. Some children become terrified; some have increasing behavior problems within and outside the home; others seem on the surface to accept the situation calmly.[1]

During periods of the husband's drinking, the hostility, resentment and frustrations felt by the couple are allowed expression. Both may resort to violence— the wife in self-defense or because she can find no other outlet for her feelings. In those cases in which the wife retaliates to violence in kind, she feels a mixture of relief and intense shame at having deviated so far from what she conceives to be "the behavior of a normal woman."

When the wife looks at her present behavior, she worries about her "normality." In comparing the person she was in the early years of her marriage with the person she has become, she is

---

[1] Some effects of alcoholism of the father on children have been discussed by Newell (8).

frightened. She finds herself nagging and unable to control herself. She resolves to stand up to her husband when he is belligerent but instead finds herself cringing in terror and then despises herself for her lack of courage. If she retaliates with violence, she is filled with self-loathing at behaving in an "unwomanly" manner. She finds herself compulsively searching for bottles, knowing full well that finding them will change nothing, and is worried because she engages in such senseless behavior. She worries about her inability to take constructive action of any kind. She is confused about where her loyalty lies, whether with her husband or her children. She feels she is a failure as a wife, mother and person. She believes she should be strong in the face of adversity and instead feels herself weak.

The wife begins to find herself avoiding sexual contact with her husband when he has been drinking. Sex under these circumstances, she feels, is sex for its own sake rather than an indication of affection for her. Her husband's lack of consideration of her needs to be satisfied leaves her feeling frustrated. The lack of sexual responsiveness reflects her emotional withdrawal from him in other areas of family life. Her husband, on his part, feels frustrated and rejected; he accuses her of frigidity and this adds to her concern about her adequacy as a woman.[2]

By this time the opening wedge has been inserted into the self-sufficiency of the family. The husband has often been in difficulty with the police and the wife has learned that police protection is available. An emergency has occurred in which the seeking of outside help was the only possible action to take; subsequent calls for aid from outsiders do not require the same degree of urgency before they can be undertaken. However, guilt and a lessening of self-respect and self-confidence accompany this method of resolving emergencies. The husband intensifies these feelings by speaking of the interference of outsiders, or of his night in jail.

In Stage 3 all is chaos. Few problems are met constructively. The husband and wife both feel trapped in an intolerable, unstructured situation which offers no way out. The wife's self-assurance is almost completely gone. She is afraid to take action and afraid to let things remain as they are. Fear is one of the major characteristics of this stage: fear of violence, fear of personality damage to the children, fear for her own sanity, fear that relatives will interfere, and fear that they will not help in an emergency. Added to this, the family feels alone in the world and helpless. The problems, and the behavior of family members in attempting to cope with them, seem so shameful that help from others is unthinkable. They feel that attempts to get help would meet only with rebuff, and that communication of the situation will engender disgust.

At this point the clinical picture which the wife presents is very similar to what Whalen (5) has described as "The Waverer."

Stage 4. Attempts to Reorganize in Spite of the Problem

Stage 4 begins when a crisis occurs which necessitates that action be taken. There may be no money or food in the

[2] It is of interest here that marriage counselors and students of marital adjustment are of the opinion that unhappy marriage results in poor sexual adjustment more often than poor sexual adjustment leads to unhappy marriage. If this proves to be true, it would be expected that most wives of alcoholics would find sex distasteful while their husbands are drinking. The wives of the inactive alcoholics report that their sexual adjustments with their husbands are currently satisfactory; many of those whose husbands are still drinking state that they enjoyed sexual relationships before the alcoholism was established.

house; the husband may have been violent to the children; or life on the level of Stage 3 may have become intolerable. At this point some wives leave, thus entering directly into Stage 5.

The wife who passes through Stage 4 usually begins to ease her husband out of his family roles. She assumes husband and father roles. This involves strengthening her role as mother and putting aside her role as wife. She becomes the manager of the home, the discipliner of the children, the decision-maker; she becomes somewhat like Whalen's (5) "Controller." She either ignores her husband as much as possible or treats him as her most recalcitrant child. Techniques are worked out for getting control of his pay check, if there still is one, and money is doled out to her husband on the condition of his good behavior. When he drinks, she threatens to leave him, locks him out of the house, refuses to pay his taxi bills, leaves him in jail overnight rather than pay his bail. Where her obligations to her husband conflict with those to her children, she decides in favor of the latter. As she views her husband increasingly as a child, pity and a sense of being desperately needed by him enter. Her inconsistent behavior toward him deriving from the lack of predictability inherent in the situation up to now, becomes reinforced by her mixed feelings toward him.

In this stage the husband often tries to set his will against hers in decisions about the children. If the children have been permitted to stay with a friend overnight, he may threaten to create a scene unless they return immediately. He may make almost desperate efforts to gain their affection and respect, his behavior ranging from getting them up in the middle of the night to fondle them, to giving them stiff lectures on children's obligations to fathers. Sometimes he will attempt to align the males of the family with him against the females. He may

openly express resentment of the children and become belligerent toward them physically or verbally.

Much of the husband's behavior can be conceptualized as resulting from an increasing awareness of his isolation from the other members of the family and their steady withdrawal of respect and affection. It seems to be a desperate effort to regain what he has lost, but without any clear idea of how this can be accomplished—an effort to change a situation in which everyone is seen as against him; and, in reality, this is becoming more and more true. As the wife has taken over control of the family with some degree of success, he feels, and becomes, less and less necessary to the ongoing activity of the family. There are fewer and fewer roles left for him to play. He becomes aware that members of the family enjoy each other's company without him. When he is home he tries to enter this circle of warmth or to smash it. Either way he isolates himself further. He finds that the children discuss with the mother how to manage him and he sees the children acting on the basis of their mother's idea of him. The children refuse to pay attention to his demands: they talk back to him in the same way that they talk back to one another, adding pressure on him to assume the role of just another child. All this leaves him frustrated and, as a result, often aggressive or increasingly absent from home.

The children, on the whole, become more settled in their behavior as the wife takes over the family responsibilities. Decisions are made by her and upheld in the face of their father's attempts to interfere. Participation in activities outside the home is encouraged. Their patterns of interaction with their father are supported by the mother. Whereas in earlier stages the children often felt that there were causal connections between their actions and their father's drinking, they now accept his unpredictability.

"Well," says a 6-year old, "I'll just have to get used to it. I have a drunken father."

The family is more stabilized in one way but in other ways insecurities are multiplied. Pay checks are received less and less regularly. The violence or withdrawal of the father increases. When he is away the wife worries about automobile accidents or injury in fights, which become more and more probable as time passes. The husband may begin to be seriously ill from time to time; his behavior may become quite bizarre. Both of these signs of increasing illness arouse anxiety in the family.

During this stage hopes may rise high for father's "reform" when he begins to verbalize wishes to stop drinking, admits off and on his inability to stop, and sounds desperate for doing something about his drinking. Now may begin the trek to sanitariums for the middle-class alcoholic, to doctors, or to Alcoholics Anonymous. Where just the promise to stop drinking has failed to revive hope, sobriety through outside agencies has the ability to rekindle it brightly. There is the feeling that at last he is "taking really constructive action." In failure the discouragement is deeper. Here another wedge has been inserted into the self-sufficiency of the family.

By this time the wedges are many. The wife, finding she has managed to bring some semblance of order and stability to her family, while not exactly becoming a self-assured person, has regained some sense of worth which grows a little with each crisis she meets successfully. In addition, the very fact of taking action to stabilize the situation brings relief. On some occasion she may be able to approach social agencies for financial help, often during a period when the husband has temporarily deserted or is incarcerated. She may have gone to the family court; she may have consulted a lawyer about getting a restraining order when the husband was in a particularly belligerent state. She has begun to learn her way around among the many agencies which offer help.

Often she has had a talk with an Alcoholics Anonymous member and has begun to look into what is known about alcoholism. If she has attended a few Alcoholics Anonymous meetings, her sense of shame has been greatly alleviated as she finds so many others in the same boat. Her hopes rise as she meets alcoholics who have stopped drinking, and she feels relieved at being able to discuss her problems openly for the first time with an audience which understands fully. She begins to gain perspective on her problem and learns that she herself is involved in what happens to her husband, and that she must change. She exchanges techniques of management with other wives and receives their support in her decisions.

She learns that her husband is ill rather than merely "ornery," and this often serves to quell for the time being thoughts about leaving him which have begun to germinate as she has gained more self-confidence. She learns that help is available but also that her efforts to push him into help are unavailing. She is not only supported in her recently evolved behavior of thinking first of her family, but now this course also emerges from the realm of the unconceptualized and is set in an accepted rationale. She feels more secure in having a reason and a certainty that the group accepts her as "doing the right thing." When she reports deviations from what the group thinks is the "right way," her reasons are understood; she receives solid support but there is also pressure on her to alter her behavior again toward the acceptable. Blaming and self-pity are actively discouraged. In group discussions she still admits to such feelings but learns to recognize them as they arise and to go beyond them to more productive thinking.

How much her altered behavior changes the family situation is uncertain, but it helps her and gives her security from which to venture forth to further actions of a consistent and constructive type, constructive at least from the point of view of keeping her family on as even a keel as possible in the face of the disruptive influence of the husband. With new friends whom she can use as a sounding board for plans, and with her growing acquaintance with the alternatives and possible patterns of behavior, her thinking ceases to be circular and unproductive. Her anxiety about her own sanity is alleviated as she is reassured by others that they have experienced the same concern and that the remedy is to get her own life and her family under better control. As she accomplishes this, the difference in her feelings about herself convinces her that this is so.

Whether or not she has had a contact with wives of Alcoholics Anonymous members or other wives who have been through a similar experience and have emerged successfully, the very fact of taking hold of her situation and gradually making it more manageable adds to her self-confidence. As her husband is less and less able to care for himself or his family, she begins to feel that he needs her and that without her he would be destroyed. Such a feeling makes it difficult for her to think of leaving him. His almost complete social isolation at this point and his cries for help reinforce this conviction of being needed.

The drinking behavior is no longer hidden. Others obviously know about it, and this becomes accepted by the wife and children. Already isolated and insulated against possible rejection, the wife is often surprised to find that she has exaggerated her fears of what would happen were the situation known. However, the unpredictability of her husband's behavior makes her reluctant to form social relationships which could be violently disrupted or to involve others in the possible consequences of his behavior.

Stage 5. Efforts to Escape the Problem

Stage 5 may be the terminal one for the marriage. In this stage the wife separates from her husband. Sometimes the marriage is reestablished after a period of sobriety, when it appears certain that the husband will not drink again. If he does revert to drinking, the marriage is sometimes finally terminated but with less emotional stress than the first time. If the husband deserts, being no longer able to tolerate his lack of status in his family, Stage 6 may be entered abruptly.

The events precipitating the decision to terminate the marriage may be near-catastrophic, as when there is an attempt by the husband to kill the wife or children, or they may appear trivial to outsiders, being only the last straw to an accumulation of years.

The problems in coming to the decision to terminate the marriage cannot be underestimated. Some of these problems derive from emotional conflicts; some are related to very practical circumstances in the situation; some are precipitated by the conflicting advice of outsiders. With several children dependent on her, the wife must decide whether the present situation is more detrimental to them than future situations she can see arising if she should leave her husband. The question of where the money to live on will come from must be thought out. If she can get a job, will there be enough to provide for child care also while she is away from home? Should the children, who have already experienced such an unsettled life, be separated from her to be cared for by others? If the family still owns its own home, how can she retain control of it? If she leaves, where can she go? What can be done to tide the family over until her first earnings come in? How can she ensure her husband's continued absence from the home and thus be certain of the safety of individuals and property in her absence? These are only a small sample of the practical issues that must be dealt with in trying to think her way through to a decision to terminate the marriage.

Other pressures act on her to impede the decision-making process. "If he would only stay drunk till I carry out what I intend to do," is a frequent statement. When the husband realizes that his wife really means to leave, he frequently sobers up, watches his behavior in the home, plays on her latent and sometimes conscious feelings of her responsibility for the situation, stresses his need for her and that without her he is lost, tears away at any confidence she has that she will be able to manage by herself, and threatens her and the children with injury or with his own suicide if she carries out her intention.

The children, in the meantime, are pulling and pushing on her emotions. They think she is "spineless" to stay but unfair to father's chances for ultimate recovery if she leaves. Relatives, who were earlier alienated in her attempts to shield her family but now know of the situation, do not believe in its full ramifications. They often feel she is exaggerating and persuade her to stay with him. Especially is this true in the case of a "solitary drinker." His drinking has been so well concealed that the relatives have no way of knowing the true nature of the situation. Other relatives, afraid that they will be called on for support, exert pressure to keep the marriage intact and the husband thereby responsible for debts. Relatives who feel she should leave him overplay their hands by berating the husband in such a manner as to evoke her defense of him. This makes conscious the positive aspects of her relationship with him, causing her to waver in her decision. If she consults organized agencies, she often gets conflicting advice. The agencies concerned with the well-being of the family may counsel leaving; those concerned with rehabilitating the husband may press her to stay. In addition, help from public organizations almost always involves delay and is frequently not forthcoming at the point where she needs it most.

The wife must come to terms with her own mixed feelings about her husband, her marriage and herself before she can decide on such a step as breaking up the marriage. She must give up hope that she can be of any help to her husband. She must command enough self-confidence, after years of having it eroded, to be able to face an unknown future and leave the security of an unpalatable but familiar past and present. She must accept that she has failed in her marriage, not an easy thing to do after having devoted years to stopping up the cracks in the family structure as they appeared. Breaking up the marriage involves a complete alteration in the life goals toward which all her behavior has been oriented. It is hard for her to rid herself of the feeling that she married him and he is her responsibility. Having thought and planned for so long on a day-to-day basis, it is difficult to plan for a long-term future.

Her taking over of the family raises her self-confidence, but failure to carry through on decisions undermines the new gains that she has made. Vacillation in her decisions tends to exasperate the agencies trying to help her, and she begins to feel that help from them may not be forthcoming if she finally decides to leave.

Some events, however, help her to arrive at a decision. During the absences of her husband she has seen how manageable life can be and how smoothly her family can run. She finds that life goes on without him. The wife who is working comes to feel that "my husband is a luxury I can no longer afford." After a few short-term separations in which she tries out her wings successfully, leaving comes to look more possible. Another step on the path to leaving is the acceptance of the idea that, although she cannot help her husband, she can help her family. She often reaches a state of such emotional isolation from her husband that his behavior no longer disturbs her emotionally but is only something annoying which upsets daily routines and plans.

Stage 6. Reorganization of Part of the Family

The wife is without her husband and must reorganize her family on this basis. Substantially the process is similar to that in other divorced families, but with some additions. The divorce rarely cuts her relationship to her husband. Unless she and her family disappear, her husband may make attempts to come back. When drunk, he may endanger her job by calls at her place of work. He may attempt violence against members of the family, or he may contact the children and work to gain their loyalty so that pressure is put on the mother to accept him again. Looking back on her marriage, she forgets the full impact of the problem situation on her and on the children and feels more warmly toward her husband, and these feelings can still be manipulated by him. The wide circulation of information on alcoholism as an illness engenders guilt about having deserted a sick man. Gradually, however, the family becomes reorganized.

Stage 7. Recovery and Reorganization of the Whole Family

Stage 7 is entered if the husband achieves sobriety, whether or not separation has preceded. It was pointed out that in earlier stages most of the problems in the marriage were attributed to the alcoholism of the husband, and thus problems in adjustment not related directly to the drinking were unrecognized and unmet. Also, the "sober personality" of the husband was thought of as the "real" personality, with a resulting lack of recognition of other factors involved in his sober behavior, such as remorse and guilt over his actions, leading him to act to the best of his ability like "the ideal husband" when sober. Irritation or other signs of growing tension were viewed as indicators of further drinking, and hence the problems giving rise to them were walked around gingerly rather than faced and resolved. Lack of conflict and lack of drinking were defined as indicating a perfect adjustment. For the wife and husband facing a sober marriage after many years of an alcoholic marriage, the expectations of what marriage without alcoholism will be are unrealistically idealistic, and the reality of marriage almost inevitably brings disillusionments. The expectation that all would go well and that all problems be resolved with the cessation of the husband's drinking cannot be met and this threatens the marriage from time to time.

The beginning of sobriety for the husband does not bring too great hope to the family at first. They have been through this before but are willing to help him along and stand by him in the new attempt. As the length of sobriety increases, so do the hopes for its permanence and efforts to be of help. The wife at first finds it difficult to think more than in terms of today, waking each morning with fear of what the day will bring and sighing with relief at the end of each sober day.

With the continuation of sobriety, many problems begin to crop up. Mother has for years managed the family, and now father again wishes to be reinstated in his former roles. Usually the first role reestablished is that of breadwinner, and the economic problems of the family begin to be alleviated as debts are gradually paid and there is enough left over for current needs. With the resumption of this role, the husband feels that the family should also accept him at least as a partner in the management of the family. Even if the wife is willing to hand over some of the control of the children, for example, the children often are not able to accept this change easily. Their mother has been both parents for so long that it takes time to get used to the idea of consulting their father on problems and asking for his decisions. Often the father tries too hard to manage this change overnight, and the very pressure put on the children toward this end defeats him. In addition, he is unable to meet many of the demands the children make on him because he has never really become acquainted with them or learned to understand them and is lacking in much necessary background knowledge of their lives.

The wife, who finds it difficult to conceive of her husband as permanently sober, feels an unwillingness to let control slip from her hands. At the same time she realizes that reinstatement of her husband in his family roles is necessary to his sobriety. She also realizes that the closer his involvement in the family the greater the probability of his remaining sober. Yet she remembers events in the past in which his failure to handle his responsibilities was catastrophic to the family. Used to avoiding anything which might upset him, the wife often hesitates to discuss problems openly. At times, if she is successful in helping him to regain his roles as father, she feels resentful of his intrusion into territory she has come to regard as hers. If he makes errors in judgment which affect the family adversely, her former feelings of being his superior may come to the fore and affect her interaction with him. If the children begin to turn to him, she may feel a resurgence of self-pity at being left out and find herself attempting to swing the children back toward her-

self. Above all, however, she finds herself feeling resentful that some other agency achieved what she and the children could not.

Often the husband makes demands for obedience, for consideration and for pampering which members of the family feel unable to meet. He may become rather euphoric as his sobriety continues and feel superior for a time.

Gradually, however, the drinking problem sinks into the past and marital adjustment at some level is achieved. Even when this has occurred, the drinking problem crops up occasionally, as when the time comes for a decision about whether the children should be permitted to drink. The mother at such times becomes anxious, sees in the child traits which remind her of her husband, worries whether these are the traits which mean future alcoholism. At parties, at first, she is watchful and concerned about whether her husband will take a drink or not. Relatives and friends may, in a party mood, make the husband the center of attention by emphasizing his nondrinking. They may unwittingly cast aspersions on his character by trying to convince him that he can now "drink like a man." Some relatives and friends have gone so far as secretly to "spike" a non-alcoholic drink and then cry "bottoms up!" without realizing the risk of reactivating patterns from the past.

If sobriety has come through Alcoholics Anonymous, the husband frequently throws himself so wholeheartedly into A.A. activities that his wife sees little of him and feels neglected. As she worries less about his drinking, she may press him to cut down on these activities. That this is dangerous, since A.A. activity is correlated with success in Alcoholics Anonymous, has been shown by Lahey (9). Also, the wife discovers that, though she has a sober husband, she is by no means free of alcoholics. In his

Twelfth Step work, he may keep the house filled with men he is helping. In the past her husband has avoided self-searching; and now he may become excessively introspective, and it may be difficult for her to deal with this.

If the husband becomes sober through Alcoholics Anonymous and the wife participates actively in groups open to her, the thoughts of what is happening to her, to her husband and to her family will be verbalized and interpreted within the framework of the Alcoholics Anonymous philosophy and the situation will probably be more tolerable and more easily worked out. . . .

SUMMARY

The onset of alcoholism in a family member has been viewed as precipitating a cumulative crisis for the family. Seven critical stages have been delineated. Each stage affects the form which the following one will take. The family finds itself in an unstructured situation which is undefined by the culture. Thus it is forced to evolve techniques of adjustment by trial and error. The unpredictability of the situation, added to its lack of structure, engenders anxiety in family members which gives rise to personality difficulties. Factors in the culture, in the environment and within the family situation prolong the crisis and deter the working out of permanent adjustment patterns. With the arrest of the alcoholism, the crisis enters its final stage. The family attempts to reorganize to include the ex-alcoholic and makes adjustments to the changes which have occurred in him.

It has been suggested that the clinical picture presented by the wife to helping agencies is not only indicative of a type of basic personality structure but also of the stage in family adjustment to an alcoholic. That the wives of alcoholics represent a rather limited number of personality types can be interpreted in two ways, which are not mutually exclusive.

(*a*) That women with certain personality attributes tend to select alcoholics or potential alcoholics as husbands in order to satisfy unconscious personality needs;

(*b*) That women undergoing similar experiences of stress, within similarly unstructured situations, defined by the culture and reacted to by members of the society in such a manner as to place limits on the range of possible behavior, will emerge from this experience showing many similar neurotic personality traits. As the situation evolves some of these personality traits will also change. Changes have been observed in the women studied which correlate with altered family interaction patterns. This hypothesis is supported also by observations on the behavior of individuals in other unstructured situations, in situations in which they were isolated from supporting group interaction. It is congruent also with the theory of reactions to increased and decreased stress.

REFERENCES
1. Mowrer, H. R. "A Psychocultural Analysis of the Alcoholic." *Amer. Sociol. Rev.* 5:546–557, 1940.
2. Bacon, S. D. "Excessive Drinking and the Institution of the Family." In: Alcohol, Science and Society; Lecture 16. New Haven; *Quarterly Journal of Studies on Alcohol*, 1945.
3. Baker, S. M. "Social Case Work with Inebriates." In: Alcohol, Science and Society; Lecture 27. New Haven; *Quarterly Journal of Studies on Alcohol*, 1945.
4. Futterman, S. "Personality Trends in Wives of Alcoholics." *J. Psychiat. Soc. Work* 23:37–41, 1953.
5. Whalen, T. "Wives of Alcoholics: Four Types Observed in a Family Service Agency." *Quart. J. Stud. Alc.* 14:632–641, 1953.

6. Price, G. M. "A Study of the Wives of 20 Alcoholics." *Quart. J. Stud. Alc.* 5: 620–627, 1945.
7. Club and Educational Bureaus of Newsweek. "Is Alcoholism Everyone's Problem?" Platform, N.Y., p. 3, Jan. 1950.
8. Newell, N. "Alcoholism and the Father-image." *Quart. J. Stud. Alc.* 11:92–96, 1950.
9. Lahey, W. W. *A Comparison of Social and Personal Factors Identified with Selected Members of Alcoholics Anonymous.* Master's Thesis; University of Southern California; 1950.

3 | *the cultural context*

Cultures include ideas about different types of people. While most of these ideas deal with conventional types, many deal with deviant types. In analyzing these ideas about deviance, a number of questions can be posed. What definitions of deviance are found in a particular culture? Who formulates these definitions? Who has the right to apply these labels, and what norms affect the application and consequence of these labels? Finally, whose interests are served by these definitions of deviance?

Lofland, in the first selection, discusses cultural definitions of deviance, specialists who apply the definition, and the role of cultural stereotypes in deviant typing. Next Conrad discusses the implications of doctors' renaming over-activity in children as the "hyperkinetic syndrome." In the following selection Mercer claims that because high-status people have a clearer definition of mental retardation than do low-status people, high-status parents are more likely to label one of their children retarded and to institutionalize the child. Scheff then discusses the role cultural stereotypes play in mental illness. Finally, Currie shows that the prevalence of "witches" during the Middle Ages was related to social and cultural conditions in Europe.

Social Identification

JOHN LOFLAND

We want to inquire . . . into the circumstances that will increase the probability that an imputation of pivotal deviance will be made by anyone at all and, if made, into the circumstances which will promote the acceptance of it by yet other persons in Actor's milieu.

KNOWLEDGE

Historical Variability

An obvious but fundamental first circumstance is that, whatever the pivotal deviant category, it must appear among the repertoire of types of possible persons possessed by a possibly imputing set of Others. If possibly imputing Others do not *know* of the pivotal category, they can hardly interpret experience in terms of it. Thus, for example, part of the reason for past differences in rural-urban rates of delinquency may have to do with the failure of rural people to employ the pivotal category of juvenile delinquent in coding juvenile misconduct. If rural folk tend to view such misconduct as merely an expression of normal youthful exuberance, and if they are unaware that the same acts could be viewed as indicative of a pivotal category called "juvenile delinquent," then rates of official delinquency and the number of "delinquent boys" will be low in rural areas. Recent increases in rates of rural delinquency may as well reflect an increasing awareness of the pivotal

category of juvenile delinquent as a way to identify those involved in youthful misconduct, as much as a change in the true rate of offenses.

In a modern society characterized by almost universal state education and by exposure of the population to mass communication, the number of such universally known deviant pivotal categroies may be increasing. Local pockets of ignorance and provincialism, both urban and rural, crumble under the penetrative power of large organizations of all kinds. It becomes possible under these circumstances to create (or abolish) deviant (and other) identities in relatively short periods of time. At the same time that the pivotal category "witch" is disappearing and "Negro' is under assault, other types are swiftly being created and disseminated. Most recently the pivotal categories of "high school dropout," "bigot," "hippy" and "Hell's Angel" (Thompson, 1967) have entered the popular lexicon of disapproved types of persons. Further, the psychiatric establishment and its allies vigorously disseminate conceptions of certain acts as criteria of various kinds of mental illnesses, categories of mental illness being themselves of relatively recent vintage, although of growing currency. Surveys taken between 1950 and the early sixties, in which people were invited to impute mental illness to fictitious portraits of "juvenile character disorder," "anxiety character neurotic," "alcoholic," "simple

From John Lofland, *Deviance and Identity,* © 1969, pp. 131–144. Reprinted by permission of Prentice-Hall, Inc., Englewood Cliffs, New Jersey.

schizophrenic" and others have demonstrated a rather marked increase in "the public's readiness to see . . . behavior [in the presented sketches] as mentally ill" (Dohrenwend and Chin-Shong, 1967:422).

Social Organizational Sources

. . . Prior to the advent of a category in public consciousness, there is, *sociologically speaking,* no deviance (in the sense of deviant identities) of the particular kind. That is, it does not exist when it has not been "worked up" or articulated such that it is possible to identify human bodies as instances of it. One of the more interesting facets of the sociology of deviance is the concern with historical circumstances and processes by which a category enters the coding scheme of the participants in a society. Although still scattered, a number of works have attempted to trace the development of such categories as drug addict, marijuana user, vagrant, mentally ill and thief.[1] One key pattern highlighted in such sociohistorical studies has been that of social enterprise or *moral entrepreneurship,* wherein some people come to feel that there is "X" deviant in the world and set about vigorously propagandizing others as to his existence and evil character and as to the necessity to do something about him. That is, categories of deviants do not just appear naturally. Social action has to be mobilized and zealously prosecuted if a new conception is to be foisted upon the larger mass of indifferent and otherwise preoccupied members of the body politic (H. S. Becker, 1963:Chaps. 7 and 8; Erikson, 1966). . . .

Appropriate [conditions include] . . . the organization of the economy, the family, the distribution of ethnic and religious groups, the rate of urbanization and the like—the range of variables conventionally identified as the central subject of sociology. Thus with reference to the questions posed, it has been argued that a belief in the special nature and treatment of children arises under conditions of their progressive exclusion from the economic process under the impact of increasing complexity of technology and in response to the coming of labor unions (which had to worry more about fathers working steadily for a living wage than about the employment of sons). The label "juvenile delinquent" arose in the context of the introduction of a wide range of "child welfare" legislation which, among other things, excluded children from many kinds of gainful employment and forced them to attend public schools. Not having access to the former and disinclined to the latter, children were set free like an army upon the land. Juvenile delinquency labels and laws were one formal way to attempt to control this newly created under-enmeshed stratum. . . .

With reference to the coming of legal restrictions on alcohol, some sociologists have suggested that Prohibition was a by-product or symbolic expression of larger shifts in power taking place in America in the early part of the century. While 19th-century America was dominated by the rural, Protestant, northern European agrarian sectors of the country, the influx of Catholic and southern European immigrants at the turn of the century and afterward began a shift of power to the urban industrial sectors. The Catholic and southern European immigrants happened to have somewhat different attitudes toward alcoholic bev-

---

[1] See H. S. Becker, 1963:Chap. 7; Chambliss, 1964; Hall, 1939; Davis, 1938; Gursslin, Hunt and Roach, 1959–60; Foucault, 1967; Szasz, 1961:Part I; Sutherland, 1950; Dickson, 1968; Lindesmith and Strauss, 1968:401–5; Lindesmith, 1968:Part II; Cohen, 1966:31–36; Erikson, 1966. See also, the description provided by Thompson (1967) of how the mass media were able in 1964–65 to create the category "motorcycle outlaw" or Hell's Angel.

erages than did the rural Protestants. In the power struggles that ensued (and still furtively survive), the rural elements came to define the use of alcohol as epitomizing what they saw as the debilitating and dissolute characteristics of the urban population. Thus there arose organized expressions of such moral sentiments in such famous movements as the Anti-Saloon League and the Women's Christian Temperance Union (Gusfield, 1963, 1967).

Sociologists who have undertaken analyses of this type have been particularly fond of noting that moral entrepreneurs often have a narrower and more self-interested concern with the deviants they seek to create than they are willing to acknowledge. Moral enterprise often predicates its legitimacy on a concern for "problem people" who are doing harm to themselves or others or who are being victimized or harmed by someone else. Scrutinizing the social interests of those who proclaim this about others, more cynical sociologists have suggested that a weighty element of self-interest often underlies this altruism (H. S. Becker, 1963:147–52). So it can be suggested that moral concern over the welfare of children among unionists was conveniently congruent with union interest in cutting down the labor supply, thereby forcing up the level of wages and the availability of jobs. Moral concern among rural Protestants over the "self-destructive" doings of urban Catholics was conveniently congruent with reasserting and maintaining the dominance of Protestant small-town America (Gusfield, 1963).

REASONABLENESS

It is possible, however, to know of a given pivotal category but still not to believe that it is "real" or "reasonable" or ever relevant for purposes of identifying known others. The classic category of "witch" is thus well known but has of late lost its "reasonableness". . . . As is perhaps most evident in contemporary America, some persons who have knowledge of psychiatric pivotal categories do not accept them as reasonable constructions of "kinds of people." It is necessary, therefore, for those who know a category to have a certain amount of faith in it, or, at least, if they are not personally taken with its validity, to be cynical enough to use it to manipulate others. So it is that some hypercynical sophisticates who spurn psychiatric categories may nevertheless use them in the presence of believing Others to discredit a third party. It is perhaps more typical for "knowers," especially lay knowers, to be rather ambivalent about the reasonableness of a category of deviance. They may alternate between thinking that there really is such a thing and wondering if it is not, in some sense, an "artificial" construction. However, under the press of managing the Actors of their world, such Others seem likely to squelch such doubts in favor of the social control gains derived from having a firm faith in a category.

A belief among a population at large in the "reality" or "reasonableness" of a category seems best fostered under circumstances of the adoption and promotion of the category by well-financed elite groups, especially elite groups which control the means of mass communication. Such elites speak, in some sense, with authority. It well behooves the recipients of their messages to accept these messages as true facts about the world. The degree to which special groups, promoting one or another conception of what is deviant, complain about the difficulties in getting their messages across should not detract attention from the rather major successes they have enjoyed. The rather widespread beliefs that there are obviously mentally ill persons and that there are obviously juvenile delinquents are among their more recent successes in making constructions seem reasonable.[2]

PREVALENT SENSITIVITY

The collective bearers of a category or categories of deviance are likely to vary in the degree to which they are disposed to find instances of even that which everyone knows about and feels to be reasonable. In a complex society, social differentiation by occupation and other pursuits may result in segments of the population being rather insensitive in their everyday lives to discovering instances of those deviant categories they know about and feel to be reasonable. They can be "turned off" for coding, such that much escapes their attention. The greater the number of Others in a society who are not "turned off"—who are sensitively disposed to coding—and the larger the portion of their days they are so disposed, the greater the probability that Actor will be identified as an instance of a deviant category.

Imputational Specialists: Numbers

It would appear dubiously facilitative to rely completely on everyday citizens for imputations of pivotal deviance. They appear too ready to code potentially "deviant" emissions as simple variants of normality (e.g., Yarrow *et al.,* 1955). Immersed in conventional pursuits, the man on the street has too little time or interest to be a fully effective coder, except, perhaps, during periods of

"crackdown" on some form of deviance (cf. Erikson, 1966). In all of social life, a high probability for the occurrence of a set of activities is best ensured by giving a set of Others some interest in, and pay-off for, performing them. In the same way that profit in industrial manufacture ensures a flow of goods, the flow of imputations of pivotal deviance can be facilitated by paying people to spend a major portion of their time making them. As the number of *imputational specialists* increases in a society, it is likely that the number of people imputed as deviant will also increase. A study of juvenile justice in two southern California communities thus found that although

one of the two communities . . . (Community A) had both a slightly larger population and a higher adult crime rate . . . [it] had . . . 3200 current cases of juveniles suspected or confirmed to be offenders . . . [while] Community B, on the other hand, had approximately 8000 current suspected or confirmed juvenile cases. Community A has two juvenile officers on its staff, while Community B has five juvenile officers. (Kitsuse and Cicourel, 1963:138.)

The growing army of social workers, psychologists, psychiatrists, police, etc., constitutes a stratum with a precise interest in ensuring a flow of persons defined as deviant. The training undergone by such specialists creates a stratum whose aim it is to discover "out there" in the empirical world those sorts of people they have been trained to see.[3] As more of them become better trained and

[2] See further, Clinard's (1968:702–14) review of general public education.

[3] And, ironically, at least some imputational specialists become so sensitive and so zealous that they code well beyond their occupational obligation to do so—as with those social workers and psychiatrists who impute their friends and spouses in addition to the humans presented professionally. An obligation is thus translated into a mandate. In so doing, they exercise the mantle bequeathed by Sigmund Freud, the modern initiator of promiscuous imputation. His talent has been delightfully epitomized in this account of the young Gordon Allport's encounter with him in 1920.

With a callow forwardness characteristic of age twenty-two, I wrote to Freud announcing that I was in Vienna and implied that no doubt he would be glad to make

organized—that is, more professional—their sensitivity could well increase. This possibility is suggested by a study of two police systems which varied in whether or not they had developed specialized juvenile bureaus.

The department whose juvenile officers had more advanced and professional training (and thus were more prepared to consider delinquents as problem children) . . . had much higher rates of arrest for juveniles than a department in which these conditions did not hold true. (Wheeler, 1967:662; Wilson, 1968.)

Imputational Specialists: Strategic Dispersion

In addition to their sheer numbers, the facilitative significance of sensitive specialists is increased by their institutional and territorial dispersion. The psychiatrist in the factory and the social worker (or even policeman) in the school, by their penetration of new institutional spheres, increase the visibility of the conduct of a larger number of Actors. They thereby collectively increase the number and range of Actors who are likely to be imputed. Such a dispersion of specialists gives rise, in turn, to opportunities for collaboration and cooperation among them, even further increasing the possibilities for imputation. . . .

SIMPLE INDICATIONS

As schemes for the identification of human bodies, pivotal categories and their correlative features may be viewed as a set of instructions for the coding of the raw emissions of persons. Similar to coding schemes of other sorts, they can vary as to the number of qualitative features of the information necessary to accomplish a given placement. Given this variance, it can be asked, what organization of indicators most increases the likelihood that human bodies will be coded as instances of a widely known and believed in category? Phrased generally, imputation of pivotal deviance is most facilitated under conditions of minimal indicators, minimal here being used in two senses.

Small Number Required

First, imputation is facilitated through having a very small number of necessary indicators . . . [e.g.,] the use of only one or a few indicators as sufficient for making a pivotal imputation. The following coding practice, said to have ex-

my acquaintance. I received a kind reply in his own handwriting inviting me to come to his office at a certain time. Soon after I had entered the famous red burlap room with pictures of dreams on the wall, he summoned me to his inner office. He did not speak to me but sat in an expectant silence, for me to state my mission. I was not prepared for silence and had to think fast to find a suitable conversation gambit. I told him of an episode on the tram car on my way to his office. A small boy about four years of age had displayed a conspicuous dirt phobia. He kept saying to his mother, "I don't want to sit there . . . don't let that dirty man sit beside me." To him everything was *schmutzig*. His mother was a well-starched *Hausfrau*, so dominant and purposive looking that I thought the cause and effect apparent.

When I finished my story, Freud fixed his kindly therapeutic eyes upon me and said, "And was that little boy you?" Flabbergasted and feeling a bit guilty, I contrived to change the subject. While Freud's misunderstanding of my motivation was amusing, it also started a deep train of thought. I realized that he was accustomed to neurotic defenses and that my manifest motivation (a sort of rude curiosity and youthful ambition) escaped him. For therapeutic progress he would have to cut through my defenses, but it so happened that therapeutic progress was not here an issue. (Allport, 1968:383–84.)

isted among some ethnic groups at one time, seems rather well constructed for the facilitation of the imputation of "prostitute."

In some . . . ethnic groups, such as the Italian, a rigid dichotomy was culturally drawn between "good" girls and "bad" girls. Parents customarily refused to forgive a single misstep, even assuming that if a girl stayed away from home overnight she was guilty of illicit sex behavior. The behavior consequently was unequivocally reflected in the parental reaction as that of the "bad" girl or the folk equivalent of the prostitute. (Lemert, 1951:269) . . .

Large Number Alternatively Sufficient

Second, coding as deviant is facilitated if there are available for use in small numbers a large number of alternatively sufficient indicators. One of the most effective features of some psychiatric coding schemes is their ability to use only a few of a very large number of alternative indicators in order to code Actors as pivotally deviant. . . .

Social Organizational Sources

It can be suggested that coding schemes relying heavily upon a small number of necessary indicators, with a large number of alternatively sufficient indicators, are likely to predominate in social orders where a high proportion of the population are in necessary contact but are relative strangers to one another. Under conditions of rapid social change and territorial mobility, there is created a situation in which persons have little information about one another, yet need to deal with and manage each other (L. H. Lofland, 1966). A reasonable, at least short-run, adaptation to this situation is to squeeze from meager amounts of available information a large amount of "indicativeness" (giving rise, perhaps, to a popular concern with managing impressions, a concern most poignantly explored by David Riesman *et al.,* [1950]

and Erving Goffman [1959]). When some doubt is raised as to the standing of a given Actor under conditions of anonymity and, therefore, under conditions of a measure of distrust and fear, the safest course is quickly to presume the worst, that is, to code for pivotal deviance using a large number of alternatively sufficient indicators in small numbers. . . .

Conditions of anonymity, distrust and fear create a demand for simple and direct characterizations of types of persons, a demand catered to in no small measure by those who call themselves medical and social scientists. It is their mission to come up with "essential findings" and essential correlates and features or indicators, the better and easier to identify various sets of "them" toward whom one should be on guard. . . .

DIFFERENTIAL VULNERABILITY TO IMPUTATION AS DEVIANT

As almost everyone wants to believe, items that can be indicative of pivotal deviance are probably not evenly or even randomly distributed throughout the population of a society. Models of deviant categories are founded precisely upon the assumption that particular classes of people are more likely to perform deviant acts and to be particular types of deviant persons. I have tried in the above to hold in abeyance that proposition in order to point up the possibility that imputation of Actors as deviant can have as much or more to do with who is coding with what category under what circumstances than with simple discernment of specially differentiated deviant persons. But, as is popularly believed, some Actors are, to a degree, likely to be specially differentiated from the general population in their acts and activities in a way that makes it more likely that they will be imputed. Others have probed this possibility so thoroughly[4] that I need not pursue it here. I will . . . note only that information known about Actors tends to be highly selective relative to the total amount that can be known. This fact poses the question of the extent to which almost anyone might be "informationally sampled" so as to effect identification as some type of pivotal deviant. . . .

REFERENCES

Allport, G., *The Person in Psychology: Selected Essays.* Boston: Beacon Press, Inc., 1968.

Becker, H. S., *Outsiders: Studies in the Sociology of Deviance.* New York: The Free Press of Glencoe, Inc., 1963.

Black, D. J., "Police Encounters and Social Organizations." Unpublished Ph.D. dissertation, Department of Sociology, University of Michigan, 1968.

Chambliss, W. J., "A Sociological Analysis of the Law of Vagrancy." *Social Problems,* 12:67–77 (Summer, 1964).

Cicourel, A. V., *The Social Organization of Juvenile Justice.* New York: John Wiley & Sons, Inc., 1968.

Clinard, M. B., *Sociology of Deviant Behavior.* New York: Holt, Rinehart & Winston, Inc. (3rd ed.), 1968.

Cohen, A. K., *Deviance and Control.* Englewood Cliffs, N.J.: Prentice-Hall, Inc., 1966.

Davis, K., "Mental Hygiene and the Class Structure." *Psychiatry,* 1:55–65 (February, 1938).

Dickson, D. T., "Bureaucracy and Morality: An Organizational Perspective on a Moral Crusade." *Social Problems,* 16: 143–56 (1968).

Dohrenwend, B. P., and E. Chin-Shong, "Social Status and Attitudes Toward Psychological Disorder: The Problem of Tolerance of Deviance." *American Sociological Review,* 32:417–33 (June, 1967).

Erikson, K. T., *Wayward Puritans: A Study in the Sociology of Deviance.* New York: John Wiley & Sons, Inc., 1966.

Foucault, M., *Madness and Civilization: A History of Insanity in the Age of Reason.* New York: New American Library, 1967.

Goffman, E., *The Presentation of Self in Everyday Life.* New York: Doubleday Anchor, Inc., 1959.

Goldman, N., *The Differential Selection of Offenders for Court Appearance.* Washington, D.C.: National Research and Information Center and National Council on Crime and Delinquency, 1963.

Gursslin, O. R., R. G. Hunt and J. L. Roach, "Social Class and the Mental Health Movement." *Social Problems,* 7:210–18 (Winter, 1959–60).

[4] Aside from the theories of psychiatry, psychology and sociology precisely intended to discover the underlying or correlative features of "deviant people," attention has been called to matters such as (1) the Actor's demeanor during contact with imputation specialists (Black, 1968; Goldman, 1963:106; Piliavin and Briar, 1964); (2) the degree of his previous contact with authorities (Cicourel, 1968; Werthman, 1967:167); (3) the degree of incongruity of a current act against the background of a given biography, especially social-class biography (Werthman and Piliavin, 1967; Cicourel, 1968; Erikson, 1966:141–53; President's Commission, . . . *Assessment* . . . , 1967:106–9); (4) the existence of a "segmental or checkered pattern" of "interpersonal difficulties" (Lemert, 1962:7–8); (5) the circumstance of Actor being situationally disoriented (Scheff, 1966:39–54; Chap. 8 of J. Lofland, 1969) and (6) the fact of being male rather than female (e.g., Johnson, 1964:76–81) as affecting ease with which pivotal deviance will be imputed, that is, the degree to which Actor is vulnerable to imputation. These and other factors relevant to the general topic of social identification have been placed in appropriate general perspective by Erikson (1966). The organization of his analysis of witches around issues of their "functional necessity" among the Puritans of the Massachusetts Bay Colony should not detract attention from the potential usefulness of the historical materials in answering other kinds of questions. See also Reckless' helpful conception of "categoric risks" (1961:Chap. 3).

Gusfield, J. R., *Symbolic Crusade: Status Politics and the American Temperance Movement.* Urbana, Ill.: University of Illinois Press, 1963.

———, "Moral Passage: The Symbolic Process in Public Designations of Deviance." *Social Problems,* 15:175–88 (Fall, 1967).

Hall, J., *Theft, Law, and Society.* Indianapolis, Ind.: The Bobbs-Merrill Co., Inc., 1939.

Johnson, E. H., *Crime, Correction and Society.* Homewood, Ill.: The Dorsey Press, 1964.

Kitsuse, J. I., and A. V. Cicourel, "A Note on the Uses of Official Statistics." *Social Problems,* 11:131–39 (Fall, 1963).

Lemert, E. M., *Social Pathology.* New York: McGraw-Hill Book Company, 1951.

———, "Paranoia and the Dynamics of Exclusion." *Sociometry,* 25:2–20 (March, 1962).

Lindesmith, A. R., *Addiction and Opiates.* Chicago: Aldine Publishing Company, 1968.

Lindesmith, A. R., and A. L. Strauss, *Social Psychology.* New York: Holt, Rinehart & Winston, Inc. (3rd ed.), 1968.

Lofland, J., *Deviance and Identity,* Englewood Cliffs, N.J.: Prentice-Hall, 1969.

Lofland, L. H., "In the Presence of Strangers: A Study of Behavior in Public Settings." Working Paper Number 19, Center for Research on Social Organizations, The University of Michigan, December 1966.

Piliavin, I., and S. Briar, "Police Encounters with Juveniles." *American Journal of Sociology,* 70:206–14 (September, 1964).

President's Commission on Law Enforcement and Administration of Justice, *Task Force Report: Crime and Its Impact—An Assessment.* Washington, D.C.: U.S. Government Printing Office, 1967.

Reckless, W. C., *The Crime Problem.* New York: Appleton-Century & Appleton-Century-Crofts (3rd ed.), 1961.

Riesman, D., N. Glazer and R. Denney, *The Lonely Crowd: A Study of the Changing American Character.* New Haven, Conn.: Yale University Press, 1950.

Scheff, T. J., *Being Mentally Ill.* Chicago: Aldine Publishing Company, 1966.

Sutherland, E. H., "The Diffusion of Sexual Psychopath Laws." *American Journal of Sociology,* 56:142–48 (1950).

Szasz, T. S., *The Myth of Mental Illness.* New York: Hoeber-Harper Books, 1961.

Thompson, H. S., *Hell's Angels.* New York: Ballantine Books, 1967.

Werthman, C., "The Function of Social Definitions in the Development of Delinquent Careers," in The President's Commission on Law Enforcement and Administration of Justice, *Task Force Report: Juvenile Delinquency and Youth Crime.* Washington, D.C.: U.S. Government Printing Office, 1967, Appendix J, pp. 155–70.

Werthman, C., and I. Piliavin, "Gang Members and the Police," in D. Bordua, editor, *The Police: Six Sociological Essays.* New York: John Wiley & Sons, Inc., 1967, pp. 56–98.

Wheeler, S. "Deviant Behavior," in N. J. Smelser, editor, *Sociology.* New York: John Wiley & Sons, Inc., 1967, pp. 601–66.

Wilson, J. Q., "The Police and the Delinquent in Two Cities," in S. Wheeler, editor, *Controlling Delinquents.* New York: John Wiley & Sons, Inc., 1968, pp. 9–30.

Yarrow, M., C. Schwartz, H. Murphy, and L. Deasy, "The Psychological Meaning of Mental Illness in the Family." *The Journal of Social Issues,* 11:12–24 (1955).

The Medicalization of Deviance in American Culture

PETER CONRAD

INTRODUCTION

The increasing medicalization of deviant behavior and the medical institution's role as an agent of social control has gained considerable notice (Friedson, 1970; Pitts, 1971; Kitterie, 1971; Zola, 1972). By medicalization we mean defining behavior as a medical problem or illness and mandating or licensing the medical profession to provide some type of treatment for it. Examples include alcoholism, drug addiction and treating violence as a genetic or brain disorder. This redefinition is not a new function of the medical institution: psychiatry and public health have always been concerned with social behavior and have traditionally functioned as agents of social control (Foucault, 1965; Szasz, 1970; Rosen, 1972). . . .

This paper describes how certain forms of behavior in children have become defined as a medical problem and how medicine has become a major agent for their social control since the discovery of hyperkinesis. By discovery we mean both origin of the diagnosis and treatment for this disorder; and discovery of children who exhibit this behavior. The first section analyzes the discovery of hyperkinesis and why it suddenly became popular in the 1960's. The second section will discuss the medicalization of deviant behavior and its ramifications.

THE MEDICAL DIAGNOSIS OF HYPERKINESIS

Hyperkinesis is a relatively recent phenomenon as a medical diagnostic category. Only in the past two decades has it been available as a recognized diagnostic category and only in the last decade has it received widespread notice and medical popularity. However, the roots of the diagnosis and treatment of this clinical entity are found earlier.

Hyperkinesis is also known as Minimal Brain Dysfunction, Hyperactive Syndrome, Hyperkinetic Disorder of Childhood, and by several other diagnostic categories. Although the symptoms and the presumed etiology vary, in general the behaviors are quite similar and greatly overlap.[1] Typical symptom patterns for diagnosing the disorder include: extreme excess of motor activity (hyperactivity); very short attention span (the child flits from activity to ac-

Reprinted from *Social Problems*, Vol. 23, No. 1 (October 1975), pp. 12–21, by permission of the Society for the Study of Social Problems and the author.

[1] The U.S.P.H.S. report (Clements, 1966) included 38 terms that were used to describe or distinguish the conditions that it labeled Minimal Brain Dysfunction. Although the literature attempts to differentiate M.B.D., hyperkinesis, hyperactive syndrome, and several other diagnostic labels, it is our belief that in practice they are almost interchangeable.

tivity); restlessness; fidgetiness; often wildly oscillating mood swings (he's fine one day, a terror the next); clumsiness; aggressive-like behavior; impulsivity; in school he cannot sit still, cannot comply with rules, has low frustration level; frequently there may be sleeping problems and acquisition of speech may be delayed (Stewart, 1966, 1970; Wender, 1971). Most of the symptoms for the disorder are deviant behaviors.[2] It is six times as prevalent among boys as among girls. We use the term hyperkinesis to represent all the diagnostic categories of this disorder.

THE DISCOVERY OF HYPERKINESIS

It is useful to divide the analysis into what might be considered *clinical factors* directly related to the diagnosis and treatment of hyperkinesis and *social factors* that set the context for the emergence of the new diagnostic category.

Clinical Factors

Bradley (1937) observed that amphetamine drugs had a spectacular effect in altering the behavior of school children who exhibited behavior disorders or learning disabilities. Fifteen of the thirty children he treated actually became more subdued in their behavior. Bradley termed the effect of this medication paradoxical, since he expected that amphetamines would stimulate children as they stimulated adults. After the medication was discontinued the children's behavior returned to premedication level.

A scattering of reports in the medical literature on the utility of stimulant medications for "childhood behavior disorders" appeared in the next two decades. The next significant contribution was the work of Strauss and his associates (Strauss and Lehtinen, 1947) who

found certain behavior (including hyperkinesis behaviors) in postencephaletic children suffering from what they called minimal brain injury (damage). This was the first time these behaviors were attributed to the new organic distinction of minimal brain damage.

This disorder still remained unnamed or else it was called a variety of names (usually just "childhood behavior disorder"). It did not appear as a specific diagnostic category until Laufer, et al. (1957) described it as the "hyperkinetic impulse disorder" in 1957. Upon finding "the salient characteristics of the behavior pattern . . . are strikingly similar to those with clear cut organic causation" these researchers described a disorder with no clear-cut history or evidence for organicity (Laufer, et al., 1957).

In 1966 a task force sponsored by the U.S. Public Health Service and the National Association for Crippled Children and Adults attempted to clarify the ambiguity and confusion in terminology and symptomology in diagnosing children's behavior and learning disorders. From over three dozen diagnoses, they agreed on the term "minimal brain dysfunction" as an overriding diagnosis that would include hyperkinesis and other disorders (Clements, 1966). Since this time M.B.D. has been the primary formal diagnosis or label.

In the middle 1950's a new drug, Ritalin, was synthesized, that has many qualities of amphetamines without some of their more undesirable side effects. In 1961 this drug was approved by the F.D.A. for use with children. Since this time there has been much research published on the use of Ritalin in the treatment of childhood behavior disorders. This medication became the "treatment of choice" for treating children with hyperkinesis.

[2] For a fuller discussion of the construction of the diagnosis of hyperkinesis, see Conrad (forthcoming), especially Chapter 6.

Since the early sixties, more research appeared on the etiology, diagnosis and treatment of hyperkinesis (cf. DeLong, 1972; Grinspoon and Singer, 1973; Cole, 1975)—as much as three-quarters concerned with drug treatment of the disorder. There had been increasing publicity of the disorder in the mass media as well. The *Reader's Guide to Periodical Literature* had no articles on hyperkinesis before 1967, one each in 1968 and 1969 and a total of forty for 1970 through 1974 (a mean of eight per year).

Now hyperkinesis has become the most common child psychiatric problem (Gross and Wilson, 1974: 142); special pediatric clinics have been established to treat hyperkinetic children, and substantial federal funds have been invested in etiological and treatment research. Outside the medical profession, teachers have developed a working clinical knowledge of hyperkinesis' symptoms and treatment (cf. Robin and Bosco, 1973); articles appear regularly in mass circulation magazines and newspapers so that parents often come to clinics with knowledge of this diagnosis. Hyperkinesis is no longer the relatively esoteric diagnostic category it may have been twenty years ago, it is now a well-known clinical disorder.

Social Factors

The social factors affecting the discovery of hyperkinesis can be divided into two areas: (1) The Pharmaceutical Revolution; (2) Government Action.

(1) *The Pharmaceutical Revolution.* Since the 1930's the pharmaceutical industry has been synthesizing and manufacturing a large number of psychoactive drugs, contributing to a virtual revolution in drug making and drug taking in America (Silverman and Lee, 1974).

Psychoactive drugs are agents that affect the central nervous system. Benzedrine, Ritalin, and Dexedrine are all synthesized psychoactive stimulants which were indicated for narcolepsy, appetite control (as "diet pills"), mild depression, fatigue, and more recently hyperkinetic children.

Until the early sixties there was little or no promotion and advertisement of any of these medications for use with childhood disorders.[3] Then two major pharmaceutical firms (Smith, Kline and French, manufacturer of Dexedrine and CIBA, manufacturer of Ritalin) began to advertise in medical journals and through direct mailing and efforts of the "detail men." Most of this advertising of the pharmaceutical treatment of hyperkinesis was directed to the medical sphere; but some of the promotion was targeted for the educational sector also (Hentoff, 1972). This promotion was probably significant in disseminating information concerning the diagnosis and treatment of this newly discovered disorder.[4] Since 1955 the use of psychoactive medications (especially phenothiazines) for the treatment of persons who are mentally ill, along with the concurrent dramatic decline in inpatient populations, has made psychopharmacology an integral part of treatment for mental disorders. It has also undoubtedly increased the confidence in the medical profession for the pharmaceutical ap-

[3] The American Medical Association's change in policy in accepting more pharmaceutical advertising in the late fifties may have been important. Probably the F.D.A. approval of the use of Ritalin for children in 1961 was more significant. Until 1970, Ritalin was advertised for treatment of "functional behavior problems in children." Since then, because of an F.D.A. order, it has only been promoted for treatment of M.B.D.

[4] The drug industry spends fully 25 percent of its budget on promotion and advertising. See Coleman et al. (1966) for the role of the detail men and how physicians rely upon them for information.

proach to mental and behavioral problems.

(2) *Government Action.* Since the publication of the U.S.P.H.S. report on M.B.D. there have been at least two significant governmental reports on treating school children with stimulant medications for behavior disorders. Both of these came as a response to the national publicity created by the *Washington Post* report (1970) that five to ten percent of the 62,000 grammar school children in Omaha, Nebraska were being treated with "behavior modification drugs to improve deportment and increase learning potential" (quoted in Grinspoon and Singer, 1973). Although the figures were later found to be a little exaggerated, it nevertheless spurred a Congressional investigation (U.S. Government Printing Office, 1970) and a conference sponsored by the Office of Child Development (1971) on the use of stimulant drugs in the treatment of behaviorally disturbed school children.

The Congressional Subcommittee on Privacy chaired by Congressman Cornelius E. Gallagher held hearings on the issue of prescribing drugs for hyperactive school children. In general, the committee showed great concern over the facility in which the medication was prescribed; more specifically that some children at least were receiving drugs from general practitioners whose primary diagnosis was based on teachers' and parents' reports that the child was doing poorly in school. There was also a concern with the absence of follow-up studies on the long-term effects of treatment.

The H.E.W. committee was a rather hastily convened group of professionals (a majority were M.D.'s) many of whom already had commitments to drug treatment for children's behavior problems. They recommended that only M.D.'s make the diagnosis and prescribe treatment, that the pharmaceutical companies promote the treatment of the disorder only through medical channels, that parents should not be coerced to accept any particular treatment and that long-term follow-up research should be done. This report served as blue ribbon approval for treating hyperkinesis with psychoactive medications.

DISCUSSION

We will focus discussion on three issues: How children's deviant behavior became conceptualized as a medical problem; why this occurred when it did; and what are some of the implications of the medicalization of deviant behavior.

How does deviant behavior become conceptualized as a medical problem? We assume that before the discovery of hyperkinesis this type of deviance was seen as disruptive, disobedient, rebellious, anti-social or deviant behavior. Perhaps the label "emotionally disturbed" was sometimes used, when it was in vogue in the early sixties, and the child was usually managed in the context of the family or the school or in extreme cases, the child guidance clinic. How then did this constellation of deviant behaviors become a medical disorder?

The treatment was available long before the disorder treated was clearly conceptualized. It was twenty years after Bradley's discovery of the "paradoxical effect" of stimulants on certain deviant children that Laufer named the disorder and described its characteristic symptoms. Only in the late fifties were both the diagnostic label and the pharmaceutical treatment available. The pharmaceutical revolution in mental health and the increased interest in child psychiatry provided a favorable background for the dissemination of knowledge about this new disorder. The latter probably made the medical profession more likely to consider behavior problems in children as within their clinical jurisdiction.

There were agents outside the medical profession itself that were significant in "promoting" hyperkinesis as a disorder within the medical framework. These agents might be conceptualized in Becker's terms as "moral entrepreneurs," those who crusade for creation and enforcement of the rules (Becker, 1963).[5] In this case the moral entrepreneurs were the pharmaceutical companies and the Association for Children with Learning Disabilities.

The pharmaceutical companies spent considerable time and money promoting stimulant medications for this new disorder. From the middle 1960's on, medical journals and the free "throwaway" magazines contained elaborate advertising for Ritalin and Dexedrine. These ads explained the utility of treating hyperkinesis and urged the physician to diagnose and treat hyperkinetic children. The ads run from one to six pages. For example, a two-page ad in 1971 stated:

MBD . . . MEDICAL MYTH OR DIAGNOSABLE DISEASE ENTITY What medical practitioner has not, at one time or another, been called upon to examine an impulsive, excitable hyperkinetic child? A child with difficulty in concentrating. Easily frustrated. Unusually aggressive. A classroom rebel. In the absence of any organic pathology, the conduct of such children was, until a few short years ago, usually dismissed as . . . spunkiness, or evidence of youthful vitality. But it is now evident that in many of these children the hyperkinetic syndrome exists as a distinct medical entity. This syndrome is readily diagnosed through patient histories, neurologic signs, and psychometric testing—has been classified by an expert panel convened by the United States Department of Health, Education and Welfare as Minimal Brain Dysfunction, MBD.

The pharmaceutical firms also supplied sophisticated packets of "diagnostic and treatment" information on hyperkinesis to physicians, paid for professional conferences on the subject, and supported research in the identification and treatment of the disorder. Clearly these corporations had a vested interest in the labeling and treatment of hyperkinesis; CIBA had $13 million profit from Ritalin alone in 1971, which was 15 percent of the total gross profits (Charles, 1971; Hentoff, 1972).

The other moral entrepreneur, less powerful than the pharmaceutical companies, but nevertheless influential, is the Association for Children with Learning Disabilities. Although their focus is not specifically on hyperkinetic children, they do include it in their conception of Learning Disabilities along with aphasia, reading problems like dyslexia and perceptual motor problems. Founded in the early 1950's by parents and professionals, it has functioned much as the National Association for Mental Health does for mental illness: promoting conferences, sponsoring legislation, providing social support. One of the main functions has been to disseminate information concerning this relatively new area in education, Learning Disabilities. While the organization does have a more educational than medical perspective, most of the literature indicates that for hyperkinesis members have adopted the medical model and the medical approach to the problem. They have sensitized

---

[5] Freidson also notes the medical professional role as moral entrepreneur in this process also:

The profession does treat the illnesses laymen take to it, but it also seeks to discover illness of which the laymen may not even be aware. One of the greatest ambitions of the physician is to discover and describe a "new" disease or syndrome . . . (1970: 252).

teachers and schools to the conception of hyperkinesis as a medical problem.

The medical model of hyperactive behavior has become very well accepted in our society. Physicians find treatment relatively simple and the results sometimes spectacular. Hyperkinesis minimizes parents' guilt by emphasizing "it's not their fault, it's an organic problem" and allows for nonpunitive management or control of deviance. Medication often makes a child less disruptive in the classroom and sometimes aids a child in learning. Children often like their "magic pills" which make their behavior more socially acceptable and they probably benefit from a reduced stigma also. There are, however, some other, perhaps more subtle ramifications of the medicalization of deviant behavior.

THE MEDICALIZATION OF DEVIANT BEHAVIOR

Pitts has commented that "medicalization is one of the most effective means of social control and that it is destined to become the main mode of *formal* social control" (1971:391). Kitterie (1971) has termed it "the coming of the therapeutic state."

Medicalization of mental illness dates at least from the seventeenth century (Foucault, 1965; Szasz, 1970). Even slaves who ran away were once considered to be suffering from the disease *drapedomania* (Chorover, 1973). In recent years alcoholism, violence, and drug addiction as well as hyperactive behavior in children have all become defined as medical problems, both in etiology or explanation of the behavior and the means of social control or treatment.

There are many reasons why this medicalization has occurred. Much scientific research, especially in pharmacology and genetics, has become technologically more sophisticated, and found more subtle correlates with human behavior. Sometimes these findings (as in the case of XYY chromosomes and violence) become etiological explanations for deviance. Pharmacological technology that makes new discoveries affecting behavior (e.g., antibuse, methadone and stimulants) are used as treatment for deviance. In part this application is encouraged by the prestige of the medical profession and its attachment to science. As Freidson notes, the medical profession has first claim to jurisdiction over anything that deals with the functioning of the body and especially anything that can be labeled illness (1970: 251). Advances in genetics, pharmacology and "psychosurgery" also may advance medicine's jurisdiction over deviant behavior.

Second, the application of pharmacological technology is related to the humanitarian trend in the conception and control of deviant behavior. Alcoholism is no longer sin or even moral weakness, it is now a disease. Alcoholics are no longer arrested in many places for "public drunkenness," they are now somehow "treated," even if it is only to be dried out. Hyperactive children are now considered to have an illness rather than to be disruptive, disobedient, overactive problem children. They are not as likely to be the "bad boy" of the classroom; they are children with a medical disorder. Clearly there are some real humanitarian benefits to be gained by such a medical conceptualization of deviant behavior. There is less condemnation of the deviants (they have an illness, it is not their fault) and perhaps less social stigma. In some cases, even the medical treatment itself is more humanitarian social control than the criminal justice system.

There is, however, another side to the medicalization of deviant behavior. The four aspects of this side of the issue include (1) the problem of expert control; (2) medical social control; (3) the individualization of social problems; and (4) the "depoliticization" of deviant behavior.

1. The problem of expert control. The medical profession is a profession of experts; they have a monopoly on anything that can be conceptualized as illness. Because of the way the medical profession is organized and the mandate it has from society, decisions related to medical diagnoses and treatment are virtually controlled by medical professionals.

Some conditions that enter the medical domain are not *ipso facto* medical problems, especially deviant behavior, whether alcoholism, hyperactivity or drug addiction. By defining a problem as medical it is removed from the public realm where there can be discussion by ordinary people and put on a plane where only medical people can discuss it. As Reynolds states,

The increasing acceptance, especially among the more educated segments of our populace, of technical solutions—solutions administered by disinterested politically and morally neutral experts—results in the withdrawal of more and more areas of human experience from the realm of public discussion. For when drunkenness, juvenile delinquency, sub par performance and extreme political beliefs are seen as symptoms of an underlying illness or biological defect the merits and drawbacks of such behavior or beliefs need not be evaluated (1973:200–221).

The public may have their own conceptions of deviant behavior but that of the experts is usually dominant.

2. Medical social control. Defining deviant behavior as a medical problem allows certain things to be done that could not otherwise be considered; for example, the body may be cut open or psychoactive medications may be given. This treatment can be a form of social control.

In regard to drug treatment Lennard points out: "Psychoactive drugs, especially those legally prescribed, tend to restrain individuals from behavior and experience that are not complementary to the requirements of the dominant value system" (1971:57). These forms of medical social control presume a prior definition of deviance as a medical problem. Psychosurgery on an individual prone to violent outbursts requires a diagnosis that there was something wrong with his brain or nervous system. Similarly, prescribing drugs to restless, overactive and disruptive school children requires a diagnosis of hyperkinesis. These forms of social control, what Chorover (1973) has called "psychotechnology," are very powerful and often very efficient means of controlling deviance. These relatively new and increasingly popular forms of social control could not be utilized without the medicalization of deviant behavior. As is suggested from the discovery of hyperkinesis, if a mechanism of medical social control seems useful, then the deviant behavior it modifies will develop a medical label or diagnosis. No overt malevolence on the part of the medical profession is implied: rather it is part of a complex process, of which the medical profession is only a part. The larger process might be called the individualization of social problems.

3. The individualization of social problems. The medicalization of deviant behavior is part of a larger phenomenon that is prevalent in our society, the individualization of social problems. We tend to look for causes and solutions to complex social problems in the individual rather than in the social system. This view resembles Ryan's (1971) notion of "blaming the victim;" seeing the causes of the problem in individuals rather than in the society where they live. We then seek to change the "victim" rather than the society. The medical perspective of diagnosing an illness in an individual lends itself to the individualization of social problems. Rather than seeing certain deviant behaviors as symptomatic of problems in the social system, the medical perspective focuses on the individual diagnosing and treating the illness, generally ignoring the social situation.

Hyperkinesis serves as a good example. Both the school and the parents are concerned with the child's behavior; the child is very difficult at home and disruptive in school. No punishments or rewards seem consistently to work in modifying the behavior; and both parents and school are at their wits' end. A medical evaluation is suggested. The diagnoses of hyperkinetic behavior leads to prescribing stimulant medications. The child's behavior seems to become more socially acceptable, reducing problems in school and at home.

But there is an alternate perspective. By focusing on the symptoms and defining them as hyperkinesis we ignore the possibility that behavior is not an illness but an adaptation to a social situation. It diverts our attention from the family or school and from seriously entertaining the idea that the "problem" could be in the structure of the social system. And by giving medications we are essentially supporting the existing systems and do not allow this behavior to be a factor of change in the system.

4. The depoliticization of deviant behavior. Depoliticization of deviant behavior is a result of both the process of medicalization and individualization of social problems. To our western world, probably one of the clearest examples of such a depoliticization of deviant behavior occurred when political dissenters in the Soviet Union were declared mentally ill and confined in mental hospitals (cf. Conrad, 1972). This strategy served to neutralize the meaning of political protest and dissent, rendering it the ravings of mad persons.

The medicalization of deviant behavior depoliticizes deviance in the same manner. By defining the overactive, restless and disruptive child as hyperkinetic we ignore the meaning of behavior in the context of the social system. If we focused our analysis on the school system we might see the child's behavior as symptomatic of some "disorder" in the school or classroom situation, rather than symptomatic of an individual neurological disorder.

CONCLUSION

I have discussed the social ramifications of the medicalization of deviant behavior, using hyperkinesis as the example. A number of consequences of this medicalization have been outlined, including the depoliticization of deviant behavior, decision-making power of experts, and the role of medicine as an agent of social control. In the last analysis medical social control may be the central issue, as in this role medicine becomes à *de facto* agent of the *status quo.* The medical profession may not have entirely sought this role, but its members have been, in general, disturbingly unconcerned and unquestioning in their acceptance of it. With the increasing medical knowledge and technology it is likely that more deviant behavior will be medicalized and medicine's social control function will expand.

REFERENCES
Becker, Howard S. (1963). *Outsiders.* New York: Free Press.

Bradley, Charles (1937). "The behavior of children receiving Benzedrine." *American Journal of Psychiatry* 94 (March): 577–585.

Charles, Alan (1971). "The case of Ritalin." *New Republic* 23 (October): 17–19.

Chorover, Stephen L. (1973). "Big brother and psychotechnology." *Psychology Today* (October): 43–54.

Clements, Samuel D. (1966). "Task force I: Minimal brain dysfunction in children." National Institute of Neurological Diseases and Blindness, Monograph no.

3. Washington, D.C.: U.S. Department of Health, Education, and Welfare.

Cole, Sherwood (1975). "Hyperactive children: The use of stimulant drugs evaluated." *American Journal of Orthopsychiatry* 45 (January): 28–37.

Coleman, James, Elihu Katz, and Herbert Menzel (1966). *Medical Innovation.* Indianapolis: Bobbs-Merrill.

Conrad, Peter (1972). "Ideological deviance: An analysis of the Soviet use of mental hospitals for political dissenters." Unpublished manuscript.

———— Forthcoming. "Identifying hyperactive children: A study in the medicalization of deviant behavior." Unpublished Ph.D. dissertation, Boston University.

DeLong, Arthur R. (1972). "What have we learned from psychoactive drugs research with hyperactives?" *American Journal of Diseases in Children* 123 (February): 177–180.

Foucault, Michel (1965). *Madness and Civilization.* New York: Pantheon.

Grinspoon, Lester and Susan Singer (1973). "Amphetamines in the treatment of hyperactive children." *Harvard Educational Review* 43 (November): 515–555.

Gross, Mortimer B. and William E. Wilson (1974). *Minimal Brain Dysfunction.* New York: Brunner Mazel.

Hentoff, Nat (1972). "Drug pushing in the schools: The professionals." *The Village Voice* 22 (May): 21–23.

Kitterie, Nicholas (1971). *The Right to Be Different.* Baltimore: Johns Hopkins Press.

Laufer, M. W., Denhoff, E., and Solomons, G. (1975). "Hyperkinetic impulse disorder in children's behavior problems." *Psychosomatic Medicine* 19 (January): 38–49.

Lennard, Henry L. and Associates (1971). *Mystification and Drug Misuse.* New York: Harper and Row.

Office of Child Development (1971). "Report of the conference on the use of stimulant drugs in treatment of behaviorally disturbed children." Washington, D.C.: Office of Child Development, Department of Health, Education and Welfare, January 11–12.

Pitts, Jesse (1968). "Social control: The concept." In David Sills (ed.), *International Encyclopedia of the Social Sciences,* Volume 14. New York: Macmillan.

Reynolds, Janice M. (1973). "The medical institution." Pp. 198–324 in Larry T. Reynolds and James M. Henslin, *American Society: A Critical Analysis.* New York: David McKay.

Robin, Stanley S. and James J. Bosco (1973). "Ritalin for school children: The teacher's perspective." *Journal of School Health* 47 (December): 624–628.

Rosen, George (1972). "The evolution of social medicine." Pp. 30–60 in Howard E. Freeman, Sol Levine, and Leo Reeder, *Handbook of Medical Sociology.* Englewood Cliffs, N. J.: Prentice-Hall.

Ryan, William (1970). *Blaming the Victim.* New York: Vintage.

Silverman, Milton and Philip R. Lee (1974). *Pills, Profits and Politics.* Berkeley: University of California Press.

Sroufe, L. Alan and Mark Stewart (1973). "Treating problem children with stimulant drugs." *New England Journal of Medicine* 289 (August 23): 407–421.

Stewart, Mark A. (1970). "Hyperactive Children." *Scientific American* 222 (April): 794–798.

Stewart, Mark A., A. Ferris, N. P. Pitts and A. G. Craig (1966). "The hyperactive child syndrome." *American Journal of Orthopsychiatry* 36 (October): 861–867.

Strauss, A. A. and L. E. Lehtinen (1947). *Psychopathology and Education of the Brain-Injured Child.* Vol. 1. New York: Grune and Stratton.

U.S. Government Printing Office (1970). "Federal involvement in the use of behavior modification drugs on grammar school children of the right to privacy inquiry: Hearing before a subcommittee of the committee on government operations." Washington, D.C.: 91st Congress, 2nd session (September 29).

Wender, Paul (1971). *Minimal Brain Dysfunction in Children.* New York: John Wiley and Sons.

Zola, Irving (1972). "Medicine as an institution of social control." *Sociological Review* 20 (November): 487–504.

Cultural Stereotypes and Mental Illness

THOMAS J. SCHEFF

THE SYMPTOMS OF "MENTAL ILLNESS" AS RESIDUALLY DEVIANT BEHAVIOR

One source of immediate embarrassment to any social theory of "mental illness" is that the terms used in referring to these phenomena in our society prejudge the issue. The medical metaphor "mental illness" suggests a determinate process which occurs within the individual: the unfolding and development of disease. It is convenient, therefore, to drop terms derived from the disease metaphor in favor of a standard sociological concept, deviant behavior, which signifies behavior that violates a social norm in a given society.

If the symptoms of mental illness are to be construed as violations of social norms, it is necessary to specify the type of norms involved. Most norm violations do not cause the violator to be labeled as mentally ill, but as ill-mannered, ignorant, sinful, criminal, or perhaps just harried, depending on the type of norm involved. There are innumerable norms, however, over which consensus is so complete that the members of a group appear to take them for granted. A host of such norms surround even the simplest conversation: a person engaged in conversation is expected to face toward his partner, rather than directly away from him; if his gaze is toward the part-

ner, he is expected to look toward his eyes, rather than, say, toward his forehead; to stand at a proper conversational distance, neither one inch away nor across the room, and so on. A person who regularly violated these expectations probably would not be thought to be merely ill-bred, but as strange, bizarre, and frightening, because his behavior violates the assumptive world of the group, the world that is construed to be the only one that is natural, decent, and possible.

The culture of the group provides a vocabulary of terms for categorizing many norm violations: crime, perversion, drunkenness, and bad manners are familiar examples. Each of these terms is derived from the type of norm broken, and ultimately, from the type of behavior involved. After exhausting these categories, however, there is always a residue of the most diverse kinds of violations, for which the culture provides no explicit label. For example, although there is great cultural variation in what is defined as decent or real, each culture tends to reify its definition of decency and reality, and so provide no way of handling violations of its expectations in these areas. The typical norm governing decency or reality, therefore, literally "goes without saying" and its violation is unthinkable for most of its members. For the convenience of the society in

Reprinted from *Sociometry,* Vol. 26 (1963), pp. 438–452, by permission of The American Sociological Association and the author.

construing those instances of unnamable deviance which are called to its attention, these violations may be lumped together into a residual category: witchcraft, spirit possession, or, in our own society, mental illness. In this paper, the diverse kinds of deviation for which our society provides no explicit label, and which, therefore, sometimes lead to the labeling of the violator as mentally ill, will be considered to be technically *residual deviance.*

THE ORIGINS, PREVALENCE AND COURSE OF RESIDUAL DEVIANCE

The first proposition concerns the origins of residual deviance. *1. Residual deviance arises from fundamentally diverse sources.* It has been demonstrated that some types of mental disorder are the result of organic causes. It appears likely, therefore, that there are genetic, biochemical or physiological origins for residual deviance. It also appears that residual deviance can arise from individual psychological peculiarities and from differences in upbringing and training. Residual deviance can also probably be produced by various kinds of external stress: the sustained fear and hardship of combat, and deprivation of food, sleep, and even sensory experience.[1] Residual deviance, finally, can be a volitional act of innovation or defiance. The kinds of behavior deemed typical of mental illness, such as hallucinations, delusions, depression, and mania, can all arise from these diverse sources.

The second proposition concerns the prevalence of residual deviance which is analogous to the "total" or "true" prevalence of mental disorder (in contrast to the "treated" prevalence). *2. Relative to the rate of treated mental illness, the rate of unrecorded residual deviance is extremely high.* There is evidence that grossly deviant behavior is often not noticed or, if it is noticed, it is rationalized as eccentricity. Apparently, many persons who are extremely withdrawn, or who "fly off the handle" for extended periods of time, who imagine fantastic events, or who hear voices or see visions, are not labeled as insane either by themselves or others.[2] Their deviance, rather, is unrecognized, ignored, or rationalized. This pattern of inattention and rationalization will be called "denial."[3] . . .

[It] seems plausible that residual deviant behavior is usually transitory, which is the substance of the third proposition. *3. Most residual deviance is "denied" and is transitory.* The high rates of total prevalence suggest that most residual deviancy is unrecognized or rationalized away. For this type of deviance, which is amorphous and uncrystallized, Lemert uses the term "primary deviation."[4] Balint describes similar behavior as "the unorganized phase of illness."[5] Although Balint assumes that patients in this phase ultimately "settle

---

[1] Philip Solomon, *et al.* (eds.), *Sensory Deprivation,* Cambridge: Harvard, 1961; E. L. Bliss, *et al.,* "Studies of Sleep Deprivation—Relationship to Schizophrenia," *A.M.A. Archives of Neurology and Psychiatry,* 81 (March, 1959), pp. 348–359.

[2] See, for example, John A. Clausen and Marian R. Yarrow, "Paths to the Mental Hospital," *Journal of Social Issues,* 11 (December, 1955), pp. 25–32; August B. Hollingshead and Frederick C. Redlich, *Social Class and Mental Illness,* New York: Wiley, 1958, pp. 172–176; and Elaine Cumming and John Cumming, *Closed Ranks,* Cambridge: Harvard, 1957, pp. 92–103.

[3] The term "denial" is used in the same sense as in Cumming and Cumming, *ibid.,* Chap. VII.

[4] Edwin M. Lemert, *Social Pathology,* New York: McGraw-Hill, 1951, Chap. 4.

[5] Michael Balint, *The Doctor, His Patient, and the Illness,* New York: International Universities Press, 1957, p. 18.

down" to an "organized illness," other outcomes are possible. A person in this stage may "organize" his deviance in other than illness terms, e.g., as eccentricity or genius, or the deviant acts may terminate when situational stress is removed.

SOCIAL CONTROL: INDIVIDUAL AND SOCIAL SYSTEMS OF BEHAVIOR

. . . One of Szasz's very apt formulations touches upon the social systemic aspects of role-playing. He draws an analogy between the role of the mentally ill and the "type-casting" of actors.[6] Some actors get a reputation for playing one type of role, and find it difficult to obtain other roles. Although they may be displeased, they may also come to incorporate aspects of the type-cast role into their self-conceptions, and ultimately into their behavior. Findings in several social psychological studies suggest that an individual's role behavior may be shaped by the kinds of "deference" that he regularly receives from others.[7]

One aspect of the voluntariness of role-playing is the extent to which the actor believes in the part he is playing.

Although a role may be played cynically, with no belief, or completely sincerely, with whole-hearted belief, many roles are played on the basis of an intricate mixture of belief and disbelief. During the course of a study of a large public mental hospital, several patients told the author in confidence about their cynical use of their symptoms—to frighten new personnel, to escape from unpleasant work details, and so on. Yet these *same* patients, at other times, appear to have been sincere in their symptomatic behavior. Apparently it was sometimes difficult for them to tell whether they were playing the role or the role was playing them. Certain types of symptomatology are quite interesting in this connection. In simulation of previous psychotic states, and in the behavior pattern known to psychiatrists as the Ganser syndrome, it is apparently almost impossible for the observer to separate feigning of symptoms from involuntary acts with any degree of certainty.[8] In accordance with what has been said so far, the difficulty is probably that the patient is just as confused by his own behavior as is the observer. . . .

What are the beliefs and practices that constitute the social institution of insanity?[9] And how do they figure in the de-

---

[6] Thomas S. Szasz, *The Myth of Mental Illness,* New York: Hoeber-Harper, 1961, p. 252. For discussion of type-casting see Orrin E. Klapp, *Heroes, Villains, and Fools,* Englewood Cliffs, New Jersey: Prentice-Hall, 1962, pp. 5–8 and *passim.*

[7] Cf. Zena S. Blau, "Changes in Status and Age Identification," *American Sociological Review,* 21 (April, 1956), pp. 198–203; James Benjamins, "Changes in Performance in Relation to Influences upon Self-Conceptualization," *Journal of Abnormal and Social Psychology,* 45 (July, 1950), pp. 473–480; Albert Ellis, "The Sexual Psychology of Human Hermaphrodites," *Psychosomatic Medicine,* 7 (March, 1945), pp. 108–125; S. Lieberman, "The Effect of Changes in Roles on the Attitudes of Role Occupants," *Human Relations,* 9 (1956), pp. 385–402. For a review of experimental evidence, see John H. Mann, "Experimental Evaluations of Role Playing," *Psychological Bulletin,* 53 (May, 1956), pp. 227–234. For an interesting demonstration of the inter-relations between the symptoms of patients on the same ward, see Sheppard G. Kellam and J. B. Chassan, "Social Context and Symptom Fluctuation," *Psychiatry,* 25 (November, 1962), pp. 370–381.

[8] Leo Sadow and Alvin Suslick, "Simulation of a Previous Psychotic State," *A.M.A. Archives of General Psychiatry,* 4 (May, 1961), pp. 452–458.

[9] The Cummings describe the social institution of insanity (the "patterned response" to deviance) in terms of denial, isolation, and insulation. Cumming and Cumming, *loc. cit.*

velopment of mental disorder? Two propositions concerning beliefs about mental disorder in the general public will now be considered.

4. *Stereotyped imagery of mental disorder is learned in early childhood.* Although there are no substantiating studies in this area, scattered observations lead the author to conclude that children learn a considerable amount of imagery concerning deviance very early, and that much of the imagery comes from their peers rather than from adults. The literal meaning of "crazy," a term now used in a wide variety of contexts, is probably grasped by children during the first years of elementary school. Since adults are often vague and evasive in their responses to questions in this area, an aura of mystery surrounds it. In this socialization the grossest stereotypes which are heir to childhood fears, e.g., of the "boogie man," survive. These conclusions are quite speculative, of course, and need to be investigated systematically, possibly with techniques similar to those used in studies of the early learning of racial stereotypes. . . .

5. *The stereotypes of insanity are continually reaffirmed, inadvertently, in ordinary social interaction.* Although many adults become acquainted with medical concepts of mental illness, the traditional stereotypes are not discarded, but continue to exist alongside the medical conceptions, because the stereotypes receive almost continual support from the mass media and in ordinary social discourse. In newspapers, it is a common practice to mention that a rapist or a murderer was once a mental patient. This negative information, however, is seldom offset by positive reports. An item like the following is almost inconceivable:

Mrs. Ralph Jones, an ex-mental patient, was elected president of the Fairview Home and Garden Society in their meeting last Thursday.

Because of highly biased reporting, the reader is free to make the unwarranted inference that murder and rape occur more frequently among ex-mental patients than among the population at large. Actually, it has been demonstrated that the incidence of crimes of violence, or of any crime, is much lower among ex-mental patients than among the general population.[10] Yet, this is not the picture presented to the public.

Reaffirmation of the stereotype of insanity occurs not only in the mass media, but also in ordinary conversation, in jokes, anecdotes, and even in conventional phrases. Such phrases as "Are you crazy?", or "It would be a madhouse," "It's driving me out of my mind," or "It's driving me distracted," and hundreds of others occur frequently in informal conversations. In this usage insanity itself is seldom the topic of conversation; the phrases are so much a part of ordinary language that only the person who considers each word carefully can eliminate them from his speech. Through verbal usages the stereotypes of insanity are a relatively permanent part of the social structure. . . .

DENIAL AND LABELING

According to the analysis presented here, the traditional stereotypes of mental disorder are solidly entrenched in the population because they are learned early in childhood and are continuously reaffirmed in the mass media and in every-

[10] Henry Brill and Benjamin Malzberg, "Statistical Report Based on the Arrest Record of 5354 Male Ex-patients Released from New York State Mental Hospitals During the Period 1946–48," mimeographed document available from the authors; L. H. Cohen and H. Freeman, "How Dangerous to the Community Are State Hospital Patients?" *Connecticut State Medical Journal,* 9 (September, 1945), pp. 697–701.

day conversation. How do these beliefs function in the processes leading to mental disorder? This question will be considered by first referring to the earlier discussion of the societal reaction to residual deviance.

It was stated that the usual reaction to residual deviance is denial, and that in these cases most residual deviance is transitory. The societal reaction to deviance is not always denial, however. In a small proportion of cases the reaction goes the other way, exaggerating and, at times distorting the extent and degree of deviation. This pattern of exaggeration, which we will call "labeling," has been noted by Garfinkel in his discussion of the "degradation" of officially recognized criminals.[11] Goffman makes a similar point in his description of the "discrediting" of mental patients.[12] Apparently under some conditions the societal reaction to deviance is to seek out signs of abnormality in the deviant's history to show that he was always essentially a deviant.

The contrasting social reactions of denial and labeling provide a means of answering two fundamental questions. If deviance arises from diverse sources—physical, psychological, and situational—how does the uniformity of behavior that is associated with insanity develop? Secondly, if deviance is usually transitory, how does it become stabilized in those patients who became chronically deviant? To summarize, what are the sources of uniformity and stability of deviant behavior?

In the approach taken here the answer to this question is based on hypotheses Nos. 4 and 5, that the role imagery of insanity is learned early in childhood, and is reaffirmed in social interaction. In a crisis, when the deviance of an individual becomes a public issue, the traditional stereotypes of insanity, his amorphous and unstructured deviant behavior tends to crystallize in conformity to these expections, thus becoming similar to the behavior of other deviants classified as mentally ill, and stable over time. The process of becoming uniform and stable is completed when the traditional imagery becomes a part of the deviant's orientation for guiding his own behavior.

The idea that cultural stereotypes may stabilize primary deviance, and tend to produce uniformity in symptoms, is supported by cross-cultural studies of mental disorder. Although some observers insist there are underlying similarities, most agree that there are enormous differences in the manifest symptoms of stable mental disorder *between* societies, and great similarity *within* societies.[13]

These considerations suggest that the labeling process is a crucial contingency in most careers of residual deviance. Thus Glass, who observed that neuropsychiatric casualties may not become mentally ill if they are kept with their unit, goes on to say that military experience with psychotherapy has been disappointing. Soldiers who are removed from their unit to a hospital, he states, often go on to become chronically impaired.[14] That is, their deviance is stabilized by the labeling process, which is

[11] Harold Garfinkel, "Conditions of Successful Degradation Ceremonies," *American Journal of Sociology,* 61 (March, 1956), pp. 420–424.

[12] Erving Goffman, "The Moral Career of the Mental Patient," in his *Asylums,* New York: Doubleday-Anchor, 1961, pp. 125–171.

[13] P. M. Yap, "Mental Diseases Peculiar to Certain Cultures: A Survey of Comparative Psychiatry," *Journal of Mental Science,* 97 (April, 1951), pp. 313–327; Paul E. Benedict and Irving Jacks, "Mental Illness in Primitive Societies," *Psychiatry,* 17 (November, 1954), pp. 377–389.

[14] Albert J. Glass, "Psychotherapy in the Combat Zone," in *Symposium on Stress,* Washington, D.C.: Army Medical Service Graduate School, 1953.

implicit in their removal and hospitalization. . . .

ACCEPTANCE OF THE DEVIANT ROLE

From this point of view, then, most mental disorder can be considered to be a social role. This social role complements and reflects the status of the insane in the social structure. It is through the social processes which maintain the statue of the insane that the varied deviancies from which mental disorder arises are made uniform and stable. The stabilization and uniformization of residual deviance are completed when the deviant accepts the role of the insane as the framework within which he organizes his own behavior. Three hypotheses are stated below which suggest some of the processes which cause the deviant to accept such a stigmatized role.

6. *Labeled deviants may be rewarded for playing the stereotyped deviant role.* Ordinarily patients who display "insight" are rewarded by psychiatrists and other personnel. That is, patients who manage to find evidence of "their illness" in their past and present behavior, confirming the medical and societal diagnosis, receive benefits. This pattern of behavior is a special case of a more general pattern that has been called the "apostolic function" by Balint, in which the physician and others inadvertently cause the patient to display symptoms of the illness the physician thinks the patient has.[15] Not only physicians but other hospital personnel and even other patients, reward the deviant for conforming to the stereotypes.[16]

7. *Labeled deviants are punished when they attempt the return to conventional roles.* The second process operative is the systematic blockage of entry to nondeviant roles once the label has been publicly applied. Thus the ex-mental patient, although he is urged to rehabilitate himself in the community, usually finds himself discriminated against in seeking to return to his old status, and on trying to find a new one in the occupational, marital, social, and other spheres.[17] Thus, to a degree, the labeled deviant is rewarded for deviating, and punished for attempting to conform.

8. *In the crisis occurring when a primary deviant is publicly labeled, the deviant is highly suggestible, and may accept the proffered role of the insane as the only alternative.* When gross deviancy is publicly recognized and made an issue, the primary deviant may be profoundly confused, anxious, and ashamed. In this crisis it seems reasonable to assume that the deviant will be suggestible to the cues that he gets from the reactions of others toward him.[18] But those around him are also in a crisis; the incomprehensible nature of the deviance, and the seeming need for immediate action lead them to take collective action against the deviant on the basis of the attitude which all share—the traditional

[15] Balint, *op. cit.,* pp. 215–239. Cf. Thomas J. Scheff, "Decision Rules, Types of Error and Their Consequences in Medical Diagnosis," *Behavioral Science,* 8 (April, 1963), pp. 97–107.

[16] William Caudill, F. C. Redlich, H. R. Bilmore, and E. B. Brody, "Social Structure and the Interaction Processes on a Psychiatric Ward," *American Journal of Orthopsychiatry,* 22 (April, 1952), pp. 314–334.

[17] Lemert, *op. cit.,* provides an extensive discussion of this process under the heading of "Limitation of Participation," pp. 434–440.

[18] This proposition receives support from Erikson's observations: Kai T. Erikson, "Patient Role and Social Uncertainty—A Dilemma of the Mentally Ill," *Psychiatry,* 20 (August, 1957), pp. 263–274.

stereotypes of insanity. The deviant is sensitive to the cues provided by these others and begins to think of himself in terms of the stereotyped role of insanity, which is part of his own role vocabulary also, since he, like those reacting to him, learned it early in childhood. In this situation his behavior may begin to follow the pattern suggested by his own stereotypes and the reactions of others. That is, when a primary deviant organizes his behavior within the framework of mental disorder, and when his organization is validated by others, particularly prestigeful others such as physicians, he is "hooked" and will proceed on a career of chronic deviance. . . .

For a person who has acquired an image of himself as lacking the ability to control his own actions, the process of self-control is likely to break down under stress. Such a person may feel that he has reached his "breaking-point" under circumstances which would be endured by a person with a "normal" self-conception. This is to say, a greater lack of self-control than can be explained by stress tends to appear in those roles for which the culture transmits imagery which emphasizes lack of self-control. In American society such imagery is transmitted for the roles of the very young and very old, drunkards and drug addicts, gamblers, and the mentally ill.

Thus, the social role of the mentally ill has a different significance at different phases of residual deviance. When labeling first occurs, it merely gives a name to primary deviation which has other roots. When (and if) the primary deviance becomes an issue, and is not ignored or rationalized away, labeling may create a social type, a pattern of "symptomatic" behavior in conformity with the stereotyped expectations of others. Finally, to the extent that the deviant role becomes a part of the deviant's self-conception, his ability to control his own behavior may be impaired under stress, resulting in episodes of compulsive behavior.

The preceding eight hypotheses form the basis for the final causal hypothesis. *9. Among residual deviants, labeling is the single most important cause of careers of residual deviance.* This hypothesis assumes that most residual deviance, if it does not become the basis for entry into the sick role, will not lead to a deviant career. Most deviant careers, according to this point of view, arise out of career contingencies, and are therefore not directly connected with the origins of the initial deviance.[19] Although there are a wide variety of contingencies which lead to labeling rather than denial, these contingencies can be usefully classified in terms of the nature of the deviant behavior, the person who commits the deviant acts, and the community in which the deviance occurs. Other things being equal, the severity of the societal reaction to deviance is a function of, first, the degree, amount, and visibility of the deviant behavior; second, the power of the deviant, and the social distance between the deviant and the agents of social control; and finally, the tolerance level of the community, and the availability in the culture of the community of alternative

---

[19] It should be noted, however, that these contingencies are causal only because they become part of a dynamic system: the reciprocal and cumulative inter-relation between the deviant's behavior and the societal reaction. For example, the more the deviant enters the role of the mentally ill, the more he is defined by others as mentally ill; but the more he is defined as mentally ill, the more fully he enters the role, and so on. By representing this theory in the form of a flow chart, Walter Buckley pointed out that there are numerous such feedback loops implied here. For an explicit treatment of feedback see Edwin M. Lemert, "Paranoia and the Dynamics of Exclusion," *Sociometry,* 25 (March, 1962), pp. 2–20.

nondeviant roles.[20] Particularly crucial for future research is the importance of the first two contingencies (the amount and degree of deviance), which are characteristics of the deviant, relative to the remaining five contingencies, which are characteristics of the social system.[21] To the extent that these five factors are found empirically to be independent determinants of labeling and denial, the status of the mental patient can be considered a partly ascribed rather than a completely achieved status. The dynamics of treated mental illness could then be profitably studied quite apart from the individual dynamics of mental disorder. . . .

[20] Cf. Lemert, *op. cit.*, pp. 51–53, 55–68; Goffman, "The Moral Career of the Mental Patient," in *Asylums, op. cit.*, pp. 134–135; David Mechanic, "Some Facts in Identifying and Defining Mental Illness," *Mental Hygiene*, 46 (January, 1962), pp. 66–74; for a list of similar factors in the reaction to physical illness, see Earl L. Koos, *The Health of Regionville*, New York: Columbia University Press, 1954, pp. 30–38.

[21] Cf. Thomas J. Scheff, "Psychiatric and Social Contingencies in the Release of Mental Patients in a Midwestern State," forthcoming; Simon Dinitz, Mark Lefton, Shirley Angrist, and Benjamin Pasamanick, "Psychiatric and Social Attributes as Predictors of Case Outcome in Mental Hospitalization," *Social Problems*, 8 (Spring, 1961), pp. 322–328.

Labeling the Mentally Retarded

JANE R. MERCER

The clinical perspective is the frame of reference most commonly adopted in studies of mental deficiency, mental illness, drug addiction, and other areas which the students of deviance choose to investigate.[1,2] This viewpoint is readily identified by several distinguishing characteristics.

First, the investigator accepts as the focus for study those individuals who have been labelled deviant. In so doing, he adopts the values of whatever social system has defined the person as deviant and assumes that its judgments are the valid measure of deviance. . . . Groups in the social structure sharing the values of the core culture tend to accept the labels attached as a consequence of the application of these values without serious questioning. . . .

A second distinguishing characteristic of the clinical perspective is the tendency to perceive deviance as an attribute of the person, as a meaning inherent in his behavior, appearance, or performance. Mental retardation, for example, is viewed as a characteristic of the person, a lack to be explained. This viewpoint results in a quest for etiology. Thus, the clinical perspective is essentially a medical frame of reference, for it sees deviance as individual pathology requiring diagnostic classification and etiological analysis for the purpose of determining proper treatment procedures and probable prognosis.

Three additional characteristics of the clinical perspective are the development of a diagnostic nomenclature, the creation of diagnostic instruments, and the professionalization of the diagnostic function.

When the investigator begins his research with the diagnostic designations assigned by official defining agents, he tends to assume that all individuals placed in a given category are essentially equivalent in respect to their deviance. . . . Individuals assigned to different categories of deviance are compared with each other or with a "normal" population consisting of persons who, for whatever reason, have escaped being labelled. The focus is on the individual.

Another characteristic of the clinical perspective is its assumption that the official definition is somehow the "right" definition. . . .

Reprinted from *Social Problems*, Vol. 13, No. 1 (Summer 1965), pp. 21–30, 33–34.

Supported in part by the National Institute of Mental Health, Grant No. 3M-9130: Population Movement of Mental Defectives and Related Physical, Behavioral, Social, and Cultural Factors; and Grant No. MH-5687: Mental Retardation in a Community, Pacific State Hospital, Pomona, California. Appreciation for assistance is expressed to the Western Data Processing Center, Division of the Graduate School of Business Administration, University of California, Los Angeles.

[1] August B. Hollingshead and Frederick C. Redlich, *Social Class and Mental Illness*, New York: John Wiley and Sons, 1958, Chapter 11.

[2] H. E. Freeman and O. G. Simmons, "Social Class and Posthospital Performance Levels," *American Sociological Review*, 2 (June, 1959), p. 348.

Finally, when deviance is perceived as individual pathology, social action tends to center upon changing the individual or, that failing, removing him from participation in society. Prevention and cure become the primary social goals. . . .

The social system perspective, on the other hand, attempts to see the definition of an individual's behavior as a function of the values of the social system within which he is being evaluated. The professional definers are studied as one of the most important of the evaluating social systems but within the context of other social systems which may or may not concur with official definitions.

Defining an individual as mentally ill, delinquent, or mentally retarded is viewed as an interpersonal process in which the definer makes a value judgment about the behavior of the persons being defined. . . . Deviation is not seen as a characteristic of the individual or as a meaning inherent in his behavior, but as a socially derived label which may be attached to his behavior by some social systems and not by others.[3]

. . . Thus, it follows that a person may be mentally retarded in one system and not mentally retarded in another. He may change his label by changing his social group. This viewpoint frees us from the necessity of seeing the person as permanently stigmatized by a deviant label and makes it possible to understand otherwise obscure patterns in the life careers of individuals. . . . The research reported in this paper attempts to answer these questions about a group of persons who shared the common experience of having been labelled retarded by official defining agencies and placed in a public institution for the retarded. . . .

The specific question which this study seeks to investigate within the above framework is: "Why do the families of some individuals take them back home after a period of institutionalization in a hospital for the retarded while other families do not, when, according to official evaluations, these individuals show similar degrees of deviance, that is, have comparable intelligence test scores, and are of equivalent age, sex, ethnic status, and length of hospitalization?" . . .

METHOD

Two groups of labelled retardates were studied. One group consisted of patients who had been released to their families from a state hospital for the retarded and the other group consisted of a matched group of patients still resident in the hospital at the time of the study.[4]

Specifically, the released group was made up of all patients released to their families during a three year period (1957–59), who had not been readmitted to another institution for the retarded at the time of the study, and who were reported to be living within a one hundred mile radius of the hospital. Only those cases in which the family had assumed responsibility for the patient were included. Of the 76 patients who met these qualifications, it was possible to complete interviews with 63 of the families. Six families refused to be interviewed and seven could not be located.

The resident group was selected to match the released group in intelligence quotient, age, sex, ethnic status, and year of admission, other studies having

[3] Howard S. Becker, editor, *The Other Side: Perspectives on Deviance*, New York: The Free Press, 1964.
[4] Pacific State Hospital, Pomona, California, is a state supported hospital for the mentally retarded with a population of approximately 3,000 patients.

TABLE 1 Comparison of Interviewed Cases by Birth Year, Intelligence Quotient, and Year of Admission

Matched Variable	Released (63)	Resident (70)	Significance Level
Birth Year			
Before 1920	4	5	
1921–1930	13	12	
1931–1940	33	34	> .05 [1]
1941–1950	12	17	
1951–1960	1	2	
Intelligence Quotient			
0–9	2	4	
10–19	2	1	
20–29	4	3	
30–39	6	4	> .05 [1]
40–49	13	15	
50–59	14	18	
60–69	19	19	
70+	3	6	
Year of Admission			
Before 1945	5	9	
1945–1950	20	14	
1951–1956	33	31	> .05 [1]
1957 and later	5	16	

1. The Kolmogorov-Simirnov Test of two independent samples was used.

demonstrated that these factors are related to the probability of release.[5]

The matched group of resident patients was selected in the following manner: all patients on the hospital rolls were sorted into two groups by sex, two groups by age, three groups by ethnic status, three groups by intelligence quotient, and two groups by year of admission. All released patients were likewise assigned to the proper category. Resident patients were then chosen at random from within each cell in sufficient numbers to correspond to the number of discharged patients also falling in that cell. Each resident case was required to have a family living within a one hundred mile radius of the hospital. If a case did not meet this requirement, another case was drawn randomly from the appropriate cell until there were an equal number of discharged and resident cases in each cell. Sex distribution in each group was 53 males and 23 females, ethnic distribution, 47 Caucasians, 20 Mexicans, and 9 Negroes.

. . . Table 1 presents the distribution of intelligence quotients, birth years, and years of admission for the interviewed cases. Of the 76 resident cases selected to match the released cases, interviews were completed with 70 families. Two refused to be interviewed and four fami-

[5] G. Tarjan, S. W. Wright, M. Kramer, P. H. Person, Jr., and R. Morgan, "The Natural History of Mental Deficiency in a State Hospital. I: Probabilities of Release and Death by Age, Intelligence Quotients, and Diagnosis," *AMA J. dis. Childr.*, 96 (1958), pp. 64–70.

TABLE 2 The Release Process as Reported by the Families of Released Patients

	f	%
Hospital Initiated Releases	12	19
Family Initiated Releases		
Family opposed to placement from beginning	9	14
Parents lonely without patient or need him for some practical reason, e.g., to help with younger children, earn money, etc.	8	13
Patient was unhappy in the hospital. Hospital Failure: Mistreated patient, made him work too hard, etc.	6	9
Hospital Success: Patient improved enough to come home	9	14
Home conditions changed to permit return, e.g., found patient a job, mother's health better, etc.	10	16
Total Released Cases	63	

lies could not be located. Using a Kolmogorov-Smirnov Test of two independent samples, we found that all differences between the interviewed groups could be accounted for by chance.

When the 19 non-interviewed cases were compared with the 133 interviewed cases, no significant differences were found in the sex, age, I.Q., or ethnic status of the patients, or the socioeconomic level of the families. . . .

The hospital file for each patient selected for study was searched for relevant data and an interview was held with a family member. In 75 per cent of the cases the mother was interviewed; in 8 per cent the father was interviewed; and in the remaining cases some other relative served as informant. . . .

To clarify the circumstances under which the released group returned to their families, the respondent was asked two questions: "Who was the most important person in getting you to take _____out of the hospital?" and "What were the main reasons you decided to have_____discharged from the hospital?"

In 12 cases the parents reported that someone in the hospital, i.e., a social worker, family care mother, or a ward technician, had first suggested that the patient could be released to the family. In the 51 remaining cases the families were the active agents in release. Reasons given by the family for seeking a discharge are described in Table 2.

It is clear from this table that most of the patients who returned to their families returned because the family made an effort to secure their release. . . .

FINDINGS

Social Status of Released Patients

Several indices were used to measure the socioeconomic level of the family of each retardate. A socioeconomic index score based on the occupation and education of the head of the household, weighted according to Hollingshead's system, was used as the basic measure. In addition, the interviewer rated the economic status of the street on which the patient's home was located, rated the physical condition of the housing unit, and completed a checklist of equipment present in the household. As can be seen in Table 3, the families of the released patients rated significantly lower than the families of the resident patients on every measure. The heads of the households in

TABLE 3 Socioeconomic Differences Between Patients Released to Their Families and Those Still Resident in the State Hospital

Socioeconomic Measure		Released Living at Home (63) %	Resident in State Hospital (70) %	Significance Level
Socioeconomic Index	Above Median	36.5	61.4	
Score of Head of	Below Median	61.9	38.6	< .01 [3]
Household	Unknown	1.6	0.0	
Economic Status	Housing Value	29.0	55.1	
of Street [1]	$10,000 and Above			
	Housing Value Less Than $10,000	71.0	44.9	< .05 [3]
Condition of Housing	Run Down	48.4	23.2	
Unit [1]	Average	46.8	57.2	< .05 [3]
	Above Average	4.8	18.8	
Household Equipment	0–2	19.0	11.9	
Scale [1]	3–5	27.6	20.9	< .05 [2]
	6–8	43.1	41.8	
	9–11	10.3	25.4	

1. Some cases are not included because data were not available.
2. Test of significance of difference between unrelated means was used.
3. Chi Square test was used.

the families of released patients had less education and lower level jobs, the family residence was located among less affluent dwellings, the housing unit was in a poorer state of repair, and the dwelling was less elaborately furnished and equipped. Contrary to the pattern found in studies of those placed as mentally ill,[6] it is the "retardate" from lower socioeconomic background who is most likely to be released to his family while higher status "retardates" are more likely to remain in the hospital.

From the clinical perspective, several explanations may be proposed for these differences. It has been found in hospital populations that patients with an I.Q. below 50 are more likely to come from families which represent a cross-section of social levels, while those with an I.Q. between 50 and 70 are more likely to come from low status families.[7] Since persons with higher I.Q.'s have a higher probability of release, this could account for higher rates of release for low status persons. However, in the present study, the tested level of intelligence was equal for both groups, and this hypothesis cannot be used as an explanation.

A second possible explanation from a

[6] August B. Hollingshead and Frederick C. Redlich, 1958, *op. cit.*, Chapter 11.

[7] Georges Sabagh, Harvey F. Dingman, George Tarjan, and Stanley W. Wright, "Social Class and Ethnic Status of Patients Admitted to a State Hospital for the Retarded," *Pacific Sociological Review,* 2 (Fall, 1959), pp. 76–80.

clinical perspective might be based on the fact that persons who have more physical handicaps tend to be institutionalized for longer periods of time than persons with few handicaps.[8] Should it be found that high status patients have more physical handicaps than low status patients, then this could account for the latter's shorter hospitalization. Data from the present sample were analyzed to determine whether there was a significant relationship between physical handicap and social status. Although released patients tended to have fewer physical handicaps than resident patients, this was irrespective of social status. When high status patients were compared with low status patients, 50% of the high status and 56% of the low status patients had no physical handicaps. A chi square of 1.9 indicates these differences could be accounted for by chance variation.

A third explanation from the clinical perspective may hinge on differences in the diagnostic categories to which retardates of different social status were assigned. . . . A diagnostic label of "familial" or "undifferentiated" ordinarily indicates that the individual has few or no physical stigmata and is essentially normal in body structure. All other categories ordinarily indicate that he has some type of physical symptomatology. Although released patients were more likely to be diagnosed as familial or undifferentiated than resident patients ($x^2 = 7.08$, p $<$ .01), this, like physical handicap, was irrespective of social status. Fifty-seven per cent of the high status retardates, and 69% of the low status retardates were classified as either undifferentiated or familial, a difference which could be accounted for by chance. . . .

Divergent Definitions

In analyzing social status, four types of situations were identified. The modal category for resident patients was high social status with a smaller number of resident patients coming from low status families. The modal category for released patients was low status with a smaller number of released patients coming from higher status families. If we are correct in our hypothesis (that higher release rates for low status patients are related to the fact that the family social system is structurally more distant from the core culture and that its style of life, values, and definitions of the patient are more divergent from official definitions than that of high status families), we would expect the largest differences to occur when high status resident families are compared to low status released families. The two non-modal categories would be expected to fall at some intermediate point. For this reason, the analysis of all subsequent variables has retained these four basic classifications.

Table 4 presents the responses made to three questions asked to determine the extent to which the family concurred in the official label of "retardation," the extent to which they believed the patient's condition amenable to change, and the extent to which they anticipated that the individual could live outside the hospital and, perhaps, fill adult roles. The patterns of the divergent definitions of the situation which emerged for each group are illuminating.

When asked whether *he* believed the patient to be retarded, the high status parent more frequently concurred with the definitions of the official defining agencies while the low status parent was more prone to disagree outright or to be uncertain. This tendency is especially

---

[8] G. Tarjan, S. W. Wright, M. Kramer, R. H. Person, Jr., and R. Morgan, 96, 1958, *op. cit.,* pp. 64–70.

TABLE 4 Patterns of Deviant Definitions

Question	Response Categories	High Status Resident (43) %	High Status Released (23) %	Low Status Resident (27) %	Low Status Released (39) %	Significance Levels — High Status / Low Status	Significance Levels — High Status Resident / Low Status Released	Significance Levels — High Status Resident / High Status Released	Significance Levels — Low Status Resident / Low Status Released
1. We know that many people have told you ____ is retarded but we want to know what you think. Do you think he/she is retarded?	Yes	74.4	47.8	66.6	41.0				
	Uncertain	20.9	39.1	14.8	25.6	< .02 [1]	< .02 [1]	NS [1]	NS [1]
	No	4.6	13.0	18.5	33.3				
2. Do you believe anything can change ____'s condition?	Nothing	74.3	39.0	66.6	33.3				
	Uncertain	2.3	17.2	11.1	38.4	< .02 [2]	< .001 [2]	< .01 [2]	< .01 [2]
	Training, Medical Care, etc.	23.2	43.4	22.2	28.2				
3. What do you see in the future for ____?	Dependent in Institution	83.7	13.0	74.0	2.5				
	Dependent at Home	9.3	60.8	22.2	48.7	< .02 [2]	< .001 [2]	< .001 [2]	< .001 [2]
	Normal Adult Roles	6.9	26.0	3.7	46.1				

1. The Kolmogorov—Smirnov Test of two independent samples was used.
2. The Log-Likelihood Ratio Test was used. (Barnett, Wolf, "The Log-Likelihood Ratio Test [The G-Test]: Methods and Tables for a Test of Heterogeneity in Contingency Tables," *Annals of Human Genetics*, Vol. 21, Part 4, June 1957, pp. 397–409.)

marked when the two modal categories are compared. While 33.3% of the parents of the low status released patients stated that they did not think the patient was retarded and 25.6% were uncertain whether he was retarded, only 4.6% of the parents of high status resident patients felt he was not retarded and 20.9% were uncertain.

When parents were asked whether they believed anything could change the patient's condition, the differences between all groups were significant at the .02 level or beyond. The high status parent was most likely to believe that nothing could change his child's condition, and this was significantly more characteristic of parents whose children were still in the hospital than those who had taken their child from the hospital on both status levels.

When asked what they saw in the future for their child, all groups again differed significantly in the expected direction. The modal, high status group was least optimistic and the modal, low status group, most optimistic about the future. Fully 46% of the parents of the latter group expressed the expectation that their child would get a job, marry, and fulfill the usual adult roles while only 6.9% of the modal, high status group responded in this fashion. High status parents, as a group, more frequently see their child playing dependent roles. It is interesting to note that, although a large percentage of parents of released patients believe the patient will be dependent, they demonstrate their willingness to accept responsibility for the retarded child themselves by their responding that they foresee him having a future in which he is dependent at home. Only 9.3% of the high status and 22.2% of the low status parents of the resident patients see this as a future prospect. Release to the family clearly appears to be contingent upon the willingness of the family to accept the patient's dependency, if they do not foresee him assuming independent adult roles.

Factors in the Labeling Process

From the social system perspective, retardation is viewed as a label placed upon an individual after someone has evaluated his behavior within a specific set of norms. Retardation is not a meaning necessarily inherent in the behavior of the individual. We have seen that the parents of low status, released patients tend to reject the label of retardation and to be optimistic about the future. We surmised that this divergent definition could well be related to factors in the process by which the child was first categorized as subnormal, such as his age at the time, the type of behavior which was used as a basis for making the evaluation, and the persons doing the labelling. Consequently, parents were asked specifically about these factors. Table 5 records their responses.

Children from lower status families were labelled as mentally subnormal at a significant later age than children from high status families. Seventy-nine per cent of the patients in the high status, modal group were classified as retarded by the age of six while only 36.1% of those in the low status, modal group were identified at such an early age. The largest percentage of low status retardates were first classified after they reached public school age. This indicates that relatives and friends, who are the individuals most likely to observe and evaluate the behavior of young children, seldom saw anything deviant in the early development of lower status children later labelled retarded, but that the primary groups of higher status children did perceive early deviation.

This is related to the responses made when parents were asked what first prompted someone to believe the patient retarded. The modal, high status group reported slow development in 48.8% of the cases and various types of physical

TABLE 5 Factors in the Labeling Process

Question	Response Categories	High Status Resident (43) %	High Status Released (23) %	Low Status Resident (27) %	Low Status Released (39) %	Significance Levels High Status / Low Status	Significance Levels Resident High / Released Low	Significance Levels Resident High / Released High	Significance Levels Resident Low / Released Low
1. How old was ——— when someone first said he was retarded?	1–2 years	44.1	18.1	23.2	16.7	< .001 [1]	< .02 [1]	NS [1]	NS [1]
	3–6 years	34.8	50.0	30.2	19.4				
	7–10 years	9.3	22.7	11.5	30.5				
	11–14 years	4.6	0.0	11.5	16.7				
	15 or over	6.9	9.1	23.2	16.7				
2. What was there about ——— that made you/them think he/she might be retarded?	Slow Development	48.8	30.4	19.2	14.7	< .005 [2]	< .001 [2]	NS [2]	NS [2]
	Physical Symptoms	20.9	17.3	26.9	11.8				
	Behavioral Problems	20.9	21.7	15.4	17.6				
	Couldn't Learn in School	9.3	30.4	38.5	55.9				
3. Who was the most important person in getting you to place ——— in the hospital?	Family	27.9	43.4	48.1	25.6	< .01 [2]	< .001 [2]	NS [2]	< .01 [2]
	Medical or Psychological Person	37.2	30.4	11.1	2.5				
	Police or Welfare	13.9	17.3	18.5	64.1				
	Schools or Other	20.9	8.6	22.2	7.6				

1. The Kolmogorov-Smirnov Test of two independent samples were used.
2. The Log-Likelihood Ratio Test was used. (Barnett, Wolf, "The Log-Likelihood Ratio Test [The G-Test]: Methods and Tables for a Test of Heterogeneity in Contingency Tables," Annals of Human Genetics, Vol. 21, Part 4, June 1957, pp. 397–409.)

symptoms in an additional 20.9%, while only 14.7% and 11.8% of the modal, low status parents gave these responses. On the other hand, 55.9% of the modal, low status group were first labelled because they had problems learning in school, while this was true of only 9.3% of the modal high status group.

When parents were asked who was the most important person influencing them in placing the child in the hospital, a parallel pattern emerged. Medical persons are the most important single group for the modal high status persons while the police and welfare agencies loom very significant in 64.1% of the cases in the modal, low status group. These findings are similar to those of Hollingshead and Redlich in their study of paths to the hospital for the mentally ill.[9] Of additional interest is the fact that the person important in placement differentiates the low status released from the low status resident patient at the .01 level. The resident low status patient's path to the hospital is similar to that of the high status patient and markedly different from released low status persons. When authoritative figures such as police and welfare are primary forces in placement, the patient is more likely to return home.

We interpret these findings to mean that when the family—or persons whose advice is solicited by the family, i.e., medical persons—is "most important" in placing a person in a hospital for the retarded, the primary groups have themselves first defined the individual as a deviant and sought professional counsel. When their own suspicions are supported by official definitions, they are more likely to leave the patient in an institution.

Conversely, when a person is labelled retarded by an authoritative, governmental agency whose advice is not solicited and who, in the case of the police,

may be perceived as a punishing agent, the family frequently rejects the official definition of the child as retarded and withdraws him from the institution at the first opportunity. This attitude was clearly exemplified by one mother who, when asked why the family had taken the child from the hospital, replied, "Why not? He had served his time."

The influence of the police as a factor in labelling the low status person as retarded may actually be greater than that shown in Table 5. Fifty per cent of the low status retardates had some type of police record while only 23% of the high status subnormals were known to the police, a difference significant beyond the .01 level. . . .

DISCUSSION AND CONCLUSIONS

The life space of the individual may be viewed as a vast network of interlocking social systems through which the person moves during the course of his lifetime. Those systems which exist close to one another in the social structure tend, because of overlapping memberships and frequent communication, to evolve similar patterns of norms. Most individuals are born and live out their lives in a relatively limited segment of this social network and tend to contact mainly social systems which share common norms. When an individual's contacts are restricted to a circumscribed segment of the structure, this gives some stability to the evaluations which are made of his behavior and to the labels which are attached to him.

However, when the person's life career takes him into segments of the social network which are located at a distance from his point of origin, as when a Mexican-American child enters the public school or a Negro child gets picked

[9] August B. Hollingshead and Frederick C. Redlich, 1958, *op. cit.*, Chapter 11.

up by the police, he is then judged by a new and different set of norms. Behavior which was perfectly acceptable in his primary social systems may now be judged as evidence of "mental retardation." At this point, he is caught up in the web of official definitions. However, because he has primary social systems which may not agree with these official labels, he may be able to return to that segment of the social structure which does not label him as deviant after he has fulfilled the minimal requirements of the official system. That is, he can drop out of school or he can "serve his time" in the state hospital and then go home. By changing his location in social space, he can change his label from "retarded" to "not much different from the rest of us." For example, the mother of a Mexican-American, male, adult patient who had been released from the hospital after being committed following an incident in which he allegedly made sexual advances to a young girl, told the author, "There is nothing wrong with Benny. He just can't read or write." Since the mother spoke only broken English, had no formal schooling, and could not read or write, Benny did not appear deviant to her. From her perspective, he didn't have anything wrong with him.

The child from a high status family has no such recourse. His primary social systems lie structurally close to the official social systems and tend to concur on what is acceptable. Definitions of his subnormality appear early in his life and are more universal in all his social groups. He cannot escape the retarded label because all his associates agree that he is a deviant.[10]

In conclusion, tentative answers may be given to the three questions raised earlier in this discussion. "Who sees whom as retarded?" Within the social system perspective, it becomes clear that persons who are clinically similar may be defined quite differently by their primary social systems. The person from lower status social systems is less likely to be perceived as mentally subnormal.

"What impact does this differential definition have on the life career of the person?" Apparently, these differential definitions do make a difference because the group which diverges most widely from official definitions is the group in which the most individuals are released from the institution to their families.

Finally, "What are the characteristics of the social systems which diverge most widely from official definitions?" These social systems seem to be characterized by low educational achievement, high levels of dependency, and high concentrations of ethnic minorities.

A social system perspective adds a useful dimension to the label "mental retardation" by its focus on the varied definitions which may be applied to behavior by different groups in society. For those interested in the care and treatment of persons officially labelled as mentally subnormal, it may be beneficial in some cases to seek systematically to relocate such individuals in the social structure in groups which will not define them as deviant. Rather than insisting that a family adopt official definitions of abnormality, we may frequently find it advisable to permit them to continue to view the patient within their own frame of reference and thus make it easier for them to accept him.

---

[10] Lewis Anthony Dexter, "On the Politics and Sociology of Stupidity in Our Society" in *The Other Side: Perspectives on Deviance,* edited by Howard S. Becker, New York: The Free Press, 1964, pp. 37–49.

Witchcraft and Its Control

ELLIOTT P. CURRIE

Something labeled witchcraft can be found in many societies, but the particular definition of the crime of witchcraft which emerged in Renaissance Europe was unique. It consisted of the individual's making, for whatever reason and to whatever end, a pact or covenant with the Devil, thereby gaining the power to manipulate supernatural forces for antisocial and un-Christian ends. What was critical was the pact itself; not the assumption or use of the powers which it supposedly conferred, but the willful renunciation of the Faith implied by the act of Covenant with the Devil. Thus, on the Continent, witchcraft was usually prosecuted as a form of heresy, and in England as a felony whose essence was primarily mental.[1] Witchcraft, then, came to be defined as a sort of thought-crime. It was not necessarily related to the practice of magic, which was widespread and had many legitimate forms. There were statutes forbidding witchcraft before the Renaissance, but the new conception of witchcraft involved important changes in both the nature and the seriousness of the crime. Early legislation, throughout Europe, had tended to lump witchcraft and magic in the same category, and to deal with them as minor offenses. . . . In no sense were

witches considered by ecclesiastical or secular authorities to be a serious problem, until the 15th century. . . . [During] the 15th and 16th centuries a new logical and legal conception of witchcraft emerged, which amounted to an official recognition of a hitherto unknown form of deviance. . . . At this point, the witch persecutions in continental Europe entered a peak phase which lasted into the 18th century. Estimates of the number of witches executed in Western Europe vary, but half a million is an average count.[2] Although there were consistently dissident voices both within and outside of the Church, the prevalence of witches was a fact widely accepted by the majority, including a number of the most powerful intellects of the time. Luther and Calvin were believers, as was Jean Bodin, who wrote an extremely influential book on witches in which he argued, among other things, that those who scoffed at the reality of witches were usually witches themselves.[3] Witchcraft was used as an explanation for virtually everything drastic or unpleasant that occurred; leading one Jesuit critic of the persecutions to declare: "God and Nature no longer do anything; witches, everything."[4] In the 15th century, a delayed winter in the province

---

Reprinted from Elliot P. Currie, "Crimes Without Criminals: Witchcraft and Its Control in Renaissance Europe," *Law and Society Review*, 3, I (August 1968), pp. 297–308, 310–13, 315–16. Reprinted by permission of The Law and Society Association.

[1] Elizabeth's statute of 1563 made witchcraft punishable by death only if it resulted in the death of the bewitched; witchcraft unconnected with death was a lesser offense. However, in 1604 James I revised the statute to invoke the death penalty for witchcraft regardless of result. On this point see R. T. Davies, *Four Centuries of Witch Beliefs* 15, 41–42 (1947).

[2] This estimate is from G. L. Kittredge, *Notes on Witchcraft* 59 (1907).

[3] Davies, *supra* note 1, at 25, 5–9.

[4] Father Friedrich Spee, quoted in Kittredge, *supra* note 2, at 47.

of Treves brought over a hundred people to the stake as witches.[5]

Once officially recognized, the crime of witchcraft presented serious problems for those systems of control through which it was to be hunted down and suppressed. The fact that no one had ever been seen making a pact with the Devil made ordinary sources of evidence rather worthless. Ordinary people, indeed, were in theory unable to see the Devil at all; as an eminent jurist, Sinistrari, phrased the problem, "There can be no witness of that crime, since the Devil, visible to the witch, escapes the sight of all beside."[6] The attendant acts—flying by night, attending witches' Sabbaths, and so on—were of such nature that little reliable evidence of their occurrence could be gathered through normal procedures. The difficulty of proving that the crime had ever taken place severely taxed the competence of European legal institutions, and two different responses emerged. In England, the response to witchcraft took place within a framework of effective limitations on the suppressive power of the legal order and a relatively advanced conception of due process of law; on the Continent, the response took place within a framework of minimal limitations on the activity of the legal system, in which due process and legal restraint tended to go by the board.

CONTINENTAL EUROPE: REPRESSIVE CONTROL

In continental Europe, people accused of witchcraft were brought before the elaborate machinery of a specialized bureaucratic agency with unusual powers and what amounted to a nearly complete absence of institutional restraints on its activity. Originally, the control of witchcraft was the responsibility of the Inquisition. After the disappearance, for practical purposes, of the Inquisition in most of Western Europe in the 16th century, witches were tried before secular courts which retained for the most part the methods which the Inquisition had pioneered.[7] . . .

Ordinary continental criminal procedure approximated the "inquisitorial" process, in which accusation, detection, prosecution and judgment are all in the hands of the official control system, rather than in those of private persons; and all of these functions reside basically in one individual.[8] The trial was not, as it was in the "accusatorial" procedure of English law, a confrontative combat between the accuser and the accused, but an attack by the judge and his staff upon the suspect, who carried with him a heavy presumption of guilt. Litigation was played down or rejected.[9] . . .

Nevertheless, certain powerful safeguards existed, in theory, for the accused. Chief among these was a rigorous conception of proof, especially in the case of capital crimes. In general, continental criminal procedure, at least from the 15th century onward, demanded a "complete proof" as warrant for capital punishment. "Complete proof" generally implied evidence on the order of testimony of two eyewitnesses to the criminal act or, in the case of certain crimes which otherwise would be difficult to establish, like heresy or conspiracy against the Prince, written proofs bound by rigorous standards of authenticity.[10]

[5] H. C. Lea, *A History of the Inquisition in the Middle Ages 493* (1888) at 549.

[6] Quoted in G. Parrinder, *Witchcraft: European and African* 76 (1958).

[7] Lea, *supra* note 5, at 244.

[8] *See* A. Esmein, *A History of Continental Criminal Procedure* 8 *passim* (1913).

[9] *Ibid.* at 9.

[10] *Ibid.* at 622–23.

In most cases of heresy and of witchcraft generally, proof of this order was hard, if not impossible, to come by, for obvious reasons. As a result, it was necessary to form a complete proof through combining confession, which was strong but not complete evidence, with another indication, such as testimony by one witness.[11] The result was tremendous pressure for confession at all costs, as well as a pressure for the relaxation of standards for witnesses and other sources of lesser evidence. The pressure for confession put a premium on the regular and systematic use of torture. In this manner, the procedural safeguard of rigorous proof broke down in practice through the allowance of extraordinary procedures which became necessary to circumvent it.[12] . . .

Besides being virtually required for the death penalty, confession was useful in two other important ways, which consequently increased the usefulness of torture. First, confession involved the denunciation of accomplices, which assured a steady flow of accused witches into the courts.[13] Secondly, confessions were publicly read at executions, and distributed to the populace at large, which reinforced the legitimacy of the trials themselves and recreated in the public mind the reality of witchcraft itself. If people *said* they flew by night to dance with the devil, then surely there was evil in the land, and the authorities were more than justified in their zeal to root it out. In extorting confessions from accused witches, the court also made use of means other than torture. Confession was usually required if the accused were to receive the last sacraments and avoid damnation,[14] and the accused, further, were frequently promised pardon if they confessed, a promise which was rarely kept.[15]

In line with the tendency to relax other standards of evidence, there was a considerable weakening of safeguards regarding testimony of witnesses. Heretics could testify, which went against established ecclesiastical policy;

[11] *Ibid.* at 625. It would still, of course, have been difficult to get even one reliable witness to an act of witchcraft; in practice, the testimony of one accused, under torture, was used for this purpose.

[12] *See* Esmein, *supra* note 8, at 625. In a study of the criminal process in China, Cohen relates, in a similar vein, that the requirement of confession for conviction in Manchu China reinforced the temptation to use torture on the accused. *See* J. A. Cohen, "The Criminal Process in the People's Republic of China; an Introduction," 79 *Harv. L. Rev.* 473 (1966). It should be noted that the employment of torture by the Inquisition was a retrograde step in continental criminal procedure. The Church explicitly condemned torture; after it had been used by the Romans, torture was not again a standard procedure in Western Europe until it was reactivated in the 1200s in the offensive against heresy. *See* Esmein, *supra* note 8 at 9. It was early laid down as an accepted rule of Canon Law that no confession should be extracted by torment; but the elimination of trials by ordeal in the 13th century coupled with the rise of powerful heretical movements put strong pressure on the Church to modify its approach. Originally, torture was left to the secular authorities to carry out, but a Bull of Pope Alexander IV in 1256 authorized Inquisitors to absolve each other for using it directly, and to grant each other dispensation for irregularities in its use. *See* Lea, *supra* note 1, at 421.

[13] 2 H. C. Lea, *Materials Toward a History of Witchcraft* (1939), at 885.

[14] 3 Lea, *Supra* note 5, at 506.

[15] *Ibid.* at 514; 2 Lea, *supra* note 13, at 895. Deception by the court in witchcraft cases was widely approved. Bodin argued that the court should use lying and deception of the accused whenever possible; the authors of the *Malleus Maleficarum* felt that it was a good idea for the courts to promise life to the accused, since the fear of execution often prevented confession.

so could excommunicates, perjurors, harlots, children and others who ordinarily were not allowed to bear witness. Witnesses themselves were liable to torture if they equivocated or appeared unwilling to testify; and, contrary to established procedure in ordinary continental courts, names of witnesses were withheld from the accused.[16]

In general, prisoners were not provided with information on their case.[17] Most of the proceedings were held in secret.[18] The stubborn prisoner who managed to hold to a denial of guilt was almost never released from custody[19] and frequently spent years in prison.[20] Acquittal, in witchcraft and heresy cases, was virtually impossible. Lacking enough evidence for conviction, the court could hold an accused in prison indefinitely at its discretion. In general, innocence was virtually never the verdict in such cases; the best one could hope for was "not proven."[21]

Legal counsel for the accused under the Inquisition was often prohibited, again contrary to ordinary continental procedure.[22] Where counsel was allowed, it was with the disturbing understanding that successful or overly eager defense laid the counsel himself open to charges of heresy or of conspiracy to aid heretics.[23] Moreover, counsel was appointed by the court, was warned not to assume a defense he "knew to be unjust," and could be summoned by the court as a witness and made to turn over all his information to the court.[24]

Lesser indications of guilt were supplied through the court's use of impossible dilemmas. If the accused was found to be in good repute among the populace, he or she was clearly a witch, since witches invariably sought to be highly thought of; if in bad repute, then he or she was also clearly a witch, since no one approves of witches. If the accused was especially regular in worship or morals, it was argued that the worst witches made the greatest show of piety.[25] Stubbornness in refusing to confess was considered a sure sign of alliance with the Devil, who was known to be taciturn.[26] Virtually the only de-

---

[16] Esmein, *supra* note 8, at 91–94; Lea, *supra* note 5, at 434–37.

[17] Esmein, *supra* note 8, at 129.

[18] Lea, *supra* note 5, at 406.

[19] *Ibid.* at 419.

[20] *Ibid.* at 419.

[21] *Ibid.* at 453. The following quote from the period shows one important motive behind the absence of outright release:

> If by torture he will say nothing nor confess, and is not convicted by witnesses . . . he should be released at the discretion of the judge on pain of being attained and convicted of the matters with which he is charged and of which he is presumed guilty . . . for if he be freed absolutely, *it would seem that he had been held prisoner without charge.*

Quoted in Esmein, *supra* note 8, at 130 (emphasis added).

[22] Esmein, *supra* note 8, at 91–94. This was particularly critical in continental procedure, where presumption of guilt made the defense difficult in any case; it was less critical in England, where the burden of proof was on the court. The Church well knew the vital importance of counsel in criminal trials; *free counsel* was provided, in many kinds of ordinary cases, to those unable to afford it. *See* Lea, *supra* note 5, at 444–45.

[23] J. Sprenger & H. Kramer, *Malleus Maleficarum* (M. Summers transl. 1948) at 218; Lea, *supra* note 5, at 444–45.

[24] 2 Lea, *supra* note 5, at 517–18.

[25] 2 Lea, *supra* note 13, at 858.

[26] Lea, *supra* note 5, at 509.

fense available to accused witches was in disabling hostile witnesses on the grounds of violent enmity; this provision was rendered almost useless through the assumption that witches were naturally odious to everyone, so that an exceptionally great degree of enmity was required.[27]

A final and highly significant characteristic of the continental witch trial was the power of the court to confiscate the property of the accused, whether or not he was led to confess.[28] The chief consequence of this practice was to join to a system of virtually unlimited power a powerful motive for persecution. This coincidence of power and vested interest put an indelible stamp on every aspect of witchcraft in continental Europe.

All things considered, the continental procedure in the witch trials was an enormously effective machine for the systematic and massive production of confessed deviants. As such, it approximates a type of deviance-management which may be called repressive control. Three main characteristics of such a system may be noted, all of which were present in the continental legal order's handling of the witch trials:

1. Invulnerability to restraint from other social institutions

2. Systematic establishment of extraordinary powers for suppressing deviance, with a concomitant lack of internal restraints

3. A high degree of structured interest in the apprehension and processing of deviants. . . .

ENGLAND: RESTRAINED CONTROL

There was no Inquisition in Renaissance England, and the common law tradition provided a variety of institutional restraints on the conduct of the witch trials. As a consequence, there were fewer witches in England, vastly fewer executions, and the rise of a fundamentally different set of activities around the control of witchcraft.

Witchcraft was apparently never prosecuted as a heresy in England, but after a statute of Elizabeth in 1563 it was prosecuted as a felony in secular courts.[29] The relatively monolithic ecclesiastical apparatus, so crucial in the determination of the shape of witch trials on the Continent, did not exist in England; the new definition of witchcraft came to England late and under rather different circumstances.[30] . . .

---

[27] *Ibid.* at 517.

[28] 2 Lea, *supra* note 13, at 808–811; Lea, *supra* note 5, at 529.

[29] The statute is 5 Eliz., c. 16 (1563); see Davies, *supra* note 1, at 15, for a partial quote of this statute; and p. 42, for a quote from James I's 1604 statute making witchcraft per se, without involving the death of another person, a capital offense.

An earlier statute (33 Hen. 8, c. 8 [1541]) made witchcraft a felony, but was repealed in 1547 and probably used only sporadically and for largely political purposes. Before that, too, there were occasional trials for witchcraft or sorcery, and witchcraft of a sort, as I have shown, appears in the earliest English law. But this was the older conception of witchcraft, blurring into that of magic; and it was not until Elizabeth's statute that witch trials began in earnest. *See* W. Notestein, *A History of Witchcraft in England* ch. 1 (1911).

[30] Two of these circumstances may be mentioned. One was the general atmosphere of social and political turmoil surrounding the accession of Elizabeth to the throne; another was the return to England, with Elizabeth's crowning, of a number of exiled Protestant leaders who had been exposed to the witch trials in Geneva and elsewhere and had ab-

(Continued)

[The] English laws were enforced in a relatively restrained fashion through a system of primarily local courts of limited power, accountable to higher courts and characterized by a high degree of internal restraint.

. . . English courts operated primarily on the accusatory principle, stressing above all the separation of the functions of prosecution and judgment, trial by jury, and the presumption of the innocence of the accused.[31] Accuser and accused assumed the role of equal combatants before the judge and jury; prosecution of offenses generally required a private accuser.[32] The English trial was confrontative and public, and the English judge did not take the initiative in investigation or prosecution of the case.[33] Again unlike the situation on the Continent, the accused witch could appeal to higher authority from a lower court, and could sue an accuser for defamation. . . . Reprieves were often granted.[34] From the middle of the 17th century, the accused in capital cases could call witnesses in their defense.[35] In general, the English courts managed to remain relatively autonomous and to avoid degeneration into a tool of ideological or moral interests: Voltaire was to remark, in the 18th century, that "In France the Criminal Code seems framed purposely for the destruction of the people; in England it is their safeguard."[36]

There were, nevertheless, important limitations to this picture of the English courts as defenders of the accused. Accusatory ideals were not always met in practice, and many elements of a developed adversary system were only latent. Defendants were not allowed counsel until 1836.[37] In general, since the defendant entered court with a presumption of innocence, the English courts did not demand such rigorous proofs for conviction as did the continental courts. Testimony of one witness was usually sufficient for conviction in felony cases; children were frequently allowed to testify.[38] In practice, however, this worked out differently than might be expected. The lack of complex, rigid standards of proof in English courts meant that there was little pressure to subvert the series of safeguards surrounding the accused through granting the court extraordinary powers of interrogation, and it went hand-in-hand with a certain care on the part of the courts

---

sorbed the continental attitudes toward witchcraft. One of these, Bishop John Jewel of Salisbury, argued before the Queen that

> This kind of people (I mean witches and sorcerers) within the last few years are marvelously increased within your Grace's realm. These eyes have seen the most evident and manifest marks of their wickedness. Your Grace's subjects pine away even unto death, their color fadeth, their speech is benumbed, their senses are bereft. Wherefore your poor subject's most humble petition to your Highness is, that the laws touching such malefactors may be put in due execution. Davies, *supra* note 1, at 17; *cf.* Notestein, *supra* note 29.

[31] *See* Esmein, *supra* note 8, at Introduction. Esmein notes the similarity between the politically-oriented Star Chamber and the typical continental court. A few cases of witchcraft, notably those with political overtones, were processed there; *see* C. L'Estrange Ewen, *Witchcraft in the Star Chamber* esp. 11 (1938).

[32] Esmein, *supra* note 8, at 107, 336.

[33] *Ibid.* at 3, 6.

[34] C. L'Estrange Ewen, *Witch Hunting and Witch Trials* 32 (1929).

[35] Esmein, *supra* note 8, at 342.

[36] Quoted in Esmein, *supra* note 8, at 361.

[37] *Ibid.* at 342.

[38] Ewen, *supra* note 34, at 58.

for the rights of the defendant. Torture, except in highly limited circumstances as an act of Royal prerogative, was illegal in England, and was never lawfully or systematically used on accused witches in the lower courts.[39]

Given the nature of the crime of witchcraft, witnesses were not always easily found; given the illegality of torture, confessions were also relatively rare. In this difficult situation, alternative methods of obtaining evidence were required. As a consequence, a variety of external evidence emerged.

Three sources of external evidence became especially significant in English witch trials. These are pricking, swimming, and watching.[40] Pricking was based on the theory that witches invariably possessed a "Devil's Mark," which was insensitive to pain. Hence, the discovery of witches involved searching the accused for unusual marks on the skin and pricking such marks with an instrument designed for that purpose. If the accused did not feel pain, guilt was indicated. Often, pricking alone was considered sufficient evidence for conviction.

Swimming was based on the notion that the Devil's agents could not sink in water, and was related to the "ordeal by water" common in early European law.[41]

The victim was stripped naked and bound with her right thumb to her left toe, and her left thumb to her right toe, and was then cast into the pond or river. If she sank, she was frequently drowned; if she swam she was declared guilty without any further evidence being required.[42]

The third source of evidence, watching, reflected the theory that the Devil provided witches with imps or familiars which performed useful services, and which the witch was charged with suckling. The familiars could therefore be expected to appear at some point during the detention of the suspected witch, who was therefore placed in a cell, usually on a stool, and watched for a number of hours or days, until the appointed watchers observed familiars in the room.

A number of other kinds of evidence were accepted in the English trials. Besides the testimony of witnesses, especially those who claimed to have been bewitched, these included the discovery of familiars, waxen or clay images, or other implements in the suspect's home, and of extra teats on the body, presumably used for suckling familiars.[43]

These methods were called for by the lack of more coercive techniques of obtaining evidence within the ambit of English law. In general, the discovery and trial of English witches was an unsystematic and inefficient process, resembling the well-oiled machinery of the continental trial only remotely. The English trial tended to have an ad hoc aspect in which new practices, techniques and

---

[39] Torture may have been used on some witches in the Star Chamber. Notestein, *supra* note 29, at 167, 204 suggests that it may have been used illegally in a number of cases; nevertheless, torture was not an established part of English criminal procedure, except in the limited sense noted above. *See* 2 Sir J. F. Stephen, *History of the Criminal Law in England* 434 (1883); Ewen, *supra* note 34, at 65. It was allowed in Scotland, where, predictably, there were more executions; several thousand witches were burned there during this period. *See* G. F. Black, *A Calendar of Cases of Witchcraft in Scotland, 1510–1727*, 13–18 (1938); Notestein, *supra* note 29, at 95–96.

[40] This discussion is taken from Ewen, *supra* note 34, at 60–71, and from remarks at various places in Notestein, *supra* note 29.

[41] *See* M. Hopkins, *The Discovery of Witches* 38 (1928).

[42] Quoted in Ewen, *supra* note 34, at 68; Ewen argues, though, that swimming alone was probably not usually sufficient evidence for the death penalty.

[43] *Ibid.* at 68.

theories were continually being evolved or sought out.

Finally, the confiscation of the property of suspected witches did not occur in England. . . . As a consequence, unlike the continental authorities, the English officials had no continuous vested interest in the discovery and conviction of witches. Thus, they had neither the power nor the motive for large-scale persecution. The English control system, then, was of a "restrained" type, involving the following main characteristics:

1. Accountability to, and restraint by, other social institutions

2. A high degree of internal restraint, precluding the assumption of extraordinary powers

3. A low degree of structured interests in the apprehension and processing of deviants

The English and continental systems, then, were located at nearly opposite ends of a continuum from restrained to repressive control of deviance. We may now look at the effects of these differing control systems on the character of witchcraft in the two regions.

WITCHCRAFT CONTROL AS INDUSTRY: THE CONTINENT

On the Continent, the convergence of a repressive control system with a powerful economic motive created something very much like a largescale industry based on the mass stigmatization of witches and the confiscation of their property. This gave distinct character to the *rate* of witchcraft in Europe, the kinds of people who were convicted as witches, and the entire complex of activities which grew up around witchcraft. . . .

Like any large enterprise, the witchcraft industry was subject to the need for continual expansion in order to maintain its level of gain. A mechanism for increasing profit was built into the structure of the trials, whereby, through the use of torture to extract names of accomplices from the accused, legitimate new suspects became available. . . .

Its effect on the scope or rate of the deviance is the most striking at first glance. Several hundred thousand witches were burned in continental Europe during the main period of activity, creating a picture of the tremendous extent of witchcraft in Europe. The large number of witches frightened the population and legitimized ever more stringent suppression. Thus, a cycle developed in which rigorous control brought about the appearance of high rates of deviance, which were the basis for more extreme control, which in turn sent the rates even higher, and so on.

A second major effect was the selection of particular categories of people for accusation and conviction. A significant proportion of continental witches were men, and an even more significant proportion of men and women were people of wealth and/or property. This is not surprising, given the material advantages to the official control apparatus of attributing the crime to heads of prosperous households. . . .

WITCHCRAFT CONTROL AS RACKET: ENGLAND

The restrained nature of the English legal system precluded the rise of the kind of mass witchcraft industry which grew up on the Continent. What the structure of that system did provide was a context in which individual entrepreneurs, acting from below, were able to profit through the discovery of witches. Hence, in England, there developed a series of rackets through which individuals manipulated the general climate of distrust, within the framework of a control structure which was frequently reluctant to approve of their activities. Because of its accusatorial character, the English court could not systematically initiate the prosecution of witches; because of its limited character generally, it could not have processed masses of presumed witches even had it had the power to initiate such prosecutions; and because of the absence of authority to confiscate witches' property, it had no interest in doing so even had it been able to. Witch prosecutions in England were initiated by private persons who stood to make a small profit in a rather precarious enterprise. As a result, there were fewer witches in England than on the Continent, and their sex and status tended to be different as well.

Given the lack of torture and the consequent need to circumvent the difficulty of obtaining confessions, a number of kinds of external evidence, some of which were noted above, became recognized. Around these sources of evidence there grew up a number of trades, in which men who claimed to be expert in the various arts of witchfinding—pricking, watching, and so on—found a ready field of profit. They were paid by a credulous populace, and often credulous officials, for their expertise in ferreting out witches. . . . Several devices were used by prickers to increase the probability of discovery and conviction. One was the use of pricking knives with retractable blades and hollow handles, which could be counted on to produce no pain while appearing to be embodied in the flesh—thus demonstrating the presence of an insensible "Devil's Mark."[44] Professional "watchers," too, thrived in this climate. . . .

An essential characteristic of all these rackets was their precariousness. To profess special knowledge of the demonic and its agents opened the entrepreneur to charges of fraud or witchcraft; money could be made, but one could also be hanged, depending on the prevailing climate of opinion. . . .

The peculiar and restrained character of the English control of witches led to characteristic features of the behavior system of English witchcraft. The lack of vested interest from above, coupled with the absence of torture and other extraordinary procedures, was largely responsible for the small number of witches executed in England from 1563 to 1736.[45] Of those indicted for witchcraft, a relatively small percentage was actually executed—again in contrast to the inexorable machinery of prosecution in continental Europe. . . .

Further, English witches were usually women and usually lower class. Again, this was a consequence of the nature of the control structure. English courts did not have the power or the motive to systematically stigmatize the wealthy and propertied; the accusations came from below, specifically from the lower and more credulous strata or those who manipulated them, and were directed against socially marginal and undesirable individuals who were powerless to defend themselves. The process through which the witch was brought to justice involved the often reluctant capitulation of the courts to popular sentiment fueled by the activities of the witchfinders; the witches were usually borderline deviants already in disfavor with their neighbors. Household servants, poor tenants, and others of lower status predominated. Women who worked as midwives were especially singled out, particularly when it became necessary to explain stillbirths. . . .

The decline of witchcraft in England, too, was the result of a different process from that on the Continent, where the decline of witchcraft was closely related to the imposition of restraints on court

---

[44] Ewen, *supra* note 34, at 62.

[45] Cf. Ewen, *supra* note 5, at 112; G. L. Kittredge, *Notes on Witchcraft* 59 (1907).

procedure. In England, the decline was related to a general shift of opinion, in which the belief in witchcraft itself waned, particularly in the upper strata, as a result of which the courts began to treat witchcraft as illusory or at best unprovable. English judges began refusing to execute witches well before the witch laws were repealed in 1736; and although there were occasional popular lynchings of witches into the 18th century, the legal system had effectively relinquished the attempt to control witchcraft.[46] With this shift of opinion, the entire structure of witchcraft collapsed, for all practical purposes, at the end of the 17th century.[47]

CONCLUSION

If one broad conclusion emerges from this discussion, it is that the phenomenon of witchcraft in Renaissance Europe strongly reinforces on one level the argument that deviance is what officials say it is, and deviants are those so designated by officials. Where the deviant act is nonexistent, it is necessarily true that the criteria for designating people as deviant do not lie in the deviant act itself, but in the interests, needs, and capacities of the relevant official and unofficial agencies of control, and their relation to extraneous characteristics of the presumptive deviant. . . .

Because of their combination of power and interest, repressive control systems tend to concentrate most heavily on stigmatizing people whose successful prosecution will be most useful in terms of the system's own needs and goals. This is true whether the goal is economic profit or the elimination of sources of moral or political dissent, or a combination of these. Consequently, the deviant population under a system of repressive control will contain an unusually large number of relatively wealthy and/or powerful people, and of solid citizens generally. Under a restrained control system, on the other hand, the typical deviant will be lower-class; the deviant population will be most heavily represented by the relatively powerless, who lack the resources necessary to make successful use of those safeguards which the restrained system provides, and who are particularly vulnerable to abuse.

[46] See Davies, *supra* note 1, at 182–203.

[47] An incident supposedly involving the anatomist William Harvey is indicative of this change of opinion. Harvey, on hearing that a local woman was reputed to be a witch, took it upon himself to dissect one of her familiars, which took the shape of a toad; he found it to be exactly like any other toad, and a minor blow was struck for the Enlightenment. *See* Notestein, *supra* note 29, at 111.

the role of third parties

4

As we noted in Chapter 1, deviance reflects a process of social definition. Such definition is often effected or facilitated by third parties. Family members, for example, may enlist an outside defining agent to help them define deviance. And people may appeal to the law to define certain others officially as deviant. In any event, how successful the labeling will be depends on how much consensus the defining agent can muster, and consensus is much easier to attain when significant outsiders cooperate in the labeling.

In the first reading Goffman points out how family members and outside defining agents collaborate in a process that culminates in a person's being committed to a mental hospital. Next, Lemert shows how people actually do conspire to exclude so-called paranoids. Garfinkel then describes the things that must be communicated for a defining agent to be able to denounce another person successfully. In the final reading Bustamante describes the wetbacks' labor situation, and how the failure of the Border Patrol to enforce immigration laws is related to the economic interests of powerful farmers; thus, in this case, the farmers, as third parties, are "antilaw entrepreneurs."

The Moral Career of the Mental Patient

ERVING GOFFMAN

Traditionally the term *career* has been reserved for those who expect to enjoy the rises laid out within a respectable profession. The term is coming to be used, however, in a broadened sense to refer to any social strand of any person's course through life. The perspective of natural history is taken: unique outcomes are neglected in favor of such changes over time as are basic and common to the members of a social category, although occurring independently to each of them. Such a career is not a thing that can be brilliant or disappointing; it can no more be a success than a failure. In this light, I want to consider the mental patient, drawing mainly upon data collected during a year's participant observation of patient social life in a public mental hospital,[1] wherein an attempt was made to take the patient's point of view.

One value of the concept of career is its two-sidedness. One side is linked to internal matters held dearly and closely, such as image of self and felt identity; the other side concerns official position, jural relations, and style of life, and is part of a publicly accessible institutional complex. The concept of career, then, allows one to move back and forth between the personal and the public, between the self and its significant society, without having overly to rely for data upon what the person says he thinks he imagines himself to be.

This paper, then, is an exercise in the institutional approach to the study of self. The main concern will be with the *moral* aspects of career—that is, the regular sequence of changes that career entails in the person's self and in his framework of imagery for judging himself and others.[2]

Reprinted by special permission of the author and The William Alanson White Psychiatric Foundation, Inc., from *Psychiatry: Journal for the Study of Interpersonal Processes,* Vol. 22 (May 1959), pp. 123–135. Copyright 1959 by The William Alanson White Psychiatric Foundation, Inc.

[1] The study was conducted during 1955–56 under the auspices of the Laboratory of Socio-environmental Studies of the National Institute of Mental Health. I am grateful to the Laboratory Chief, John A. Clausen, and to Dr. Winfred Overholser, Superintendent, and the late Dr. Jay Hoffman, then First Assistant Physician of Saint Elizabeth's Hospital, Washington, D.C., for the ideal cooperation they freely provided. A preliminary report is contained in Goffman, "Interpersonal Persuasion," pp. 117–193; in *Group Processes: Transactions of the Third Conference,* edited by Bertram Schaffner; New York, Josiah Macy, Jr. Foundation, 1957. A shorter version of this paper was presented at the Annual Meeting of the American Sociological Society, Washington, D.C., August, 1957.

[2] Material on moral career can be found in early social anthropological work on ceremonies of status transition, and in classic social psychological descriptions of those spectacular changes in one's view of self that can accompany participation in social movements

The category "mental patient" itself will be understood in one strictly sociological sense. In this perspective, the psychiatric view of a person becomes significant only in so far as this view itself alters his social fate—an alteration which seems to become fundamental in our society when, and only when, the person is put through the process of hospitalization.[3] I therefore exclude certain neighboring categories: the undiscovered candidates who would be judged "sick" by psychiatric standards but who never come to be viewed as such by themselves or others, although they may cause everyone a great deal of trouble;[4] the office patient whom a psychiatrist feels he can handle with drugs or shock on the outside; the mental client who engages in psychotherapeutic relationships. And I include anyone, however robust in temperament, who somehow gets caught up in the heavy machinery of mental hospital servicing. In this way the effects of being treated as a mental patient can be kept quite distinct from the effects upon a person's life of traits a clinician would view as psychopathological.[5] Persons who become mental hospital patients vary widely in the kind and degree of illness that a psychiatrist would impute to them, and in the attributes by which laymen would describe them. But once started on the way, they are confronted by some importantly similar circumstances and respond to these in some importantly similar ways. Since these similarities do not come from mental illness, they would seem to occur in spite of it. It is thus a tribute to the power of social forces that the uniform status of mental patient can not only assure an aggregate of persons a common fate and eventually, because of this, a common character, but that this social reworking can be done upon what is perhaps the most obstinate diversity of human materials that can be brought together by society. Here there lacks only the frequent forming of a protective group-life by ex-patients to illustrate in full the classic cycle of response by which deviant sub-groupings are psychodynamically formed in society.

---

and sects. Recently new kinds of relevant data have been suggested by psychiatric interest in the problem of "identity" and sociological studies of work careers and "adult socialization."

[3] This point has recently been made by Elaine and John Cumming, *Closed Ranks:* Cambridge, Commonwealth Fund, Harvard Univ. Press, 1957; pp. 101–102. "Clinical experience supports the impression that many people define mental illness as 'That condition for which a person is treated in a mental hospital.'. . . Mental illness, it seems, is a condition which afflicts people who must go to a mental institution, but until they do almost anything they do is normal." Leila Deasy has pointed out to me the correspondence here with the situation in white collar crime. Of those who are detected in this activity, only the ones who do not manage to avoid going to prison find themselves accorded the social role of the criminal.

[4] Case records in mental hospitals are just now coming to be exploited to show the incredible amount of trouble a person may cause for himself and others before anyone begins to think about him psychiatrically, let alone take psychiatric action against him. See John A. Clausen and Marian Radke Yarrow, "Paths to the Mental Hospital," *J. Social Issues* (1955) 11:25–32; August B. Hollingshead and Frederick C. Redlich, *Social Class and Mental Illness;* New York, Wiley, 1958; pp. 173–174.

[5] An illustration of how this perspective may be taken to all forms of deviancy may be found in Edwin Lemert, *Social Pathology;* New York, McGraw-Hill, 1951; see especially pp. 74–76. A specific application to mental defectives may be found in Stewart E. Perry, "Some Theoretic Problems of Mental Deficiency and Their Action Implications," *Psychiatry* (1954) 17:45–73; see especially p. 68.

This general sociological perspective is heavily reinforced by one key finding of sociologically oriented students in mental hospital research. As has been repeatedly shown in the study of nonliterate societies, the awesomeness, distastefulness, and barbarity of a foreign culture can decrease in the degree that the student becomes familiar with the point of view to life that is taken by his subjects. Similarly, the student of mental hospitals can discover that the craziness or "sick behavior" claimed for the mental patient is by and large a product of the claimant's social distance from the situation that the patient is in, and is not primarily a product of mental illness. Whatever the refinements of the various patient's psychiatric diagnoses, and whatever the special ways in which social life on the "inside" is unique, the researcher can find that he is participating in a community not significantly different from any other he has studied.[6] Of course, while restricting himself to the off-ward grounds community of paroled patients, he may feel, as some patients do, that life in the locked wards is bizarre; and while on a locked admissions or convalescent ward, he may feel that chronic "back" wards are socially crazy places. But he need only move his sphere of sympathetic participation to the "worst" ward in the hospital, and this too can come into social focus as a place with a livable and continuously meaningful social world. This in no way denies that he will find a minority in any ward or patient group that continues to seem quite beyond the capacity to follow rules of social organization, or that the orderly fulfilment of normative expectations in patient society is partly made possible by strategic measures that have somehow come to be institutionalized in mental hospitals.

The career of the mental patient falls popularly and naturalistically into three main phases: the period prior to entering the hospital, which I shall call the *prepatient phase;* the period in the hospital, the *inpatient phase;* the period after discharge from the hospital, should this occur, namely, the *ex-patient phase.*[7] This paper will deal only with the first . . . [phase].

THE PREPATIENT PHASE

A relatively small group of prepatients come into the mental hospital willingly, because of their own idea of what will be good for them, or because of wholehearted agreement with the relevant members of their family. Presumably these recruits have found themselves acting in a way which is evidence to them that they are losing their minds or losing control of themselves. This view of oneself would seem to be one of the most pervasively threatening things that can happen to the self in our society, especially since it is likely to occur at a time when the person is in any case sufficiently troubled to exhibit the kind of symptom which he himself can see. As Sullivan described it,

What we discover in the self-system of a person undergoing schizophrenic changes or schizophrenic processes, is then, in its simplest form, an extremely fear-marked puzzlement, consisting of the use of rather generalized and anything but exquisitely refined referential processes in an attempt to cope with what is essentially a failure at

---

[6] Conscientious objectors who voluntarily went to jail sometimes arrived at the same conclusion regarding criminal inmates. See, for example, Alfred Hassler, *Diary of a Self-made Convict;* Chicago, Regnery, 1954; p. 74.

[7] This simple picture is complicated by the somewhat special experience of roughly a third of ex-patients—namely, readmission to the hospital, this being the recidivist or "re-patient" phase.

being human—a failure at being anything that one could respect as worth being.[8]

Coupled with the person's disintegrative re-evaluation of himself will be the new, almost equally pervasive circumstance of attempting to conceal from others what he takes to be the new fundamental facts about himself, and attempting to discover whether others too have discovered them.[9] Here I want to stress that perception of losing one's mind is based on culturally derived and socially engrained stereotypes as to the significance of symptoms such as hearing voices, losing temporal and spatial orientation, and sensing that one is being followed, and that many of the most spectacular and convincing of these symptoms in some instances psychiatrically signify merely a temporary emotional upset in a stressful situation, however terrifying to the person at the time. Similarly, the anxiety consequent upon this perception of oneself, and the strategies devised to reduce this anxiety, are not a product of abnormal psychology, but would be exhibited by any person socialized into our culture who came to conceive of himself as someone losing his mind. Interestingly, subcultures in American society apparently differ in the amount of ready imagery and encouragement they supply for such self-views, leading to differential rates of *self*-referral; the capacity to take this disintegrative view of oneself without psychiatric prompting seems to be one of the questionable cultural privileges of the upper classes.[10]

For the person who has come to see himself—with whatever justification—as mentally unbalanced, entrance to the mental hospital can sometimes bring relief, perhaps in part because of the sudden transformation in the structure of his basic social situations; instead of being to himself a questionable person trying to maintain a role as a full one, he can become an officially questioned person known to himself to be not so questionable as that. In other cases, hospitalization can make matters worse for the willing patient, confirming by the objective situation what has theretofore been a matter of the private experience of self.

Once the willing prepatient enters the hospital, he may go through the same routine of experiences as do those who enter unwillingly. In any case, it is the latter that I mainly want to consider, since in America at present these are by far the more numerous kind.[11] Their approach to the institution takes one of three classic forms: they come because they have been implored by their family or threatened with the abrogation of family ties unless they go "willingly"; they come by force under police escort; they come under misapprehension purposely induced by others, this last restricted mainly to youthful prepatients.

[8] Harry Stack Sullivan, *Clinical Studies in Psychiatry;* edited by Helen Swick Perry, Mary Ladd Gavel, and Martha Gibbon: New York, Norton, 1956; pp. 184–185.

[9] This moral experience can be contrasted with that of a person learning to become a marihuana . . . [user], whose discovery that he can be "high" and still "op" effectively without being detected apparently leads to a new level of use. See Howard S. Becker, "Marihuana Use and Social Control," *Social Problems* (1955) 3:35–44; see especially pp. 40–41.

[10] See footnote 2; Hollingshead and Redlich, p. 187, Table 6, where relative frequency is given of self-referral by social class grouping.

[11] The distinction employed here between willing and unwilling patients cuts across the legal one, of voluntary and committed, since some persons who are glad to come to the mental hospital may be legally committed, and of those who come only because of strong familial pressure, some may sign themselves in as voluntary patients.

The prepatient's career may be seen in terms of an extrusory model; he starts out with relationships and rights, and ends up, at the beginning of his hospital stay, with hardly any of either. The moral aspects of this career, then, typically begin with the experience of abandonment, disloyalty, and embitterment. This is the case even though to others it may be obvious that he was in need of treatment, and even though in the hospital he may soon come to agree.

The case histories of most mental patients document offense against some arrangement for face-to-face living—a domestic establishment, a work place, a semipublic organization such as a church or store, a public region such as a street or park. Often there is also a record of some *complainant,* some figure who takes that action against the offender which eventually leads to his hospitalization. This may not be the person who makes the first move, but it is the person who makes what turns out to be the first effective move. Here is the *social* beginning of the patient's career, regardless of where one might locate the psychological beginning of his mental illness.

The kinds of offenses which lead to hospitalization are felt to differ in nature from those which lead to other extrusory consequences—to imprisonment, divorce, loss of job, disownment, regional exile, noninstitutional psychiatric treatment, and so forth. But little seems known about these differentiating factors; and when one studies actual commitments, alternate outcomes frequently appear to have been possible. It seems true, moreover, that for every offense that leads to an effective complaint, there are many psychiatrically similar ones that never do. No action is taken; or action is taken which leads to other extrusory outcomes; or ineffective action is taken, leading to the mere pacifying or putting off of the person who complains. Thus, as Clausen and Yarrow have nicely shown, even offenders who are eventually hospitalized are likely to have had a long series of ineffective actions taken against them.[12]

Separating those offenses which could have been used as grounds for hospitalizing the offender from those that are so used, one finds a vast number of what students of occupation call career contingencies.[13] Some of these contingencies in the mental patient's career have been suggested, if not explored, such as socioeconomic status, visibility of the offense, proximity to a mental hospital, amount of treatment facilities available, community regard for the type of treatment given in available hospitals, and so on.[14] For information about other contingencies one must rely on atrocity tales: a psychotic man is tolerated by his wife until she finds herself a boy friend, or by his adult children until they move from a house to an apartment; an alcoholic is sent to a mental hospital because the jail is full, and a drug addict because he declines to avail himself of psychiatric treatment on the outside; a rebellious adolescent daughter can no longer be managed at home because she now threatens to have an open affair with an unsuitable companion; and so on. Corre-

[12] Clausen and Yarrow: see footnote 4.

[13] An explicit application of this notion to the field of mental health may be found in Edwin M. Lemert, "Legal Commitment and Social Control," *Sociology and Social Research* (1946) 30:370–378.

[14] For example, Jerome K. Meyers and Leslie Schaffer, "Social Stratification and Psychiatric Practice: A Study of an Outpatient Clinic," *Amer. Sociological Rev.* (1954) 19: 307–310. Lemert, see footnote 5; pp. 402–403. *Patients in Mental Institutions, 1941;* Washington, D.C., Department of Commerce, Bureau of the Census, 1941; p. 2.

spondingly there is an equally important set of contingencies causing the person to by-pass this fate. And should the person enter the hospital, still another set of contingencies will help determine when he is to obtain a discharge—such as the desire of his family for his return, the availability of a "manageable" job, and so on. The society's official view is that inmates of mental hospitals are there primarily because they are suffering from mental illness. However, in the degree that the "mentally ill" outside hospitals numerically approach or surpass those inside hospitals, one could say that mental patients *distinctively* suffer not from mental illness, but from contingencies.

Career contingencies occur in conjunction with a second feature of the prepatient's career—the *circuit of agents*—and agencies—that participate fatefully in his passage from civilian to patient status.[15] Here is an instance of that increasingly important class of social system whose elements are agents and agencies, which are brought into systemic connection through having to take up and send on the same persons. Some of these agent-roles will be cited now, with the understanding that in any concrete circuit a role may be filled more than once, and a single person may fill more than one of them.

First is the *next-of-relation*—the person whom the prepatient sees as the most available of those upon whom he should be able to most depend in times of trouble; in this instance the last to doubt his sanity and the first to have done everything to save him from the fate which, it transpires, he has been approaching. The patient's next-of-relation is usually his next of kin; the special term is introduced because he need not be.

Second is the *complainant,* the person who retrospectively appears to have started the person on his way to the hospital. Third are the *mediators*—the sequence of agents and agencies to which the prepatient is referred and through which he is relayed and processed on his way to the hospital. Here are included police, clergy, general medical practitioners, office psychiatrists, personnel in public clinics, lawyers, social service workers, school teachers, and so on. One of these agents will have the legal mandate to sanction commitment and will exercise it, and so those agents who precede him in the process will be involved in something whose outcome is not yet settled. When the mediators retire from the scene, the prepatient has become an inpatient, and the significant agent has become the hospital administrator.

While the complainant usually takes action in a lay capacity as a citizen, an employer, a neighbor, or a kinsman, mediators tend to be specialists and differ from those they serve in significant ways. They have experience in handling trouble, and some professional distance from what they handle. Except in the case of policemen, and perhaps some clergy, they tend to be more psychiatrically oriented than the lay public, and will see the need for treatment at times when the public does not.[16]

An interesting feature of these roles is the functional effects of their interdigitation. For example, the feelings of the patient will be influenced by whether or not the person who fills the role of complainant also has the role of next-of-relation—an embarrassing combination more prevalent, apparently, in the higher classes than in the lower.[17] Some of

---

[15] For one circuit of agents and its bearing on career contingencies, see Oswald Hall, "The Stages of a Medical Career," *Amer. J. Sociology* (1948) 53:327–336.

[16] See Cumming, footnote 3; p. 92.

[17] Hollingshead and Redlich, footnote 4; p. 187.

these emergent effects will be considered now.[18]

In the prepatient's progress from home to the hospital he may participate as a third person in what he may come to experience as a kind of *alienative co-alition*. His next-of-relation presses him into coming to "talk things over" with a medical practitioner, an office psychiatrist, or some other counselor. Disinclination on his part may be met by threatening him with desertion, disownment, or other legal action, or by stressing the joint and explorative nature of the interview. But typically the next-of-relation will have set the interview up, in the sense of selecting the professional, arranging for time, telling the professional something about the case, and so on. This move effectively tends to establish the next-of-relation as the responsible person to whom pertinent findings can be divulged, while effectively establishing the other as the patient. The prepatient often goes to the interview with the understanding that he is going as an equal of someone who is so bound together with him that a third person could not come between them in fundamental matters; this after all, is one way in which close relationships are defined in our society. Upon arrival at the office the prepatient suddenly finds that he and his next-of-relation have not been accorded the same roles, and apparently that a prior understanding between the professional and the next-of-relation has been put in operation against him. In the extreme but common case the professional first sees the prepatient alone, in the role of advisor, while carefully avoiding talking things over seriously with them both together.[19] And even in those nonconsultative cases where public officials must forcibly extract a person from a family that wants to tolerate him, the next-of-relation is likely to be induced to "go along" with the official action, so that even here the prepatient may feel that an alienative coalition has been formed against him.

The moral experience of being third man in such a coalition is likely to embitter the prepatient, especially since his troubles have already probably led to some estrangement from his next-of-relation. After he enters the hospital, continued visits by his next-of-relation can give the patient the "insight" that his own best interests were being served. But the initial visits may temporarily strengthen his feeling of abandonment; he is likely to beg his visitor to get him out or at least to get him more privileges and to sympathize with the monstrousness of his plight—to which the visitor ordinarily can respond only by trying to maintain a hopeful note, by not "hearing" the requests, or by assuring the patient that the medical authorities know about these things and are doing what is medically best. The visitor then nonchalantly goes back into a world that the patient has learned is incredibly thick with freedom and privileges, causing the patient to feel that his next-of-relation is merely adding a pious gloss to a clear case of traitorous desertion.

The depth to which the patient may feel betrayed by his next-of-relation seems to be increased by the fact that another witnesses his betrayal—a factor

---

[18] For an analysis of some of these circuit implications for the inpatient, see Leila C. Deasy and Olive W. Quinn, "The Wife of the Mental Patient and the Hospital Psychiatrist," *J. Social Issues* (1955) 11:49–60. An interesting illustration of this kind of analysis may also be found in Alan G. Gowman, "Blindness and the Role of Companion," *Social Problems* (1956) 4:68–75. A general statement may be found in Robert Merton, "The Role Set: Problems in Sociological Theory," *British J. Sociology* (1957) 8:106–120.

[19] I have one case record of a man who claims he thought *he* was taking his wife to see the psychiatrist, not realizing until too late that his wife had made the arrangements.

which is apparently significant in many three-party situations. An offended person may well act forbearantly and accommodatively toward an offender when the two are alone, choosing peace ahead of justice. The presence of a witness, however, seems to add something to the implications of the offense. For then it is beyond the power of the offended and offender to forget about, erase, or suppress what has happened; the offense has become a public social fact.[20] When the witness is a mental health commission as is sometimes the case, the witnessed betrayal can verge on a "degradation ceremony."[21] In such circumstances, the offended patient may feel that some kind of extensive reparative action is required before witnesses, if his honor and social weight are to be restored.

Two other aspects of sensed betrayal should be mentioned. First, those who suggest the possibility of another's entering a mental hospital are not likely to provide a realistic picture of how in fact it may strike him when he arrives. Often he is told that he will get required medical treatment and a rest, and may well be out in a few months or so. In some cases they may thus be concealing what they know, but I think, in general, they will be telling what they see as the truth. For here there is a quite relevant difference between patients and mediating professionals; mediators, more so than the public at large, may conceive of mental hospitals as short-term medical establishments where required rest and attention can be voluntarily obtained, and not as places of coerced exile. When the prepatient finally arrives he is likely to learn quite quickly, quite differently. He then finds that the information given him about life in the hospital has had the effect of his having put up less resistance to entering than he now sees he would have put up had he known the facts. Whatever the intentions of those who participated in his transition from person to patient, he may sense they have in effect "conned" him into his present predicament.

I am suggesting that the prepatient starts out with at least a portion of the rights, liberties, and satisfactions of the civilian and ends up on a psychiatric ward stripped of almost everything. The question here is *how* this stripping is managed. This is the second aspect of betrayal I want to consider.

As the prepatient may see it, the circuit of significant figures can function as a kind of *betrayal funnel*. Passage from person to patient may be effected through a series of linked stages, each managed by a different agent. While each stage tends to bring a sharp decrease in adult free status, each agent may try to maintain the fiction that no further decrease will occur. He may even manage to turn the prepatient over to the next agent while sustaining this note. Further, through words, cues, and gestures, the prepatient is implicitly asked by the current agent to join with him in sustaining a running line of polite small talk that tactfully avoids the administrative facts of the situation, becoming, with each stage, progressively more at odds with these facts. The spouse would rather not have to cry to get the prepatient to visit a psychiatrist; psychiatrists would rather not have a scene when the prepatient learns that he and his spouse are being seen separately and in different ways; the police infrequently bring a prepatient to the hospital in a strait jacket, finding it much easier all around to give him a cigarette, some kindly words, and freedom to relax in the back seat of the

[20] A paraphrase from Kurt Riezler, "The Social Psychology of Shame," *Amer. J. Sociology* (1943) 48:458.

[21] See Harold Garfinkel, "Conditions of Successful Degradation Ceremonies," *Amer. J. Sociology* (1956) 61:420–424.

patrol car; and finally, the admitting psychiatrist finds he can do his work better in the relative quiet and luxury of the "admission suite" where, as an incidental consequence, the notion can survive that a mental hospital is indeed a comforting place. If the prepatient heeds all of these implied requests and is reasonably decent about the whole thing, he can travel the whole circuit from home to hospital without forcing anyone to look directly at what is happening or to deal with the raw emotion that his situation might well cause him to express. His showing consideration for those who are moving him toward the hospital allows them to show consideration for him, with the joint result that these interactions can be sustained with some of the protective harmony characteristic of ordinary face-to-face dealings. But should the new patient cast his mind back over the sequence of steps leading to hospitalization, he may feel that everyone's *current* comfort was being busily sustained while his long-range welfare was being undermined. This realization may constitute a moral experience that further separates him for the time from the people on the outside.[22]

I would now like to look at the circuit of career agents from the point of view of the agents themselves. Mediators in the person's transition from civil to patient status—as well as his keepers, once he is in the hospital—have an interest in establishing a responsible next-of-relation as the patient's deputy or *guardian;* should there be no obvious candidate for the role, someone may be sought out and pressed into it. Thus while a person is gradually being transformed into a patient, a next-of-relation is gradually being transformed into a guardian. With a guardian on the scene, the whole transition process can be kept tidy. He is likely to be familiar with the prepatient's civil involvements and business, and can tie up loose ends that might otherwise be left to entangle the hospital. Some of the prepatient's abrogated civil rights can be transferred to him, thus helping to sustain the legal fiction that while the prepatient does not actually have his rights he somehow actually has not lost them.

Inpatients commonly sense, at least for a time, that hospitalization is a massive unjust deprivation, and sometimes succeed in convincing a few persons on the outside that this is the case. It often turns out to be useful, then, for those identified with inflicting these deprivations, however justifiably, to be able to point to the cooperation and agreement of someone whose relationship to the patient places him above suspicion, firmly defining him as the person most likely to have the patient's personal interest at heart. If the guardian is satisfied with what is happening to the new inpatient, the world ought to be.[23]

Now it would seem that the greater the legitimate personal stake one party has in another, the better he can take the

---

[22] Concentration camp practices provide a good example of the function of the betrayal funnel in inducing cooperation and reducing struggle and fuss, although here the mediators could not be said to be acting in the best interests of the inmates. Police picking up persons from their homes would sometimes joke good-naturedly and offer to wait while coffee was being served. Gas chambers were fitted out like delousing rooms, and victims taking off their clothes were told to note where they were leaving them. The sick, aged, weak, or insane who were selected for extermination were sometimes driven away in Red Cross ambulances to camps referred to by terms such as "observation hospital." See David Boder, *I Did Not Interview the Dead;* Urbana, Univ. of Illinois Press, 1949; p. 81; and Elie A. Cohen, *Human Behavior in the Concentration Camp;* London, Cape, 1954; pp. 32, 37, 107.

[23] Interviews collected by the Clausen group at NIMH suggest that when a wife comes to be a guardian the responsibility may disrupt previous distance from in-laws, leading either to a new supportive coalition with them or to a marked withdrawal from them.

role of guardian to the other. But the structural arrangements in society which lead to the acknowledged merging of two persons' interests lead to additional consequences. For the person to whom the patient turns for help—for protection against such threats as involuntary commitment—is just the person to whom the mediators and hospital administrators logically turn for authorization. It is understandable, then, that some patients will come to sense, at least for a time, that the closeness of a relationship tells nothing of its trustworthiness.

There are still other functional effects emerging from this complement of roles. If and when the next-of-relation appeals to mediators for help in the trouble he is having with the prepatient, hospitalization may not, in fact, be in his mind. He may not even perceive the prepatient as mentally sick, or, if he does, he may not consistently hold to this view.[24] It is the circuit of mediators, with their great psychiatric sophistication and their belief in the medical character of mental hospitals, that will often define the situation for the next-of-relation, assuring him that hospitalization is a possible solution and a good one, that it involves no betrayal, but is rather a medical action taken in the best interests of the prepatient. Here the next-of-relation may learn that doing his duty to the prepatient may cause the prepatient to distrust and even hate him for the time. But the fact that this course of action may have had to be pointed out and prescribed by professionals, and be defined by them as a moral duty, relieves the next-of-relation of some of the guilt he may feel.[25] It is a poignant fact that an adult son or daughter may be pressed into the role of mediator, so that the hostility that might otherwise be directed against the spouse is passed on to the child.[26]

Once the prepatient is in the hospital, the same guilt-carrying function may become a significant part of the staff's job in regard to the next-of-relation.[27] These reasons for feeling that he himself has not betrayed the patient, even though the patient may then think so, can later provide the next-of-relation with a defensible line to take when visiting the patient in the hospital and a basis for hoping that the relationship can be re-established after its hospital moratorium. And of course this position, when sensed by the patient, can provide him with excuses for the next-of-relation, when and if he comes to look for them.[28]

[24] For an analysis of these nonpsychiatric kinds of perception, see Marian Radke Yarrow, Charlotte Green Schwartz, Harriet S. Murphy, and Leila Calhoun Deasy, "The Psychological Meaning of Mental Illness in the Family," *J. Social Issues* (1955) 11:12–24; Charlotte Green Schwartz, "Perspectives on Deviance—Wives' Definitions of their Husbands' Mental Illness," *Psychiatry* (1957) 20:275–291.

[25] This guilt-carrying function is found, of course, in other role-complexes. Thus, when a middle-class couple engages in the process of legal separation or divorce, each of their lawyers usually takes the position that his job is to acquaint his client with all of the potential claims and rights, pressing his client into demanding these, in spite of any nicety of feelings about the rights and honorableness of the ex-partner. The client, in all good faith, can then say to self and to the ex-partner that the demands are being made only because the lawyer insists it is best to do so.

[26] Recorded in the Clausen data.

[27] This point is made by Cumming, see footnote 3; p. 129.

[28] There is an interesting contrast here with the moral career of the tuberculosis patient. I am told by Julius Roth that tuberculous patients are likely to come to the hospital willingly, agreeing with their next-of-relation about treatment. Later in their hospital career, when they learn how long they yet have to stay and how depriving and irrational some of the hospital rulings are, they may seek to leave, be advised against this by the staff and by relatives, and only then begin to feel betrayed.

Thus while the next-of-relation can perform important functions for the mediators and hospital administrators, they in turn can perform important functions for him. One finds, then, an emergent unintended exchange or reciprocation of functions, these functions themselves being often unintended.

The final point I want to consider about the prepatient's moral career is its peculiarly *retroactive* character. Until a person actually arrives at the hospital there usually seems no way of knowing for sure that he is destined to do so, given the determinative role of career contingencies. And until the point of hospitalization is reached, he or others may not conceive of him as a person who is becoming a mental patient. However, since he will be held against his will in the hospital, his next-of-relation and the hospital staff will be in great need of a rationale for the hardships they are sponsoring. The medical elements of the staff will also need evidence that they are still in the trade they were trained for. These problems are eased, no doubt unintentionally, by the case-history construction that is placed on the patient's past life, this having the effect of demonstrating that all along he had been becoming sick, that he finally became very sick, and that if he had not been hospitalized much worse things would have happened to him—all of which, of course, may be true. Incidentally, if the patient wants to make sense out of his stay in the hospital, and, as already suggested, keep alive the possibility of once again conceiving of his next-of-relation as a decent, well-meaning person, then he too will have reason to believe some of this psychiatric work-up of his past.

Here is a very ticklish point for the sociology of careers. An important aspect of every career is the view the person constructs when he looks backward over his progress; in a sense, however, the whole of the prepatient career derives from this reconstruction. The fact of having had a prepatient career, starting with an effective complaint, becomes an important part of the mental patient's orientation, but this part can begin to be played only after hospitalization proves that what he had been having, but no longer has, is a career as a prepatient. . . .

Paranoia and the Dynamics of Exclusion

EDWIN M. LEMERT

One of the few generalizations about psychotic behavior which sociologists have been able to make with a modicum of agreement and assurance is that such behavior is a result or manifestation of a disorder in communication between the individual and society. The generalization, of course, is a large one, and, while it can be illustrated easily with case history materials, the need for its conceptual refinement and detailing of the process by which disruption of communication occurs in the dynamics of mental disorder has for some time been apparent. Among the more carefully reasoned attacks upon this problem is Cameron's formulation of the paranoid pseudocommunity (1).

In essence, the conception of the paranoid pseudocommunity can be stated as follows:[1]

Paranoid persons are those whose inadequate social learning leads them in situations of unusual stress to incompetent social reactions. Out of the fragments of the social behavior of others the paranoid person symbolically organizes a pseudocommunity whose functions he perceives as focused on him. His reac-

tions to this *supposed community* of response which he sees loaded with threat to himself bring him into open conflict with the actual community and lead to his temporary or permanent isolation from its affairs. The "real" community, which is unable to share in his attitudes and reactions, takes action through forcible restraint or retaliation *after* the paranoid person "bursts into defensive or vengeful activity" (1).

That the community to which the paranoid reacts is "pseudo" or without existential reality is made unequivocal by Cameron when he says:

As he [the paranoid person] begins attributing to others the attitudes which he has towards himself, he unintentionally organizes these others into a functional community, a group unified in their supposed reactions, attitudes and plans with respect to him. He in this way organizes individuals, some of whom are actual persons and some only inferred or imagined, into a whole which satisfies for the time being his immediate need for explanation but which brings no assurance with it, and usually serves to increase his tensions. The community he forms not only fails to corre-

Reprinted from *Sociometry*, Vol. 25, No. 1 (March 1962), pp. 2–5, 7–15, 18–20, by permission of the author and the American Sociological Association.

The research for this paper was in part supported by a grant from the California State Department of Mental Hygiene, arranged with the assistance of Dr. W. A. Oliver, Associate Superintendent of Napa State Hospital, who also helped as a critical consultant and made the facilities of the hospital available.

[1] In a subsequent article Cameron (2) modified his original conception, but not of the social aspects of paranoia, which mainly concern us.

spond to any organization shared by others but actually contradicts this consensus. More than this, the actions ascribed by him to its personnel are not actually performed or maintained by them; *they are united in no common undertaking against him* (1). [Italics ours.]

The general insightfulness of Cameron's analysis cannot be gainsaid and the usefulness of some of his concepts is easily granted. Yet a serious question must be raised, based upon empirical inquiry, as to whether in actuality the insidious qualities of the community to which the paranoid reacts are pseudo or a symbolic fabrication. There is an alternative point of view, which is the burden of this paper, namely that, while the paranoid person reacts differentially to his social environment, it is also true that "others" react differentially to him and this reaction commonly if not typically involves covertly organized action and conspiratorial behavior in a very real sense. A further extension of our thesis is that these differential reactions are reciprocals of one another, being interwoven and concatenated at each and all phases of a process of exclusion which arises in a special kind of relationship. Delusions and associated behavior must be understood in a context of exclusion which attenuates this relationship and disrupts communication. . . .

From what has been said thus far, it should be clear that our formulation and analysis will deal primarily with what Tyhurst (8) calls paranoid patterns of behavior rather than with a clinical entity in the classical Kraepelinian sense. Paranoid reactions, paranoid states, paranoid personality disturbances, as well as the seldom-diagnosed "true paranoia," which are found superimposed or associated with a wide variety of individual behavior or "symptoms," all provide a body of data for study so long as they assume priority over other behavior in meaningful social interaction. The elements of behavior upon which paranoid diagnoses are based—delusions, hostility, aggressiveness, suspicion, envy, stubbornness, jealousy, and ideas of reference—are readily comprehended and to some extent empathized by others as social reactions, in contrast to the bizarre, manneristic behavior of schizophrenia or the tempo and affect changes stressed in manic-depressive diagnoses. It is for this reason that paranoia suggests, more than any other forms of mental disorder, the possibility of fruitful sociological analysis.

DATA AND PROCEDURE

The first tentative conclusions which are presented here were drawn from a study of factors influencing decisions to commit mentally disordered persons to hospitals, undertaken with the cooperation of the Los Angeles County Department of Health in 1952. This included interviews by means of schedules with members of 44 families in Los Angeles County who were active petitioners in commitment proceedings and the study of 35 case records of public health officer commitments. In 16 of the former cases and in seven of the latter, paranoid symptoms were conspicuously present. In these cases family members and others had plainly accepted or "normalized" paranoid behavior, in some instances longstanding, until other kinds of behavior or exigencies led to critical judgments that "there was something wrong" with the person in question, and, later, that hospitalization was necessary. Furthermore, these critical judgments seemed to signal changes in the family attitudes and behavior towards the affected persons which could be interpreted as contributing in different ways to the form and intensity of the paranoid symptoms.

In 1958 a more refined and hypothesis-directed study was made of eight cases of persons with prominent paranoid characteristics. Four of these had been admitted to the state hospital at Napa, California, where they were diagnosed as paranoid schizophrenic. Two other cases were located and investigated with the assistance of the district attorney in Martinez, California. One of the persons had previously been committed to a California state hospital, and the other had been held on an insanity petition but was freed after a jury trial. Added to these was one so-called "White House case," which had involved threats to a President of the United States, resulting in the person's commitment to St. Elizabeth's Hospital in Washington, D.C. A final case was that of a professional person with a history of chronic job difficulties, who was designated and regarded by his associates as "brash," "queer," "irritating," "hypercritical," and "thoroughly unlikeable."

In a very rough way the cases made up a continuum ranging from one with very elaborate delusions, through those in which fact and misinterpretation were difficult to separate, down to the last case, which comes closer to what some would call paranoid personality disturbance. A requirement for the selection of the cases was that there be no history or evidence of hallucinations and also that the persons be intellectually unimpaired. Seven of the cases were of males, five of whom were over 40 years of age. Three of the persons had been involved in repeated litigations. One man published a small, independent paper devoted to exposures of psychiatry and mental hospitals. Five of the men had been or were associated with organizations, as follows: a small-town high school, a government research bureau, an association of agricultural producers, a university, and a contracting business.

The investigations of the cases were as exhaustive as it was possible to make them, reaching relatives, work associates, employers, attorneys, police, physicians, public officials and any others who played significant roles in the lives of the persons involved. As many as 200 hours each were given to collecting data on some of the cases. Written materials, legal documents, publications and psychiatric histories were studied in addition to the interview data. Our procedure in the large was to adopt an interactional perspective which sensitized us to sociologically relevant behavior underlying or associated with the more apparent and formal contexts of mental disorder. In particular we were concerned to establish the order in which delusions and social exclusion occur and to determine whether exclusion takes conspiratorial form. . . .

THE GENERIC PROCESS OF EXCLUSION

The paranoid process begins with persistent interpersonal difficulties between the individual and his family, or his work associates and superiors, or neighbors, or other persons in the community. These frequently or even typically arise out of bona fide or recognizable issues centering upon some actual or threatened loss of status for the individual. This is related to such things as the death of relatives, loss of a position, loss of professional certification, failure to be promoted, age and physiological life cycle changes, mutilations, and changes in family and marital relationships. The status changes are distinguished by the fact that they leave no alternative acceptable to the individual, from whence comes their "intolerable" or "unendurable" quality. For example: the man trained to be a teacher who loses his certificate, which means he can never teach; or the man of 50 years of age who is faced with loss of promotion which is a regular order of upward mobility in an organization, who knows that he can't "start over"; or the wife undergoing hysterectomy, which mutilates her image as a woman.

In cases where no dramatic status loss can be discovered, a series of failures often is present, failures which may have been accepted or adjusted to, but with progressive tension as each new status situation is entered. The unendurability of the current status loss, which may appear unimportant to others, is a function of an intensified commitment, in some cases born of an awareness that there is a quota placed on failures in our society. Under some such circumstances, failures have followed the person, and his reputation as a "difficult person" has preceded him. This means that he often has the status of a stranger on trial in each new group he enters, and that the groups or organizations willing to take a chance on him are marginal from the standpoint of their probable tolerance for his actions.

The behavior of the individual—arrogance, insults, presumption of privilege and exploitation of weaknesses in others —initially has a segmental or checkered pattern in that it is confined to status-committing interactions. Outside of these, the person's behavior may be quite acceptable—courteous, considerate, kind, even indulgent. Likewise, other persons and members of groups vary considerably in their tolerance for the relevant behavior, depending on the extent to which it threatens individual and organizational values, impedes functions, or sets in motion embarrassing sequences of social actions. In the early generic period, tolerance by others for the individual's aggressive behavior generally speaking is broad, and it is very likely to be interpreted as a variation of normal behavior, particularly in the absence of biographical knowledge of the person. At most, people observe that "there is something odd about him," or "he must be upset," or "he is just ornery," or "I don't quite understand him" (3).

At some point in the chain of interactions, a new configuration takes place in perceptions others have of the individual, with shifts in figure-ground relations. The individual, as we have already indicated, is an ambiguous figure, comparable to textbook figures of stairs or outlined cubes which reverse themselves when studied intently. From a normal variant the person becomes "unreliable," "untrustworthy," "dangerous," or someone with whom others "do not wish to be involved." An illustration nicely apropos of this came out in the reaction of the head of a music department in a university when he granted an interview to a man who had worked for years on a theory to compose music mathematically:

When he asked to be placed on the staff so that he could use the electronic computers of the University *I shifted my ground* . . . when I offered an objection to his theory, he became disturbed, so I changed my reaction to "yes and no."

As is clear from this, once the perceptual reorientation takes place, either as the outcome of continuous interaction or through the receipt of biographical information, interaction changes qualitatively. In our words it becomes *spurious,* distinguished by patronizing, evasion, "humoring," guiding conversation onto selected topics, underreaction, and silence, all calculated either to prevent intense interaction or to protect individual and group values by restricting access to them. When the interaction is between two or more persons it is cued by a whole repertoire of subtle expressive signs which are meaningful only to them.

The net effects of spurious interaction are to:

1. stop the flow of information to ego;

2. create a discrepancy between expressed ideas and affect among those with whom he interacts;

3. make the situation or the group image an ambiguous one for ego, much as he is for others.

Needless to say this kind of spurious interaction is one of the most difficult for an adult in our society to cope with, because it complicates or makes decisions impossible for him and also because it is morally invidious.[2]

The process from inclusion to exclusion is by no means an even one. Both individuals and members of groups change their perceptions and reactions, and vacillation is common, depending upon the interplay of values, anxieties and guilt on both sides. Members of an excluding group may decide they have been unfair and seek to bring the individual back into their confidence. This overture may be rejected or used by ego as a means of further attack. We have also found that ego may capitulate, sometimes abjectly, to others and seek group reentry, only to be rejected. In some cases compromises are struck and a partial reintegration of ego into informal social relations is achieved. The direction which informal exclusion takes depends upon ego's reactions, the degree of communication between his interactors, the composition and structure of the informal groups, and the perceptions of "key others" at points of interaction which directly affect ego's status.

ORGANIZATIONAL CRISIS AND FORMAL EXCLUSION

Thus far we have discussed exclusion as an informal process. Informal exclusion may take place but leave ego's formal status in an organization intact. So long as this status is preserved and rewards are sufficient to validate it on his terms, an uneasy peace between him and others may prevail. Yet ego's social isolation and his strong commitments make him an unpredictable factor; furthermore the rate of change and internal power struggles, especially in large and complex organizations, means that preconditions of stability may be short lived.

Organizational crises involving a paranoid relationship arise in several ways. The individual may act in ways which arouse intolerable anxieties in others, who demand that "something be done." Again, by going to higher authority or making appeals outside the organization, he may set in motion procedures which leave those in power no other choice than to take action. In some situations ego remains relatively quiescent and does not openly attack the organization. Action against him is set off by growing anxieties or calculated motives of associates—in some cases his immediate superiors. Finally, regular organizational procedures incidental to promotion, retirement or reassignment may precipitate the crisis.

Assuming a critical situation in which the conflict between the individual and members of the organization leads to action to formally exclude him, several possibilities exist. One is the transfer of ego from one department, branch or division of the organization to another, a device frequently resorted to in the armed services or in large corporations. This requires that the individual be persuaded to make the change and that some department will accept him. While this may be accomplished in different ways, not infrequently artifice, withholding information, bribery, or thinly disguised threats figure conspicuously among the means by which the transfer is brought about. Needless to say, there

---

[2] The interaction in some ways is similar to that used with children, particularly the "enfant terrible." The function of language in such interactions was studied by Sapir (7) years ago.

is a limit to which transfers can be employed as a solution to the problem, contingent upon the size of the organization and the previous diffusion of knowledge about the transferee.

Solution number two we call encapsulation, which, in brief, is a reorganization and redefinition of ego's status. This has the effect of isolating him from the organization and making him directly responsible to one or two superiors who act as his intermediators. The change is often made palatable to ego by enhancing some of the material rewards of his status. He may be nominally promoted or "kicked upstairs," given a larger office, or a separate secretary, or relieved of onerous duties. Sometimes a special status is created for him.

This type of solution often works because it is a kind of formal recognition by the organization of ego's intense commitment to his status and in part a victory for him over his enemies. It bypasses them and puts him into direct communication with higher authority who may communicate with him in a more direct manner. It also relieves his associates of further need to connive against him. This solution is sometimes used to dispose of troublesome corporation executives, high-ranking military officers, and academic *personae non gratae* in universities.

A third variety of solutions to the problem of paranoia in an organization is outright discharge, forced resignation or non-renewal of appointment. Finally, there may be an organized move to have the individual in the paranoid relationship placed on sick leave, or to compel him to take psychiatric treatment. The extreme expression of this is pressure (as on the family) or direct action to have the person committed to a mental hospital.

The order of the enumerated solutions to the paranoid problem in a rough way reflects the amount of risk associated with the alternatives, both as to the probabilities of failure and of damaging repercussions to the organization. Generally, organizations seem to show a good deal of resistance to making or carrying out decisions which require expulsion of the individual or forcing hospitalization, regardless of his mental condition. One reason for this is that the person may have power within the organization, based upon his position, or monopolized skills and information,[3] and unless there is a strong coalition against him the general conservatism of administrative judgments will run in his favor. Herman Wouk's novel of *The Caine Mutiny* dramatizes some of the difficulties of cashiering a person from a position of power in an essentially conservative military organization. An extreme of this conservatism is illustrated by one case in which we found a department head retained in his position in an organization even though he was actively hallucinating as well as expressing paranoid delusions.[4] Another factor working on the individual's side is that discharge of a person in a position of power reflects unfavorably upon those who placed him there. Ingroup solidarity of administrators may be involved, and the methods of the opposition may create sympathy for ego at higher levels.

Even when the person is almost totally excluded and informally isolated within an organization, he may have power outside. This weighs heavily when the external power can be invoked in some way, or when it automatically leads to raising questions as to the internal workings of the organization. This touches upon the more salient reason for reluctance to eject an uncooperative and

[3] For a systematic analysis of the organizational difficulties in removing an "unpromotable" person from a position see (5).

[4] One of the cases in the first study.

retaliatory person, even when he is relatively unimportant to the organization. We refer to a kind of negative power derived from the vulnerability of organizations to unfavorable publicity and exposure of their private lives that are likely if the crisis proceeds to formal hearings, case review or litigation. This is an imminent possibility where paranoia exists. If hospital commitment is attempted, there is possibility that a jury trial will be demanded, which will force leaders of the organization to defend their actions. If the crisis turns into a legal contest of this sort, it is not easy to prove insanity, and there may be damage suits. Even if the facts heavily support the petitioners, such contests can only throw unfavorable light upon the organization.

THE CONSPIRATORIAL NATURE OF EXCLUSION

A conclusion from the foregoing is that organizational vulnerability as well as anticipations of retaliations from the paranoid person lay a functional basis for conspiracy among those seeking to contain or oust him. Probabilities are strong that a coalition will appear within the organization, integrated by a common commitment to oppose the paranoid person. This, the exclusionist group, demands loyalty, solidarity and secrecy from its members; it acts in accord with a common scheme and in varying degrees utilizes techniques of manipulation and misrepresentation.

Conspiracy in rudimentary form can be detected in informal exclusion apart from an organizational crisis. This was illustrated in an office research team in which staff members huddled around a water cooler to discuss the unwanted associate. They also used office telephones to arrange coffee breaks without him and employed symbolic cues in his presence, such as humming the Dragnet theme song when he approached the group. An office rule against extraneous conversation was introduced with the collusion of supervisors, ostensibly for everyone, actually to restrict the behavior of the isolated worker. In another case an interview schedule designed by a researcher was changed at a conference arranged without him. When he sought an explanation at a subsequent conference, his associates pretended to have no knowledge of the changes.

Conspiratorial behavior comes into sharpest focus during organizational crises in which the exclusionists who initiate action become an embattled group. There is a concerted effort to gain consensus for this view, to solidify the group and to halt close interaction with those unwilling to completely join the coalition. Efforts are also made to neutralize those who remain uncommitted but who can't be kept ignorant of the plans afoot. Thus an external appearance of unanimity is given even if it doesn't exist.

Much of the behavior of the group at this time is strategic in nature, with determined calculations as to "what we will do if he does this or that." In one of our cases, a member on a board of trustees spoke of the "game being played" with the person in controversy with them. Planned action may be carried to the length of agreeing upon the exact words to be used when confronted or challenged by the paranoid individual. Above all there is continuous, precise communication among exclusionists, exemplified in one case by mutual exchanging of copies of all letters sent and received from ego.

Concern about secrecy in such groups is revealed by such things as carefully closing doors and lowering of voices when ego is brought under discussion. Meeting places and times may be varied from normal procedures; documents may be filed in unusual places and certain telephones may not be used during a paranoid crisis.

The visibility of the individual's behavior is greatly magnified during this period; often he is the main topic of conversation among the exclusionists, while rumors of the difficulties spread to other groups, which in some cases may be drawn into the controversy. At a certain juncture steps are taken to keep the members of the ingroup continually informed of the individual's movements and, if possible, of his plans. In effect, if not in form, this amounts to spying. Members of one embattled group, for example, hired an outside person unknown to their accuser to take notes on a speech he delivered to enlist a community organization on his side. In another case, a person having an office opening onto that of a department head was persuaded to act as an informant for the nucleus of persons working to depose the head from his position of authority. This group also seriously debated placing an all-night watch in front of their perceived malefactor's house.

Concomitant with the magnified visibility of the paranoid individual, come distortions of his image, most pronounced in the inner coterie of exclusionists. His size, physical strength, cunning, and anecdotes of his outrages are exaggerated, with a central thematic emphasis on the fact that he is dangerous. Some individuals give cause for such beliefs in that previously they have engaged in violence or threats, others do not. One encounters characteristic contradictions in interviews on this point, such as: "No, he has never struck anyone around here—just fought with the policemen at the State Capitol," or "No, I am not afraid of him, but one of these days he will explode."

It can be said parenthetically that the alleged dangerousness of paranoid persons storied in fiction and drama has never been systematically demonstrated. As a matter of fact, the only substantial data on this, from a study of delayed admissions, largely paranoid, to a mental hospital in Norway, disclosed that "neither the paranoiacs nor paranoids have been dangerous, and most not particularly troublesome" (6). Our interpretation of this, as suggested earlier, is that the imputed dangerousness of the paranoid individual does not come from physical fear but from the organizational threat he presents and the need to justify collective action against him.[5]

However, this is not entirely tactical behavior—as is demonstrated by anxieties and tensions which mount among those in the coalition during the more critical phases of their interaction. Participants may develop fears quite analogous to those of classic conspirators. One leader in such a group spoke of the period of the paranoid crisis as a "week of terror," during which he was wracked with insomnia and "had to take his stomach pills." Projection was revealed by a trustee who, during a school crisis occasioned by discharge of an aggressive teacher, stated that he "watched his shadows," and "wondered if all would be well when he returned home at night." Such tensional states, working along with a kind of closure of communication within the group, are both a cause and an effect of amplified group interaction which distorts or symbolically rearranges the image of the person against whom they act.

Once the battle is won by the exclusionists, their version of the individual as dangerous becomes a crystallized rationale for official action. At this point misrepresentation becomes part of a more deliberate manipulation of ego. Gross misstatements, most frequently called "pretexts," become justifiable ways of

---

[5] *Supra*, p. 3.

getting his cooperation, for example, to get him to submit to psychiatric examination or detention preliminary to hospital commitment. This aspect of the process has been effectively detailed by Goffman, with his concept of a "betrayal funnel" through which a patient enters a hospital (4). We need not elaborate on this, other than to confirm its occurrence in the exclusion process, complicated in our cases by legal strictures and the ubiquitous risk of litigation.

THE GROWTH OF DELUSION

The general idea that the paranoid person symbolically fabricates the conspiracy against him is in our estimation incorrect or incomplete. Nor can we agree that he lacks insight, as is so frequently claimed. To the contrary, many paranoid persons properly realize that they are being isolated and excluded by concerted interaction, or that they are being manipulated. However, they are at a loss to estimate accurately or realistically the dimensions and form of the coalition arrayed against them.

As channels of communication are closed to the paranoid person, he has no means of getting feedback on consequences of his behavior, which is essential for correcting his interpretations of the social relationships and organization which he must rely on to define his status and give him identity. He can only read overt behavior without the informal context. Although he may properly infer that people are organized against him, he can only use confrontation or formal inquisitorial procedures to try to prove this. The paranoid person must provoke strong feelings in order to receive any kind of meaningful communication from others—hence his accusations, his bluntness, his insults. Ordinarily this is nondeliberate; nevertheless, in one complex case we found the person consciously provoking discussions to get readings from others on his behavior. This man said of himself: "Some people would describe me as very perceptive, others would describe me as very imperceptive."

The need for communication and the identity which goes with it does a good deal to explain the preference of paranoid persons for formal, legalistic, written communications, and the care with which many of them preserve records of their contracts with others. In some ways the resort to litigation is best interpreted as the effort of the individual to compel selected others to interact directly with him as equals, to engineer a situation in which evasion is impossible. The fact that the person is seldom satisfied with the outcome of his letters, his petitions, complaints and writs testifies to their function as devices for establishing contact and interaction with others, as well as "setting the record straight." The wide professional tolerance of lawyers for aggressive behavior in court and the nature of Anglo-Saxon legal institutions, which grew out of a revolt against conspiratorial or star-chamber justice, mean that the individual will be heard. Furthermore his charges must be answered; otherwise he wins by default. Sometimes he wins small victories, even if he loses the big ones. He may earn grudging respect as an adversary, and sometimes shares a kind of legal camaraderie with others in the courts. He gains an identity through notoriety. . . .

CONCLUDING COMMENT

We have been concerned with a process of social exclusion and with the ways in which it contributes to the development of paranoid patterns of behavior. While the data emphasize the organizational forms of exclusion, we nevertheless believe that these are expressions of a generic process whose correlates will emerge from the study of paranoia in the family and other groups.

The differential responses of the individual to the exigencies of organized exclusion are significant in the development of paranoid reactions only insofar as they partially determine the "intolerable" or "unendurable" quality of the status changes confronting him. Idiosyncratic life history factors of the sort stressed in more conventional psychiatric analyses may be involved, but equally important in our estimation are those which inhere in the status changes themselves, age being one of the more salient of these. In either case, once situational intolerability appears, the stage is set for the interactional process we have described.

Our cases, it will be noted, were all people who remained undeteriorated, in contact with others and carrying on militant activities oriented towards recognizable social values and institutions. Generalized suspiciousness in public places and unprovoked aggression against strangers were absent from their experiences. These facts, plus the relative absence of "true paranoia" among mental-hospital populations, leads us to conclude that the "pseudocommunity" associated with random aggression (in Cameron's sense) is a sequel rather than an integral part of paranoid patterns. They are likely products of deterioration and fragmentation of personality appearing, when and if they do, in the paranoid person after long or intense periods of stress and complete social isolation.

REFERENCES

1. Cameron, N., "The Paranoid Pseudo-community," *American Journal of Sociology,* 1943, 46, 33–38.
2. Cameron, N., "The Paranoid Pseudo-community Revisited," *American Journal of Sociology,* 1959, 65, 52–58.
3. Cumming, E., and J. Cumming, *Closed Ranks,* Cambridge, Mass.: Harvard Press, 1957, Ch. VI.
4. Goffman, E., "The Moral Career of the Mental Patient," *Psychiatry,* 1959, 22, 127 ff.
5. Levenson, B., "Bureaucratic Succession," in *Complex Organizations,* A. Etzioni (ed.), New York: Holt, Rinehart and Winston, 1961, 362–395.
6. Ödegard, Ö., "A Clinical Study of Delayed Admissions to a Mental Hospital," *Mental Hygiene,* 1958, 42, 66–67.
7. Sapir, E., "Abnormal Types of Speech in Nootka," *Canada Department of Mines, Memoir 62,* 1915, No. 5.
8. Tyhurst, J. S., "Paranoid Patterns," in A. H. Leighton, J. A. Clausen, and R. Wilson (eds.), *Explorations in Social Psychiatry,* New York: Basic Books, 1957, Ch. II.

Conditions of Successful Degradation Ceremonies

HAROLD GARFINKEL

Any communicative work between persons, whereby the public identity of an actor is transformed into something looked on as lower in the local scheme of social types, will be called a "status degradation ceremony." Some restrictions on this definition may increase its usefulness. The identities referred to must be "total" identities. That is, these identities must refer to persons as "motivational" types rather than as "behavioral" types,[1] not to what a person may be expected to have done or to do (in Parsons' term,[2] to his "performances") but to what the group holds to be the ultimate "grounds" or "reasons" for his performance.[3]

The grounds on which a participant achieves what for him is adequate understanding of why he or another acted as he did are not treated by him in a utilitarian manner. Rather, the correctness of an imputation is decided by the participant in accordance with socially valid and institutionally recommended standards of "preference." With reference to these standards, he makes the crucial distinctions between appearances and reality, truth and falsity, triviality and importance, accident and essence, coincidence and cause. Taken together, the grounds, as well as the behavior that the grounds make explicable as the other person's conduct, constitute a person's identity. Together, they constitute the other as a social object. Persons identified by means of the ultimate "reasons" for their socially categorized and socially understood behavior will be said to be "totally" identified. The degradation ceremonies here discussed are those that are concerned with the alteration of total identities.

It is proposed that only in societies that are completely demoralized, will an observer be unable to find such ceremonies, since only in total anomie are the conditions of degradation ceremonies

Reprinted by permission of the author and *The American Journal of Sociology,* Vol. 61 (March 1956), pp. 420–24. Copyright, 1956, The University of Chicago. All rights reserved.

[1] These terms are borrowed from Alfred Schutz, "Common Sense and Scientific Interpretation of Human Action," *Philosophy and Phenomenological Research,* Vol. XIV, No. 1 (September, 1953).

[2] Talcott Parsons and Edward Shils, "Values, Motives, and Systems of Action," in Parsons and Shils (eds.), *Toward a General Theory of Action* (Cambridge: Harvard University Press, 1951).

[3] Cf. the writings of Kenneth Burke, particularly *Permanence and Change* (Los Altos, Calif.: Hermes Publications, 1954), and *A Grammar of Motives* (New York: Prentice-Hall, Inc., 1945).

lacking. Max Scheler[4] argued that there is no society that does not provide in the very features of its organization the conditions sufficient for inducing shame. It will be treated here as axiomatic that there is no society whose social structure does not provide, in its routine features, the conditions of identity degradation. Just as the structural conditions of shame are universal to all societies by the very fact of their being organized, so the structural conditions of status degradation are universal to all societies. In this framework the critical question is not whether status degradation occurs or can occur within any given society. Instead, the question is: Starting from any state of a society's organization, what program of communicative tactics will get the work of status degradation done?

First of all, two questions will have to be decided, at least tentatively: *What are we referring to behaviorially when we propose the product of successful degradation work to be a changed total identity?* And *what are we to conceive the work of status degradation to have itself accomplished or to have assumed as the conditions of its success?*

I

Degradation ceremonies fall within the scope of the sociology of moral indignation. Moral indignation is a social affect. Roughly speaking, it is an instance of a class of feelings particular to the more or less organized ways that human beings develop as they live out their lives in one another's company. Shame, guilt, and boredom are further important instances of such affects.

Any affect has its behavioral paradigm. That of shame is found in the withdrawal and covering of the portion of the body that socially defines one's public appearance—prominently, in our society, the eyes and face. The paradigm of shame is found in the phrases that denote removal of the self from public view, i.e., removal from the regard of the publicly identified other: "I could have sunk through the floor; I wanted to run away and hide; I wanted the earth to open up and swallow me." The feeling of guilt finds its paradigm in the behavior of self-abnegation, disgust, the rejection of further contact with or withdrawal from, and the bodily and symbolic expulsion of the foreign body, as when we cough, blow, gag, vomit, spit, etc.

The paradigm of moral indignation is *public* denunciation. We publicly deliver the curse: "I call upon all men to bear witness that he is not as he appears but is otherwise and *in essence*[5] of a lower species."

The social affects serve various functions both for the person as well as for the collectivity. A prominent function of shame for the person is that of preserving the ego from further onslaughts by withdrawing entirely its contact with the outside. For the collectivity shame is an "individuator." One experiences shame in his own time.

Moral indignation serves to effect the ritual destruction of the person denounced. Unlike shame, which does not bind persons together, moral indignation may reinforce group solidarity. In the market and in politics, a degradation ceremony must be counted as a secular form of communism. Structurally a deg-

---

[4] Richard Hays Williams, "Scheler's Contributions to the Sociology of Affective Action, with Special Attention to the Problem of Shame," *Philosophy and Phenomenological Research,* Vol. II, No. 3 (March, 1942).

[5] The man at whose hands a neighbor suffered death becomes a "murderer." The person who passes on information to enemies is really, i.e., "in essence," "in the first place," "all along," "in the final analysis," "originally," an informer.

radation ceremony bears close resemblance to ceremonies of investiture and elevation. How such a ceremony may bind persons to the collectivity we shall see when we take up the conditions of a successful denunciation. Our immediate question concerns the meaning of ritual destruction.

In the statement that moral indignation brings about the ritual destruction of the person being denounced, destruction is intended literally. The transformation of identities is the destruction of one social object and the constitution of another. The transformation does not involve the substitution of one identity for another, with the terms of the old one loitering about like the overlooked parts of a fresh assembly, any more than the woman we see in the department-store window that turns out to be a dummy carries with it the possibilities of a woman. It is not that the old object has been overhauled; rather it is replaced by another. One declares, *"Now,* it was otherwise in the first place."

The work of the denunciation effects the recasting of the objective character of the perceived other: The other person becomes in the eyes of his condemners literally a different and *new* person. It is not that the new attributes are added to the old "nucleus." He is not changed, he is reconstituted. The former identity, at best, receives the accent of mere appearance. In the social calculus of reality representations and test, the former identity stands as accidental; the new identity is the "basic reality." What he is now is what, "after all," he was all along.[6]

The public denunciation effects such a transformation of essence by substituting another socially validated motivational scheme for that previously used to name and order the performances of the denounced. It is with reference to this substituted, socially validated motivational scheme as the essential grounds, i.e., the *first principles,* that his performances, past, present, and prospective, according to the witnesses, are to be properly and necessarily understood.[7] Through the interpretive work that respects this rule, the denounced person becomes in the eyes of the witnesses a different person.

II

How can one make a good denunciation?[8]

To be successful, the denunciation

---

[6] Two themes commonly stand out in the rhetoric of denunciation: (1) the irony between what the denounced appeared to be and what he is seen now really to be where the new motivational scheme is taken as the standard and (2) a re-examination and re-definition of origins of the denounced. For the sociological relevance of the relationship between concerns for essence and concerns for origins see particularly Kenneth Burke, *A Grammar of Motives.*

[7] While constructions like "substantially a something" or "essentially a something" have been banished from the domain of scientific discourse, such constructions have prominent and honored places in the theories of motives, persons, and conduct that are employed in handling the affairs of daily life. Reasons can be given to justify the hypothesis that such constructions may be lost to a group's "terminology of motives" only if the relevance of socially sanctioned theories to practical problems is suspended. This can occur where interpersonal relations are trivial (such as during play) or, more interestingly, under severe demoralization of a system of activities. In such organizational states the frequency of status degradation is low.

[8] Because the paper is short the risk must be run that, as a result of excluding certain considerations, the treated topics may appear exaggerated. It would be desirable, for ex-

(Continued)

must redefine the situations of those that are witnesses to the denunciation work. The denouncer, the party to be denounced (let us call him the "perpetrator"), and the thing that is being blamed on the perpetrator (let us call it the "event") must be transformed as follows:[9]

1. Both event and perpetrator must be removed from the realm of their everyday character and be made to stand as "out of the ordinary."

2. Both event and perpetrator must be placed within a scheme of preferences that shows the following properties:

A. The preferences must not be for event A over event B, but for event of *type* A over *type* B. The same typing must be accomplished for the perpetrator. Event and perpetrator must be defined as instances of a uniformity and must be treated as a uniformity throughout the work of the denunciation. The unique, never recurring character of the event or perpetrator should be lost. Similarly, any sense of accident, coincidence, indeterminism, chance, or momentary occurrence must not merely be minimized. Ideally, such measures should be inconceivable; at least they should be made false.

B. The witnesses must appreciate the characteristics of the typed person and event by referring the type to a dialectical counterpart. Ideally, the witnesses should not be able to contemplate the features of the denounced person without reference to the counterconception, as the profanity of an occurrence or a desire or a character trait, for example, is clarified by the references it bears to its opposite, the sacred. The features of the mad-dog murderer reverse the features of the peaceful citizen. The confessions of the Red can be read to teach the meanings of patriotism. There are many contrasts available, and any aggregate of witnesses this side of a complete war of each against all will have a plethora of such schemata for effecting a "familiar," "natural," "proper," ordering of motives, qualities, and other events.

From such contrasts, the following is to be learned. If the denunciation is to take effect, the scheme must not be one in which the witness is allowed to elect the preferred. Rather, the alternatives must be such that the preferred is morally required. Matters must be so arranged that the validity of his choice, its justification, is maintained by the fact that he makes it.[10] The scheme of alternatives must be

---

ample, to take account of the multitude of hedges that will be found against false denunciation; of the rights to denounce; of the differential apportionment of these rights, as well as the ways in which a claim, once staked out, may become a vested interest and may tie into the contests for economic and political advantage. Further, there are questions centering around the appropriate arenas of denunciation. For example, in our society the tribal council has fallen into secondary importance; among lay persons the denunciation has given way to the complaint to the authorities.

[9] These are the effects that the communicative tactics of the denouncer must be designed to accomplish. Put otherwise, in so far as the denouncer's tactics accomplish the reordering of the definitions of the situation of the witnesses to the denunciatory performances, the denouncer will have succeeded in effecting the transformation of the public identity of his victim. The list of conditions of this degrading effect are the determinants of the effect. Viewed in the scheme of a project to be rationally pursued, they are the adequate means. One would have to choose one's tactics for their efficiency in accomplishing these effects.

[10] Cf. Gregory Bateson and Jurgen Ruesch, *Communication: The Social Matrix of Psychiatry* (New York: W. W. Norton & Co., 1951), pp. 212–27.

such as to place constraints upon his making a selection "for a purpose." Nor will the denunciation succeed if the witness is free to look beyond the fact that he makes the selection for evidence that the correct alternative has been chosen, as, for example, by the test of empirical consequences of the choice. The alternatives must be such that, in "choosing," he takes it for granted and beyond any motive for doubt that not choosing can mean only preference for its opposite.

3. The denouncer must so identify himself to the witnesses that during the denunciation they regard him not as a private but as a publicly known person. He must not portray himself as acting according to his personal, unique experiences. He must rather be regarded as acting in his capacity as a public figure, drawing upon communally entertained and verified experience. He must act as a bona fide participant in the tribal relationships to which the witnesses subscribe. What he says must not be regarded as true for him alone, not even in the sense that it can be regarded by denouncer and witnesses as matters upon which they can become agreed. In no case, except in a most ironical sense, can the convention of true-for-reasonable-men be invoked. What the denouncer says must be regarded by the witnesses as true on the grounds of a socially employed metaphysics whereby witnesses assume that witnesses and denouncer are alike in essence.[11]

4. The denouncer must make the dig-nity of the supra-personal values of the tribe salient and accessible to view, and his denunciation must be delivered in their name.

5. The denouncer must arrange to be invested with the right to speak in the name of these ultimate values. The success of the denunciation will be undermined if, for his authority to denounce, the denouncer invokes the personal interests that he may have acquired by virtue of the wrong done to him or someone else. He must rather use the wrong he has suffered as a tribal member to invoke the authority to speak in the name of these ultimate values.

6. The denouncer must get himself so defined by the witnesses that they locate him as a supporter of these values.

7. Not only must the denouncer fix his distance from the person being denounced, but the witnesses must be made to experience their distance from him also.

8. Finally, the denounced person must be ritually separated from a place in the legitimate order, i.e., he must be defined as standing at a place opposed to it. He must be placed "outside," he must be made "strange."

These are the conditions that must be fulfilled for a successful denunciation. If they are absent, the denunciation will fail. Regardless of the situation when the denouncer enters, if he is to succeed in degrading the other man, it is necessary to introduce these features.[12]

---

[11] For bona fide members it is not that these are the grounds upon which we are agreed but upon which we are *alike,* consubstantial, in origin the same.

[12] Neither of the problems of possible communicative or organizational conditions of their effectiveness have been treated here in systematic fashion. However, the problem of communicative tactics in degradation ceremonies is set in the light of systematically related conceptions. These conceptions may be listed in the following statements:

1. The definition of the situation of the witnesses (for ease of discourse we shall use the letter S) always bears a time qualification.

2. The S at t_2 is a function of the S at t_1. This function is described as an operator that transforms the S at t_1.

(*Continued*)

Not all degradation ceremonies are carried on in accordance with publicly prescribed and publicly validated measures. Quarrels which seek the humiliation of the opponent through personal invective may achieve degrading on a limited scale. Comparatively few persons at a time enter into this form of communion, few benefit from it, and the fact of participation does not give the witness a definition of the other that is standardized beyond the particular group or scene of its occurrence.

The devices for effecting degradation vary in the feature and effectiveness according to the organization and operation of the system of action in which they occur. In our society, the arena of degradation whose product, the redefined person, enjoys the widest transferability between groups has been rationalized, at least as to the institutional measures for carrying it out. The court and its officers have something like a fair monopoly over such ceremonies, and there they have become an occupational routine. This is to be contrasted with degradation undertaken as an immediate kinship and tribal obligation and carried out by those who, unlike our professional degraders in the law courts, acquire both right and obligation to engage in it through being themselves the injured parties or kin to the injured parties.

Factors conditioning the effectiveness of degradation tactics are provided in the organization and operation of the system of action within which the degradation occurs. For example, timing rules that provide for serial or reciprocal "conversations" would have much to do with the kinds of tactics that one might be best advised to use. The tactics advisable for an accused who can answer the charge as soon as it is made are in contrast with those recommended for one who had to wait out the denunciation before replying. Face-to-face contact is a different situation from that wherein the denunciation and reply are conducted by radio and newspaper. Whether the denunciation must be accomplished on a single occasion or is to be carried out over a sequence of "tries," factors like the territorial arrangements and movements of persons at the scene of the denunciation, the numbers of persons involved as accused, degraders, and witnesses, status claims of the contenders, prestige and power allocations among participants, all should influence the outcome.

In short, the factors that condition the

---

3. The operator is conceived as communicative work.

4. For a successful denunciation, it is required that the S at t_2 show specific properties. These have been specified previously.

5. The task of the denouncer is to alter the S's of the witnesses so that these S's will show the specified properties.

6. The "rationality" of the denouncer's tactics, i.e., their adequacy as a means for effecting the set of transformations necessary for effecting the identity transformation, is decided by the rule that the organizational and operational properties of the communicative net (the social system) are determinative of the size of the discrepancy between an intended and an actual effect of the communicative work. Put otherwise, the question is not that of the temporal origin of the situation but always and only how it is altered over time. The view is recommended that the definition of the situation at time 2 is a function of the definition at time 1 where this function consists of the communicative work conceived as a set of operations whereby the altered situation at time 1 is the situation at time 2. In strategy terms the function consists of the program of procedures that a denouncer should follow to effect the change of state S_{t_1} to S_{t_2}. In this paper S_{t_1} is treated as an unspecified state.

success of the work of degradation are those that we point to when we conceive the actions of a number of persons as group-governed. Only some of the more obvious structural variables that may be expected to serve as predictors of the characteristics of denunciatory communicative tactics have been mentioned. They tell us not only how to construct an effective denunciation but also how to render denunciation useless.

The "Wetback" As Deviant

JORGE A. BUSTAMANTE

INTRODUCTION

Those who illegally stream across the Mexico-U.S. border are called "wetbacks" because they cross the Rio Grande without the benefit of a bridge. All other illegal migrants from Mexico are referred to by the same term. Thus, wetback characterizes anyone who enters illegally from Mexico. The term, then, carries an unavoidable connotation—one who has broken the law. This paper will deal with some of the questions that arise from that connotation. In the first part, we describe the historical emergence of the wetback, discussing the roles of the persons involved in the violation of the immigration law and some of the socioeconomic consequences of the wetback as a deviant. In the second part, we examine the wetback as a case of deviance through labeling theory. In this approach the deviant character of the wetback is analyzed as a process of interaction. Each role in this process will be discussed in terms of its interests, power, and consequences with respect to those of the roles of the other participants. Finally, the concept of "antilaw entrepreneur" is introduced, and its explanatory potential is indicated.

HISTORICAL BACKGROUND

In 1882, during President Arthur's administration, the first immigration law was passed following a strong nativist movement. The same year the first "Chinese exclusion act" established significant limits to what was considered an "invasion of Orientals" who had been a preferred source of cheap labor for West Coast employers (Wittke 1949, p. 13). The search for cheap labor turned to Japanese and Filipino immigrants, who then became the target of "exclusionists." Campaigns like the "swat the Jap" campaign in Los Angeles and those inspired by the writings of Madison Grant and Lothrop Stoddard led to further restrictions of immigration from the Orient. The "Asian barred zone" provisions excluded immigration from Oriental countries as a source for cheap labor (Daniels and Kitano 1970, p. 53).

In the first decade of the century, eastern and southern European immigration became the focus of nativist and exclusionist crusades. Pressure generated by those movements crystallized in the appointment of a commission by the U.S. Congress to study immigration; the result of that study is known as the Dillingham Commission Report (1907–10). Throughout this voluminous report a long-debated distinction between the "old" and "new" immigration was made. It was argued that the values and occupations of the "old immigrants" (Anglo-Saxons and Nordics) were threatened by the "newer immigrants," southern and eastern Europeans and Asians (Hourwich 1912, p. 19). The distinction between new and old immigration created a dichotomy about which many pages of "scientific" reports were written in support of the undesirability of the new immigration.

Campaigns demanding restriction of the new immigration finally crystallized in the immigration laws of 1921 and 1924, which established quotas restricting immigration from all countries except those in the western hemisphere.

In the meantime, social scientists conducted research on the immigration phenomenon; they found empirical evidence showing that immigration to the United States has consistently supplied cheap labor (Eckler and Zoltnick 1949, p. 16; Hourwich 1912, pp. 167–72).

All countries which provided cheap labor for the United States were affected by the quota system established by the Immigration Act of 1921. Thus, the search for cheap labor turned to the western hemisphere, to which the quota system did not apply (Marden and Meyer 1968, p. 104); Mexican immigrants were found to be the most suitable replacement (Samora and Bustamante 1971). The suitability of Mexican labor rested on (1) geographical proximity; (2) the uninterrupted tradition of immigration, which was internal when most of the southwestern United States was still part of Mexico (McWilliams 1968, pp. 162–69); and (3) unemployment and unrest in Mexico, created by several years of revolution (Bustamante, in press).

A tremendous increase in Mexican immigration during the first quarter of the century (Grebler 1966, p. 20) corresponded to the increased demand for unskilled labor in the economic expansion of the Southwest. Mexicans crossed 1,870 miles of an almost completely open border (Gamio 1930, p. 10) to reach the steel industry in East Chicago (Samora and Lamanna 1970), railroad construction, and, most significantly, agricultural expansion in the Southwest (Samora 1971).

In this period the Mexican who wanted to legally cross the border had to go through a complicated procedure to be admitted into the United States. Those procedures included, in particular, a literacy test, "a condition which many immigrants cannot fulfill" (Gamio 1930, p. 11). Therefore, many took advantage of the "open" border policy toward Mexican laborers.

Moreover, the illegal immigrant could stay in the United States untroubled as long as he avoided the authorities who might disclose his status. Since no specific authorities were entrusted with apprehending illegal immigrants, the dangers of being caught were further minimized (Jones 1965, p. 13). Thus, the illegal immigrant's status was not visibly distinct from the legal immigrant's. The illegal entrant was able to maintain his violation in a state of "primary deviance" (Lemert 1951, pp. 70–78).

The appearance of the Border Patrol in 1924 altered the primary deviance of the illegal entrant by crystallizing a new social reaction to the violation of immigration laws. The new police force was to reveal those primary deviants, violators of immigration laws. In this process, the term "wetback," previously purely descriptive, acquired a new meaning. It became the "label" or "stigma" by which the illegal immigrant was made visible. At the same time, the label "wetback" also became the symbol by which the illegal immigrant was able to identify a new "me" for himself (Mead 1918, pp. 577–602), and a new role which better equipped him to meet the social reaction to his behavior (illegal entrance) (Lemert 1967, pp. 42–51).

The establishment of the Border Patrol in 1924 not only made the wetback more visible as a law breaker; it also brought changes in the patterns of behavior of the illegal immigrants. The freedom of interaction the illegal immigrant had had before 1924 was considerably reduced. He now had to walk, to speak, and to bear any treatment with the fear of being caught by or "turned in" to the Border Patrol.

The interaction most significantly changed was between illegal migrant worker and employer. Before 1924 labor conditions resulted from differential access to mechanisms of power and from the interplay of labor-force supply and demand. The organization of the Border Patrol brought a new factor: the illegal migrant could always be caught and sent back to Mexico. To be "turned in" became a threat always present in the migrant's mind that interfered with his social contacts. Social contacts, except for those with an employer or prospective employer, could be avoided for self-protection. The explicit or implicit threat of being denounced by the employer became a new significant element in the settlement of work contracts. It could be used to impose oppressive salaries and working conditions. In his search for a job he could no longer freely accept or reject a given offer; he always had to consider the alternative of being denounced to the Border Patrol.[1]

The importance of the "wetback problem" gains further emphasis in its numerical proportions. Although no reliable statistics exist on the actual number of wetbacks who have entered the United States, an approximate idea can be inferred from the records of expatriated wetbacks. Records for the period 1930–69 indicate that 7,486,470 apprehensions of wetbacks were made by the U.S. Immigration Authority (U.S. Immigration and Naturalization Service 1966, 1967–68). The highest rates were concentrated in the decades 1941–60, during which 5,953,210 expulsions of wetbacks were

made. The size of the population involved clearly defines the importance of the problem.

When we look at the sociocultural characteristics of the persons involved, we see that the problem is much larger. Most are poor peasants from central and northern states in Mexico who come to the United States only to find work to survive (Samora 1971, p. 102). They are willing to accept anything—good or bad treatment, illness, starvation, low wages, poor living conditions; all are taken philosophically and accepted without struggle. Their struggle is concentrated on pure survival (Saunders and Leonard 1951, p. 6).

THE NETWORK OF SOCIAL RELATIONS OF WETBACKS

Various groups of people come in contact with the wetback in the United States. In this section we will review four major groups: (1) the employer who benefits from a cheap labor pool, (2) the southwestern Mexican-American farm worker who suffers from the competition of these low-paid workers, (3) the lawmaker who is in the ambiguous position of defender of the law and protector of the "illegal" interests of farm entrepreneurs, and (4) the law enforcer who is directly responsible for enforcing the laws.

The Employer. In all economic enterprises, and in particular agricultural enterprises, labor constitutes a major segment of production costs. Rational manipulation of all instruments of production in pure economic terms requires the mimimization of costs in all areas to

[1] Data from 493 interviews that I conducted with wetbacks in 1969 show that 8% of the interviewees were "turned in" by their employers without being paid for their work. A year later, similar situations were encountered by the author during a participant observation as a "wetback" conceived to validate previous findings (a report of these experiences and the larger research project appears in Samora 1971). Further evidence of these and other kinds of exploitation of the "wetback" are reported by Sanders and Leonard 1951, p. 72; Hadley 1956, p. 352; and Jones 1965, pp. 14–20.

achieve the highest possible economic return. Workers willing to accept labor contracts below going wages clearly become a positive asset in that they assure higher returns for the entrepreneur. Moreover, other economic advantages besides low wages accrue from the employment of wetback labor. First, in some kinds of employment no strict accounting of working hours is kept, since work contracts based on daily labor may involve as many as twelve hours (Hadley 1956, p. 347). Second, little or no responsibility for disability occurs, since the wetback must assume responsibility for his own injuries and accidents. Third, the employer is under no obligation, legal or otherwise, to provide health and medical services, sanitary facilities, or even decent housing (American G.I. Forum of Texas and Texas State Federation of Labor 1953, pp. 17–27). As a result, what the wetback receives as wages and other standard "fringe benefits" is determined only by the employer's conscience and the current standards of neighbors and friends (Hadley 1956, p. 347). Even in pure economic terms, then, the position of the rural entrepreneur vis-à-vis the wetback is highly advantageous; by using wetbacks as workers, farmers can maximize possible economic gains in labor costs (Samora 1971, pp. 98–103).

The Mexican-American Farm Worker. Whereas the rural entrepreneur gains by the presence of wetbacks, the Mexican-American rural workers lose in competition for jobs. They feel that wetbacks push work contract conditions to the lowest possible level, a "charity" level out of step with living requirements in the United States. Their personal suffering from such competition is unjust, since, while being penalized by this competition, they have to pay the costs of citizenship (e.g., income and other taxes) and receive little or no benefit from such required contributions. Further, wetbacks break the possible cohesion of the rural labor force, and so they lose bargaining power with rural entrepreneurs. Finally, the manipulation of the mass media and urban lobbying groups by the rural entrepreneur creates an artificial shortage of labor which serves to ensure the permanence of wetbacks. At the same time, Mexican-American workers are prevented from speaking in the mass media to unmask the artificial labor shortage (Hadley 1956, p. 345).

The Lawmaker. The lawmaker should be the one to bridge the gap between the conflicting demands of the entrepreneur and the Mexican-American. Nevertheless, the most general pattern followed by lawmakers is to consider the wetback problem and the working situation on the border as something unavoidable or expected. Legal attempts to effectively prevent the wetback from crossing the border are stricken from proposed codes by the lawmakers on the rationale that the farmer along the border wants wetback labor (U.S. Congress, Senate 1953, p. 10). The "realistic" attitude of these lawmakers seems to be either that it is convenient to conform or worthless to struggle against the situation. Thus, the U.S. immigration law is broken in order to maintain a supply of wetbacks. For many southern, and in particular Texas, legislators, there is no evil in maintaining the influx of wetbacks.

Protection of the interests of wetback employers by lawmakers is best illustrated by a law (U.S. Congress, 8 U.S.C., section 1324, 1952) which makes it a felony to be a wetback but not to hire one.[2] This is a paradoxical situation

---

[2] That law provides that "any person who willfully or knowingly conceals, harbors, or shields from detection, in any place including any building or by any means of transportation, or who encourages or induces, or attempts to encourage or induce, either directly

(Continued)

which legitimizes the hiring of wetbacks in spite of the general recognition that it is the possibility of being hired that attracts Mexican workers to cross illegally to the United States. This situation was pointed out by Ruben Salazar (recently killed in the Chicago Moratorium in Los Angeles) in an article published in the *Los Angeles Times* (April 27, 1970): "There is no law against hiring wetbacks. There is only a law against being a wetback" (Samora 1971, p. 139).

The Law Enforcer. The Border Patrol is directly responsible for the prevention of wetback crossings and for the apprehension of wetbacks already in the United States. Theoretically, such a role would place the patrol in direct confrontation with the rural entrepreneurs using wetback labor, inasmuch as they enforce laws made in the interests of the total society. Their activities would, in part, protect the immediate interests of the legal rural workers.

Nevertheless, evidence suggests that such relationships of reciprocity are not realized (Saunders and Leonard 1951, p. 68); instead, the conflict between the Border Patrol and entrepreneurs is somehow transformed into covert cooperation through a "pattern of evasion" of the law (see Williams 1951). This transformation involves the following: first, the entrepreneurs offer little resistance to the apprehension of wetbacks, in exchange for the patrol's overlooking the wetbacks when work needs to be done. Second, wetbacks openly at work may informally legitimate their status as workers and thus remain unharassed. Third, complete enforcement of the law by state and national authorities, and with minimum cooperation from local

people, is theoretically possible (Saunders and Leonard 1951, p. 68).

THE LABELING APPROACH TO DEVIANT BEHAVIOR

Theories which view deviance as a quality of the deviant act or the actor cannot help us understand the wetback as deviant. "Wetback" became the label for a deviant after the appearance of the Border Patrol, and various social groups came to *react* differently to the presence of wetbacks. It is singularly characteristic of this deviant type that it occurs in a cross-cultural context; as a Mexican, the wetback breaks an American law and receives negative legal sanction while, at the same time, he positively fulfills the needs of specific American groups. This context of deviance fits well into the framework of labeling theory. According to Becker (1963, p. 91), deviance cannot be viewed as homogeneous because it results from interaction and consists of particular responses by various social groups to a particular behavior of the prospective deviant or outsider.

In this context, we must analyze the wetback in interaction, singling out the responses of the various groups making up the network which labels his behavior as deviant. The deviant character of the wetback, then, lies not in him nor in his behavior but in the superimposition of the deviant label on him.

Becker's use of labeling theory in deviance is of particular interest to us because of his stress on the political dimensions of the labeling processes. He emphasizes the fact that the legal norms and the behavior classified as deviant must be

or indirectly, the entry into the United States of any alien shall be guilty of a felony. Upon conviction he shall be punished by a fine not exceeding $2,000 or by imprisonment for a term not exceeding five years, or both, for each alien in respect to whom the violation occurs. *Provided, however, that for the purposes of this section, employment, including the usual and normal practices incident to employment, shall not be deemed to constitute harboring"* (italics added; Samora 1971, p. 139).

viewed as part of a political process in which group A, *in conflict* with group B, defines the rules for group B. The degree of group A's success in imposing such rules and in enforcing them depends primarily upon the political and economic power of group A. Furthermore, the will of group A is often an expression of a class interest rather than solely of individual members of group A. In such a case, enforcement of the rules becomes applicable to all members of that class, excluding members of group B whose class interests are the same as group A's.

Becker further indicates that labeling always begins with the initiative of a "moral entrepreneur" (Becker 1963, pp. 147–63), a leader (individual or group) who crusades for new rules to stop something that he views as wrong. Moral entrepreneurs are interested in the content of rules and are very often involved in what they view as humanitarian or moral reformism. In their crusades, they typically say they want to help those beneath them to achieve a better status, and in the process "they add to the power they derive from the legitimacy of their moral position the power they derive from their superior position in society" (Becker 1963, p. 149). The outcome of a successful moral crusade is the establishment of a new set of rules (i.e., the immigration laws of 1921 and 1924) and corresponding enforcement agencies and officials (i.e., the U.S. Border Patrol). The new law enforcers justify their existence by attempting to fulfill the new activities, and, in their performance, they try to win the respect of prominent persons.

Once a law and its enforcers come into existence the process of labeling becomes independent of the moral entrepreneur. The enforcer becomes the most important actor, and while enforcing the law he stigmatizes or labels certain individuals as deviants. Thus, there is a process of interaction in which some actors will enforce rules "in the service

of their own interest," whereas others, also "in the service of their own interest," commit acts labeled as deviant (Becker 1963, p. 162).

THE WETBACK LABELING PROCESS

The labeling process started with a moral crusade under the leadership of moral entrepreneurs representing the moral spirit of the American legal system. The results of the crusade were new legal codes (the immigration laws of 1921 and 1924) and the establishment of organizations and specialized personnel (e.g., the Border Patrol) to implement the new codes. The moral component of the legitimization of the new codes rest on the righteousness of the law, inasmuch as it protects the interests of nationals who otherwise would be defenseless against the threat of foreign competitors.

This organizational superstructure, whose purpose was to carry out the moral imperatives, resulted in a radical transformation of the previous interactions of foreign laborers. Of immediate concern was the reinforcement of the illegal status of immigrant workers under the deviant label of wetback. Nevertheless, moral imperatives, even those incorporated legally and implemented by specialized personnel, are not the only basis of motivation and rationalization of action. Others, especially political and economic interests, can be at variance with these new moral imperatives and influence behavior. When we examine such conflicting motivations we see that they may be selectively used, depending on the context of the action and the character of the actor—in particular his power. Thus, the rural entrepreneur in certain situations (e.g., harvest time) uses economic motivation to hire wetbacks with contracts calling for long hours of work and the lowest possible pay. In other situations (say, when he has unwanted workers) he uses the moral imperative to denounce wetbacks to the Border Patrol. A similar differential use of motivation occurs with other groups. It is necessary to specify the nature of motivations at play in the wetback case.

Looking at interests as a source of motivations, we shall focus on them at the juncture where they shape action; that is, at the point of interaction between wetbacks and the groups of actors discussed in this paper. A distinction will be made between group interests related to the presence of the wetback and group interests related only to each actor's role independent of the presence of the wetback. The latter would be those interests pertaining to the maintenance of the role played by actors of each group, that is, (1) the Mexican-American farm worker's role interest would be to maximize wages, (2) the farmer's (wetback employer's) role interest would be to maximize profit, (3) the lawmaker's role interest would be to provide legislation that meets the necessities of his constituencies and the country, (4) the law enforcer's (Border Patrol's) role interest would be to enforce immigration laws, (5) the moral entrepreneur's role interest would be to define good and evil for society. On the other hand, group interest related to the presence of the wetback seems to indicate a different dimension of each actor's role, as, respectively, (1) to stop the influx of wetbacks in order to avoid their competition for jobs and to increase bargaining power vis-à-vis the farmer, (2) to maximize profits by the use of the wetback cheap labor, (3) to gain political support from the farmers by protecting their interests, (4) to enforce immigration laws selectively, (5) to define protection of nationals against foreign competition as good and entrance to the United States without inspection as immoral.

This distinction of interests seems to promote understanding of some contradictions in the wetback phenomenon, such as (1) condemning the wetback by defining him as a deviant and, at the same time, maintaining a demand for his labor force which is reflected in a steadily increasing influx of wetbacks each year (Samora 1971, pp. 195–96); (2) penalizing a person for being a wetback, but not a farmer for hiring one (U.S. Congress, 8 U.S.C., section 1324, 1952); (3) maintaining an agency for the enforcement of immigration laws and at the same time exerting budget limitations and/or political pressures to prevent successful enforcement of the law (Hadley 1956, p. 348).

These are some of the contradictions that become apparent in the wetback case, but they are nothing less than reflections of contradictions in society at large. This is particularly obvious to us when we see the conflict of interests between the farmer and Mexican-American farm worker (each tries to maximize his economical gains at the expense of the other) and when we see the presence of the wetback kept undercover as a veil hiding deeper conflict. Indeed, when the role of the wetback is introduced in agricultural production, we see a different conflict of interests taking place—namely, that between the Mexican-American worker and the wetback. The former blames the latter for lowering working conditions and standards of living.

The nature of the two conflicts should be differentiated. Whereas the conflict of interests between the Mexican-American farm worker and the farmer is determined by the position each plays in a particular mode of agricultural production, the conflict between the Mexican-American worker and the wetback is determined primarily by a set of beliefs that are not necessarily grounded in reality, namely, that wages and working conditions are determined by external laws of supply and demand independent of the employers; that the wetback *causes* low wages and low standards of living for the farm worker, etc. It is important to note the point here that the conflicts "created" by the wetback would disappear with an unrestricted enforcement of immigration laws.

Another aspect of our discussion of group interest is the power that supports each specified interest and respective action. Since the groups themselves reflect status differentials, it is the differences in power (and possible collisions of power) that give form to the interaction. Furthermore, the power of legitimization of these actions sustains the existing form against any possible transformation.

Power differences among the various actors result from their ability to manipulate or influence interaction in the direction of their interests (see Gamson 1968). In this interpretation, the wetback employer is clearly the most powerful category, since he is able to influence all other actors. On the other extreme is the wetback. He clearly appears at a disadvantage. As an outsider he has no legitimacy. He is not eligible for public assistance or for the benefits of an eventual "moral entrepreneur," since he is not eligible to stay in the country, unless he is in jail. He is also not eligible for other benefits because of the stigma of having once broken the immigration laws. This might, technically, prevent him from acquiring legal residence or citizenship in the United States. The wetback only has the original motivation which made him cross the border (survival) and a new one resulting from the deviant label (not to be caught) which becomes another element of pure survival. As an outsider with such elemental interests he dares not complain—the only possible protest comes when his survival is in jeopardy and his only course of action is to return to Mexico.

A Conceptual Addendum to Becker's Schema. Labeling theory provides us with the concept of moral entrepreneur. Applying the elements of this type to the case under analysis, we find a new type in the role of the wetback employer. His crusade is directed toward the self-serving enforcement of existing laws. The source of his crusade is the threat of the loss of cheap labor that would occur if the laws were enforced. Evidently the characteristics of this second type are the polar opposites of those of the moral entrepreneur. The imperative he singles out as a banner is economic rather than moral. The crusade he leads is supported by power and economic interest rather than moral righteousness. This type can perhaps be characterized as an *antilaw entrepreneur.* In order to be successful he associates the law enforcer and the lawmaker in his enterprise and becomes able to manipulate the law in two ways: first, by preventing its enforcement whenever he needs cheap labor; second, by stimulating its enforcement when he needs to dispose of a complaining or useless wetback.

A view of the contradictions of society apparent in the wetback case has allowed us to introduce the antilaw entrepreneur. Such a concept is useful for the understanding of deviance because it shows that violation of a law can also become the goal of an enterprise in the same sense that the creation of a law may be the goal of an enterprise. Both crusades, to be successful, require leaders holding legitimate power, although in one case they have the added legitimization of answering to a moral imperative, whereas in the other they answer to the economic interests of a specialized group. The law enforcer, the lawmaker, and a powerful group of rural entrepreneurs can launch such a crusade against the law and yet not be "labeled" as deviants.

If a Border Patrol man states firmly that to enforce the law would "ruin the fields" (Saunders and Leonard 1951, p. 68), and a lawmaker refers to specific measures in the Senate to allow the influx of wetbacks (U.S. Congress, Senate 1953), and a former vice president of the United States (John Nance Garner) says, "If they [wetback employers] get the Mexican labor it enables them to make a profit" (Jones 1965, p. 17), then the essential objectives of the enterprise are spelled out. The continuing presence of wetbacks is in no little measure an indication of the success of the antilaw entrepreneur.

CONCLUSION

The preceding analysis leads us to see—

(1) the wetback as one who crosses the U.S.–Mexican border illegally, taking advantage of the limited enforcement of the U.S. immigration laws;

(2) the interaction process in which such a man is labeled a deviant, a label that will constitute a central element of a process of exploitation;

(3) the deviant label making the wetback more attractive as a worker than the Mexican-American (at the same time, paradoxically, such a label—an element of destitution—becomes what the wetback exchanges for an unstable taste of survival);

(4) the labeling process in which the wetback is "created," in which interests and power are arranged in an action that we have typified as an antilaw enterprise.

And finally, a human being with the alternatives of being exploited by a country forcing him to become a deviant or of facing misery in his own country by not doing so.

REFERENCES

American G.I. Forum of Texas and Texas State Federation of Labor. 1953. *What Price Wetbacks?* Austin: American G.I. Forum of Texas and Texas State Federation of Labor (AFL).

Becker, Howard S. 1963. *Outsiders: Studies in the Sociology of Deviance.* New York: Free Press.

Bustamante, Jorge A. In press. *Don Chano: Autobiografía de un Emigrante Mexicano.* Mexico City: Instituto de Investigaciones Sociales of the National University of Mexico.

Daniels, Roger, and Harry H. L. Kitano. 1970. *American Racism: Exploration of the Nature of Prejudice.* Englewood Cliffs, N.J.: Prentice-Hall.

Eckler, Ross A., and Jack Zlotnick. 1949. "Immigration and Labor Force." In *The Annals,* edited by Thorsten Sellin. Philadelphia: American Academy of Political and Social Sciences.

Gamio, Manuel. 1930. *Mexican Immigration to the United States.* Chicago: University of Chicago Press.

Gamson, William. 1968. *Power and Discontent.* Homewood, Ill.: Dorsey.

Grebler, Leo. 1966. "Mexican Immigration to the United States." Mexican American Study Project, Advanced Report No. 2. Los Angeles: University of California.

Hadley, Eleanor M. 1956. "A Critical Analysis of the Wetback Problem." *Law and Contemporary Problems* 21 (Spring): 334–57.

Hourwich, Isaac A. 1912. *Immigration and Labor.* New York: Putnam.

Jones, Lamar B. 1965. "Mexican American Labor Problems in Texas." Ph.D. dissertation, University of Texas.

Lemert, Edwin M. 1951. *Social Pathology.* New York: McGraw-Hill.

———. 1967. *Human Deviance, Social Control.* Englewood Cliffs, N.J.: Prentice-Hall.

McWilliams, Carey. 1968. *North from Mexico.* Westport, Conn.: Greenwood.

Marden, Charles F., and Gladys Meyer. 1968. *Minorities in American Society.* New York: American Book Co.

Mead, George H. 1918. "The Psychology of Punitive Justice." *American Journal of Sociology* 23 (March): 577–602.

Samora, Julian, assisted by Jorge A. Bustamante and Gilbert Cardenas. 1971. *Los Mojados, the Wetback Story.* Notre Dame, Ind.: University of Notre Dame Press.

Samora, Julian, and Jorge A. Bustamante. 1971. "Mexican Immigration and American Labor Demands." In *Migrant and Seasonal Farmworker Powerlessness.* Pt. 7B. Hearings, U.S. Senate, Committee on Labor and Public Welfare. Washington, D.C.: Government Printing Office.

Samora, Julian, and Richard A. Lamanna. 1970. "Mexican American in a Midwest Metropolis: A Study of East Chicago." In *The Mexican American People: The Nation's Second Largest Minority,* edited by V. Webb. New York: Free Press.

Saunders, Lyle, and Olen F. Leonard. 1951. *The Wetback in the Lower Rio Grande Valley of Texas.* Inter-American Education Occasional Papers, No. 7. Austin: University of Texas.

U.S. Immigration and Naturalization Service. 1966. *Annual Report of the United States Immigration and Naturalization Service.* Washington, D.C.: Government Printing Office.

―――. 1967–68. *Report of Field Operations of the Immigration and Naturalization Service.* Washington, D.C.: Government Printing Office.

U.S. Congress, Senate. 1953. Appropriation Hearings on S. 1917 before the Subcommittee of the Senate Committee of the Judiciary 83rd Cong., 1st sess., p. 123 Senator McCarran).

Williams, Robins, Jr. 1951. *American Society: A Sociological Interpretation.* New York: Knopf.

Wittke, Carl. 1949. "Immigration Policy Prior to World War I." In *The Annals,* edited by Thorsten Sellin. Philadelphia: American Academy of Political and Social Science.

the formal regulation of deviance

In addition to typing on an informal, interpersonal level, much typing of deviants occurs on a formal or official level. In fact, complex societies such as ours invariably include formal agencies whose role it is to seek out, identify, and regulate deviance. Such agencies include the police, the courts, the federal Drug Enforcement Administration, the Department of the Treasury (whose agents deal with smuggling), county and state health and welfare agencies—the list could go on and on. When these agencies of social control take action against someone adjudged deviant, the effects can be dramatic. These may include a formal confirmation of deviant typing, induction into a deviant role, and launching on a deviant career. This turning point in the deviant's life can also bring about a radical redefinition of self. What the deviant may experience as a unique personal crisis, however, is usually merely organizational routine for the agent and the agency.

The controls that such agents and agencies can impose differ significantly from those available to lay people. In terms of power, for example, the political state stands behind many agencies, while informal labelers may be no more powerful than the deviant. Likewise, the agents' control is usually legitimized by the state, whereas labeling by other people may simply represent an opposing set of norms. Finally, agents of social control usually operate according to an elaborate set of rules that provide standardized ways of dealing with deviants; other people's actions against the deviant need not be based on any plan at all.

Underlying the formal processing of deviants is usually a special perspective that the agents of social control adopt in their work. This perspective provides the agents with a system for typing or retyping so-called deviants, and it allows them to process deviants routinely and efficiently. The perspective varies, however, from one type of agency to the next, and this sometimes makes for conflict between the agencies themselves. The police and the courts, for example, occasionally clash in their views regarding the proper treatment of defendants.

Part Two

In this part of the book we consider the basic premises underlying the treatment of deviants by social control agencies, or what we term "the theory of the office"; the special perspectives police use in their police work; the logic that influences typing in the courts; and the social conditions under which lay people take the social control agencies' perspective.

THE THEORY OF THE OFFICE

In dealing with deviance as part of their occupational routine, police type some people as deviants and process them in terms of various categories. Thus the rates of deviant behavior that are officially recorded on police blotters are as dependent on the actions of the police as they are on the actions of the so-called deviants themselves. This processing in accordance with routine conceptions continues in court in a more sophisticated manner. Here again, though, the operational perspectives of the court personnel play as large a role in the administration of deviance as do the deviations of the persons being processed.

When persons first go to work in such capacities, they may begin with an unjaded perspective. Rookie police officers, for example, may be unprejudiced against minority groups. Young prosecuting attorneys may be committed to seeing persons as innocent until proven guilty. In time, though, this "naive" viewpoint is usually superseded by an operational perspective shared with veteran control agents. The agents acquire a set of simple, workable categories for defining and responding to the so-called deviants with whom they must deal. This operational perspective is called the theory of the office. The theory of the office specifies the typical characteristics of the deviants; the agents who will find, admit, and process them; and the way these agents will do so. By facilitating the management of deviance, the theory of the office enhances social order.

In primary groups unusual or nonconforming behaviors may go unlabeled as deviant for quite some time. Formal agencies, by contrast, are quicker to label people as deviants. Agencies have a set of fairly precise categories with which to type people and a set of prescribed rules for typing them in one category rather than another. Although exact procedures for doing this may differ from agency to agency, the theory of the office generally demands some kind of official categorization—and the sooner the better.

The theory of the office not only regularizes but also bureaucratizes deviance. This means that deviants come under the regulation of official hierarchy, specialization, impersonality, and systematic formal rules. The theory of the office indicates the authority relations among the agents themselves, as well as how they should relate to the deviants. It also dictates who will engage in which specific tasks (catching, processing, controlling, or treating deviants), and it dictates the procedures for handling deviants impersonally. Finally, it prescribes, often in detail, the organized rules for dealing with the deviants.

In this respect, the theory by which an office types and categorizes deviants is fundamental to its operation. Furthermore, its premises and categories are the basis for official "rates" and reports.

POLICE WORK

The police perspective—distinctly unlike other people's—is organized around "looking for trouble." Such "trouble" includes traffic violations, crimes, and observably eccentric or violent behavior. For police officers, trouble is defined by the penal code, by private citizens, and by experience with the kind of persons police define as de facto criminals.

Police culture combines legal and lay categories of deviance so as to be able to predict violations in advance. The police have advance notions of what suspects ought to look like, how they might make trouble, and how they should be typed. These routinized conceptions enable police to label suspects; thus they aid in the apprehension of deviants. In short, police perceive trouble in accordance with their working conceptions of it. Then they can regularize and deal with deviance in an orderly manner.

THE DEVIANT IN COURT

Police develop their categories of deviants from contact with a variety of suspects. When they make contact with a deviant, for example, their usual concern is the mechanics of arrest. Thus one way in which police type suspects is according to how hard or easy it will be to arrest them. By contrast, court personnel employ less pragmatic categories in dealing with suspects, because their roles are abstract and symbolic in accordance with the rules of law.

Court processing involves interaction (some of it behind the scenes) among judge, prosecuting attorney, defense attorney, bailiff, and sometimes a jury. To a very large extent it depends on legal terminology, court norms, and routine conceptions of defendants. Just as police fit suspects into a system of types, the court fits defendants into routine conceptions of typical cases. The use of these routine conceptions means that some persons who fit the court's conceptions of typical cases receive a prison sentence, while others who are guilty of the same offense (but who do not fit the court's conceptions of typical cases) may get lighter sentences or not get into court at all. Court work is rapid to the extent that court personnel can collaborate to make the facts fit their ideas of what typical cases look like.

THE EFFECTS OF FORMAL LABELS

When a person comes into contact with an agency of social control, the agency may view the person solely in terms of a deviant label. Initial contact with such an agency may suffice to call into question the person's "good name." Additional contact may give the person a definitely bad reputation.

Thus deviant typing may not end with the person's experience with a given agency. When meeting a stranger, for example, people look for information to help them type the stranger. If they find out that s/he has been in a prison or mental hospital, they may type the person primarily on the basis of that past experience, assuming that a person who has had contact with an agency of social control is likely to repeat the behavior that originally led to that contact. Accordingly, lay people feel less inclined to trust such a person. The agency perspective is so powerful that a deviant label, once formally applied, can long outlive any evidentiary basis. Once formally labeled, the so-called deviant becomes defined as the kind of person who probably did perform the imputed behaviors, or at least would if given a chance. Both the deviant and others may then organize their social relations around this belief.

the theory of the office

5

People who work with deviants in an official capacity generally develop specialized ideas about their work and the deviants with whom they deal. These ideas include notions about the nature of the deviance, what causes it, how it is best dealt with, and the role their agency should play in this regard. The readings in this chapter specify some of the bases for the official typing and treatment of deviants.

In the first reading Daniels describes the logic used by combat psychiatrists during the Vietnam War. Next Scheff proposes several generalizations about the stereotypes agencies use to define and respond to the people they are supposed to serve. Finally, Scott shows how contrasting theories of the office in two agencies for the blind affect how they deal with their clients.

The Philosophy of Combat Psychiatry

ARLENE K. DANIELS

. . . The purpose of (military) psychiatry, as for every other military support system, is to preserve the fighting strength. Psychiatrists further this purpose by refusing to support requests for release by men who want to escape from service. In the jargon of military psychiatry, the psychiatrists "support strengths" by encouraging men to be proud of themselves as adults who can take responsibility. And they "deny weakness" by refusing to see men as too weak to accept responsibility.

In combat conditions, military personnel cannot be allowed to succumb to problems which might legitimately be incapacitating to civilians. And so, the role of military psychiatrists as definers of a reality which is unpleasant but normal becomes most clear in wartime (Daniels and Clausen, 1966). The arguments they use in this definition focus upon altruistic rather than egoistic perceptions of reality. You have responsibilities to your buddies, your officers, your branch of the service, and your country.

Therefore, no one should request release and ask for special treatment. Any who nonetheless do so will be interviewed by a psychiatrist who has the authority to decide whether or not each petitioner has sufficient grounds for relief from his responsibility (i.e., because of some mental disability). Since these psychiatrists are governed by the philosophy of combat psychiatry which narrowly circumscribes the definition of mental illness, it is unlikely that they will be particularly sympathetic or lenient to such suppliants.[1]

In this respect the psychiatrists are like representatives of any bureaucratic agency. They order their expectations of the clients to be serviced according to their understanding of the goals and powers of the bureaucracy. And so they attempt to fit their clients into the well-established categories. Since the psychiatrist has the authority to do so, his definition of the situation prevails in most cases.

This excerpt from "Normal Mental Illness and Understandable Excuses: The Philosophy of Combat Psychiatry" by Arlene K. Daniels is reprinted from *American Behavioral Scientist,* Vol. 14, No. 2 (November/December 1970), pp. 169–178, by permission of the Publisher, Sage Publications, Inc., and the author.

[1] Generally speaking the career military psychiatrists who hold regular commissions are more wholeheartedly supportive of combat psychiatry philosophy than are the reserve officer psychiatrists on two-year commissions. But these psychiatrists are all members of the military and so, whatever their personal philosophy, they recognize the power of authorities to impose sanctions upon any psychiatrists who do not implement military policy as directed (Daniels, 1969, 1970b). Therefore, it can be assumed that the theory of military psychiatry is also practiced. In this respect the system resembles in many ways that within which the Soviet physician practices (see Field, 1960).

THE MENTAL HYGIENE APPROACH: STRATEGIES FOR ENFORCING A DEFINITION OF REALITY

In actual practice, the responsibility for defining the reality of combat psychiatry is most often assumed not by the psychiatrist but by his agents, "specialists," or "techs," who make the initial evaluation of those coming to the psychiatric unit. The technicians serve as screening agents who simply send some men back to duty without much comment, counsel others before and even after returning them to duty, and refer the remainder to the officers of the team for more complex decisions about treatment or disposition. Somewhat paradoxically, then, the bulk of the practice of combat psychiatry is performed not by psychiatrists (officers) but by technicians (enlisted men). It is thus mainly a medical practice turned over to the laity, performed by enlisted men for enlisted men. The officers who require attention are considered more "delicate matters" and are attended by the psychiatrists.[2]

The simplest strategy for "containing" the men (i.e., keeping them on duty) is to question their motives or intentions in requesting a psychiatric interview in the first place. Any suspicious events in their record (instances of "goldbricking" or unsatisfactory performance) may contribute to the negative interpretation of their actions. If, at this screening stage, the technician can convince the applicant that his appeal is thoroughly unworthy, the case can be closed. Here is how a psychiatrist explained the help his technicians gave him in this screening process at a division base camp in Vietnam in 1967:

For somebody who seems to be a malingerer, with a history of repeated shirking and sick call, they will often deal with him rather strenuously. . . . They will tell him in no uncertain terms to "cut out the crap." . . . It's obvious to them and to the patient that he's faking and often they'll return him to duty. If the patient wants to see the psychiatrist he still sees a psychiatrist. Most of them have seen the light at this point and go back to work. They weren't really serious, but they were just trying.

Thus, persons in positions of authority assume the social responsibility of establishing "the facts of the case." By their attribution of motives to the patient, they define the situation as one that the individual can endure if he wishes. Those in authority report that many patients readily accept this picture of themselves and thus most cases are successfully closed.[3]

For those who are still unconvinced, higher authority (the psychiatrist) can be requested to confirm the technician's perception of reality. The psychiatrist acts only as the possessor of an honorific status which should impress the wavering soldier, for as one psychiatrist said: "No psychiatrist in the world can differentiate between a soldier who cannot and one who will not perform" (Maskin, 1946: 190).

Some persons are not seen as immature, shirking, or manipulative, but as genuinely misunderstanding their own

---

[2] The management of these problems, problems of command consultation, will be discussed in a forthcoming paper.

[3] Unfortunately, it is not possible to ascertain whether this method is ultimately successful, since the measure of evaluation is simply nonreturn to that particular clinic. The possibility that such men may break down again and report to other agencies through which they are subsequently released from service has been suggested by studies of garrison troops (Datel et al., 1970). Another possibility is that men who have complained of mental illness problems may be killed in disproportionate number during combat (Glass, 1947). But this unfortunate possibility has never been tested.

ability. Such conclusions are drawn from the fact that either they have no history of attempting to escape from duty, or they have injuries or illnesses which they might consider incapacitating. Here the strategy, while it involves a more conciliatory attitude toward the petitioner, also focuses on returning the man to duty as quickly as possible. A problem is recognized; but the situation is seen as tolerable. A technician provides an example of this strategy in his discussion of newcomers:

New replacements in Vietnam—I see a lot of these people. They do have psychosomatic problems as soon as they get off the boat . . . but I normally do not send them to [the psychiatrist]. We try to handle it by getting them over it. I figure that they're going to adjust and this is part of their adjustment. They are also trying to get out of the field by remembering any sort of illness that they ever had to see whether that's going to get 'em out of it. So if we can get them over that two week period and get them into the unit . . . started to work, and forgetting about their problems and thinking about what they are doing, why that usually, I think, solves [the problems] for the new men.

In this type of situation, the established authorities show their willingness to accept the soldier's definition of himself as genuinely upset, but they deny that this upset is debilitating. They cut off any arguments for release based solely on presentation of symptoms. The world of military service is a harsh one; and so those who come to the clinic must revise their underlying assumptions or "background expectancies" (Garfinkel, 1967) about the world that they carry from civilian life. Much higher standards of endurance are taken for granted in military settings than might be the case at home. Psychiatrists and their agents reaffirm this reality when they refuse to recognize the legitimacy of illness as an excuse. They help to substantiate this

reality; for if they were sympathetic or lenient in expectations of performance the military world would not, in fact, be so harsh.

To enforce their definition of the situation as one within normal tolerance limits, the psychiatrists and their agents attempt to manipulate the environment to gain reaffirmation and support. They try to keep alternative definitions of the situation from developing. First, they try to minimize the amount of time a man spends away from the world of the battlefield when he is wavering in his belief that he can soldier. Second, they try to prevent entrenchment of the idea that reasonable or justifiable excuses for *not* soldiering could possibly be present. One technician at Chu Lai in 1968 expresses both these strategies of containment:

A very frequent case will be an individual who comes back [from the field] with physical symptoms, is sent to a hospital around here, and is given extensive tests . . . which [show] nothing. . . . He is then sent back to mental hygiene and I see him back there with a consultation by the doctors indicating some sort of functional disease. . . . He has been back [i.e., away] so long now . . . five or seven days . . . that it is very hard to get him back out to the field again. . . . [He hasn't seen a psychiatrist yet, he has just seen an ordinary physician.] So now he is [away] for quite a while and he is very hesitant to go back out again. And this is why it takes quite a bit of counseling and talking to him, to get him out there again.

From this perspective, five to seven days is a dangerous amount of time to spend away, for it gives a soldier time to realize that another reality than the battlefield exists. The hospital is also a place for the development of a counter-definition of reality—a soldier's definition of his condition as illness, as something that has happened to him for which he is not responsible and thus cannot be expected to control.

The technician's argument shows the importance of using imagery to support (or deny) a particular construction of reality. He realizes that his authority may be diluted by an array of medical tests—no matter how inconclusive—for by their number they suggest medical recognition of the symptom's importance. The soldier may reason that some additional medical tests will yet uncover the illness that *he* is sure he has to provide him with his justifiable release from Vietnam. Thus the authority of the technician to deny the relevance of the illness is weakened when the patient has been allowed to leave the field for a long time. And so special efforts must be made to reassert the military definition of the situation.

If, instead of a long absence, the crucial problem is a very bad experience in the field, the technician must argue against the reasoning that the soldier has already suffered enough and now has a justifiable reason to escape. From his point of view, the technician is persuading someone to accept his responsibility and to relax so that he will be more efficient and more likely to survive when he returns to combat. From a different perspective, it could be argued that the technician is, to garble Goffman (1952), "cooling the mark in" by persuading him to return willingly to a difficult and dangerous situation.[4]

I try to put all the emphasis on him talking to me and telling me just what is the matter with him, and why he feels this way.

And after he gets all this out and after he ventilates everything that he feels, then I explain to him that everybody out there feels the same way, and this anxiety and this tension and nervousness is normal. And that is not going to impair . . . it is probably going to enhance his functioning once he is forced into action. Most of the time I just try to appeal to their common sense. And try to force them to deal with the situation as it exists. . . . They are going to have to go out there again sooner or later. And once they get out there, it is not going to be as bad as they think. They are going to adjust, because they are able to adjust to any type of situation. . . . And it just takes quite a bit of talking between the two of us until we can get him [to do it].

All the preceding strategies for enforcing a definition of reality rely primarily upon the technician as the first line of defense. In this way the potential medical significance of the complaint is denied from the beginning.[5] Although psychiatrists minimize their medical connections in this way, they do not deny them altogether. Obviously some behavioral disorders will require more professional consideration than the technicians can provide. The psychiatrist will make these decisions as a medical specialist, but this will not mean that he will diagnose and treat mental illnesses as they are defined in civilian psychiatric nosology. His usual task will be to discriminate between understandable mental breakdowns (combat neuroses), which provide a reasonable excuse, and unacceptable

---

[4] The technician has to persuade the soldier (or mark) who has already been badly frightened (or burned) that it was not as serious a danger (or loss) as he believes. And in this process, the technician must obscure the possibility that the man may not be able to return, or that his case is sufficiently marginal so that he might escape punishment if he refuses to return (or that the mark really could complain to the police and institute proceedings which would make trouble for the con man).

[5] In general, the members of the psychiatric team de-emphasize their medical contact. They speak of counseling rather than diagnosis or treatment; everyone in the service wears battle dress rather than white coats; the service is more often named Mental Hygiene than Mental Health; and it may be officially titled a division (like any other support service) rather than a clinic (with its association of hospital service).

breakdowns (character and behavior disorders, immaturity reactions) which do not (see Daniels, 1970b).

NEGOTIATED DISTINCTIONS BETWEEN "ORDINARY" AND "TOO MUCH" TROUBLE

Once the men are actually in combat for any length of time the strains may wear them down. Studies of the combat effectiveness of men under stress suggest that there might possibly be physiological and psychological limits to the extent of time the average man can successfully remain in the combat setting (Ginzberg, 1959; Glass, 1953; Grinker and Spiegel, 1945). It also seems quite reasonable to the men that they may occasionally become hysterical or panic under the pressures they face. It is assumed that the hardships of combat life are sufficiently corrosive so that even when "physically" fit, the "mental" condition of the troops can progressively deteriorate over time. Therefore, no particular notice may be taken (no response is required) when a comrade breaks down and weeps or in other ways displays grief and rage. Such behavior is an ordinary expression in the course of war; it is not evidence of characterological weakness, immaturity, or incapacity to soldier. In fact, such displays may almost be expected from men who have fought in many battles and who are nearing their time of release. Apparently the stress of combat and the strain of anticipating release from it combine to create a terribly anxiety-provoking situation. Here is how one soldier described this process:

A few of us who were wounded returned to battle in a few weeks. And the others were sent home. You can tell now which are good soldiers when you have seen men break. They drop their weapons, lay down, and start crying. For no reason, you think. But it's just that they are tired of killing and being shot at. They are tired of seeing their friends wounded and killed. For a while you go out on patrol and make contact now and then. But you know there's a change in yourself which you have witnessed in others. You have been in combat for nine months. You are hesitant to go on . . . because the snipers, every time they fire a round, you feel they are firing at you.

This occurs when the man has less than 100 days in the country and will soon be a short timer—the two digit fidgets. . . . Can't sleep; when you should sleep you dream about dying . . . you feel alone, you think everyone is against you. . . .

When you are in camp . . . you cannot concentrate on anything and make careless mistakes that could kill you or those with you . . . then you really start getting short. Forty days till you leave. You wonder . . . if it takes 6 men to support one man in combat, why do I have to stay until I only have 20 days left to stay in the country?

This definition of the situation as intolerable uses the same criteria that the psychiatrists use in evaluating the mental deterioration in the field for which a man may be relieved from duty. These criteria include length of time in combat, the possession of an honorable combat history, an assumption that the soldier has made a genuine attempt to continue, and a belief that the soldier is becoming progressively more disturbed and less effective. If the psychiatrist finds that these social criteria (rather than classical diagnostic categories) are met, he may use the term "combat neurosis" to suggest that a form of psychiatric illness might actually be present. In this case, the commonsense view of the combat soldier and the professional evaluation of the psychiatrist coincide, both views being compatible with understandings about average tolerance limits under stress presented in empirical studies of combat. Here is a career military psychiatrist's description of "combat neurosis:"

A man should have been in combat for probably nine, ten months. There might be a little bit of range on either side. But he also has had to see some pretty severe action. He's had to see probably a lot of his friends get killed. Or he might have had to be wounded himself quite severely. . . . And he also has to be a good soldier up until that time. No problems, no character and behavior disorders at all. This man is a good man, a good soldier, is able to fight effectively, do a good job. He could be just an ordinary rifleman or a squad or platoon sergeant for that matter.

Then after experiencing the ordinary fear and anxiety that everyone in combat experiences for this period of time, finally he is triggered by this trauma of someone else getting killed, a close friend, or his unit may be overrun or himself getting severely wounded. It sets off a severe combination of anxiety, usually G.I. [gastro-intestinal] symptoms, anorexia, sometimes nausea, vomiting and bad dreams. And the nightmares are usually a recurrent type. . . . They can't sleep because their insomnia occurs. After they get enough of the bad dreams, they won't sleep by choice.

Also we find that there's a combination of this [symptomatology] with depression. Usually some guilt feelings. It's inappropriate guilt but it's guilt they feel. Maybe there's something they could have done to save their friends. . . . Or sometimes it might be a little guilt or depression that . . . after all this time they seem like they're cracking up and they can't fight effectively and they're sort of ashamed of themselves. . . .

So we have anxiety, depression, insomnia . . . G.I. symptoms, and dreams. And the anxiety is so acute that at times the guy becomes very tremulous in combat out in the field. Especially if he gets fired upon. . . . Sometimes we find the G.I. symptoms predominate. It takes just a little explosion or a rifle going off or something like that to [start] . . . severe vomiting and dry heaves. And he has to be brought back. This [symptomatology] is not dependent upon any previous psychiatric history.

This account presents a picture of a "reasonable" or "honorable" breakdown which can occur to anyone under sufficient pressure. This view requires no assumption of underlying illness or characterological weakness, only that there has been a sufficiently lengthy and successful military career prior to the event which can be seen as the cause of the breakdown. Under so much repeated, sustained, psychic, and physical punishment anyone might have broken down; there is no need to explain the situation in the traditional terminology of mental illness.

This perspective suggests that breakdown might arise after *sufficient* cause. It specifically excludes the notion that any particular encounter in wartime could be sufficient to cause breakdown (see Scott and Lyman, 1968). No single act of war or individual atrocity can be viewed as sufficiently brutalizing or terrible to induce mental incapacity. Such a view would undermine the entire picture of war as unpleasant but endurable. Should a man actually become incapacitated after such acts, a variety of other reasons for his difficulty can always be found by examining his career (Goffman, 1959).

The question of what is "enough" punishment is decided by the psychiatrist. He makes the decision according to rules that have been already formulated to a certain extent in the combat psychiatry literature from World War II. One of the best statements of how the criteria of enough punishment came to be defined on the basis of the psychiatrists' experiences in World War II is provided by Sobel (1947) in his discussion of "The 'Old Sergeant' Syndrome." Sobel suggested that men who had honorably and efficiently seen combat for long periods of time might eventually become incapacitated by all the griefs and hardships they had endured in the course of service. In effect, he was suggesting how anyone might be unable to endure any more of that kind of experience. Once their condition is recognized, it is acknowledged that such persons are "entitled" to break down, and that they are entitled to some honorable release from pressures. But, in general, this view did not supersede more traditional psychiatric views until much later.[6]

The traditional psychiatric views have officially been abandoned in military psychiatry on the basis of experience in past wars; for a focus on symptomatology as psychiatric illness rather than understandable stress reaction presented two main problems. For the man, the psychiatric diagnosis often resulted in a mental illness label. Once the label was applied, men often found it difficult or impossible ever again to shoulder normal adult responsibilities (Ginzberg, 1959). For the military, the application of the mental illness label eventually required the federal government to assume responsibility for long-term disability payments as it would for any soldier suffering from a service-related illness. Thus, the use of illness categories encouraged lifetime dependence and created a great fiscal burden for the government (Daniels, 1970a).

Today the view that soldiers may have their breaking points is accepted in military psychiatry, and so there is less necessity for singling out as possessors of a characterological weakness those who break down after long combat experience. The significance of this view is that since there is no necessary expectation of characterological weakness, there is no reason to fear that future psychotic breaks or permanent impairment to the soldier will occur. Normal recovery should follow normal breakdown, for if

there is no characterological weakness causing a collapse under severe and prolonged hardship, then there is every reason to expect spontaneous remission or remission once the situation is less oppressive. What this philosophy means in practice is that men who break down in the field are given a period of rest and sedation. They are supposed to recover quickly, forget their traumatizing experiences, and return to duty. However, if they do not recover quickly, they may be sent to some less stressful post to recover at leisure. In other words, it is reasonable to offer them some measure of escape from battle if it seems necessary to do so, even though technically they have no illness. And so disposition of the case will stress these possibilities.

Our approach . . . is that just because he has this doesn't mean that he is no longer a good soldier. He's proven himself in battle . . . and elsewhere. What he is suffering from is a temporary reaction that's curable. And we make a big point of the fact that it is curable. And also we have to make a point of the fact that he's not going crazy. He's not going to be a psychiatric case all his life. We give him encouragement that after his treatment he can return to duty and do as good a job as he did before and then we'll treat him with some medication like Librium—20 milligrams four times a day—and make sure we give give him plenty of sleeping medicine at night, like Seconal perhaps, a couple of hundred milligrams. Maybe about three days. After this we send him back to duty . . . [If his unit tells us he is not fully re-

[6] For example, a World War II psychiatrist (Lidz, 1946a) takes the traditional psychiatric perspective in describing the dreadful circumstances under which a number of marines broke down at Guadalcanal and had to be hospitalized as psychiatric casualties. These marines had to endure months of hardship in which buddies were killed by the enemy and left to decompose in plain sight and smell around the fortifications while help never came; where fear of torture and death at the hands of the enemy was realistic and ever-present; and where defeat seemed inevitable. The symptoms now termed combat neurosis are described in men who had endured such events. Yet, in this essay and elsewhere (Lidz, 1946b), this psychiatrist places greater emphasis on prior history of neurosis, unhappiness, or family instability than he does on the view that "every soldier has his breaking point."

covered and a recurrence of his symptoms appears] they should let us know and either arrange for a transfer with our recommendation backing theirs, or send him back to us sometime and we may be able directly to arrange a transfer to a non-combat unit.

The meaning of symptoms is thus dependent upon the combat history with which they are associated. They mean nothing without combat experience, something else when a soldier has little combat experience, and something else again when he has a history of nine or ten months of honorable and efficient service.

Possibly [a soldier] might come in with . . . symptoms but not with [the] full-blown syndrome. In the first place . . . we have to have our first criteria that the man has to have been a good soldier and have been in combat for some time before he develops this [symptomatology] in order to call this a combat neurosis. . . . If the guy comes in with anxiety and so on and maybe even some physiological symptoms after he has only been in combat for a month, we usually find that he had this right off from the first contact out in the field. And this seems to represent to us more of a kind of an immaturity reaction than anything [like] a true neurotic reaction.

When symptoms are presented within the wrong context, an entire reconstruction of the situation may be required. Not only are the symptoms given a different diagnosis but also the past history of the referral will be re-examined and then reconstructed. A contextual analysis of the situation permits the psychiatrist to find the necessary evidence in the moral career of the patient who shows symptoms too early in his combat experience, to label him as one who has displayed immaturity reactions from the very beginning, and thus who

deserves the disposition (no mental illness) he now receives (Goffman, 1959).

The diagnosis of "no mental illness" has an additional effect in that it reassures the soldier's superiors and peers that strong sanctions may properly be used to bring him into line. When the psychiatrist indicates that he sees no reasonable excuse in the case which might justify leniency for the man in question, the clear understanding that no alternative views will be tolerated creates additional pressure to accept the developing definition that "nothing is wrong" or that "nothing unusual is happening" (Emerson, 1970, 1969: 170). And since nothing is wrong, the soldier must eventually accept the world as a place where excuses are unacceptable.

REFERENCES

Becker, H. S. (1967) "Whose Side Are We On?" Social Problems 14 (Winter): 239–247.

Berger, P. and T. Luckmann (1967) The Social Construction of Reality. New York: Doubleday Anchor.

Blake, J. A. (1970) "The Organization as Instrument of Violence: The Military Case," Sociological Quarterly 11 (Summer): 331–350.

Bloch, H. S. (1969) "Army Clinical Psychiatry in the Combat Zone 1967–1968." Amer. J. of Psychiatry 126 (September): 289–298.

Cavan, S. (1966) Liquor License. Chicago: Aldine.

Daniels, A. K. (1970a) "A Sub-Specialty Within a Professional Specialty: Military Psychiatry," in E. Friedson and J. Lorber (eds.) Reader in Medical Sociology. New York: Atherton.

——— (1970b) "The Social Construction of Military Psychiatric Diagnoses," pp. 182–205, in H. Dreitzel (ed.) Patterns of Communicative Behavior. New York: Macmillan.

Typification in Rehabilitation Agencies

THOMAS J. SCHEFF

One particular avenue of research which would move outside of the traditional research perspective in rehabilitation is diagnostic, prognostic, and treatment stereotypes of officials and clients and the ways in which these influence rehabilitation process. Following Sudnow, this discussion will use the generic term, "normal cases." The discussion will begin with a review of Balint's concepts concerning doctor-patient relationships.

One of Balint's conclusions is that there is an apostolic function, i.e., that doctors in some ways act as apostles, seeking to proselytize their patients into having the kinds of diseases that the doctor thinks are conceivable in their cases:

Apostolic mission or function means in the first place that every doctor has a vague, but almost unshakably firm, idea of how a patient ought to behave when ill. Although this idea is anything but explicit and concrete, it is immensely powerful, and influences, as we have found, practically every detail of the doctor's work with his patients.

It was almost as if every doctor had revealed knowledge of what was right and what was wrong for patients to expect and to endure, and further, as if he had a sacred duty to convert to his faith all the ignorant and unbelieving among his patients.[1]

It would be easy to accept Balint's statement concerning apostolic mission as academic hyperbole which is used to make a subtle point concerning physical and psychiatric diagnosis. However, one can also take Balint's statement as literally true, and talk about the kinds of organizations and the kinds of situations in which diagnostic stereotypes are used in classifying clientele and become the base for action.

The literal use of such stereotypes is apparent in Sudnow's "Normal Crimes."[2] Making observations in the public defender's office in the court of a large city, he notes that the effective diagnostic unit for the public defender is the *typical* kind of crime—that is, the crime that is typical for the city that he describes at this time in history. He proceeds to describe burglary, child molestation, as-

Reprinted from "Typification in the Diagnostic Practices of Rehabilitation Agencies" in *Sociology and Rehabilitation,* Marvin B. Sussman, ed. (Washington, D.C.: American Sociological Association, 1966), pp. 139–144, by permission of the American Sociological Association and the author. Work on this paper was facilitated by grants from the Graduate Research Committee, University of California, Santa Barbara; the Social Science Research Committee, and the Center for the Study of Law and Society, U. of California, Berkeley. Arlene K. Daniels made useful criticisms of an earlier draft.

[1] Michael Balint, *The Doctor, His Patient, and the Illness,* New York: International Universities Press, 1957, p. 216.

[2] David Sudnow, "Normal Crimes: Sociological Features of the Penal Code in a Public Defender's Office," *Social Problems,* 12 (Winter 1965), pp. 255–276.

sault with a deadly weapon, and so on, in terms of the folklore which exists in the court about these crimes in that particular city. To say that this is folklore is not to say that it is completely or even mostly inaccurate. The point that is made, however, is that the thinking of the public defender is in terms of these stereotypic crimes, and his questioning of the defendant is not so much an attempt to find the particular dimensions and aspects of the situation in which the defendant finds himself, but almost entirely to discover the extent to which this defendant seems to fit into the stereotyped category of criminal which exists in the court.

This discussion will not attempt to repeat details of Sudnow's article. The point that is relevant is that these stereotypes are the functional units which are used by the public defender and, apparently to a large extent, by the public prosecutor also. In carrying out the business of the court, in this particular case, it should be noted that the aim of the public defender in using these stereotypes is not as much an attempt to get an acquittal as to get a reduction of sentence. This technique is therefore a way of maintaining smooth-running operation of the court, without gross violation of either the court's concepts of punishment, on the one hand, or the defendant's rights, on the other.

It seems likely that such diagnostic stereotypes function in many kinds of treatment, control, and welfare agencies. As the functional units in which business gets done, it is important to note, however, that these diagnostic packages are of different importance in different kinds of organizations and situations. In the kind of situation which one might find, say, in the surgical ward of an outstanding hospital, one would assume that diagnostic stereotypes are used as preliminary hypotheses which are retained or rejected on the basis of further investigation—that is, at one pole of the organizational continuum. At the other pole, in the kind of situation which Sudnow describes, these stereotypes are not only first hypotheses, but also the final result of the investigation. That is, there is a tendency to accept these stereotyped descriptions with a very minimal attempt to see if they fit the particular case at hand. Later in this discussion, some propositions will relate the type of situation, the type of organization, and the functional importance of the diagnostic stereotypes.

The idea of "normal cases" would seem to offer an entering wedge for research in the most diverse kinds of agencies. In current medical practice, the dominant perspective is the "doctrine of specific etiology."[3] This perspective, largely an outgrowth of the successful application of the germ theory of disease, gives rise to the stance of "scientific medicine" in which the conceptual model of disease is a determinate system. The four basic components of this system are a single cause, usually a pathogen in the body; a basic lesion; uniform and invariant symptoms; and regularly recurring outcome, usually damage in the body or death, if medical intervention is not forthcoming.

The model of disease in scientific medicine gives rise to "normal cases" in which diagnosis, prognosis, and treatment are somewhat standardized. (Thus diabetes mellitus is a disease in which the basic lesion is glucose intolerance; primary features are nutritional and metabolic disorders and susceptibility to infection; secondary features include retinopathy, coronary heart disease, renal disease, or neuropathy; and treatment is by routine insulin control.) An important component of this disease model is the application for treatment by the patient, with complaints which are

[3] René Dubos, *Mirage of Health,* Garden City, N.Y.: Doubleday-Anchor, 1961.

traceable to the disease. (Feinstein uses the term "lanthanic" for patients who have the disease but either do not have complaints, or whose complaints do not result in application for treatment.)[4] Cases in which the disease is present but the symptoms are not, are obvious deviations from the "normal case" and cause difficulties in medical practice and research. Equally troublesome are cases in which the primary and/or secondary features of the disease are present, but in which the basic lesion is absent. Meador has suggested, only half in jest, that such conditions be given specific medical status as "nondiseases."[5]

The concept of "normal cases" is closely connected with the notion that physicians have of "what's going around." That is, in a normal practice, a physician is not exposed to all kinds of the most diverse diseases that are described in medical textbooks, but rather only to a small sample of diseases which come in repeatedly: colds, flu, appendicitis, nervous headaches, low back pain, etc.

Proportionately as the case load increases, or inversely with the amount of time, interest, or knowledge that the physician has, one would expect that these diagnostic stereotypes would play an important role. Some of the atrocity tales of medical practice in the armed services and in industry suggest what can occur. For example, at the extreme, in some medical clinics for trainees in the army, virtually all treatments fall into one or two categories—aspirins for headaches and antihistamines for colds, and possibly a third category—a talk with the commanding officer for the residual category of malingerers.[6]

It is conceivable that the same kinds of conceptual packages would be used in other kinds of treatment, welfare, and control agencies. Surely in rehabilitation agencies, the conceptual units which the working staff uses cover only a rather limited number of contingencies of disability, placement possibilities, and client attitudes. The same minimal working concepts should be evident in such diverse areas as probation and parole, divorce cases, adoption cases, police handling of juveniles, and mental health.

PROPOSITIONS CONCERNING NORMAL CASES

Perhaps the most important characteristic of normal diagnoses, prognoses, and treatments is their validity. How accurate are the stereotypes which agency workers and patients use in considering their situations? One would guess that validity of stereotypes is related to their precision. Other things being equal, the more precise the stereotypes, the more ramified they are in the various characteristics of the client, the situation, and the community, the more accurate one would guess that they would be. The first proposition, therefore, concerns simply the number of the different stereotypes that are used in an agency. One would guess that validity and precision are correlated. That is, the more numerous the stereotypes that are actually used in the agency, the more precise they will be; and the more precise, the more valid they will be.

Proposition #2 concerns the power of clients. Using the term "marginality," in the sense used by Krause, the more marginal the patients, the less numerous, precise, and valid the stereotypes will be. That is, the more the status of the client

[4] Alvan R. Feinstein, "Boolean Algebra and Clinical Taxonomy," *New England Journal of Medicine,* 269 (October 31, 1964), pp. 929–938.

[5] Clifton K. Meador, "The Art and Science of Nondisease," *New England Journal of Medicine,* 272 (January 14, 1965), pp. 92–95.

[6] *Cf.* Philip Roth, "Novotny's Pain," *The New Yorker,* October 27, 1962, pp. 46–56.

is inferior to and different from that of the staff, whether because of economic position, ethnicity, race, education, etc., the more inaccurate and final the normal cases will be.[7]

Proposition #3: The less dependent the agent is on the client's good will, the less precise and valid the stereotypes will be. In private practice, where the physician is dependent on the patient for remuneration, one is more likely to find a situation as outlined by Balint, where decision concerning the patient's diagnosis becomes a matter of bargaining.

If the doctor has the opportunity of seeing (patients) in the first phase of their becoming ill, i.e., before they settle down to a definite organized illness, he may observe that these patients, so to speak, offer or propose various illnesses, and that they have to go on offering new illnesses until, between doctor and patient, an agreement can be reached resulting in the acceptance of both of them of one of the illnesses as justified.[8]

This discussion qualifies Balint's formulation by suggesting that bargaining or negotiation is a characteristic of a medical service in which patients are powerful, such that the diagnostic stereotypes of the physician are confronted by the diagnostic stereotypes of the patient, and that the patient has some power to regulate the final diagnosis.

A fourth proposition relates to the body of knowledge in the agency or profession which is handling the clients. One would suspect that the more substantial or scientific the body of knowledge, the less important and the more valid and accurate the conceptual packages. In areas of general medicine, for example, such as pneumonia and syphilis, the kind of stereotyping process discussed here is relatively unimportant. The same would be true in some areas of physical rehabilitation.

A fifth proposition relates the socialization of the staff member to his use of conceptual packages. A fairly accurate index of socialization into an agency might be the degree to which a staff member uses the diagnostic packages that are prevalent in that agency. This proposition suggests a final proposition which is somewhat more complicated, relating effectiveness of a staff member in diagnosis or prognosis to his use of diagnostic stereotypes. Effectiveness presumably has a curvilinear relationship to knowledge and use of stereotypes. In the beginning, a new staff member would have only theory and little experience to guide him and would find that his handling of clients is time-consuming and that his diagnoses tend to be inaccurate. As he learns the conceptual packages, he becomes more proficient and more rapid in his work, so that effectiveness increases. The crucial point comes after the time in which he has mastered the diagnostic packages, when the question becomes, is his perceptiveness of client situations and placement opportunities going to remain at his stereotypic level, where it is certainly more effective than it was when he was a novice in the organization? Is it going to become frozen at this stereotypic level, or is he going to go on to begin to use these stereotypes as hypotheses for guiding further investigation on his part? This would appear to be a crucial point in the career of any staff member in an agency, and research considering this crisis would be most beneficial. . . .[9]

[7] Elliott A. Krause, *Factors Related to Length of Mental Hospital Stay,* Community Mental Health Monograph, Massachusetts Department of Mental Health, 1967.

[8] Balint, *op. cit.,* p. 18.

[9] Charles Spaulding has suggested the proposition that typification practices in organizations are also a function of hierarchical position: the higher a person in the hierarchy (and therefore, the more removed from organizational routine), the less stereotyped are his typifications.

The Making of Blind Men

ROBERT A. SCOTT

When a blind person first comes to an organization for the blind, he usually has some specific ideas about what his primary problems are and how they can be solved. Most new clients request services that they feel will solve or ameliorate the specific problems they experience because of their visual impairment. Many want only to be able to read better, and therefore request optical aids. Others desire help with mobility problems, or with special problems of dressing, eating, or housekeeping. Some need money or medical care. A few contact agencies for the blind in search of scientific discoveries that will restore their vision. Although the exact type of help sought varies considerably, many clients feel that the substance of their problems is contained in their specific requests. . . .

The personal conceptions that blinded persons have about the nature of their problems are in sharp contrast with beliefs that workers for the blind share about the problems of blindness. The latter regard blindness as one of the most severe of all handicaps, the effects of which are long-lasting, pervasive, and extremely difficult to ameliorate. They believe that if these problems are to be solved, blind persons must understand them and all their manifestations and willingly submit themselves to a prolonged, intensive, and comprehensive program of psychological and restorative services. *Effective socialization of the client largely depends upon changing his views about his problem.* In order to do this, the client's views about the problems of blindness must be discredited. Workers must convince him that simplistic ideas about solving the problems of blindness by means of one or a few services are unrealistic. Workers regard the client's initial definition of his problems as akin to the visible portion of an iceberg. Beneath the surface of awareness lies a tremendously complicated mass of problems that must be dealt with before the surface problems can ever be successfully solved.

Discrediting the client's personal ideas about his problems is achieved in several ways. His initial statements about why he has come to the organization and what he hopes to receive from it are euphemistically termed "the presenting problem," a phrase that implies superficiality in the client's views. During the intake interview and then later with the caseworker or psychologist, the client is encouraged to discuss his feelings and aspirations. . . . However, when concrete plans are formulated, the client learns that his personal views about his problems are largely ignored. A client's request for help with a reading problem produces a recommendation by the worker for a comprehensive psychological work-up. A client's inquiries regarding the availability of financial or medical aid may elicit the suggestion that he enroll in a complicated long-term program of testing, evaluation, and training.

From *The Making of Blind Men: A Study of Adult Socialization*, by Robert A. Scott, pp. 76–87. © 1969 Russell Sage Foundation.

In short, blind persons who are acceptable to the agency for the blind will often find that intake workers listen attentively to their views but then dismiss them as superficial or inaccurate. . . . For most persons who have come this far in the process, however, dropping out is not a particularly realistic alternative, since it implies that the blind person has other resources open to him. For the most part, such resources are not available.

. . . [The] experiences a blind person has before being inducted into an agency make him vulnerable to the wishes and intentions of the workers who deal with them. The ability to withstand the pressure to act, think, and feel in conformity with the workers' concept of a model blind person is further reduced by the fact that the workers have a virtual monopoly on the rewards and punishments in the system. By manipulating these rewards and punishments, workers are able to pressure the client into rejecting personal conceptions of problems in favor of the worker's own definition of them. Much evaluative work, in fact, involves attempts to get the client to understand and accept the agency's conception of the problems of blindness. . . . In face-to-face situations, the blind person is rewarded for showing insight and subtly reprimanded for continuing to adhere to earlier notions about his problems. He is led to think that he "really" understands past and present experiences when he couches them in terms acceptable to his therapist. . . .

Psychological rewards are not the only rewards at stake in this process. A fundamental tenet of work for the blind is that a client must accept the fact of his blindness and everything implied by it before he can be effectively rehabilitated. As a result, a client must show signs of understanding his problem in the therapist's terms before he will be permitted to progress any further in the program. Since most blind persons are anxious to move along in the program as rapidly as possible, the implications of being labeled "uncooperative" are serious. Such a label prevents him from receiving basic restorative services. The uncooperative client is assigned low priority for entering preferred job programs. Workers for the blind are less willing to extend themselves on his behalf. As a result, the alert client quickly learns to become "insightful," to behave as workers expect him to.

Under these circumstances, the assumptions and theories of workers for the blind concerning blindness and rehabilitation take on new significance, for what they do is to create, shape, and mold the attitudes and behavior of the client in his role as a blind person. . . . [It] is in organizations for the blind that theories and explicit and implicit assumptions about blindness and rehabilitation become actualized in the clients' attitudes and behavior. We can therefore gain an understanding about the behavior of clients as blind people by examining the theories and assumptions about blindness and rehabilitation held by workers for the blind.

THE PRACTICE THEORIES OF BLINDNESS WORKERS

The beliefs, ideologies, and assumptions about blindness and rehabilitation that make up practice theories of work for the blind are legion. They include global and limited theories about blindness, ethical principles, commonsense ideas, and an array of specific beliefs that are unrelated, and often contradictory, to one another. Contained in this total array of ideas are two basically different approaches to the problems of blindness. The first I will call the "restorative approach"; the most complete and explicit version of this approach is contained in the writings of Father Thomas Carroll.[1] The second I will call the "accommodative approach." This approach has never been formulated into a codified practice theory; rather, it is only apparent in the programs and policies of more orthodox agencies for the blind.

The Restorative Approach

The basic premise of the restorative approach to blindness is that most blind people can be restored to a high level of independence enabling them to lead a reasonably normal life. However, these goals are attainable only if the person accepts completely the fact that he is blind, and only after he has received competent professional counseling and training. . . .

Seven basic kinds of losses resulting from blindness are identified: (1) the losses to psychological security—the losses of physical integrity, confidence in the remaining senses, reality contact with the environment, visual background, and light security; (2) the losses of the skills of mobility and techniques of daily living; (3) the communication losses, such as the loss of ease of written and spoken communication, and of information about daily events in the world; (4) the losses of appreciation, which include the loss of the visual perception of the pleasurable and of the beautiful; (5) the losses of occupational and financial status, which consist of financial security, career, vocational goals, job opportunities, and ordinary recreational activities; (6) the resulting losses to the whole personality, including the loss of personal independence, social adequacy, self-esteem, and total personality organization; and (7) the concomitant losses of sleep, of physical tone of the body, and of decision, and the sense of control over one's life.[2]

Rehabilitation, in this scheme, is the process "whereby adults in varying stages of helplessness, emotional disturbance, and dependence come to gain new understanding of themselves and their handicap, the new skills necessary for their state, and a new control of their emotions and their environment."[3] This process is not a simple one; it involves the pain and recurrent crises that accompany the acceptance of the many "deaths" to sighted life. It consists of "restorations" for each of the losses involved in blindness. The final objective of total rehabilitation involves returning and integrating the blinded person in his society.

. . . The various restorations in each of these phases correspond to the losses the person has encountered. The loss of confidence in the remaining senses is restored through deliberate training of these senses; the loss of mobility is restored through training in the use of a long cane or a guide dog; the loss of ease of written communication is restored through learning braille; and so on. The goal of this process is to reintegrate the components of the restored personality into an effectively functioning whole. . . .

[In] several rehabilitation centers and general agencies . . . the ideas contained in . . . [Father Carroll's] book are used as the basis for a formal course taught to blind people while they are obtaining services. The purpose of this course is to clarify for them what they have lost because they are blind, how they must change through the course of rehabilitation, and what their lives will be like when rehabilitation has been

[1] Thomas J. Carroll, *Blindness: What It Is, What It Does, and How to Live with It,* Little, Brown & Company, Boston, 1961.
[2] *Ibid.,* pp. 14–79.
[3] *Ibid.,* pp. 96.

completed. These ideas are given added weight by the fact that they are shared by all staff members who deal directly with the client and, in some agencies at least, by other nonservice personnel who have occasional contacts with clients. . . .

We cannot assume that there is a necessary correspondence between these beliefs regarding the limits and potentialities imposed by blindness and the blind client's self-image. The question of the full impact of the former on the latter is an empirical one on which there are no hard data. Our analysis of the client's "set" when he enters an agency for the blind does suggest, however, that such beliefs probably have a profound impact on his self-image. . ., . [When] the client comes to an agency, he is often seeking direction and guidance and, more often than not, he is in a state of crisis. Consequently, the authority of the system makes the client highly suggestible to the attitudes of those whose help he seeks.

There is evidence that some blind people resist the pressures of the environment of agencies and centers that adopt this philosophy by feigning belief in the workers' ideas for the sake of "making out" in the system.[4] In such cases, the impact of workers on the client's self-image will be attenuated. Despite this, he will learn only those skills made available to him by the agency or center. These skills, which the workers regard as opportunities for individual fulfillment, act also as limits. The choice of compensatory skills around which the theory revolves means the exclusion of a spectrum of other possibilities.

The Accommodative Approach

A basic premise of the restorative approach is that most blind people possess the capacity to function independently enough to lead normal lives. Rehabilitation centers and general service agencies that have embraced this approach therefore gear their entire service programs toward achieving this goal. In other agencies for the blind, no disagreement is voiced about the desirability of blind people's attaining independence, but there is considerable skepticism as to whether this is a feasible goal for more than a small fraction of the client population.[5] According to this view, blindness poses enormous obstacles to independence—obstacles seen as insurmountable by a majority of people. . . . Settings and programs are designed to accommodate the helpless, dependent blind person.

The physical environment in such agencies is often contrived specifically to suit certain limitations inherent in blindness. In some agencies, for example, the elevators have tape recorders that report the floor at which the elevator is stopping and the direction in which it is going, and panels of braille numbers for each floor as well. Other agencies have mounted over their front doors special bells that ring at regular intervals to indicate to blind people that they are approaching the building. Many agencies maintain fleets of cars to pick up clients at their homes and bring them to the agency for services. In the cafeterias of many agencies, special precautions are taken to serve only food that blind people can eat without awkwardness. In one agency cafeteria, for example, the food

[4] *Information Bulletin No. 59,* University of Utah, Regional Rehabilitation Research Institute, Salt Lake City, 1968.
[5] Roger G. Barker *et al., Adjustment to Physical Handicap and Illness: A Survey of the Social Psychology of Physique and Disability,* Social Science Research Council, New York, 1953.

is cut before it is served, and only spoons are provided.

Recreation programs in agencies that have adopted the accommodative approach consist of games and activities tailored to the disability. For example, bingo, a common activity in many programs, is played with the aid of a corps of volunteers who oversee the game, attending to anything the blind person is unable to do himself.

Employment training for clients in accommodative agencies involves instruction in the use of equipment specifically adapted to the disability. Work tasks, and even the entire method of production, are engineered with this disability in mind, so that there is little resemblance between an average commercial industrial setting and a sheltered workshop. Indeed, the blind person who has been taught to do industrial work in a training facility of an agency for the blind will acquire skills and methods of production that may be unknown in most commercial industries.

The general environment of such agencies is also accommodative in character. Clients are rewarded for trivial things and praised for performing tasks in a mediocre fashion. This superficial and overgenerous reward system makes it impossible for most clients to assess their accomplishments accurately. Eventually, since anything they do is praised as outstanding, many of them come to believe that the underlying assumption must be that blindness makes them incompetent.

The unstated assumption of accommodative agencies is that most of their clients will end up organizing their lives around the agency. Most will become regular participants in the agency's recreation programs, and those who can

work will obtain employment in a sheltered workshop or other agency-sponsored employment program. The accommodative approach therefore produces a blind person who can function effectively only within the confines of the agency's contrived environment. He learns skills and behavior that are necessary for participating in activities and programs of the agency, but which make it more difficult to cope with the environment of the larger community. A blind person who has been fully socialized in an accommodative agency will be maladjusted to the larger community. In most cases, he does not have the resources, the skills, the means, or the opportunity to overcome the maladaptive patterns of behavior he has learned. He has little choice but to remain a part of the environment that has been designed and engineered to accommodate him.

This portrayal of accommodative agencies suggests that the workers in them, like those in restorative agencies, make certain assumptions about the limitations that blindness imposes, and that these assumptions are manifested in expectations about attitudes and behavior that people ought to have because they are blind. . . .

Unfortunately, no hard data are available on socialization outcomes in agencies that adopt either of the two approaches I have described. However, the materials I collected from interviews with blind people suggest that a number of discernably patterned reactions occur.[6] Some clients and trainees behave according to workers' expectations of them deliberately and consciously in order to extract from the system whatever rewards it may have. Others behave according to expectations because they have accepted and internalized them as

[6] Most of this discussion applies to blind people who have been exposed to agencies that adopt an accommodative approach to rehabilitation. Little information could be gathered on those who have been trainees in restorative agencies, primarily because such agencies are comparatively few in number and recent in origin.

genuine qualities of character. The former are the "expedient" blind people, and the latter are the "true believers."

Expedient blind people consciously play a part, acting convincingly the way they sense their counselors and instructors want them to act. They develop a keen sense of timing that enables them to be at their best when circumstances call for it. When the circumstances change, the façade is discarded, much as the Negro discards his "Uncle Tomisms" in the absence of whites. As a rule, the expedient blind person is one who recognizes that few alternatives are open to him in the community; his response is an understandable effort to maximize his gains in a bad situation.

True believers are blind people for whom workers' beliefs and assumptions about blindness are unquestioned ideals toward which they feel impelled earnestly to strive. While this pattern is probably found in all agencies for the blind, it is most obvious in those which embrace the accommodative approach to blindness. Clients who become true believers in such agencies actually experience the emotions that workers believe they must feel. They experience and spontaneously verbalize the proper degree of gratitude, they genuinely believe themselves to be helpless, and they feel that their world must be one of darkness and dependency.

6 | *police work*

In occupations that routinely deal with deviants, there are often guidelines for dealing with the deviants and for compiling and using official records about them. In some occupations, such as police work, these norms are so central that they often become second nature, followed almost by rote. They prescribe how police officers should relate to deviants, as well as the form their records should take.

In the first reading Werthman and Piliavin describe the police perspective on juvenile delinquency. Skolnick then shows how police underreport some crimes and overreport others in order to establish a good job performance record. In the final reading Wilson describes how the social organization of the police affects police work in two cities.

The Police Perspective on Delinquency

CARL WERTHMAN
IRVING PILIAVIN

The juvenile officer exercises a good deal of discretion in deciding how to process offenders, a discretion that far transcends the measure of ambiguity ordinarily involved in legal assessments of motivation and intent. Although a truant may not be responsible for his behavior, may be a touch rebellious, or may be acting in complete and willful disregard for law, the nature and intent of this crime are not as important to a juvenile officer as what he learns about the attitude of the offender towards the idea of the law itself. For example, if an officer decides he is dealing with a boy who is "guilty but essentially good" or "guilty but sometimes weak," the probability is high that he will decide to let the boy go with a warning about the consequences of committing this crime again. He might feel that contact with the unsavory clientele of a juvenile hall would damage an otherwise positive attitude towards the law or that moral contamination in the eyes of parents and teachers as a result of being sent to jail

might weaken an otherwise firm commitment to conventional behavior. On the other hand, if the officer decides that the offender is a "punk," a "persistent troublemaker," or some other version of a thoroughly bad boy, he may well decide to make an arrest.[1]

A "delinquent" is therefore not a juvenile who happens to have committed an illegal act. He is a young person whose moral character has been negatively assessed. And this fact has led some observers to conclude that the transformation of young people into official "delinquents" is best looked at as an organizational rather than a legal process since policemen, probation officers, and juvenile court judges often base their dispositions on a host of criteria that are virtually unrelated to the nature of the specific offense.[2]

The *magnitude of an offense*, of course, can become a factor in dispositions. One responsibly planned and willfully executed robbery, rape, or assault can ruin the moral status of a juvenile

Reprinted by permission from Carl Werthman and Irving Piliavin, "Gang Members and the Police," *The Police: Six Sociological Essays,* David Bordua, ed. (New York: John Wiley & Sons, Inc., 1967), pp. 72–75, 80–81, 90–94. Copyright © 1967 by John Wiley and Sons, Inc.

[1] For a more complete discussion of police discretion in dealing with juveniles, see Irving Piliavin and Scott Briar, "Police Encounters with Juveniles," *The American Journal of Sociology,* Vol. LXX, No. 2 (Sept. 1964), pp. 209–211.

[2] The problem of discretion has been formulated and studied by Aaron Cicourel in these terms. See Aaron V. Circourel, *The Social Organization of Juvenile Justice,* New York: John Wiley & Sons, 1968.

indefinitely. Since 90% of the crimes committed by juveniles are minor offenses, however, this criterion is only rarely used.

The number of *previous contacts with police* has a more important effect on dispositions. These contacts are typically recorded on easily accessible files, and these files contain everything from arrests and convictions to contacts made on the flimsiest of contingent grounds. If a boy confesses to a crime and is not known to the police, he is often released. If he is caught for a third or fourth time, however, the sum total of previous contacts may be enough to affect a judgment about his moral character adversely, regardless of the nature or magnitude of the present offense and regardless of the reasons he was previously contacted. For example:

Like last night, man, me and Willy got busted for curfew. I mean I got busted for curfew. We was walkin' up the hill towards home, and these cops pull up. It was a Friday night, man, so we didn't want no trouble. When the cops ask us what we was doing and what about our names we was all nice. So then the cop gets on that radio and checks us out. There was a whole bunch of noise comin' over that box. I couldn't hear what they was sayin'. But then the cop comes out and says to Willy, "O.K., you can go." And I say, "What about me?" And the cop says, "You been in trouble before. We don't want you walkin' the streets at night. We going to take you down to the station for curfew." Then I got real mad. I almost ran. Lucky thing I didn't though. I woulda been in real trouble then.

There is even some evidence to suggest that assessments about the type and quality of *parental control* are even more important factors in dispositions than *any* of the offense-related criteria. One of the main concerns of a juvenile officer is the likelihood of future offense, and this determination is often made largely on the basis of "the kinds of parents" a boy happens to possess. Thus, the moral character of parents also passes under review; and if a house appears messy, a parent is missing, or a mother is on welfare, the probability of arrest increases. Similarly, a boy with a father and two older brothers in jail is considered a different sort of person from a boy whose immediate family is not known to the police. As Cicourel points out, these judgments about family life are particularly subject to bias by attitudes related to class.[3]

See, like if you or maybe one of your brothers, say both of you been to Y.A.,[4] or your sister, every time they see you they get on your back. They know all your family. If they ever pick you up and look at your records, they automatically take you in. They see where your sister been to jail, your brother, or if you ever went to jail. And they start saying, "Your whole family is rotten. Your whole family is jailbirds." Shit like that. And this is what really make you mad, when they tell you your mother don't know how to read!

Although the family situation of a boy and his record of prior police contacts both enter into dispositions, the most important factor affecting the decision of juvenile officers is the *attitude* displayed by the offender, both during and after the confession itself. Cicourel, for example, found that juvenile officers were strongly influenced by the style and speed with which the offender confessed.[5] If a boy blurts out his misdeeds

---

[3] Aaron Cicourel, "Social Class, Family Structure and the Administration of Juvenile Justice," Center for the Study of Law and Society, University of California at Berkeley, Working Paper, MS.

[4] The detention facilities administered by the California Youth Authority.

[5] Cicourel, *The Social Organization of Juvenile Justice, loc. cit.*

immediately, this behavior is taken as a sign that the boy "trusts" authority and is therefore "under control." If the boy proves to be a "tough nut to crack," however, he is viewed with suspicion. As soon as a juvenile is defined as "hardened," he is considered no less dangerous to society than the adult criminal.

Similarly, the boys who appear frightened, humble, penitent, and ashamed are also more likely to go free. They are often defined as "weak, troubled, and the victim of circumstances" but basically "good boys," an assessment of moral character that may win them a release.

On the other hand, if a boy shows no signs of being spiritually moved by his offense, the police deal harshly with him. Not only has he sinned against a legal rule, but he has also symbolically rejected the normative basis for conforming to it in the first place; and it is this double deviation that has fateful consequences for the way he is treated by the police. Once he gets himself defined as "the kind of person who doesn't respect the law," he becomes a perfect candidate for arrest, detention, and eventual incarceration. Most of the juvenile officers we interviewed felt that the attitude of the offender was the major determinant of dispositions in 50% of their cases, and Nathan Goldman reports that "defiance on the part of a boy will lead to juvenile court quicker than anything else."[6]

It is hardly necessary to describe the way most gang boys feel about the equity of these dispositions. One only needs to imagine the look on a boy's face when he is told that he is about to spend a year in jail for an offense committed with a friend who was sent home when he promptly confessed. . . .

In addition to the variety of *places* used to draw samples, however, the police also seem to rely on a number of physical or material *individual attributes*. Certain kinds of clothing, hair, and walking styles seem intrinsically to trigger suspicion. The general description of these styles had best be left to the boys themselves.

(Why do you think the cops pick you up all the time?) Why do they pick us up? They don't pick everybody up. They just pick up on the ones with the hats on and trench coats and conks.[7] If you got long hair and hats on, something like this one, you gonna get picked up. Especially a conk. And the way you dress. Sometimes, like if you've got on black pants, better not have on no black pants or bends[8] or Levi's.

They think you going to rob somebody. And don't have a head scarf on your head. They'll bust you for having a head scarf.[9]

(All right, so they bust you for clothes. That's one thing. Is there anything else?) The way you walk sometimes. If you walk pimp. Don't try to walk pimp. Don't try to be cool. You know. They'll bust you for that. (Could you tell me how you walk pimp?) You know. You just walk cool like. Like you got a boss high.[10] Like you got a fix or something. Last night a cop picked me up for that. He told me I had a bad walk. He say, "You think you're bad." You know.

[6] Nathan Goldman, *The Differential Selection of Juvenile Offenders for Court Appearances,* National Council on Crime and Delinquency (1963), p. 106.

[7] A "conk" is a hair straightening process used by Negroes that is similar in concept to the permanent wave.

[8] "Bends" are a form of the bell-bottom trouser which, when worn effectively, all but obscure the shoe from vision, thus creating the impression that the wearer is moving down the street with an alarmingly irresponsible shuffle.

[9] Head scarves (sometimes called "mammy rags") are worn by Negroes around the forehead to keep "conk jobs" in place.

[10] "Boss" is a synonym for "good."

Finally, the police also use *themselves* as an instrument for locating suspicious people. Every time an officer makes visible contact with a citizen, the citizen is forced to confront his status in the eyes of the law, and the police soon learn to rely on hostile *looks* and furtive *glances* as signs of possible guilt. A policeman's uniform is a potent symbolic device. It sometimes has the power to turn a patrolman into a walking test of moral identity.

It should not be construed from the above discussion that the process of locating a population of potential offenders always proceeds on such slim grounds. There are a variety of "scenes" that constitute much more obvious bases for investigation. However, since policemen rarely stumble on armed men standing over dead bodies, much of their activity involves a subtle and exceedingly tenuous reading of both appearances and events. For example, when dealing with people who possess the ecological and personal indicators of suspiciousness outlined above, patrolmen may turn a screwdriver into a "deadly weapon" and a scratch on the neck into evidence of rape.

Like you be walking. Just come from working on the car or something. And if you've got a screwdriver or something in your back pocket, hell, they may beat the shit outa you. They talk about you got a burglary tool or you got a deadly weapon on you.

Remember the time when we was getting ready to go up to the gym? We came home from school one day. He had some scratches on his neck, and the cop pull over and say, "Turn around!" The cop grabbed him. I didn't say nothing. I was walking. I got to the top of the stairs and the cop holler "Turn around" at me too. So I turn around. And the cop look at my neck and he say, "Yeah. You too. You got scratches on your neck too." So he took us down to the police station. It seem like some girl way over in another district got raped. And the girl say, "I think they live

over at Hunters Point and I scratched one of them on the neck." Some stuff like that.

Gang members are very much aware of their moral status in the eyes of the police. On most occasions, they are likely to know that the police have singled them out for interrogation because of the neighborhood they live in, because of their hair styles, or perhaps because they are temporarily "out of place." They know how the police operate, and they are particularly aware of the role played by judgments about moral character in this methodology. . . .

OUTCOMES

If a juvenile being interrogated in the situation of suspicion refuses to proffer the expected politeness or to use the words that typically denote respect and if no offense has been discovered, a patrolman finds himself in a very awkward position. He cannot arrest the boy for insolence or defiance, since for obvious reasons no charges of this nature exist. The patrolman is thus faced with the choice of three rather unpleasant alternatives.

First, he can back down, thereby allowing his authority to evaporate. If a patrolman allows his authority to escape, however, there is no guarantee that it can be recaptured the next day or any day thereafter. Since patrolmen are structurally locked into the authority role over long periods of uninterrupted time, any fleeting defeat at the hands of a gang member has the prospect of becoming permanent. In a certain sense, then, gang members have a great deal of power. With the mere hint of impiety they can sometimes manage to strip a patrolman symbolically of his authority.

For these reasons, if a patrolman does decide to back down, he must be careful to retreat strategically by withdrawing from the encounter without a public loss of face. This is usually done by communicating to the juvenile that his innocence is fortuitous, that he is the kind of person who *could* have committed an offense, and that he owes his release to the grouchy good graces of the interrogating officer. If executed artfully, comments such as "keep your nose clean or we'll run you in next time" can pave the way out of a potentially damaging encounter. From the point of view of the boys, of course, this technique simply constitutes an additional insult to moral character.

If a patrolman chooses to press his claims to authority, however, he has only two sanctions available with which to make these claims good. On the one hand, he can attempt an arrest.

One day we were standing on the corner about three blocks from school and this juvenile officer comes up. He say, "Hey, you boys! Come here!" So everybody else walked over there. But this one stud made like he didn't hear him. So the cop say, "Hey punk! Come here!" So the stud sorta look up like he hear him and start walking over. But he walking over real slow. So the cop walk over there and grab him by the collar and throw him down and put the handcuffs on him, saying, "When I call you next time come see what I want!" So everybody was standing by the car, and he say, "All right you black mother fuckers! Get your ass home!" Just like that. And he handcuffed the stud and took him to juvenile hall for nothing. Just for standing there looking at him.

On the other hand, there are a variety of curfew, vagrancy, and loitering laws that can also be used to formally or officially prosecute the informal violation of norms governing deportment in the situation of suspicion.

I got arrested once when we were just riding around in a car. There was a bunch of us in the car. A police car stopped us, and it was about ten after ten when they stopped us. They started asking us our names and wanted to see our identification. Then they called in on us. So they got through calling in on us, and they just sit in the car and wait till the call came through. Then they'd bring back your I.D. and take another one. One at a time. They held me and another boy till last. And when they got to us it was five minutes to eleven. They told everybody they could go home, but they told us it didn't make no sense for us to go home because we was just riding around and we'd never make it home in five minutes. So they busted us both for curfew.

In addition to these laws, a boy can also be charged with "suspicion" of practically anything. When the police use suspicion as a charge, however, they usually try to make the specific offense as serious as possible. This is why the criminal records of many gang boys are often heavily laced with such charges as "suspicion of robbery" and "suspicion of rape."

(Could you tell me some of the things you have been busted for?) Man, I been charged with everything from suspicion of murder to having suspicious friends. I think they call it "associates!" (laughter) They got me on all kinda trash, man, and they only make but one thing stick. (What's that?) A couple of years ago they caught me stone cold sittin' behind the wheel of a '60 Pontiac. I said it belong to my uncle, but it turn out that the name of the registration was O'Shaunessee or O'Something, some old fat name like that. The cop knew there wasn't no bloods [Negroes] named things like that.

Gang boys are aware that the police have a very difficult time making these illusory charges stick. They can always succeed in sending a boy to jail for a few hours or a few days, but most of these charges are dismissed at a preliminary hearing on recommendations from probation officers. Moreover, gang members also understand the power of probation officers, and by behaving better in front of these officials they can often embarrass the local authority of patrolmen by having decisions to arrest reversed over their heads. As far as the patrolmen are concerned, then, the boys can make a mockery of false charges as a sanction against impertinence in the situation of suspicion.

Perhaps more important, however, a patrolman's sergeant also knows that most trivial or trumped-up charges are likely to be dropped, and thus the police department itself puts a premium on ability to command authority without invoking the sanction of arrest. Unlike the juvenile officer who is judged by his skills at interrogation, a patrolman's capacity to gain respect is his greatest source of pride as well as his area of greatest vulnerability. If he is forced to make too many "weak" arrests, he stands to lose prestige among his peers and superiors on the police force and to suffer humiliation at the hands of his permanent audience of tormentors on the beat.

It is largely for these reasons that many patrolmen prefer to settle a challenge to authority on the spot, an alternative that necessarily poses the prospect of violence. As William Westley has pointed out, in the last analysis the police can always try to "coerce respect."[11]

They don't never beat you in the car. They wait until they get you to the station. And then they beat you when the first shift comes on and they beat you when the second shift comes on. I've seen it happen.

I was right there in the next cell. They had a boy. His name was Stan, and they had beat him already as soon as they brought him in. And then when they was changing shifts, you know, the detective came and looked on the paper that say what he was booked for, I think it was robbery or something like that, and they started beating on him again. See, the police are smart. They don't leave no bruises. They'll beat you somewhere where it don't show. That's the main places where they look to hit you at. And if it did show, your word wouldn't be as good as theirs. They can lie too, you know. All they have to say is that you was resisting and that's the only reason they need for doing what they do.

Resisting arrest is the one charge involving violence that seems uniquely designed to deal with improper deportment in the situation of suspicion. A policeman interviewed by Westley suggests that when the challenge to authority is not sufficiently serious to warrant this charge, the police may continue to provoke the suspect until the level of belligerence reaches proportions that legitimate invoking this category of offense.

For example, when you stop a fellow for a routine questioning, say a wise guy, and he starts talking back to you and telling you that you are no good and that sort of thing. You know you can take a man in on disorderly conduct charge, but you can practically never make it stick. So what you do in a case like this is to egg the guy on until he makes a remark where you can

---

[11] The above analysis of why policemen retaliate when the legitimacy of their authority is challenged differs somewhat from Westley's analysis of why a large percentage of the policemen he studied "believed that it was legitimate to use violence to coerce respect." Westley argues that disrespectful behavior constitutes a threat to the already low "occupational status" of policemen and therefore comes as a blow to their self-esteem. Westley's hypothesis would suggest, however, that those policemen who *accepted* their low occupational status would therefore allow their authority to be challenged. Although Westley's variables no doubt affect the behavior of patrolmen, there also seems to be more at stake than status as a workman when claims to authority are ignored. In a sense the patrolman whose authority has been successfully called into question has already abdicated a sizable chunk of his honor as well as his job. See William A. Westley, "Violence and the Police," *American Journal of Sociology*, Vol. LIX (July 1953).

justifiably slap him, and then if he fights back, you can call it resisting arrest.[12]

And from a gang member's point of view:

Another reason why they beat up on you is because they always have the advantage over you. The cop might say "You done this." And you might say, "I didn't!" And he'll say, "Don't talk back to me or I'll go upside your head!" You know, and then they say they had a right to hit you or arrest you because you were talking back to an officer or resisting arrest, and you were merely trying to explain or tell him that you hadn't done what he said you'd done. One of those kinds of things. Well, that means you in the wrong when you get downtown anyway. You're always in the wrong.

Unlike encounters between gang members and patrolmen, the confrontations between gang members and juvenile officers rarely end in violence. This is because the ability to command respect is not as crucial to a juvenile officer as it is to a patrolman. A juvenile officer is not judged by his capacity to command authority on a beat, and he can therefore leave a situation in which his authority has been challenged without having to face the challenger again the next day. Since he is evaluated largely by his skill at interrogation, he rarely finds himself structurally predisposed to "coerce respect."

[12] *Ibid.*, p. 30.

Clearance Rates

JEROME H. SKOLNICK

For detectives, the most important measure of accomplishment has come to be the "clearance rate."[1] Indeed, Griffin states that the clearance rate is the most important indication of the efficiency of the police force as a whole.[2] The clearance rate is also strongly endorsed as a control measure by the leading authority on police management and professionalization, O. W. Wilson. Wilson does not see detectives as dedicated plyers of their trade, much less as heroes; instead, his basic assumption is that investigators, unless checked on, drift into inactivity. At the same time, he is not unduly concerned by this problem, because the control mechanisms are, in his opinion, clear and effective. He says:

In no branch of police service may the accomplishment of the unit and of its individual members be so accurately evaluated as in the detective division. Rates of clearances by arrest, of property recovered, and of convictions, serve as measures of the level of performance. Current accomplishments in the same class of crime may reveal significant variations between the accomplishment of the incumbent and his predecessor, or between the present and past performance of the same detective. Similar comparisons may be made between local accomplishments and the accomplishments in comparable communities. Chance may cause an unfavorable comparison during a short period, but when the failure in performance extends over six months or a year, a conclusion of diminished effectiveness seems justified.

A detective division built of members retained on this selective basis is most likely to contain the best investigators on the force.[3]

Wilson and Griffin are by no means isolated spokesmen in their high estimation of clearance rates as a measure of police efficiency. The Federal Bureau of Investigation also compiles national statistics of clearance rates, published in an *Annual Bulletin* for the year following

Reprinted from Jerome H. Skolnick, *Justice Without Trial* (New York: John Wiley & Sons, Inc., 1966), pp. 167–181.

[1] Among educators, for instance, there are similar questions of what the goals of the profession are. Some emphasize the development of measurable skills, while others maintain a broader conception of the aims of education. One sociologist of education has suggested that the popularity of such devices as teaching machines may in part be attributed to the facilitation of evaluative and control functions. (See Martin Trow, "American Education and the New Modes of Instruction," mimeographed paper.) Thus, whatever may be said for or against "programmed" teaching and its ultimate effect not only upon knowledge and skill but also upon creativity, it does permit the administrator to rate attainment more easily.

[2] John Griffin, *Statistics Essential for Police Efficiency* (Springfield: Charles C Thomas, 1958), p. 69.

[3] O. W. Wilson, *Police Planning* (Springfield: Charles C Thomas, 1962), p. 112. Chicago Crime Commission recently lauded Wilson's work as head of the Chicago police force by stating that the improvement in police efficiency measured by the percentage of offenses cleared by arrest was "tremendous." (*New York Times*, July 19, 1964).

the date of clearance. These data are collected from 3,441 cities (population, 101,285,000) in the United States. Thus, the clearance rate has evidently been adopted by most police departments in the United States as a primary means to evaluate detectives.

What is the clearance rate? This is a simple question demanding a complicated answer. Briefly stated, it is the percentage of crimes known to the police which the police believe have been "solved." It is important to note that the clearance rate is based upon *offenses known to the police*. Thus, there can be no clearance rate for crimes without citizen complainants. Although there are difficulties in counting such crimes as homicide, robbery, and burglary, they can be counted. It is impossible, however, to count crimes without complainants. As a result, such offenses as bookmaking, the illegal use of narcotics, and prostitution cannot be analyzed by clearance rates.

In the materials that follow, I should like, mainly from observations of burglary enforcement, to illustrate two processes: (1) how the employment of these quantitative criteria—clearance rates—leads to practices that in turn attenuate the validity of the criteria themselves as measures of quality control; and (2) how emphasis on these criteria has consequences for the administration of justice that may interfere with the legality and the stated aims of law enforcement. It should be emphasized that these analytically distinct processes are closely related to each other empirically. What the policeman does in order to amplify clearance rates may have the consequence of both weakening the validity of clearance rates and interfering with legality and

aims of law enforcement. Empirically, however, these processes are not separated.

CATEGORIES OF "CLEARANCE"

. . . [The] designation "cleared" . . . [is] a police organizational term bearing no *direct* relation to the administration of criminal law. That is, no set of statistics describing the processes of criminal law—statistics on arrest and prosecution—gives rise to a similar or even a consistently related set of clearance figures. For example, of the 29 per cent of burglaries "cleared" by the Westville police, less than one-quarter (6 per cent) were "cleared" by arrest and prosecution for that offense, while almost two-fifths (11 per cent) were "cleared" through prosecution for another offense. Furthermore, the percentage for any category will vary from year to year. Thus, the designation "cleared" merely means that the police believe they know who committed the offense, *if* they believe an offense has been committed. It does not indicate, however, *how* the crime was cleared.

Two important categories do not appear in the . . . [official clearance]. One is the category "unfounded"; the other is called "suspicious circumstance." . . . [Of] the 3,719 burglary offenses *reported* to the Westville police, 3,578 were considered *actual* offenses. The "actual offense" figure, which provides the denominator for computing the clearance rate, is derived by subtracting the "unfounded" reports from the reported offenses and adding the "suspicious circumstances—changed to burglary" figure to the difference.[4]

The possibility of "unfounding" (to

---

[4] It is highly difficult to track down the number of instances in which a complaint was first recorded as a suspected crime other than burglary and then changed to burglary. Generally, the Westville police consider the difference between "offenses reported" and "actual offenses" to be "unfounded" reports.

coin an inelegant verb) suggests the first move of the detective—to determine whether in fact an offense has been committed. This procedure requires the detective to assess the motives of the complainant. In investigating a robbery, for instance, there are certain situations which indicate quite clearly to the detective that the complainant is not a victim. For instance, if a man reports that he was robbed at 11 P.M. on 7th and State, and a policeman says he saw him in another part of town at the same hour, the suspicion is that the man did something with his paycheck which he would rather his wife did not know about, and has reported a crime to police to "take off the heat from his old lady."

Seen the other way round, the complainant must be able to justify himself or herself as a victim. The situation here is a familiar one, existing in any context where a claim of victimization is made to a higher authority. To do this, the victim must be able to produce symbols of victimization to the higher authority, symbols appropriate to the victimization context. In a tennis game, for instance, chalk marks on a ball would be appropriate to show that a player's baseline shot had fallen in bounds. Thus, when called out, the player would be "victimized." In other social situations, the rules of the game are not quite so clear—the jilted suitor may consequently have more or less difficulty sustaining an impression of himself as a victim, depending on whose sympathy he is trying to get. In the criminal law context, the rules of the game are less clear than tennis rules, more clear than those between lovers.

An incident may also be recorded as a "suspicious circumstance" in Westville. The more or less official definition of a suspicious circumstance is that a crime appears to have been committed, but that one of its elements is missing. For example, the major element of the crime of burglary is "the burglarious intent, the intent to commit either grand or petit theft or any felony after the entry has been effected. This requisite intent must exist at the time of the entry."[5] There must also be entry into a building (or one of the other places listed in the statute). If some men happened to be shooting craps in the rear of a store, and entered ostensibly for that purpose, there was no burglary. The patrolman, however, may suspect that the real reason for the entry was to steal, not merely to throw dice. If so, his offense report would list a suspected burglary. Or perhaps a householder reports the theft of a watch, but the patrolman cannot find a point of entry. In such an instance, the patrolman will report a "suspicious circumstance," and an investigation will follow. Thus, complaints are typically screened by patrolmen before being presented to the detectives for further investigation.

In addition to deciding whether an offense has been committed, the patrolman must decide what the offense was, if any. The citizen often makes a general noise—which is partly why citizen complaints are referred to in many police departments as "squeals." A woman may call the police and complain that she has been raped, when in fact she has also been robbed. Because the robbery may appear easier to prove than the rape—for example, if corroborating evidence has been found on the person of the defendant—the patrolman reports a robbery and includes the surrounding circumstances.

Even when it is clear that an offense has occurred, the patrolman (usually with the advice of his sergeant, if the offense appears serious) may decide not to

[5] Fricke, *California Criminal Law* (Los Angeles: Legal Book Store, 1956), p. 310.

write up an offense report. The following notes illustrate:

It was a very quiet evening for crime. Only one interesting happening—a call that an assault had been committed. After some time trying to find the house—in one of the courtyards of a city project—Sergeant L. and I arrived on the scene after one of the "beat" patrolmen. (The Sergeant is in charge, by the way, of about nine men who cover six beats, and whenever any one of them has a special problem the Sergeant will likely arrive.) We walked into a poorly furnished house. A large, rather handsome Negro man was seated on a couch daubing at his ear with a towel and being aided by a five- or six-year-old boy.

The man looked dazed and the Sergeant inquired brusquely as to what had happened. (He knew already; before we entered the patrolman told us the man had been cut in the ear by his wife, and also that the man didn't want to file a complaint.)

"She cut me," the man mumbled.

The Sergeant flashed his light on the man's ear. It had been slashed a good half inch through right above the lobe. The beam of the flashlight revealed fingernail marks on the man's neck.

The Sergeant continued to ask the man what had happened. Answers were mumbled and incoherent. In essence, they amounted to: "Nothing really happened, she just came at me with the knife; I was drinking, she came at me with the knife."

There was discussion of whether the man wanted an ambulance. Arrangements were made with a neighboring relative to drive the man to the county hospital.

Before leaving, the Sergeant made sure the man didn't want to file a complaint. We left the house with the Sergeant admonishing him to have the ear taken care of. The patrolman remarked, "As they say, she done stuck."

No offense report is made out for such an incident. It is a family squabble with no complainant. (That the man is colored is also relevant. If the family were white, the police would take the offense more seriously. A stabbing by a white woman of her husband suggests a potential homicide to police, while a similar Negro cutting can be written off as a "North Westville battery."[6] Instead, an *assignment report* recording the incident suffices. Incidents described on assignment reports are not tabulated and are not sent for further investigation to the detective division. An incident may be unfounded only when reported as an offense or as a suspected offense.

In Westville, a large proportion (20 to 25 per cent) of burglary complaints processed by patrolmen are recorded as suspected offenses ("suspicious circumstances") for follow-up investigation by a detective. The detective is allowed wide discretion in the filing of burglary complaints as "suspicious circumstances." Not only does he record a complaint as a suspected offense when one or more of the elements of the alleged crime appears to be missing, but he also may list a complaint as a suspected offense when he believes—even in the absence of hard evidence to support his suspicion—that the complaint is unfounded. For instance, a Negro delivery boy claims to have been robbed of the money he was supposed to deposit for his employer. He shows a lump on his head and holds to his story, but the detective does not believe him. Such a complaint is filed as a suspicious circumstance, and as such does not fall into the category of "offenses reported." When a complaint is filed as a "suspicious circumstance," it is "cleared" for practical purposes. Usually the detective concentrates on "actual" offenses and ignores further investigation of "suspicious circumstances." In effect, therefore, every time a complaint is filed

[6] For a similar illustration, see Wayne R. LaFave, "The Police and Nonenforcement of the Law—Part II," *Wisconsin Law Review* (March, 1926), pp. 207–210.

as a "suspicious circumstance" instead of as a reported offense, the clearance rate rises (since it is based on the ratio of "cleared" to "actual" offenses).[7]

In Eastville, on the other hand, virtually every complaint is recorded as an actual offense. This reporting system was introduced in Eastville as a strong means of control. As form follows function, so may tight controls follow corruption. For example, during the period of my observations in Eastville, a known prostitute reported she had been assaulted and raped. A desk sergeant recorded her complaint as rape, and Eastville's crime rate was thereby heightened. In Westville, a similar complaint would have been recorded as "suspicious circumstance—rape" on the grounds that a person practicing criminality is not a reliable complainant. The complaint would therefore not appear in Westville's crime statistics as an offense known to the police.

Many of the Eastville detectives resent the requirement that every complaint be recorded as an actual offense. They feel that, as several noted to me, "It makes us look bad." I questioned one of the supervisory policemen regarding the practice of recording, and he said:

Well, we're an honest police department. All these other departments that have these fancy clearance rates—we know damned well they're stacking the cards. It's easy to show a low crime rate when you have a category like suspicious circumstance to use as a wastebasket. Here, at least we know what's going on—everything is reported. Sure the prostitute could have been lying, and probably was. But the fact is that a prostitute can be raped, and prostitutes sometimes are. After all, a prostitute has a right not to go to bed with somebody if she doesn't want to.

It is certainly possible that the number of reported offenses in many police departments may be manipulated in order to exaggerate the efficiency of the burglary division. Since approximately 20 per cent of the original reports never find their way into the crime statistics and assignment reports are not included in crime reports (thereby greatly reducing the visibility of police discretion), any small statistical changes—on the order of, say, 2 or 3 per cent per year—should be given little significance in the evaluation of a department's performance. Yet this is the order of magnitude frequently suggested—in staff meetings, conferences, to outsiders—as evidence of a department's competence. Thus, in general, 22 per cent is regarded as a low burglary clearance rate, 35 per cent is seen as a high one (the national average for 1962 was 28 per cent). A burglary clearance rate which has risen from 27 to 31 per cent, for example, is presented as an indicator of significant change.

CLEARANCE RATES AND THE ADMINISTRATION OF JUSTICE

From the above analysis, it is evident that clearance rates are a somewhat suspect method of judging the competence of an individual policeman, a division of a department, or a department as a whole, assuming for the moment that the qualities clearance rates purport to measure are appropriate indicators of police proficiency. If statistical manipulation were the only unanticipated consequence of this control mechanism, the problems created might be relatively inconsequential. To be sure, the clearance rate might not mirror "real" differences in individual ability from one year to the next,

[7] Eight hundred and five suspicious-circumstance burglaries were reported by patrolmen in Westville in 1962. Of these, two hundred and eighty-six remained as such after detective investigation and never found their way into the crime reports. Of the remaining five hundred and seventeen, an unknown number were called actual offenses and became part of the crime report; the remainder were unfounded and never entered the crime report.

as it purports to, nor might it accurately reflect differences in the proficiency of police departments when these are compared. The implications of these errors might appear serious to individual policemen or to individual police departments when invidious conclusions are drawn about their competence. When it can be shown that under certain conditions the attention paid by working detectives to clearance rates may *reverse the hierarchy of penalties* associated with substantive criminal law, the resulting issues are of greater theoretical and practical importance.

To understand the process of reversal, it is useful to ask how the burglary detective goes about obtaining clearances. The simplest answer is that he persuades a burglar to admit having committed several prior offenses. That is, the exchange principle again operates: in order to gain such admissions, the police must provide the burglar with either rewards or penalties to motivate self-incrimination. In the "professional" Westville Police Department, one sees relatively little evidence of the "stick" and much of the "carrot." In what follows, I should like to describe two cases from Westville, one a routine case, the other a "big" case, to illustrate the strategies and rewards used by burglary detectives to obtain clearances, and to analyze how these strategies may undermine legislative and judicial aims regarding law enforcement.

The first case is the routine "good pinch." Arthur C. was arrested as an auto thief and cooperated with the police by confessing to the commission of two additional thefts of autos and five "classy" burglaries. In return for this cooperation, Arthur received several assets. First, the police agreed to drop the two counts of auto theft and to charge Arthur with only one count of burglary. Secondly, Arthur's formal confession as given to the court showed that he had committed only one burglary. As the sergeant handling his case said:

We had him cop out to only one charge because we don't really want it made public that he committed the other burglaries. If it were made public, then the question might be raised as to why we didn't charge him with the other burglaries, and the public doesn't understand these things.

What the sergeant intended to indicate is that the public typically does not understand that the sentence would not be different if the defendant had confessed to one burglary or to five—and the severity of the sentence is the most important consideration to all of the active participants in the system, the judge and the attorneys as well as the defendant and the police. None is especially impressed by the "rehabilitative" capacities of the penal system. Thus, the sergeant added, when asked by the writer if the court did not realize that perhaps other offenses had been committed:

Of course the courts know. In fact we tell the judge the defendant committed other burglaries, but we don't want it put on the record. So we take the confession in such a way as to implicate the guy with only one burglary, and then that's what he gets sentenced for.

Of course, from the parole board's point of view, it might be of some significance that the defendant had actually committed five burglaries instead of one. Since an extensive burglary record could conceivably reduce the convicted defendant's chances for parole, a confession showing him to have committed only one burglary is to his advantage.

In addition to possibly receiving a reduction of charges and counts, and a recorded minimization of his appearance of criminality, the defendant who "cops out" and clears burglaries is also said to "clean" himself. The term "cleaning" in this context means that the defendant is afforded virtual immunity for future arrests on past burglaries. Thus, if the police have cleared ten burglaries with the defendant's help, he is no longer liable to be arrested for having committed them (even though the statute of limitations might permit prosecution). As a result, when the defendant completes his sentence, he need not fear apprehension for any of the crimes he committed before.

These, then, are the three basic "commodities" which the detective exchanges in return for the defendant's cooperation in admitting to prior offenses: reduction of charges and counts, concealment of actual criminality, and freedom from further investigation of prior offenses. Since it is in the interest of both the defendant and the policeman that the defendant "clear" crimes, the defendant typically cooperates with the policeman once a deal has been set in motion. Indeed, the defendant may occasionally become "too" cooperative by confessing to crimes he never committed, since liability does not increase as a result of admissions made for the purpose of clearing crimes.

It is impossible to know how often defendants claim to have committed the crimes of others. When such claims occur, however, they necessarily undermine the aims of law enforcement by presenting the police with "false positives"—"solved cases" for which synthetic solutions are reached. On the other hand, the policeman's ability to determine the truth of defendant's assertions might minimize error of this sort. Nevertheless, the pressures in the situation are clearly in the direction of overlooking or not inquiring too carefully into the defendant's representations.

CRIMINALITY AS COMMODITY FOR EXCHANGE

There is a more serious problem about clearance rates as a control mechanism. If clearances are valued, then criminality becomes a commodity for exchange. Thus, it is possible that in some cases

defendants who confess to large numbers of crimes will tend to be shown more leniency in prosecution than those who are in fact less culpable. This is not to suggest that an inverse correlation actually exists between the number of offenses which a person admits having committed and the severity of the penalty which he receives. (To test the truth of any such generalization would be difficult since it would be necessary to have an accurate accounting of the crimes for which defendants actually were responsible. Because the maintenance of such records would in itself threaten to upset the operation of the system for maximizing clearance rates, an observer would need at least to see the processing of the cases themselves.) Rather, the situation in which detectives are expected to demonstrate proficiency is structured so as to invite the policeman to undermine the hierarchy of penalties found in substantive criminal law. The following case is presented to illustrate more fully the process of undermining. This case, a "big one," is not statistically "representative," but does, I believe, fairly represent pressures inherent in the situation. It was not especially selected, but simply occurred during the period of observation.

Essentially, the undermining process in the "big" case is more conspicuous because the police "get" more and have to "give" more in exchange. The process by which the police obtain clearance in a "big" case is therefore merely an exaggerated instance of the process in the routine case. In this case (the Moore case), approximately thirty-five thousand dollars worth of jewels, furs, and other valuable objects had been stolen from a leading citizen. Partly as a result of the citizen's status, and partly because of the value of the stolen goods, the police looked upon the case as an unusually important one to "break." "Breaking it" would and did lead to praise from the general community, including the press and television. I was able to work on the case with the sergeant to whom it had been assigned, and followed him on the laborious and time-consuming round of checking out false leads, questioning neighbors and witnesses, and interviewing informants and potential informants. The description of the development of such a case would make interesting popular nonfiction. I intend to describe only that part of it relating to the analytical point of how emphasis on clearance rates as a measure of the competence of detectives can interfere with stated aims of law enforcement by creating an informal hierarchy of penalties. That part of the case follows:

After considerable investigation, two of the four suspects were "picked up on a roust," that is, they were arrested on minor charges in order to give the police an opportunity to interrogate them. After they had been placed in custody in Jonesville, an all-points bulletin was sent out which came to the attention of the Westville detectives assigned to the Moore case. The Westville detectives were given permission to interrogate the suspects by the Jonesville Police Department and especially, as a matter of courtesy, through the Jonesville detective who arranged the "roust."

In the meantime, the Westville detectives had independently gathered information which, added to the considerable information held by the Jonesville detective, pointed to the culpability of these suspects in the Moore case. The information regarding the recent activities of one of the suspects, who will be called Jerome, was especially comprehensive. As the sergeant put it in describing the interrogation to me:

We know enough to make him feel that we got him by the balls. We have enough information so that we can almost tell him

where he took a piss twenty-four hours a day for the last few days. Actually, we don't know what is what so far as real evidence is concerned, but we know so much about his general activities, that he thinks we know a lot more than we actually do.[8]

After six hours he finally says he wants to make a deal. It turns out that he's got a charge hanging over him in another state and says he'll make a deal if we don't send him back. Then he copped out and told us how he did the Moore job and who he did it with.

He agreed to work for us and so we turned him loose and told him we wanted the fence. The first thing he did was to set up Rich [another member of the burglary team; the third was James and there was also a fence]. Then James, who's in jail in Smithville, calls us up and says he wants to help us out, and with his help and Jerome's help we got the fence all wired up tight. [There was an additional reason for "helping" here. Jerome and James both mistrusted—indeed hated—the fence, since in their opinion he had cheated them by pretending to have gotten less for the stolen articles than he actually had.]

Over a period of about ten days after the arrest, burglary police from neighboring cities frequently visited the Westville jail, since, between the two of them, Jerome and James could account for more than five hundred burglaries. James himself provided the police with more than four hundred clearances. I witnessed several interrogations of James regarding burglaries he had presumably committed and, in my opinion, it was relatively simple for him to "fake" clearances. One need not have been exceptionally shrewd—and James was—to sense the detectives' pleasure at writing off old cases. This is not to say that the detectives who interviewed him were easily deceived. But from the detail with which he recalled burglaries he had com-

[8] This is a typical ploy detectives use during interrogation. By indicating to the suspect that they know more than they actually do, they frequently are able to bluff the suspect into believing that they have "hard" evidence.

mitted in the past year, the policeman could tell that James had committed numerous burglaries. When he expressed vagueness of memory as to those two or three years old, he thereby created a situation in which the police would have either to be extremely scrupulous, and thus forego potential clearances, or "feed" him information to refresh his recollection (which, to this observer, appeared to be rather easily renewed).

Rich and the fence each received substantial prison sentences. Jerome and James were charged as misdemeanants. Jerome spent four months in custody, while James was permitted to finish out sentence on another charge, for which he was already serving time, and was released after thirty days. In part, Jerome and James were given a liberal reduction in charges because they had served as informants and also because they had agreed to appear as State's witnesses. These services were an important aspect of their "cooperation" with law enforcement.

At the same time, however, the two burglars had also given the police numerous clearances. While it would be virtually impossible to separate out the effect of their "cooperation" as informants and State's witnesses as against their "cooperation" in giving clearances, it would be unrealistic to discount the importance of their providing "clearances" in accounting for their lenient treatment. James, who had certainly committed numerous burglaries and had admitted having participated in more than four hundred, received what he regarded as no sentence at all. Jerome, James, the sergeant, and I spent almost five hours reconstructing the events of the case, the backgrounds of Jerome and James, and the morality of the outcome. All agreed

that "it wasn't right" that the penalties should have been distributed as they were, although the defendants felt that rough justice had been served since they claimed to have been mistreated by law enforcement authorities in the past. The sergeant, also a shrewd observer, sensed that there was something decidedly wrong with the process. From his point of view, which was largely shared by other detectives interviewed, the society would be better served

. . . if we didn't have this clearance business hanging over our heads. We get guys like this and they hand us clearance after clearance and on FBI books we look terrific. But the fact is that large numbers of burglaries are committed by a relatively small group and when we get one of them we have to give him a good break in order to make ourselves look good. It's a ridiculous system, but that's the way they run things upstairs.

The reader may raise the question as to how the police arranged these low charges with the district attorneys of several jurisdictions. It was not always easy. In one jurisdiction, the district attorney insisted upon heavy prosecution despite the fact that a promise of leniency had already been made to one of the suspects. Eventually, the police view prevailed, on the grounds that unless the district attorney agreed to "back up" the discretionary actions of the police, they would, in future burglary investigations, be seriously impaired. It is unlikely that police discretion can, as one writer has suggested,[9] be exercised without the cooperation of the district attorney. Since the district attorney depends largely upon the policeman for evidence, the policeman has a good deal of influence over the district attorney's exercise of

---

[9] Joseph Goldstein, "Police Discretion Not to Invoke the Criminal Process; Low-Visibility Decisions in the Administration of Justice," *Yale Law Journal,* **69** (March, 1960), especially pp. 568–569.

discretionary authority. It is not that the policeman interferes with the work of the district attorney when his work is in the traditional legal domain; rather, the policeman, by gaining the cooperation of the district attorney, usurps the prerogatives of the prosecutor to control the policeman's activities.

SUMMARY AND CONCLUSIONS

This . . . [section] has described and analyzed the processes by which clearance rates are constructed, as part of the broader issue of how the ambiguous institutional character of police influences the actual administration of criminal law. Thus, the . . . [section] concentrated on the issue of how clearance rates—so important to internal control processes —may affect the penalty structure associated with substantive criminal law.

The behavior of the detectives involved should not be seen as an instance of corruption or even of inefficiency. On the contrary, their actions are to be interpreted as an unanticipated consequence of their superiors' development of a method for controlling their efficiency. The response of the detective to the clearance rate is easily understandable. It stems from a sociological tendency manifesting itself in all work organizations: the worker always tries to perform *according to his most concrete and specific understanding of the control system.* That is, in general, workers try to please those supervising *routine* activities. Thus, in prisons (or at least in the one studied by Sykes), the guard is judged according to how successfully he maintains a smoothly running cell block. Prison authorities overlook infractions in minor rules and judge the guard's competence by the composure of his cell block. As a consequence, guards permit minor rules to be broken in order to comply with their immediate superiors' over-all aim of keeping the prison under physical control.[10] (How such arrangements react upon the still more general aims of incarceration, such as building up respect for law, is a question beyond the scope of the present study, but surely significant for sanctioning policy.)

Actually, police practices about clearance rates are more strictly comparable to the practices of foremen and production line workers rather than to those of prison guards and inmates. There are numerous examples and allusions in sociological literature of "positive deviance" on the production line—of reshaping, reinterpreting, or ignoring formal rules in order to make the best possible appearance in terms of the most current and pressing demands.[11] A most dramatic recent one is contained in Bensman and Gerver's[12] description of the use of the "tap" in a wartime airplane plant. The tap is a hard steel screw used to bring nuts and bolts into a new but not true alignment on airplane wings, and its use is described as being both "the most serious crime of workmanship conceivable" and "imperative to the functioning of the production organization." The pressure, for these workers, is to show high production rate. The *ultimate* goal may be ignored under the more immediate pressures to produce. When means are found to raise production, rules are circumvented—not with

---

[10] Gresham M. Sykes, "The Corruption of Authority and Rehabilitation," *Social Forces,* 34 (March, 1956), 257–267.

[11] Probably the best-known illustration is found in George C. Homans' *The Human Group* (New York: Harcourt, Brace and Company, 1950), pp. 48–80.

[12] Joseph Bensman and Israel Gerver, "Crime and Punishment in the Factory: The Function of Deviancy in Maintaining the Social System," *American Sociological Review,* 28 (1963), 588–598.

impunity, however, but only under the strain of production quotas.

Similarly, the detective is inclined to engage in those activities improving *his* appearance as a competent worker. One cannot say that the detective is unconcerned about his work, but rather that he typically engages in practices—such as, for instance, "saving" clearances from month to month—that put the best possible light on his competence and dependability when his record is examined by superiors. Thus, the perceived necessity of measures of departmental efficiency results in the development of techniques by detectives to enlarge the magnitude of the criteria for measuring their performance. One of these techniques is to exchange the prerogative of charging crime for "clearances," with the result that in major cases criminality may inadvertently be rewarded. Thus, the statistical control system, intended to prevent detectives from drifting into inactivity, may tend to reverse the hierarchy of criminal penalties established by the legislature.[13]

These consequences do not, however, stem from the personal deficiencies either of working policemen or those men who might be termed police "efficiency experts"—men like O. W. Wilson or the personally dedicated and honest head of the Westville Police Department, who are attempting to develop methods for running a "modern and efficient" police department. Instead, the problem stems from the well-motivated attempts of such experts to develop measurable standards of efficiency. Unfortunately, meeting these standards tends to become an end in itself, a transformation found in many organizations. In this process, Blau and Scott interpret the organization's relation to its environment as a crucial factor. They write, "As long as its very survival is threatened by a hostile environment, its officers will seek to strengthen the organization by building up its administrative machinery and searching for external sources of support."[14] As an organization, the police provide a clear example of this development. Requiring a "set of books" to demonstrate a competence of performance, the "clearance rate" has been developed as a measure of the effectiveness of the police department, especially the detective branch. This concern with efficiency, however, may also have the unanticipated consequence of developing detective initiative to the point of reversing the hierarchy of penalties associated with the substantive criminal law. Thus, the standard of efficiency employed in police departments may not only undermine due process of law, but also the basic standard of justice—that those equally culpable shall be given equal punishment.[15]

[13] On the problems created by statistical records in a similar setting, see Peter M. Blau, *The Dynamics of Bureaucracy* (Chicago: University of Chicago Press, 1955), pp. 36–67.

[14] Peter M. Blau and W. Richard Scott, *Formal Organizations: A Comparative Approach* (San Francisco: Chandler Publishing Company, 1962), p. 231.

[15] It is worth noting that the findings of this chapter also strongly support the idea that rates of deviant behavior are as dependent on the actions of officials, as on the conduct of so-called deviants. For a brief and cogent development of this position see John I. Kitsuse and Aaron V. Cicourel, "A Note on the Uses of Official Statistics," *Social Problems,* 11 (Fall, 1963), 131–139.

Police Work in Two Cities

JAMES Q. WILSON

The two police departments compared here are those of what we shall call Eastern City and Western City. Both cities have substantially more than 300,000 inhabitants, they are heterogeneous in population and in economic base, both are free of domination by a political machine; and both have a substantial nonwhite population. Western City general has a mild climate, which probably contributes to rates of crimes against property that are somewhat higher than the rates of Eastern City, where severe winters assist the police in keeping thieves off the streets.

THE MEANING OF PROFESSIONALISM

The most important difference between the police of the two cities is that in Western City the police department is highly "professionalized." This does not mean that in Eastern City the police department is wholly corrupt and incompetent; far from it. But as any observer familiar with Eastern City will readily acknowledge, its police officers have been recruited, organized, and led in a way that falls considerably short of the standards set forth in the principal texts. Whether the standards of the texts are right is, of course, another matter. Since the meaning (to say nothing of the value) of professionalism is itself problematical, an effort will be made here to arrive at a general analytical definition and to specify the particular attributes of the police that professionalism implies and how the two police forces differ in these attributes.

A "professional" police department is one governed by values derived from general impersonal rules which bind all members of the organization and whose relevance is independent of circumstances of time, place or personality.[1] A nonprofessional department (what will be called a "fraternal" department), on the other hand, relies to a greater extent on particularistic judgments that is, judgments based on the significance to a particular person of his particular relations to particular others. The professional department looks outward to universal, externally valid, enduring standards; the nonprofessional department looks, so to speak, inward at the informal standards of a special group and distributes rewards and penalties according to how well a member conforms to them. The specific attributes that are consistent with these definitions include the following ones.

A professional, to a greater extent than a fraternal, department recruits members on the basis of achievement rather than ascriptive criteria. It relies more on standardized

Reprinted from James Q. Wilson, "The Police and the Delinquent in Two Cities," *Controlling Delinquents,* Stanton Wheeler, ed. (New York: John Wiley & Sons, Inc., 1968), pp. 9–30, by permission of John Wiley & Sons, Inc.

[1] The following definitions are taken from, and treated in greater detail by James Q. Wilson, "The Police and Their Problems: A Theory," *Public Policy*, XII (1962), 189–216.

formal entrance examinations, open equally to all eligible persons. Thus the professional department recruits not only impartially as to political connections, race or religion; it recruits without regard to local residence. Nonprofessional departments often insist (or laws require them to insist) on recruitment only from among local citizens. Educational standards are typically higher for entrants to professional departments.

Professional departments treat equals equally; that is, laws are enforced without respect to person. In such departments "fixing" traffic tickets is difficult or impossible and the sons of the powerful cannot expect preferential treatment. Fraternal departments have a less formal sense of justice, either because the system of which they are a part encourages favoritism or because (and this is equally important) officers believe it is proper to take into account personal circumstances in dispensing justice. Concretely, we may expect to find less difference in the professional department between the proportion of white and nonwhite juvenile offenders who are arrested, as opposed to being let off with warnings or reprimands.

Professional departments are less open to graft and corruption and their cities will be more free of "tolerated" illegal enterprises (gambling, prostitution) than will cities with nonprofessional departments.

Professional departments seek, by formal training and indoctrination, to produce a force whose members are individually committed to generally applicable standards. Their training will acquaint them with the writing and teaching of "experts" (that is, of carriers of generalized, professional norms). In fraternal departments there is less formal training and what there is of it is undertaken by departmental officers who inculcate particularistic values and suggest "how to get along" on the force.

Within the professional department, authority attaches to the role and not to the incumbent to a greater extent than in nonprofessional departments. The essentially bureaucratic distribution of authority within the professional force is necessary because, due to the reliance of achievement, young officers are often promoted rapidly to positions of considerable authority (as sergeants and lieutenants in both line and staff bureaus).[2]

By these tests Western City has a highly professionalized force and Eastern City has not. An observer's first impressions of the two departments suggest the underlying differences. The Western City force has modern, immaculate, and expensive facilities, new buildings, and shiny cars; the officers are smartly dressed in clean, well-pressed uniforms; the routine business of the department is efficiently carried out. In Eastern City, the buildings are old and in poor repair; cars are fewer, many are old and worn, the officers are sometimes unkempt; routine affairs, particularly the keeping of records, are haphazardly conducted by harried or indifferent personnel.

In Western City, three-fourths of the officers were born outside the city and one-half outside the state (this is about the same as the proportion of all males in the city who were born outside the state). In Eastern City, the vast majority of officers were born and raised within the city they now serve, many in or near neighborhoods in which they now live. In Western City, over one-third of all officers had one year or more of college education, over one-fifth have two years or more; and one-tenth a college degree or better. In Eastern City, the proportion of officers educated beyond high school is far smaller.[3]

[2] There is a general tendency for authority to adhere more to the person than to the office in a police force as compared to other kinds of public agencies. See Robert L. Peabody, "Perceptions of Organizational Authority: A Comparative Analysis," *Administrative Science Quarterly,* VI (March 1962), 477–480.

[3] These differences are characteristic of entire regions and not simply of the two departments here studied. In one study it was found that almost 90 percent of the officers in police departments in the Pacific states, but only about two-thirds of those in New England

In Western City, there was little evidence of gambling or prostitution; Eastern City, while far from "wide open," has not made it difficult for a visitor to find a bookie or a girl. For several years at least, Western City has had a department free from the suspicion of political influence and a court system noted for its "no-fix" policy. In Eastern City, *reports* of influence and fixes are not infrequent (of course, a scholar without the power of subpoena cannot confirm such charges).

The chief of the Western City police department has been a high official of the International Association of Chiefs of Police (IACP); Eastern City's force, by contrast, has been the subject of a special comprehensive report by the IACP, contracted for by the local officials and containing recommendations for extensive reorganization and improvement. In sum, whether judged by subjective impression or objective measure, the police forces of the two cities are significantly different. The crucial question is the consequences of the differences upon the handling of juvenile offenders. . . .

HANDLING THE DELINQUENT

The two police departments are systematically different both in their treatment of delinquents and in the way the members think and talk about delinquents; paradoxically, the differences in behavior do not correspond to the verbal differences. Interviews with approximately half the officers (selected at random) assigned to the juvenile bureaus of the police departments of Eastern and Western Cities reveal that Western City's officers have more complex attitudes toward delinquency and juveniles than their colleagues of Eastern City. The former's attitudes, at least superficially, tend to be less moralistic, less certain as to causal factors, more therapeutic, and more frequently couched in generalizations than in anecdotes. Eastern City's officers, by contrast, are more likely to interpret a problem as one of personal and familial morality rather than of social pathology, to urge restrictive and punitive rather than therapeutic measures, to rely on single explanations expressed with great conviction and certainty, and to confine discussions of juveniles almost exclusively to anecdotes and references to recent episodes than to generalizations, trends, or patterns.[4]

The behavior of the officers with respect to juveniles tends to be the opposite of what we might expect from their expressed sentiments. In Western City, the discretionary powers of the police are much more likely than in Eastern City to be used to restrict the freedom of the juvenile: Western City's officers process a larger proportion of the city's juvenile population as suspected offenders and, of those they process, arrest a larger proportion. . . .

Thus, a juvenile in Western City is far less likely than one in Eastern City to be let off by the police with a reprimand. . . . Police officers, social workers, and

---

and North Atlantic states, had a high school education. Similarly, 55 percent of those from the Pacific states, but only about 18 percent of those from New England and North Atlantic states, had attended college. See George W. O'Connor and Nelson A. Watson, *Juvenile Delinquency and Youth Crime: The Police Role* (Washington, D.C.: International Association of Chiefs of Police, 1964), pp. 78–79.

[4] Compare these dichotomous attitudes with those classified in Walter B. Miller, "Inter-Institutional Conflict as a Major Impediment to Delinquency Prevention," *Human Organization,* XVII, no. 3 (Fall 1958), 20–23; and Harold L. Wilensky and Charles N. Lebeaux, *Industrial Society and Social Welfare* (New York: Russell Sage Foundation, 1958), pp. 219–228.

students of delinquency in Eastern City agree that the police there are well-known for what is called by many the "pass system." Unless the youth commits what the police consider a "vicious" crime—brutally assaulting an elderly person, for example, or engaging in wanton violence—he is almost certain to be released with a reprimand or warning on his first contact with the police and quite likely to be released on the second, third, and sometimes even on the fourth contact. . . .

In Eastern City, there are, of course, officers who have the reputation for being "tough." The "toughness" may be manifested, however, not so much in more frequent court appearances of youths, but in the greater ease of getting information. "Tough" and "soft" officers work as teams, the latter persuading juveniles to talk in order to save them from the former. In any case, the net effect of police discretion in Eastern City is unambiguous; only 17.5 percent of the first offenders included in a 1/25 random sample of all juveniles processed over a four-year period by the police department were referred to court. Indeed, Eastern City's officers occasionally mentioned that it was their understanding that officers "in the West" made arrests more frequently than they: Western City's officers sometimes observed that they had been told that officers "in the East" made arrests less frequently than they.

Observation of the operation of the two departments provided considerable evidence of the effect of the preceding on the day-to-day practice of police work. While cruising the city in patrol cars, Western City's officers would frequently stop to investigate youths "hanging" on street corners; the officers would check the youths' identification, question them closely, and often ask over the radio if they were persons for any reason wanted at headquarters. In Eastern City, officers would generally ignore young persons

hanging around corners except to stop the car, lean out, and gruffly order them to "move along." "Sweeping" or "brooming" the corners was done with no real hope on the part of the police that it would accomplish much ("they'll just go around the block and come right back here in ten minutes") but they would ask, "what else can you do?"

Technically, of course, an officer in either city who takes a person into custody on the street is required by law to bring him to police headquarters or to a station house and to initiate a formal procedure whereby an arrest is effected, charges stated, certain rights guaranteed, and, if necessary, physical detention effected. In fact, and particularly with respect to juveniles, police officers sometimes take persons directly to their homes. In Eastern City this procedure is . . . much more common than in Western City.

THE CORRELATES OF DISCRETION

If, at least in this one case, a "professionalized" police department tends to expose a higher proportion of juveniles to the possibility of court action, despite the more "therapeutic" and sophisticated verbal formulas of its officers it is important to ask why this occurs. . . .

Certain structural and procedural dissimilarities undoubtedly account for some of the differences in arrests. In Eastern City the juvenile officer on the police force is also the prosecuting officer: he personally prepares and presents the case in court against the juvenile. In Western City, the juvenile officer (who, as in Eastern City, takes charge of the juvenile after a patrolman or detective has "brought him in") prepares an initial report but sends the report and, if detention seems warranted, the child himself, to an independent probation department which determines whether the suspect should be taken before the judge.

In effect, Western City officers can "pass the buck," and even if the case goes to court, the officer himself only rarely is required to appear in court. In Eastern City, the police are involved right up to the moment when the judge actually makes a disposition, a police appearance being always required if there is to be a court hearing. Moreover, the probation department is not independent, but is an arm of the court which acts only *after* a court appearance. As a result of these arrangements, Eastern City's officers may have an incentive not to send the child to court because it requires more work; to Western City's officers, on the other hand, initiating a court appearance is relatively costless. . . .

For more important, . . . [however,] are the organizational, arrangements, community attachments, and institutionalized norms which govern the daily life of the police officer himself, all of which might be referred to collectively as the "ethos" of the police force. It is this ethos which, in my judgment, decisively influences the police in the two places. In Western City, this is the ethos of a *professional* force; in Eastern City, the ethos of a *fraternal* force.

Western City's police officer works in an organizational setting which is highly centralized. Elaborate records are kept on all aspects of police work: each officer must, on a log, account for every minute of his time on duty; all contacts with citizens must be recorded in one form or another; and automatic data-processing equipment frequently issues detailed reports on police and criminal activity. The department operates out of a single headquarters; all juvenile offenders are processed in the office of the headquarters' juvenile bureau in the presence of a sergeant, a lieutenant, and, during the day shift, a captain. Dossiers on previously processed juveniles are kept and consulted at headquarters. Arresting officers bring all juveniles to headquarters for processing and their disposition is determined by officers of the juvenile bureau at that time.

In Eastern City, the force is highly decentralized. Officers are assigned to and, sometimes for their whole career, work in precinct station houses. Juvenile suspects are brought to the local station house and turned over to the officer of the juvenile bureau assigned there. These assignments are relatively constant: a patrolman who becomes a juvenile officer remains in the same station house. The juvenile officer is not supervised closely or, in many cases, not supervised at all; he works in his own office and makes his own dispositions. Whatever records the juvenile officer chooses to keep—and most keep some sort of record—is largely up to him. Once a week he is required to notify the headquarters of the juvenile bureau of his activities and to provide the bureau with the names and offenses of any juveniles he has processed. Otherwise, he is on his own.[5]

The centralized versus the decentralized mode of operations is in part dictated by differences in size of city— Eastern City has a larger population than Western City—but also in great part by a deliberate organizational strategy.

[5] The juvenile bureau of the Eastern City police department was only created after community concern over what appeared to be a serious incident involving a juvenile "gang" compelled it. The police commissioner at the time was reported to oppose the existence of such a bureau on the revealing grounds that "each beat officer should be his own juvenile officer." The fraternal force apparently resisted even the nominal degree of specialization and centralization represented by the creation of this bureau. This, again, is also a regional phenomenon. Over 80 percent of the police departments in Pacific states, but less than 58 percent of those in New England states have specialized juvenile units. O'Connor and Watson, *op. cit.*, p. 84.

Western City at one time had precincts, but they were abolished by a new, "reform" police chief as a way of centralizing control over the department in his hands. There had been some scandals before his appointment involving allegations of police brutality and corruption which he was determined would not occur again. Abolishing the precincts, centralizing the force, increasing the number and specificity of the rules and reporting procedures, and tightening supervision were all measures to achieve this objective. These actions all had consequences, many of them perhaps unintended, upon the behavior of the department. Officers felt the pressure: they were being watched, checked, supervised, and reported on. The force was becoming to a considerable extent "bureaucratized"—behavior more and more was to involve the nondiscretionary application of general rules to particular cases.[6] Some officers felt that their "productivity" was being measured—number of arrests made, citations written, field contact reports filed, and suspicious persons checked. Under these circumstances, it would be surprising if they did not feel they ought to act in such a way as to minimize any risk to themselves that might arise, not simply from being brutal or taking graft, but from failing to "make pinches" and "keep down the crime rate." In short, organizational measures intended to insure that police behave properly with respect to nondiscretionary matters (such as taking bribes) may also have the effect (perhaps unintended) of making them behave differently with respect to matters over which they *do* have discretion. More precisely, these measures tend to induce officers to convert discretionary to nondiscretionary matters—for example, to treat juveniles according to rule and without regard to person.

In Eastern City the nonprofessional, fraternal ethos of the force leads officers to treat juveniles primarily on the basis of personal judgment and only secondarily by applying formal rules. Although the department has had its full share of charges of corruption and brutality, at the time of this research there had been relatively few fundamental reforms. The local precinct captain is a man of great power; however, he rarely chooses to closely supervise the handling of juvenile offenders. His rules, though binding, are few in number and rarely systematic or extensive.

In Western City, the juvenile officers work as a unit; they meet together every morning for a line-up, briefing, and short training session; they work out of a common headquarters; they have their own patrol cars; and they work together in pairs. In Eastern City most, though not all, precincts have a single juvenile officer. He works in the station house in association with patrolmen and detectives; he has no car of his own, but must ride with other officers or borrow one of their cars; he rarely meets with other juvenile officers and there is practically no training for his job or systematic briefing while on it. In Western City, the juvenile officer's ties of association on and off the job are such that his fellow juvenile officers are his audience. He is judged by, and judges himself by, their standards and their opinions. In Eastern City, the relevant audience is much more likely to be patrolmen and detectives. In Western City, the primary relations of the juvenile officer are with "professional" colleagues; in Eastern City, the relations are with fraternal associates.

Eastern City's juvenile officer feels, and expresses to an interviewer, the conflicting and ambivalent standards arising out of his association with officers who do not handle juveniles. On

---

[6] Compare the causes and consequences of bureaucratization in an industrial setting in Alvin W. Gouldner, *Patterns of Industrial Bureaucracy* (Glencoe, Ill.: Free Press, 1954).

the one hand, almost every juvenile officer in Eastern City complained that patrolmen and detectives did not "understand" his work, that they regarded him as a man who "chased kids," that they "kissed off" juvenile cases onto him and did not take them seriously, and that they did not think arresting a "kid" constituted a "good pinch." These attitudes might, in part, be explained by the patrolmen's reluctance to bring a juvenile into the station, even if they could then turn him over to the juvenile officer on duty; bringing the boy in meant bringing him in in front of their fellow patrolmen in the squad room of the station house. . . .

Instead, the patrolmen or detectives often simply refer the juvenile's name to the juvenile officer and let the officer go out and handle the case from investigation to arrest. This not only places a larger work load on the juvenile officer, it places it on him under conditions that do not reward effective performance. He is given the "kid stuff" because patrolmen do not feel rewarded for handling it; at the same time, the patrolman lets it be known that he does not feel the juvenile officer ought to get much credit, either. . . . This being the case, the juvenile officer in Eastern City seems to allow his behavior to be influenced by associates, insofar as it is influenced by them at all, in the direction of permissive treatment.

Western City's juvenile officers, by contrast, are more insulated from or less dependent on the opinion of patrolmen and detectives. And the latter, when taking a juvenile into custody, can bring him to a central juvenile bureau staffed only by juvenile officers, rather than to a precinct station filled with fellow patrolmen and detectives. Neither juvenile officers nor arresting patrolmen are, in Western City, as directly exposed to or dependent upon the opinions of associates concerning whether a juvenile arrest is justified.

Even if Western City's officers should be so exposed, however, it is likely that they would still be more punitive than their counterparts in Eastern City. In Western City, the officer, both in and out of the juvenile bureau, is recruited and organized in a way that provides little possibility of developing a strong identification with either delinquents in general or with delinquents in some particular neighborhood. He is likely to have been raised outside the city and even outside the state; in many cases he was recruited by the representatives of the force who canvass the schools of police administration attached to western and midwestern universities. In only *one* case in Western City did I interview a juvenile officer who, when asked about his own youth, spoke of growing up in a "tough" neighborhood where juvenile gangs, juvenile misbehavior, and brushes with the police were common. There were, on the other hand, only one or two of Eastern City's officers who had *not* come from such backgrounds: they were almost all products not only of local neighborhoods but of neighborhoods where scrapes with the law were a common occurrence.

The *majority* of Eastern City's officers were not only "locals," but locals from lower or lower-middle-class backgrounds. Several times officers spoke of themselves and their friends in terms that suggested that the transition between being a street-corner rowdy and a police officer was not very abrupt. The old street-corner friends that they used to "hang" with followed different paths as adults but, to the officers, the paths were less a matter of choice than of accidents, fates which were legally but not otherwise distinct. The officers spoke proudly of the fights they used to have, of youthful wars between the Irish and the Italians, and of the old gangs, half of whose alumni went to the state prison and the other half to the police and fire departments. Each section of the city has great meaning to these officers; they are nostalgic about some where the old life continues, bitter about others where new elements—particularly Negroes—have "taken over."

The *majority* of Western City's officers who were interviewed almost without exception, described their own youth as free of violence, troubles with the police, broken homes, or gang behavior. The city in which they now serve has a particular meaning for only a very few. Many live outside it in the suburbs, and know the city's neighborhoods almost solely from their police work. Since there are no precinct stations but only radio car routes, and since these are frequently changed, there is little opportunity to build up an intimate familiarity, much less an identification, with any neighborhood. The Western City police are, in a real sense, an army of occupation organized along paramilitary lines.

It would be a mistake to exaggerate these differences or to be carried away by neighborhood romanticism that attaches an undeservedly high significance to the folklore about the "neighborhood cop" walking his rounds—king of the beat, firm arbiter of petty grievances, and gruff but kind confidant of his subjects. The "old-time beat cop," as almost all the Eastern City's officers are quick and sad to admit, is gone forever. But even short of romanticism, the differences remain and are important. Except for the downtown business district and the skid row area, there are no foot patrolmen in Western City; in Eastern City, in all the residential areas with high crime rates, officers walk their beats. Furthermore, the station houses in Eastern City receive a constant stream of local residents who bring their grievances and demands to the police; in Western City the imposing new police headquarters building is downtown and has no "front desk" where business obviously can be transacted. Although visitors are encouraged, upon entering the ground floor one is confronted by a bank of automatic elevators. Finally, officers on duty in Eastern City eat in diners and cafes in or close to their routes; in Western City officers often drive several miles to a restaurant noted for its reasonably priced food rather than for its identification with the neighborhood.

These differences in style between the two police departments can perhaps be summarized by saying that in Western City the officer has a generalized knowledge of juveniles and of delinquency and that, although he, of course, becomes familiar with some children and areas, that generalized knowledge—whether learned in college, from departmental doctrine, from the statute books, or from the popular literature on juvenile behavior—provides the premises of his decisions. He begins with general knowledge and he is subjected to fewer particularizing influences than his counterpart in Eastern City. In Eastern City, the officer's knowledge or what he takes to be his knowledge about delinquency, crime, and neighborhood affairs is, from the first, specific, particular, indeed, *personal,* and the department is organized and run in a way that maintains a particularist orientation toward relations between officer and officer and between police and citizens.[7]

[7] The findings of O'Connor and Watson are consistent with this argument. They discovered that officers in Pacific police departments tended to have "tougher" attitudes toward the *means* to be employed in handling juvenile offenders than officers in New England or North Atlantic departments. The former were more likely to favor transporting juveniles in marked rather than unmarked police cars, to favor having a curfew, to oppose having the police get involved in community affairs concerning youth matters, to oppose destroying the police records of juveniles after they become adults, and to oppose having the police try to find jobs for juveniles who come to their attention. (*Op. cit.,* pp. 91–97, 115–127.)

This Eastern City ethos exists side by side with the general moral absolutism of police attitudes toward delinquency *in general.* When asked about the cause, extent, or significance of delinquency *generally,* the officers usually respond, as has been indicated, with broad, flat, moral indictments of the modern American family, overly-indulged youth, weakened social bonds, corrupting mass media of communication, and pervasive irreligion and socialism. When the same officers are asked about delinquency in *their precinct,* they speak anecdotally of particular juveniles engaging in particular acts in particular circumstances, in dealing with whom they apply, not their expressed general moral absolutes, but their particular knowledge of the case in question and some rough standard of personal substantive justice.

The one striking exception arises when Negroes are involved. The white officer is not in any kind of systematic communication with Negroes, the Negro is the "invader," and—what may be statistically true—more likely to commit crimes. The officer sees the Negro as being often more vicious, certainly more secretive, and always alien. To the policemen of Eastern City, the Negro has no historical counterpart in his personal experience and, as a result, the Negro juvenile is more likely than the white to be treated, in accord not with particularist standards, but with the generalized and absolutist attitudes which express the officer's concern for the problem "as a whole."

One reason for the apparently higher proportion of arrests of Negro compared to white juveniles in Eastern City may have nothing to do with "prejudice." In addition to being perceived as an "alien," the Negro offender is also perceived as one who "has no home life." Eastern City officers frequently refer to (and deplore) the apparent weakness of the lower-class Negro family structure, the high proportion of female heads of households, and the alleged high incidence of welfare cases (notably Aid to Dependent Children). If a fraternal force is concerned as much with the maintenance of family authority as with breaking the law and if referring the child to the home is preferred to referring him to court, then the absence (or perceived absence) of family life among Negroes would lead to a greater resort to the courts.

Western City's officer, acting on essentially general principles, treats juveniles with more severity (concern with distinctions of person is less, though by no means entirely absent) but with less discrimination. Negroes and whites are generally treated alike and both are treated more severely. Because the officer in this city is more likely to be essentially of middle-class background and outlook and sometimes college educated as well, he is much more likely to be courteous, impersonal, and "correct" than the Eastern officer. . . .

7

the deviant in court

The court is one of the important stations through which many deviants pass during their deviant careers. Like the police, court personnel have their theories of the office to help them process deviants efficiently and effectively.

Reporting on the public defender, Sudnow shows how cases are handled according to stereotypes of different kinds of crimes and criminals. In the second selection Emerson describes how court personnel place juveniles into particular categories. Scheff then describes how during commitment hearings psychiatrists simply assume that the people in question are legally insane; otherwise, why would their families seek to commit them? In the final selection Wiseman delineates the criteria judges use to deal with Skid Row men charged with public drunkenness.

Normal Crimes

DAVID SUDNOW

Two stances toward the utility of official classificatory schema for criminological research have been debated for years. One position, which might be termed that of the "revisionist" school, has it that the categories of the criminal law, e.g., "burglary," "petty theft," "homicide," etc., are not "homogeneous in respect to causation."[1] From an inspection of penal code descriptions of crimes, it is argued that the way persons seem to be assembled under the auspices of criminal law procedure is such as to produce classes of criminals who are, at least on theoretical grounds, as dissimilar in their social backgrounds and styles of activity as they are similar. The entries in the penal code, this school argues, require revision if sociological use is to be made of categories of crime and a classificatory scheme of etiological relevance is to be developed. Common attempts at such revision have included notions such as *"white collar* crime," and *"systematic* check forger," these conceptions constituting attempts to institute sociologically meaningful specifications which the

operations of criminal law procedure and statutory legislation "fail" to achieve.

The other major perspective toward the sociologist's use of official categories and the criminal statistics compiled under their heading derives less from a concern with etiologically useful schema than from an interest in understanding the actual operations of the administrative legal system. Here, the categories of the criminal law are not regarded as useful or not, as objects to be either adopted, adapted, or ignored; rather, they are seen as constituting the basic conceptual equipment with which such people as judges, lawyers, policemen, and probation workers organize their everyday activities. The study of the actual use of official classification systems by actually employed administrative personnel regards the penal code as data, to be preserved intact; its use, both in organizing the work of legal representation, accusation, adjudication, and prognostication, and in compiling tallies of legal occurrences, is to be examined as one would examine any social activity.

Reprinted from *Social Problems,* Vol. 12 (Winter 1965), pp. 255–264, 269–270.

This investigation is based on field observations of a Public Defender Office in a metropolitan California community. The research was conducted while the author was associated with the Center for the Study of Law and Society, University of California, Berkeley. I am grateful to the Center for financial support. Erving Goffman, Sheldon Messinger, Harvey Sacks, and Emanuel Schegloff contributed valuable suggestions and criticisms to an earlier draft.

[1] D. R. Cressey, "Criminological Research and the Definition of Crimes," *American Journal of Sociology,* Vol. 61 (No. 6), 1951, p. 548. See also J. Hall, *Theft, Law and Society,* second edition, Indianapolis: Bobbs-Merrill, 1952; and E. Sutherland, *Principles of Criminology,* New York: Lippincott, 1947, p. 218. An extensive review of "typological developments" is available in D. C. Gibbons and D. L. Garrity, "Some Suggestions for the Development of Etiological and Treatment Theory in Criminology," *Social Forces,* Vol. 38 (No. 1), 1959.

By sociologically regarding, rather than criticizing, rates of statistics and the categories employed to assemble them, one learns, it is promised, about the "rate producing agencies" and the assembling process.[2]

While the former perspective, the "revisionist" position, has yielded several fruitful products, the latter stance (commonly identified with what is rather loosely known as the "labelling" perspective), has been on the whole more promissory than productive, more programmatic than empirical. The present report will examine the operations of a Public Defender system in an effort to assess the warrant for the continued theoretical and empirical development of the position argued by Kitsuse and Cicourel. It will address the question: what of import for the sociological analysis of legal administration can be learned by describing the actual way the penal code is employed in the daily activities of legal representation? First, I shall consider the "guilty plea" as a way of handling criminal cases, focusing on some features of the penal code as a description of a population of defendants. Then I shall describe the Public Defender operation with special attention to the way defendants are represented. The place of the guilty plea and penal code in this representation will be examined. Lastly, I shall briefly analyze the fashion in which the Public Defender prepares and conducts a "defense." The latter section will attempt to indicate the connection between certain prominent organizational features of the Public Defender system and the penal code's place in the routine operation of that system.

GUILTY PLEAS, INCLUSION, AND NORMAL CRIMES

It is a commonly noted fact about the criminal court system generally, that the greatest proportion of cases are "settled" by a guilty plea.[3] In the county from which the following material is drawn, over 80 per cent of all cases "never go to trial." To describe the method of obtaining a guilty plea disposition, essential for the discussion to follow, I must distinguish between what shall be termed "necessarily-included-lesser-offenses" and "situationally-included-lesser-offenses." Of two offenses designated in the penal code, the lesser is considered to be that for which the length of required incarceration is the shorter period of time. *Inclusion* refers to the relation between two or more offenses. The "necessarily-included-lesser-offense" is a strictly legal notion:

Whether a lesser offense is included in the crime charged is a question of law to be determined solely from the definition and corpus delicti of the offense charged and of the lesser offense. . . . If all the elements of the corpus delicti of a lesser crime can be found in a list of all the elements of the offense charged, then only is the lesser included in the greater.[4]

[2] The most thorough statement of this position, borrowing from the writings of Harold Garfinkel, can be found in the recent critical article by J. I. Kitsuse and A. V. Cicourel, "A Note on the Official Use of Statistics," *Social Problems,* Vol. 11, No. 2 (Fall, 1963), pp. 131–139.

[3] See D. J. Newman, "Pleading Guilty for Considerations," *The Journal of Criminal Law, Criminology and Police Science,* Vol. 46, No. 6 (March–April, 1956), pp. 780–790. Also, M. Schwartz, *Cases and Materials on Professional Responsibility and the Administration of Criminal Justice,* San Francisco: Matthew Bender and Co., 1961, esp. pp. 79–105.

[4] C. W. Fricke, *California Criminal Law,* Los Angeles: The Legal Book Store, 1961, p. 41.

Stated alternatively:

The test in this state of necessarily included offenses is simply that where an offense cannot be committed without necessarily committing another offense, the latter is a necessarily included offense.[5]

The implied negative is put: could Smith have committed A and not B? If the answer is yes, then B is not necessarily included in A. If the answer is no, B is necessarily included. While in a given case a battery might be committed in the course of a robbery, battery is not necessarily included in robbery. Petty theft is necessarily included in robbery but not in burglary. Burglary primarily involves the "intent" to acquire another's goods illegally (e.g., by breaking and entering); the consummation of the act need not occur for burglary to be committed. Theft, like robbery, requires that some item be stolen.

I shall call *lesser* offenses that are not necessarily but "only" *actually* included, "situationally-included-lesser-offenses." By statutory definition, necessarily included offenses are "actually" included. By actual here, I refer to the "way it occurs as a course of action." In the instance of necessary inclusion, the "way it occurs" is irrelevant. With situational inclusion, the "way it occurs" is definitive. In the former case, no particular course of action is referred to. In the latter, the scene and progress of the criminal activity would be analyzed.

The issue of necessary inclusion has special relevance for two procedural matters:

A. A man cannot be charged and/or convicted of two or more crimes any one of which is necessarily included in the others, unless the several crimes occur on separate occasions.

If a murder occurs, the defendant cannot be charged and/or convicted of both "homicide" and "intent to commit a murder," the latter of which is necessarily included in first degree murder. If, however, a defendant "intends to commit a homicide" against one person and commits a "homicide" against another, both offenses may be properly charged. While it is an extremely complex question as to the scope and definition of "in the course of," in most instances the rule is easily applied.

B. The judge cannot instruct the jury to consider as alternative crimes of which to find a defendant guilty, crimes that are not necessarily included in the charged crime or crimes.

If a man is charged with "statutory rape" the judge may instruct the jury to consider as a possible alternative conviction "contributing to the delinquency of a minor," as this offense is necessarily included in "statutory rape." He cannot however suggest that the alternative "intent to commit murder" be considered and the jury cannot find the defendant guilty of this latter crime, unless it is charged as a distinct offense in the complaint.

It is crucial to note that these restrictions apply only to (a) the relation between several charged offenses in a formal allegation, and (b) the alternatives allowable in a jury instruction. At any time before a case "goes to trial," alterations in the charging complaint may be made by the district attorney. The issue of necessary inclusion has no required bearing on (a) what offense(s) will be charged initially by the prosecutor, (b) what the relation is between the charge initially made and "what happened," or (c) what modifications may be made after the initial charge and the

[5] People v. Greer, 30 Cal. 2d, 589.

relation between initially charged offenses and those charged in modified complaints. It is this latter operation, the modification of the complaint, that is central to the guilty plea disposition.

Complaint alterations are made when a defendant agrees to plead guilty to an offense and thereby avoid a trial. The alteration occurs in the context of a "deal" consisting of an offer from the district attorney to alter the original charge in such a fashion that a lighter sentence will be incurred with a guilty plea than would be the case if the defendant were sentenced on the original charge. In return for this manipulation, the defendant agrees to plead guilty. The arrangement is proposed in this following format: "if you plead guilty to this new lesser offense, you will get less time in prison than if you plead not guilty to the original, greater charge and lose the trial." The decision must then be made whether or not the chances of obtaining complete acquittal at trial are great enough to warrant the risk of a loss and higher sentence if found guilty on the original charge. As we shall see below, it is a major job of the Public Defender, who mediates between the district attorney and the defendant, to convince his "client" that the chances of acquittal are too slight to warrant this risk.

If a man is charged with "drunkenness" and the Public Defender and Public Prosecutor (hereafter P.D. and D.A.) prefer not to have a trial, they seek to have the defendant agree to plead guilty. While it is occasionally possible, particularly with first offenders, for the P.D. to convince the defendant to plead guilty to the originally charged offense, most often it is felt that some "exchange" or "consideration" should be offered, i.e., a lesser offense charged.

To what offense can "drunkenness" be reduced? There is no statutorily designated crime that is necessarily included in the crime of "drunkenness." That is, if any of the statutorily required com-ponents of drunk behavior (its corpus delicti) are absent, there remains no offense of which the resultant description is a definition. For drunkenness there is, however, an offense that while not necessarily included is "typically-situationally-included," i.e., "typically" occurs as a feature of the way drunk persons are seen to behave—"disturbing the peace." The range of possible sentences is such that of the two offenses, "disturbing the peace" cannot call for as long a prison sentence as "drunkenness." If, in the course of going on a binge a person does so in such a fashion that "disturbing the peace" may be employed to describe some of his behavior, it would be considered as an alternative offense to offer in return for a guilty plea. A central question for the following analysis will be: in what fashion would he have to behave so that disturbing the peace would be considered a suitable reduction?

If a man is charged with "molesting a minor," there are not any necessarily included lesser offenses with which to charge him. Yet an alternative charge—"loitering around a schoolyard"—is often used as a reduction. As above, and central to our analysis the question is: what would the defendant's behavior be such that "loitering around a schoolyard" would constitute an appropriate alternative?

If a person is charged with "burglary," "petty theft" is not necessarily included. Routinely, however, "petty theft" is employed for reducing the charge of burglary. Again, we shall ask: what is the relation between burglary and petty theft and the *manner in which the former occurs* that warrants this reduction?

Offenses are regularly reduced to other offenses the latter of which are not necessarily or situationally included in the former. As I have already said the determination of whether or not offense X was situationally included in Y involves an analysis of the course of action that constitutes the criminal behavior. I must now turn to examine this mode of behavioral analysis.

When encountering a defendant who is charged with "assault with a deadly weapon," the P.D. asks: "what can this offense be reduced to so as to arrange for a guilty plea?" As the reduction is only to be proposed by the P.D. and accepted or not by the D.A., his question becomes "what reduction will be allowable?" (As shall be seen below, the P.D. and D.A. have institutionalized a common orientation to allowable reductions.) The method of reduction involves, as a general feature, the fact that the particular case in question is scrutinized to decide its membership in a class of similar cases. But *the penal code does not provide the reference for deciding the correspondence between the instant event and the general case; that is, it does not define the classes of offense types.* To decide, for purposes of finding a suitable reduction, if the instant case involves a "burglary," reference is not made to the statutory definition of "burglary." To decide what the situationally included offenses are in the instant case, the instant case is not analyzed as a *statutorily* referable course of action; rather, reference is made to a *non-statutorily* conceived class "burglary" and offenses that are typically situationally included in it, taken as a class of behavioral events. Stated again: in searching an instant case to decide what to *reduce it to,* there is no analysis of the statutorily referable elements of the instant case; instead, its membership in a class of events, the features of which cannot be described by the penal code, must be decided. An example will be useful. If a defendant is charged with burglary and the P.D. is concerned to propose a reduction to a lesser offense, he might search the elements of the burglary at hand to decide what other offenses were committed. The other offenses he might "discover" would be of two sorts: those necessarily and those situationally included. In attempt-

ing to decide those other offenses situationally included in the instant event, the instant event might be analyzed as a statutorily referable course of action. Or, as is the case with the P.D., the instant case might be analyzed to decide if it is a "burglary" in common with other "burglaries" conceived of in terms other than those provided by the statute.

Burglaries are routinely reduced to petty theft. If we were to analyze the way burglaries typically occur, petty theft is neither situationally nor necessarily included; when a burglary is committed, money or other goods are seldom illegally removed from some person's body. If we therefore analyzed burglaries, employing the penal code as our reference, and then searched the P.D.'s records to see how burglaries are reduced in the guilty plea, we could not establish a rule that would describe the transformation between the burglary cases statutorily described and the reductions routinely made (i.e., to "petty theft"). The rule must be sought elsewhere, in the character of the non-statutorily defined class of "burglaries," which I shall term *normal burglaries.*

NORMAL CRIMES

In the course of routinely encountering persons charged with "petty theft," "burglary," "assault with a deadly weapon," "rape," "possession of marijuana," etc., the P.D. gains knowledge of the typical manner in which offenses of given classes are committed, the social characteristics of the persons who regularly commit them, the features of the settings in which they occur, the types of victims often involved, and the like. He learns to speak knowledgeably of "burglars," "petty thieves," "drunks," "rapists," "narcos," etc., and to attribute to them personal biographies, modes of usual criminal activity, criminal histories, psychological characteristics, and social backgrounds. The following characterizations are illustrative:

Most ADWs [assault with deadly weapon] start with fights over some girl.

These sex fiends [child molestation cases] usually hang around parks or schoolyards. But we often get fathers charged with these crimes. Usually the old man is out of work and stays at home when the wife goes to work and he plays around with his little daughter or something. A lot of these cases start when there is some marital trouble and the woman gets mad.

I don't know why most of them don't rob the big stores. They usually break into some cheap department store and steal some crummy item like a $9.95 record player you know.

Kids who start taking this stuff [narcotics] usually start out when some buddy gives them a cigarette and they smoke it for kicks. For some reason they always get caught in their cars, for speeding or something.

They can anticipate that point when persons are likely to get into trouble:

Dope addicts do O.K. until they lose a job or something and get back on the streets and, you know, meet the old boys. Someone tells them where to get some and there they are.

In the springtime, that's when we get all these sex crimes. You know, these kids play out in the schoolyard all day and these old men sit around and watch them jumping up and down. They get their ideas.

The P.D. learns that some kinds of offenders are likely to repeat the same offense while others are not repeat violators or, if they do commit crimes frequently, the crimes vary from occasion to occasion:

You almost never see a check man get caught for anything but checks—only an occasional drunk charge.

Burglars are usually multiple offenders, most times just burglaries or petty thefts. Petty thefts get started for almost anything—joy riding, drinking, all kinds of little things.

These narcos are usually through after the second violation or so. After the first time some stop, but when they start on the heavy stuff, they've had it.

I shall call *normal crimes* those occurrences whose typical features, e.g., the ways they usually occur and the characteristics of persons who commit them (as well as the typical victims and typical scenes), are known and attended to by the P.D. For any of a series of offense types the P.D. can provide some form of proverbial characterization. For example, *burglary* is seen as involving regular violators, no weapons, low-priced items, little property damage, lower class establishments, largely Negro defendants, independent operators, and a non-professional orientation to the crime. *Child molesting* is seen as typically entailing middle-aged strangers or lower class middle-aged fathers (few women), no actual physical penetration or severe tissue damage, mild fondling, petting, and stimulation, bad marriage circumstances, multiple offenders with the same offense repeatedly committed, a child complainant, via the mother, etc. *Narcotics* defendants are usually Negroes, not syndicated, persons who start by using small stuff, hostile with police officers, caught by some form of entrapment technique, etc. *Petty thefts* are about 50-50 Negro-white, unplanned offenses, generally committed on lower class persons and don't get much money, don't often employ weapons, don't make living from thievery, usually younger defendants with long juvenile assaultive records, etc. *Drunkenness* offenders are lower class white and Negro, get drunk on wine and beer, have long histories of repeated drunkeness, don't hold down jobs, are usually arrested on the streets, seldom violate other penal code sections, etc.

Some general features of the normal crime as a way of attending to a category of persons and events may be mentioned:

1. The focus, in these characterizations, is not on particular individuals, but offense types. If asked "What are burglars like?" or "How are burglaries usually committed?", the P.D. does not feel obliged to refer to particular burglars and burglaries as the material for his answer.

2. The features attributed to offenders and offenses are often not of import for the statutory conception. In burglary, it is "irrelevant" for the statutory determination whether or not much damage was done to the premises (except where, for example, explosives were employed and a new statute could be invoked). Whether a defendant breaks a window or not, destroys property within the house or not, etc., does not affect his statutory classification as a burglar. While for robbery the presence or absence of a weapon sets the degree, whether the weapon is a machine gun or pocket knife is "immaterial." Whether the residence or business establishment in a burglary is located in a higher income area of the city is of no issue for the code requirements. And, generally, the defendant's race, class position, criminal history (in most offenses), personal attributes, and in particular style of committing offenses are features specifically not definitive of crimes under the auspices of the penal code. For deciding "Is this a 'burglary' case I have before me," however, the P.D.'s reference to this range of non-statutorily referable personal and social attributes, modes of operation, etc., is crucial for the arrangement of a guilty plea bargain.

3. The features attributed to offenders and offenses are, in their content, specific to the community in which the P.D. works. In other communities and historical periods the lists would presumably differ. Narcotics violators in certain areas, for example, are syndicated in dope rackets or engage in systematic robbery as professional criminals, features which are not commonly encountered (or, at least, evidence for which is not systematically sought) in this community. Burglary in some cities will more often occur at large industrial plants, banking establishments, warehouses, etc. The P.D. refers to the population of defendants in the county as "our defendants" and qualifies his prototypical portrayals and knowledge of the typically operative social structures, "for our county." An older P.D., remembering the "old days," commented:

We used to have a lot more rapes than we do now, and they used to be much more violent. Things are duller now in. . . .

4. Offenses whose normal features are readily attended to are those which are routinely encountered in the courtroom. This feature is related to the last point. For embezzlement, bank robbery, gambling, prostitution, murder, arson, and some other uncommon offenses, the P.D. cannot readily supply anecdotal and proverbial characterizations. While there is some change in the frequencies of offense-type convictions over time, certain offenses are continually more common and others remain stably infrequent. . . . Troubles (are) created for the P.D. when offenses whose features are not readily known occur, and whose typicality is not easily constructed. . . .

5. Offenses are ecologically specified and attended to as normal or not according to the locales within which they are committed. The P.D. learns that burglaries usually occur in such and such areas of the city, petty thefts around this or that park, ADWs in these bars. Ecological patterns are seen as related to socio-economic variables and these in

turn to typical modes of criminal and non-criminal activities. Knowing where an offense took place is thus, for the P.D., knowledge of the likely persons involved, the kind of scene in which the offense occurred, and the pattern of activity characteristic of such a place:

Almost all of our ADWs are in the same half a dozen bars. These places are Negro bars where laborers come after hanging around the union halls trying to get some work. Nobody has any money and they drink too much. Tempers are high and almost anything can start happening.

6. One further important feature can be noted at this point. . . . The P.D. office consists of a staff of twelve full time attorneys. Knowledge of the properties of offense types of offenders, i.e., their normal, typical, or familiar attributes, constitutes the mark of any given attorney's competence. A major task in socializing the new P.D. deputy attorney consists in teaching him to recognize these attributes and to come to do so naturally. The achievement of competence as a P.D. is signalled by the gradual acquisition of professional command not simply of local penal code peculiarities and courtroom folklore, but, as importantly, of relevant features of the social structure and criminological wisdom. His grasp of that knowledge over the course of time is a key indication of his expertise. Below, in our brief account of some relevant organizational properties of the P.D. system, we shall have occasion to re-emphasize the competence-attesting aspects of the attorney's proper use of established sociological knowledge. Let us return to the mechanics of the guilty plea procedure as an example of the operation of the notion of normal crimes.

Over the course of their interaction and repeated "bargaining" discussions, the P.D. and D.A. have developed a set of unstated recipes for reducing original charges to lesser offenses. These recipes are specifically appropriate for use in instances of normal crimes and in such instances alone. "Typical" burglaries are reduced to petty theft, "typical" ADWs to simple assault, "typical" child molestation to loitering around a schoolyard, etc. The character of these recipes deserves attention.

The specific content of any reduction, i.e., what particular offense class X offenses will be reduced to, is such that the reduced offense may bear no obvious relation (neither situationally nor necessarily included) to the originally charged offense. The reduction of burglary to petty theft is an example. The important relation between the reduced offense and the original charge is such that the reduction from one to the other is considered "reasonable." At this point we shall only state what seems to be the general principle involved in deciding this reasonableness. The underlying premises cannot be explored at the present time, as that would involve a political analysis beyond the scope of the present report. *Both P.D. and D.A. are concerned to obtain a guilty plea wherever possible and thereby avoid a trial. At the same time, each party is concerned that the defendant "receive his due." The reduction of offense X to Y must be of such a character that the new sentence will depart from the anticipated sentence for the original charge to such a degree that the defendant is likely to plead guilty to the the new charge and, at the same time, not so great that the defendant does not "get his due."*

In a homicide, while battery is a necessarily included offense, it will not be considered as a possible reduction. For a conviction of second degree murder a defendant could receive a life sentence in the penitentiary. For a battery conviction he would spend no more than six months in the county jail. In a homicide, however, "felony manslaughter," or "assault with a deadly weapon," whatever their relation to homicide as regards inclusion, would more closely approximate the sentence outcome that could be expected on a trial conviction of second degree murder. These alternatives would be considered. For burglary, a typically situationally included offense might be "disturbing the peace," "breaking and entering" or "destroying public property." "Petty theft," however, constitutes a reasonable lesser alternative to burglary as the sentence for petty theft will often range between six months and one year in the county jail and burglary regularly does not carry higher than two years in the state prison. "Disturbing the peace" would be a thirty-day sentence offense.

While the present purposes make the exposition of this calculus unnecessary, it can be noted and stressed that the particular content of the reduction does not necessarily correspond to a relation between the original and altered charge that could be described in either the terms of necessary or situational inclusion. Whatever the relation between the original and reduced charge, its essential feature resides in the spread between sentence likelihoods and the reasonableness of that spread, i.e., the balance it strikes between the defendant "getting his due" and at the same time "getting something less than he might so that he will plead guilty."

The procedure we want to clarify now, at the risk of some repetition, is the manner in which an instant case is examined to decide its membership in a class of "crimes such as this" (the category *normal crimes*). Let us start with an obvious case, burglary. As the typical reduction for burglary is petty theft and as petty theft is neither situationally nor necessarily included in burglary, the examination of the instant case is clearly not undertaken to decide whether petty theft is an appropriate statutory description. The concern is to establish the

relation between the instant burglary and the normal category "burglaries" and, having decided a "sufficient correspondence," to now employ petty theft as the proposed reduction.

In scrutinizing the present burglary case, the P.D. seeks to establish that "this is a burglary just like any other." If that correspondence is not established, regardless of whether or not petty theft in fact was a feature of the way the crime was enacted, the reduction to petty theft would not be proposed. *The propriety of proposing petty theft as a reduction does not derive from its in-fact-existence in the present case, but is warranted or not by the relation of the present burglary to "burglaries," normally conceived.*

In a case of "child molestation" (officially called "lewd conduct with a minor"), the concern is to decide if this is a "typical child molestation case." While "loitering around a schoolyard" is frequently a feature of the way such crimes are instigated, establishing that the present defendant *did in fact loiter around a schoolyard* is secondary to the more general question "Is this a typical child molestation case?" What appears as a contradiction must be clarified by examining the status of "loitering around a schoolyard" as a typical feature of such child molestations. The typical character of "child molesting cases" does not stand or fall on the fact that "loitering around a schoolyard" is a feature of the way they are in fact committed. It is *not* that "loitering around a schoolyard" as a *statutorily referable behavior sequence* is part of typical "child molesting cases" but that "loitering around a schoolyard" as a *socially distinct mode of committing child molestations typifies the way such offenses are enacted.* "Strictly speaking," i.e., under the auspices of the statutory *corpus delicti,* "loitering around a schoolyard," requires *loitering, around, a schoolyard;* if one loiters around a ball park or a public recreation area, he "cannot," within a proper reading of the statute, be charged with loitering around a *schoolyard.* Yet "loitering around a schoolyard," as a feature of the typical way such offenses as child molestations are committed, has the status not of a description of the way in *fact* (*fact,* statutorily decided) it occurred or typically occurs, but "the kind-of-social-activity-typically-associated-with-such-offenses." It is not its statutorily conceived features but its socially relevant attributes that gives "loitering around a schoolyard" its status as a feature of the class "normal child molestations." Whether the defendant loitered around a schoolyard or a ball park, and whether he loitered or "was passing by," "loitering around a schoolyard" as a reduction will be made if the defendant's activity was such that "he was hanging around some public place or another" and "was the kind of guy who hangs around schoolyards." As a component of the class of normal child molestation cases (of the variety where the victim is a stranger), "loitering around a schoolyard" typifies a mode of committing such offenses, the class of "such persons who do such things as hang around schoolyards and the like." A large variety of actual offenses could thus be nonetheless reduced to "loitering" if, as kinds of social activity, "loitering," conceived of as typifying a way of life, pattern of daily activity, social psychological circumstances, etc., characterized the conduct of the defendant. The young P.D. who would object "You can't reduce it to 'loitering'—he didn't really 'loiter,' " would be reprimanded: "Fella, you don't know how to use that term; he might as well have 'loitered'—it's the same kind of case as the others. . . ."

The P.D.'s activity is seldom geared to securing acquittals for clients. He and the D.A., as co-workers in the same courts, take it for granted that the persons who come before the courts are guilty of crimes and are to be treated accordingly:

Most of them have records as you can see. Almost all of them have been through our courts before. And the police just don't make mistakes in this town. That's one thing about _____, we've got the best police force in the state.

As we shall argue below, the way defendants are "represented" (the station manning rather than assignment of counselors to clients), the way trials are conducted, the way interviews are held and the penal code employed—all of the P.D.'s work is premised on the supposition that people charged with crimes—have committed crimes.

This presupposition makes such first questions as "Why don't you start by telling me where this place was . . . ?" reasonable questions. When the answer comes: "What place? I don't know what you are talking about," the defendant is taken to be a phony, making an innocent pitch." The conceivable first question: "Did you do it?" is not asked because it is felt that this gives the defendant the notion that he can try an "innocent pitch":

I never ask them, "did you do it?" because on one hand I know they did and mainly because then they think that they can play games with us. We can always check their records and usually they have a string of offenses. You don't have to, though, because in a day or two they change their story and plead guilty. Except for the stubborn ones.

Of the possible answers to an opening question, bewilderment, the inability to answer or silence are taken to indicate that the defendant is putting the P.D. on. For defendants who refuse to admit anything, the P.D. threatens:

Look, if you don't want to talk, that's your business. I can't help you. All I can say is that if you go to trial on this beef you're going to spend a long time in the joint. When you get ready to tell me the story straight, then we can see what can be done.

If the puzzlement comes because the wrong question is asked, e.g., "There wasn't any fight—that's not the way it happened," the defendant will start to fill in the story. The P.D. awaits to see if, how far, and in what ways the instant case is deviant. If the defendant is charged with burglary and a middle class establishment was burglarized, windows shattered, a large payroll sought after and a gun used, then the reduction to petty theft, generally employed for "normal burglaries," would be more difficult to arrange.

Generally, the P.D. doesn't have to discover the atypical kinds of cases through questioning. Rather, the D.A., in writing the original complaint, provides the P.D. with clues that the typical recipe, given the way the event occurred, will not be allowable. Where the way it occurs is such that it does not resemble normal burglaries and the routinely used penalty would reduce it *too far* commensurate with the way the crime occurred, the D.A. frequently charges various situationally included offenses, indicating to the P.D. that the procedure to employ here is to suggest "dropping" some of the charges, leaving the originally charged greatest offense as it stands.

In the general case he doesn't charge all those offenses that he legally might. He might charge "child molesting" and "loitering around a schoolyard" but typically only the greater charge is made. The D.A. does so, so as to provide for a later reduction that will appear particularly lenient in that it seemingly involves a *change* in the charge. Were he to charge both molesting and loitering, he would be obliged, moreover, should the case come to trial, to introduce evidence for both offenses. The D.A. is thus always constrained not to set overly high charges or not situationally included multiple offenses by the possibility that the defendant will not plead guilty to a lesser offense and the case will go to trial. Of

primary importance is that he doesn't charge multiple offenses so that the P.D. will be in the best position vis-à-vis the defendant. He thus charges the first complaint so as to provide for a "setup."

The alteration of charges must be made in open court. The P.D. requests to have a new plea entered:

P.D.: Your honor, in the interests of justice, my client would like to change his plea of not guilty to the charge of burglary and enter a plea of guilty to the charge of petty theft.
Judge: Is this new plea acceptable to the prosecution?
D.A.: Yes, your honor.

The prosecutor knows beforehand that the request will be made, and has agreed in advance to allow it.

I asked a P.D. how they felt about making such requests in open court, i.e., asking for a reduction from one offense to another when the latter is obviously not necessarily included and often (as is the case in burglary-to-petty theft) not situationally included. He summarized the office's feeling:

. . . in the old days, ten or so years ago, we didn't like to do it in front of the judge. What we used to do when we made a deal was that the D.A. would dismiss the original charge and write up a new complaint altogether. That took a lot of time. We had to re-arraign him all over again back in the muni court and everything. Besides, in the same courtroom, everyone used to know what was going on anyway. Now, we just ask for a change of plea to the lesser charge regardless of whether it's included or not. Nobody thinks twice about asking for petty theft on burglary or drunkenness on car theft, or something like that. It's just the way it's done.

Some restrictions are felt. Assaultive crimes (e.g., ADW, simple assault, attempted murder, etc.) will not be reduced to or from "money offenses" (burglary, robbery, theft) unless the latter involve weapons or some violence. Also, victimless crimes (narcotics, drunkenness) are not reduced to or from assaultive or "money offenses," unless there is some factual relation, e.g., drunkenness with a fight might turn out to be simple assault reduced to drunkenness.

For most cases that come before their courts, the P.D. and D.A. are able to employ reductions that are formulated for handling typical cases. While some burglaries, rapes, narcotics violations and petty thefts are instigated in strange ways and involve atypical facts, some manipulation in the way the initial charge is made can be used to set up a procedure to replace the simple charge-alteration form of reducing. . . .

Court Responses to Juveniles

ROBERT M. EMERSON

A NOTE ON TOTAL DENUNCIATION

Consideration of the structural features of total denunciation provides additional insight into the processes of establishing moral character in the juvenile court. For a successful total denunciation must transcend routine denunciation by *foreclosing* all possible defenses and by *neutralizing* all possible sources of support.

Foreclosure of defenses available to the delinquent . . . has two related elements. First, in order to discredit moral character totally, it must be clearly demonstrated that the denounced delinquent has been given a great many "breaks" or "chances" which he has, however, rejected and spoiled. Such a demonstration is necessary to prove that the case is "hopeless," that the delinquent youth's character is so ruined as to preclude any possibility of reform. The role of the disregarded "chance" is clearly seen in the following case, where a probation officer convinces both judge and public defender to go along with his punitive recommendation by proving that the youth has received chances not even officially reported:

Two escapees from reform school were brought into court on a series of new complaints taken out by the police. Public defender argued that these complaints should be dismissed and the boys simply returned to the school. The probation officer, however, argued strongly that boys should be found delinquent on the new complaints (this would require reconsideration of their cases by the Youth Correction Authority, perhaps leading to an extension of their commitment). The probation officer described how one of his colleagues had worked hard on one of these cases earlier, giving the boy a great many chances, none of which did any good. The judge accepted the probation officer's recommendation.

After the hearing, the public defender admitted that he felt the probation officer had been right, acknowledging the validity of his picture of the character of this boy: "I did not realize he was such a bastard. . . . Apparently one of the probation officers had given him a lot of breaks. He had him on so many cases that he should be shot."

Second, it must be made to appear that the delinquent himself "messed up" the chances that he had been given. It should be established not only that the youth misbehaved on numerous occasions, but also that he did so in full knowledge of the possible consequences and with no valid excuse or extenuating circumstances. In this way, responsibility or "fault" for the imminent incarceration must fall completely on the denounced delinquent. Any official contribution to the youth's "messing up" (e.g., an official's intolerance) must be glossed over so that the delinquent bears total blame.

Court probation is in fact constructed so that responsibility for "messing up," should it occur, unavoidably falls on the delinquent. . . . Probationers are con-

Reprinted from Robert M. Emerson, *Judging Delinquents* (Chicago: Aldine Publishing Company, 1969), pp. 137–41, 155–63; copyright © 1969 by Robert M. Emerson. Reprinted by permission of the author and Aldine • Atherton, Inc.

stantly warned that they will be committed if there is any further misconduct, and they are given a number of "breaks" on this condition. As one probation officer commented about a youth who had been "given a break" by the judge: "This way, if he gets committed, he knows he has it coming." Furthermore, the constant warnings and lectures against getting into trouble that occur throughout probation tend to undermine in advance the possibility of defending subsequent misbehavior. For example, it is difficult for a youth to excuse a new offense as the product of peer group influence when he has continually been warned to stay away from "bad friends."

A second key element in a successful total denunciation is the neutralization of all possible sources of support. There are several components in this neutralization. First, the assessment of discredited and "hopeless" character must be made to appear as a general consensus among all those concerned in the case. A delinquent without a spokesman—with no one to put in a good word for him—stands in a fundamentally discredited position.

Here the stance taken by the delinquent's lawyer, normally a public defender, becomes crucial. A vigorous defense and pitch by a lawyer often might dispel the appearance of consensus and weaken the denunciation. This occurs very rarely, however, because of court cooptation of the public defender. Working closely with the probation staff, the public defender comes to share their values and indexes of success and failure in delinquency cases. Consequently, he will generally concur with the court's highly negative assessments of delinquent moral character. As a public defender noted in response to a question about how he usually handled his cases in the juvenile court:

Generally I would find the probation officer handling the case and ask him: "What do you have on this kid? How bad is he?"

He'll say: "Oh, he's bad!" Then he opens the probation folder to me, and I'll see he's got quite a record. Then I'll ask him, "What are you going to recommend?" He'll say, "Give him another chance. Or probation. Or we've got to put him away."

But probation officers don't make this last recommendation lightly. Generally they try to find a parent in the home,"someone who can keep him under control, someone who can watch him." But if the probation officer has given the kid a number of chances, it is a different story: "He's giving the kid chances and he keeps screwing up. . . . [Commitment will then be recommended.] And I say the kid deserves it. Before a kid goes away he's really got to be obnoxious—he will deserve it."

Adoption of probation standards for assessing delinquent character becomes crucial in total denunciation. The public defender is then in the position of arguing on behalf of a youth whose moral character has been totally discredited in his eyes and who he feels should indeed be committed. His courtroom defense will generally reflect this assessment. He will make only the most perfunctory motions of arguing that the delinquent be let off, and he will do so in a way that communicates an utter lack of conviction that this is a desirable course of action. Or, as in the following case, he will not even go through the motions of making a defense but will explicitly concur with the recommended incarceration and the grounds on which it rests:

A policeman told of finding an 11-year-old Negro boy in a laundry where a coin box had been looted. The officer reported that the boy had admitted committing the offense. Public defender waived cross-examination, and the judge found the youth delinquent.

Probation officer then delivered a rather lengthy report on the case. The boy had been sent to the Boys' Training Program and, while no great trouble, did not attend regularly. He had also recently been transferred to the Harris School and had been in trouble there. Probation officer recommended that the prior suspended sentence be revoked and the boy committed to the Youth Correction Authority.

Judge then asked the public defender if he had anything he wanted to say. Public defender: "The record more or less speaks for itself. He does not seem to have taken advantage of the opportunities the court has given him to straighten out." Then, after briefly reconferring with the probation officer, the judge ordered the commitment. Public defender waived the right of appeal.

Second, the denouncer must establish that in "messing up" and not taking advantage of the chances provided him, the denounced has created a situation in which there is *no other alternative open* but commitment to the Youth Correction Authority. In some cases, this may involve showing that the youth is so dangerous that commitment to the Authority is the only effective way he can be restrained; in others, demonstration that by his misbehavior the youth has completely destroyed all possible placements, including the one he has been in. It is only by dramatically showing in these ways that "there is nothing we can do with him" that the proposed commitment can be made to appear as an inevitable and objective necessity.

The fact that many total denunciations concentrate on proving that nothing else can be done with the case reflects the court's basic resistance to unwarrantable agency attempts to "dump" undesirable cases onto them for incarceration. The court feels that most of these institutions are too ready to give up on cases that from the court's point of view are still salvageable. To overcome this suspiciousness, the denouncer must not only present the youth's character as essentially corrupt and "hopeless," but also show that every effort has been made to work with him and every possible opportunity afforded him. The denouncer, in other words, must take pains to avoid appearing to be merely getting rid of a difficult and troublesome case simply to make his own work easier. This requires showing both that persistent efforts have been made to work with the case and that at the present time even extraordinary efforts cannot come up with anything as an alternative to incarceration.

A final aspect of demonstrating that there is no viable alternative to incarceration involves isolating the denounced delinquent from any kind of reputable sponsorship. In the usual case, where a parent acts as sponsor, successful total denunciation requires either that the parent be induced to denounce the youth and declare him fit only for incerceration or that the parent be discredited. In other cases, where the sponsor is a parental substitute, this sponsor must similarly be led to denounce the youth or be discredited. In this way, for example, sponsors who seek too aggressively to save delinquents considered overripe for commitment by other officials may encounter attacks on their motives, wisdom, or general moral character. This not only undermines the viability of any defense of character made by the sponsor, but also effectively isolates the delinquent by showing the unsuitability of his sponsorship as an alternative to commitment. . . .

COUNTER-DENUNCIATION

As noted earlier, the courtroom proceeding routinely comes to involve a denunciation of the accused delinquent in the course of a confrontation between him and his accusers. This fact creates the conditions for the use of *counter-denunciation* as a defensive strategy. This strategy seeks to undermine the discrediting implications of the accusation by attacking the actions, motives and/or character of one's accusers.

The underlying phenomenon is counter-denunciation has been noted in a number of other contexts. McCorkle and Korn, for example, have analyzed the concept of the "rejection of the rejectors" as a defensive reaction to imprisonment (1964, p. 520). Similarly, Sykes and Matza explain the "condemnation of the condemners" in the process of neutralization in the following terms: "The delinquent shifts the focus of attention from his own deviant acts to the motives and behaviors of those who disapprove of his violations" (1957, p. 668). The concept of counter-denunciation, in contrast, focuses on the communicative work which accomplishes this shift of attention. Furthermore, it gains relevance as a defense against attempted character discrediting. Use of this strategy, however, is extremely risky in the court setting. While counter-denunciation may appear to the delinquent as a "natural" defense as he perceives the circumstances of his case, it tends to challenge fundamental court commitments and hence, even when handled with extreme care, often only confirms the denunciation.

It is striking that counter-denunciation has the greatest likelihood of success in cases where the complainant or denouncer lacks official stature or where the initiative rests predominantly with private parties who have clearly forced official action. Under these circumstances the wrongful quality of the offense can be greatly reduced if not wholly eliminated by showing that the initiator of the complaint was at least partially to blame for the illegal act. For example:

A 16-year-old Negro boy, Johnny Haskin, was charged with assault and battery on two teenaged girls who lived near his family in a public housing project. Although a juvenile officer brought the case into court, he was clearly acting on the initiative of the two girls and their mother, for he had had no direct contact with the incident and did not testify about it. He simply put the two girls on the stand and let them tell about what happened. This was fairly confused, but eventually it appeared that Johnny Haskin had been slapping the younger sister in the hall of the project when the older

girl had pulled him off. He had then threatened her with a knife. The girls admitted that there had been fighting in the hall for some time, and that they had been involved, but put the blame on Johnny for starting it. Mrs. Haskin, however, spoke up from the back of the room, and told about a gang of boys coming around to get her son (apparently justifying Johnny's carrying a knife). And Johnny himself denied that he had started the fighting, claiming that the younger girl had hit him with a bat and threatened him first.

Judge then lectured both families for fighting, and placed Johnny on probation for nine months, despite a rather long prior record.

In this case, by establishing that the girls had also been fighting, the boy was at least partially exonerated. The success of this strategy is seen in the fact that the judge lectured both families, and then gave the boy what was a mild sentence in light of his prior court record.

Similarly, the possibility of discrediting the victim, thereby invalidating the complaint, becomes apparent in the following "rape" case:

Two Negro boys, ages 12 and 13, had admitted forcing "relations" on a 12-year-old girl in a schoolyard, the police reported. After a full report on the incidents surrounding the offense, the judge asked the policemen: "What kind of girl is she?" Officer: "I checked with Reverend Frost [the girl's minister and the person instrumental in reporting this incident] and he said she was a good girl."

As the judge's query implies, the reprehensibility of this act can only be determined in relation to the assessed character of the girl victim. Had the police or the accused brought up evidence of a bad reputation or incidents suggesting "loose" or "promiscuous" behavior, the force of the complaint would have been undermined.

In the above cases, successful counter-denunciation of the complainants would undermine the moral basis of their involvement in the incident, thereby discrediting their grounds for initiating the complaint. But this merely shifts part of the responsibility for an offense onto the complaining party and does not affect the wrongful nature of the act per se. Thus, by denouncing the general character of the complainant and the nature of his involvement in the offense, the accused does not so much clear himself as diminish his guilt. If the offense involved is serious enough and the culpability of the complainant not directly related to the offense, therefore, this strategy may have little impact.

For example, in the homosexuality-tinged case of car theft . . . both the accused and his father tried to support their contention that the car owner was lying by pointing to his discredited character. But the "victim's" homosexuality had no real connection with the act of stealing the car nor with the threatened physical violence it entailed, and hence did not affect the judge's evaluation of the act and of the delinquent's character. Under these circumstances, the soiled nature of the victim simply was not considered sufficiently extenuating to dissolve the reprehensibility of the act.[1]

In general, then, a successful counter-denunciation must discredit not only the general character of the denouncer but also his immediate purpose or motive in making the complaint. Only in this way can the counter-denunciation cut the ground out from under the wrongfulness of the alleged offense. For example:

An 11-year-old Negro boy was charged with wantonly damaging the car of an older Negro man, Frankie Williams, with a BB gun. With the boy was his mother, a respectably dressed woman, a white lawyer, and a white couple who served as character witnesses.

A juvenile officer brought the case in and then called Mr. Williams up to testify. The witness told of going outside to shovel his car out of the snow several weeks previously and finding his windshield damaged in several places. He had noticed the boy at this time leaning out of the window of his house with a BB gun. Lawyer then cross-examined, getting Williams to admit that he had been bickering with the family for some time, and that a year before the mother had accused him of swearing at her son and had tried to get a court complaint against him. (Judge ruled this irrelevant after Williams had acknowledged it.) Williams seemed flustered, and grew angry under the questioning, claiming that because of the boy's shooting he would not be able to get an inspection sticker for his car.

Juvenile officer then told judge that although he had not investigated the case, his partner reported that the marks on the windshield were not consistent with a BB gun. Williams had also admitted that he had not looked for any BB pellets. On the basis of this evidence, the judge found the boy not delinquent. He then severely warned all parties in the case: "I'm going to tell you I do not want any more contests between these two families. Do you understand?"

Here, by showing that the complainant had both a selfish motive for complaining about his damaged windshield (to help get it repaired) and a grudge against the defendant and his family, as well as bringing out the lack of concrete evidence to substantiate the charge, the lawyer was able to get the complaint totally dismissed. . . .

Finally, successful counter-denuncia-

[1] Note, however, that even though this denunciation succeeded, the denouncer suffered both discrediting and penalty. Immediately after the delinquency case had been decided the police took out a complaint for "contributing to the delinquency of a minor" against him, based on his admitted homosexual activities with the youth. This "contributing" case was brought before the juvenile court later that same morning, complainant and accused changed places, and the first denouncer was found guilty, primarily from what he had revealed about his behavior earlier in establishing the delinquency complaint.

tion requires that the denounced provide a convincing account for what he claims is an illegitimate accusation. The court will reject any implication that one person will gratuitously accuse another of something he has not done. The youth in the following case can provide this kind of account:

Five young boys were charged with vandalism and with starting a fire in a public school. Juvenile officer explained that he had investigated the incident with the school principal, getting two of the boys to admit their part in the vandalism. These two boys had implicated the other three, all of whom denied the charge.

The judge then took over the questioning, trying to determine whether the three accused had in fact been in the school. In this he leaned heavily on finding out why the first two boys should lie. One of the accused, Ralph Kent, defended himself by saying he had not been at the school and did not know the boy who had named him. Judge asked how this boy had then been able to identify him. Kent replied that he had been a monitor at school, and one of his accusers might have seen him there. And he used to take the other accuser to the basement [lavatory] because the teacher would not trust him alone for fear he would leave the school.

The two other boys continued to deny any involvement in the incident, but could provide no reason why they should be accused unjustly. The judge told them he felt they were lying, and asked several times: "Can you give me a good reason why these boys would put you in it?" Finally he pointed toward Kent and commented: "He's the only one I'm convinced wasn't there." He then asked Kent several questions about what he did as a monitor. When it came to dispositions, Kent was continued without a finding while the four other boys were found delinquent.

In this situation an accused delinquent was able to establish his own reputable character in school (later confirmed by the probation report on his school record), the discredited character of one of his accusers, and a probable motive for their denunciation of him (resentment toward his privileges and position in school) in a few brief sentences. It should be noted, however, that this successful counter-denunciation was undoubtedly facilitated by the fact that denouncers and denounced were peers. It is incomparably more difficult for a youth to establish any acceptable reason why an adult should want to accuse and discredit him wrongfully.

Counter-denunciation occurs most routinely with offenses arising out of the family situation and involving complaints initiated by parents against their own children. Here again it is possible for the child to cast doubt on the parents' motives in taking court action, and on the parents' general character:

A Negro woman with a strong West Indian accent had brought an incorrigible child complaint against her 16-year-old daughter. The mother reported: "She never says anything to me, only to ask, 'Gimme car fare, gimme lunch money.' . . . As for the respect she gave me I don't think I have to tolerate her!" The daughter countered that her mother never let her do anything, and simply made things unbearable for her around the house. She went out nights, as her mother claimed, but only to go over to a girl friend's house to sleep.

This case was continued for several months, during which time a probation officer worked with the girl and the court clinic saw mother and daughter. The psychiatrist there felt that the mother was "very angry and cold." Eventually an arrangement was made to let the girl move in with an older sister.

In this case the daughter was effectively able to blame her mother and her intolerance for the troubled situation in the home. But in addition, counter-denunciation may also shift the focus of the court inquiry from the misconduct charged to the youth onto incidents involving the parents. This shift of attention facilitated the successful counter-denunciation in the following case:

A 16-year-old white girl from a town some distance from the city was charged with shoplifting. But as the incident was described by the police, it became clear that this offense had occurred because the girl had run away from home and needed clean clothes. Police related what the girl had said about running away: She had been babysitting at home and was visited by her boyfriend, who had been forbidden in the house. Her father had come home, discovered this, and beaten her with a strap. (The girl's face still appeared somewhat battered with a large black-and-blue mark on one cheek, although the court session occurred at least three days after the beating.) She had run away that night.

The rest of the hearing centered not on the theft but on the running away and the incident which precipitated it. After the police evidence, the judge asked the girl: "How did you get that mark on your face?" Girl: "My father hit me." Judge: "With his fist?" Girl (hesitating): "Yes, it must have been his fist." Later in the proceeding, the judge asked the girl specifically why she had run away. She emphasized that she had not tried to hide anything; the kids had been up until eleven and the boy had left his bike out front. "I didn't try to hide it. I told them he'd been there."

With this her father rose to defend himself, arguing with some agitation: ". . . His clothes were loose. Her clothes were loose. Her bra was on the floor. . . . She was not punished for the boy being in the house, but for what she did." Girl (turning toward her father): "What about my eye?" Father: "She got that when she fell out of the bed (angrily, but directed toward the judge)." Girl (just as angrily): "What about the black and blue marks?" Father: "Those must have been from the strap."

The relatively high probability of successful counter-denunciation in cases arising from family situations points up the most critical contingency in the use of this protective strategy, the choice of an appropriate object. Denouncers with close and permanent relations with the denounced are particularly vulnerable to counter-denunciation, as the accusation is apt to rest solely on their word and illegitimate motives for the denunciation may be readily apparent. But again, where relations between the two parties are more distant, counter-denunciation has more chance of success where the denouncer is of more or less equivalent status with the denounced. Thus, the judge can be easily convinced that a schoolmate might unjustly accuse one from jealousy, but will reject any contention that an adult woman would lie about an attempted purse-snatching incident.

While a denounced youth has a fair chance of successfully discrediting a complainant of his own age, and some chance where the complainant is a family member, counter-denunciations directed against officials, particularly against the most frequent complainants in the juvenile court, the police, almost inevitably fail. In fact, to attempt to counterattack the police, and to a lesser extent, other officials, is to risk fundamentally discrediting moral character, for the court recoils against all attacks on the moral authority of any part of the official legal system.

One reflection of this is the court's routine refusal to acknowledge complaints of *unfair* treatment at the hands of the police. On occasion, for example, parents complain that their children were arrested and brought to court while others involved in the incident were not. Judges regularly refuse to inquire into such practices:

Two young Puerto Rican boys were charged with shooting a BB gun. After police testimony, their mother said something in Spanish, and their priest-translator explained to the judge: "What they've been asking all morning is why they did not bring the other two boys." The judge replied: "I can only deal with those cases that are before me. I can't go beyond that and ask about these other boys that are not here."

Similarly, in this same case the judge refused to inquire into a complaint of police brutality when the mother complained that one boy had been hit on the head, saying: "The question of whether he was injured is not the question for me right now."

But beyond this, the court will often go to great lengths to protect and defend the public character of the police when it is attacked during a formal proceeding. To accuse a policeman of acting for personal motives, or of dishonesty in the course of his duties, not only brings immediate sanctions from the court, but also tends to discredit basically the character of the delinquent accuser. Accusations of this nature threaten the basic ceremonial order of the court proceeding and hence the legitimacy of the legal order itself. . . .

REFERENCES

McCorkle, Lloyd W., and Richard Korn. 1964. "Resocialization Within Walls." In David Dressler (ed.), *Readings in Criminology and Penology*. New York: Columbia University Press.

Sykes, Gresham M., and David Matza. 1957. "Techniques of Neutralization: A Theory of Delinquency." *American Sociological Review*, 22:664–70.

Screening Mental Patients

THOMAS J. SCHEFF

The case for making the societal reaction to deviance a major independent variable in studies of deviant behavior has been succinctly stated by Kitsuse:

A sociological theory of deviance must focus specifically upon the interactions which not only define behaviors as deviant but also organize and activate the application of sanctions by individuals, groups, or agencies. For in modern society, the socially significant differentiation of deviants from the non-deviant population is increasingly contingent upon circumstances of situation, place, social and personal biography, and the bureaucratically organized activities of agencies of control.[1]

In the case of mental disorder, psychiatric diagnosis is one of the crucial steps which "organizes and activates" the societal reaction, since the state is legally empowered to segregate and isolate those persons whom psychiatrists find to be commitable because of mental illness.

Recently, however, it has been argued that mental illness may be more usefully considered to be a social status than a disease, since the symptoms of mental illness are vaguely defined and widely distributed, and the definition of behavior as symptomatic of mental illness is usually dependent upon social rather than medical contingencies.[2] Furthermore, the argument continues, the status of the mental patient is more often an ascribed status with conditions for status entry external to the patient, than an achieved status, with conditions for status entry dependent upon the patient's own behavior. According to this argument, the societal reaction is a fundamentally important variable in all stages of a deviant career.

The actual usefulness of a theory of mental disorder based on the societal reaction is largely an empirical question: to what extent is entry to the status of mental patient independent of the behavior or "condition" of the patient? The present paper will explore this question for one phase of the societal reaction: the legal screening of persons alleged to be mentally ill. This screening represents the official phase of the societal reaction, which occurs after the alleged deviance has been called to the attention of the community by a complainant. This report will make no ref-

Reprinted from "The Societal Reaction to Deviance: Ascriptive Elements in the Psychiatric Screening of Mental Patients in a Midwestern State" in *Social Problems,* Vol. 11, No. 4 (Spring 1964), pp. 401–413, by permission of the author and *Social Problems.*

With the assistance of Daniel M. Culver this report is part of a larger study, made possible by a grant from The Advisory Mental Health Committee of Midwestern State. By prior agreement, the state in which the study was conducted is not identified in publications.

[1] John I. Kitsuse, "Societal Reaction to Deviant Behavior: Problems of Theory and Method," *Social Problems,* 9 (Winter, 1962), pp. 247–257.

[2] Edwin M. Lemert, *Social Pathology,* New York: McGraw-Hill, 1951; Erving Goffman, *Asylums,* Chicago: Aldine, 1962.

erence to the initial deviance or other situation which resulted in the complaint, but will deal entirely with procedures used by the courts after the complaint has occurred.

The purpose of the description that follows is to determine the extent of uncertainty that exists concerning new patients' qualifications for involuntary confinement in a mental hospital, and the reactions of the courts to this type of uncertainty. The data presented here indicate that, in the face of uncertainty, there is a strong presumption of illness by the court and the court psychiatrists.[3] In the discussion that follows the presentation of findings, some of the causes, consequences and implications of the presumption of illness are suggested.

The data upon which this report is based were drawn from psychiatrists' ratings of a sample of patients newly admitted to the public mental hospitals in a Midwestern state, official court records, interviews with court officials and psychiatrists, and our observations of psychiatric examinations in four courts. The psychiatrists' ratings of new patients will be considered first.

In order to obtain a rough measure of the incoming patient's qualifications for involuntary confinement, a survey of newly admitted patients was conducted with the cooperation of the hospital psychiatrists. All psychiatrists who made admission examinations in the three large mental hospitals in the state filled out a questionnaire for the first ten consecutive patients they examined in the month of June, 1962. A total of 223 questionnaires were returned by the 25 admission psychiatrists. Although these returns do not constitute a probability sample of all

new patients admitted during the year, there were no obvious biases in the drawing of the sample. For this reason, this group of patients will be taken to be typical of the newly admitted patients in Midwestern State.

The two principal legal grounds for involuntary confinement in the United States are the police power of the state (the State's right to protect itself from dangerous persons) and *parens patriae* (the State's right to assist those persons who, because of their own incapacity, may not be able to assist themselves).[4] As a measure of the first ground, the potential dangerousness of the patient, the questionnaire contained this item: "In your opinion, if this patient were released at the present time, is it likely he would harm himself or others?" The psychiatrists were given six options, ranging from Very Likely to Very Unlikely. Their responses were: Very Likely, 5%, Likely, 4%, Somewhat Likely, 14%, Somewhat Unlikely, 20%, Unlikely 37%, Verly Unlikely, 18%. Three patients were not rated (1%).

As a measure of the second ground, *parens patriae,* the questionnaire contained the item: "Based on your observations of the patient's behavior, his present degree of mental impairment is: None _____ Minimal _____ Moderate _____ Severe _____." The psychiatrists' responses were: None, 2%; Minimal, 12%; Mild, 25%; Moderate, 42%; Severe, 17%. Three patients were not rated (1%).

To be clearly qualified for involuntary confinement, a patient should be rated as likely to harm self or others (Very Likely, Likely, or Somewhat Likely) and /or as Severely Mentally Impaired. How-

---

[3] For a more general discussion of the presumption of illness in medicine, and some of its possible causes and consequences, see the author's "Decision Rules, Types of Error and Their Consequences in Medical Diagnosis," *Behavioral Science,* 8 (April, 1963), pp. 97–107.

[4] Hugh Allen Ross, "Commitment of the Mentally Ill: Problems of Law and Policy," *Michigan Law Review,* 57 (May, 1959), pp. 945–1018.

ever, voluntary patients should be excluded from this analysis, since the court is not required to assess their qualifications for confinement. Excluding the 59 voluntary admissions (26% of the sample) leaves a sample of 164 involuntary confined patients. Of these patients, 10 were rated as meeting both qualifications for involuntary confinement, 21 were rated as being severely mentally impaired, but not dangerous, 28 were rated as dangerous but not severely mentally impaired, and 102 were rated as not dangerous nor as severely mentally impaired. (Three patients were not rated.)

According to these ratings, there is considerable uncertainty connected with the screening of newly admitted involuntary patients in the state, since a substantial majority (63%) of the patients did not clearly meet the statutory requirements for involuntary confinement. How does the agency responsible for assessing the qualifications for confinement, the court, react in the large numbers of cases involving uncertainty?

On the one hand, the legal rulings on this point by higher courts are quite clear. They have repeatedly held that there should be a presumption of sanity. The burden of proof of insanity is to be on the petitioners, there must be a preponderance of evidence, and the evidence should be of a "clear and unexceptionable" nature.[5]

On the other hand, existing studies suggest that there is a presumption of illness by mental health officials. In a discussion of the "discrediting" of patients by the hospital staff, based on observations at St. Elizabeth's Hospital, Washington, D.C., Goffman states:

[The patient's case record] is apparently not regularly used to record occasions when the patient showed capacity to cope honorably and effectively with difficult life situations. Nor is the case record typically used to provide a rough average or sampling of his past conduct. [Rather, it extracts] from his whole life course a list of those incidents that have or might have had "symptomatic" significance. . . . I think that most of the information gathered in case records is quite true, although it might seem also to be true that almost anyone's life course could yield up enough denigrating facts to provide grounds for the record's justification of commitment.[6]

Mechanic makes a similar statement in his discussion of two large mental hospitals located in an urban area in California:

In the crowded state or county hospitals, which is the most typical situation, the psychiatrist does not have sufficient time to make a very complete psychiatric diagnosis, nor do his psychiatric tools provide him with the equipment for an expeditious screening of the patient. . . .

In the two mental hospitals studied over a period of three months, the investigator never observed a case where the psychiatrist advised the patient that he did not need treatment. Rather, all persons who appeared at the hospital were absorbed into the patient population regardless of their ability to function adequately outside the hospital.[7]

A comment by Brown suggests that it is a fairly general understanding among mental health workers that state mental hospitals in the U.S. accept all comers.[8]

Kutner, describing commitment procedures in Chicago in 1962, also reports

[5] This is the typical phrasing in cases in the *Dicennial Legal Digest,* found under the heading "Mental Illness."

[6] Goffman, *op. cit.,* pp. 155, 159.

[7] David Mechanic, "Some Factors in Identifying and Defining Mental Illness," *Mental Hygiene* 46 (January, 1962), pp. 66–75.

[8] Esther Lucile Brown, *Newer Dimensions of Patient Care,* Part I, New York: Russell Sage, 1961, p. 60, fn.

a strong presumption of illness by the staff of the Cook County Mental Health Clinic:

Certificates are signed as a matter of course by staff physicians after little or no examination. . . . The so-called examinations are made on an assembly-line basis, often being completed in two or three minutes, and never taking more than ten minutes. Although psychiatrists agree that it is practically impossible to determine a person's sanity on the basis of such a short and hurried interview, the doctors recommend confinement in 77% of the cases. It appears in practice that the alleged-mentally-ill is presumed to be insane and bears the burden of proving his sanity in the few minutes allotted to him. . . .[9]

These citations suggest that mental health officials handle uncertainty by presuming illness. To ascertain if the presumption of illness occurred in Midwestern State, intensive observations of screening procedures were conducted in the four courts with the largest volume of mental cases in the state. These courts were located in the two most populous cities in the state. Before giving the results of these observations, it is necessary to describe the steps in the legal procedures for hospitalization and commitment.

STEPS IN THE SCREENING OF PERSONS ALLEGED TO BE MENTALLY ILL

The process of screening can be visualized as containing five steps in Midwestern State:

1. The application for judicial inquiry, made by three citizens. This application is heard by deputy clerks in two of the courts (C and D), by a court reporter in the third court, and by a commissioner in the fourth court.
2. The intake examination conducted by a hospital psychiatrist.
3. The psychiatric examination, conducted by two psychiatrists appointed by the court.
4. The interview of the patient by the guardian *ad litem,* a lawyer appointed in three of the courts to represent the patient. (Court A did not use guardians *ad litem.*)
5. The judicial hearing conducted by a judge.

These five steps take place roughly in the order listed, although in many cases (those cases designated as emergencies) step No. 2, the intake examination, may occur before step No. 1. Steps No. 1 and No. 2 usually take place on the same day or the day after hospitalization. Steps No. 3, No. 4, and No. 5 usually take place within a week of hospitalization. (In courts C and D, however, the judicial hearing is held only once a month.)

This series of steps would seem to provide ample opportunity for the presumption of health, and a thorough assessment, therefore, of the patient's qualifications for involuntary confinement, since there are five separate points at which discharge could occur. According to our findings, however, these procedures usually do not serve the function of screening out persons who do not meet statutory requirements. At most of these decision points, in most of the courts, retention of the patient in the hospital was virtually automatic. A notable exception to this pattern was found in one of the three state hospitals; this hospital attempted to use step No. 2, the intake examination, as a screening point to discharge patients that the superintendent described as "illegitimate," i.e., patients who do not qualify for involun-

[9] Luis Kutner, "The Illusion of Due Process in Commitment Proceedings," *Northwestern University Law Review,* 57 (Sept., 1962), pp. 383–399.

tary confinement. In the other two hospitals, however, this examination was perfunctory and virtually never resulted in a finding of health and a recommendation of discharge.[10] In a similar manner, the other steps were largely ceremonial in character. For example, in court B, we observed twenty-two judicial hearings, all of which were conducted perfunctorily and with lightning rapidity. (The mean time of these hearings was 1.6 minutes.) The judge asked each patient two or three routine questions. Whatever the patient answered, however, the judge always ended the hearings and retained the patient in the hospital.

What appeared to be the key role in justifying these procedures was played by step No. 3, the examination by the court-appointed psychiatrists. In our informal discussions of screening with the judges and other court officials, these officials made it clear that although the statutes give the court the responsibility for the decision to confine or release persons alleged to be mentally ill, they would rarely if ever take the responsibility for releasing a mental patient without a medical recommendation to that effect. The question which is crucial, therefore, for the entire screening process is whether or not the court-appointed psychiatric examiners presume illness. The remainder of the paper will consider this question.

Our observations of 116 judicial hearings raised the question of the adequacy of the psychiatric examination. Eighty-six of the hearings failed to establish that the patients were "mentally ill" (according to the criteria stated by the judges in interviews).[11] Indeed, the behavior and responses of 48 of the patients at the hearings seemed completely unexceptionable. Yet the psychiatric examiners had not recommended the release of a single one of these patients. Examining the court records of 80 additional cases, there was still not a single recommendation for release.

Although the recommendation for treatment of 196 out of 196 consecutive cases strongly suggests that the psychiatric examiners were presuming illness, particularly when we observed 48 of these patients to be responding appropriately, it is conceivable that this is not the case. The observer for this study was not a psychiatrist (he was a first year graduate student in social work) and it is possible that he could have missed evidence of disorder which a psychiatrist might have seen. It was therefore arranged for the observer to be present at a series of psychiatric examinations, in order to determine whether the examinations appeared to be merely formalities or whether, on the other hand, through careful examination and interrogation, the psychiatrists were able to establish illness even in patients whose appearance and responses were not obviously disordered. The observer was instructed to note the examiners' procedures, the criteria they appeared to use in arriving at their decision, and their reaction to uncertainty.

Each of the courts discussed here employs the services of a panel of physicians as medical examiners. The physicians are paid a flat fee of ten dollars per examination, and are usually assigned

---

[10] Other exceptions occurred as follows: the deputy clerks in courts C and D appeared to exercise some discretion in turning away applications they considered improper or incomplete, at step No. 1; the judge in court D appeared also to perform some screening at step No. 5. For further description of these exceptions see "Social Conditions for Rationality: How Urban and Rural Courts Deal with the Mentally Ill," *American Behavioral Scientist,* 7 (March, 1964), pp. 21–24.

[11] In interviews with the judges, the following criteria were named: Appropriateness of behavior and speech, understanding of the situation, and orientation.

from three to five patients for each trip to the hospital. In court A, most of the examinations are performed by two psychiatrists, who went to the hospital once a week, seeing from five to ten patients a trip. In courts B, C and D, a panel of local physicians was used. These courts seek to arrange the examinations so that one of the examiners is a psychiatrist, the other a general practitioner. Court B has a list of four such pairs, and appoints each pair for a month at a time. Courts C and D have a similar list, apparently with some of the same names as court B.

To obtain physicians who were representative of the panel used in these courts, we arranged to observe the examinations of the two psychiatrists employed by court A, and one of the four pairs of physicians used in court B, one a psychiatrist, the other a general practitioner. We observed 13 examinations in court A and 13 examinations in court B. The judges in courts C and D refused to give us the names of the physicians on their panels, and we were unable to observe examinations in these courts. (The judge in court D stated that he did not want these physicians harassed in their work, since it was difficult to obtain their services even under the best of circumstances.) In addition to observing the examinations by four psychiatrists, three other psychiatrists used by these courts were interviewed.

The medical examiners followed two lines of questioning. One line was to inquire about the circumstances which led to the patient's hospitalization, the other was to ask standard questions to test the patient's orientation and his capacity for abstract thinking by asking him the date, the President, Governor, proverbs, and problems requiring arithmetic calculation. These questions were often asked very rapidly, and the patient was usually allowed only a very brief time to answer.

It should be noted that the psychiatrists in these courts had access to the patient's record (which usually contained the Application for Judicial Inquiry and the hospital chart notes on the patient's behavior), and that several of the psychiatrists stated that they almost always familiarized themselves with this record before making the examination. To the extent that they were familiar with the patient's circumstances from such outside information, it is possible that the psychiatrists were basing their diagnoses of illness less on the rapid and peremptory examination than on this other information. Although this was true to some extent, the importance of the record can easily be exaggerated, both because of the deficiencies in the typical record, and because of the way it is usually utilized by the examiners.

The deficiencies of the typical record were easily discerned in the approximately one hundred applications and hospital charts which the author read. Both the applications and charts were extremely brief and sometimes garbled. Moreover, in some of the cases where the author and interviewer were familiar with the circumstances involved in the hospitalization, it was not clear that the complainant's testimony was any more accurate than the version presented by the patient. Often the original complaint was so paraphrased and condensed that the application seemed to have little meaning.

The attitude of the examiners toward the record was such that even in those cases where the record was ample, it often did not figure in their decision. Disparaging remarks about the quality and usefulness of the record were made by several of the psychiatrists. One of the examiners was apologetic about his use of the record, giving us the impression that he thought that a good psychiatrist would not need to resort to any information outside his own personal examination of the patient. A casual attitude toward the record was openly displayed in 6 of the 26 examinations we observed. In these 6 examinations, the psychiatrist could not (or in 3 cases, did not bother to) locate the record and conducted the examination without it, with one psychiatrist making it a point of pride that he could easily diagnose most cases "blind."

In his observations of the examinations, the interviewer was instructed to rate how well the patient responded by noting his behavior during the interview, whether he answered the orientation and concept questions correctly, and whether he denied and explained the allegations which resulted in his hospitalization. If the patient's behavior during the interview obviously departed from conventional social standards (e.g., in one case the patient refused to speak), if he answered the orientation questions incorrectly, or if he did not deny and explain the petitioners' allegations, the case was rated as meeting the statutory requirements for hospitalization. Of the 26 examinations observed, eight were rated as Criteria Met.

If, on the other hand, the patient's behavior was appropriate, his answers correct, and he denied and explained the petitioners' allegations, the interviewer rated the case as not meeting the statutory criteria. Of the 26 cases, seven were rated as Criteria Not Met. Finally, if the examination was inconclusive, but the interviewer felt that more extensive investigation might have established that the criteria were met, he rated the cases

as Criteria Possibly Met. Of the 26 examined, 11 were rated this way. The interviewer's instructions were that whenever he was in doubt he should avoid using the rating Criteria Not Met.

Even giving the examiners the benefit of the doubt, the interviewer's ratings were that in a substantial majority of the cases he observed, the examination failed to establish that the statutory criteria were met. The relationship between the examiners' recommendations and the interviewer's ratings are shown in the following table.

The interviewer's ratings suggest that the examinations established that the statutory criteria were met in only eight cases, but the examiners recommended that the patient be retained in the hospital in 24 cases, leaving 16 cases which the interviewer rated as uncertain, and in which retention was recommended by the examiners. The observer also rated the patient's expressed desires regarding staying in the hospital, and the time taken by the examination. The ratings of the patient's desire concerning staying or leaving the hospital were: Leave, 14 cases; Indifferent, 1 case; Stay, 9 cases; and Not Ascertained, 2 cases. In only one of the 14 cases in which the patient wished to leave was the interviewer's rating Criteria Met.

The interviews ranged in length from five minutes to 17 minutes, with the mean time being 10.2 minutes. Most of the interviews were hurried, with the

TABLE 1 Observer's Ratings and Examiners' Recommendations

Observer's Ratings		Criteria Met	Criteria Possibly Met	Criteria Not Met	Total
Examiners'	Commitment	7	9	2	18
Recommendations	30-Day Observation	1	2	3	6
	Release	0	0	2	2
	Total	8	11	7	26

questions of the examiners coming so rapidly that the examiner often interrupted the patient, or one examiner interrupted the other. All of the examiners seemed quite hurried. One psychiatrist, after stating in an interview (before we observed his examinations) that he usually took about thirty minutes, stated:

It's not remunerative. I'm taking a hell of a cut. I can't spend 45 minutes with a patient. I don't have the time, it doesn't pay.

In the examinations that we observed, this physician actually spent 8, 10, 5, 8, 8, 7, 17, and 11 minutes with the patients, or an average of 9.2 minutes.

In these short time periods, it is virtually impossible for the examiner to extend his investigation beyond the standard orientation questions, and a short discussion of the circumstances which brought the patient to the hospital. In those cases where the patient answered the orientation questions correctly, behaved appropriately, and explained his presence at the hospital satisfactorily, the examiners did not attempt to assess the reliability of the petitioner's complaints, or to probe further into the patient's answers. Given the fact that in most of these instances the examiners were faced with borderline cases, that they took little time in the examinations, and that they usually recommended commitment, we can only conclude that their decisions were based largely on a presumption of illness. Supplementary observations reported by the interviewer support this conclusion.

After each examination, the observer asked the examiner to explain the criteria he used in arriving at his decision. The observer also had access to the examiner's official report, so that he could compare what the examiner said about the case with the record of what actually occurred during the interview. This supplementary information supports the conclusions that the examiner's decisions are based on the presumption of illness, and sheds light on the manner in which these decisions are reached:

1. The "evidence" upon which the examiners based their decision to retain often seemed arbitrary.

2. In some cases, the decision to retain was made even when no evidence could be found.

3. Some of the psychiatrists' remarks suggest prejudgment of the cases.

4. Many of the examinations were characterized by carelessness and haste. The first question, concerning the arbitrariness of the psychiatric evidence, will now be considered.

In the weighing of the patient's responses during the interview, the physician appeared not to give the patient credit for the large number of correct answers he gave. In the typical interview, the examiner might ask the patient fifteen or twenty questions: the date, time, place, who is President, Governor, etc., what is 11×10, 11×11, etc., explain "Don't put all your eggs in one basket," "A rolling stone gathers no moss," etc. The examiners appeared to feel that a wrong answer established lack of orientation, even when it was preceded by a series of correct answers. In other words, the examiners do not establish any standard score on the orientation questions, which would give an objective picture of the degree to which the patient answered the questions correctly, but seem at times to search until they find an incorrect answer.

For those questions which were answered incorrectly, it was not always clear whether the incorrect answers were due to the patient's "mental illness," or to the time pressure in the interview, the patient's lack of education, or other causes. Some of the questions used to establish orientation were sufficiently difficult that persons not mentally ill might have difficulty with them. Thus one of the examiners always asked, in a rapid-fire manner: "What year is it? What year was it seven years ago? Seventeen years before that?" etc. Only two of the five patients who were asked this series of questions were able to answer it correctly. However, it is a moot question whether a higher percentage of persons in a household survey would be able to do any better. To my knowledge, none of the orientation questions that are used have been checked in a normal population.

Finally, the interpretations of some of the evidence as showing mental illness seemed capricious. Thus one of the patients, when asked, "In what way are a banana, an orange, and an apple alike?" answered, "They are all something to eat." This answer was used by the examiner in explaining his recommendation to commit. The observer had noted that the patient's behavior and responses seemed appropriate and asked why the recommendation to commit had been made. The doctor stated that her behavior had been bizarre (possibly referring to her alleged promiscuity), her affect inappropriate ("When she talked about being pregnant, it was without feeling,") and with regard to the question above:

She wasn't able to say a banana and an orange were fruit. She couldn't take it one step further, she had to say it was something to eat.

In other words, this psychiatrist was suggesting that the patient manifested concreteness in her thinking, which is held to be a symptom of mental illness. Yet in her other answers to classification questions, and to proverb interpretations, concreteness was not apparent, suggesting that the examiner's application of this test was arbitrary. In another case, the physician stated that he thought the

patient was suspicious and distrustful, because he had asked about the possibility of being represented by counsel at the judicial hearing. The observer felt these and other similar interpretations might possibly be correct, but that further investigation of the supposedly incorrect responses would be needed to establish that they were manifestations of disorientation.

In several cases where even this type of evidence was not available, the examiners still recommended retention in the hospital. Thus, one examiner, employed by court A, stated that he had recommended 30-day observation for a patient whom he had thought *not* to be mentally ill, on the grounds that the patient, a young man, could not get along with his parents, and "might get into trouble." This examiner went on to say:

We always take the conservative side [commitment or observation]. Suppose a patient should commit suicide. We always make the conservative decision. I had rather play it safe. There's no harm in doing it that way.

It appeared to the observer that "playing safe" meant that even in those cases where the examination established nothing, the psychiatrists did not consider recommending release. Thus in one case the examination had established that the patient had a very good memory, was oriented and spoke quietly and seriously. The observer recorded his discussion with the physician after the examination as follows:

When the doctor told me he was recommending commitment for this patient too (he had also recommended commitment in the two examinations held earlier that day) he laughed because he could see what my next question was going to be. He said, "I already recommended the release of two patients this month." This sounded like it was the maximum amount the way he said it.

Apparently this examiner felt that he had a very limited quota on the number of patients he could recommend for release (less than two percent of those examined).

The language used by these physicians tends to intimate that mental illness was found, even when reporting the opposite. Thus in one case the recommendation stated "No gross evidence of delusions or hallucinations." This statement is misleading, since not only was there no gross evidence, there was not any evidence, not even the slightest suggestion of delusions or hallucinations, brought out by the interview.

These remarks suggest that the examiners prejudge the cases they examine. Several further comments indicate prejudgment. One physician stated that he thought that most crimes of violence were committed by patients released too early from mental hospitals. (This is an erroneous belief.)[12] He went on to say that he thought that all mental patients should be kept in the hospital at least three months, indicating prejudgment concerning his examinations. Another physician after a very short interview (8 minutes), told the observer:

On the schizophrenics, I don't bother asking them more questions when I can see they're schizophrenic because *I know what they are going to say.* You could talk to them another half hour and not learn any more.

Another physician, finally, contrasted cases in which the patient's family or other initiated hospitalization ("petition cases," the great majority of cases) with those cases initiated by the court:

The petition cases are pretty *automatic.* If the patient's own family wants to get rid of him you know there is something wrong.

The lack of care which characterized the examinations is evident in the forms on which the examiners make their recommendations. On most of these forms, whole sections have been left unanswered. Others are answered in a peremptory and uninformative way. For example, in the section entitled Physical Examination, the question is asked: "Have you made a physical examination of the patient? State fully what is the present physical condition.", a typical answer is "Yes. Fair.", or, "Is apparently in good health." Since in none of the examinations we observed was the patient actually physically examined, these answers appear to be mere guesses. One of the examiners used regularly in court B, to the question "On what subject or in what way is derangment now manifested?" always wrote in "Is mentally ill." The omissions, and the almost flippant brevity of these forms, together with the arbitrariness, lack of evidence, and prejudicial character of the examinations, discussed above, all support the observer's conclusion that, except in very unusual cases, the psychiatric examiner's recommendation to retain the patient is virtually automatic.

Lest it be thought that these results are unique to a particularly backward Midwestern state, it should be pointed out that this state is noted for its pro-

[12] The rate of crimes of violence, or any crime, appears to be less among ex-mental patients than in the general population. Henry Brill and Benjamin Maltzberg, "Statistical Report Based on the Arrest Record of 5354 Ex-patients Released from New York State Mental Hospitals During the Period 1946–48." Mimeo available from the authors; Louis H. Cohen and Henry Freeman, "How Dangerous to the Community Are State Hospital Patients?," *Connecticut State Medical Journal,* 9 (Sept., 1945), pp. 697–700, Donald W. Hastings, "Follow-up Results in Psychiatric Illness," *Amer. Journal of Psychiatry,* 118 (June, 1962), pp. 1078–1086.

gressive psychiatric practices. It will be recalled that a number of the psychiatrists employed by the court as examiners had finished their psychiatric residencies, which is not always the case in many other states. A still common practice in other states is to employ, as members of the "Lunacy Panel," partially retired physicians with no psychiatric training whatever. This was the case in Stockton, California, in 1959, where the author observed hundreds of hearings at which these physicians were present. It may be indicative of some of the larger issues underlying the question of civil commitment that, in these hearings, the physicians played very little part; the judge controlled the questioning of the relatives and patients, and the hearings were often a model of impartial and thorough investigation.

DISCUSSION

Ratings of the qualifications for involuntary confinement of patients newly admitted to the public mental hospitals in a Midwestern state, together with observations of judicial hearings and psychiatric examinations by the observer connected with the present study, both suggest that the decision as to the mental condition of a majority of the patients is an uncertain one. The fact that the courts seldom release patients, and the perfunctory manner in which the legal and medical procedures are carried out, suggest that the judicial decision to retain patients in the hospital for treatment is routine and largely based on the presumption of illness. Three reasons for this presumption will be discussed: financial, ideological, and political.

Our discussions with the examiners indicated that one reason that they perform biased "examinations" is that their rate of pay is determined by the length of time spent with the patient. In recommending retention, the examiners are refraining from interrupting the hospitalization and commitment procedures already in progress, and thereby allowing someone else, usually the hospital, to make the effective decision to release or commit. In order to recommend release, however, they would have to build a case showing why these procedures should be interrupted. Building such a case would take much more time than is presently expended by the examiners, thereby reducing their rate of pay.

A more fundamental reason for the presumption of illness by the examiners, and perhaps the reason why this practice is allowed by the courts, is the interpretation of current psychiatric doctrine by the examiners and court officials. These officials make a number of assumptions, which are now thought to be of doubtful validity:

1. The condition of mentally ill persons deteriorates rapidly without psychiatric assistance.
2. Effective psychiatric treatments exist for most mental illnesses.
3. Unlike surgery, there are no risks involved in involuntary psychiatric treatment: it either helps or is neutral, it can't hurt.
4. Exposing a prospective mental patient to questioning, cross-examination, and other screening procedures exposes him to the unnecessary stigma of trial-like procedures, and may do further damage to his mental condition.
5. There is an element of danger to self or others in most mental illness. It is better to risk unnecessary hospitalization than the harm the patient might do himself or others.

Many psychiatrists and others now argue that none of these assumptions are necessarily correct.

1. The assumption that psychiatric disorders usually get worse without treatment rests on very little other than evi-

dence of an anecdotal character. There is just as much evidence that most acute psychological and emotional upsets are self-terminating.[13]

2. It is still not clear, according to systematic studies evaluating psychotherapy, drugs, etc., that most psychiatric interventions are any more effective, on the average, than no treatment at all.[14]

3. There is very good evidence that involuntary hospitalization and social isolation may affect the patient's life: his job, his family affairs, etc. There is some evidence that too hasty exposure to psychiatric treatment may convince the patient that he is "sick," prolonging what might have been an otherwise transitory episode.[15]

4. This assumption is correct, as far as it goes. But it is misleading because it fails to consider what occurs when the patient who does not wish to be hospitalized is forcibly treated. Such patients often become extremely indignant and angry, particularly in the case, as often happens, when they are deceived into coming to the hospital on some pretext.

5. The element of danger is usually exaggerated both in amount and degree. In the psychiatric survey of new patients in state mental hospitals, danger to self or others was mentioned in about a fourth of the cases. Furthermore, in those cases where danger is mentioned, it is not always clear that the risks involved are greater than those encountered in ordinary social life. This issue has been discussed by Ross, an attorney:

A truck driver with a mild neurosis who is "accident prone" is probably a greater danger to society than most psychotics; yet, he will not be committed for treatment, even if he would be benefited. The community expects a certain amount of dangerous activity. I suspect that as a class, drinking drivers are a greater danger than the mentally ill, and yet the drivers are tolerated or punished with small fines rather than indeterminate imprisonment.[16]

From our observations of the medical examinations and other commitment procedures, we formed a very strong impression that the doctrines of danger to self or others, early treatment, and the avoidance of stigma were invoked partly because the officials believed them to be true, and partly because they provided convenient justification for a pre-existing policy of summary action, minimal investigation, avoidance of responsibility and, after the patient is in the hospital, indecisiveness and delay.

The policy of presuming illness is probably both cause and effect of political pressure on the court from the com-

---

[13] For a review of epidemiological studies of mental disorder see Richard J. Plunkett and John E. Gordon, *Epidemiology and Mental Illness,* New York: Basic Books, 1960. Most of these studies suggest that at any given point in time, psychiatrists find a substantial proportion of persons in normal populations to be "mentally ill." One interpretation of this finding is that much of the deviance detected in these studies is self-limiting.

[14] For an assessment of the evidence regarding the effectiveness of electroshock, drugs, psychotherapy, and other psychiatric treatments, see H. J. Eysenck, *Handbook of Abnormal Psychology,* New York: Basic Books, 1961, Part III.

[15] For examples from military psychiatry, see Albert J. Glass, "Psychotherapy in the Combat Zone," in *Symposium on Stress,* Washington, D.C., Army Medical Service Graduate School, 1953, and B. L. Bushard, "The U.S. Army's Mental Hygiene Consultation Service," in *Symposium on Preventive and Social Psychiatry,* 15–17 (April, 1957), Washington, D.C.: Walter Reed Army Institute of Research, pp. 431–443. For a discussion of essentially the same problem in the context of a civilian mental hospital, cf. Kai T. Erikson, "Patient Role and Social Uncertainty—A Dilemma of the Mentally Ill," *Psychiatry,* 20 (August, 1957), pp. 263–275.

[16] Ross, *op. cit.,* p. 962.

munity. The judge, an elected official, runs the risk of being more heavily penalized for erroneously releasing than for erroneously retaining patients. Since the judge personally appoints the panel of psychiatrists to serve as examiners, he can easily transmit the community pressure to them, by failing to reappoint a psychiatrist whose examinations were inconveniently thorough.

Some of the implications of these findings for the sociology of deviant behavior will be briefly summarized. The discussion above, of the reasons that the psychiatrists tend to presume illness, suggests that the motivations of the key decision-makers in the screening process may be significant in determining the extent and direction of the societal reaction. In the case of psychiatric screening of persons alleged to be mentally ill, the social differentiation of the deviant from the non-deviant population appears to be materially affected by the financial, ideological, and political position of the psychiatrists, who are in this instance the key agents of social control.

Under these circumstances the character of the societal reaction appears to undergo a marked change from the pattern of denial which occurs in the community. The official societal reaction appears to reverse the presumption of normality reported by the Cummings as a characteristic of informal societal reaction, and instead exaggerates both the amount and degree of deviance.[17] Thus, one extremely important contingency influencing the severity of the societal reaction may be whether or not the original deviance comes to official notice. This paper suggests that in the area of mental disorder, perhaps in contrast to other areas of deviant behavior, if the official societal reaction is invoked, for whatever reason, social differentiation of the deviant from the non-deviant population will usually occur.

CONCLUSION

This paper has described the screening of patients who were admitted to public mental hospitals in early June, 1962, in a Midwestern state. The data presented here suggest that the screening is usually perfunctory, and that in the crucial screening examination by the court-appointed psychiatrists, there is a presumption of illness. Since most court decisions appear to hinge on the recommendation of these psychiatrists, there appears to be a large element of status ascription in the official societal reaction to persons alleged to be mentally ill, as exemplified by the court's actions. This finding points to the importance of lay definitions of mental illness in the community, since the "diagnosis" of mental illness by laymen in the community initiates the official societal reaction, and to the necessity of analyzing social processes connected with the recognition and reaction to the deviant behavior that is called mental illness in our society.

[17] Elaine Cumming and John Cumming, *Closed Ranks,* Cambridge, Mass.: Harvard University Press, 1957, 102; for further discussion of the bipolarization of the societal reaction into denial and labeling, see the author's "The Role of the Mentally Ill and the Dynamics of Mental Disorder: A Research Framework," *Sociometry,* 26 (December, 1963), pp. 436–453.

Court Treatment of
Skid Row Alcoholics

JACQUELINE P. WISEMAN

Matching sentences with men who plead guilty is . . . the judge's true concern. This task must be handled within the pressures created by restricting drunk court to a morning session in one court room, regardless of the number of men scheduled to be seen that day.

Up until last year (when drunk arrests were temporarily reduced because of the large number of hippies and civil rights demonstrators in jail), 50 to 250 men were often sentenced with a few hours. Appearance before the judge was handled in platoons of five to 50. This meant the judge decided the fate of each defendant within a few short minutes. Thus judicial compassion attained assembly-line organization and speed.

As a court observer noted:

The Court generally disposes of between 50 and 100 cases per day, but on any Monday there are 200 to 250 and on Monday mornings after holiday weekends the Court may handle as many as 350 cases. I would estimate that, on the average, cases take between 45 seconds and one minute to dispose of.[1]

Later, with drunk arrests drastically curtailed, the court handled no more than 50 cases in an average morning, and perhaps 125 on the weekends, according to the observer.[2] Right after a civil rights demonstration that resulted in many arrests, only 33 persons were observed in drunk court. This reduction in the quantity of defendants, however, did not appear to increase the length of time spent on each person. Rather, it seemed to reduce it. The observer noted the average length of time per person was 30 seconds, although the size of platoons was reduced from 50 to 15 or 20.

SENTENCING CRITERIA

How is the judge able to classify and sentence a large, unwieldy group of defendants so quickly? The answer is he utilizes social characteristics as indicators to signify drinking status—just as in an arrest situation the policeman looked for social characteristics to identify alcoholic troublemaking potential, combined with the arrestee's legal impotence. The effect is essentially the same: the men are objectified into social types for easy classification. In the case of the judge, the legal decision process must be more refined than for a policeman's arrest, no-arrest

From Jacqueline P. Wiseman, *Stations of the Lost: The Treatment of Skid Row Alcoholics,* pp. 88–91, 94–95, 97–100, © 1970. Reprinted by permission of Prentice-Hall, Inc., Englewood Cliffs, New Jersey.

[1] Frederic S. LeClercq, "Field Observations in Drunk Court of the Pacific City Municipal Court" (unpublished memorandum, 1966), p. 1.

[2] These observations were made almost two years after LeClercq made his.

decision. Therefore, the judge's sentencing criteria are more complex, as they must include all possible decision combinations.

From court observations, plus interviews with court officers and judges, three primary criteria for typing defendants in drunk court emerge:

The General Physical Appearance of the Man. Is he shaky and obviously in need of drying out? Here, some of the judges ask the men to extend their hands before sentencing and decide the sentence on the degree of trembling.

Physical appearance may actually be the most potent deciding factor. As one court officer put it, when asked how the judges decide on a sentence:

Primarily by appearance. You can tell what kind of shape they're in. If they're shaking and obviously need drying out, you know some are on the verge of the DT's so these get 10 or 15 days [in jail] to dry out. . . .

One of the seasoned judges said that his criteria were as follows:

I rely on his record and also his "looks." Their "looks" are very important. I make them put their hands out—see if they are dirty and bloody in appearance.[3]

Past Performance. How many times have they been up before the court on a drunk charge before? A record of past arrests is considered to be indicative of the defendant's general attitude toward drinking. The longer and more recent the record, the greater the need for a sentence to aid the defendant to improve his outlook on excessive liquor consumption. (This is in some contradiction to the presumed greater need the man must have for drying out, since previous recent jailings mean that he could not have been drinking for long.)

The previous comment, plus the answer by a court officer to the question, "Who gets dismissed?" illustrate this criteria for sentencing:

A person with no previous arrests [gets dismissed]. If they have had no arrests, then the judge hates for them to have a conviction on their record. *The more arrests they've had and the more recently they've had them, the more likely they are to get another sentence.* (Emphasis mine.) . . .

The Man's Social Position. Does he have a job he could go to? Is he married? Does he have a permanent address, or will he literally be on the streets if he receives a dismissal?

For these data, dress is an all-important clue, age a secondary one. A man who looks down-and-out is more likely to receive a sentence than the well-dressed man. According to a court officer:

If they look pretty beat—clothes dirty and in rags, then you figure that they need some help to stop drinking before they kill themselves. . . .

If they're under 21 we usually give them a kick-out. If they are a business man or a lawyer we have them sign a civil release so they can't sue and let them go. . . .

An observer reports that a judge freed a young man with the following remarks:

I am going to give you a suspended sentence and hope that this experience will be a warning to you. I don't want you to get caught up in the cycle. . . .

Transients form a category of their own and get a special package deal—if they will promise to leave town, they draw a suspended sentence or probation. The parallel between this practice and the police policy of telling some Skid Row drunks to "take a walk" need only be

---

[3] LeClercq, "Field Observations in Drunk Court," p. 12.

mentioned. The following interchanges are illustrative:

Judge: I thought you told me the last time you were here that you were going to leave Pacific City.

Defendant: I was supposed to have left town yesterday. I just got through doing time.

Judge: Go back to Woodland. Don't let me see you in here again or we are going to put you away. Thirty days suspended. . . .

Defendant: I am supposed to leave with the circus tomorrow. If I don't go, I will be out of work for the whole season.

Judge: You promised to leave three times before. Thirty days in the County Jail.

By combining the variables of physical appearance, past performance and social position, a rough description of social types expected in drunk court, and matching sentences for each type is shown in Table [1]. . . .

OTHER SENTENCING ASSISTANCE

Even with the aid of a simplified mental guide, the judge cannot be expected to assemble and assimilate sufficient material on each man, review it, mentally type the man, and then make a sentencing decision in less than a minute. Thus,

TABLE [1] Paradigm of Social Types and Sentences in Drunk Court

Social Type	Probable Sentence
A young man who drank too much: a man under 40, with a job, and perhaps a wife, who has not appeared in court before.	A kick-out or a suspended sentence.
The young repeater: same as above, but has been before the judge several times (may be on way to being an alcoholic).	Suspended sentence or short sentence (five–ten days) to scare him, or possible attendance at Alcoholism School.
The repeater who still looks fairly respectable. (Image vacillating between an alcoholic and a drunk.)	30-day suspended sentence, with possible attendance at Alcoholism School.
Out-of-towner (social characteristics not important as they have nonlocal roots). Therefore not important as to whether overindulged, a chronic drunk, or an alcoholic.	Suspended sentence on condition he leave town. Purpose is to discourage him from getting on local loop and adding to taxpayer's load.
The middle-aged repeater who has not been up for some time. (May be an alcoholic who has relapsed.)	Suspended sentence with required attendance at Alcoholism School or given to custody of Christian Missionaries.
The derelict-drunk who looks "rough," i.e., suffering withdrawal, a hangover, has cuts and bruises, may have malnutrition or some diseases connected with heavy drinking and little eating; a chronic drunk, seedy clothing, stubble beard, etc.	30–60–90 day sentence depending on number of prior arrests and physical condition at time of arrest. (Has probably attended Alcoholism School already.)
The man who looks gravely ill (probably a chronic alcoholic).	County hospital under suspended sentence.

it is not surprising that almost all drunk court judges employ the aid of one assistant and sometimes two court attachés who are familiar with the Row and its inhabitants. These men are known as court liaison officers. Because of personal familiarity with chronic drunkenness offenders, the liaison officers are able to answer questions about each accused person quickly and to recommend a case disposition. Such persons obviously operate as an informal screening board.

The most important court helper in Pacific City is a man who knows most of the Row men by sight and claims also to know their general outlook on alcohol and life. Known to the defendants as "the Rapper," this man often sits behind the judge and suggests informally who would benefit most from probation and assignment to Alcoholism School, who might need the "shaking-up" that jail provides, and who ought to be sent to alcoholic screening at City Hospital and perhaps on to State Mental Hospital. As each man is named, the Rapper whispers to the judge, who then passes sentence.[4]

In Pacific City, the man who was the Rapper for a period of time was an ex-alcoholic who could claim intimate knowledge of the chronic drunkenness offender because he had drunk with them. A relative of the Rapper was highly placed in city politics, and the Rapper made no secret of the fact that his appointment was politically engineered.[5] During the course of the study (several times in fact), the Rapper himself "fell off the wagon" and underwent treatment at Northern State Mental Hospital. . . . While there, the Rapper told about his recent job with the court and how he helped the judge:

Each man arrested has a card with the whole record on it. We would go over the cards before the case came up. We see how many times he's been arrested. I could advise the judge to give them probation or a sentence. Many times, the family would call and request a sentence. I would often arrange for them to get probation plus clothes and a place to stay at one of the halfway houses. Oh, I'll help and help, but when they keep falling off—I get disgusted. . . .[6]

The Christian Missionaries also send a liaison man to the drunk court sessions. He acts as Rapper at special times and thereby also serves in an informal screening capacity. Sponsorship by this organization appears to guarantee that the defendant will get a suspended sentence. For instance, this interchange was observed in court several times:

Judge, turing to Missionary representative: "Do you want him [this defendant]?" (Meaning, "Will you take him at one of your facilities?")
Missionary: (Nods "Yes.")
Judge: "Suspended sentence." . . .

Another observer discussed this arrangement with a veteran judge:

Interviewer: Isn't there any attempt made to consider the men for rehabilitation? The men are screened by the Christian Missionaries usually. The Christian Mis-

---

[4] The use of a "Rapper" is apparently not a local phenomenon. Bogue notes it also in his study of the Chicago Skid Row. See Donald J. Bogue, *Skid Row in American Cities* (Chicago: University of Chicago, 1963), p. 414.

[5] When the Rapper started drinking again, he was not replaced; rather, court officers and an official of the Christian Missionaries, fulfilled his duties.

[6] The Rapper was under treatment again for alcoholism at State Mental Hospital when he made this statement. . . . Kurt Lewin discusses this phenomenon of rejection of one's own (if they are a minority group of some type) in "Self-Hatred Among Jews," Chap. 12 of *Resolving Social Conflict* (New York: Harper Publishing Company, 1945).

sionaries send someone down to the jail who tries to help them. They talk with the men and screen them. Nobody does the job that the Christian Missionaries do in the jails.

Interviewer: The Court abdicates the screening of defendants to the Christian Missionaries, then?

Not completely. We try to keep a record. Some of these men we can help, but most we can't. I know by heart all of their alibis and stories.[7]

Another important informal court post is filled by an employee who is known to some of the men as "the Knocker." The job of the Knocker is to maintain the personal records of the men who appear before drunk court and to supply the judge with this information. A court observer reported the following:

The Knocker spoke to the judge in just about every case. However, I do not know what he said. He may just be reading to the judge the official records, or he may be giving his personal judgment about the possibility of the defendant being picked up again in the near future. One thing seems clear: the judge receives his information from the Knocker just before he hands out the sentence.

Sometimes it is difficult to distinguish the Knocker (who merely gives information to the judge) from the Rapper (who "suggests" the proper sentence). . . .

The operational ideology of the judge in drunk court, although much like that of juvenile court, is lacking in the compassion often shown for juveniles. An attempt is made to sentence the man in terms of his characteristics and not the criminal act he is accused of. Extenuating circumstances of all types are used in arriving at decision. There is no lawyer or advocacy system in operation. The defendant may be discharged to "responsible" persons in the community (this means some member of his family if he has one, or the Christian Missionaries if they exhibit an interest in him.)[8]

Far from freeing the judge to make idiosyncratic personalized decisions, the result of the drunk court system is to standardize drunks on the basis of social types and then with the assistance of court aides objectify them in such a way as to fit the predetermined types. Thus the decision of the patrolman in typification of the Skid Row drinker is not only accepted in the court without question—it is reinforced and embellished.

JUSTIFYING THE SENTENCING PROCESS

How does the municipal court judge, serving in drunk court sessions, allow himself to be a party to such extra-legal activities as platoon sentencing, the heavy reliance on advice from "friends of the court," and the utilization of extraneous social characteristics in setting the sentence? Why is there not a conflict with his self-image of judicial compassion for the individual and scrupulous attention to legal niceties?

For some judges, this conflict is resolved by falling back on the alcoholism-as-an-illness view of drunkenness, and by

[7] LeClercq, "Field Observations in Drunk Court," p. 11.

[8] "The fundamental idea of the (juvenile court) law is that the state must step in and exercise guardianship over a child found under such adverse social or individual conditions as develop crime. . . . It proposes a plan whereby he may be treated, not as a criminal, or legally charged with crime, but as a ward of the state, to receive practically the care, custody, and discipline that are accorded the neglected and dependent child. . . ." *Report Committee of Chicago Bar*, 1899, footnote in Gustav L. Schramm, "Philosophy of the Juvenile Court," in Petersen and Matza (eds.), *Social Controversy* (Belmont, Calif.: Wadsworth Publishing Company, 1963), p. 109.

redefining many of the men who appear before him as *patients* rather than defendants. Thus, when asked to describe their duties, drunk court judges often sound like physicians dealing with troublesome patients for whom they must prescribe unpleasant but necessary medicine, rather than judges punishing men for being a public annoyance. As an example of this:

I know that jail isn't the best place for these men, but we have to do something for them. We need to put them someplace where they can dry out. You can't just let a man go out and kill himself. . . .

This is a grave and almost hopeless problem. But you have to try some kind of treatment. Often they are better off in jail than out on the street. . . .

The drunk court judges sometimes add the wish that the city provided a more palatable alternative to the County Jail, but then reiterate the view that it is better than no help at all.

Court attachés have essentially the same attitude:

Some of these guys are so loaded that they will fall and break their skull if you don't lock them up. Half of these guys have no place to stay anyway except a dingy heap. They are better off in jail. . . .

The whole purpose of the law is to try to help them. It's for the protection of themselves and for others, that's the way the law reads. For example, say you're driving through here [Skid Row] and you hit a drunk. He could get killed and if you don't stop and render aid, you could become a criminal. . . .

Giving them 30 days in County Jail is sometimes a kindness. *You are doing them a favor, like a diabetic who won't take his insulin. Sometimes you must hurt him to help him.* [Emphasis mine.]

Like the Skid Row police, the officers, the judge and his coterie are reinforced

in their definition of the situation as clinical, and of themselves as diagnosticians and social internists, by the fact that relatives often call the court and ask that a man be given time in jail for his own good. The judge usually complies. Furthermore, as has been mentioned, there is at the jail a branch of the Out-Patient Therapy Center that was originally established to work for the rehabilitation of alcoholics. . . . Having this jail clinic allows the drunk court judge to say:

I sentence you to 30 days and I will get in touch with the social worker at the County Jail and she will help you. . . .[9]

I sentence you to therapy with the psychologists at the County Jail. . . . [Also reported by court observers.]

Creation of the Pacific City Alcoholism School also allows the judge to feel that he is fulfilling both judicial and therapeutic duties, giving the defendant a suspended sentence on the condition that he will attend the lecture sessions.

Where the name of the social worker or psychologist of Alcoholism School is not invoked as part of the sentence, an awareness of alcoholism as an illness is frequently used as an introductory statement to indicate the reasoning of the courts for giving a jail sentence.

We realize that you men are sick and need help. Any action I might take, therefore, should not in any sense be construed as punishment. Jail in this case is not a punitive measure, but to help you with your alcoholism problem. . . .

However, the uneasiness of the judge with the jailing of alcoholics has other indicators. The captain of the County Jail, for instance, reports that inmates serving time for public drunkenness have only to write a letter requesting modifica-

[9] Reported by inmate in County Jail on public drunkenness charge.

tion and it is almost automatically forth-coming, something not true for modification requests of prisoners convicted of other misdemeanors.[10]

That drunk court's methods and procedures of handling Row men go against the judicial grain also seems to be indicated by the fact court officers claim a new judge must be "broken in" to drunk court before he operates efficiently. When the judge first arrives, he will sentence differently from an experienced judge and in the direction of greater leniency. This upsets the established pattern.

The result is he is taken in hand and guided to do "the right thing" by the veteran court aids. As one court aid put it:

Most of the judges are pretty good—they rely on us. Sometimes you get a new judge who wants to do things his way. We have to break them in, train them. This court is very different. We have to break new judges in. It takes some of them some time to get adjusted to the way we do things.[11]

The high rate of recidivism of chronic drunkenness offenders leads some experts to question the value of jail as a cure for alcoholism or chronic drunkenness.[12] Publicly, at least, the judges appear to hold to the view that the current arrest and incarceration process *can* be helpful, but that often the alcoholic simply does not respond to "treatment" permanently and needs periodic "doses" of jail-therapy. As one judge put it:

Some men have simply gone so far that you can't do anything for them. They are hopeless. All we can do is send them to jail to dry out from time to time. . . .[13]

[10] Source: Captain, County Jail.

[11] LeClercq, "Field Observations in Drunk Court," p. 7.

[12] As previously mentioned, the chief deputy of County Jail puts the number of recidivists at 85 percent of the total admissions in any one year. A small "loop," made by a chronic drunkenness offender who goes between municipal jail and Skid Row, has been well chronicled by Pittman and Gordon in *The Revolving Door* (Glencoe, Ill.: The Free Press, 1958).

[13] Statement made by Municipal Judge from city near Pacific City.

the effects of formal labels

8

The careers of many deviants take them through correctional or treatment institutions. Some are arrested, charged, tried, sentenced, and sent to prison. Others are processed through a network of health and welfare agencies. Passage through such institutions can have both dramatic and subtle effects. Once it is known, for example, that a person has had contact with such institutions, other people may regard that person as permanently suspect.

In the first reading Rosenhan shows the difficulty mental patients have in disproving a label of insanity. Schwartz and Skolnick show that prospective employers may discriminate against persons who have been accused of a crime, even though later found innocent; thus they illustrate how a deviant status may transcend time, organizational setting, and factual basis. In the final selection, by contrast, Williams and Weinberg, in discussing less than honorable discharge from the military, show that such a situation does not automatically produce lasting stigma or discrimination. Official labeling is not necessarily made public, and labeling that people do not find out about is unlikely to have these effects.

Being Sane in Insane Places

D. L. ROSENHAN

If sanity and insanity exist, how shall we know them?

The question is neither capricious nor itself insane. However much we may be personally convinced that we can tell the normal from the abnormal, the evidence is simply not compelling. It is commonplace, for example, to read about murder trials wherein eminent psychiatrists for the defense are contradicted by equally eminent psychiatrists for the prosecution on the matter of the defendant's sanity. More generally, there are a great deal of conflicting data on the reliability, utility, and meaning of such terms as "sanity," "insanity," "mental illness," and "schizophrenia" (1). Finally, as early as 1934, Benedict suggested that normality and abnormality are not universal (2). What is viewed as normal in one culture may be seen as quite aberrant in another. Thus, notions of normality and abnormality may not be quite as accurate as people believe they are.

To raise questions regarding normality and abnormality is in no way to question the fact that some behaviors are deviant or odd. Murder is deviant. So, too, are hallucinations. Nor does raising such questions deny the existence of the personal anguish that is often associated with "mental illness." Anxiety and depression exist. Psychological suffering exists. But normality and abnormality, sanity and insanity, and the diagnoses that flow from them may be less substantive than many believe them to be.

At its heart, the question of whether the sane can be distinguished from the insane (and whether degrees of insanity can be distinguished from each other) is a simple matter: do the salient characteristics that lead to diagnoses reside in the patients themselves or in the environments and contexts in which observers find them? . . . [T]he belief has been strong that patients present symptoms, that those symptoms can be categorized, and, implicitly, that the sane are distinguishable from the insane. More recently, however, this belief has been questioned. . . . [T]he view has grown that psychological categorization of mental illness is useless at best and downright harmful, misleading, and pejorative at worst. Psychiatric diagnoses, in this view, are in the minds of the observers and are not valid summaries of characteristics displayed by the observed (3–5).

Gains can be made in deciding which of these is more nearly accurate by getting normal people (that is, people who do not have, and have never suffered, symptoms of serious psychiatric disorders) admitted to psychiatric hospitals and then determining whether they were discovered to be sane and, if so, how. If the sanity of such pseudopatients were always detected, there would be prima facie evidence that a sane individual can be distinguished from the insane context in which he is found. . . . If, on the other hand, the sanity of the pseudopatients were never discovered, serious difficulties would arise for those who support traditional modes of psychiatric diagnosis. Given that the hospital staff was not incompetent, that the pseudopatient had been behaving as sanely as he had been outside of the hospital, and that it had never been previously suggested that he belonged in a psychiatric hospital, such an unlikely outcome would support the view that psychiatric diagnosis betrays little about the patient but much about the environment in which an observer finds him.

This article describes such an experiment. Eight sane people gained secret admission to 12 different hospitals (6). Their diagnostic experiences constitute the data of the first part of this article; the remainder is devoted to a description of their experiences in psychiatric institutions. . . .

PSEUDOPATIENTS AND THEIR SETTINGS

The eight pseudopatients were a varied group. One was a psychology graduate student in his 20's. The remaining seven were older and "established." Among them were three psychologists, a pediatrician, a psychiatrist, a painter, and a housewife. Three pseudopatients were women, five were men. All of them employed pseudonyms, lest their alleged diagnoses embarrass them later. Those who were in mental health professions alleged another occupation in order to avoid the special attentions that might be accorded by staff, as a matter of courtesy or caution, to ailing colleagues (7). With the exception of myself (I was the first pseudopatient and my presence was known to the hospital administrator and chief psychologist and, so far as I can tell, to them alone), the presence of pseudopatients and the nature of the re-

search program was not known to the hospital staffs (8).

The settings were similarly varied. In order to generalize the findings, admission into a variety of hospitals was sought. The 12 hospitals in the sample were located in five different states on the East and West coasts. Some were old and shabby, some were quite new. Some were research-oriented, others not. Some had good staff-patient ratios, others were quite understaffed. Only one was a strictly private hospital. All of the others were supported by state or federal funds or, in one instance, by university funds.

After calling the hospital for an appointment, the pseudopatient arrived at the admissions office complaining that he had been hearing voices. Asked what the voices said, he replied that they were often unclear, but as far as he could tell they said "empty," "hollow," and "thud." The voices were unfamiliar and were of the same sex as the pseudopatient. . . .

Beyond alleging the symptoms and falsifying name, vocation, and employment, no further alterations of person, history, or circumstances were made. The significant events of the pseudopatient's life history were presented as they had actually occurred. Relationships with parents and siblings, with spouse and children, with people at work and in school, consistent with the aforementioned exceptions, were described as they were or had been. Frustrations and upsets were described along with joys and satisfactions. These facts are important to remember. If anything, they strongly biased the subsequent results in favor of detecting sanity, since none of their histories or current behaviors were seriously pathological in any way.

Immediately upon admission to the psychiatric ward, the pseudopatient ceased simulating any symptoms of abnormality. In some cases, there was a brief period of mild nervousness and anxiety, since none of the pseudopatients really believed that they would be admitted so easily. Indeed, their shared fear was that they would be immediately exposed as frauds and greatly embarrassed. Moreover, many of them had never visited a psychiatric ward; even those who had, nevertheless had some genuine fears about what might happen to them. Their nervousness, then, was quite appropriate to the novelty of the hospital setting, and it abated rapidly.

Apart from that short-lived nervousness, the pseudopatient behaved on the ward as he "normally" behaved. The pseudopatient spoke to patients and staff as he might ordinarily. Because there is uncommonly little to do on a psychiatric ward, he attempted to engage others in conversation. When asked by staff how he was feeling, he indicated that he was fine, that he no longer experienced symptoms. He responded to instructions from attendants, to calls for medication (which was not swallowed), and to dining-hall instructions. Beyond such activities as were available to him on the admissions ward, he spent his time writing down his observations about the ward, its patients, and the staff. Initially these notes were written "secretly," but as it soon became clear that no one much cared, they were subsequently written on standard tablets of paper in such public places as the dayroom. No secret was made of these activities.

The pseudopatient, very much as a true psychiatric patient, entered a hospital with no foreknowledge of when he would be discharged. Each was told that he would have to get out by his own devices, essentially by convincing the staff that he was sane. The psychological stresses associated with hospitalization were considerable, and all but one of the pseudopatients desired to be discharged almost immediately after being admitted. They were, therefore, motivated not only to behave sanely, but to be paragons of cooperation. That their

behavior was in no way disruptive is confirmed by nursing reports, which have been obtained on most of the patients. These reports uniformly indicate that the patients were "friendly," "cooperative," and "exhibited no abnormal indications."

THE NORMAL ARE NOT DETECTABLY SANE

Despite their public "show" of sanity, the pseudopatients were never detected. Admitted, except in one case, with a diagnosis of schizophrenia (9), each was discharged with a diagnosis of schizophrenia "in remission." The label "in remission" should in no way be dismissed as a formality, for at no time during any hospitalization had any question been raised about any pseudopatient's simulation. Nor are there any indications in the hospital records that the pseudopatient's status was suspect. Rather, the evidence is strong that, once labeled schizophrenic, the pseudopatient was stuck with that label. If the pseudopatient was to be discharged, he must naturally be "in remission"; but he was not sane, nor, in the institution's view, had he ever been sane.

The uniform failure to recognize sanity cannot be attributed to the quality of the hospitals. . . . Nor can it be alleged that there was simply not enough time to observe the pseudopatients. Length of hospitalization ranged from 7 to 52 days, with an average of 19 days. The pseudopatients were not, in fact, carefully observed, but this failure clearly speaks more to traditions within psychiatric hospitals than to lack of opportunity.

Finally, it cannot be said that the failure to recognize the pseudopatients' sanity was due to the fact that they were not behaving sanely. While there was clearly some tension present in all of them, their daily visitors could detect no serious behavioral consequences—nor, indeed, could other patients. It was quite common for the patients to "detect" the pseudopatients' sanity. . . . "You're not crazy. You're a journalist, or a professor [referring to the continual note-taking]. You're checking up on the hospital." While most of the patients were reassured by the pseudopatient's insistence that he had been sick before he came in but was fine now, some continued to believe that the pseudopatient was sane throughout his hospitalization (10). The fact that the patients often recognized normality when staff did not raises important questions.

Failure to detect sanity during the course of hospitalization may be due to the fact that . . . physicians are more inclined to call a healthy person sick . . . than a sick person healthy . . . . The reasons for this are not hard to find: it is clearly more dangerous to misdiagnose illness than health. Better to err on the side of caution, to suspect illness even among the healthy.

But what holds for medicine does not hold equally well for psychiatry. Medical illnesses, while unfortunate, are not commonly pejorative. Psychiatric diagnoses, on the contrary, carry with them personal, legal, and social stigmas (11). It was therefore important to see whether the tendency toward diagnosing the sane insane could be reversed. The following experiment was arranged at a research and teaching hospital whose staff had heard these findings but doubted that such an error could occur in their hospital. The staff was informed that at some time during the following 3 months, one or more pseudopatients would attempt to be admitted into the psychiatric hospital. Each staff member was asked to rate each patient who presented himself at admissions or on the ward according to the likelihood that the patient was a pseudopatient. . . .

Judgments were obtained on 193 patients who were admitted for psychi-

atric treatment. All staff who had had sustained contact with or primary responsibility for the patient—attendants, nurses, psychiatrists, physicians, and psychologists—were asked to make judgments. Forty-one patients were alleged, with high confidence, to be pseudopatients by at least one member of the staff. Twenty-three were considered suspect by at least one psychiatrist. Nineteen were suspected by one psychiatrist *and* one other staff member. Actually, no genuine pseudopatient (at least from my group) presented himself during this period.

The experiment is instructive. It indicates that the tendency to designate sane people as insane can be reversed when the stakes (in this case, prestige and diagnostic acumen) are high. But what can be said of the 19 people who were suspected of being "sane" by one psychiatrist and another staff member? Were these people truly "sane?" . . . There is no way of knowing. But one thing is certain: any diagnostic process that lends itself so readily to massive errors of this sort cannot be a very reliable one.

THE STICKINESS OF PSYCHODIAGNOSTIC LABELS

Beyond the tendency to call the healthy sick—a tendency that accounts better for diagnostic behavior on admission than it does for such behavior after a lengthy period of exposure—the data speak to the massive role of labeling in psychiatric assessment. Having once been labeled schizophrenic, there is nothing the pseudopatient can do to overcome the tag. The tag profoundly colors others' perceptions of him and his behavior.

From one viewpoint, these data are hardly surprising, for it has long been known that elements are given meaning by the context in which they occur. . . . Once a person is designated abnormal, all of his other behaviors and characteristics are colored by that label. Indeed, that label is so powerful that many of the pseudopatients' normal behaviors were overlooked entirely or profoundly misinterpreted. Some examples may clarify this issue.

Earlier I indicated that there were no changes in the pseudopatient's personal history and current status beyond those of name, employment, and, where necessary, vocation. Otherwise, a veridical description of personal history and circumstances was offered. Those circumstances were not psychotic. How were they made consonant with the diagnosis of psychosis? Or were those diagnoses modified in such a way as to bring them into accord with the circumstances of the pseudopatient's life, as described by him?

As far as I can determine, diagnoses were in no way affected by the relative health of the circumstances of a pseudopatient's life. Rather, the reverse occurred: the perception of his circumstances was shaped entirely by the diagnosis. A clear example of such translation is found in the case of a pseudopatient who had had a close relationship with his mother but was rather remote from his father during his early childhood. During adolescence and beyond, however, his father became a close friend, while his relationship with his mother cooled. His present relationship with his wife was characteristically close and warm. Apart from occasional angry exchanges, friction was minimal. The children had rarely been spanked. Surely there is nothing especially pathological about such a history. . . . Observe, however, how such a history was translated in the psychopathological context, this from the case summary prepared after the patient was discharged.

This white 39-year-old male . . . manifests a long history of considerable ambivalence in close relationships, which began in early childhood. A warm relationship with his mother cools during his adolescence. A distant relationship to his father is described as becoming very intense. Affective stability is absent. His attempts to control emotionality with his wife and children are punctuated by angry outbursts and, in the case of the children, spankings. And while he says that he has several good friends, one senses considerable ambivalence embedded in those relationships also. . . .

The facts of the case were unintentionally distorted by the staff to achieve consistency with a popular theory of the dynamics of a schizophrenic reaction (12). Nothing of an ambivalent nature had been described in relations with parents, spouse, or friends. . . . Clearly, the meaning ascribed to his verbalizations (that is, ambivalence, affective instability) was determined by the diagnosis: schizophrenia. An entirely different meaning would have been ascribed if it were known that the man was "normal."

All pseudopatients took extensive notes publicly. Under ordinary circumstances, such behavior would have raised questions in the minds of observers, as, in fact, it did among patients. Indeed, it seemed so certain that the notes would elicit suspicion that elaborate precautions were taken to remove them from the ward each day. But the precautions proved needless. The closest any staff member came to questioning these notes occurred when one pseudopatient asked his physician what kind of medication he was receiving and began to write down the response. "You needn't write it," he was told gently. "If you have trouble remembering, just ask me again."

If no questions were asked of the pseudopatients, how was their writing interpreted? Nursing records for three patients indicate that the writing was seen as an aspect of their pathological behavior. . . . Given that the patient is in the hospital, he must be psychologically disturbed. And given that he is disturbed, continuous writing must be a behavioral manifestation of that disturbance, perhaps a subset of the compulsive behaviors that are sometimes correlated with schizophrenia.

One tacit characteristic of psychiatric diagnosis is that it locates the sources of aberration within the individual and only rarely within the complex of stimuli that surrounds him. Consequently, behaviors that are stimulated by the environment are commonly misattributed to the patient's disorder. For example, one kindly nurse found a pseudopatient pacing the long hospital corridors. "Nervous, Mr. X?" she asked. "No, bored," he said.

The notes kept by pseudopatients are full of patient behaviors that were misinterpreted by well-intentioned staff. Often enough, a patient would go "berserk" because he had, wittingly or unwittingly, been mistreated by, say, an attendant. A nurse coming upon the scene would rarely inquire even cursorily into the environmental stimuli of the patient's behavior. Rather, she assumed that his upset derived from his pathology, not from his present interactions with other staff members. . . . [N]ever were the staff found to assume that one of themselves or the structure of the hospital had anything to do with a patient's behavior. One psychiatrist pointed to a group of patients who were sitting outside the cafeteria entrance half an hour before lunchtime. To a group of young residents he indicated that such behavior was characteristic of the oral-acquisitive nature of the syndrome. It seemed not to occur to him that there were very few things to anticipate in a psychiatric hospital besides eating.

A psychiatric label has a life and an influence of its own. Once the impression has been formed that the patient is schizophrenic, the expectation is that he will continue to be schizophrenic. When a sufficient amount of time has passed, during which the patient has done nothing bizarre, he is considered to be in remission and available for discharge. But the label endures beyond discharge, with the unconfirmed expectation that he will behave as a schizophrenic again. Such labels, conferred by mental health professionals, are as influential on the patient as they are on his relatives and friends, and it should not surprise anyone that the diagnosis acts on all of them as a self-fulfilling prophecy. Eventually, the patient himself accepts the diagnosis, with all of its surplus meanings and expectations, and behaves accordingly (5). . . .

POWERLESSNESS AND DEPERSONALIZATION

Eye contact and verbal contact reflect concern and individuation; their absence, avoidance and depersonalization. The data I have presented do not do justice to the rich daily encounters that grew up around matters of depersonalization and avoidance. I have records of patients who were beaten by staff for the sin of having initiated verbal contact. During my own experience, for example, one patient was beaten in the presence of other patients for having approached an attendant and told him, "I like you." Occasionally, punishment meted out to patients for misdemeanors seemed so excessive that it could not be justified by the most radical interpretations of psychiatric canon. Nevertheless, they appeared to go unquestioned. Tempers were often short. A patient who had not heard a call for medication would be roundly excoriated, and the morning attendants would often wake patients with, "Come on, you m-----f-----s, out of bed!"

Neither anecdotal nor "hard" data can convey the overwhelming sense of powerlessness which invades the individual as he is continually exposed to the depersonalization of the psychiatric hospital. . . .

Powerlessness was evident everywhere. The patient is deprived of many of his legal rights by dint of his psychiatric commitment (13). He is shorn of credibility by virtue of his psychiatric label. His freedom of movement is restricted. He cannot initiate contact with the staff, but may only respond to such overtures as they make. Personal privacy is minimal. Patient quarters and possessions can be entered and examined by any staff member, for whatever reason. His personal history and anguish is available to any staff member (often including the "grey lady" and "candy striper" volunteer) who chooses to read his folder, regardless of their therapeutic relationship to him. His personal hygiene and waste evacuation are often monitored. The [toilets] may have no doors.

At times, depersonalization reached such proportions that pseudopatients had the sense that they were invisible, or at least unworthy of account. Upon being admitted, I and other pseudopatients took the initial physical examinations in a semipublic room, where staff members went about their own business as if we were not there.

On the ward, attendants delivered verbal and occasionally serious physical abuse to patients in the presence of other observing patients, some of whom (the pseudopatients) were writing it all down. Abusive behavior, on the other hand, terminated quite abruptly when other staff members were known to be coming. Staff are credible witnesses. Patients are not.

A nurse unbuttoned her uniform to adjust her brassiere in the presence of an entire ward of viewing men. One did not have the sense that she was being seductive. Rather, she didn't notice us. A group of staff persons might point to a patient in the dayroom and discuss him animatedly, as if he were not there.

One illuminating instance of depersonalization and invisibility occurred with regard to medications. All told,

the pseudopatients were administered nearly 2100 pills . . . Only two were swallowed. The rest were either pocketed or deposited in the toilet. The pseudopatients were not alone in this. Although I have no precise records on how many patients rejected their medications, the pseudopatients frequently found the medications of other patients in the toilet before they deposited their own. As long as they were cooperative, their behavior and the pseudopatients' own in this matter, as in other important matters, went unnoticed throughout.

Reactions to such depersonalization among pseudopatients were intense. Although they had come to the hospital as participant observers and were fully aware that they did not "belong," they nevertheless found themselves caught up in and fighting the process of depersonalization. . . .

THE CONSEQUENCES OF LABELING AND DEPERSONALIZATION

Whenever the ratio of what is known to what needs to be known approaches zero, we tend to invent "knowledge" and assume that we understand more than we actually do. We seem unable to acknowledge that we simply don't know. The needs for diagnosis and remediation of behavioral and emotional problems are enormous. But rather than acknowledge that we are just embarking on understanding, we continue to label patients "schizophrenic," "manic-depressive," and "insane," as if in those words we had captured the essence of understanding. The facts of the matter are that we have known for a long time that diagnoses are often not useful or reliable, but we have nevertheless continued to use them. We now know that we cannot distinguish insanity from sanity. It is depressing to consider how that information will be used.

Not merely depressing, but frightening. How many people, one wonders, are sane but not recognized as such in our psychiatric institutions? How many have been needlessly stripped of their privileges of citizenship, from the right to vote and drive to that of handling their own accounts? How many have feigned insanity in order to avoid the criminal consequences of their behavior, and, conversely, how many would rather stand trial than live interminably in a psychiatric hospital—but are wrongly thought to be mentally ill? How many have been stigmatized by well-intentioned, but nevertheless erroneous, diagnoses? . . . [P]sychiatric diagnoses are rarely found to be in error. The label sticks, a mark of inadequacy forever.

Finally, how many patients might be "sane" outside the psychiatric hospital but seem insane in it—not because craziness resides in them, as it were, but because they are responding to a bizarre setting, one that may be unique to institutions which harbor nether people? Goffman (4) calls the process of socialization to such institutions "mortification"—an apt metaphor that includes the processes of depersonalization that have been described here. And while it is impossible to know whether the pseudopatients' responses to these processes are characteristic of all inmates—they were, after all, not real patients—it is difficult to believe that these processes of socialization to a psychiatric hospital provide useful attitudes or habits of response for living in the "real world."

REFERENCES AND NOTES

1. P. Ash, *J. Abnorm. Soc. Psychol,* 44, 272 (1949); A. T. Beck, *Amer. J. Psychiat.* 119, 210 (1962); A. T. Boisen, *Psychiatry* 2, 233 (1938); N. Kreitman, *J. Ment. Sci.* 107, 876 (1961); N. Kreitman, P. Sainsbury, J. Morrisey, J. Towers, J. Scrivener, *ibid.,* p. 887; H. O. Schmitt and C. P. Fonda, *J. Abnorm. Soc. Psychol.* 52, 262 (1956); W. Seeman, *J. Nerv. Ment.* *Dis.* 118, 541 (1953). For an analysis of these artifacts and summaries of the disputes, see J. Zubin, *Annu. Rev. Psychol,* 18, 373 (1967); L. Phillips and J. G. Draguns, *ibid.,* 22, 447 (1971).

2. R. Benedict, *J. Gen. Psychol.* 10, 59 (1934).

3. See in this regard H. Becker, *Outsiders: Studies in the Sociology of Deviance* (Free Press, New York, 1963); B. M. Braginsky, D. D. Branginsky, K. Ring, *Methods of Madness: The Mental Hospital as a Last Resort* (Holt, Rinehart & Winston, New York, 1969); G. M. Crocetti and P. V. Lemkau, *Amer. Sociol. Rev.* 30, 577 (1965); E. Goffman, *Behavior in Public Places* (Free Press, New York, 1964); R. D. Laing, *The Divided Self: A Study of Sanity and Madness* (Quadrangle, Chicago, 1960); D. L. Phillips, *Amer. Sociol. Rev.* 28, 963 (1963); T. R. Sarbin, *Psychol. Today* 6, 18 (1972); E. Schur, *Amer. J. Sociol.* 75, 309 (1969); T. Szasz, *Law, Liberty and Psychiatry* (Macmillan, New York, 1963); *The Myth of Mental Illness: Foundations of a Theory of Mental Illness* (Hoeber Harper, New York, 1963). For a critique of some of these views, see W. R. Gove, *Amer. Sociol. Rev.* 35, 873 (1970).

4. E. Goffman, *Asylums* (Doubleday, Garden City, N.Y., 1961).

5. T. J. Scheff, *Being Mentally Ill: A Sociological Theory* (Aldine, Chicago, 1966).

6. Data from a ninth pseudopatient are not incorporated in this report because, although his sanity went undetected, he falsified aspects of his personal history, including his marital status and parental relationships. His experimental behaviors therefore were not identical to those of the other pseudopatients.

7. Beyond the personal difficulties that the pseudopatient is likely to experience in the hospital, there are legal and social ones that, combined, require considerable attention before entry. For example, once admitted to a psychiatric institution, it is difficult, if not impossible, to be discharged on short notice, state law to the contrary notwithstand-

ing. I was not sensitive to these difficulties at the outset of the project, nor to the personal and situational emergencies that can arise, but later a writ of habeas corpus was prepared for each of the entering pseudopatients and an attroney was kept "on call" during every hospitalization. I am grateful to John Kaplan and Robert Bartels for legal advice and assistance in these matters.

8. However distasteful such concealment is, it was a necessary first step to examining these questions. Without concealment, there would have been no way to know how valid these experiences were; nor was there any way of knowing whether whatever detections occurred were a tribute to the diagnostic acumen of the staff or to the hospital's rumor network. Obviously, since my concerns are general ones that cut across individual hospitals and staffs, I have respected their anonymity and have eliminated clues that might lead to their identification.

9. Interestingly, of the 12 admissions, 11 were diagnosed as schizophrenic and one, with the identical symptomatology, as manic-depressive psychosis. This diagnosis has a more favorable prognosis, and it was given by the only private hospital in our sample. On the relations between social class and psychiatric diagnosis, see A. deB. Hollingshead and F. C. Redlich, *Social Class and Mental Illness: A Community Study* (Wiley, New York, 1958).

10. It is possible, of course, that patients have quite broad latitudes in diagnosis and therefore are inclined to call many people sane, even those whose behavior is patently aberrant. However, although we have no hard data on this matter, it was our distinct impression that this was not the case. In many instances, patients not only singled us out for attention, but came to imitate our behaviors and styles.

11. J. Cumming and E. Cumming, *Community Ment. Health* 1, 135 (1965); A. Farina and K. Ring, *J. Abnorm. Psychol.* 70, 47 (1965); H. E. Freeman and O. G. Simmons, *The Mental Patient Comes Home* (Wiley, New York, 1963): W. J. Johannsen, *Ment. Hygiene* 53, 218 (1969); A. S. Linsky, *Soc. Psychiat.* 5, 166 (1970).

12. For an example of a similar self-fulfilling prophecy, in this instance dealing with the "central" trait of intelligence, see R. Rosenthal and L. Jacobson, *Pygmalion in the Classroom* (Holt, Rinehart & Winston, New York, 1968).

13. D. B. Wexler and S. E. Scoville, *Ariz. Law Rev.* 13, 1 (1971).

Legal Stigma

RICHARD D. SCHWARTZ
JEROME H. SKOLNICK

Legal thinking has moved increasingly toward a sociologically meaningful view of the legal system. Sanctions, in particular, have come to be regarded in functional terms.[1] In criminal law, for instance, sanctions are said to be designed to prevent recidivism by rehabilitating, restraining, or executing the offender. They are also said to deter others from the performance of similar acts and, sometimes, to provide a channel for the expression of retaliatory motives. In such civil actions as tort or contract, monetary awards may be intended as retributive and deterrent, as in the use of punitive damages, or may be ragarded as a *quid pro quo* to compensate the plaintiff for his wrongful loss.

While these goals comprise an integral part of the rationale of law, little is known about the extent to which they are fulfilled in practice. Lawmen do not as a rule make such studies, because their traditions and techniques are not designed for a systematic examination of the operation of the legal system in action, especially outside the courtroom. Thus, when extra-legal consequences—e.g., the social stigma of a prison sentence—are taken into account at all, it is through the discretionary actions of police, prosecutor, judge, and jury. Systematic information on a variety of unanticipated outcomes, those which benefit the accused as well as those which hurt him, might help to inform these decision makers and perhaps lead to changes in substantive law as well. The present paper is an attempt to study the consequences of stigma associated with legal accusation. . . .

THE EFFECTS OF A CRIMINAL COURT RECORD ON THE EMPLOYMENT OPPORTUNITIES OF UNSKILLED WORKERS

In [a] field experiment, four employment folders were prepared, the same in all respects except for the criminal court record of the applicant. In all of the folders he was described as a thirty-two year old single male of unspecified race, with a high school training in mechanical trades, and a record of successive short term jobs as a kitchen helper, maintenance worker, and handyman. These characteristics are roughly typical of applicants for unskilled hotel jobs in the Catskill resort area of New York State where employment opportunities were tested.[2]

Reprinted from "Two Studies of Legal Stigma" in *Social Problems,* Vol. 10 (Fall, 1962), pp. 133–38, by permission of the authors and *Social Problems.*

[1] Legal sanctions are defined as changes in life conditions imposed through court action.

[2] The generality of these results remains to be determined. The effects of criminal involvement in the Catskill area are probably diminished, however, by the temporary nature of employment, the generally poor qualifications of the work force, and the excess of demand over supply of unskilled labor there. Accordingly, the employment differences among the four treatment groups found in this study are likely, if anything to be *smaller* than would be expected in industries and areas where workers are more carefully selected.

The four folders differed only in the applicant's reported record of criminal court involvement. The first folder indicated that the applicant had been convicted and sentenced for assault; the second, that he had been tried for assault and acquitted; the third, also tried for assault and acquitted, but with a letter from the judge certifying the finding of not guilty and reaffirming the legal presumption of innocence. The fourth folder made no mention of any criminal record.

A sample of one hundred employers was utilized. Each employer was assigned to one of four "treatment" groups.[3] To each employer only one folder was shown; this folder was one of the four kinds mentioned above, the selection of the folder being determined by the treatment group to which the potential employer was assigned. The employer was asked whether he could "use" the man described in the folder. To preserve the reality of the situation and make it a true field experiment, employers were never given any indication that they were participating in an experiment. So far as they knew, a legitimate offer to work was being made in each showing of the folder by the "employment agent."

The experiment was designed to determine what employers would do in fact if confronted with an employment applicant with a criminal record. The questionnaire approach used in earlier studies[4] seemed ill-adapted to the problem since respondents confronted with hypothetical situations might be particularly prone to answer in what they considered a socially acceptable manner. The second alternative—studying job opportunities of individuals who had been involved with the law—would have made

it very difficult to find comparable groups of applicants and potential employers. For these reasons, the field experiment reported here was utilized.

Some deception was involved in the study. The "employment agent"—the same individual in all hundred cases—was in fact a law student who was working in the Catskills during the summer of 1959 as an insurance adjuster. In representing himself as being both an adjuster and an employement agent, he was assuming a combination of roles which is not uncommon there. The adjuster role gave him an opportunity to introduce a single application for employment casually and naturally. To the extent that the experiment worked, however, it was inevitable that some employers should be led to believe that they had immediate prospects of filling a job opening. In those instances where an offer to hire was made, the "agent" called a few hours later to say that the applicant had taken another job. The field experimenter attempted in such instances to locate a satisfactory replacement by contacting an employment agency in the area. Because this procedure was used and since the jobs involved were of relatively minor consequence, we believe that the deception caused little economic harm.

As mentioned, each treatment group of twenty-five employers was approached with one type of folder. Responses were dichotomized: those who expressed a willingness to consider the applicant in any way were termed positive, those who made no response or who explicitly refused to consider the candidate were termed negative. Our results consist of comparisons between positive and nega-

[3] Employers were not approached in pre-selected random order, due to a misunderstanding of instructions on the part of the law student who carried out the experiment during a three and one-half week period. Because of this flaw in the experimental procedure, the results should be treated with appropriate caution. Thus, chi-squared analysis may not properly be utilized. (For those used to this measure, $P < .05$ for Table 1.)

[4] Sol Rubin, *Crime and Juvenile Delinquency*, New York: Oceana, 1958, pp. 151–56.

tive responses, thus defined, for the treatment groups.

Of the twenty-five employers shown the "no record" folder, nine gave positive reponses. Subject to reservations arising from chance variations in sampling, we take this as indicative of the "ceiling" of jobs available for this kind of applicant under the given field conditions. Positive responses by these employers may be compared with those in the other treatment groups to obtain an indication of job opportunities lost because of the various legal records.

Of the twenty-five employers approached with the "convict" folder, only one expressed interest in the applicant. This is a rather graphic indication of the effect which a criminal record may have on job opportunities. Care must be exercised, of course, in generalizing the conclusions to other settings. In this context, however, the criminal record made a major difference.

From a theoretical point of view, the finding leads toward the conclusion that conviction constitutes a powerful form of "status degradation"[5] which continues to operate after the time when, according to the generalized theory of justice underlying punishment in our society, the individual's "debt" has been paid. A record of conviction produces a durable if not permanent loss of status. For purposes of effective social control, this state of affairs may heighten the deterrent effect of conviction—though that remains to be established. Any such contribution to social control, however, must be balanced against the barriers imposed upon rehabilitation of the convict. If the exprisoner finds difficulty in securing menial kinds of legitimate work, further crime may become an increasingly attractive alternative.[6]

Another important finding of this study concerns the small number of positive responses elicited by the "accused but acquitted" applicant. Of the twenty-five employers approached with this folder, three offered jobs. Thus, the individual accused but acquitted of assault has almost as much trouble finding even an unskilled job as the one who was not only accused of the same offense, but also convicted.

From a theoretical point of view, this result indicates that permanent lowering of status is not limited to those explicitly singled out by being convicted of a crime. As an ideal outcome of American justice, criminal procedure is supposed to distinguish between the "guilty" and those who have been acquitted. Legally controlled consequences which follow the judgment are consistent with this purpose. Thus, the "guilty" are subject to fine and imprisonment, while those who are acquitted are immune from these sanctions. But deprivations may be

---

[5] Harold Garfinkel, "Conditions of Successful Degradation Ceremonies," *American Journal of Sociology,* 61 (March, 1956), pp. 420–24.

[6] Severe negative effects of conviction on employment opportunities have been noted by Sol Rubin, *Crime and Juvenile Delinquency,* New York: Oceana, 1958. A further source of employment difficulty is inherent in licensing statutes and security regulations which sometimes preclude convicts from being employed in their pre-conviction occupation or even in the trades which they may have acquired during imprisonment. These effects, may, however, be counteracted by bonding arrangement, prison associations, and publicity programs aimed at increasing confidence in, and sympathy for, exconvicts. See also, B. F. McSally, "Finding Jobs for Released Offenders," *Federal Probation,* 24 (June, 1960), pp. 12–17; Harold D. Lasswell and Richard C. Donnelly, "The Continuing Debate over Responsibility: An Introduction to Isolating the Condemnation Sanction," *Yale Law Journal,* 68 (April, 1959), pp. 869–99; Johs Andenaes, "General Prevention—Illusion or Reality?", *J. Criminal Law, Criminology and Police Science,* 43 (July–August, 1952), pp. 176–98.

imposed on the acquitted, both before and after victory in court. Before trial, legal rules either permit or require arrest and detention. The suspect may be faced with the expense of an attorney and a bail bond if he is to mitigate these limitations on his privacy and freedom. In addition, some pre-trial deprivations are imposed without formal legal permission. These may include coercive questioning, use of violence, and stigmatization. And, as this study indicates, some deprivations not under the direct control of the legal process may develop or persist after an official decision of acquittal has been made.

Thus two legal principles conflict in practice. On the one hand, "a man is innocent until proven guilty." On the other, the accused is systematically treated as guilty under the administration of criminal law until a functionary or official body—police, magistrate, prosecuting attorney or trial judge—decides that he is entitled to be free. Even then, the results of treating him as guilty persist and may lead to serious consequences.

The conflict could be eased by measures aimed at reducing the deprivations imposed on the accused, before and after acquittal. Some legal attention has been focused on pre-trial deprivations. The provision of bail and counsel, the availability of habeas corpus, limitations on the admissibility of coerced confessions, and civil actions for false arrest are examples of measures aimed at protecting the rights of the accused before trial. Although these are often limited in effectiveness, especially for individuals of lower socioeconomic status, they at least represent some concern with implementing the presumption of innocence at the pre-trial stage.

By contrast, the courts have done little toward alleviating the post-acquittal consequences of legal accusation. One effort along these lines has been employed in the federal courts, however. Where an individual has been accused and exonerated of a crime, he may petition the federal courts for a "Certificate of Innocence" certifying this fact.[7] Possession of such a document might be expected to alleviate post-acquittal deprivations.

Some indication of the effectiveness of such a measure is found in the responses of the final treatment group. Their folder, it will be recalled, contained information on the accusation and acquittal of the applicant, but also included a letter from the judge addressed "To whom it may concern" certifying the applicant's acquittal and reminding the reader of the presumption of innocence. Such a letter might have had a boomerang effect, by reemphasizing the legal involvement of the applicant. It was important, therefore, to determine empirically whether such a communication would improve or harm the chances of employment. Our findings indicate that it increased employment opportunities, since the letter folder elicited six positive responses. Even though this fell short of the nine responses to the "no record" folder, it doubled the number for the "accused but acquitted" and created a significantly greater number of job offers than those elicited by the convicted record. This suggests that the procedure merits consideration as a means of offsetting the occupational loss resulting from accusation. It should be noted, however, that repeated use of this device might reduce its effectiveness.

The results of the experiment are summarized in Table 1. The differences in outcome found there indicate that various types of legal records are systematically related to job opportunities. It seems fair to infer also that the trend of job losses corresponds with the apparent punitive intent of the authorities.

[7] 28 United States Code, Secs, 1495, 2513.

TABLE 1 Effect of Four Types of Legal Folder on Job Opportunities (in per cent)

	No Record	Acquitted With Letter	Acquitted Without Letter	Convicted	Total
	(N = 25)	(N = 25)	(N = 25)	(N = 25)	(N = 100)
Positive	36	24	12	4	19
Negative response	64	76	88	96	81
Total	100	100	100	100	100

Where the man is convicted, that intent is presumably greatest. It is less where he is accused but acquitted and still less where the court makes an effort to emphasize the absence of a finding of guilt. Nevertheless, where the difference in punitive intent is ideally greatest, between conviction and acquittal, the difference in occupational harm is very slight. . . .

Homosexuals and the Military

COLIN J. WILLIAMS

MARTIN S. WEINBERG

This selection examines one instance of official labeling: less than honorable discharge from the military for reasons that concern homosexuality. One set of questions that guided the research was: What are the consequences of being officially labeled, of leaving the military with a less than honorable discharge? What are the effects upon a person's perception of himself and others now that he has been adjudged "undesirable"? What are the consequences regarding his life chances, his deviant career, and his relationship to the conventional world?

METHOD

The research design involved comparing male homosexuals who had been less than honorably discharged from the military with homosexuals who received honorable discharges. Two sample sources were utilized: the Mattachine Society of New York and the Society for Individual Rights in San Francisco. Both are homophile organizations with large memberships. Using their mailing lists, those persons who lived in the New York or San Francisco metropolitan areas were respectively selected out.

A short questionnaire was sent to each of these persons. From the responses to this questionnaire it was possible to separate out those who had received a less than honorable discharge due to homosexuality (hereinafter referred to as the LHD group) and a comparison group of homosexuals who had served in the military but who had received honorable discharges (the HD group). It was also possible to estimate the equivalence of the groups at the time of their military service.

Of the 136 respondents who had served in the military and who agreed to be interviewed, we then interviewed 31 who had received less than honorable discharges (LHD) due to their homosexuality and 32 who had received honorable discharges (HD). Included in the personal interview were questions designed to tap the consequences of a less than honorable discharge. On both the initial questionnaire and in the interview a large number of other questions that had nothing to do with the military were also included. These were asked to gather data on other aspects of the homosexual's social and psychological situation. These other questions also concealed the fact that military experiences were the main focus of interest and thereby limited some of the bias that could appear, for example, through the creation of a "sad tale." Thus questions on the military were the last questions to be asked.

Whenever possible, replication was attempted, with data gathered in Chicago by the Institute for Sex Research.

RESULTS

We looked for two main consequences of receiving a less than honorable discharge. The first, which we called subjective effects, involved the way in which the deviant typified himself and others as a result of being officially labeled undesirable. The second, which we called objective effects, involved his behavior, the extent and nature of his social relationships, and the like. If the discharge did have an effect, then the LHD group should be different from the HD group in certain predicted ways.

First, however, *we directly asked the LHD group how they had been affected by their discharge.* From their replies it seemed that in most cases the effects were short-lived, centering mainly on employment difficulties. Those who said the discharge had little or no effect were persons in certain of the professions or who had jobs that did not require an honorable discharge from the military as part of their credentials. Those who said the discharge had effects upon their employment were (a) persons who had problems initially getting employment after discharge, but who eventually found satisfactory jobs after which their discharge was no problem, and (b) persons who by their qualifications or experience had to have security clearances and/or desired employment in federal or local government jobs. For this group the effects of discharge were more enduring in that they could not take advantage of their skills or experience and often were working in jobs they disliked. A second major effect described by many in the LHD group was a feeling of injustice over the way they had been treated by the military.

In addition to examining the LHDs' own analysis of the consequences of a less than honorable discharge, we also compared the HD and LHD groups on a number of subjective measures to see how the groups might differ. Few differences appeared, and of the small differences that did appear, no corroboration appeared in the Chicago data.

With regard to objective differences between the HD and LHD groups the following were found. First, the members of the LHD group were more likely than were members of the HD group to report that they were known to be homosexual (specifically, by their fathers and employers). This can be attributed to one or both of two things. The individual's family and other associates may discover his homosexuality directly as a result of the discharge. Either by an investigation carried out in his hometown or by the curtailment of his service time, suspicion may be aroused and questions asked, resulting in the admission of his homosexuality. Although this did occur in a few cases, we feel this is limited as an explanation. Another explanation is the pressure that can ensue from having a secret differentness that is a matter of public record. The person does not know when this knowledge will appear and discredit him. Thus, in order to gain control of the situation, he may reveal his deviance to others.

In general, these findings were given support from the Chicago replication. The LHD group was more likely than the HD group to report that their fathers, mothers, co-workers, and/or male heterosexual friends knew they were homosexual.

Another difference is that the LHD group was more likely to have considered and attempted suicide than the HD group. Although these differences were not significant for our sample, in the Chicago replication they were highly significant. (The interviews from our sample show that most of the LHD suicide considerations and attempts occurred around the time of their separation from the military.)

The over-all findings, however, were not of a consistency to vitiate our conclusion that while less than honorable discharge may be very traumatic in the short term, *generally* its long-term effects for the majority of respondents are not readily apparent.

How might we explain this?

1. *The Nature of the Deviant Label.* Some deviant labels are more widespread in their consequences than others. In our case, it seems that a less than honorable discharge was restricted in its effects; in other words, the mere fact that a person is officially labeled deviant does not tell us much unless we know the nature of the label and its disruptive potential for those who carry it. With regard to this latter point, we need to know *the conditions under which the stigmatic potential of deviant labels is realized.* For the majority of respondents, managing the stigma of their discharge did not pose insurmountable problems. This we feel is due mainly to the nature of the label itself having little influence outside of certain occupations and appearing on the official records of few of the organizations that circumscribe a person's life.

2. *The Nature of the Labelers.* It is also necessary to know more about those organizations or persons engaged in defining and processing the deviant. In connection with the previous point, *it is important to know the publicity given the labeling and the extent of the interconnectedness of organizations of social control*—that is, whether there is a communication network (formal or informal) whereby the knowledge of a person's deviance held by one such organization is passed on to another. In the case of the military, it was shown that publicity was not evident and information on deviants was seldom passed on to other official agencies as a matter

of course. Consequently, *not all official labeling represents public labeling.*

3. *The Nature of the Deviance. Labeling might have extensive effects upon some forms of deviance but relatively little effect on certain aspects of other forms of deviance.* It is tentatively suggested that this may be true for homosexuals as well as, for example, drug addicts. That is, the simple problem of "supply" can lead addicts, as well as homosexuals, into subcultural involvement, leading to results (change in self-image, etc.) without official labeling that are similar to those that are expected to be a consequence of labeling.

4. *Temporal Features.* Labeling theory deals with the problems caused by labeling as well as with their resolution (e.g., through subcultural or group participation). Consequently, when the investigator comes on the scene, and what segment of the theory s/he links into, is crucial. *Studying similarly labeled deviants at different points in their deviant careers, one can arrive at opposite hypotheses that follow from the labeling perspective (e.g., regarding self-acceptance).* For instance, the newly labeled homosexual, according to one part of the theory, is subject to low self-acceptance, etc., whereas the labeled homosexual who has resolved identity problems by involvement in the homosexual subculture, according to another part of the theory, would be a self-accepting systematic deviant. Thus, even where the theoretical implications of labeling theory seem to be clear and simple their testing can be a complex matter.

5. *Positive, Negative, or Neutral Consequences. It should also be recognized that the consequences of labeling are varied and can be either positive, negative, or neutral.* Being labeled deviant can have positive effects for the secret deviant in that it can resolve his problems of identity. Furthermore, he can use his self-label to get a social label which from his point of view has posi-

tive consequences—homosexuals relatively advanced in their homosexual careers prior to induction who admitted their homosexuality in order to get out of the military are a case in point. The negative consequences of being labeled deviant are very real. In our research, such consequences were especially experienced by those persons who could not work at jobs they were trained for because of the discharge they received. Also, it should be recognized that labeling can have neutral consequences in that no lasting effects are forthcoming. This seemed to be the case for the majority of our sample.

It seems, therefore, that labeling theory is presently an oversimplified conception. The revitalization of the theory by Becker was widely accepted as an antidote to current reified models of deviant behavior. Yet, reification seems to be the fate of labeling theory itself. Lemert's original presentation of the theory involved two elements: (a) the idea of social reaction to deviance—its sociological element—and (b) the idea of socialization to deviance through the production of secondary deviance and deviant self-concept—its social psychological element. The first element has been relatively neglected, whereas the second element has been trivialized. Labeling theory often has been reduced to a theory of stigma determinism, of people locked into deviant careers, never to escape. If the labeling approach is to continue to excite sociologists, the intricacies of social reality must be faced—its social psychological aspect must increase in sophistication, and its sociological aspect must be extended to fulfill its most important promise.

deviant subcultures

Despite popular stereotype, deviant careers are not unilinear; nor do they have fixed and inevitable stages. Some people who commit deviant acts may never be typed as deviant and/or may discontinue those acts, while others may become "hard-core" career deviants. And even those who do become career deviants may do so through widely different routes. Thus there is no single natural history of deviant careers; there are many career histories. One hypothetical deviant career might proceed as follows. A person lives in a culture where certain acts are viewed as deviant. This person is believed, rightly or wrongly, to have committed such deviance. Someone (e.g., teacher, neighbor) types the person as a certain type of deviant. The person comes to the attention of an official agency (e.g., juvenile authorities) and becomes an official case. This social processing propels the person into organized deviant life (e.g., the person is now a "hoodlum"—ostracized by "good kids" and accepted only in disreputable circles). Finally, in self-redefinition, the person assumes the deviant role (i.e., actually becomes a "hood"), thus confirming the initial typing.

This, however, is only one developmental model. Another hypothetical deviant career (which is probably more characteristic of certain kinds of deviance such as professional crime) might proceed along opposite lines. First, the person defines himself or herself as a certain kind of deviant, then enters a deviant world to confirm that identity, comes to official notice, becomes an official case, and engages in more persistent and patterned deviations, thus reinforcing the system of social types. Still other types of deviant careers may require different models. In fact, deviant careers vary so widely that a person might enter the deviance process at any one of the various stages and move forward, backward, or out of the process completely.

Perhaps a visual image will help. Suppose we visualize deviant careers as a long corridor. Each segment of the corridor represents one stage in a deviant career, with doors that allow people to directly enter into or exit from that stage. Some people can enter the deviance corridor from a side door, without previous experience in a deviant career. Others can leave by a side door, thus terminating their deviant careers. Finally, there are some who will enter at one end of the corridor and proceed through all the stages to the other end. The following diagram shows how the traffic of deviance may flow.

Part Three

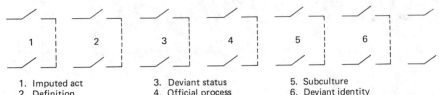

The deviance corridor

| 1 | 2 | 3 | 4 | 5 | 6 |

1. Imputed act
2. Definition
3. Deviant status
4. Official process
5. Subculture
6. Deviant identity

The dotted lines represent the invisible boundaries marking stages of a person's deviant career. At each of these symbolic boundaries there are defining agents who speed certain people farther along the corridor and usher others out the side doors or back to where they started.

The rate and direction of a person's progress through the corridor are based largely on the person's responses to others' symbolic definitions of him or her. In addition to conventional people, those who type and respond to the deviant often include members of the deviant subculture; thus these people can be an important influence in solidifying a person's deviant career.

The fact that a person has been assigned a deviant label does not mean that s/he will automatically be drawn into a deviant subculture. Nonetheless, dilettantes in deviance and career deviants alike are likely to become involved with a deviant subculture at some time. Thus Part Three of this book examines the rise and nature of deviant subcultures. It then goes on to examine how people enter deviant worlds, and how they learn subcultural traditions. Finally, it considers social variations within and among deviant subcultures.

THE RISE AND NATURE OF DEVIANT SUBCULTURES

A subculture is apt to come into being when people are in contact with one another, suffer a common fate, and have common interests. These common interests generally arise from their social situation and are shared because these people face more or less the same dilemma.

The general dilemma for the persons who ultimately become involved in deviant subcultures is that they want to continue activities that the society labels deviant but at the same time they want to avoid punishment. When enough people become aware that they share such a problem, a deviant subculture can arise to provide a solution.

When these people are especially concerned with continuing their activities, the deviant group forms on the basis of a common attraction; an example would be the gay subculture. When people are thrust together because of official typing, on the other hand, the deviant group forms on the basis of shared punishment; the prison subculture is one example. Finally, if it is merely by chance that the persons engage together in deviant activities, they do not actually form a subculture. Race riots provide an example.

ENTRY AND ACCULTURATION

Entry refers to the ways in which a person comes to participate in and gain admittance to a deviant world. *Acculturation* refers to the new ways and meanings a person acquires from that world. Entry can be clearly defined (where a person clearly is or is not a member of the subculture), or it can be rather loose in character. Likewise, acculturation can be highly specialized or casual and offhand. Like colleges, subcultures vary in how hard they are to get into and how hard they are to stay in. Much of this depends on the complexity of the activities involved, on how much commitment others in the subculture expect from newcomers, and on how much they must rely on them for their own safety and welfare. With a team of pickpockets, for example, entry and socialization are rigorous. On the other hand, admission and socialization to a Skid Row bottle gang are relatively simple. Here all a person needs is a few coins to "go in on a bottle," and there is relatively little to learn.

SUBCULTURAL VARIATIONS

Some deviants become highly involved in deviant worlds, but this is not true for all deviants. Within a particular subculture (e.g., the "hippie" subculture) some people may be highly immersed while others (e.g., weekend visitors) may participate only occasionally. Also, some forms of deviance lend themselves to more involvement in a subculture than do others. Because they have to be highly mobile, check forgers, for example, may be marginal to any kind of social group, conventional or deviant. Skid Row drunks, on the other hand, are freer to immerse themselves in a subculture. In addition, covert deviants (e.g., "closet queens") are generally less engulfed in an unconventional way of life and engage in the deviant world sporadically and secretly. Overt deviants (e.g., gay activists) ordinarily find themselves more involved in an unconventional way of life that stipulates a regular schedule of activities and a circle of intimate and deviant acquaintances.

Sanctions that deviants bring against one another are also important. Social control operates in deviant ways of life just as it does in the conventional world. How well do deviant groups control members? In general, it seems that in some subcultures (e.g., organized crime) members are subject to more social control than in others (e.g., the gay subculture). Also, it seems that within a subculture more social control is exerted over some members (e.g., a novice) than over others (e.g., a leader in the group).

Subcultures have beliefs, values, and norms that are supposed to regulate conduct. These prescriptions contribute to a form of social order. Deviant groups vary in the extent to which they organize their activities and define them by subcultural rules: some have elaborate rules that specify beliefs and actions; others have simpler codes. A simple, tightly organized code leads to one set of consequences, a complex, loosely organized code to another. In addition, some deviant subcultures have rules and beliefs that protect and dignify their members while others spawn normlessness, induce exploitation, and set deviants against one another.

Within a subculture some members show more commitment to the deviant way of life than do others. How dependent the person is on the deviant subculture, the person's identity, how much the person shares the viewpoints of others in the subculture—all these seem to be factors influencing a person's commitment to the subculture.

the rise and nature of deviant subcultures

9

In most cases a so-called deviant is not unique or alone. There are often many other people who have been similarly typed; they may also have been similarly punished (e.g., imprisoned) for their alleged deviance and thus further differentiated from conventional society. If such people come into contact with one another, they may form their own subculture in which to gain acceptance and support. Also, when they are interested in continuing their "deviant ways," a subculture may arise to offer good opportunities for them to do so. These conditions and others discussed in the readings to follow, then, may lead to the rise of deviant subcultures.

In the first reading Cohen lists some of the general conditions that are necessary for the development of subcultures. In the second reading he describes the social situation faced by working-class youths and how this gave rise to the delinquent subculture. Simmons then examines the nature of deviant subcultures, and in the next reading Yablonsky illustrates Simmons' points with research on delinquent gangs. Finally, Matza describes the misconceptions surrounding the subculture of juvenile delinquency and argues that the subculture of delinquency is really supported by the larger society as a "subterranean" tradition.

A Theory of Subcultures

ALBERT K. COHEN

. . . The crucial condition for the emergence of new cultural forms is the existence, *in effective interaction with one another, of a number of actors with similar problems of adjustment.* These may be the entire membership of a group or only certain members, similarly circumstanced, within the group. Among the conceivable solutions to their problems may be one which is not yet embodied in action and which does not therefore exist as a cultural model. This solution, except for the fact that it does not already carry the social criteria of validity and promise the social rewards of consensus, might well answer more neatly to the problems of this group and appeal to its members more effectively than any of the solutions already institutionalized. For each participant, this solution would be adjustive and adequately motivated provided that he could anticipate a simultaneous and corresponding transformation in the frames of reference of his fellows. Each would welcome a sign from the others that a new departure in this direction would receive approval and support. But how does one *know* whether a gesture toward innovation will strike a responsive and sympathetic chord in others or whether it will elicit hostility, ridicule and punishment? *Potential* concurrence is always problematical and innovation or the impulse to innovate a stimulus for anxiety.

The paradox is resolved when the innovation is broached in such a manner as to elicit from others reactions suggesting their receptivity, and when, at the same time, the innovation occurs by increments so small, tentative and ambiguous as to permit the actor to retreat, if the signs be unfavorable, without having become identified with an unpopular position. Perhaps all social actions have, in addition to their instrumental, communicative and expressive functions, this quality of being *exploratory gestures*. For the actor with problems of adjustment which cannot be resolved within the frame of reference of the established culture, each response of the other to what the actor says and does is a clue to the directions in which change may proceed further in a way congenial to the other and to the direction in which change will lack social support. And if the probing gesture is motivated by tensions common to other participants it is likely to initiate a process of *mutual* exploration and *joint* elaboration of a new solution. My exploratory gesture functions as a cue to you, your exploratory gesture as a cue to me. By a casual semi-serious, noncommittal or tangential remark I may stick my neck out just a little way, but I will quickly withdraw it unless you, by some sign of affirmation, stick *yours* out. I will permit myself to become progressively committed but only as others, by some visible sign, become likewise committed. The final product, to which we are jointly committed, is likely to be a compromise formation of all the participants to what we may call a cultural process, a formation perhaps unanticipated by any of them. Each actor may contribute directly to the growing product, but he may also contribute indirectly by encouraging others to advance, inducing them to retreat, and suggesting new avenues to be explored. The product cannot be ascribed to any one of the participants; it is a real "emergent" on a group level. . . .

The emergence of these "group standards" of this shared frame of reference, is the emergence of a new subculture. It is cultural because each actor's participation in this system of norms is influenced by his perception of the same norms in other actors. It is *sub*cultural because the norms are shared only among those actors who stand somehow to profit from them and who find in one another a sympathetic moral climate within which these norms may come to fruition and persist. In this fashion culture is continually being created, re-created and modified wherever individuals sense in one another like needs, generated by like circumstances, not shared generally in the larger social system. Once established, such a subcultural system may persist, but not by sheer inertia. It may achieve a life which outlasts that of the individuals who participated in its creation, but only so long as it continues to serve the needs of those who succeed its creators.

One variant of this cultural process interests us especially because it provides the model for our explanation of the delinquent subculture. Status problems are problems of achieving respect in the eyes of one's fellows. Our ability to achieve status depends upon the criteria of status applied by our fellows, that is, the standards or norms they go by in evaluating people. These criteria are an aspect of their cultural frames of reference. If we lack the characteristics or capacities which give status in terms of these criteria, we are beset by one of the most typical and yet distressing of human problems of adjustment. One solution is for individuals who share such problems to gravitate toward one another and jointly to establish new norms, new criteria of status which define as meritorious the characteristics they *do* possess, the kinds of conduct of which they *are* capable. It is clearly necessary for each participant, if the innovation is to solve his status problem, that these new criteria be shared with others, that the solution be a group and not a private solution. If he "goes it alone" he succeeds only in further estranging himself from his fellows. Such new status criteria would represent new subcultural values different from or even antithetical to those of the larger social system.

The Delinquent Subculture

ALBERT K. COHEN

. . . I have addressed the question: Why is delinquency disproportionately frequent among lower-class youth, and why does so much of it have no manifest point or utility, but seem rather to proceed from a spirit of pure meanness, negativism, contrariness, and the like?[1] Very briefly summarized, my argument states that young people's self-feelings depend very largely upon how they are judged by others. In this country the stages on which they perform and the situations in which they are judged—most notably, the school situation—are largely dominated by middle-class people, and the standards or measuring rods by which they are judged are those current among middle-class people. They are not, however, exclusively middle-class standards. They express the dominant American value system; they pervade the mass media, and they are also applied, although in a less thoroughgoing way, by "respectable" working-class people. These standards include such criteria as verbal fluency, academic intelligence, high levels of aspiration, drives for achievement, capacity for sustained effort in the service of long-run goals, the ability to delay gratification, neatness, cleanliness, polished manners, and others. It is also a characteristic of American culture generally—an aspect of its "democratic" ethos—that young people of different origins and backgrounds tend to be judged by the same

standards, so that young people of different social class, race, and ethnicity find themselves competing with one another for status and approval under the same set of rules. However, they are not all equally well-equipped for success in this status game. In particular, different patterns of socialization are associated with the different social classes and middle-class socialization is far more effective in training children for such success than is lower-class socialization. For this and other reasons, lower-class children are more likely to experience failure and humiliation. In brief, they are caught up in a game in which others are typically the winners and they are the losers and the also-rans.

One way they can deal with this problem is to repudiate and withdraw from the game, to refuse to recognize the rules as having any application to them, and to set up new games with their own rules or criteria of status—rules by which they *can* perform satisfactorily. It is not, however, quite that simple. The dominant value system is also, to a degree, *their* value system. They can *tell* themselves that they don't really care about what people think of them, and about the things these people think are important, but their internalized values, even if repressed, threaten always to break through and dilute their satisfaction with the alternative they have chosen. Therefore, to buttress this

Reprinted from *Deviance and Control* by Albert K. Cohen, pp. 65–66; © 1966, by permission of the author and Prentice-Hall, Inc., Englewood Cliffs, N.J.
[1] Albert K. Cohen, *Delinquent Boys: The Culture of the Gang* (New York: The Free Press, 1955).

choice, to protect it from incursions from "the enemy within as well as the enemy without," they resort to reaction-formation. They not only reject the dominant value system, but do so with a vengeance. They "stand it on its head"; they exalt its opposition; they engage in malicious, spiteful, "ornery" behavior of all sorts to demonstrate not only to others, but to themselves as well, their contempt for the game they have rejected. . . .

The Nature of Deviant Subcultures

J. L. SIMMONS

In response to society's disapproval and harassment deviants usually band together with others in the same plight. Beyond the ties of similar interests and views which lie at the base of most human associations, deviants find that establishing fairly stable relationships with other deviants does much to ease procurement and coping problems and to provide a more stable and reliable source of direct support and interaction. In these indirect ways, society's condemnation "creates" the deviant subculture. When disapproval eases, the "subculture" may attenuate or even disintegrate. For example, the present subculture of [drug] users is something like the subculture of alcohol drinkers during Prohibition.

"Deviant subculture" is a stripped-down scientific abstraction for a very real and concrete thing—most deviants live in connection with other deviants and "sympathizers," even if this be only half a dozen people in a little Midwestern town. And such subcultures evolve their own little communities or social worlds, each with its own local myths (the county attorney goes easy with us cause he's an old head himself), its own legendary heroes (remember Max—what a crazy one he was), its own honorary members (Blaine the druggist or Sophie at the cafe), its own scale of reputations (Garth's all right, he's just a little slow about some things), and its own social routine (probably see you at the Totem later on tonight).

The term is useful because it points to something important; deviants tend to get together. There are deviant traditions and ideologies, deviant prestige systems, commitment and conformity to deviant codes, deviant recruitment and missionary work, and deviant utopian dreams.

But the social scientists have also been taken in by their own word game. My conclusion from field research with two rural delinquent gangs, a health food coterie, two mystic groups, several beatnik and hippie groups, and various student fringe groups is that "deviant subcultures" are in actuality far from the tightly-knit, highly cohesive, clearly structured entities they are pictured to be in social science literature, police records, or the press. These misconceptions are projected onto what, in reality, is usually no more than a bunch of people with ever-shifting, overlapping relationships. Such groups are amorphous and quite unstable through time. Goals and purposes, moral codes, and even memberships are often only semi-conscious. Commitment and loyalties to the group wax and wane, and they are seldom dependable. I recall the remark of a mischievous teenager in Cedar Rapids, Iowa: "I had no idea I belonged to a

From J. L. Simmons, *Deviants* (Berkeley, Calif.: The Glendessary Press, 1969), pp. 88–92. Copyright © 1969 by The Glendessary Press.

delinquent gang until the cops told me."

The notion of "deviant subculture," therefore, is itself a stereotype which is partly true but also false in several important respects. Lewis Yablonsky's concept, "near-group"—a collectivity of people whose degree of cohesion and organization falls somewhere between a mob and a true group—applies, I think, far more accurately to the realities of deviants associating together. There are shared understandings among the participants, but their interpersonal relations are also shot through with many misunderstandings and miscarried intentions. Any "organization" is usually informal, uncrystallized and unstable beyond a few weeks.

With a few notable exceptions, such as the Hell's Angels, the commitment of the participants to one another and to the group as a whole is tenuous and half-hearted. For individual "members" it varies. On one occasion it may be an intense brotherhood; on the next the individuals may be willing to sell each other out to save themselves or to obtain some small personal gain. (Sometimes this personal gain may be no more than the undivided attention of a reporter or a bit of flattery from an investigator.)

Membership itself is often vague, and the line between "us" and "them" wavers and changes. . . . The dichotomy of members and nonmembers is oversimple; usually a few core members are unequivocally committed, a larger circle of part-time members drift back and forth between conventionality and deviance, and an even larger circle are only tangentially acquainted or involved. These last two circles, and sometimes even the few at the core, constantly move in and out of the subculture. They are occupied with a variety of conventional as well as deviant activities and commitments. Rather than being the essential part of their lives, the deviance may be only a casual weekend thing or the result of an occasional spree.

The supposed members are often not very clear in their own minds on what the group is about, who else is in it, what it attempts to accomplish. And different members will give conflicting views on these matters.

Even leadership and other designations of functions are vague and constantly changing. Factionalism and incessant internal shifts in personal status are the rule rather than the exception. Internal statuses tend to be negotiated and temporary, so control of individual members by the group isn't really all that extensive.

These vagaries are why drug use or black radicalism or homosexuality can't be eradicated by dealing with the supposed leaders. There are eminent people in these and similar fringe movements but there is no "head to lop off." A teacher in one of the depressed schools of Wichita, Kansas, exclaimed after the assassination of Martin Luther King, "Good, that'll be the end of all this trouble and unrest." I could only feel sorry for her on various counts.

We mustn't, however, err in the opposite direction by suggesting that the whole subculture notion is false. A deviant's closer associates are statistically most likely to be other fringe people. There are discernible deviant social worlds, partially insulated and estranged from the society at large, each with its subterranean traditions, its own literature and slang, its own beliefs and ways of looking at things. All these things exist but in varying degrees, not as hard and fast characteristics.

The ambivalence of the participants is the main thing that keeps deviant subcultures from becoming more solid. Most members are of two minds about deviating and most of them still have many conventional commitments. My observations suggest that the vast majority of deviants inhabit dual worlds of deviance/ conventionality and when things aren't going well in the one they turn to the other. They vacillate between the two as situations and opportunities shift. . . .

A visible deviant group is the symptom and surface of some larger and more widespread fringe drift within the society. The Women's Christian Temperance Union, for instance, was only the organized spearhead of a Prohibition backlash against the perceived moral decline of urbanism—the Prohibition mood was felt by far more people than were members of this organization, and it spread beyond a fight against liquor into action against illicit drugs, sex, political liberalism and so on. Delinquent gangs were only the more spectacular aspects of the failure of the huge metropolis to take humane care of its inhabitants. The hippies are only the more far out examples of the pervasive unrest and disillusionment of a whole generation of youth with standard-brand America. And the Black Panthers are but a more vocal and visible swell on the surface of a deep militant thrust of twenty million blacks for a place in the sun.

Sometimes changes in these fringe drifts will leave particular deviant groups aground to flounder and finally expire for lack of underlying support. This seems to be the fate of the old Marxist radicals in the United States, younger radicals have gone beyond Communism as well as capitalism. . . .

More often there is a number of different . . . groups expressing a range of different positions in the fringe drift. Most such groups are more fleeting and unstable than the underlying deviant subcultural drift that spawned them. Wife-swapping clubs, sexual freedom leagues . . . are only facets of the erotic revolution in our time.

Societal condemnation gives powerful support to the creation and continuation of these deviant groups. Even when the members don't altogether agree with or even like each other they are thrown together because they may have nowhere else to turn for help and support. But just about everything else is against them. Unlike conventional associations, deviant groups must solve their internal conflicts and problems without any supports from the larger society. . . .

The Delinquent Gang As a Near-Group

LEWIS YABLONSKY

. . . Some recent sociological theory and discourse on gangs suffers from distortions of gang structure to fit a group rather than a near-group conception. Most gang theorizing begins with an automatic assumption that gangs are defined sociological groups. Many of these misconceived theories about gangs in sociological treatises are derived from the popular and traditional image of gangs held by the general public as reported in the press, rather than as based upon empirical scientific investigation. The following cast material reveals the disparities between popular reports of gang war behavior and their organization as revealed by more systematic study.

The official report of a gang fight, which made headlines in New York papers as the biggest in the city's history, detailed a gang war between six gangs over a territorial dispute.[1] The police, social workers, the press, and the public accepted a defined version of groups meeting in battle over territory. Research into this gang war incident, utilizing a near-group concept of gangs, indicates another picture of the situation.

N.Y. Daily News
NIP 200—PUNK FIGHT NEAR COLUMBIA CAMPUS
by Grover Ryder and Jack Smee
A flying squad of 25 cops, alerted by a civilian's tip, broke up the makings of one of the biggest gang rumbles in the city's turbulent teen history last night at the edge of Columbia University campus on Morningside Heights.

N.Y. Herald Tribune
POLICE SEIZE 38, AVERT GANG BATTLE—RIVERSIDE PARK RULE WAS GOAL
Police broke up what they said might have been "a very serious" battle between two juvenile factions last night as they intercepted thirty-eight youths.

N.Y. Times
GANG WAR OVER PARK BROKEN BY POLICE
The West Side police broke up an impending gang fight near Columbia University last night as 200 teen-agers were massing for battle over exclusive rights to the use of Riverside Park.

N.Y. Journal-American
6–GANG BATTLE FOR PARK AVERTED NEAR GRANT'S TOMB COPS PATROL TROUBLE SPOT
Police reinforcements today patrolled Morningside Heights to prevent a teen-aged gang war for "control" of Riverside Park.

World-Telegram and Sun
HOODLUM WAR AVERTED AS COPS ACT FAST
38 to 200 Seized Near Columbia
by Richard Graf
Fast police action averted what threatened to be one of the biggest street gang fights in the city's history as some 200

Reprinted from *Social Problems*, Vol. 7, No. 2 (Fall 1959), pp. 108–117 by permission of the author and *Social Problems*. This is a revised version of a paper delivered at The Eastern Sociological Meetings in New York City, April 11, 1959. [A larger version of the theory of near-groups and gang data presented in this paper can be found in *The Violent Gang*, Baltimore, Md.: Penguin Books, 1966.]

[1] New York newspaper headlines—June 11, 1955.

hoodlums massed last light on the upper West Side to battle over "exclusive rights" to Riverside Park.

Depth interviews with 40 gang boys, most of whom had been arrested at the scene of the gang fight, revealed a variety of reasons for attendance at the battle. There were also varied perceptions of the event and the gangs involved reported simply in the press as "gangs battling over territory." Some of the following recurring themes were revealed in the gang boys' responses.

Estimates of number of gang boys present varied from 80 to 5,000.

Gang boys interviewed explained their presence at the "battle" as follows:

I didn't have anything to do that night and wanted to see what was going to happen.

Those guys called me a Spic and I was going to get even. [He made this comment even though the "rival" gangs were mostly Puerto Ricans.]

They always picked on us. [The "they" is usually a vague reference.]

I always like a fight; it keeps up my rep.

My father threw me out of the house; I wanted to get somebody and heard about the fight.

The youth who was responsible for "calling on" the gang war—the reputed Balkan Gang leader—presented this version of the event:

That night I was out walkin' my dog about 7:30. Then I saw all these guys coming from different directions. I couldn't figure out what was happening. Then I saw some of the guys I know and I remembered we had called it on for that night.

I never really figured the Politicians [a supposed "brother Gang" he had called] would show.

Another boy added another dimension to "gang war organization":

How did we get our name? Well, when we were in the police station, the cops kept askin' us who we were. Jay was studying history in school—so he said how about The Balkans. Let's call ourselves the Balkans. So we told the cops—we're the Balkans—and that was it.

Extensive data revealed this was not a case of two organized groups meeting in battle. The press, public, police, social workers, and others projected group conceptions onto a near-group activity. Most of the youths at the scene of the gang war were, in fact, participating in a kind of mob action. Most had no real concept of belonging to any gang or group; however, they were interested in a situation which might be exciting and possibly a channel for expressing some of their aggressions and hostilities. Although it was not necessarily a defined war, the possibilities of a stabbing or even a killing were high—with a few hundred disturbed and fearful youths milling around in the undefined situation. The gang war was not a social situation of two structured teen-aged armies meeting on a battlefield to act out a defined situation; it was a case of two near-groups in action.

Another boy's participation in this gang war further reveals its structure. The evening of the fight he had nothing to do, heard about this event and decided that he would wander up to see what was going to happen. On his way to the scene of the rumored gang fight he thought it might be a good idea to invite a few friends "just to be on the safe side." This swelled the final number of youths arriving at the scene of the gang fight, since other boys did the same. He denied (and I had no reason to disbelieve him) belonging to either of the gangs and the same applied to his friends. He was arrested at the scene of "battle" for disorderly conduct and weapon-carrying.

I asked him why he had carried a knife and a zip gun on his person when he went to the gang fight if he did not belong to either of the reputed gangs and intended to be merely a "peaceful observer." His response: "Man, I'm not going to a rumble without packin'." The boy took along weapons for self-defense in the event he was attacked. The possibilities of his being attacked in an hysterical situation involving hundreds of youths who had no clear idea of what they were doing at the scene of a gang fight was, of course, great. Therefore, he was correct (within his social framework) in taking along a weapon for self-protection.

These characteristic responses to the situation when multiplied by the numbers of others present characterize the problem. What may be a confused situation involving many aggressive youths (belonging to near-groups) is often defined as a case of two highly mechanized and organized gang groups battling each other with definition to their activities.

In another "gang war case" which made headlines, a psychotic youth acted out his syndrome by stabbing another youth. When arrested and questioned about committing the offense, the youth stated that he was a member of a gang carrying out retaliation against another gang, which was out to get him. He attributed his assault to gang affiliation.

The psychotic youth used the malleable near-group, the gang, *as his psychotic syndrome.* Napoleon, God, Christ, and other psychotic syndromes, so popular over the years, may have been replaced on city streets by gang membership. Not only is it a convenient syndrome, but some disturbed youths find their behavior as rational, accepted, and even aggrandized by many representatives of society. Officials such as police officers and social workers, in their interpretation of the incident, often amplify this individual behavior by a youth

into a group gang war condition because it is a seemingly more logical explanation of a senseless act.

In the case of the Balkans, the societal response of viewing them as a group rather than a near-group solidified their structure. After the incident, as one leader stated it, "lots more kids wanted to join."

Another gang war event further reveals the near-group structure of the gang. On the night of July 30, 1957, a polio victim named Michael Farmer was beaten and stabbed to death by a gang varyingly known as the Egyptian Kings and the Dragons. The boys who participated in this homicide came from the upper West Side of Manhattan. I had contact with many of these boys prior to the event and was known to others through the community program I directed. Because of this prior relationship the boys cooperated and responded openly when I interviewed them in the institutions where they were being held in custody.[2]

Responses to my interviews indicated the near-group nature of the gang. Some of the pertinent responses which reveal this characteristic of the Egyptian King gang structure are somewhat demonstrated by the following comments made by five of the participants in the killing. (These are representative comments selected from over ten hours of recorded interviews.)

I was walking uptown with a couple of friends and we ran into Magician [one of the Egyptian King gang leaders] and them there. They asked us if we wanted to go to a fight, and we said yes. When he asked me if I wanted to go to a fight, I couldn't say no. I mean, I could say no, but for old time's sake, I said yes.

[2] The research and interviewing at this time was combined with my role as consultant to the Columbia Broadcasting System. I assisted in the production of a gang war documentary narrated by Edward R. Murrow, entitled "Who Killed Michael Farmer?" The documentary tells the story of the killing through the actual voices of the boys who committed the act.

Everyone was pushin' and I pulled out my knife. I saw this face—I never seen it before, so I stabbed it.

He was laying on the ground lookin' up at us. Everyone was kicking, punching, stabbing. I kicked him on the jaw or someplace; then I kicked him in the stomach. That was the least I could do was kick 'im.

They have guys watching you and if you don't stab or hit somebody, they get you later. I hit him over the head with a bat. [Gang youths are unable to articulate specific individuals of the vague "they" who watch over them.]

I don't know how many guys are in the gang. They tell me maybe a hundred or a thousand. I don't know them all. [Each boy interviewed had a different image of the gang.]

These comments and others revealed the gang youths' somewhat different perceptions and rationale of gang war activity. There is a limited consensus of participants as to the nature of the gang war situations because the gang structure—the collectivity which defines gang war behavior—is amorphous, diffuse, and malleable.

Despite the fact of gang phenomena taking a diffuse form, theoreticians, social workers, the police, the press, and the public autistically distort gangs and gang behavior toward a gestalt of clarity. The rigid frame of perceiving gangs as groups should shift to the fact of gangs as near-groups. This basic redefinition is necessary if progress is to be made in sociological diagnosis as a foundation for delinquent gang prevention and correction. . . .

NEAR-GROUP STRUCTURE

Research into the structure of 30 groups revealed three characteristic levels of membership organization. In the center of the gang, on the first level, are the most psychologically disturbed members—the leaders. It is these youths who require and need the gang most of all. This core of disturbed youths provides the gang's more cohesive force. In a gang of some 30 boys there may be five or six who are central or core members because they desperately need the gang in order to deal with their personal problems of inadequacy. These are youths always working to keep the gang together and in action, always drafting, plotting, and talking gang warfare. They are the center of the near-group activity.

At a second level of near-group organization in the gang, we have youths who claim affiliation to the gang but only participate in it according to their emotional needs at given times. For example, one of the Egyptian Kings reported that if his father had not given him a "bad time" and kicked him out of the house the night of the homicide, he would not have gone to the corner and become involved in the Michael Farmer killing. This second-level gang member's participation in the gang killing was a function of his disturbance on that particular evening. This temporal gang need is a usual occurrence.

At a third level of gang participation, we have peripheral members who will join in with gang activity on occasion, although they seldom identify themselves as members of the gang at times. This type of gang member is illustrated by the youth who went along with the Egyptian Kings on the night of the Farmer killing, as he put it, "for old time's sake." He just happened to be around on that particular evening and went along due to a situational condition. He never really "belonged" to the gang nor was he defined by himself or others as a gang member.

The size of gangs is determined in great measure by the emotional needs of its members at any given point. It is not a measure of actual and live membership. Many of the members exist only on the thought level. In the gang, if the boys feel particularly hemmed in (for paranoid reasons), they will expand the number of their near-group. On the other hand, at other times when they feel secure, the gang's size is reduced to include only those youths known on a face-to-face basis. The research revealed that, unlike an actual group, no member of a near-group can accurately determine the number of its membership at a particular point in time.

For example, most any university department member will tell you the number of other individuals who comprise the faculty of their department. It is apparent that if there are eight members in a department of psychology, each member will know each other member, his role, and the total number of members of the department. In contrast, in examining the size of gangs or near-group participation, the size increases in almost direct relationship to the lack of membership clarity. That is, the second- and third-level members are modified numerically with greater ease than the central members. Third level members are distorted at times to an almost infinite number.

In one interview, a gang leader distorted the size and affiliations of the gang as his emotional state shifted. In an hour interview, the size of his gang varied from 100 members to 4,000, from five brother gangs or alliances to 60, from about ten square blocks of territorial control to include jurisdiction over the five boroughs of New York City, New Jersey, and part of Philadelphia.

Another characteristic of the gang is its lack of role definition. Gang boys exhibit considerable difficulty and contradiction in their roles in the gang. They may say that the gang is organized for protection and that one role of a gang is to fight. How, when, whom, and for what reason he is to fight are seldom clear. The rights, duties, and obligations associated with the gang member's role in

the gang varies from gang boy to gang boy.

One gang boy may define himself as a protector of the younger boys in the neighborhood. Another defines his role in the gang as "We are going to get all those guys who call us Spics." Still other gang boys define their participation in the gang as involuntarily forced upon them, through their being "drafted." Moreover, few gang members maintain a consistent function or role within the gang organization.

Definition of membership is vague and indefinite. A youth will say he belongs one day and will quit the next without necessarily telling any other gang member. I would ask one gang boy who came into my office daily whether he was a Balkan. This was comparable to asking him, "How do you feel today?"

Because of limited social ability to assume rights, duties, and obligations in constructive solidified groups, the gang boy attaches himself to a structure which requires limited social ability and can itself be modified to fit his momentary needs. This malleability factor is characteristic of the near-group membership. As roles are building blocks of a group, diffuse role definitions fit in adequately to the near-group which itself has diverse and diffuse objectives and goals. The near-group, unlike a true group, has norms, roles, functions, cohesion, size, and goals which are shaped by the emotional needs of its members.

GANG LEADERSHIP CHARACTERISTICS

Another aspect of near-groups is the factor of self-appointed leadership, usually of a dictatorial, authoritarian type. In interviewing hundreds of gang members one finds that many of them give themselves some role of leadership. For example, in the Egyptian Kings, approximately five boys defined themselves as "war counsellors." It is equally apparent that, except on specific occasions, no one will argue with this self-defined role. Consequently, leadership in the gang may be assumed by practically any member of the gang if he so determines and emotionally needs the power of being a leader at the time. It is not necessary to have his leadership role ratified by his constituents.

Another aspect of leadership in the gang is the procedure of "drafting" or enlisting new members. In many instances, this pattern of coercion to get another youth to join or belong to the gang becomes an end in itself, rather than a means to an end. In short, the process of inducing, coercing, and threatening violence upon another youth, under the guise of getting him to join, is an important gang leader activity. The gang boy is not truly concerned with acquiring another gang member, since the meaning of membership is vague at best; however, acting the power role of a leader forcing another youth to do something against his will becomes meaningful to the "drafter."

GANG FUNCTIONS

In most groups some function is performed or believed to be performed. The function which it performs may be a constructive one, as in an industrial organization, a P.T.A. group, or a political party. On the other hand, it may be a socially destructive group, such as a drug syndicate, a group of bookies, or a subversive political party. There is usually a consensus of objectives and goals shared by the membership, and their behavior tends to be essentially organized group action.

The structure of a near-group is such that its functions not only vary greatly and shift considerably from time to time, but its primary function is unclear. The gang may on one occasion be organized to protect the neighborhood; on another occasion, to take over a particular territory, and on still another, it may be organized in response to or for the purpose of racial discrimination.

The function of near-groups, moreover, is not one which is clearly understood, known, and communicated among all of its members. There is no consensus in this near-group of goals, objectives, or functions of the collectivity—much near-group behavior is individualistic and flows from emotional distrubance.

A prime function of the gang is to provide a channel to act out hostility and aggression to satisfy the continuing and momentary emotional needs of its members. The gang is a convenient and malleable structure quickly adaptable to the needs of emotionally disturbed youths, who are unable to fulfill the responsibility and demands required for participation in constructive groups. He belongs to the gang because he lacks the social ability to relate to others and to assume responsibility for the relationship, not because the gang gives him a "feeling of belonging."

Because of the gang youth's limited "social ability," he constructs a social organization which enables him to relate and to function at his limited level of performance. In this structure norms are adjusted so that the gang youth can function and achieve despite his limited ability to relate to others.

An example of this is the function of violence in the near-group of the gang. Violence in the gang is highly valued as a means for the achievement of reputation or "rep." This inversion of societal norms is a means for quick upward social mobility in the gang. He can acquire and maintain a position in the gang through establishing a violent reputation.

The following comments by members of the Egyptian Kings illustrate this point:

If I would of got the knife, I would have stabbed him. That would have gave me more of a build-up. People would have respected me for what I've done and things like that. They would say, "There goes a cold killer."

It makes you feel like a big shot. You know some guys think they're big shots and all that. They think, you know, they got the power to do everything they feel like doing.

They say, like, "I wanna stab a guy," and the other guy says, "Oh, I wouldn't dare to do that." You know, he thinks I'm acting like a big shot. That's the way he feels. He probably thinks in his mind, "Oh, he probably won't do that." Then, when we go to a fight, you know, he finds out what I do.

Momentarily, I started to thinking about it inside: den I have my mind made up I'm not going to be in no gang. Then I go on inside. Something comes up den here come all my friends coming to me. Like I said before, I'm intelligent and so forth. They be coming to me—then they talk to me about what they gonna do. Like, "Man, we'll go out here and kill this guy." I say, "Yeah." They kept on talkin' and talkin'. I said, "Man, I just gotta go with you." Myself, I don't want to go, but when they start talkin' about what they gonna do, I say, "So, he isn't gonna take over my rep. I ain't gonna let him be known more than me." And I go ahead just for selfishness.

The near-group of the gang, with its diffuse and malleable structure, can function as a convenient vehicle for the acting out of varied individual needs and problems. For the gang leader it can be a super-powered organization through which (in his phantasy) he dominates and controls "divisions" of thousands of members. For gang members, unable to achieve in more demanding social organizations, swift and sudden violence is a means for quick upward social mobility and the achievement of a reputation. For less disturbed youths, the gang may function as a convenient temporary escape from the dull and rigid requirements of a difficult and demanding society. These are only some of the functions the near-group of the gang performs for its membership.

NEAR-GROUP THEORY AND SOCIAL PROBLEMS

The concept of the near-group may be of importance in the analysis of other collectivities which reflect and produce social problems. The analysis of other social structures may reveal similar distortions of their organization. To operate on an assumption that individuals in interaction with each other, around some function, with some shared mutual expectation, in a particular normative system as always being a group formation is to project a degree of distortion onto certain types of collectivities. Groups are social structures at one end of a continuum; mobs are social structures at another end; and at the center are near-groups which have some of the characteristics of both, and yet are characterized by factors not found fully in either.

In summary, these factors may include the following:

1. Individualized role definition to fit momentary needs.
2. Diffuse and differential definitions of membership.
3. Emotion-motivated behavior.
4. A decrease of cohesiveness as one moves from the center of the collectivity to the periphery.
5. Limited responsibility and sociability required for membership and belonging.
6. Self-appointed and disturbed leadership.
7. A limited consensus among participants of the collectivities' functions or goals.

8. A shifting and personalized stratification system.

9. Shifting membership.

10. The inclusion in size of phantasy membership.

11. Limited consensus of normative expectations.

12. Norms in conflict with the inclusive social system's prescriptions.

Although the gang was the primary type of near-group appraised in this analysis, there are perhaps other collectivities whose structure is distorted by autistic observers. Their organization might become clearer if subjected to this conceptual scheme. Specifically, in the area of criminal behavior, these might very well include adult gangs varyingly called the "Mafia," the "National Crime Syndicate," and so-called International Crime Cartels. There are indications that these social organizations are comparable in organization to the delinquent gang. They might fit the near-group category if closely analyzed in this context, rather than aggrandized and distorted by mass media and even Senate Committees.

Other more institutionalized collectivities might fit the near-group pattern. As a possible example, "the family in transition" may not be in transition at all. The family, as a social institution, may be suffering from near-groupism. Moreover, such standardized escape hatches of alcoholism, psychoses, and addictions may be too prosaic for the sophisticated intellectual to utilize in escape from himself. For him, the creation and perpetuation of near-groups requiring limited responsibility and personal commitment may be a more attractive contemporary form of expressing social and personal pathology. The measure of organization or disorganization of an inclusive social system may possibly be assessed by the prevalence of near-group collectivities in its midst. The delinquent gang may be only one type of near-group in American Society.

The Nature of Delinquent Commitment

DAVID MATZA

. . . A distinctive feature of the subculture of delinquency is that its beliefs are imbedded in action. This is partially true of all traditions but never as much so as in delinquency. We speak of the delinquent code as if it existed somewhere clearly displayed. There are such patent codes in modern society. Their hallmark is that they are written. The code of delinquency is relatively latent. It is not written, except by sociologists, nor is it even well verbalized. Delinquency is well characterized as a relatively inarticulate oral tradition. Its precepts are neither codified nor formally transmitted. Rather, they are inferred from action which obviously includes speech. An ideology of delinquency in the sense of a coherent viewpoint is implicit in delinquent action, but this ideology is not known to delinquents. They are not conscious of an ideology because they have not bothered to work it out. Thus, they infer ideology from each other. This is the primary relevance of the situation of company. It is that context in which the subculture of delinquency is mutually inferred. Mutual inference is accomplished through concrete verbal directives, hints, sentiments, gestures, and activities. But as long as the subculture is inferred, it is not taught in the usual sense of the term. Instead, it is cued.[1] Each member of the company infers the subculture from the cues of others. The company is in a state of acute mutual dependence since there is no coherent ideology which may be consulted. There are only specific and concrete slogans. But there is no explicit general theory.

The mutual inference is a delinquent subculture. Each member believes that others are committed to their delinquencies. But what about each member, what does he believe of himself? Has he not revealed in a variety of other situations that he is not so committed? Possibly, he is transformed in the situation of company to a committed delinquent by dint of the cues he has received from others. Possibly, however, each member believes himself to be an exception in the company of committed delinquents. The intricate system of cues may be miscues. Since the subculture must be constructed from the situation of company, it may be misconstructed. But is this not implausible? All that would be necessary to straighten out the mess would be a discussion. The company consists of friends, and surely if delinquency is public, attitudes toward it could similarly become part of the common knowledge. But that does not necessarily follow. In every public, there is the realm of privacy. There are things that are not openly discussed, and thus

Reprinted from *Delinquency and Drift* by David Matza (New York: John Wiley & Sons, Inc., 1964), pp. 51–59, 62–64, by permission of the author and John Wiley & Sons, Inc.

[1] Albert K. Cohen, *Delinquent Boys,* New York: Free Press, 1955, pp. 59–62.

do not become part of the common knowledge. Frequently, the basis of privacy is *status anxiety*.[2] As such, it may preface a system of shared misunderstanding.

Status anxiety is not likely to attain publicity. Its distinctive feature is that the dissipation of anxiety may occur only through reassurance from those parties whose perceived rebuff initiated anxiety. The anxiety is about status, about how one *stands* within a specific or general company. A person suffering such anxiety may either put the question—how do I stand with you?—or, anticipating rebuff, he may indefinitely postpone it, in which case the anxiety is never dissipated, but instead is expressed in one way or another. Why does the delinquent suffer status anxiety, of what sort, and why does he not put the question?

The situation of delinquent company elicits two related anxieties. One reason for both may be found in an innocent pastime—sounding. Sounding is a daily and almost incessant activity of the delinquent company. But because of its mundane and legal quality, its effects have remained unconsidered. Sounding reflects the delinquent's status anxieties, and it aggravates them by minimizing the likelihood that they will be publicized and thus dissipated.

Sounding . . . is a probing of one's depth, taking the form of insult. One's depth is never definitively certified. It is sounded almost daily. One's depth is probed along a number of dimensions, but two loom most important. Most sounding is a probing of one's manliness and one's membership. Are you really a man, or just a kid? Are you really one of us, or just faking it? Thus, each delinquent in the situation of company suffers generally from masculinity anxiety and specifically from membership anxiety. He can hardly avoid these anxieties. He is sounded daily by a jury of peers. Note, there is initially nothing different about the substance of delinquent anxiety. Most boys suffer some degree of masculinity and membership anxiety. But sounding which may or may not reflect greater initial anxiety eventuates in either case in an increase in the level of anxiety. Note, also, that the consequence of masculinity and membership anxiety is not delinquency, but only the prevention of publicity regarding the evaluation of delinquent acts. The function of anxiety is the limitation of discussion and common knowledge. Thus, it is a key fact in the emergence of the possibility of mutual misconception culminating in a system of shared misunderstanding. Each thinks others are committed to delinquency.

Why are the questions of masculinity and membership not put? And assuming my answer to be plausible, why does it follow that the question of delinquency is not put? The questions of membership and masculinity are not put because given the history of sounding one can anticipate the following kinds of responses: "Do I really like you? Yea, come here and suck and I'll show you how much I like you." "Are you really a man? Well, I don't know, man, sometimes I think you a kid and sometimes you a fag." The anticipation of these sorts of response makes good sense since one excellent way of temporarily alleviating one's own anxiety is the invidious derogation of others. Sounding is both a source of anxiety and a vehicle by which it may be temporarily alleviated.

The question of evaluation of delinquency is not put because it is almost immediately translated into a question of masculinity or membership. "Do I think that stealing a car is a good thing? Man,

---

[2] For a more extensive use of a conception of status anxiety with respect to politics, see the essays in Daniel Bell, *The New American Right,* New York: Criterion, 1955.

you a fag or something? Ain't you one of the boys?" The serious discussion of sentiments regarding delinquency is prevented by frivolous replies whose motive is a demonstration of depth and thus a suggestion that a formal sounding is unnecessary. Thus, the delinquent in the situation of company *does not consider his* misdeeds. Instead, he infers the assessments of others from barbed remarks whose basic motive is not an exposition of the subculture but an alleviation of status anxiety. Whatever the motive, however, the function of such remarks is to mislead the delinquent into believing that his subculture is committed to delinquency.

Is the delinquent forever trapped in this comedy of errors? I think not. Moreover, I believe that the ways out may be taken as partial confirmation of what surely seems a strange and implausible hypothesis. . . . The majority of delinquents do not become adult criminals. Among the manifold and complex reasons for the drift out of delinquency is one that is immediately pertinent. The serious evaluation of delinquency does attain publicity but not in the situations of company thus far described. There are two situations of company, one crescive and mundane, the other contrived and esoteric in which the public evaluation of delinquency may occur. Publicity and its implicit potential for correcting possible misconceptions and misunderstandings is commonly a preface to the drift out of delinquency.

The occasion for crescive and mundane publicity is friendship ideally involving two buddies. Why two? Sounding is a public display of feud. Since the couple are friendly they are not given to feuding except for appearance sake. When they are alone there is no wider company before whom to perform. Public evaluation of delinquency is possible in the situation of isolated couples. Though possible, it is not probable until

the anxieties which soundings reflect as well as aggravate subside.

Masculinity anxiety is somewhat reduced when someone becomes a man rather than being a mere aspirant. Boys are less driven to prove manhood unconventionally through deeds or misdeeds when with the passing of time they may effortlessly exhibit the conventional signposts of manhood—physical appearance, the completion of school, job, marriage, and perhaps even children. Adulthood may not in all social circles definitively prove manhood, but it is always good *prima facie* evidence. In a revealing reversal, the incumbent of manhood may exempt himself from the demand to engage in delinquencies emanating from mere aspirants by condescendingly observing that it is, after all, kid stuff. This applies not only to rumbling but also to many forms of theft.

The reduction of membership anxiety is coincident with that of masculinity anxiety. The approach of adulthood is marked by the addition of new affiliations. One is less anxious about membership in the company of peers because there are new alternative affiliations. There were always alternatives but the new ones are more tenable since they are adult. They cannot be slandered as kid stuff and thus dismissed. Work, marriage, and other conventional adult statuses may be considered stupid or "square" but they are obviously not kid stuff. To that extent they invite affiliation. Their very existence serves to reduce the membership anxiety inherent in the subculture of juvenile delinquency.

Thus, the approach of adulthood converts the possibility of public evaluation of delinquency to a probability. In the majority of cases, pairs of delinquents discover one after the other that they had shared misunderstandings. They had not really been committed to delinquency—it was fun and each thought that others demanded it, but *they* had never really believed in it. However, this does not always happen. A very small proportion may discover that they are in fact committed to their misdeeds.[3] These *decide* to be criminals. A larger proportion never publicly evaluate delinquency and continue through adult life guided by their misconception of the subculture deriving from the system of shared misunderstandings. Each is privately uncommitted but publicly a receiver and transmitter of miscues suggesting commitment. Why does this group maintain its pluralistic ignorance?

There are many contingencies, but the pertinent factors are inherent in the conditions of publicity already described. They are merely the reverse side of the conditions converting the possibility of publicity to a probability: the frequency and intensity of the coupled relationship and the level of status anxiety. It is not the fact of coupling that is crucial but what can be said about delinquency. Everyone or almost everyone in the subculture of delinquency has a close buddy at one time or another. However, friendship varies according to intimacy and frequency. Thus, disliked adherents who less frequently enter into close coupled relationships are less likely than others to discover their misconception regarding the subculture of delinquency. But even if one is liked and thus involved in a series of close coupled relationships, the level of status anxiety sets limits on what may be discussed. Normally, the level of both status anxieties is reduced with the approach of adulthood. Sometimes, however, the membership anxiety remains high because the additional

affiliations ordinarily inherent in adulthood do not occur. For a variety of reasons some members do not join a woman in marriage; other, and frequently the same members, do not join the labor force. Thus, the membership anxiety persists.

What of masculinity anxiety? Did I not suggest that the approach of adulthood is *prima facie* evidence of masculinity? Ordinarily, this is so but occasionally an additional and weighty piece of evidence may offset whatever reassurance of manhood one may find in the approach of adulthood. Often, the dwindling remnants of the old gang affiliate with younger cohorts. Obviously, this is quite functional in the transmission of the subculture. But what of its effect on the bearded adolescent? The increment of assurance painfully gained through the slow passage of years is cruelly offset by the humiliation of hanging around with mere kids. The level of masculinity anxiety persists or is heightened.[4]

Thus, the persistence of misconceptions ideally depends on the interrelated circumstances of superficial friendship, abstinence from the affiliations of work and marriage, and a chronologic descent into the still densely populated cohorts of the subculture of delinquency. Those who never discover their misconception become criminals, but they never decide to do so. They simply continue the drift into adulthood.

The occasion for contrived and esoteric publicity is commonly called group therapy but more accurately termed guided group interaction.[5] Public evaluation of delinquency may occur in guided

[3] The couple is the ideal situation of publicity and discovery of misconception, but slightly large cliques may also undergo this process.

[4] Other patterns of accommodating to declining gang membership are well described in Richard Cloward and Lloyd Ohlin, *Delinquency and Opportunity*, New York: Free Press, 1960.

[5] See, for instance, Lloyd McCorkle, Albert Elias, and F. Lovell Bixby, *The Highfield Story*, New York: Holt, 1958, and Lamar T. Empey and Jerome Rabow, "The Provo Experiment in Delinquency Rehabilitation," *American Sociological Review*, October 1961, pp. 679–695.

group interaction, either in a street or institutional setting. Guided group interaction is pertinent because it may help confirm the initially implausible thesis of shared misunderstandings. The limited success of this technique may derive from the discovery of misconception during the many hours of public discussion. Given this interpretation, it is not insight into self that is the critical contribution of guided group interaction; rather, the discovery of the outlook of others.

The two settings of guided group interaction have offsetting advantages and disadvantages that set limits on its effectiveness. In the institutional setting, two possible ways of interpreting the discovery that others share one's private outlook may interfere with applying the knowledge gained. The participant may feel that his companions in therapy are simply responding in tactical fashion to the situation of incarceration. According to reports on guided group interaction, this feeling is dispelled in the initial stages of the process. These reports are credible if we assume the initially implausible assertion that delinquents are involved in a system of shared misunderstanding in which commitment to delinquency is a common misunderstanding. The reports on the dissipation of doubt are less credible, perhaps incredible, if we assume the initially plausible assertion that delinquents are committed to their misdeeds. Being more gullible about reported observations than speculative theory, but also for self-serving reasons, I prefer to assume that the reports on the dissipation of doubt are credible.

But even if the delinquent surrenders the belief that the outlook on delinquency expressed by institutional companions is a tactical response to the situation of incarceration, he is still left with the possibility that his civilian peers are different. This is the fundamental limita-tion of guided group interaction in an institutional setting.[6] Unless the delinquent assumes the unity of subcultural delinquency—the essential similarity of delinquents throughout a large territory —he may not easily apply his institutional discovery to mates in civil society. He may assume the unity of subcultural delinquency, but that is a risky and not entirely warranted choice. The delinquent is not a trained theorist and the generalization implicit in such a notion may elude him. Moreover, an assumption of the unity of subcultural delinquency flies in the face of the well-known enmities that abound in this world. True, he is confused on the term unity and takes it to mean cooperation rather than like-mindedness. But such equivocation is the stuff of social misconception. Finally, he may be unwilling to hazard the application of his discovery when he returns to his civilian mates. Even if the unity of subcultural delinquency becomes explicit through guidance or intuition, it is, after all, just a theory. The delinquent is surely capable of that observation. He may not be willing to risk his status as man and member to test so undocumented a notion. Thus, the guided group interaction of institutional setting is fundamentally limited in the transfer of discoveries to civilian life.

Guided group interaction, less formal to be sure, may also occur on a street setting. Here, too, the public evaluation of delinquency is not the focused aim of gang work. Here, too, effort is dissipated in a hundred directions. But just as in the institutional setting, public evaluation of delinquency is an almost inevitable by-product of the gang worker's larger enterprise.

The limitations inherent in the street setting are just the reverse of those in the institution. On the street, the limitation derives from the fact that this is *his*

[6] A highly local institution which more or less coincides with the civilian street setting is limited because it quickly confronts the fundamental restriction of the street setting.

company of peers. The obstacle to the public evaluation of delinquency and the subsequent discovery of misconception—status anxiety regarding masculinity and membership—are all here despite the intervention of the street worker. It is the relative absence of masculinity but especially membership anxiety that makes the discovery of misconception easy and rapid in the institutional setting, but also helps account for the frequently premature prognosis of reformation. The situation of incarceration is not simply an extension of the situation of authentic company. Minimal masculinity is demonstrated but one may easily claim the desire to do quick time. Membership anxiety is even less warranted since this is not his company of peers. The pace and ease of attaining public evaluation and the discovery of previously shared misunderstandings is slow and uncertain in the street setting. More of one's investments are here. That is the fundamental disadvantage of the street setting. Its advantage is obvious. Accomplishment of publicity, discovery, and the drift out of delinquency when attained are of more durable consequence than in the institutional setting.

In summary, my thesis is that even in the situation of company, commitment to delinquency is a misconception—first of delinquents and later of the sociologists who study them. Instead, there is a system of shared misunderstandings, based on miscues, which leads delinquents to believe that all others situated in their company are committed to their misdeeds. Thus, the situation of company perhaps does not result in a posture toward delinquency radically different from that revealed in the situations previously discussed. If in all situations the delinquent reveals a basic ambivalence toward his behavior, a new conception of his subculture may be warranted. . . .

The continued existence of the subculture is facilitated and perhaps even dependent on support and reinforcement from conventional sources. The subculture is buttressed by beliefs that flourish in influential sectors of the normative order. These views, which include the professional ideology of criminology, psychiatry, and social work, an emergent ideology of leisure, a celebration of the primitive in Bohemia and anthropology, the cult of cowboy masculinity in the mass media, and the persistence of provincial sentiments in insulated sections of metropolis, all reflect at critical points precepts in the subculture of delinquency. But we cannot point to these obscure but consequential similarities unless we first discontinue the current sociological practice of confusing a richly pluralistic American normative system with a simple puritanism. Puritanism or its routinized equivalent, middle-class morality, is one tradition among many in American life. No one has documented its continued dominance. *Les bourgeoises* have undergone such steady and militant attack since an allegedly grubby ascent to power that the persistence of their moral dominance would be quite surprising, except perhaps in the suburbs of Boston. The morality of the historical bourgeoisie has undergone drastic modification. Moreover, it has encountered moral rivals in the spirit of modern corporate enterprise, the influence of intellectuals in an increasingly educated society, and in the rise of specialized professions of welfare. Moreover, its ancient rival, the sentiments of feudal provincialism, was never more than partially vanquished. Unless the proliferation of important moral traditions in a pluralistic America is understood and granted, the sustenance of the subculture of delinquency by conventional beliefs is implausible. To be consequential, the new traditions and the very old must be in the moral atmosphere of society. They need not reach the adherents of subcultural delinquency in pure and sophisticated form to support and reinforce it.

On the contrary, the function of reinforcement and sustenance is best served if these beliefs are grossly vulgarized. But to be consequential, they must in some form be heard by members of the subculture.

The subculture of delinquency receives cultural support from conventional traditions. Moreover, it receives considerable social and persona reinforcement if we conceive of support as a range rather than an attribute. Thus, an apparently tenuous and precarious subculture delicately balanced between crime and convention has an additional source of stability. It is itself a subterranean tradition in American life.

A subterranean tradition is characterized by contemporary adherents linked to the past through local legacies and to the wider social structure by a range of support. It is an ideal case of an integrated subculture. Thus, it is an advancing of the fundamental sociological notion of the *relation* between society and its deviants.

The major contribution of sociology to the understanding of deviance has consisted of two fundamental insights. First, persistent deviance typically is not a solitary enterprise; rather, it best flourishes when it receives group support. Second, deviance typically is not an individual or group innovation; rather, it has a history in particular locales. Thus, according to the sociological view, the deviant is linked to society in minimal form through companies of deviants and through local traditions. When these minimal links appear we speak of a deviant subculture. The view of sociology is extended if additionally we explore the relations between that subculture and the wider cultural system. That extension is the essence of the idea of subterranean analysis. Such analysis requires the exploration of *connections* between localized deviant traditions and the variety of traditions in conventional society. More-

over, subterranean analysis implies an ongoing dialectic among a variety of conventional and deviant viewpoints, and that in the process of exchange each of the traditions is simultaneously stabilized and modified. The paradox of simultaneous stability and modification is the fundamental meaning of cultural pluralism.

Subterranean tradition may be defined by specification of key points along the range of support. It is deviant, which is to say that it is publicly denounced by authorized spokesmen. However, the tradition is viewed with ambivalence in the privacy of contemplation and in intimate publics by most conventional citizens. The spirit and substance of subterranean traditions are familiar and within limits tolerated by broad segments of the adult population. Adolescent immersion in the delinquent tradition, or flirtation with it, is a suitable subject of nostalgic reminiscence and recreation. So popular is the pastime that surviving puritans are sometimes forced to either falsify a biography or ludicrously confuse their innocent naughtiness with the precepts of a subculture which under proper conditions countenances murder. Among youth, conventional versions of subterranean tradition—reasonable facsimiles stripped of the more intolerable aspects—are experienced by broad segments of the population. Teenage culture consists of the frivolous and mindless pursuit of fun and thrill. The experiences encountered in this pursuit ordinarily include many of the juvenile status offenses. Its spirit is a modification of that implicit in the subculture of delinquency. Thus, teenage culture may be conceived as a conventional version, a reasonable facsimile, of subcultural delinquency. Finally, of course, subterranean traditions have bands of adherents. These adherents are the bona fide members of the subculture. They are the carriers of its theory and the perpetrators of its practice.

10

getting into deviant worlds

Entry into a deviant world is not always simple or automatic.
A person may have to learn new beliefs, values, and norms before
s/he can successfully participate. Moreover, the factors that
initially lead one to become involved may differ considerably
from the factors that keep the person involved at a later point
in time. Also, of course, different factors may be involved in
different types of deviation.

In the first reading Wallace discusses the stages men go
through in becoming Skid Row "bums." Next Weinberg deals
with how people become nudists and how segmental that involvement remains. Bryan then describes the period of apprenticeship
that beginning call girls go through. In the last selection Lofland
describes the processes involved in conversion to a religious
cult.

The Road to Skid Row

SAMUEL E. WALLACE

. . . Skid row, that familiar aggregate of flop houses, bars, cheap restaurants, second-hand stores, pawnshops, and missions has existed as a distinct ecological area of almost every major American city since the close of the Civil War. Since its establishment, it has become more than a rundown and quarantined neighborhood catering to the random needs of the down-and-outer. Through isolation and the mutual interaction partially fostered by ecological separation from the larger community, a web of skid row institutions emerged to support the basic features of the skid row way of life—its attitudes, beliefs and opinions about the world, its special language, its traditions—to support, in other words, the subculture of skid row.

If skid row, then, may be defined as an isolated and deviant subcultural community expressing the features of a distinct and recognizable way of life, the skid rower may be viewed as one who shares this way of life. Not only is the skid rower an outcast and a deviant, he is also the member of an outcast and deviant community.

In terms of its basic institutions and the process of socialization, skid row is a subculture. Recruitment into the skid row way of life may be divided into four phases with component community and social psychological characteristics. The incipient phase involves the *dislocation* from the basic social network of society accompanied by a sense of rootlessness. *Exposure* to skid row subculture follows, accompanied by isolation and desocialization. The third phase—*regular participation* in skid row institutions—witnesses the beginnings of submergence into skid row subculture. The final phase in the natural history of the skid rower is marked by his *integration* into the skid row community, and by his acculturation.

DISLOCATION

Dislocation from the basic social network of society at large may be the result of either ecological or normative isolation, or both. Historically, ecological isolation was forced upon some—at least on a temporary basis—by the exigencies of certain kinds of itinerant and migratory labor, on others as a result of privation, infirmity, or need. Normative isolation, on the other hand, refers to a pattern of individual deviancy preceding arrival on skid row.

In the early years of this century and at the close of the last, a vast number of men, and sometimes women and children, became separated from home and community simply by the nature of their work. There were, for example, apprentices to guilds who were required to travel for a number of years learning the basic skills of their trades, soldiers who did not enjoy the benefits of a permanent encampment, seamen whose voyages often lasted several years, entertainers who journeyed from settlement to settle-

Reprinted from *Social Problems*, Vol. 16, No. 1 (Summer 1968), pp. 96–102, by permission of the Society for the Study of Social Problems and the author.

ment, and a variety of unskilled or semi-skilled laborers—lumber, harvest, railroad, and dam and river levee workmen. All had one characteristic in common. They had been separated from familiar places and from familiar ways. Whereas some returned to renew family and community ties, many did not. For these, *ecological* isolation led to permanent dislocation from society and its norms.[1]

A similar pattern of isolation and dislocation confronted the destitute. Those seeking relief—in the wake of old age and infirmity, natural disasters, financial and civil disorders—were forced to take to the road in search of help, charity, new jobs, or relief. Cut off from their former communities, the disinherited of former days—the displaced poor—also became prime candidates for the skid row way of life.

Until recent changes in welfare policy and administration, even the organized and continuing relief programs brought the destitute into contact with skid row subculture. During the depression of the 1930's this pattern of ecological isola-

tion followed by recruitment into skid row was so widespread that social workers referred to it as "shelterization": a process whereby in exchange for relief in a municipal shelter, the "reliefer" found himself ineluctably drawn into commitment to the skid row way of life.[2]

The middle-class alcoholic who ultimately commits himself to the skid row way of life is on the other hand following the process of *normative* isolation, dislocation, and recruitment. To escape the social consequences of his excessive drinking, to conceal his alcoholism from friends, family, and employer, he seeks out situations, bars, where he is unknown and where excessive drinking is the rule rather than the exception.[3] In skid row bars, the alcoholic is able to curtail, as Becker phrases it, some of the contingencies in his career pattern.[4] Although every alcoholic does not become a skid rower, the essential features of the recruitment process are ever present—his normative isolation through deviancy threatens to dislocate him from his own community and eventually put him in

[1] Numerous studies report the occupational histories of homeless men, but those focusing upon the work camp itself most clearly indicate the isolation. See: Edmund W. Bradwin, *The Bunkhouse Man,* New York, unpublished Ph.D. thesis, Columbia University, 1928; William Z. Foster, *Pages from a Worker's Life,* New York: International Publishers, 1939; Marion Hathway, *The Migratory Worker and Family Life,* Chicago: University of Chicago, 1934; Carleton H. Parker, *The Casual Laborer, and Other Essays,* New York: Harcourt, Brace and Howe, 1920; Louisa R. Shotwell, *The Harvesters: The Story of the Migrant People,* New York: Doubleday, 1961; Margaret Mary Wood, *Paths of Loneliness,* New York: Columbia University, 1953.

[2] Edward E. Hale, "Report on Tramps," Conference of Charities and American Social Science Association, New Haven: Hoggson and Robinson, 1877, pp. 102–110; Philip Klein, *The Burden of Unemployment,* New York: Russell Sage Foundation, 1923; Mariner J. Kent, "The Making of a Tramp," *The Independent,* 55 (January–December, 1903), pp. 667–670; George Orwell, *Down and Out in Paris and London,* Avon, 1933; Alvin Roseman, *Shelter Care and the Local Homeless Man,* Chicago: Public Administration Service, 46 (1935).

[3] Elmer Bendiner, *The Bowery Man,* New York: Nelson, 1961; Edmund G. Love, *Subways Are for Sleeping,* New York: New American Library, 1958; Harris E. Hill, "The Social Deviant and Initial Addiction to Narcotics and Alcohol," *Quarterly Journal of Studies on Alcohol,* 23 (1962), pp. 562–582; Robert Straus, "Some Sociological Concomitants of Excessive Drinking, as Revealed in the Life History of an Itinerant Inebriate," *Quarterly Journal of Studies on Alcohol,* 9 (1948), pp. 1–52.

[4] Howard S. Becker, *Outsiders: Studies in the Sociology of Deviance,* Glencoe: Free Press, 1963.

touch with skid row subculture. A similar pattern is also characteristic of the last stages in the professional career of some prostitutes, petty racketeers, and other minor criminal types.

EXPOSURE

The incipient phase gradually evolves into the second phase of *exposure* to skid row. Since ecological and normative isolation from the community may be simultaneously accompanied by exposure to skid row subculture, this second phase is only analytically distinct and, in the life history of any particular individual, may be indistinguishable from the first.

The quasi-simultaneity of the processes of isolation, dislocation and exposure to skid row subculture, is particularly characteristic of those whose initial separation from society was forced upon them by the nature of their work or by the circumstances under which relief was formerly administered. The migratory agricultural worker, the lumberjack, seaman, construction worker, and those who follow equally itinerant trades come into direct contact with the skid rower and the skid row way of life on the job itself. All of these work sites are virtually isolated from stable communities and from communication with the world at large. There is little or no contact with educational, religious, and civic institutions; and the low literacy rate of the unskilled laborer combined with his constant mobility make communication through the mails a remote possibility, effectively cutting individual ties to former communities, friends, and kin.[5]

This kind of isolation inevitably produces a state of alienation from society. Not only is the individual desocialized from the basic patterns in which he was raised, but the socialization or reinforcement he would experience were he living in his original community setting has been forcibly interrupted. He does not continue to learn, nor is he reinforced in the basic norms he would need were he to rejoin the wider community.

The young male of the itinerant work world, for instance, increasingly deprived of experience in dealing with women, tends to forget what he once knew or had begun to learn in his former world. His bachelorhood, in turn, further isolates him from the basic life patterns of society. Thus, when the adult or middle-aged male approaches the threshold of skid row society, he is already decommitted and to a large degree desocialized.

The person who enters skid row in the course of securing relief experiences a parallel process. Depression, natural disaster, or war and its aftermath have initiated his isolation, and the location of relief agencies within skid row areas carries it one step further. The temporarily unemployed white collar worker, forced to take up residence in a municipal shelter, soon discovers that the skid row world is very different from his former one. Previously aceeptable behavior meets with disapproval in his new world, while his old one increasingly labels him a failure. As he withdraws from the basic and continuing socializing process of the wider community, he experiences the same kind of desocialization (and interrupted socialization) as does the mobile worker.

The alcoholic, prostitute, or racketeer whose prior deviancy leads to skid row

[5] In addition to the studies of labor camps cited earlier, see also: Paul F. Brissenden, *The I.W.W. A Study of American Syndicalism,* New York: Russell and Russell, 1919; Ralph Chaplin, *Wobbly: The Rough-and-Tumble Story of an American Radical,* Chicago, University of Chicago, 1948; Steward H. Holbrook, *The Story of American Railroads,* New York: Crown, 1947; Allan Pinkerton, *Strikers, Communists, Tramps and Detectives,* New York: Dillingham, 1878.

provides but a third variation on the same theme. For these normatively isolated individuals, recruitment to the skid row way of life may provide a solution to some of the undesirable consequences of another deviant career. Thus itinerant worker and reliefer were first isolated ecologically, while the skid row "aficionado"[6]—alcoholic, prostitute, racketeer, or even brain surgeon—was initially isolated normatively before coming to skid row.

REGULAR PARTICIPATION

Some degree of participation in skid row institutions and initial socialization into skid row norms and values inevitably accompany exposure to the skid row way of life. The mobile or casual laborers, for example, may have begun to use skid row as a regular source of contacts with employers, and the flophouse as a residence between jobs. The reliefer finds himself living among men whom the community condemns and despises. The middle-class alcoholic, the prostitute, the small rackets man, and other deviants and discards have begun to drift more and more often to skid row bars and cheap cafes.

Whereas anxiety and curiosity may have marked initial contact with skid row, the third phase of recruitment into the skid row way of life is marked by the beginning of commitment—regular participation. The stage of regular participation in the skid row way of life embodies, perhaps, the core of the re-socialization process—the interval in a neophyte skid rower's life when he gradually ceases to occupy a status recognized by the outside community and begins to occupy one recognized only by skid row subculture.

The status of the newcomer to skid row is one objectively supported by society. He can still produce the necessary credentials to validate his self-image as: a member of the migrant or casual labor force if he has entered skid row by this route; a temporary member of the unemployed if he has entered by the relief route; or a poet, writer, priest, sociologist, or surgeon if his route has been via the bottle or one of the other paths followed by the deviant loner.

However, as time goes on, only fellow associates on skid row continue to assure each other of the validity of these status claims. In fact, as Rooney[7] points out, much of the conversation on skid row centers around this subject. No one else supports the delusion. To the community at large all men living on skid row (and/or participating in its institutions) are bums, i.e., nonworkers; and the fact that they have generally worked little, if at all, over a period of several years necessarily strengthens this conviction. The fact that the harvest hand who no longer works in the field calls himself a "bindle stiff", that—in short—skid rowers claim legitimate status long after they have ceased to occupy legitimate roles in society at large makes no sizeable impression on anyone—ultimately even on their fellow skid rowers.

Every day in his contact with the out-

[6] "Aficionados" are those attracted to the skid row way of life because of its tolerance and isolation. It is worthwhile to point out that when ecological isolation is added to their already established normative isolation, their deviancy is in effect compounded—effectively removing all possibility of "rescue" by any of the many rehabilitation agencies operating outside—but not inside—skid row.

[7] James F. Rooney, "Group Processes Among Skid Row Winos: A Re-evaluation of the Undersocialization Hypothesis," *Quarterly Journal of Studies on Alcohol*, 22 (1961), pp. 444–460.

side community the skid rower is told he is no good, a failure, a misfit, a bum; and this pressure of community condemnation forces the newcomer on skid row to make increasing use of skid row attitudes in an attempt to neutralize what the rest of the world is saying about him. For the problem of dealing with a society which punishes, derides, and condemns you is partially solved by condemning, deriding, and even punishing that society in return.

Thus, turning the tables, the skid rower condemns his condemners as foolish, ignorant, and contemptible.[8] He glorifies the skid row way of life. Or he adopts a more punitive tactic to neutralize the community attitudes against him. He demands that all relationships between insider and outsider—himself and the community—be based on material exchange. Since there are no shared values, there can be no relationships based on deference, or the mutual pleasures of association. The skid rower demands to be paid even for talking to an outsider, whether he be researcher, citizen or tourist.[9] Or he derides the outsider by "putting him on." He invents stories of his past designed to fit the preconceptions of his audience. The journalist goes to skid row to find colorful types which will make good newspaper copy, and he

is obliged. The sociologist arrives on skid row with pretested, pre-coded questionnaires in hand, and the skid rower gives "safe-average" answers.

As the neophyte skid rower begins to accept, even to embrace these subcultural attitudes towards the community at large, he is pushed into further acceptance of the skid row way of life. Laborer, pensioner, reliefer, clerk, and poet all find that they are no longer what they thought they were. What, or rather who, are they then?

INTEGRATION

The final stage in the process of becoming a skid rower is marked by integration into the skid row community and acculturation into the subculture.[10] As the new recruit moves into the final stage in his natural life history, he masters skid row argot. Proper use of skid row terms quickly identifies him as a genuine insider. As he becomes an insider, he participates less and less in the outside world. Family, friends, and neighbors are replaced by fellow skid rowers; work is replaced by relief, panhandling, and begging; homosexuality takes the place of heterosexuality; police, judge, and social worker become familiar figures; a

[8] See, for example, C. J. Ribton–Turner, *A History of Vagrants and Vagrancy and Beggars and Begging,* London: Chapman and Hall, 1887, p. 647; and William Edge, *The Main Stem,* New York: Vanguard, 1927, pp. 6–7 and 198.

[9] Sara Harris, Donald Bogue, and those conducting the Philadelphia study conceded to this demand by paying their skid row interviewees. Sara Harris and Donald Bogue, *Skid Row, U.S.A.,* New York: Doubleday, 1956; Philadelphia, The Department of Psychiatry of Temple University School of Medicine, *The Men on Skid Row,* Philadelphia: Mimeographed Report, Temple University, 1960.

[10] The rich subculture of skid row is indicated in numerous publications. Among those dealing specifically with the language, lore, and literature of skid row are: Robert H. Cowdrey, *A Tramp in Society,* Chicago: Francis J. Schulte, 1891; William H. Davies, *True Travellers,* London: Jonathan Cape, 1923; William DeVere, *Tramp Poems of the West,* Tacoma, Washington: Cromwell, 1891; George Milburn, *The Hobo's Hornbook: A Repertory for a Gutter Jongleur,* New York: Ives Washburn, 1930; Arthur Compton Rickett, *The Vagabond in Literature,* London: J. M. Dent, 1906.

jug of wine satisfies all other needs.[11]

From the point of view of responsible society, the skid rower has become desocialized. From the point of view of skid row society he has become socialized and acculturated. It is in this phase that the individual may be publicly labeled a deviant through arrest, sentence, and incarceration. Incarceration throws him into intimate contact with fellow associates from skid row and intensifies his socialization into the subculture. The label of "deviant" serves as an important credential for the admission to the innermost circle of skid rowers and at the same time additionally isolates our recruit from his society. Private self-acceptance must inevitably follow public recognition and that most important element of all emerges—the individual now thinks of himself as a skid rower.

When individuals are fully integrated into the skid row community, they occupy statuses recognized exclusively by skid row and quite unfamiliar to members of the outside community. Viewed in terms of what the outside community considers acceptable behavior, the status hierarchy of skid row is an inverted one, revealing with utmost clarity the fact that the isolation first forced on the skid rower is then ultimately valued most by him. One's "progress" in a skid row career is a matter of working one's way downhill, departing further and further from contact with the outside world and from conformity to its standards. . . .

[11] One paragraph from Edge's autobiography, *op. cit.,* will perhaps portray this final stage. "How I changed . . . I had developed the strange fears of the migratory worker. I feared policemen above all things. I felt like an outcast of society, a man to whom good things are permanently denied. I was so accustomed to coarse words and nasty living quarters that I mistrusted, almost to the point of being psychopathic, good meals, clean blankets, a pleasant room. Perhaps I realized this more keenly because of Charlie. He had not developed the cautions and apprehensions of a proletarian. He was a free American with civil rights of which he felt quite confident. I looked at Charlie. I was thinking. Too damn goodlooking for a migratory worker, attracts too much attention. Talks about the wrong thing on the job. On the job a fellow ought not talk about books and theories and things. Ought to talk about the same thing as other workers—whiskey, women, jobs, flophouses." Pp. 152–153.

Becoming a Nudist

MARTIN S. WEINBERG

In order to better understand deviant life styles and the meanings they have for those engaged in them, it is often useful to conceptualize a life-style as a career, consisting of various stages. We can then study the interpersonal processes that draw and sustain people at each of these various stages. In this way, we can appreciate the motivations, perceptions, and experiences that characterize involvement in that way of life at various points in time—e.g., these may differ for novices, "veterans," etc.

Using such a career model, this paper deals with the interpersonal processes and phases involved in nudist camp membership. Specifically, it deals with the processes by which people come to contemplate a visit to a nudist camp, attend for the first time, and then continue attending over a period of time. The data come from three sources—101 interviews with nudists in the Chicago area; two successive summers of participant observation in nudist camps; and 617 mailed questionnaires completed by nudists located throughout the United States and Canada.[1]

PRENUDIST ATTITUDES TOWARD NUDISM

Most people seldom give much thought to the subject of nudism.[2] Responses in the interviews indicated that nudism is not a prominent object of thought even for many persons who will later become nudists. Thus when nudist members were asked what they had thought of nudism before visiting a camp, many stated that they had never really given it any thought. Until their initial experience, the interviewees' con-

Reprinted by special permission of The William Alanson White Psychiatric Foundation, Inc., from *Psychiatry: Journal for the Study of Interpersonal Processes*, Vol. 29, No. 1 (February 1966), pp. 15–24. Copyright 1966 by The William Alanson White Psychiatric Foundation, Inc.

This investigation was supported in part by a Public Health Service fellowship (No. 7–F1–MH–14, 660–01A1 BEH) from the National Institute of Mental Health, and in part by contributions from Mr. O. B. E. and from the National Nudist Council. I wish to acknowledge my appreciation to the individuals and organizations who helped me in carrying out my research. I am also grateful to John I. Kitsuse for his encouragement, suggestions, and criticisms.

[1] Interviews were the primary source of data, and all of the quotations and quantifications in this paper, unless otherwise specified, are drawn from interviews. All known nudists in the vicinity of Chicago were contacted for an interview; the mean interview time was three and one-half hours. Approximately one hundred camps were represented in the interviews and questionnaires. A detailed discussion of my methodology may be found in "Sex, Modesty, and Deviants," Ph.D. Dissertation, Northwestern University, June, 1965.

[2] This statement is based on the results of a questionnaire study of social response to nudism.

ceptions of nudism had been vague stereotypes, much like those held by the general public. In the words of a now active nudist:

I never gave it too much thought. I thought it was a cult—a nut-eating, berry-chewing bunch of vegetarians, doing calisthenics all day, a gymno-physical society. I thought they were carrying health to an extreme, being egomaniacs about their body.

Many of those who had thought about the subject conceived of nudists' camps as more exclusive, luxurious, and expensive than they actually are. Others had different conceptions:

I'm afraid I had the prevailing notion that they were undignified, untidy places populated (a) by the very poor, and (b) by languishing bleached blonds, and (c) by greasy, leering bachelors.

Table 1 sums up the attitudes that nudists reported themselves to have taken before their affiliation.

TABLE 1 Prenudist Attitudes Toward Nudism*

Attitude	Percentage of Interviewees
Positive	35
Live and let live	16
Negative	19
Very negative	1
Does not know	29

* For coding purposes, "positive" was defined as a desire to participate in nudism or to become a nudist. "Live and let live" included those who did not desire participation in nudism, but did not think ill of those who did participate; however, some of these respondents would have imposed social distance from nudists, and some would not.

THE INITIAL INTEREST IN NUDISM

If prenudist attitudes are of the nature indicated by Table 1, how does one become interested enough to make a first visit to a nudist camp? As shown in Table 2, the highest percentage of men mentioned magazines as the source of their interest, and the next largest source was other persons (exclusive of parents or parents-in-law). For women, the pattern was different; the highest percentage were first informed about nudism by their husbands. In 78 percent of the families, the husband had been more

TABLE 2 Source of Initial Interest in Nudism

Source	Male	Female
Magazines	47%	14%
Movies	6	6
Newspapers	6	0
Spouse	0	47
Parents or parents-in-law	2	8
Other person	31	23
Medical advice from physician	0	2
Other source	8	0

interested in visiting a camp. In all other cases both spouses had equally wanted to go. There were no cases in which the wife had wanted to go more than the husband.

The fact that the overwhelming majority of women became interested in nudism through their relationships with other people, rather than through the mass media which played such an important part with men, was reflected in the finding that interpersonal trust had to be sustained in order to evoke the women's interest.[3] This was indicated in

[3] My thanks are due to James L. Wilkins for initially pointing this pattern out in his analysis of the additional data on the response of college students to nudists.

the content of many interviews. The interviews also indicated that common-sense justifications and "derivations"[4] were important in overcoming the women's anxieties.

The following quotation is from an interview with a woman who became interested in nudism after being informed about it by a male friend. Here she was describing what her feelings would have been prior to that time. (In this quotation, as in others in this paper, Q is used to signify a neutral probe by the interviewer that follows the course of the last reply—such as "Could you tell me some more about that?" or "How's that?" or "What do you mean?" Other questions by the interviewer are given in full.)

. . . [Whether or not I would go to a nudist camp would] depend on who asked me. If a friend, I probably would have gone along with it. . . . [Q] If an acquaintance, I wouldn't have been interested. [Q] I don't know, I think it would depend on who was asking me to go. [Q] If it was someone you liked or had confidence in, you'd go along with it. If you didn't think they were morally upright you probably wouldn't have anything to do with it.

A man described how he had persuaded his wife to become interested in nudism:

I expected difficulty with my wife. I presented it to her in a wholesome manner. [Q] I had to convince her it was a wholesome thing, and that the people there were sincere. . . . [Q] That they were sincere in efforts to sunbathe together and had only good purposes in mind when they did that. [Q] All the things that nudism stands for: a healthy body and a cleansed mind by killing sex curiosities.

The anxieties that enter into the anticipation of public nudity were de-

scribed in the following interview excerpts:

I was nervous. . . . [Q] It's different. It's not a daily practice. . . . I'm heavy, that added to the nervousness.

They said they were ashamed of their builds. They think everyone there is perfection. [Q] They think everyone will look at them.

He [a friend] said he'd never go, but that he could understand it. He saw nothing wrong in it. [Q] He said he wouldn't want other men looking at his wife.

Even though they had enough confidence to make the decision to visit a camp, the respondents did not necessarily anticipate becoming nudists themselves. For many the first trip was merely a joke, a lark, or a new experience, and the main motivation was curiosity. They visited the camp as one might make a trip to the zoo, to see what it was like and what kind of characters would belong to such a group. There was also curiosity, on the part of many of the respondents, about seeing nude members of the opposite sex.

The original thought was that we were going to see a bunch of nuts. It was a joke going out there.

I thought they must be a little nutty. Eccentric. I didn't think there'd be so many normal people. . . . [Q] I felt that people that are nudists are a little bohemian or strange. [Q] I don't feel that way now. I thought we'd be the only sane people there. I thought it was kind of an adventure. . . . [Q] I like feeling I'm doing something unusual that no one knows about. It's a big secret. . . . [Q] The novelty, the excitement of driving up in the car; no one knew we were going. . . .

Table 3 presents the motivations given by interviewees for their first trip to a nudist camp.

[4] For a discussion of Pareto's concept of derivation, see Talcott Parsons, *The Structure of Social Action* (second edition); Glencoe, Ill., Free Press, 1949; pp. 198 *ff.*

TABLE 3 Motivations for the First Visit to a Nudist Camp

Motivation	Male	Female
Curiosity over what it was like	33%	25%
Sexual curiosity	16	2
To satisfy spouse or relative	2	38
Combination of curiosity and to satisfy spouse	0	13
For relaxation	2	4
For health	12	6
To sunbathe	8	2
To make friends	6	0
Other	21	10

THE FIRST VISIT

The first trip to camp was frequently accompanied by extreme nervousness. Part of this might be attributed simply to the experience of entering a new group. The visitors did not know the patterns common to the group, and they were uncertain about their acceptance by group members. For example, a nudist said, referring to his participation in a nudist camp in which he was not well known:

I guess I'm a little nervous when I get there, 'cause I'm not recognized as a member of the group.[5]

But, in the instance of a first visit to a nudist camp, this anxiety on entering a new group was considerably heightened by the unknown nature of the experience that lay ahead. Mead, in his discussion of the "social psychology of the act," has described how people, in planning an action, imaginatively rehearse it and its anticipated consequences.[6] The nudist camp, however, presents a totally unfamiliar situation; the person planning a visit has no past of similar situations, and usually no one has effectively described the situation to him in advance. This gap in effective imagination produces apprehension, anxiety, and nervousness.

[On the trip up] I was very nervous. [Q] Because the idea was foreign. [Q] . . . The unknown factor. Just seeing a lot of people without clothes on is an unusual situation. Different or new experiences make one nervous.

You're nervous and apprehensive. You don't know what to expect. . . . I was very nervous. . . . I thought of everything under the sun. . . . I didn't know what to expect.

I felt a little inferior at first, because I had no knowledge of nudist camps. . . . I started to enjoy myself, but I couldn't quite feel comfortable. [Q] In the nude. In front of a lot of people. A lack of confidence, self-confidence. [Q] By not having a complete knowledge. I really didn't know what to expect.

I was afraid of the unknown. I didn't know what to expect. If we had known nudists, I wouldn't have had those fears.

In most instances, the initial nervousness dissipated soon after the newcomer's

[5] It is this very fact of an established social system, however, that prevents a disruption of social order in nudist camps. Traditions and norms are stabilized, and even neophytes who think of themselves as leader-types are forced to fall into the pattern or be rejected. (For a small-group experiment that studies this phenomenon, see Ferenc Merei, "Group Leadership and Institutionalization," *Human Relations* [1949] 2:23–39.) In another paper I have shown how some of these traditions function to sustain a nonsexual definition of the nudist situation. See Martin S. Weinberg, "Sexual Modesty, Social Meanings, and the Nudist Camp," *Social Problems* (1965) 12:311–318.

[6] Anselm Strauss, editor, *The Social Psychology of George Herbert Mead;* Chicago, Univ. of Chicago Press, 1956; p. xiii.

arrival. Forty-six percent of the interviewees said that they were not nervous at all after arriving at camp. An additional 31 percent felt at ease in less than three hours. Thus most visitors adjusted rapidly to the nudist way of life. Seventy-one percent of those interviewed reported that *no* major adjustment was necessary. Sixteen percent of the residual group reported that undressing for the first time, or becoming used to being nude, was the only adjustment. Of these people who had to adjust, only 15 percent found the adjustment to be difficult.

I really was afraid and shy and I didn't feel too well. We had discussed going, but when the time came to go I couldn't sleep that night. . . . Once we got nude then everything just seemed to come natural. I was surprised at how at ease I felt.

A variety of other response patterns, which I shall not discuss in detail, were characteristic of the initial visit. For example, one pattern related to the visitor's socioeconomic position.[7] Because facilities in many camps are relatively primitive, those used to more comfortable circumstances were likely to be disappointed. One professional man said:

I was disappointed to see it was as rustic and unkempt as it was. . . . If people wore clothes and nothing else changed it would be a fourth-class resort. [Q] Everything there is shabby and not well cared for.

THE ADOPTION OF NUDISM AS A WAY OF LIFE

Coaching and Social Validation

The newcomers to camps received no formal indoctrination in the nudist perspective, but acquired it almost imperceptibly as the result of a subtle social process. Informal coaching, either prior to or after arrival, appears to have eased adjustment problems.[8]

My husband said the men are gentlemen. He told me I'd have fun, like play in the sun, play games, and swim.

She didn't want to undress. . . . [Q] I tried to talk to her and her husband did; she finally got convinced. [Q] I told her you feel better with them off, and that no one will pay any attention.

The consensus of 95 percent of the interviewees was that, as one of them put it, "Things run along very smoothly when you first become a nudist." Asked if they ever had any doubts that becoming a nudist was the right decision, once they had made up their minds, 77 percent reported that they had never had any doubts. Fourteen percent had doubts at the time of the interview. The following quotations illustrate the process of social validation that tends to quell doubts:[9]

I do and I don't [have doubts], because of my religion. [Q] Nobody knows about

[7] At the time of the interviews, the interviewers, making a common-sense judgment, placed 54 percent of the nudist respondents in the lower-middle class. This was the modal and median placement.

[8] For a discussion of "coaching" relationships, see Anselm Strauss, *Mirrors and Masks: The Search for Identity;* New York, Free Press, 1959; pp. 109–118.

[9] By "social validation," I mean the process by which the subjective comes to be considered objective—that is, true. The views of others (especially those considered to have more extensive knowledge) provide a social yardstick by which to measure truth. Pareto reaches a similar view of objectivity. Note the following statement: ". . . we apply the term 'logical actions' to actions that logically conjoin means to ends not only from the standpoint of the subject performing them, but from the standpoint of other persons who have more extensive knowledge—in other words, to actions that are logical both subjectively and objectively in the sense just explained." See Vilfredo Pareto, *The Mind and Society,* Vol. 1; New York, Harcourt, Brace, 1935; p. 77.

it, and I wonder about that. [Q] Whether it's the right thing. But as I read the pamphlets [nudist literature] I realize it's up to the individual. God made Adam and Eve and they had no clothes. You don't have to be ashamed of your body. Some are fat and some are thin, but it doesn't matter; it's your personality that matters. I don't know, if my minister found out, I'd defend it. We don't use bad language. Sometimes I wonder, but down underneath I think it's all right. We've just been taught to hide our bodies. Sometimes I wonder, but then I think what the pamphlets say. [Q: At what time do you have these doubts?] When I'm in church. [Q] Yes, when I get to thinking about religion. Not very often. Sometimes I just wonder. [Q: Do you ever have these doubts while at camp?] No, I forget about everything. I'm having too much fun. I remind myself that this is something good for the children. My children won't become Peeping Toms or sex maniacs.

[At first] I felt ridiculous. I thought all those people looked so funny. [Q: Why's that?] All your life you've seen people with their clothes on; now they all have them off. After a while, you feel ridiculous with your clothes on. [Q] I liked the people. They were all very nice. They came from nice families. It couldn't just be something anyone would do, or just people from a lower class.

The nudist way of life becomes a different reality, a new world:

It seems like a different world from the world we live in every day. No washing, ironing, worries. You feel so free there. The people are friendly there, interested in each other. But not nosy. You can relax among them more easily than in the city.

And this new reality imposes a different meaning on the everyday life of the outside world:

My daughter told us today the boys and girls don't sit together at school, but it makes no difference to her. Several times they're out playing and the boys get excited when they see their panties. My children don't understand that. They have a different state of mind toward different sexes.

Motives for Becoming a Nudist

Persons who became nudists—that is, became members of a camp and conceived of themselves as nudists—usually demonstrated an autonomy of motives,[10] in the sense that their motives for doing so differed from their motives for first visiting a camp. That is to say, participation in different stages of the "nudist career" were usually characterized by different sets of motives. Hence the curiosity that had often been the overriding motive for initial visits was satisfied, and the incentive for affiliating with a nudist camp was based on the person's experiences at the camp, experiences which may not have been anticipated before visiting the camp.[11] It should be noted, however, that the decision was sometimes prompted by the owner's insistence that visitors join if they wished to return. As Table 4 shows, there was a consider-

TABLE 4 Comparative Desires of Male and Female Members of Couples to Visit a Nudist Camp*

	Male Wanted To Go More	Male and Female Wanted To Go Equally	Female Wanted To Go More
First visit	79%	21%	0%
Return visits	40	51	9

* Two unmarried couples are included in these data.

[10] This concept was developed by Gordon Allport, "The Functional Autonomy of Motives," *Amer. J. Psychology* (1937) 50:141–156.

[11] Attendance is usually confined to summer weekends, and sexual curiosity may arise again between seasons.

able change, after the first visit, in the pattern of male versus female desire to attend the camp.

The following quotations are illustrative of the autonomous motives of respondents for the first and subsequent visits:

[*Q: What was your main reason for wanting to attend camp the first time?*] Curiosity. [*Q*] To see how people behave under such circumstances, and maybe also looking at the girls. [*Q*] Just that it's interesting to see girls in the nude. [*Q: What is the main reason you continue to attend?*] I found it very relaxing. [*Q*] It's more comfortable to swim without a wet suit, and not wearing clothes when it's real warm is more comfortable and relaxing.

[I went up the first time] to satisfy my husband. He wanted me to go and I fought it. But he does a lot for me, so why not do him a favor. [She had told him that people went to nudist camps only for thrills and that she would divorce him before she would go. Although he talked her into it, she cried all the way to camp. Asked why she continued to attend, she looked surprised and replied:] Why, because I thoroughly enjoy it!

This last quotation describes a common pattern for women, which appears also in the following recollection:

[I went the first time] because my husband wanted me to go. [*Q: What is the main reason that you continue to attend?*] Because we had fun . . . and we met a lot of nice people.

The interviewees were asked what they liked most about nudism, with the results shown in Table 5. Three of the benefits cited are of special sociological interest—the concept of nudist freedom, the family-centered nature of the recreation, and the emphasis on friendliness and sociability.

"*Freedom.*" Echoing the nudist ideology, many respondents mentioned

TABLE 5 What Interviewees Liked Most About Nudism

	Percent of Sample Mentioning the Item
Friendliness, sociability	60%
Relaxation, getting away from the city	47
Enjoyment of outdoors and sports	36
Freedom	31
Sunbathing	26
Physical health	26
Children becoming informed about the human body	11
Mental health	8
Economical vacations	4
Family recreation, keeping family together	4
Seeing people nude	1
Other aspects	15

"freedom"—using the term in various contexts—as a major benefit. There were varied definitions of this freedom and its meaning for the participant. Some defined it in terms of free body action, of being unhindered by clothing.

Nudism . . . gives me an opportunity to be in the sunshine and fresh air. Also to take a swim nude gives me free expression of body. [*Q*] I'm not hindered by clothes, a freedom of body movement and I can feel the water all over my body.

Nothing was binding; no socks, no tight belt, nothing clothing-wise touching me.

You don't have garter belts or bras. Your body can breathe.

With perspiration your clothes start to bind and you develop rashes. [*Q*] You just feel more relaxed when you're nude, and more comfortable from hot, sticky clothing.

Others interpreted freedom from clothing in a different way:

Freedom from a convention of society. It's a relief to get away from it. [Q] A physical relief in that wearing clothes is something you must do. I hate wearing a choking tie at a dinner party, but I have to because it is a society convention.

Yon don't have to dress appropriate for the occasion. You aren't looking for the smartest slacks and sports clothes.

The freedom. . . . You don't have to worry about the way you're dressed. You don't try to outdo someone with a thirty-dollar bathing suit.

For others, freedom meant the absence of routine and restraint:

A nudist camp has a lot more freedom [than a summer resort]. You do just as you want. . . . [Q] Just to do what you want to do, there is nothing you have to do. At a resort you have to participate in activities.

The freedom. [Q] You can do as you please. [Q] I can read or just lay in the sun.

The freedom. [Q] You can go any place you want in the camp. You can walk anywhere nude.

The range of conceptions of freedom is indicated by the following examples:

I felt free in the water. No one staring at you.

I like the complete freedom of . . . expression. With nudist people, I find them more frank and outspoken, not two-faced. You don't have to be cagey and worry about saying the wrong thing.

Feeling free with your body. [Q] I can't really explain it. Feeling more confident, I guess.

The varying constructions of nudist freedom support Schutz's model of man as a commonsense actor.[12] According to Schutz, man lives very naively in his world; clear and distinct experiences are mixed with vague conjectures, and "cookbook" descriptions of experiences are uncritically adopted from others. When these standard descriptions are vague, and are called into question—for example, by an interviewer who asks what is meant by "freedom"—a wide variety of constructions is elicited from respondents. Nudists, as devotees to a "cause," resemble other commonsense actors in their frequent inability to understand their stock answers critically.

Family Cohesion. As shown in Table 5, some respondents gave, as the feature of nudism they like most, its function in providing family recreation. One of the interview sample expressed this as follows:

Nudism tends to keep the family together. In the nonnudist society the family tends to split into different organizations; all have different interests. You can still do different things in camp, but you still have a common interest. And all your plans are made together.

One would expect that nudism would lead to family cohesiveness, as a result of this common interest, and also as a result of a tendency for the family members to conceal their nudist involvements in their dealings with the outside world. In regard to the element of secrecy, Simmel has pointed out how a group's intensified seclusion results in heightened cohesiveness.[13] Participation in nudism did not, however, always lead to increased family cohesiveness. For ex-

---

[12] See Alfred Schutz, "The Dimensions of the Social World," in *Collected Papers, II: Studies in Social Theory,* edited by Arvid Broderson; The Hague, Martinus Nijhoff, 1964; pp. 48 *ff.*

[13] Kurt H. Wolff, *The Sociology of Georg Simmel;* New York, Free Press, 1950; see Part IV.

ample, if one spouse did not appreciate the experience, the family's continued participation resulted in increased strain. And although nudist ideology claims that nudist participation brings the family closer together, 78 percent of the interviewees, and 82 percent of the questionnaire respondents, reported no change in their family relationships.

Relationships with Others. Friendliness and sociability were the characteristics of the nudist experience mentioned most often by interviewees. In addition, nudists extended the concept of "family" to include fellow nudists; they cited a "togetherness" that is rare in the clothed society. Some insight into this cohesiveness was displayed in the following remarks by an interviewee:

Camaraderie and congeniality . . . comes in any minority group that supports an unpopular position. [Q] Feelings develop by these in-groups because you are brought together by one idea which you share. On the street you may run into people you share no ideas with.

The interviewees were asked how the camp situation would change if everything remained constant except that clothes were required. Most of them anticipated that their bond would be dissolved.

They would lose the common bond. They have a bond that automatically is a bond. They are in a minority. They are glad you're here. You are welcome there; they're glad you're one of us.

I think the people would be less friendly. When you're all nude you feel the same as them. You all came here to be nude. . . .

[Q] Everybody feels the other is the same; you have something in common to be doing this unusual thing.

A number of interviewees, supporting the nudist contention that social distinctions diminish in the nudist camp, believed that class distinctions would reappear if clothing were donned.[14] A 19-year-old respondent cited both class and age distinctions:

You would have . . . your classes, and age. [Q] I wouldn't feel as close to B and G.

There is a great age difference. Knowing them this way, though, gives us a common bond. You just don't think about their ages or anything else about them.

Several blue-collar workers remarked that one of the things they liked about nudism was that, without their uniforms or customary clothes, they and their families could associate with a better class of people. Status striving decreases with the removal of these important props of impression management.

[If everyone in the camp wore clothes] everything I detest about country clubs I've seen would immediately become manifest. Namely: (1) social climbing with all its accompanying insincerity and ostentation; (2) wolves tracking down virgins; (3) highly formalized activities such as golf; (4) gambling and drinking; (5) embarrassment of having to swim under the appraising gaze of a gallery full of people sipping cocktails. This is the paradox, the curious thing; it doesn't embarrass me to swim at . . . [a nudist camp] whereas I can't be coaxed into the swimming pool at the country club in my hometown. [Q] I think that the reason is the fact that so much in that country club is so calculated to make

---

[14] For discussions of clothes as "sign equipment," see Erving Goffman, "Symbols of Class Status," *British J. Sociology* (1951) 2:294–304; and *The Presentation of Self in Everyday Life;* Garden City, N.Y., Doubleday, 1959; pp. 24 ff. Also see Gregory Stone, "Appearance and the Self," in *Human Behavior and Social Processes: An Interactionist Approach,* edited by Arnold Rose; Boston, Houghton Mifflin, 1962; pp. 86–118.

tableaux or pictures, in which only the young and the handsome can really be a part. That's terribly true.

Another interviewee, when asked what he liked most about social nudism, replied:

It is the best way to relax. [Q] Once you take your clothes off, people are on the same basis. [Q] Everyone is a person. There are no distinctions between a doctor or a mechanic because of clothing. [Q] . . . It's hard to describe. It's just that all have an equal basis, no distinctions because of clothing. That helps you to relax.

Although these statements may be somewhat idealized, the nudist camp does effectively break down patterns common to country clubs, resorts, and other settings in the outside society. Sex, class, and power lose much of their relevance in the nudist camp, and the suspension of the barriers they create effects a greater unity among the participants. This is not to say, however, that there is no social hierarchy—a point to which I shall return shortly.

The suspension of clothing modesty reinforces the atmoshpere of "one big family" in another way. Clothing modesty is a *ceremony* of everyday life that sustains a nonintimate definition of relationships, and with its voluntary suspension relationships are usually defined as closer in character. However, for this to occur, trust must not be called into question, and each person must take for granted that he is differentiated from other social objects. Camp relationships usually meet these conditions. For example, they are differentiated from relationships elsewhere; being undressed in front of others is still out of the ordinary, since nudists do not appear nude among outsiders.

The social effect was significant enough to prompt members to describe the nudist way of life as a discovery that had brought new meaning to their lives.

The experience provided many of them with "a sense of belonging." As one respondent put it:

. . . you feel like you're part of a whole family. You feel very close. That's how I feel.

The feeling of being part of "one big family" was, of course, more common to the smaller camps. But even in the large camps, participants in camp activities felt themselves to be a part of a special group.

As I have suggested, however, the "togetherness" of nudists is exaggerated. Personality clashes, cliques, and intergroup disagreements exist, and social stratification remains in evidence. In the words of an unmarried neophyte:

Sometimes I think there is a hierarchy at . . . [a large nudist camp]. [Q] In any organization there are cliques. [Q] These cliques I believe are formed by seniority. [Q] Those who have been there the longest. [Q: *What makes you think this?*] Something that is in the air. [Q] Just an impression you get. It's hard to say; it's just a feeling. [Q] As a newcomer I felt not at ease. [Q] There is an air of suspicion; people are not really friendly. [Q] They are not really unfriendly, just suspicious, I suppose, of single men. . . . They suspect single men are coming for Peeping Tom purposes. [Q] Just to see the nude women. . . . Single men, I think, are the lowest class at camp.

This attitude was borne out in the interviews with other single men; rarely did they describe nudism in *gemeinschaftlich* terms. The meaning of a person's experiences still depends on his position in the system.

Furthermore, it is doubtful that many people find a Utopia in nudism. The nudists interviewed were asked how seriously they felt that they would be affected if nudist camps were closed. As Table 6 shows, 30 percent of the interviewees considered that they would be

Closing Camps Would Affect Respondent	Percent of Respondents
Very much	43
Somewhat	26
Not too much	17
Not at all	13

* Vague categories, such as those presented in this table, were occasionally used for their descriptive value in grossly delineating some point. In this case, respondents were asked to classify themselves (after completing their open-end response). In other cases, the coders used a large group of indicators in constructing such gross scales. Although these scales lacked intrinsic rigor, reliability between coders was high.

relatively unaffected. When they were asked to identify their three best friends, almost half of the interviewees did not name another nudist.[15] Table 7 details this information, as well as the degree of social involvement with other nudists, as rated by coders.

NUDISTS AND THE CLOTHED SOCIETY

Nudists envision themselves as being labeled deviant by members of the clothed society. In both the interviews and the questionnaires, the respondents were asked to conceptualize the view of nudists taken by the general public, and by their parents. No consistent difference was found between the views of the two groups, as described by the nudists.[16] Approximately one-third of the respondents conceptualized a live-and-let-live attitude on the part of parents and public. Two-thirds conceptualized a negative or very negative attitude.

They think we're fanatics. [Q] That we go overboard on something. That we're out of line.

If I went by what the guys say at work, you'd have to be pretty crazy, off your head a little bit. [Q] They think you almost have to be . . . a sex fiend or something like that. They think there's sex orgies, or wife-swapping, or something.

They think we're a bunch of nuts. [Q] They just think that anyone who runs around without clothes is nuts. If they stopped to investigate, they'd find we weren't.

People think the body should be clothed and not exposed at any time. They associate that with vulgarity, indecency, and abnormality. [Q] Vulgarity is something that is unacceptable to the general public. [Q] Indecency in this respect would be exposing portions of the body which normally we hide. [Q] Abnormality? Well, the general public feels it's abnormal for the body to be undressed around other people, in a social group.

[15] Although 59 percent of the interviewees had been nudists for over two years, and 27 percent of this group had been nudists for over ten years, involvement did not appear to be particularly high. Also, an estimated 17 percent of the membership drops out every year.

[16] Although a positive versus negative differentiation of parents and general public was not found, there was a difference in the character of the typifications involved. In the case of parents, the typifications were derived from a history of experiences with an acting personality and were relatively concrete. In contrast, typifications of the general public were highly anonymous. Because such a collectivity could never be experienced directly, there was a much larger region of taken-for-granteds. This is due to the great number of substrata typifications underlying the general whole. This phenomenon is discussed by Alfred Schutz (see footnote 12).

TABLE 7 Social Involvement with Other Nudists*

Best Friends Who Are Nudists	Degree of Social Involvement					
	Very Low	Moderately Low	Neither High Nor Low	Moderately High	Very High	Totals
None	13	9	12	5	7	46 (47%)
One	3	2	6	9	5	25 (26%)
Two		1	3	3	10	17 (18%)
Three					9	9 (9%)
Total	16	12	21	17	31	97 (100%)
	(16%)	(12%)	(22%)	(18%)	(32%)	

* The data on the number of best friends who are nudists were drawn from the replies of interviewees. The degree of social involvement was rated by coders on the basis of the following instructions: Code the degree of social involvement with nudists throughout the year on the basis of answers to Question 40 (b and c). Think of this as a scale or continuum: (1) Very low involvement (no contact at all); (2) moderately low involvement (just write or phone occasionally); (3) neither low nor high involvement (get together every couple of months—or attend New Year's party or splash party together); (4) moderately high involvement (visit once a month); (5) very high involvement (visit every week or two).

The fact that nudists were able to participate in a group which they viewed as stigmatized (and also the sense of belonging they claimed to have found in nudism) suggested that nudists might be isolated in the larger society. If they were isolated they could more easily participate in such a deviant group, being insulated from social controls.

A comparison of nudist interviewees with a sample of the general population[17] did show the nudists to fall substantially below the general population in frequency of informal association,[18] as shown in Table 8. Further, while members of the general population got together most often with relatives, nudists got together most often with friends,[19]

as Table 9 indicates. The fact that 34 percent of the nudist sample got together with relatives less than once a month may reflect a considerable insulation from informal controls, since it is

TABLE 8 Frequency of Informal Group Participation

	Nudists	General Population
At least twice a week	17%	30%
Every 4 or 5 days	4	35
Once a week	12	16
Less often or never	67	19

[17] In this comparison, Axelrod's data on a sample of the general population in the Detroit area were used. See Morris Axelrod, "Urban Structure and Social Participation," *Amer. Sociol. Review* (1956) 21:13–18.

[18] A major limitation in this comparison, however, is that Axelrod has collapsed frequencies of association that are less than once a week into the category of "less often or never."

[19] Axelrod finds this greater participation with friends only for members of his sample with high income or high educational or social status.

TABLE 9 Frequency of Association with Several Types of Informal Groups

	Relatives		Friends		Neighbors		Co-workers	
	Nudists	General Popula- tion	Nudists	General Popula- tion	Nudists	General Popula- tion	Nudists	General Popula- tion
At least once a week	38%	51%	49%	29%	26%	30%	17%	13%
A few times a month	16	13	21	20	11	9	10	8
About once a month	11	13	8	19	6	9	7	15
Less often	34	23	20	32	56	52	63	65

relatives who would probably provide the greatest pressure in inhibiting participation in such deviant groups.[20]

The degree to which nudists were isolated in the clothed society was found to be related to the length of time they

TABLE 10 Social Isolation of Nudists According to Their Length of Time In Nudism

Degree of Social Isolation*	Years in Nudism			
	1–2	3–5	6–9	10 and Over
Moderately or very isolated	22%	38%	44%	54%
Neither isolated nor active	39	31	25	35
Very or moderately active	39	31	32	12

* As rated by coders.

had been nudists. As shown in Table 10, the longer a person had been in nudism, the more likely he was to be isolated. This may be interpreted in different ways. For example, there may be a tendency to become more isolated with continued participation, perhaps to avoid sanctions. (Yet, in regard to formal organizations nudists did *not* drop out or become less active.) Or, in the past it is likely that nudism was considered even more deviant than it is today and therefore it may have appealed primarily to more isolated types of people.

Regardless of which interpretation is correct, as previously discussed, many nudists found a sense of belonging in nudism.[21]

People are lonely. It gives them a sense of belonging.

Until I started going out . . . [to camp] I never felt like I was part of a crowd. But I

[20] Also the absolute frequency of association with friends includes association with nudist friends. This reduces the apparent social-control function of their friendship associations.

Curiously, members of the nudist sample belonged to more formal organizations than did members of Axelrod's sample of the general population. The comparison was as follows: Membership in no group—general population, 37 percent; nudists, 18 percent. One group—general population, 31 percent; nudists, 27 percent. Two groups—general population, 16 percent; nudists, 19 percent.

[21] Some nudists also viewed themselves as members of an elite, superior to clothed society because they had suspended the body taboo.

do out there. I was surprised. [Q] Well, like I said, I was never part of a crowd . . . I had friends, but never outstanding. My wife and I were [camp] King and Queen.

However, while the nudist experience helps solve this life problem for some, it creates this same problem for others. For the latter group, nudism may only ease the problem that it creates—that is, the isolation that results from concealing one's affiliation with a deviant group.[22]

---

[22] For a discussion of information control, see Erving Goffman, *Stigma: The Management of Spoiled Identity;* Englewood Cliffs, N.J., Prentice-Hall, 1963; pp. 41–104.

Apprenticeships in Prostitution

JAMES H. BRYAN

. . . This paper provides some detailed, albeit preliminary, information concerning induction and training in a particular type of deviant career: prostitution, at the call girl level. It describes the order of events, and their surrounding structure, which future call girls experience in entering their occupation.

The respondents in this study were 33 prostitutes, all currently or previously working in the Los Angeles area. They ranged in age from 18 to 32, most being in their mid-twenties. None of the interviewees were obtained through official law enforcement agencies, but seven were found within the context of a neuropsychiatric hospital. The remaining respondents were gathered primarily through individual referrals from previous participants in the study. There were no obvious differences between the "psychiatric sample" and the other interviewees on the data to be reported.

All subjects in the sample were call girls. That is, they typically obtained their clients by individual referrals, primarily by telephone, and enacted the sexual contract in their own or their clients' place of residence or employment. They did not initiate contact with their customers in bars, streets, or houses of prostitution, although they might meet their customers at any number of locations by prearrangement. The minimum fee charged per sexual encounter was $20.00. As an adjunct to the call girl interviews, three pimps and two "call boys" were interviewed as well.[1]

Approximately two thirds of the sample were what are sometimes known as "outlaw broads"; that is, they were not under the supervision of a pimp when interviewed. There is evidence that the majority of pimps who were aware of the study prohibited the girls under their direction from participating in it. It should be noted that many members of the sample belonged to one or another clique; their individually expressed opinions may not be independent. . . .

THE ENTRANCE

I had been thinking about it [becoming a call girl] before a lot. . . . Thinking about wanting to do it, but I had no connections. Had I not had a connection, I probably wouldn't have started working. . . . I thought about starting out. . . . Once I tried it [without a contact]. . . . I met this guy at a bar and I tried to make him pay me, but the thing is, you can't do it that way because they are romantically interested in you, and they don't think that it is on that kind of basis. You can't all of a sudden come up and want money for it, you have to be known beforehand. . . . I think that is what holds a lot of girls back who might work. I think I might have

Reprinted from *Social Problems,* Vol. 12, No. 3 (Winter 1965), pp. 287–97.

[1] This definition departs somewhat from that offered by Clinard. He defines the call girl as one dependent upon an organization for recruiting patrons and one who typically works in lower-class hotels. The present sample is best described by Clinard's category high-class independent professional prostitute. M. D. Clinard, *Sociology of Deviant Behavior,* New York: Rinehart & Co., Inc., 1957.

started a year sooner had I had a connection. You seem to make one contact or another . . . if it's another girl or a pimp or just someone who will set you up and get you a client. . . . You can't just, say, get an apartment and get a phone in and everything and say, "Well, I'm gonna start business," because you gotta get clients from somewhere. There has to be a contact.

Immediately prior to entrance into the occupation, all but one girl had personal contact with someone professionally involved in call girl activities (pimps or other call girls). The one exception had contact with a customer of call girls. While various occupational groups (e.g., photographers) seem to be peripherally involved, often unwittingly, with the call girl, there was no report of individuals involved in such occupations being contacts for new recruits. The novice's initial contact is someone at the level at which she will eventually enter the occupation: not a street-walker, but a call girl; not a pimp who manages girls out of a house of prostitution, but a pimp who manages call girls.

Approximately half of the girls reported that their initial contact for entrance into the profession was another "working girl." The nature of these relationships is quite variable. In some cases, the girls have been long standing friends. Other initial contacts involved sexual relationships between a Lesbian and the novice. Most, however, had known each other less than a year, and did not appear to have a very close relationship, either in the sense of time spent together or of biographical information exchanged. The relationship may begin with the aspiring call girl soliciting the contact. That is, if a professional is known to others as a call girl, she will be sought out and approached by females who are strangers.[2]

I haven't ever gone out and looked for one. All of these have fell right into my hands. . . . They turned themselves out. . . . They come to me for help.

Whatever their relationship, whenever the professional agrees to aid the beginner, she also, it appears, implicitly assumes responsibility for training her. This is evidenced by the fact that only one such female contact referred the aspirant to another girl for any type of help. Data are not available as to the reason for this unusual referral.

If the original contact was not another call girl but a pimp, a much different relationship is developed and the career follows a somewhat different course. The relationship between pimp and girl is typically one of lovers, not friends:

. . . because I love him very much. Obviously, I'm doing this mostly for him. . . . I'd do anything for him. I'm not just saying I will, I am. . . . [After discussing his affair with another woman] I just decided that I knew what he was when I decided to do this for him and I decided I had two choices—either accept it or not, and I accepted it, and I have no excuse.

Occasionally, however, a strictly business relationship will be formed:

Right now I am buying properties, and as soon as I can afford it, I am buying stocks. . . . It is strictly a business deal. This man and I are friends, our relationship ends there. He handles all the money, he is making all the investments and I trust him. We have a legal document drawn up which states that half the investments are mine, half of them his, so I am protected.

[2] A point also made in the autobiographical account of a retired call girl, Virginia McManus, *Not For Love,* New York: Dell Publishing Co., Inc., 1960, p. 160.

Whether the relationship is love or business, the pimp solicits the new girl.[3] It is usually agreed that the male will have an important managerial role in the course of the girl's career, and that both will enjoy the gains from the girl's activities for an indefinite period:

Actually a pimp has to have complete control or else it's like trouble with him. Because if a pimp doesn't, if she is not madly in love with him or something in some way, a pimp won't keep a girl.

Once the girl agrees to function as a call girl, the male, like his female counterpart, undertakes the training of the girl, or refers the girl to another call girl for training. Either course seems equally probable. Referrals, when employed, are typically to friends and, in some cases, wives or ex-wives.

Although the data are limited, it appears that the pimp retains his dominance over the trainee even when the latter is being trained by a call girl. The girl trainer remains deferential to the pimp's wishes regarding the novice.

APPRENTICESHIP

Once a contact is acquired and the decision to become a call girl made, the recruit moves to the next stage in the career sequence: the apprenticeship period. The structure of the apprenticeship will be described, followed by a description of the content most frequently communicated during this period.

The apprenticeship is typically served under the direction of another call girl, but may occasionally be supervised by a pimp. Twenty-four girls in the sample initially worked under the supervision of other girls. The classroom is, like the future place of work, an apartment. The apprentice typically serves in the trainer's apartment, either temporarily residing with the trainer or commuting there almost daily. The novice rarely serves her apprenticeship in such places as a house of prostitution, motel, or on the street. It is also infrequent that the girl is transported out of her own city to serve an apprenticeship. Although the data are not extensive, the number of girls being trained simultaneously by a particular trainer has rarely been reported to be greater than three. Girls sometimes report spending up to eight months in training, but the average stay seems to be two or three months. The trainer controls all referrals and appointments, novices seemingly not having much control over the type of sexual contact made or the circumstances surrounding the enactment of the contract.

The structure of training under the direction of a pimp seems similar, though information is more limited. The girls are trained in an apartment in the city they intend to work and for a short period of time. There is some evidence that the pimp and the novice often do not share the same apartment as might the novice and the girl trainer. There appear to be two reasons for the separation of pimp and girl. First, it is not uncommonly thought that cues which suggest the presence of other men displease the girl's customers:

Well, I would never let them know that I had a lover, which is something that you never ever let a john know, because this makes them very reticent to give you money, because they think you are going

---

[3] Two of the pimps denied that this was very often so and maintained that the girls will solicit them. The degree to which they are solicited seems to depend upon the nature and extent of the reputations. It is difficult to judge the accuracy of these reports as there appears to be a strong taboo against admitting to such solicitation.

to go and spend it with your lover, which is what usually happens.

(Interestingly, the work of Winick suggests that such prejudices may not actually be held by many customers.[4]) Secondly, the legal repercussions are much greater, of course, for the pimp who lives with his girl than for two girls rooming together. As one pimp of 19 years' experience puts it:

It is because of the law. There is a law that is called the illegal cohabitation that they rarely use unless the man becomes big in stature. If he is a big man in the hustling world, the law then employs any means at their command. . . .

Because of the convenience in separation of housing, it is quite likely that the pimp is less directly involved with the day-to-day training of girls than the call girl trainer.

The content of the training period seems to consist of two broad, interrelated dimensions, one philosophical, the other interpersonal. The former refers to the imparting of a value structure, the latter to "do's" and "don'ts" of relating to customers and, secondarily, to other "working girls" and pimps. The latter teaching is perhaps best described by the concept of a short range perspective. That is, most of the "do's" and "don'ts" pertain to ideas and actions that the call girl uses in problematic situations.[5] Not all girls absorb these teachings, and those who do incorporate them in varying degrees.

Insofar as a value structure is transmitted it is that of maximizing gains while minimizing effort, even if this requires transgressions of either a legal or moral nature. Frequently, it is postulated that people, particularly men, are corrupt or easily corruptible, that all social relationships are but a reflection of a "con," and that prostitution is simply a more honest or at least no more dishonest act than the everyday behavior of "squares." Furthermore, not only are "johns" basically exploitative, but they are easily exploited; hence they are, in some respects, stupid. As explained by a pimp:

. . . [in the hustling world] the trick or the john is known as a fool . . . this is not the truth. . . . He [the younger pimp] would teach his woman that a trick was a fool.

Since the male is corrupt, or honest only because he lacks the opportunity to be corrupt, then it is only appropriate that he be exploited as he exploits.

Girls first start making their "scores"—say one guy keeps them for a while or maybe she gets, you know, three or four grand out of him, say a car or a coat. These are your scores. . . .

The general assumption that man is corrupt is empirically confirmed when the married male betrays his wife, when the moralist, secular or religious, betrays his publicly stated values, or when the "john" "stiffs" (cheats) the girl. An example of the latter is described by a girl as she reflects upon her disillusionment during her training period.

It is pretty rough when you are starting out. You get stiffed a lot of times. . . . Oh sure. They'll take advantage of you anytime they can. And I'm a trusting soul, I really am. I'll believe anybody till they prove different. I've made a lot of mistakes that way. You get to the point, well, Christ, what the heck can I believe in people, they tell me one thing and here's what they do to me.

---

[4] C. Winick, "Prostitutes' Clients' Perception of the Prostitute and Themselves," *International Journal of Social Psychiatry*, 8 (1961–62), pp, 289–297.

[5] H. S. Becker, Blanche Geer, E. C. Hughes, and A. L. Strauss, *Boys in White,* Chicago: University of Chicago Press, 1961.

Values such as fairness with other working girls, or fidelity to a pimp, may occasionally be taught. To quote a pimp:

So when you ask me if I teach a kind of basic philosophy, I would say that you could say that. Because you try to teach them in an amoral way that there is a right and wrong way as pertains to this game . . . and then you teach them that when working with other girls to try to treat the other girl fairly because a woman's worst enemy in the street [used in both a literal and figurative sense] is the other woman and only by treating the other women decently can she expect to get along. . . . Therefore the basic philosophy I guess would consist of a form of honesty, a form of sincerity and complete fidelity to her man [pimp].

It should be noted, however, that behavior based on enlightened self-interest with concomitant exploitation is not limited to customer relationships. Interviewees frequently mentioned a pervasive feeling of distrust between trainer and trainee, and such incidents as thefts or betrayal of confidences are occasionally reported and chronically guarded against.

Even though there may be considerable pressure upon the girl to accept this value structure, many of them (perhaps the majority of the sample) reject it.

People have told me that I wasn't turned out, but turned loose instead. . . . Someone who is turned out is turned out to believe in a certain code of behavior, and this involves having a pimp, for one thing. It also involves never experiencing anything but hatred or revulsion for "tricks"

for another thing. It involves always getting the money in front [before the sexual act] and a million little things that are very strictly adhered to by those in the "in group," which I am not. . . . Never being nice or pleasant to a trick unless you are doing it for the money, getting more money. [How did you learn that?] It was explained to me over a period of about six months. I learned that you were doing it to make money for yourself so that you could have nice things and security. . . . [Who would teach you this?] [The trainer] would teach me this.[6]

It seems reasonable to assume that the value structure serves, in general, to create in-group solidarity and to alienate the girl from "square" society, and that this structure serves the political advantage of the trainer and the economic gains of the trainee more than it allays the personal anxieties of either. In fact, failure to adopt these values at the outset does not appear to be correlated with much personal distress.[7] As one girl describes her educational experiences:

Some moral code. We're taught, as a culture . . . it's there and after a while you live, breathe, and eat it. Now, what makes you go completely against everything that's inside you, everything that you have been taught, and the whole society, to do things like this?

Good empirical evidence, however, concerning the functions and effectiveness of this value structure with regard to subjective comfort is lacking.

A series of deductions derived from the premises indicated above serve to

---

[6] The statements made by prostitutes to previous investigators and mental helpers may have been parroting this particular value structure and perhaps have misled previous investigators into making the assumption that "all whores hate men." While space prohibits a complete presentation of the data, neither our questionnaire nor interview data suggest that this is a predominant attitude among call girls.

[7] There is, from the present study, little support for the hypothesis of Reckless concerning the association of experienced trauma and guilt with abruptness of entry into the occupation. W. C. Reckless, *The Crime Problem,* New York: Appleton-Century-Crofts, Inc., 1950.

provide, in part, the "rules" of interpersonal contact with the customer. Each customer is to be seen as a "mark," and "pitches" are to be made.

[Did you have a standard pitch?] It's sort of amusing. I used to listen to my girl friend [trainer]. She was the greatest at this telephone type of situation. She would call up and cry and say that people had come to her door. . . . She'd cry and she'd complain and she'd say "I have a bad check at the liquor store, and they sent the police over," and really . . . a girl has a story she tells the man. . . . Anything, you know, so he'll help her out. Either it's the rent or she needs a car, or doctor's bills, or any number of things.

Any unnecessary interaction with the customer is typically frowned upon, and the trainee will receive exhortations to be quick about her business. One girl in her fourth week of work explains:

[What are some of the other don't's that you have learned about?] Don't take so much time. . . . The idea is to get rid of them as quickly as possible.

Other content taught concerns specific information about specific customers.

. . . she would go around the bar and say, now look at that man over there, he's this way and that way, and this is what he would like and these are what his problems are. . . .

. . . she would teach me what the men wanted and how much to get, what to say when I got there . . . just a line to hand them.

Training may also include proprieties concerning consuming alcohol and drugs, when and how to obtain the fee, how to converse with the customers and, occasionally, physical and sexual hygiene. As a girl trainer explains:

First, of all, impress cleanliness. Because, on the whole, the majority of girls, I would say, I don't believe there are any cleaner women walking the streets, because they've got to be aware of any type of body odor. . . . You teach them to French [fellatio] and how to talk to men.

[Do they [pimps] teach you during the turning out period how to make a telephone call?] Oh, usually, yes. They don't teach you, they just tell you how to do it and you do it with your good common sense, but if you have trouble, they tell you more about it.

Interestingly, the specific act of telephoning a client is often distressing to the novice and is of importance in her training. Unfortunately for the girl, it is an act she must perform with regularity as she does considerable soliciting.[8] One suspects that such behavior is embarrassing for her because it is an unaccustomed role for her to play—she has so recently come from a culture where young women do *not* telephone men for dates. Inappropriate sex-role behavior seems to produce greater personal distress than does appropriate sex-role behavior even when it it morally reprehensible.

Well, it is rather difficult to get on the telephone, when you've never worked before, and talk to a man about a subject like that, and it is very new to you.

What is omitted from the training should be noted as well. There seems to be little instruction concerning sexual techniques as such, even though the previous sexual experience of the trainee may have been quite limited. What instruction there is typically revolves around the practice of fellatio. There seems to be some encouragement not to experience sexual orgasm with the client, though this may be quite variable with the trainer.

[8] The topic of solicitation will be dealt with in a forthcoming paper.

. . . and sometimes, I don't know if its a set rule or maybe it's an unspoken rule, you don't enjoy your dates.

Yes, he did [teach attitudes]. He taught me to be cold. . . .

It should be stressed that, if the girls originally accepted such instructions and values, many of them, at least at the time of interviewing, verbalized a rejection of these values and reported behavior which departed considerably from the interpersonal rules stipulated as "correct" by their trainers. Some experience orgasms with the customer, some show considerable affect toward "johns," others remain drunk or "high" throughout the contact.[9] While there seems to be general agreement as to what the rules of interpersonal conduct are, there appears to be considerable variation in the adoption of such rules.

A variety of methods are employed to communicate the content described above. The trainer may arrange to eavesdrop on the interactions of girl and client and then discuss the interaction with her. One trainer, for example, listened through a closed door to the interaction of a new girl with a customer, then immediately after he left, discussed, in a rather heated way, methods by which his exit may have been facilitated. A pimp relates:

The best way to do this [teaching conversation] is, in the beginning, when the phone rings, for instance . . . is to listen to what she says and then check and see how big a trick he is and then correct her from there.

. . . with every one of them [trainees] I would make it a point to see two guys to see how they [the girls] operate.

In one case a girl reported that her pimp left a written list of rules pertaining to relating to "johns." Direct teaching, however, seems to be uncommon. The bulk of whatever learning takes place seems to take place through observation.

It's hard to tell you, because we learn through observations.

But I watched her and listened to what her bit was on the telephone.

To summarize, the structure of the apprenticeship period seems quite standard. The novice receives her training either from a pimp or from another more experienced call girl, more often the latter. She serves her initial two to eight months of work under the trainer's supervision and often serves this period in the trainer's apartment. The trainer assumes responsibility for arranging contacts and negotiating the type and place of the sexual encounter.

The content of the training pertains both to a general philosophical stance and to some specifics (usually not sexual) of interpersonal behavior with customers and colleagues. The philosophy is one of exploiting the exploiters (customers) by whatever means necessary and defining the colleagues of the call girl as being intelligent, self-interested and, in certain important respects, basically honest individuals. The interpersonal techniques addressed during the learning period consist primarily of "pitches," telephone conversations, personal and occasionally sexual hygiene, prohibitions against alcohol and dope while with a "john," how and when to obtain the fee, and specifics concerning the sexual habits of particular customers. Specific sexual techniques are very rarely taught. The current sample included a considerable number of girls who, although capable of articulating this value structure, were not particularly inclined to adopt it.

[9] In the unpublished paper referred to above, Pomeroy has indicated that, of 31 call girls interviewed, only 23% reported never experiencing orgasms with customers.

CONTACTS AND CONTRACTS

While the imparting of ideologies and proprieties to the prospective call girl is emphasized during the apprenticeship period, it appears that the primary function of the apprenticeship, at least for the trainee, is building a clientele. Since this latter function limits the degree of occupational socialization, the process of developing the clientele and the arrangements made between trainer and trainee will be discussed.

Lists ("books") with the names and telephone numbers of customers are available for purchase from other call girls or pimps, but such books are often considered unreliable. While it is also true that an occasional pimp will refer customers to girls, this does not appear to be a frequent practice. The most frequent method of obtaining such names seems to be through contacts developed during the apprenticeship. The trainer refers customers to the apprentice and oversees the latter in terms of her responsibility and adequacy in dealing with the customer. For referring the customer, the trainer receives forty to fifty per cent of the total price agreed upon in the contract negotiated by the trainer and customer.[10] The trainer and trainees further agree, most often explicitly, on the apprentice's "right" to obtain and to use, on further occasions, information necessary for arranging another sexual contract with the "john" without the obligation of further "kick-back" to the trainer. That is, if she can obtain the name and telephone number of the customer, she can negotiate another contract without fee-splitting. During this period, then,

the girl is not only introduced to other working colleagues (pimps and girls alike) but also develops a clientele.

There are two obvious advantages for a call girl in assuming the trainer role. First, since there seems to be an abundant demand for new girls, and since certain service requirements demand more than one girl, even the well established call girl chronically confronts the necessity for making referrals. It is then reasonable to assume that the extra profit derived from the fee-splitting activities, together with the added conveniences of having a girl "on call," allows the trainer to profit considerably from this arrangement. Secondly, contacts with customers are reputedly extremely difficult to maintain if services are not rendered on demand. Thus, the adoption of the trainer role enables the girl to maintain contacts with "fickle" customers under circumstances where she may wish a respite from the sexual encounter without terminating the contacts necessary for re-entry into the call girl role. It is also possible that the financial gains may conceivably be much greater for most trainers than for most call girls, but this is a moot point.

A final aspect of the apprenticeship period that should be noted is the novice's income. It is possible for the novice, under the supervision of a competent and efficient trainer, to earn a great deal of money, or at least to get a favorable glimpse of the great financial possibilities of the occupation and, in effect, be heavily rewarded for her decision to enter it. Even though the novice may be inexperienced in both the sexual and interpersonal techniques of prostitu-

---

[10] The fee-splitting arrangement is quite common at all levels of career activity. For example, cooperative activity between two girls is often required for a particular type of sexual contract. In these cases, the girl who has contracted with the customer will contact a colleague, usually a friend, and will obtain 40%–50% of the latter's earnings. There is suggestive evidence that fee-splitting activities vary according to geographical areas and that Los Angeles is unique for both its fee-splitting patterns and the rigidity of its fee-splitting structure.

tion, her novelty on the market gives her an immediate advantage over her more experienced competitors. It seems quite likely that the new girl, irrespective of her particular physical or mental qualities, has considerable drawing power because she provides new sexual experience to the customer. Early success and financial reward may well provide considerable incentive to continue in the occupation.

A final word is needed regarding the position of the pimp vis-à-vis the call girl during the apprenticeship period. While some pimps assume the responsibility for training the girl personally, as indicated above, as many send the novice to another girl. The most apparent reason for such referral is that it facilitates the development of the "book." Purposes of training appear to be secondary for two reasons: (1) The pimp often lacks direct contact with the customers, so he personally cannot aid directly in the development of the girl's clientele; (2) When the pimp withdraws his girl from the training context, it is rarely because she has obtained adequate knowledge of the profession. This is not to say that all pimps are totally unconcerned with the type of knowledge being imparted to the girl. Rather, the primary concern of the pimp is the girl's developing a clientele, not learning the techniques of sex or conversation.

The apprenticeship period usually ends abruptly, not smoothly. Its termination may be but a reflection of interpersonal difficulties between trainer and trainee, novice and pimp, or between two novices. Occasionally termination of training is brought about through the novice's discovery and subsequent theft of the trainer's "book." Quite frequently, the termination is due to the novice's developing a sufficient trade or other business opportunities. The point is, however, that no respondent has reported that the final disruption of the apprenticeship was the result of the com-pletion of adequate training. While disruptions of this relationship may be due to personal or impersonal events, termination is not directly due to the development of sufficient skills.

DISCUSSION AND SUMMARY

On the basis of interviews with 33 call girls in the Los Angeles area, information was obtained about entrance into the call girl occupation and the initial training period or apprenticeship therein.

The novice call girl is acclimated to her new job primarily by being thoroughly immersed in the call girl subculture, where she learns the trade through imitation as much as through explicit tutoring. The outstanding concern at this stage is the development of a sizeable and lucrative clientele. The specific skills and values which are acquired during this period are rather simple and quickly learned.

In spite of the girls' protests and their extensive folklore, the art of prostitution, at least at this level, seems to be technically a low-level skill. That is, it seems to be an occupation which requires little formal knowledge or practice for its successful pursuit and appears best categorized as an unskilled job. Evidence for this point comes from two separate sources. First, there seems to be little technical training during this period, and the training seems of little importance to the career progress. Length or type of training does not appear correlated with success (i.e., money earned, lack of subjective distress, minimum fee per "trick," etc.). Secondly, the termination of the apprenticeship period is often brought about for reasons unrelated to training. It seems that the need for an apprenticeship period is created more by the secrecy surrounding the rendering or the utilization of the call girl service than by the complexity of the role. In fact, it is reasonable to assume that the complexity of the job confronting a street-walker may be considerably greater than that confronting a call girl. The tasks of avoiding the police, sampling among strangers for potential customers, and arrangements for the completion of the sexual contract not only require different skills on the part of the street-walker, but are performances requiring a higher degree of professional "know-how" than is generally required of the call girl.[11]

As a pimp who manages both call girls and "high class" street-walkers explains:

The girl that goes out into the street is the sharper of the two, because she is capable of handling herself in the street, getting around the law, picking out the trick that is not absolutely psycho . . . and capable of getting along in the street. . . . The street-walker, as you term her, is really a prima donna of the prostitutes . . . her field is unlimited, she goes to all of the top places so she meets the top people. . . .

The fact that the enactment of the call girl role requires little training, and the introduction of the girl to clients and colleagues alike is rather rapid, gives little time or incentive for adequate occupational socialization. It is perhaps for this reason rather than, for example, reasons related to personality factors, that occupational instability is great and cultural homogeneity small.

In closing, while it appears that there is a rather well defined apprenticeship period in the career of the call girl, it seems that it is the secrecy rather than the complexity of the occupation which generates such a period. While there is good evidence that initial contacts, primarily with other "working girls," are necessary for entrance into this career, there seems no reason, at this point, to assume that the primary intent of the participants in training is anything but the development of an adequate clientele.

---

[11] Needless to say, however, all of the sample of call girls who were asked for status hierarchies of prostitution felt that the street-walker had both less status and a less complex job. It *may* well be that the verbal exchange required of the call girl requires greater knowledge than that required of a street-walker, but the non-verbal skills required of the street-walker may be considerably greater than those of the call girl.

Conversion to the Doomsday Cult

JOHN LOFLAND

The logical and methodological structure of . . . [this] analysis is based on a developmental conception.[1] That is, I will offer a series of more or less successively accumulating factors, which in their total combination would seem to account for conversion to the DP's [Divine Precepts]. Seven such factors will be presented, all of which together seem both necessary and sufficient causes for conversion to occur. . . .

A MODEL OF CONVERSION

To account for the process by which persons come to be world savers for the DP, I shall be concerned with two types of conditions or factors. The first type, which may be called *predisposing conditions,* comprises attributes of persons *prior* to their contact with the cult. . . .

The second type of conditions concerns . . . the contingencies of social situations. By *situational contingencies* I refer to those conditions that develop through direct confrontation and interaction between the potential convert and DP members, conditions that can lead to the successful recruitment of persons already well disposed toward the enterprise. Many of those who qualified for conversion on the basis of predisposi-tional factors entered into interpersonal relationships with the DP's, but because the proper situational conditions were not met, they did not convert.

Let us now turn to a discussion of each of the factors operating within these two classes.

I. Tension

It would seem that no model of human conduct entirely escapes some concept of tension, strain, frustration, deprivation, or the like, as a factor in accounting for action. And not surprisingly, even the most cursory examination of the life situations of converts over the years before they embraced the DP reveals that they labored under what they at least *perceived* to be considerable tension.

This tension is best characterized as a felt discrepancy between some imaginary, ideal state of affairs and the circumstances in which they actually saw themselves. It is suggested that such acutely felt tension is a necessary, but far from sufficient condition for conversion. It provides some disposition to act. But tension may be resolved in a number of ways (or remain unresolved). Hence to know that these people were in a tension situation says little about *what* action they might take. . . .

From John Lofland, *Doomsday Cult,* © 1966. Excerpt from pp. 31–62. Reprinted by permission of the author.

[1] Cf. Ralph Turner, "The Quest for Universals in Sociological Research," *American Sociological Review,* Vol. XVIII (December, 1953), 604–611; Howard S. Becker, *Outsiders* (New York: The Free Press of Glencoe, Inc., 1963), esp. pp. 22–25; and, Neil J. Smelser, *Theory of Collective Behavior* (New York: The Free Press of Glencoe, Inc., 1963), pp. 12–21.

It would appear that problems we find among [pre-converts] . . . are not *qualitatively* different or distinct from those presumably experienced by a significant, albeit unknown, proportion of the general population. Their peculiarity, if any, appears to be *quantitative;* that is, pre-converts felt their problems to be acute and experienced high levels of tension concerning them over rather long periods of time.

It might in fact be said that from the point of view of an outside observer, their circumstances were in general not massively oppressive. One can probably find among the general population large numbers of people laboring under tensions that would seem to be considerably more acute and prolonged.

Perhaps the strongest qualitative characterization of tension supportable by the data is that pre-converts felt themselves frustrated in their various aspirations and *experienced* the tension rather more acutely and over longer periods than most do. . . .

II. Types of Problem-Solving Perspectives

On the basis of the first factor alone, only those without enduring, acute tensions are ruled out as potential DP converts. Since conversion is hardly the only response to problems, it is important to ask what else these people could have done, and why they didn't.

It seems likely that there were very few converts to the DP's for the simple reason that people have a number of conventional and readily available alternative ways of defining and coping with their problems. By this I mean that they have alternative perspectives, or rhetorics, that specify the nature and sources of problems and offer some program for their resolution. There are many such alternatives in modern society, but I shall briefly describe three particular types: the *psychiatric,* the *political,* and the *religious.* In the first, the origin of problems is typically traced to the psyche, and manipulation of the self is advocated as a resolution to problems. Political solutions, mainly radical, locate the sources of problems in the social structure and advocate its reorganization as a solution. The religious perspective tends to see both sources and solutions to difficulties as emanating from an unseen, and in principle unseeable, realm.

The first two rhetorics are both secular and are the most often used in contemporary society. It is no longer appropriate to regard recalcitrant and aberrant actors as possessed of devils. Indeed, modern religious institutions, in significant measure, offer secular, frequently psychiatric rhetorics concerning problems in living. The predominance of secular definitions of tension is a major source of loss of potential converts to the DP. Most people with acute tensions "get the psychiatric word" especially, either by defining themselves as grist for its mill or by being forced into it. Several persons met other conditions of the model but had adopted a psychiatric definition of their tensions and failed to convert. . . .

All pre-converts seemed surprisingly uninformed about conventional psychiatric and political perspectives for defining their problems. Perhaps largely because of their backgrounds (many were from small towns and rural communities), they had long been accustomed to defining the world in religious terms. Although conventional religious outlooks had been discarded by all pre-converts as inadequate, "spiritless," "dead," etc., prior to contact with the DP's, *the general propensity to impose religious meaning on events had been retained.*

Even within these constrictions in the available solutions for acutely felt problems, a number of alternative responses still remain. First, it must be recognized that people can persist in stressful situations and do little or nothing to reduce their discomfort. This is something that students of social life too often tend to underestimate. . . .

Second, people often take specifically problem-directed action to change those portions of their lives that are troublesome, without at the same time adopting a different world view to interpret them. . . .

Third, there exists a range of maneuvers that "put the problem out of mind." In general these constitute compensations for, or distractions from, problems in living. Such maneuvers include addiction to the mass media, preoccupation with childrearing, or immersion in work. More spectacular bypass routes are alcoholism, suicide, promiscuity, and the like. . . .

In any event, it may be assumed not only that many people with tensions explore these strategies, but also that some succeed and hence become unavailable as potential DP recruits.[2]

III. Religious Seekership

Whatever the reasons, pre-converts failed in their attempts to find a successful way out of their difficulties through any of the strategies outlined above. Thus their need for solutions persisted, and their problem-solving perspective was restricted to a religious outlook. However, all pre-converts found that conventional religious institutions failed to provide adequate solutions. Subsequently, each came to see himself as a seeker, a person searching for some satisfactory system for interpreting and resolving his discontent. Given their generally religious view of the world, all pre-converts had, to a greater or lesser extent, defined themselves as looking for an adequate religious perspective and had taken some action to achieve this end.

Some went from church to church and prayer group to prayer group, routing their religious seeking through relatively conventional institutions. . . .

The necessary attributes of pre-converts stated thus far could all have persisted for some time before these people encountered the DP and can be thought of as background factors, or predispositions. Although they appeared to have arisen and been active in the order specified, they are important here as accumulated and simultaneously active factors during the development of succeeding conditions.

IV. The Turning Point

We now turn to situational factors in which timing becomes significant. The first of these is the striking universal circumstance that at the time when they first encountered the DP, all pre-converts had reached or were about to reach what they perceived as a turning point in their lives. That is, each had come to a moment when old lines of action were complete, had failed, or had been or were about to be disrupted, and when they were faced with the opportunity or necessity for doing something different with their lives.[3] . . .

Turning points in general derived from having recently migrated, lost or

---

[2] It perhaps needs to be noted that this discussion is confined to isolating the elements of the conversion sequence. Extended analysis would have to give attention to the factors that *in turn* bring each conversion condition into existence—that is, to develop a theory for each of the seven elements, specifying the conditions under which they develop. On the form that this would likely take see Ralph Turner's discussion of "the intrusive factor," *op. cit.*, 609–611.

[3] Everett C. Hughes, *Men and Their Work* (New York: The Free Press of Glencoe, Inc., 1958), Chap. 1; Anselm Strauss, "Transformations of Identity," in Arnold Rose, ed., *Human Behavior and Social Processes* (Boston: Houghton Mifflin Company, 1962), pp. 67–71. Cf. the oft-noted "cultural dislocation" and migration pattern found in the background of converts to many groups, especially cults.

quit a job . . . or graduated from, failed in, or quit an educational institution. Perhaps because most converts were young adults, turning points involving educational institutions were relatively frequent. . . .

The significance of . . . [the] various kinds of turning points lies in their having produced an increased awareness of and desire to take some action on their problems, *combined with a new opportunity to do so.* Turning points were circumstances in which old obligations and lines of action had diminished, and new involvements had become desirable and possible.

V. Cult-Affective Bonds

We come now to the moments of contact between a potential recruit and the DP's. In order for persons who meet all four of the previously activated steps to be further drawn down the road to full conversion, an affective bond must develop or already exist between the potential recruit and one or more of the DP members. The development or presence of some positive, emotive, interpersonal response seems necessary to bridge the gap between first exposure to the message and coming to accept its truth. That is, persons developed affective ties with the group or some of its members while they still regarded the DP perspective as problematic, or even "way out." In a manner of speaking, final conversion was coming to accept the opinions of one's friends.[4] . . .

It is particularly important to note that conversions frequently moved through *pre-existing* friendship pairs or nets. . . .

The building of bonds that were unsupported by previous friendships with a new convert often took the form of a sense of instant and powerful rapport with a believer. . . .

It is suggested, then, that although potential converts might have difficulty in taking up the DP perspective, when the four previous conditions *and* an affective tie were present, they came to consider the DP seriously and to begin to accept it as their personal construction of reality.

VI. Extra-Cult-Affective Bonds

It may be supposed that non-DP associates of the convert-in-process would not be entirely neutral to the now live possibility of his taking up with the DP's. We must inquire, then, into the conditions under which extra-cult controls in the form of emotional attachments are activated, and how they restrain or fail to restrain persons from DP conversion.

By virtue of recent migration, disaffection with geographically distant families and spouses, and very few proximate, extra-cult acquaintances, a few converts were "social atoms" in the classic sense. For them extra-cult attachments were irrelevant. . . .

More typically, converts were effectively without opposition because, although they were acquainted with persons, no one was intimate enough with them to become aware that a conversion was in progress, or, if they knew, did not feel that there was a sufficient mutual attachment to justify intervention. . . .

Ironically, in many cases positive extra-cult attachments were to other re-

[4] Cf. Tamatsu Shibutani, *Society and Personality* (Englewood Cliffs, N.J.: Prentice-Hall, Inc., 1961), pp. 523–532, 588–592. Edgar Schein reports that in prison "the most potent source of influence in coercive persuasion was the identification which arose between a prisoner and his more reformed cellmate" [*Coercive Persuasion* (New York: W. W. Norton & Company, Inc., 1961), p. 277]. See also Alan Kerckhoff, Kurt Back, and Norman Miller, "Sociometric Patterns in Hysterical Contagion," *Sociometry*, Vol. XXVIII (March, 1965), 2–15.

ligious seekers, who, even though not yet budding converts themselves, provided impetus to continue investigation or entertainment of the DP rather than exercising a countervailing force. Indeed, such extra-cult persons might only be slightly behind their friend or friends in their own conversion process. . . .

In the relatively few cases where there were positive attachments between conventional extra-cult persons and a convert-in-process, control was minimized or not activated because of geographical distance and intentional avoidance of contact or communication about the topic during the period when the convert was solidifying his faith. . . .

When there were emotional attachments to extra-cult, nonseeking persons, and when these persons were physically present and cognizant of the incipient transformation, conversion became a nip and tuck affair. Pulled upon by competing emotional loyalties and their discordant versions of reality, pre-converts were thrown into intense emotional strain. . . .

When extra-cult bonds withstood the period of affective and ideological flirtation with the DP's, conversion failed to be consummated. However, most converts did not seem to have the kind of external affiliations in which the informal control over belief that is exerted among close friends could be exercised. They were so effectively unintegrated into any network of conventional people that for the most part they could simply fall out of relatively routine society virtually unnoticed and take their co-seeker friends (if any) with them.

VII. Intensive Interaction

The combination of the six previous factors seems sufficient to bring a person to *verbal conversion* to the DP, but one more contingency must be met if he is to become a deployable agent,[5] or what I have termed a *total convert*.

. . . [Most,] but not all, verbal converts ultimately put their lives at the disposal of the cult. It is suggested that such commitment took place as a result of intensive interaction with DP's and failed to result when such interaction was absent. By intensive interaction is meant actual daily, and even hourly physical accessibility to DP total converts. Such intense exposure offers the opportunity to reinforce and elaborate upon the initial, tentative assent that has been granted the DP world view. It is in such prolonged association that the perspective comes alive as a device for interpreting the moment-to-moment events in the verbal convert's life.

The DP doctrine has a variety of resources for explaining the most minor everyday events and for relating them to a cosmic battle between good and evil spirits in a way that places the convert at the center of this war. Since all DP interpretations point to the imminence of the end, to participate in these explanations of daily life is more and more to come to see the necessity of one's personal participation as a totally committed agent in this cosmic struggle.[6]

The need to make other converts and to support the cause in all ways was the main theme of verbal exchanges between the tentatively accepting and the total converts—and, indeed, among the total converts themselves. Without this close association with those already totally committed, such an appreciation of the need for one's transformation into a total convert failed to develop. In recognition of this fact, the DP's gave greatest priority to attempting to get verbal converts

---

[5] On the concept of the "deployable agent" or "deployable personnel" in social movements, see Philip Selznick, *The Organizational Weapon* (New York: The Free Press of Glencoe, Inc., 1959), pp. 18–29.

[6] Cf. Schein, *op. cit.,* pp. 136–139, 280–282.

(and even the merely interested) to move into the cult's communal dwellings. . . .

Thus it is that verbal conversion and resolutions to reorganize one's life for the DP's are not automatically translated into total conversion. One must be intensively exposed to the group supporting these new standards of conduct. The DP's did not find proselytizing, the primary task of total converts, a very easy activity to perform. But in the presence of people who supported one another and balmed their collective wounds, such a transformation became possible. Those who accepted the truth of the doctrine but lacked intensive interaction with the core group remained partisan spectators and failed to play an active part in the battle to usher in God's kingdom. . . .

CONCLUDING REMARK

In view of the character of the set of conditions outlined, it might be wondered what competitive advantage the DP's had over other unusual religious groups. In terms of background conditions, I am suggesting that they had little, if any, advantage. In terms of situational conditions, their advantage lay merely in the fact that they got there and actually made their pitch, developed affective bonds, and induced people into intensive interaction. As with so much in life one may say that "there but for the grace of God go I"—within the limits of the conditions specified. It is to be hoped that the present effort will contribute to dispelling the tendency to think that there must be some deep, almost mystical connection between world views and their carriers. Like conceptions which hold that criminals and delinquents must be different from others, so our thinking about other types of deviants has too often assumed some extensive characterological conjunction between participant and pattern of participation.

learning the culture

11

Deviant worlds generally have their own distinctive traditions; these include general outlooks, beliefs, values, and norms. Newcomers must learn these traditions, and deviant groups must work to sustain their ideas against the countervailing influences of the dominant culture.

In the first selection Sherman describes how police rookies learn the ways of the subculture of police corruption. Weinberg then delineates the norms nudists learn and how these norms sustain the official nudist perspective. Bryan shows that call girls learn the ideology of prostitution but are unlikely to become totally committed to that ideology. Finally, examining a mystic religious sect, Simmons outlines the techniques a deviant group may use to sustain what they have learned in the face of contradictory evidence.

The Subculture of Police Corruption

LAWRENCE W. SHERMAN

My task here is to describe the process by which policemen become corrupt in two specific ways: how they come to accept bribes, and how they come to commit burglary. The central argument of this paper is that police grafters and burglars only "get that way" through a painful process of choices, and not because they are pathological "rotten apples." Though *which* choices will be taken cannot be predicted, the process should become clearer through a picture of how the choices are presented to policemen. . . .

BECOMING A POLICEMAN

The most important context for police moral careers, both in terms of situation and frame of reference, is of course the fact that the individual has become a policeman. Perhaps a key contingency in a policeman's moral careers is the system of appointment he must deal with. Wittels (1949) describes the great disillusionment of a young police applicant when he was visited by the ward (political) boss and told his application stood no chance without a six-hundred-dollar "contribution" to the party and the reregistration of his entire family to the "right" party. Few cities maintain such a system today, but Royko (1971) suggests it may persist in Chicago.

Recruit school, when there is one—and in half of our cases there was not—is usually an experience of great idealism and anticipation of an exciting career. Westley (1970) describes the recruit school as a *rite de passage* which detaches a man from his old experience and prepares him for the new by teaching the rough outlines of the job as it appears on the books (p. 156). But Niederhoffer (1969) describes the New York recruit school's "unrealistic" stress on ethics and professionalism as the first source of cynicism about the job.

Both Westley and Niederhoffer agree that contact with older police officers in the first day on duty teaches the recruit that the formal rules are largely a sham—a situation which is true for virtually all police departments and many bureaucracies (see Gouldner, 1954). From the older officers, the recruit learns what the *real* rules of the police subculture are, often in apocryphal form. While these rules vary widely, one universal rule of police departments is secrecy and not reporting the misdeeds of brother officers (Westley, 1970; Vollmer, 1930).

Though taking on this new peer definition of police work is something of a reality shock, more traumatic is the first contact with hostility from the public. As he begins to take responsibility for his actions, the rookie becomes emotionally involved in maintaining respect for his

Reprinted from "Moral Careers of Corrupt Policemen," from *Police Corruption* by Lawrence Sherman, pp. 191, 196–205. Copyright © 1974 by Lawrence Sherman. Reprinted by permission of Doubleday & Company, Inc.

authority. From bitter experience, he sees that his lot is with other policemen, and that nonpolicemen are enemies. As Westley notes, "The rookie has then become a cop, and the group has gained a new member."

Thus, *allowing for individual differences,* the process of becoming a policeman is one of facing a set of contingencies that produce moral experiences which change a man's frame of reference. With his new uniform and group membership, he feels society has labeled him an "outsider"—and he in turn labels nonpolicemen as outsiders (Becker, 1963). As Becker's dance musicians hate "squares," so policemen hate "civilians." Since not very long ago the police recruit was a civilian himself, he has undergone a radical redefinition of self in a very short time. That change is even reflected in his life outside the job, which often relies exclusively on other police families for social contact.

BECOMING A GRAFTER

While the process of becoming a policeman is fairly universal to police work, the process of becoming a grafter is not. The key contingency for entering a moral career of grafting—i.e., accepting bribes—is the extent to which grafting already occurs in the work group the rookie is assigned to. This is not the place to explain why grafting subcultures arise in some police departments and not others . . . , but we should again note that there are wide differences in the phenomena. Our two case studies of grafters both took place within a context of well-organized police graft, run by a corrupt political machine. The first is Max Schmittberger of the nineteenth century New York police, as told by Steffens (1931). The second is "Gus Blawker," a composite character of policemen known by Wittels (1949) between 1930 and 1949. Summaries of their cases follow:

CASE NO. 1. Max Schmittberger was a tall, handsome, but naïve baker's apprentice in the 1880s when some Tammany (political) leaders offered to get this fine specimen on the police force—free! Without understanding, Max joined up and was soon directing traffic on Broadway. Since he pleased his superiors, he was transferred to the "fat" Tenderloin precinct, the major vice market of New York.

One night a brothel owner pressed ten dollars in his hand. Confused, he presented it to his captain. Angered by Max's honesty, the captain explained graft to him and began to assign him to posts more and more crucial to the graft system. He moved from liaison with the hack thieves to regulation of the brothels, finally to be promoted to the job of "bagman"—collecting twenty thousand dollars a month for the captain.

When the Lexow investigation began (1894), he was jarred back to honesty. As the star witness, he told the commission all of the details of the graft system. Though punished by his peers for years after, the forces of reform eventually had him appointed chief of police.

CASE NO. 2. Gus Blawker had an idealistic conception of police work in 1930 when the ward boss told him the conditions of appointment to the force. Disillusioned, but desperately needing a job, he borrowed the necessary money.

In the first days on the beat, he witnessed the vice squad shake down a speakeasy that had skipped a payment. His attempts to arrest politically influential men for traffic violations were severely reprimanded, and he was assigned to a boring suburban beat.

Through luck he made a much publicized arrest of a famous robber, for which he was promoted to detective. But his zeal in raiding a protected gambling house was rewarded with demotion to his old beat.

When his son needed an expensive operation, he appealed to the ward leader for a promotion with a promise to "play the game." As head of a detective squad, he took no graft until the machine required him to fix an important case. When his payoff arrived, he stared at the envelope for an hour before taking out the money. When his son needed another operation, he shook down a gambling joint.

From that point on he collected regularly from gamblers. The next step was to shake down brothels and then drug pushers. When he was arrested ten years later, he was rich enough to fix the case against him and retire in luxury.

Though Blawker's experience is probably more representative than Schmittberger's, we may derive similar conclusions from both. Most important is the process of increased involvement by which they become grafters. That is, they became more accustomed to taking graft as the graft organization tested them with first petty graft, then graft for allowing more serious offenses. Most people would agree that drug pushing is a more serious crime than gambling; we may assume that neither Gus Blawker's morality (self-definition) nor the policies of the graft organization would let him begin his grafting career with drug pushers. Rather, he worked up a ladder of increasing self-perceived social harm of offenses, neutralizing any moral objection to the (crime-specific) graft at each rung of the ladder—each stage of his moral career. The same seemed to happen with Schmittberger.

If we generalize these cases to all possible sources of graft, we may hypothesize a continuum of graft stages which follows a policeman's initial frame of reference about the social harm of each source of graft. The first stage is police "perks"—free coffee and meals from restaurants on his beat. The moral experience about accepting these perks usually occurs in the recruit's first days on duty, and the peer pressure to accept them is great. If he does accept the minor perks, he then has a different image of self to contend with when a bar owner operating after closing hours offers him a drink. Again a moral experience; a decision to accept the drink and let the place stay open redefines the policeman's self, if only slightly.

The third step in the grafting career may be another regulative bribe—a motorist handing him a driver's license with a five-dollar bill in it or a construction foreman giving him ten dollars to overlook materials left illegally on the sidewalk. He may either accept or reject the bribe, but acceptance is made easier if he is used to taking gifts from restaurants and bars.

If there are regular payoffs made by a local gambling operation, and if the rookie has passed the tests of accepting minor graft, the other policemen receiving the gambling payoffs may offer to cut him in. This moral experience is particularly difficult, because it is an invitation to solidarity with his, by now, *only* "significant others," an invitation he is loath to reject. Indeed, policemen I knew in New York who rejected the offer soon transferred out of the work unit to graft-free "inside" jobs. But most New York policemen seem to accept the offer (Knapp, 1972).

The fifth step in a grafting career may be prostitutes' bribes, either from pimps, lone streetwalkers, or more regularly, brothel operators. The relationships established in prostitution graft can lead easily into narcotics graft, since drug traffic is often closely linked with prostitution (Knapp, 1972). Accepting narcotics graft, however, is the most difficult moral experience of all, since the initial frame of reference of most policemen would abhor the thought of helping drug pushers. If that graft is accepted, though, it is not unknown for policemen to go on to selling drugs themselves.

To summarize the hypothetical stages of the moral career of a grafter:

1. Minor "perks"
2. Bar closing hours
3. Regulative crimes (traffic, construction)
4. Gambling
5. Prostitution
6. Narcotics

Again, the hypothesis is only that this career will be followed when situational contingencies make it available and then *only if the policeman accepts the invitation to bribery*. Even when all of the graft sources are available, a policeman may stop at a middle rung of his self-perceived ladder of social harm. The stage at which he stops can become a key element in his apologia: "I might take money from gamblers, and whores, 'cause they don't hurt anybody—but I won't mess around with pushers!" Put another way: "I might be bad, but I'm not *that* bad."

Stoddard (1968) suggests that most policemen stop at a certain stage of deviance on the basis of group definition of "limits." An English police official told me that Manchester constables in the 1930s might brag about bribes from pub owners and gamblers, but they would never mention bribes from prostitutes. Cook (1971) notes the 1950s distinction between clean graft (gamblers, prostitutes) and dirty graft (drugs) in the New York police (that gradually disappeared during the 1960s).

Assuming there are group limits to bribery, some policemen go beyond them. A characteristic of deviance from group bribery norms is the switch from pure bribery to extortion, or from "reactive" to "proactive" graft (Reiss, 1971). The Knapp Commission has labeled the two kinds of grafters as "grass-eaters" (reactive) and "meat-eaters" (proactive). One possible explanation of the shift from grass to meat is that of secondary deviance (Lemert, 1967). In this case, the agent defining the individual as deviant is the individual himself, without the intervention of (another) agent of social control. Assuming the initial frame of reference of the grafter was morally opposed to graft, one of the moral experiences may be so severe that, if resulting in a decision for more graft, it may produce a "What the hell, I'm a crook, so I'll make the most

of it" reaction. Subsequent career stages will then become proactive. Blawker, on the day that he received "the envelope," sought out a friend in tears and got very drunk. From then on he was a proactive grafter.

Individual differences in the initial frame of reference are important, since the switch from reactive to proactive graft does not occur at any particular stage of the grafting career. Policemen in vice-ridden Harlem have progressed to the extreme stages of grafting on an entirely reactive basis (virtually just standing on the corners and holding out their hands). Those more given to personality explanations of crime would of course suggest that individual differences are paramount: some policemen join the force with an entrepreneurial affinity for proactive graft. But the data available so far suggest that secondary deviation is a more likely explanation.

One final contingency in the moral career of a grafter should be checked in future case study research. Both Schmittberger and Blawker (as well as the burglars described below) experienced a negative social reaction in their work group to acts of honesty or honest enforcement. This moral experience tends to occur early in the police career, and it clearly redefines the self in terms of perceived definitions of being a policeman. Future research should examine the extent to which such an experience is a necessary element in a grafting career.

BECOMING A BURGLAR

If individual differences and choice was important to stress in the moral careers of the grafter, it is an even more important caveat in the moral career of the police burglar. And as important as different frames of reference are the differences in situational contingencies.

Police burglary is not nearly as persistent a phenomenon as police graft.

This is not the place to explain differences in the extent of burglary (see Wilson, 1963), but we should note that there was (1) a series of police burglary scandals all over the United States in the early 1960s, with few reports of it since, and (2) a police burglary group discovered in London in the mid-1960s, with no reports of it since.

Cook (1966), reviewing the 1961 Denver scandal, suggests a pattern that fits Cohen's (1955) description of the evolution of deviant subcultures. To re-state Cook's analysis in Cohen's terms, policemen collectively face a status problem that can best be solved by acquiring more money. Many alternative means of supplementing a salary are available, but an easy route is to pick up "lying around" loot at the scene of a burglary. "Exploratory gestures" among the policemen are made at the scene of a burglary, and some goods or money is also pocketed. Further gestures (suggestions) are made, and if well received, a burglary is planned. A successful burglary makes the idea more attractive to other policemen who are invited to join in. In Denver, when a transfer program inadvertently broke up the initial burglary subculture, its members spread the innovation to other partol districts—making the exploratory gestures that established new subcultures.

Seen in this context, we may summarize the moral careers of two police burglars: the first from Denver, interviewed by Smith (1965), the second from another midwestern city, interviewed by Stoddard (1968).

CASE NO. 3. Patrolman Hastings joined the Denver police to be an "eager beaver" cop, but discovered two policemen committing a burglary while he was still a probationary patrolman. Keeping his mouth shut, he stayed with honest, good police work.

His slated promotion to detective fell through when he arrested a politically influential man, who was immediately let off by the court.

Disillusioned, he agreed to his partner's suggestion one night to pick up "lying around " loot at the scene of a burglary, and his sergeant later took a cut of the loot.

A few nights later, they were called to a fur warehouse burglary, which turned out to be an insurance fraud done by the owner. The lieutenant's presence and the owner's offer of a free mink stole induced Hastings to "go along."

From then on he committed burglary on a regular basis, often at the request of insurance swindling businessmen.

CASE NO. 4. Patrolman Smith began his police career with free meals at Sam Paisano's restaurant and immediately learned that Paisano was virtually immune from any kind of protection.

While still a rookie, he observed his partner steal candy bars from a supermarket. Refusing to share the loot, he was advised he should "go along" or face the consequence—social isolation.

When he did pass his "test," he joined in on picking up "lying around" loot. Eventually, his group began planning burglaries. When he was finally caught, he was surprised how alone he was, and he realized that "lying around" loot was the limit of theft by police standards; planned burglary was deviant.

A key contingency in Hastings' moral career was that he entered a police subculture of planned burglary and was invited to join it. In Smith's case, he was invited to join a subculture of "shopping" (picking up lying-around loot) and participated in the evolution of a subculture that exceeded the general group limits of theft. In both cases, they learned, while still rookies, that certain people had immunity from arrest and that other policemen committed criminal acts.

Whether a policeman joins an external burglary subculture or helps to form one, the case studies suggest the following stages in the moral career of the police burglar:

1. Learning the fallacy of impartial enforcement of the law

2. Learning that other policemen are dishonest

3. Picking up lying-around loot at the scene of a burglary ("shopping")

4. Joining in a planned burglary

5. Committing planned burglary on a regular basis

Evidence from the original case studies suggest that, just as in graft, the progression to each new stage in a burglary career depends upon a change in the frame of reference that allows a consistency with basic societal values. After the Denver scandal, several police burglars stressed in public interviews that "only the big chains and insurance companies, institutions that could afford it, had been hurt." And in Smith's case, where the peer influence had been stronger than rationalizations about insurance companies, his apologia was a perception of more policemen involved in planned burglary than was in fact the case. The societal value he used for justification of burglary was solidarity with his brother officers.

Again, individual differences are important. Some policemen may refuse even to "shop"; others may shop without ever planning a burglary; still others might pull off one planned burglary and then turn honest. As in the switch from reactive to proactive grafting, the switch from occasional to regular planned burglary may possibly be explained as *secondary* deviation. Whatever the individual moral experiences are, however, any progression is along the sequence of stages outlined here. . . .

REFERENCES

Becker, Howard L. (1963). *Outsiders.* Glencoe, Ill.: Free Press.

Cohen, Albert K. (1955). *Delinquent Boys: The Culture of the Gang.* New York: Free Press.

Cook, Fred J. (1966). *The Corrupted Land.* London: Jonathan Cape, 1967.

——— (1971). "The Pusher Cop: The Institutionalization of Police Corruption." *New York,* August 16, 1971.

Gouldner, Alvin (1954). *Patterns of Industrial Bureaucracy.* New York: Free Press.

Knapp, Whitman, et al. (1972). *Report of the Commission to Investigate Alleged Police Corruption* (City of New York). New York: George Braziller.

Lemert, Edwin (1967). *Human Deviance, Social Problems, and Social Control.* Englewood Cliffs, N.J.: Prentice-Hall, Inc.

Niederhoffer, Arthur (1969). *Behind the Shield: The Police in Urban Society.* Garden City, N.Y.: Anchor Books.

Reiss, Albert J., Jr. (1971). *The Police and the Public.* New Haven, Conn.: Yale University Press.

Royko, Mike (1971). *Boss.* London: Paladin, 1972.

Smith, Ralph L. (1965). *The Tarnished Badge.* New York: T. Y. Crowell.

Steffens, Lincoln (1931). *The Autobiography of Lincoln Steffens.* New York: Harcourt, Brace.

Stoddard, Elwyn R. (1968). " 'The Informal Code' of Police Deviancy: A Group Approach to 'Blue-Coat Crime.' " *Journal of Criminal Law, Criminology and Police Science* 59, no. 2.

Vollmer, August (1930). To the U.S. National Committee of Law Observance and Enforcement. *Report on the Police.* Washington, D.C.: U.S. Government Printing Office.

Westley, William (1970). *Violence and the Police.* Cambridge, Mass.: Massachusetts Institute of Technology Press.

Wilson, James Q. (1963). "The Police and Their Problems: A Theory." *Public Policy.*

Wittels, David J. (1949). "Why Cops Turn Crooked." *Saturday Evening Post,* April 23, 1949.

The Nudist Management of Respectability

MARTIN S. WEINBERG

Public nudity is taboo in our society. Yet there is a group who breach this moral rule. They call themselves "social nudists."

A number of questions may be asked about these people. For example, how can they see their behavior as morally appropriate? Have they constructed their own morality? If so, what characterizes this morality and what are its consequences?[1]

This article will attempt to answer these questions through a study of social interaction in nudist camps. The data come from three sources: two summers of participant observation in nudist camps; 101 interviews with nudists in the Chicago area; and 617 mailed questionnaires completed by nudists in the United States and Canada.[2]

THE CONSTRUCTION OF SITUATED MORAL MEANINGS: THE NUDIST MORALITY

The construction of morality in nudist camps is based on the official interpretations that camps provide regarding the moral meanings of public heterosexual nudity. These are (1) that nudity and sexuality are unrelated, (2) that there is nothing shameful about the human body, (3) that nudity promotes a feeling of freedom and natural pleasure, and (4) that nude exposure to the sun promotes physical, mental, and spiritual well-being.

This official perspective is sustained in nudist camps to an extraordinary degree, illustrating the extent to which adult socialization can affect traditional

[1] In my previous papers, I have dealt with other questions that are commonly asked about nudists. How persons become nudists is discussed in my "Becoming a Nudist," *Psychiatry*, XXIX (February, 1966), 15–24. A report on the nudist way of life and social structure can be found in my article in *Human Organization*, XXVI (Fall, 1967), 91–99.

[2] Approximately one hundred camps were represented in the interviews and questionnaires. Interviews were conducted in the homes of nudists during the off season. Arrangements for the interviews were initially made with these nudists during the first summer of participant observation; selection of respondents was limited to those living within a one-hundred-mile radius of Chicago. The questionnaires were sent to all members of the National Nudist Council. The different techniques of data collection provided a test of convergent validation.

moral meanings. (This is especially true with regard to the first two points of the nudist perspective, which will be our primary concern since these are its "deviant" aspects.) The assumption in the larger society that nudity and sexuality are related, and the resulting emphasis on covering the sexual organs, make the nudist perspective a specifically situated morality. My field work, interview, and questionnaire research show that nudists routinely use a special system of rules to create, sustain, and enforce this situated morality.

STRATEGIES FOR SUSTAINING A SITUATED MORALITY

The first strategy used by the nudist camp to anesthetize any relationship between nudity and sexuality[3] involves a system of organizational precautions regarding who can come into the camp. Most camps, for example, regard unmarried people, especially single men, as a threat to the nudist morality. They suspect that singles may indeed see nudity as something sexual. Thus, most camps either exclude unmarried people (especially men), or allow only a small quota of them. Camps that do allow single men may charge them up to 35 percent more than they charge families. (This is intended to discourage single men, but since the cost is still relatively low compared with other resorts, this measure is not very effective. It seems to do little more than create resentment among the singles, and by giving formal organizational backing to the definition that singles are not especially desirable, it may contribute to the segregation of single and married members in nudist camps.)

Certification by the camp owner is another requirement for admission to camp grounds, and three letters of recommendation regarding the applicant's character are sometimes required. These regulations help preclude people whom members regard as a threat to the nudist morality.

[The camp owner] invited us over to see if we were *desirable* people. Then after we did this, he invited us to camp on probation; then they voted us into camp. [Q: Could you tell me what you mean by desirable people?] Well, not people who are inclined to drink, or people who go there for a peep show. Then they don't want you there. They feel you out in conversation. They want people for mental and physical health reasons.

Whom to admit [is the biggest problem of the camp]. [Q][4] Because the world is so full of people whose attitudes on nudity are hopelessy warped. [Q: Has this always been the biggest problem in camp?] Yes. Every time anybody comes, a decision has to be made. [Q] . . . The lady sitting at the gate decides about admittance. The director decides on membership.

A limit is sometimes set on the number of trial visits a non-member may make to camp. In addition, there is usually a limit on how long a person can remain clothed. This is a strategy to mark guests who may not sincerely accept the nudist perspective.

The second strategy for sustaining the nudist morality involves norms of interpersonal behavior. These norms are as follows:

---

[3] For a discussion of the essence of such relationships, see Alfred Schutz, *Collected Papers: The Problem of Social Reality,* Maurice Natanson, ed. (The Hague: Nijhoff, 1962), I, 287 ff.

[4] [Q] is used to signify a neutral probe by the interviewer that follows the course of the last reply, such as "Could you tell me some more about that?" or "How is that?" or "What do you mean?" Other questions by the interviewer are given in full.

No Staring. This rule controls overt signs of overinvolvement. As the publisher of one nudist magazine said, "They all look up to the heavens and never look below." Such studied inattention is most exaggerated among women, who usually show no recognition that the male is unclothed. Women also recount that they had expected men to look at their nude bodies, only to find, when they finally did get up the courage to undress, that no one seemed to notice. As one woman states: "I got so mad because my husband wanted me to undress in front of other men that I just pulled my clothes right off thinking everyone would look at me." She was amazed (and appeared somewhat disappointed) when no one did.

The following statements illustrate the constraints that result:

[Q: Have you ever observed or heard about anyone staring at someone's body while at camp?] I've heard stories, particularly about men that stare. Since I heard these stories, I tried not to, and have even done away with my sunglasses after someone said, half-joking, that I hide behind sunglasses to stare. Toward the end of the summer I stopped wearing sunglasses. And you know what, it was a child who told me this.

[Q: Would you stare. . . ?] Probably not, 'cause you can get in trouble and get thrown out. If I thought I could stare unobserved I might. They might not throw you out, but it wouldn't do you any good. [Q] The girl might tell others and they might not want to talk to me. . . . [Q] They disapprove by not talking to you, ignoring you, etc.

[Someone who stares] wouldn't belong there. [Q] If he does that he is just going to camp to see the opposite sex. [Q] He is just coming to stare. [Q] You go there to swim and relax.

I try very hard to look at them from the jaw up—even more than you would normally.[5]

No Sex Talk. Sex talk, or telling "dirty jokes," is uncommon in camp. The owner of a large camp in the Midwest stated: "It is usually expected that members of a nudist camp will not talk about sex, politics, or religion." Or as one single male explained: "It is taboo to make sexual remarks here." During my field work, it was rare to hear "sexual" joking such as one hears at most other types of resort. Interview respondents who mentioned that they had talked about sex qualified this by explaining that such talk was restricted to close friends, was of a "scientific nature," or, if a joke, was a "cute sort."

Asked what they would think of someone who breached this rule, respondents indicated that such behavior would cast doubt on the situated morality of the nudist camp:

One would expect to hear less of that at camp than at other places. [Q] Because you expect that the members are screened in their attitude for nudism—and this isn't one who prefers sexual jokes.

I've never heard anyone swear or tell a dirty joke out there.

No. Not at camp. You're not supposed to. You bend over backwards not to.

[5] The King and Queen contest, which takes place at conventions, allows for a patterned evasion of the staring rule. Applicants stand before the crowd in front of the royal platform, and applause is used for selecting the winners. Photography is allowed during the contest, and no one is permitted to enter the contest unless willing to be photographed. The major reason for this is that this is a major camp event, and contest pictures are used in nudist magazines. At the same time, the large number of photographs sometimes taken by lay photographers (that is, not working for the magazines), makes many nudists uncomfortable by calling into question a nonsexual definition of the situation.

They probably don't belong there. They're there to see what they can find to observe. [Q] Well, their mind isn't on being a nudist, but to see so and so nude.

No Body Contact. Although the extent to which this is enforced varies from camp to camp, there is at least some degree of informal enforcement in nearly every camp. Nudists mention that they are particularly careful not to brush against anyone or have any body contact for fear of how it might be interpreted:

I stay clear of the opposite sex. They're so sensitive, they imagine things.

People don't get too close to you. Even when they talk. They sit close to you, but they don't get close enough to touch you.

We have a minimum of contact. There are more restrictions [at a nudist camp]. [Q] Just a feeling I had. I would openly show my affection more readily someplace else.

And when asked to conceptualize a breach of this rule, the following response is typical:

They are in the wrong place. [Q] That's not part of nudism. [Q] I think they are there for some sort of sex thrill. They are certainly not there to enjoy the sun.

Also, in photographs taken for nudist magazines, the subjects usually have only limited body contact. One female nudist explained: "We don't want anyone to think we're immoral." Outsiders' interpretations, then, can also constitute a threat.

Associated with the body contact taboo is a prohibition of nude dancing. Nudists cite this as a separate rule. This rule is often talked about by members in a way that indicates organizational strain —that is, the rule itself makes evident that a strategy is in operation to sustain their situated morality.

This reflects a contradiction in our beliefs. But it's self-protection. One incident and we'd be closed.

No Alcoholic Beverages in American Camps. This rule guards against breakdowns in inhibition, and even respondents who admitted that they had "snuck a beer" before going to bed went on to say that they fully favor the rule.

Yes. We have [drunk at camp]. We keep a can of beer in the refrigerator since we're out of the main area. We're not young people or carousers. . . . I still most generally approve of it as a camp rule and would disapprove of anyone going to extremes. [Q] For common-sense reasons. People who overindulge lose their inhibitions, and there is no denying that the atmosphere of a nudist camp makes one bend over backwards to keep people who are so inclined from going beyond the bounds of propriety.

Anyone who drinks in camp is jeopardizing their membership and they shouldn't. Anyone who drinks in camp could get reckless. [Q] Well, when guys and girls drink they're a lot bolder—they might get fresh with someone else's girl. That's why it isn't permitted, I guess.

Rules Regarding Photography. Photography in a nudist camp is controlled by the camp management. Unless the photographer works for a nudist magazine, his (or her) moral perspective is sometimes suspect. One photographer's remark to a woman that led to his being so typed was, "Do you think you could open your legs a little more?"

Aside from a general restriction on the use of cameras, when cameras are allowed, it is expected that no pictures will be taken without the subject's permission. Members blame the misuse of cameras especially on single men. As one nudist said: "You always see the singles poppin' around out of nowhere snappin' pictures." In general, control is maintained, and any infractions that take place are not blatant or obvious. Over-indulgence in picture-taking communicates an overinvolvement in the subjects' nudity and casts doubt on the assumption that nudity and sexuality are unrelated.

Photographers dressed only in cameras and light exposure meters. I don't like them. I think they only go out for pictures. Their motives should be questioned.

Photographers for nudist magazines recognize the signs that strain the situated morality that characterizes nudist camps. As one such photographer commented:

I never let a girl look straight at the camera. It looks too suggestive. I always have her look off to the side.

Similarly, a nudist model showed the writer a pin-up magazine to point out how a model could make a nude picture "sexy"—through the use of various stagings, props, and expressions—and in contrast, how the nudist model eliminates these techniques to make her pictures "natural." Although it may be questionable that a nudist model completely eliminates a sexual perspective for the non-nudist, the model discussed how she attempts to do this.

It depends on the way you look. Your eyes and your smile can make you look sexy. The way they're looking at you. Here, she's on a bed. It wouldn't be sexy if she were on a beach with kids running around. They always have some clothes on too. See how she's "looking" sexy? Like an "oh dear!" look. A different look can change the whole picture.

Now here's a decent pose. . . . Outdoors makes it "nature." Here she's giving you "the eye," or is undressing. It's cheesecake. It depends on the expression on her face. Having nature behind it makes it better.

Don't smile like "come on honey!" It's that look and the lace thing she has on. . . . Like when you half-close your eyes, like "oh baby," a Marilyn Monroe look. Art is when you don't look like you're hiding it halfway.

The element of trust plays a particularly strong role in socializing women to the nudist perspective. Consider this in the following statements made by another model for nudist magazines. She and her husband had been indoctrinated in the nudist ideology by friends. At the time of the interview, however, the couple had not yet been to camp, although they had posed indoors for nudist magazines.

[Three months ago, before I was married] I never knew a man had any pubic hairs. I was shocked when I was married. . . . I wouldn't think of getting undressed in front of my husband. I wouldn't make love with a light on, or in the daytime.

With regard to being a nudist model, this woman commented:

None of the pictures are sexually seductive. [Q] The pose, the look—you can have a pose that's completely nothing, till you get a look that's not too hard to do. [Q: How do you do that?] I've never tried. By putting on a certain air about a person; a picture that couldn't be submitted to a nudist magazine—using _____ [the nudist photographer's] language. . . . [Q: Will your parents see your pictures in the magazine?] Possibly. I don't really care. . . . My mother might take it all right. But they've been married twenty years and she's never seen my dad undressed.[6]

No Accentuation of the Body. Accentuating the body is regarded as incongruent with the nudist morality. Thus, a woman who had shaved her pubic area

---

[6] I was amazed at how many young female nudists described a similar pattern of extreme clothing modesty among their parents and in their own married life. Included in this group was another nudist model, one of the most photographed of nudist models. Perhaps there are some fruitful data here for cognitive-dissonance psychologists.

was labeled "disgusting" by other members. There was a similar reaction to women who sat in a blatantly "unladylike" manner.

I'd think she was inviting remarks. [Q] I don't know. It seems strange to think of it. It's strange you ask it. Out there, they're not unconscious about their posture. Most women there are very circumspect even though in the nude.

For a girl, . . . [sitting with your legs open] is just not feminine or ladylike. The hair doesn't always cover it. [Q] Men get away with so many things. But, it would look dirty for a girl, like she was waiting for something. When I'm in a secluded area I've spread my legs to sun, but I kept an eye open and if anyone came I'd close my legs and sit up a little. It's just not ladylike.

You can lay on your back or side, or with your knees under your chin. But not with your legs spread apart. It would look to other people like you're there for other reasons. [Q: What other reasons?] . . . To stare and get an eyeful. . . . not to enjoy the sun and people.

No Unnatural Attempts at Covering the Body. "Unnatural attempts" at covering the body are ridiculed since they call into question the assumption that there is no shame in exposing any area of the body. If such behavior occurs early in one's nudist career, however, members usually have more compassion, assuming that the person just has not yet fully assimilated the new morality.

It is how members interpret the behavior, however, rather than the behavior per se, that determines whether covering up is disapproved.

If they're cold or sunburned, it's understandable. If it's because they don't agree with the philosophy, they don't belong there.

I would feel their motives for becoming nudists were not well founded. That they were not true nudists, not idealistic enough.

A third strategy that is sometimes employed to sustain the nudist reality is the use of communal toilets. Not all the camps have communal toilets, but the large camp where I did most of my field work did have such a facility, which was marked, "Little Girls Room and Little Boys Too." Although the stalls had three-quarter-length doors, this combined facility still helped to provide an element of consistency; as the owner said, "If you are not ashamed of any part of your body or any of its natural functions, men and women do not need separate toilets." Thus, even the physical ecology of the nudist camp was designed to be consistent with the nudist morality. For some, however, communal toilets were going too far.

I think they should be separated. For myself it's all right. But there are varied opinions, and for the satisfaction of all, I think they should separate them. There are niceties of life we often like to maintain, and for some people this is embarrassing. . . . [Q] You know, in a bowel movement it always isn't silent.

THE ROUTINIZATION OF NUDITY

In the nudist camp, nudity becomes routinized; its attention-provoking quality recedes, and nudity becomes a taken-for-granted state of affairs. Thus, when asked questions about staring ("While at camp, have you ever stared at anyone's body? Do you think you would stare at anyone's body?") nudists indicate that nudity generally does not invoke their attention.

Nudists don't care what bodies are like. They're out there for themselves. It's a matter-of-fact thing. After a while you feel like you're sitting with a full suit of clothes on.

To nudists the body becomes so matter-of-fact, whether clothed or unclothed, when you make it an undue point of interest it becomes an abnormal thing.

[Q: What would you think of someone staring?] I would feel bad and let down. [Q] I have it set up on a high standard. I have never seen it happen. . . . [Q] Because it's not done there. It's above that; you don't stare. . . . If I saw it happen, I'd be startled. There's no inclination to do that. Why would they?

There are two types—male and female. I couldn't see why they were staring. I wouldn't understand it.

In fact, these questions about staring elicit from nudists a frame of possibilities in which what is relevant to staring is ordinarily not nudity itself. Rather, what evokes attention is something unusual, something the observer seldom sees and thus is not routinized to.[7]

There was a red-haired man. He had red pubic hair. I had never seen this before. . . . He didn't see me. If anyone did, I would turn the other way.

Well, once I was staring at a pregnant woman. It was the first time I ever saw this. I was curious, her stomach stretched, the shape. . . . I also have stared at extremely obese people, cripples. All this is due to curiosity, just a novel sight. [Q] . . . I was discreet. [Q] I didn't look at them when their eyes were fixed in a direction so they could tell I was.

[Q: While at camp have you ever stared at someone's body?] Yes. [Q] A little girl. She has a birthmark on her back, at the base of her spine.

[Q: Do you think you would ever stare at someone's body while at camp?] No. I don't like that. I think it's silly. . . . What people are is not their fault if they are deformed.

I don't think it would be very nice, very polite. [Q] I can't see anything to stare at, whether it's a scar or anything else. [Q] It just isn't done.

I've looked, but not stared. I'm careful about that, because you could get in bad about that. [Q] Get thrown out by the owner. I was curious when I once had a perfect view of a girl's sex organs, because her legs were spread when she was sitting on a chair. I sat in the chair across from her in perfect view of her organs. [Q] For about ten or fifteen minutes. [Q] Nobody noticed. [Q] It's not often you get that opportunity.[8]

[Q: How would you feel if you were alone in a secluded area of camp sunning yourself, and then noticed that other nudists were staring at your body?] I would think I had some mud on me. [Q] . . . I would just ask them why they were staring at me. Probably I was getting sunburn and they wanted to tell me to turn over, or maybe I had a speck of mud on me. [Q] These are the only two reasons I can think of why they were staring.

In the nudist camp, the arousal of attention by nudity is usually regarded as *unnatural*. Thus, staring is unnatural, especially after a period of grace in which to adjust to the new meanings.

If he did it when he was first there, I'd figure he's normal. If he kept it up I'd stay away from him, or suggest to the owner that he be thrown out. [Q] At first it's a new experience, so he might be staring. [Q] He wouldn't know how to react to it. [Q] The first time seeing nudes of the opposite sex. [Q] I'd think if he kept staring, that he's thinking of something, like grabbing someone, running to the bushes and raping them. [Q] Maybe he's mentally unbalanced.

He just sat there watching the women. You can forgive it the first time, because of

---

[7] Cf. Schutz, *op. cit.,* p. 74.

[8] For some respondents, the female genitals, because of their hidden character, never become a routinized part of camp nudity; thus their visible exposure does not lose an attention-provoking quality.

curiosity. But not every weekend. [Q] The owner asked him to leave.

These women made comments on some men's shapes. They said, "He has a hairy body or ugly bones," or "Boy his wife must like him because he's hung big." That was embarrassing. . . . I thought they were terrible. [Q] Because I realized they were walking around looking. I can't see that.

ORGANIZATIONS AND THE CONSTITUTION OF NORMALITY

The rules-in-use of an organization *and the reality they sustain* form the basis on which behaviors are interpreted as "unnatural."[9] Overinvolvement in nudity, for example, is interpreted by nudists as unnatural (and not simply immoral). Similarly, erotic stimuli or responses, which breach the nudist morality, are defined as unnatural.

They let one single in. He acted peculiar. . . . He got up and had a big erection. I didn't know what he'd do at night. He might molest a child or anybody. . . . My husband went and told the owner.

I told you about this one on the sundeck with her legs spread. She made no bones about closing up. Maybe it was an error, but I doubt it. It wasn't a normal position. Normally you wouldn't lay like this. It's like standing on your head. She had sufficient time and there were people around.

She sat there with her legs like they were straddling a horse. I don't know how else to describe it. [Q] She was just sitting on the ground. [Q] I think she's a dirty pig. [Q] If you sit that way, everyone don't want to know what she had for breakfast. [Q] It's just the wrong way to sit. You keep your legs together even with clothes on.

[Q: Do you think it is possible for a person to be modest in a nudist camp?] I think so. [Q] If a person acts natural. . . . An immodest person would be an exhibitionist, and you find them in nudism too. . . . Most people's conduct is all right.

When behaviors are constituted as *unnatural,* attempts to understand them are usually suspended, and reciprocity of perspectives is called into question. (The "reciprocity of perspectives" involves the assumption that if one changed places with the other, one would, for all practical purposes, see the world as the other sees it.[10])

[Q: What would you think of a man who had an erection at camp?] Maybe they can't control themselves. [Q] Better watch out for him. [Q] I would tell the camp director to keep an eye on him. And the children would question that. [Q: What would you tell them?] I'd tell them the man is sick or something.

[Q: What would you think of a Peeping Tom—a non-nudist trespasser?] They should be reported and sent out. [Q] I think they shouldn't be there. They're sick. [Q] Mentally. [Q] Because anyone who wants to look at someone else's body, well, is a Peeping Tom, is sick in the first place. He looks at you differently than a normal person would. [Q] With ideas of sex. [A trespasser] . . . is sick. He probably uses this as a source of sexual stimulation.

Such occurrences call into question the taken-for-granted character of nudity in the nudist camp and the situated morality that is officially set forth.

INHIBITING BREAKDOWNS IN THE NUDIST MORALITY

Organized nudism promulgates a nonsexual perspective toward nudity, and breakdowns in that perspective are in-

[9] Compare Harold Garfinkel, "A Conception of, and Experiments with, 'Trust' as a Condition of Stable Concreted Actions," in O. J. Harvey, ed., *Motivation and Social Interaction* (New York: Ronald, 1963).

[10] See: Schutz, *op. cit.,* I, 11, for his definition of reciprocity of perspectives.

hibited by (1) controlling erotic actions and (2) controlling erotic reactions. Nudity is partitioned off from other forms of "immodesty" (e.g., verbal immodesty, erotic overtures). In this way, a person can learn more easily to attribute a new meaning to nudity.[11] When behaviors occur that reflect other forms of "immodesty," however, nudists often fear a voiding of the nonsexual meaning that they impose on nudity.

This woman with a sexy walk would shake her hips and try to arouse the men. . . . [Q] These men went to the camp director to complain that the woman had purposely tried to arouse them. The camp director told this woman to leave.

Nudists are sensitive to the possibility of a breakdown in the nudist morality. Thus, they have a low threshold for interpreting acts as "sexual."

Playing badminton, this teenager was hitting the birdie up and down and she said, "What do you think of that?" I said, "Kind of sexy." _____ [the president of the camp] said I shouldn't talk like that, but I was only kidding.

Note the following description of "mauling":

I don't like to see a man and a girl mauling each other in the nude before others. . . . [Q: Did you ever see this at camp?] I saw it once. . . . [Q: What do you mean by mauling?] Just, well, I never saw him put his hands on her breast, but he was running his hands along her arms.

This sensitivity to "sexual" signs also sensitizes nudists to the possibility that certain of their own acts, although not intended as "sexual," might nonetheless be interpreted that way.

Sometimes you're resting and you spread your legs unknowingly. [Q] My husband just told me not to sit that way. [Q] I put my legs together.

Since "immodesty" is defined as an unnatural manner of behavior, such behaviors are easily interpreted as being motivated by "dishonorable" intent. When the individual is thought to be in physical control of the "immodest" behavior and to know the behavior's meaning within the nudist scheme of interpretation, sexual intentions are assigned. Referring to a quotation that was presented earlier, one man said that a woman who was lying with her legs spread may have been doing so unintentionally, "but I doubt it. [Q] It wasn't a normal position. Normally you wouldn't lay like this. It's like standing on your head."

Erotic reactions, as well as erotic actions, are controlled in camp. Thus, even when erotic stimuli come into play, erotic responses may be inhibited.

When lying on the grass already hiding my penis, I got erotic thoughts. And then one realizes it can't happen here. With fear there isn't much erection.

Yes, once I started to have an erection. Once. [Q] A friend told me how he was invited by some young lady to go to bed. [Q] I started to picture the situation and I felt the erection coming on; so I immediately jumped in the pool. It went away.

I was once in the woods alone and ran into a woman. I felt myself getting excited. A secluded spot in the bushes which was an ideal place for procreation. [Q] Nothing happened, though.

When breaches of the nudist morality do occur, other nudists' sense of modesty may inhibit sanctioning. The immediate breach may go unsanctioned. The observers may feign inattention or withdraw from the scene. The occurrence is usually communicated, however, via the grapevine, and it may reach the camp director.

We were shooting a series of pictures and my wife was getting out of her clothes. _____ [the photographer] had an erection

[11] This corresponds with the findings of learning-theory psychologists.

but went ahead like nothing was happening. [Q] It was over kind of fast. . . . [Q] Nothing. We tried to avoid the issue. . . . Later we went to see _____ [the camp director] and _____ [the photographer] denied it.

[If a man had an erection] people would probably pretend they didn't see it.

[Q: What do you think of someone this happens to?] They should try to get rid of it fast. It don't look nice. Nudists are prudists. They are more prudish. Because they take their clothes off they are more careful. [Q] They become more prudish than people with clothes. They won't let anything out of the way happen.

As indicated in the remark, "nudists are prudists," nudists may at times become aware of the fragility of their situated moral meanings.

At _____ [camp], this family had a small boy no more than ten years old who had an erection. Mrs. _____ [the owner's wife] saw him and told his parents that they should keep him in check, and tell him what had happpened to him and to watch himself. This was silly, for such a little kid who didn't know what happened.

DEVIANCE AND MULTIPLE REALITIES

There are basic social processes that underlie responses to deviance. Collectivities control thresholds of response to various behaviors, determining the relevance, meaning, and importance of the behavior. In the nudist camp, as pointed out previously, erotic overtures and erotic responses are regarded as unnatural, and reciprocity of perspectives is called into question by such behaviors.

We thought this single was all right, until others clued us in that he had brought girls up to camp. [Then we recalled that] . . .

he was kind of weird. The way he'd look at you. He had glassy eyes, like he could see through you.[12]

Such a response to deviance in the nudist camp is a result of effective socialization to the new system of moral meanings. The deviant's behavior, on the other hand, can be construed as reflecting an ineffective socialization to the new system of meanings.

I think it's impossible [to have an erection in a nudist camp]. [Q] In a nudist camp you must have some physical contact and a desire to have one.

He isn't thinking like a nudist. [Q] The body is wholesome, not . . . a sex object. He'd have to do that—think of sex.

Sex isn't supposed to be in your mind, as far as the body. He doesn't belong there. [Q] If you go in thinking about sex, naturally it's going to happen. . . . You're not supposed to think about going to bed with anyone, not even your wife.

As these quotes illustrate, the unnaturalness or deviance of a behavior is ordinarily determined by relating it to an institutionalized scheme of interpretation. Occurrences that are "not understandable" in the reality of one collectivity may, however, be quite understandable in the reality of another collectivity.[13] Thus, what are "deviant" occurrences in nudist camps probably would be regarded by members of the clothed society as natural and understandable rather than unnatural and difficult to understand.

Finally, a group of people may subscribe to different and conflicting interpretive schemes. Thus, the low threshold of nudists to anything "sexual" is a function of their marginality; the fact that they have not completely suspended the moral meanings of the clothed society is what leads them to constitute many events as "sexual" in purpose.

[12] For a study of the process of doublethink, see James L. Wilkins, "Doublethink: A Study of Erasure of the Social Past," unpublished doctoral dissertation, Northwestern University, 1964.

[13] Cf. Schutz, op. cit., pp. 229 ff.

Occupational Ideologies and Individual Attitudes of Call Girls

JAMES H. BRYAN

Students of deviance emphasize the importance of group perspectives and values and socialization into them in the development and maintenance of deviant behavior. They agree that when behavior is stigmatized, the deviant group will propagate attitudes and moralities counter to dominant cultural values.[1] While individual deviants are thought to vary in their degree of socialization, professionals are said to be developed.[2] The ideologies of deviant groups, according to Backer, "tend to contain a general repudiation of conventional moral rules, conventional institutions, and the entire conventional world."[3] Further, students agree that deviant groups stress in-group loyalties and minimize the moral nature of their transgressions.[4]

Few data have been collected which assess the impact of professional perspectives upon the individual deviant, the degree to which ideology is incorporated into the personal belief system. The present study was concerned, therefore, with the ideological stance of the professional prostitute and its impact upon the individual practitioners.

While it is commonly thought that prostitutes' ideologies play an important role in the continuation of their behavior, these beliefs have rested as much on faith as on fact.[5] The perspectives of prostitutes have generally been ignored

Reprinted from *Social Problems,* Vol. 13, No. 4 (Spring, 1966), pp. 441–50, by permission of the author and *Social Problems.*

[1] H. S. Becker, *Outsiders: Studies in the Sociology of Deviance,* New York: The Free Press of Glencoe, 1963; H. S. Becker (ed.), *The Other Side,* New York: The Free Press of Glencoe, 1964; M. B. Clinard, *Sociology of Deviant Behavior,* New York: Rinehart and Company, 1957; D. R. Cressey, "Social Psychological Theory for Using Deviants to Control Deviation," *Report of Proceedings, Conference on the Use of a Social Problem in Coping with the Problem,* Norco, California, July, 1963. See also E. Goffman, *Stigma,* Englewood Cliffs, N.J.: Prentice-Hall, 1963; Evelyn Hooker, "The Homosexual Community," *Proceedings, XIVth International Congress of Applied Psychology,* 1961; M. B. Ray, "The Cycle of Abstinence and Relapse among Heroin Addicts," Becker, *The Other Side, op. cit.;* T. J. Scheff, "The Role of the Mentally Ill and the Dynamics of Mental Disorder: A Research Framework," *Sociometry,* 26 (1963), pp. 436–453.

[2] Goffman, *op. cit.*

[3] H. S. Becker, *Outsiders, op. cit.,* pp. 38–39.

[4] See, for example, G. Sykes and D. Matza, "Techniques of Neutralization: A Theory of Delinquency," *American Sociological Review,* 22 (1957), pp. 664–670.

[5] As an example, see M. B. Clinard, *op. cit.;* W. C. Reckless, *The Crime Problem,* New York: Appleton-Century-Crofts, 1950.

in favor of motivational states and, when not ignored, are often inferred from very limited samples or anecdotal material.[6] Among those so concerned, Hirschi, in an excellent review of the available autobiographical material, indicated that the ideology of the prostitute contains justifications based upon functionalistic premises (prostitution is needed) and impugning the "squares'" integrity (they are prostitutes themselves).[7] Ross, on the basis of interviews with three respondents directly involved with both prostitution and other "hustling" activities, indicated the belief that at least the more professional prostitutes emphasized the value of "craftiness" and in-group loyalties.[8]

Unfortunately, albeit understandably, there are no available data which directly relate attitudes of the individual prostitute to the perspectives of the group in question. It has not yet been demonstrated that such occupationally endorsed values have an impact at the individual level. More importantly, because of the restricted number of respondents heretofore employed and the necessarily limited nature of the controls under which the data have been collected, inferences concerning the values customarily associated with the occupation of prostitution are necessarily suspect. It is well known that such inferences may be unreliable, reliable but invalid, or valid but method specific. To the degree that inferences concerning such ideologies lead to valid predictions, there is evidence that such inferences are correct and that such occupational socialization

has occurred. Conversely, the failure of such predictions suggests that either the original inferences were incorrect or that such perspectives have little impact upon the individual actor.

Assuming, however, that individuals acquire occupational ideologies during socialization, it nonetheless remains to be demonstrated that such ideologies are related to *sustained* acts of prostitution. Indeed, to assert that occupationally sanctioned ideologies are important in sustaining deviant behavior requires as minimal evidence correlational data relating time in the deviant behavior to the presence or absence of such views. As yet, no such data exist.

The present study had two purposes: (1) to assess the relationship between an occupational perspective and individually endorsed attitudes toward relevant objects; and (2) to examine the relationship between such attitudes and opportunities for socialization as measured by length of time in prostitution.

METHOD

The respondents were 52 active or previously active prostitutes who volunteered to be interviewed, who were not paid, and who, with one exception defined themselves as "call girls."[9] No member of the sample was under the supervision of a police agency; eight were outpatients in a psychiatric hospital. The respondents ranged in age from 18–40, the average being 22. Their average

---

[6] For a brief review of the hypothesized motive forces affecting prostitution, see J. H. Bryan, "Apprenticeships in Prostitution," *Social Problems,* 12 (1965), pp. 287–297; for an extended review see V. L. Bullough, "Prostitution and Behavioral Research: A Biographical Essay," *Journal of History of Behavioral Science,* 1 (1965), pp. 244–251.

[7] T. Hirschi, "The Professional Prostitute," *Berkeley Journal of Sociology,* 7 (1962), pp. 33–49.

[8] H. L. Ross, "The 'Hustler' in Chicago," *Journal of Student Research,* 1 (1959), pp. 13–19.

[9] The single exception met all other criteria.

length of time as an active prostitute was 27 months. The informants obtained their clients through individual referrals, primarily by telephone, and the sexual contract was enacted in their or the clients' place of residence or employment. The respondents did not initiate contact with their customers in bars, streets, or houses of prostitution, although they might meet by pre-arrangement at such locations. With five exceptions, the minimum fee ever charged by the girl per sexual encounter was $20. This suggests that the respondents were, in fact, "upper class" prostitutes. Of the five exceptions, all had charged no less than $10 per sexual contract and all but one at the time of interview had eventually set a price of $20. Thirty-nine of the respondents worked primarily in Los Angeles, six in Chicago, three in Las Vegas, and one each in San Francisco and Miami. Many of the respondents, however, worked in more than one city.

All but two interviews were, with the respondent's prior knowledge, tape recorded. Most interviews were conducted at the girl's place of work and/or residence. Interviews were semi-structured and employed open-ended questions.

THE IDEOLOGY

While the data pertaining to ideologies are necessarily impressionistic, certain roughly specifiable criteria were used to select that material relevant to occupational perspectives. First, of course, the material was used by the girls in such a manner as to explain and justify the occupation of prostitution. For example, responses to such questions as "What are the advantages of prostitution for society [self]?" and "Should prostitution be legalized [why]?" were heavily relied upon, as they repeatedly elicited such stereotyped justifying answers. Additionally, such responses had to be known to the majority of respondents. Considerable consensus existed, for example, in response to the abovementioned questions. Certain views also were repeatedly attributed "pro," part of the "in-group," of those who had been in the profession for a lengthy period. For example, and not infrequently, a respondent would indicate how one should perceive, feel, or act, if one were to be a real professional. Hence attributed professional views, if there was agreement as to their nature, were used as the basis for inferring occupationally sanctioned ideologies.

A major element in the occupational perspective, indicated by virtually all respondents, was that prostitution served important social functions because of man's extensive and varied sexual needs, protecting both individuals and social institutions alike from destructive ruptures.

We girls see, like I guess you call them perverts of some sort, you know, little freaky people and if they didn't have girls to come to like us that are able to handle them and make it a nice thing, there would be so many rapes and . . . nutty people really.

I think that a lot less rapes and murders if it were (legalized).

I believe that there should be more prostitution houses and what have you, and then we wouldn't have so many of these perverted idiots, sex maniacs, all sorts of weird people running around.

Marriages are thought to be more enduring because of prostitution!

I could say that a prostitute has held more marriages together as part of their profession than any divorce counselor.

Respondents also commonly indicated that prostitutes serve as important psychotherapeutic agents, giving comfort, insight, and satisfaction to those men too embarrassed, lonely, or isolated to obtain interpersonal gratification in other ways.

I don't regret doing it because I feel I help people. A lot of men that come over to see me don't come over for sex. They come over for companionship, someone to talk to. . . . They talk about sex. . . . A lot of them have problems.

While the foregoing positions are commonly stated, the professional, as opposed to the novice, holds additional views. Both trainers and professionals appear to encourage a view that makes exploitation of the "john" less morally reprehensible. The customer is exploitative, hence should be exploited. Customers are to be cultivated through extensive contacts, such that repeated "scores" can be made, often to the customer's disadvantage. The professional also tends to devalue men in general. Interestingly, this position is often felt to be the natural outcome of sustained acts of prostitution so that extensive experience with customers is thought to produce the "hard and cold" girl who has developed a "very crude attitude toward it [the professional]" and ends being "bitter and hating men [clients]." Of the conceptions of the consequences of being a prostitute held by the girls, this is perhaps the one that produces the most personal anxiety.

The prostitute should see her customers as exploitative, cutting each corner of the financial contract, and herself as a potential victim: "So he [trainer] taught me to get my money out in front a lot of times . . . [if] you accept clothes from them, they'll buy you a $10.00 dress and the whole deal is worth fifty."

In addition, girls recognize occupationally-sanctioned attitudes toward women and colleagues alike. They sometimes say that the "in-group" is unique, special, more honest: "I feel that people in the life are more honest with themselves and with others."

Occasionally the trainer will exhort the novice to join the "in-group." As one prostitute of two weeks explains her reaction to her trainer's exhortations to "Get with it; do what we do": "It has to do with being a swinger or hip. Going out and more or less cheating on your boyfriend or carousing around with a fast crowd and looking hot. . . . I won't do it."

Another view, popular at both the novice and professional level, is that interpersonal relationships between the sexes are, in essence, acts of prostitution. This position stems from the assumption that within such relationships gains are often derived from intentional manipulations, deceptions, and sex. The housewife then is no less guilty than the prostitute: ". . . actually all women are whores in my opinion whether they get married for it or whatever it is. There are just different ways of being a whore." The square's hypocrisy may be further compounded by envy. "They [the public] resent them because the working girl [call girl] can do things that other women can't do."

In sum, the professional perspective argues that customers can and should be exploited, that the role of the prostitute is no more immoral than the role of the "square," and that colleagues are more honest and helpful than women outside the profession. Furthermore, since it is a necessary, indeed therapeutic, practice, prostitution should not be stigmatized, and one should not look down upon oneself for being a prostitute. These simple rules may, perhaps, justify exploitation, sustain what cooperative behavior is necessary for occupational functioning, and reduce both public and personal stigma, real or potential, attached to the actor.

INDIVIDUAL ATTITUDES

Given these perspectives, the issue remains as to how much impact they have upon the individual respondent. The interview material suggests that individual respondents do not, in fact, personally endorse the above-mentioned perspectives. While the respondents know them, they do not believe them. For example, many of the individual respondents, not surprisingly, refuse to stereotype the customer: "I've never found two alike." Or stereotyping may be more benign than that suggested by the occupation's ideology: "Most of them are very, very nice people, like overly nice." Reality soon appears to break down the ideology, occasionally to the discomfort of the actor: "Even though they're tricks, and I hate tricks, they are still people and they have as many hang-ups a lot of times as I do, therefore, I have been able to empathize with them in most cases which is bad when you try to take somebody for all they're worth. It gives you guilt feelings." Not infrequently, personal friendships with customers are reported: "Some of them are nice clients who become very good friends of mine." On the other hand, while friendships are formed with "squares," personal disputations with colleagues are frequent. Speaking of her colleagues, one call girl says that most "could cut your throat." Respondents frequently mentioned that they had been robbed, conned, or otherwise exploited by their call girl friends. Interpersonal distrust between call girls appears to be considerable. While respondents tend to deny that they or their fellow workers fulfill the usual conceptions of the tight-skirted, hip-swinging, customer-rolling street-walker, they do characteristically indicate that their relationships with other call girls are marked by interpersonal conflict, disloyalties, and mutual exploitation.

To more formally assess individually endorsed attitudes, the last 28 respondents, all currently active in prostitution, were administered a rating scale. Each

was asked to rate, on the semantic differential (to be described below), herself, other call girls, women-in-general, "johns," and men-in-general.[10] If occupational socialization occurred, then individually held attitudes toward such groups should be predictable from the occupational ideology. The three audiences of primary concern were: self, "johns," and other working girls. These groups were chosen as they appeared relevant to the girls' occupational success and because occupationally-supported perspectives pertaining to them existed. If occupational socialization does occur, then, on the basis of the described ideology, we can predict that the distribution of attitudes toward these groups would not only not be random, but that particular groups would be more favorably evaluated than others. If the ideological justifications have the effect of reducing the girls' personal distress, the self should be rated, relative to other groups, as more worthwhile. Conversely, due to the johns' "perverted" sexual nature and economic avarice, they should be held in relatively low esteem. The call girl colleague, a necessary adjunct to the daily round of affairs for most call girls, should be held in greater esteem than the customer. In addition to these groups, girls were also asked to rate women-in-general and men-in-general. These ratings allow us to avoid confounding attitudes toward specific groups with those toward a specific gender. Additionally, in light of the perspective that all women are in spirit if not in practice prostitutes, the latter ratings also served as an additional test of the effects of socialization.

The respondent rated each group on the following nine bi-polar items: good-bad, cruel-kind, valuable-worthless, fast-slow, passive-active, dull-sharp, hard-soft, large-small, weak-strong. These nine

[10] For a description of the procedure, see C. E. Osgood, G. J. Suci, and P. H. Tannenbaum, *The Measurement of Meaning,* Urbana, Ill.: University of Illinois Press, 1957.

TABLE 1 Analysis of Variance of Semantic Differential Ratings

Source	df	SS	MS	Error Term	F
Groups (G)	4	187.31	46.83	Ss × G	3.303*
Dimension (D)	2	254.957	127.48	Ss × D	8.66**
G × D	8	282.233	35.28	Ss × G × D	5.378**
Subjects (Ss)	27	605.817	22.44		
Ss × G	108	1531.623	14.18		
Ss × D	54	794.776	14.72		
Ss × G × D	216	1418.03	6.56		
Total		5074.75			

* $p < .05$.
** $p < .01$.

items have been shown previously to load on one of three factors subsequently labelled evaluation, activity, potency.[11] The first three items load heavily on evaluation, the next three on activity, and the remaining on the potency dimension. The respondent indicated her rating by checking one of seven spaces spatially separating the bi-polar units of the item. For example, ratings were made by checking one of seven spaces separating the word good from the word bad. If the respondent thought the group in question was good, she checked the space closest to the word good. This procedure was followed for each of the items.

Since it is well known that single items on such scales may not be highly reliable, ratings on items loading heavily on one dimension were summed for each respondent and treated as the primary score for that dimension. For example, the ratings of a particular group on the items good-bad, cruel-kind, and valuable-worthless were summed, thus forming the evaluative ratings on that specific group. Since there were three items per dimension, each item having a one to seven scale, summed scores could range only from three to 21 on any one dimension.

Scoring was such that the higher the score, the greater the attributed dimension. For example, high scores on the evaluative factor indicated high esteem.

In the present study, the dimension of primary concern was the evaluative factor, because occupational ideologies appear to deal with stereotypes having clear-cut implications for the evaluative rather than activity or potency dimensions. The latter dimensions were included, however, so as to provide evidence that discriminations were being made in the ratings along these dimensions.

In order to assess whether the respondents held differential attitudes toward the several groups rated, variance for correlated measures was analyzed.[12] The results of the analysis are presented in Table 1.

Mean ratings of the groups were reliably different. Respondents did discriminate between groups as evidenced by the significant main effect for groups. The significant main effect of dimensions further indicates that when ratings of the groups are combined, ratings are reliably different across each dimension. Clusters of items were being responded to differ-

[11] C. E. Osgood, *et al., op. cit.*
[12] B. J. Winer, *Statistical Principles in Experimental Design,* New York: McGraw-Hill, 1962.

TABLE 2 Mean Rating of Groups on the Evaluative and Activity Dimensions

	Self	Johns	Men	Women	Call Girls
Evaluation	14.78	14.18	13.78	13.10	11.96
Activity	14.71	11.39	13.11	11.53	14.18

entially. The significant interaction of groups by dimensions indicates that groups were rated differently on the different dimensions. The latter finding is of importance because it makes untenable the suggestion that general test-taking habits or artifacts (halo effects, position rating habits, etc.) could account for the results. If, for example, halo effects were operating, differential ratings of groups across such dimensions would not be expected. In sum, then, respondents discriminated, in their ratings, both across different groups and dimensions.

The mean ratings of the groups, within a particular dimension, are presented in Table 2. Since there were no significant mean differences between the ratings of the potency for any of the groups, these results are not presented.

The Newman-Keuls analysis was employed to test mean differences in ratings across groups.[13] By this method, each mean rating of a particular group is compared to the mean ratings of all other groups and tested for statistical significance.

While mean differences were found in the ratings of the groups, the rank ordering of the groups on the basis of evaluative ratings was not predictable from the occupational ideology. While the call girl rated herself significantly more worthwhile than her colleagues, her ratings of self did not differ, on the evaluative dimension, from her ratings of men-in-general, women-in-general, or "johns." Only call girls were rated as being significantly less worthwhile than

the self. Further, the only other group that was rated reliably as being more worthwhile than call girls were "johns." Indeed, customers were evaluated by the call girl as being as worthwhile as herself, and as significantly better than her colleagues. This particular ranking could not be predicted from knowledge of occupational beliefs. The ratings of men-in-general and of women-in-general fell just short of being reliably different from ratings of call girls.

In passing, it might be noted that call girls rate themselves as being significantly more active than either "johns" or "women-in-general." These findings suggest that "johns" are seen as more passive than most males, and that self is busier and more active than most women.

The impact of the socialization aside, if the prostitute is exposed to some sort of uniform ideological training, then attitudes toward these groups, whatever their various nature, should be correlated with opportunities for learning. One, admittedly crude, measure of such opportunity is the time the respondent has been working as a prostitute. During the course of the interview each respondent was asked how many months she had been working as a prostitute, and this estimate was then correlated with ratings of the groups for each dimension. These correlations are presented in Table 3.

As can be seen, the only significant correlation is the positive correlation found between time in the profession and esteem of men-in-general. This correlation may well be a result of chance. If it

[13] B. J. Winer, *op. cit.*

TABLE 3 Product-moment Correlations of Semantic Differential Ratings and Time in the Occupation

	Evaluation	*Activity*	*Potency*
Self	−.09	.02	−.20
Other Call Girls	.04	.09	.11
Women	.19	.19	−.16
Johns	.19	.33	.09
Men	.46*	.06	−.13

* p < .05.

is not, however, the position held by at least some girls, that one becomes hard, cold, and hateful of men, is clearly refuted. At least for girls who stay in the profession, the current ratings do not indicate such attitudes.

DISCUSSION

While the data indicate that there are differential attitudes toward the relevant audiences, correct predictions as to their nature were not deduced from knowledge of the occupational ideology. The respondents know the ideology but they do not endorse it. It is, of course, possible that the description of the occupational perspective may be incorrect, but the consensus in both the scientific and lay literature suggests otherwise. Assuming that the occupationally sanctioned ideology is as described, why do so many know the perspectives and yet not adopt them privately?

It seems reasonable to assume that such ideologies serve a variety of purposes for both the individual prostitute and her related audiences, and do so with varying importance over time. For example, the belief that in-group affiliations are more real, warm, honest, and right than other relationships provides for more cooperative and consequently more lucrative business, isolates the novice from influences hostile to prostitute activities, and provides a group in which passing and duplicity are not required of the actor. Additionally, the myth of man's exploitative nature suits not only the economic aspirations of the novice, but also those of her trainer.[14] The belief that women are hypocrites and that prostitution provides a valuable social service may not only reduce moral conflicts, but serve additionally as a defense against public stigma. It has heretofore been assumed, however, that the functions of these perspectives are served with equal efficiency across the individual prostitute's career span. It appears more likely, in light of the current data, that such orientations are learned during the initial few months of her career and during her apprenticeship period and are taught directly by the trainer. While the professional ideology is learned and perhaps serves a function during this apprenticeship period, it is doubtful that it remains of equal importance throughout the call girl's career.

Once entrance into prostitution has been accomplished, there are many reasons to reject such beliefs. First, prostitution at the call girl level, particularly for pimpless and madamless girls as in this study, is loosely organized. While training periods do exist, the train-

[14] J. H. Bryan, *op. cit.*

ing appears more oriented toward the acquisition of skills than ideology. Co-operative interaction with colleagues is required for only short periods of time and usually within restricted circumstances.[15] For example, the most frequent activity of this nature is that of "putting on a show." This refers to two girls simulating homosexual activities while the customer observes. These activities, however, frequently last a short time. Additionally, many girls are usually available to a particular prostitute for this purpose, each being an actor of equal utility. No critical dependence upon particular individuals is developed.

The everyday interaction of the call girl with her colleagues dramatically belies notions concerning her good character. Respondents are suspicious of one another, being less concerned with competition than simple exploitation.[16] Interview data, as well as personal observation, demonstrate that extensive disloyalty and exploitation characterize the interpersonal relationships among call girls. As one girl suggests: "But yet there's never a real close friendship. . . . I mean they will do anything for each other. But still at times when they're taking pills and things, they'll go against you . . . they'll slit your throat at times."

If the adoption of counter-moralities is a function of public visibility and stigma, as is often implied, could it be that prostitution is, in fact, not heavily burdened with reproach? The finding of J. Nunnally that the general public holds in higher esteem the mental hospital attendant than the psychoanalyst makes any *a priori* assumption of stigma or status somewhat suspect.[17] Furthermore, despite general cultural sanctions, the everyday life of the call girl is to a great extent designed to avoid public revelation, and is generally successful in this effort. Unlike the effeminate male homosexual, the arm-marked heroin addict, or the physically disabled, the call girl carries no tell-tale insignia of her occupational status. Nor is she forced into the job market where biographies are demanded and accounts may be checked. Moreover, much of the interaction of "john" with girl is specifically oriented toward the reduction of the stigma attached to both roles, each pretending that the other is fulfilling a role more obscure than that which is apparent. While role definitions (whore and "john") are rare, when they do occur they are delicately put, stemming from motives more benevolent than otherwise. The call girl rarely experiences moral condemnation through interpersonal relations, thus reducing the need for justification. This may further lessen the impact of attempts at occupational socialization.

In accounting for the evaluative rankings found, the most parsimonious explanation is that they reflect the general culturally supported double standard. While Nunnally, using semantic differential techniques, failed to find women rating the "average man" as being better than the "average woman," McKee and Sherriffs found, using a variety of rating techniques, that women college students consistently rated men as being superior or "more worthy" than females.[18] A

---

[15] J. H. Bryan, *op. cit.*

[16] W. C. Reckless, *op. cit.* has suggested that competition disrupts group cohesiveness among streetwalkers. Competition appears to play a minor role in determining relationships among call girls.

[17] J. C. Nunnally, *Popular Conceptions of Mental Health,* New York: Holt, Rinehart and Winston, 1961.

[18] J. P. McKee and A. C. Sherriffs, "The Differential Evaluation of Males and Females," *Journal of Personality,* 25 (1957), pp. 356–371.

plausible hunch, then, is that such rank- ing might well be found in any randomly selected representative sample of this age group.

In light of the commonplace assumption by the psychological professions that the prostitute must be emotionally disturbed, it is of interest to note that if such emotional disurbance is present, it is not reflected in at least one measure of self-esteem.[19] When compared to the self-ratings of Nunnally's sample, chosen to be representative of the U.S. population on the usual demographic variables, call girls' self-ratings on the dimensions of goodness are only slightly below those of his sample.[20] Indeed, the group as a whole fails to identify with their colleagues, each supposing herself to be more worthwhile than the others.

Whatever the reasons, however, it appears that prostitution, at this level, does not require extensive socialization of its members, nor do the members re- quire such socialization for its continuing practice. While stereotypes exist, they play a limited role in the individually held perspectives of the pimpless or independent call girl. Whether independence of the socialization model is due to the lack of cohesiveness of the occupation, the personality of the participants, or the absence of severe stigma, cannot be deduced from the present data.

If the absence of occupational socialization is, in fact, the result of the lack of stigma, then further support is given those hypotheses concerning the role of stigma in producing countermoralities of deviant groups.

No evidence has been gathered which suggests that specific attitudes toward relevant audiences are related to the continuing practice of prostitution. The effects of such activity upon the attitudes of the participants remain to be determined.

[19] H. Greenwald, *The Call Girl,* New York: Ballantine Books, 1960. See also review by V. L. Bullough, *op. cit.*

[20] Ruth C. Wylie has provided an excellent review of the theoretical and methodological difficulties pertaining to self theories and measurement: *The Self Concept,* Lincoln, Nebraska: University of Nebraska Press, 1961.

Maintaining Deviant Beliefs

J. L. SIMMONS

The present paper explores some selected aspects of a belief system shared by a small group of "mystics" located in southeastern United States. Its major concern is the means through which these divergent beliefs are maintained in the face of a disbelieving society.

Data for the report were gathered from intimate association and many lengthy conversations with a prominent member of the group and from much briefer conversations with four other members. Pamphlets and newsletters of the group were also examined. Observations from a number of other fringe groups have also been drawn upon.

The concept "belief system" is here defined as the set of notions with which individuals and groups interpret the physical and social reality around them and within themselves. No classification of these notions, such as the psychoanalytic one of conscious vs. unconscious, or Parsons' distinction among cognitive, expressive, and evaluative symbols[1] will be made here since it is neither feasible nor necessary for the purposes of this paper. The term "system" will call the reader's attention to the important fact that beliefs do not exist as a heap of disconnected items, but are related into some kind of "coherent" and "consistent" pattern.

THE ESPERS

The group, which we will call Esper, has its headquarters in a semi-isolated mountainous area of Georgia. This location was picked partly for its relative seclusion and for the natural protection it would afford in the event of a nuclear war. Several members have sold their business and properties in other locations to settle here permanently. The buildings and grounds are extensive, including housing for perhaps two hundred people, ample garden space, springs, and so forth. Several other fringe groups which share many beliefs with Esper are located within a few miles and there seem to be institutional and informal ties with these other groups. However, multiple membership seems to be relatively rare. The ties seem to be based on shared beliefs, admiration of the same fringe heroes, shared knowledge of fringe literature, and similar attitudes of suspicion and benevolent contempt toward the culture at large.

The writer was unable to get exact figures on the size of membership of Esper. Estimates clustered around fifty full members and perhaps half a hundred marginal associates. About twenty-five of these lived in or near the headquarters and most other members lived in eastern

Reprinted from "On Maintaining Deviant Belief Systems: A Case Study" in *Social Problems,* Vol. 11, No. 3 (Winter, 1964), pp. 250–56, by permission of the author and *Social Problems.*

[1] Talcott Parsons, *The Social System,* New York: Free Press, 1951, pp. 326–383.

United States. There were over three hundred subscribers to the Esper monthly newsletter; subscription price was five dollars per year. Membership dues were thirty dollars the first year and five dollars per year thereafter. The two other major sources of income for the organization and its salaried members were fees for the use of cabins, boats, etc., and fees charged for courses of training in psychic powers. Individual members made other monies through faith-healing, the practice of "natural" medicine, "reading" of an individual's psyche through photographs and signatures, etc.

At this point the reader may wonder about the possibility of fraud, the cynical manipulation of the membership by a few individuals for financial gain. The writer sought evidence for this possibility but concluded that there was no deliberate hoaxing involved. A number of the members earned their living through "mystic" work but their incomes would be judged barely above subsistence level by ordinary American standards. The Elmer Gantry type of personality seemed conspicuously absent and the leaders seemed to believe in what they were doing.

Members ranged in age from fourteen into the seventies and seemed to include roughly as many women as men. In some cases entire families were members but in other cases only one or two individuals from a family would be Espers.

The educational level of the group seemed average at best. However, the group was unmistakably far above average in amount and variety of reading. This included fringe literature, such as books and magazines on flying saucers, hypnotism, mythology, the health food publications of Rodale Press, the writings of Mary Baker Eddy, Pak Subud, and J. B. Rhine. Many of the members were also consumers of popular magazines, general paperback books, and "serious literature."

Most members seem to have had atypical life-histories. These included experiences such as loss of one or both parents, atypical relations with parents, parents who were themselves members of fringe groups, interaction with unusual significant others, and abnormal workhistories.

Such atypical life-histories, combined with breadth of reading, produce broad, though unsystematic, knowledge of the world. Among Espers and similar fringe groups, one may easily meet individuals acquainted with the Sanskrit poets, Norse mythology, medieval painting or German Idealist philosophy. However, they tend not to be "cultured" in the sense of having a broad scholarship in the humanities. They also seem to lack the rigor or critical ability which formal education tends to produce. Members seemed to be most inadequate in appraising the reliability of sources and in the forms of logical argument. At the same time, they possessed an inquiring attitude and openness of mind which would probably have delighted Bacon.

Espers interpret happenings in ways which would seem fantastic to the ordinary layman. Their view of human nature is an echo of the Hindu conception that Man is a creature blinded by external events, who is largely unaware of his real make-up or potentialities. Most of man's "spiritual" life goes on independently of the conscious individual and largely without his awareness. The world is peopled with disembodied spirits, good and bad, and with psychic manifestations of the living. All men possess psychic powers, at least in rudimentary form, and these may be cultivated and formally trained. Telepathy, clairvoyance, telekinesis, communication with spirits, reincarnation, mystical intuition, dowsing, the manipulation of events through faith and magical procedures such as pagan Hawaiian *hunna,* are real and everyday occurrences to the Espers and similar groups. Espers and similar groups are adamant in their disagreement with the world-view presented in conventional scientific and historical writings. Mystic enlightenment is considered a more valid source of knowledge than the techniques of science.

THE MAINTENANCE OF ESPER BELIEFS

The reader may wonder how individuals can continue to accept the truth of such a "crazy" belief system. For one who has been socialized into conventional American culture it may seem incredible that anyone could believe such things in the face of so much contrary evidence. As we explore some of the processes involved in confirming and maintaining Esper beliefs, it may become apparent that *all* belief systems are to some extent arbitrary and that the same mechanisms are involved in maintaining them.

The concept of the self-fulfilling prophecy, first advanced by W. I. Thomas, is particularly useful in this exploration.[2]

First, as Bruner has pointed out,[3] we tend to select that part of the total influx of incoming sense perceptions which is congruent with our expectations. This may even involve the active supplying of perceptions which are "not really there," as in the case of geometric illusions. Also, most situations are only semi-structured, so that the individual has some degrees of freedom in structuring them to come true.

Examples may clarify these points. I was sitting in a coffee shop with my main Esper informant when a young woman sat down at a table within conversation distance from us. Her hair was a neutral brown and short-cut, her features angular and her hands long and thin. The most striking aspect of her physical appearance was the bright shade of her lipstick and matching nail polish. My informant leaned forward with some agitation and told me in a low voice that she was a hunting demon who drained men of their psychic energy and left them empty hulks. Her true nature was reflected in her aura which he could plainly read. His distress seemed genuine when he asked me to extend psychic protection over him. A few minutes later a young man joined her at the table and we were able to overhear their conversation. They talked for perhaps three-quarters of an hour before leaving. A content analysis of the girl's conversation would reveal statements describing a wide variety of attitudes toward different social objects. But after they had gone, my informant cited, as corroboration of his judgment, only those statements which might bespeak a manipulative attitude toward the world. Other statements, which expressed admiration for certain people, an appreciation of music, and sympathy for the plight of the American Negro, seem to have been ignored by the Esper.

The second aspect of the self-fulfilling prophecy is more subtle, but it is a process which the writer has seen many times with Espers and other fringe group members. It might be described by the following paradigm:

A. Ego makes an inference about alter.

B. Ego acts toward alter in terms of this inference.

[2] W. I. Thomas, "The Definition of the Situation," in Lewis Coser and Bernard Rosenberg, editors, *Sociological Theory,* New York: Macmillan, 1957, pp. 209–211.
[3] Jerome Bruner, "Social Psychology and Perception," in Eleanor Maccoby, *et al.,* editors, *Readings in Social Psychology,* 3rd Ed., New York: Holt, 1958, pp. 85–94.

C. Alter makes inferences about ego in terms of this action.

D. Alter tends to react toward ego in terms of his action.

E. Thus ego's inferences tend to be confirmed by alter's reaction.

This paradigm is merely a slight modification of many social psychological models of the interpersonal process,[4] but the self-fulfilling aspect of it seems often to be missed. If a situation is rigidly structured, the self-fulfilling aspect will, of course, be limited, i.e., it would be difficult to interpret and confirm a minister's actions at a funeral as a sexual advance. But, as Kuhn has pointed out,[5] all situations are to some extent flexible so that the actors have some freedom in defining them.

To choose an example among many possible ones, my informant rented a room for several days from a middle-aged woman. After seeing her only briefly, and before he had spoken with her, he "intuited" that she was a warm accepting person who was filled with psychic strength and goodness. When he first talked with her a couple of hours later, his manner was far more friendly and patronizing than usual. He showed interest in her collection of antiques, asked about her children, and ended up by saying he felt she was a wonderful person and he wanted to rent from her, partly because they would have a chance to talk together. During the next few days, the writer had a chance to question other tenants and neighbors about the landlady. They described a fairly caustic gossiper who was unreasonably strict about the use of electricity, and of her property and grounds. Her attitude toward the writer was taciturn. But she responded graciously to my informant's open friendliness. She sought him out to talk with on several occasions, she inquired if there was enough light in his room for late reading and supplied him with a table lamp, etc. In her behavior toward him, my informant's intuition certainly seemed correct.

It seems a safe generalization that no individual can maintain beliefs when a large amount of contrary evidence is *perceived*. This is perhaps why the layman finds it difficult to see how fringers can believe "all that crazy stuff" (or why the Russian people are so easily "duped" by Communist propaganda) when common sense so easily shows them wrong. The important point is that "common sense" varies rather arbitrarily from group to group.

Extending some notions developed by Rokeach et al.,[6] we may say that groups and total cultures build up belief systems which tend toward a fairly coherent and consistent portrait of the world. To what extent do these portraits represent faithfully the "real world"? In past intellectual history, these judgments have usually been made ethnocentrically, in terms of the judge's own portrait. Now the institution of science has attempted to set up criteria for evaluating beliefs about reality which will be free of such biases.

Physics and engineering may have advanced to the point that assertions about building a bridge can be readily tested for their realism. But in the behavioral sciences the variance as yet unaccounted for is still so large that it is difficult to invalidate almost any assertion about human behavior conclusively.

To put it another way, confirming evidence for particular beliefs about

---

[4] A classic statement of such a model is Cooley's "looking-glass self," C. H. Cooley, *Human Nature and the Social Order,* New York: Scribner, 1902, p. 184.

[5] Lecture by Manford Kuhn.

[6] Milton Rokeach, *The Open and Closed Mind,* New York: Basic Books, 1960, pp. 31–71.

social reality are sought and *found* because most situations are ambiguous enough to allow them to be *interpreted as* confirming evidence. We need not bring in fringe groups as examples, since this seems to be a more widespread mechanism. For instance, any Russian offer for disarmament is automatically interpreted as a propaganda move by the American press. Lack of information makes this interpretation possible, whether it truly and always represents the real motives of the Russian government or not. In fact, it is difficult to imagine what action the Communists might take which would be accepted as an honest move for peace by our people. It is also probably true that the Russians interpret any actions of ours similarly.[7]

It is difficult to break into this circle of confirmation, to re-educate an individual who is firmly entrenched in a particular belief system, because situations are *defined* by the very notions ego is seeking to confirm and alter is seeking to discredit. For instance, Espers define man as a spiritual being who possesses a psychic aura from which certain inferences can be made about his *spiritual* nature. One cannot demonstrate that individuals do not have psychic auras; in fact, it is ironic that modern science, with its sensitive devices for measuring organic electrical fields, has indirectly lent support to the Esper argument. Fringe group members have often cited such evidence in support of their claims, although the scientific findings are freely interpreted.

A further means by which the Esper is able to maintain his beliefs is through differential association and differential identification with Espers and relative insulation from non-Espers.[8] As an interacting group, Espers provide support for the individual member in his view of the world. As a number of fringe group members have put it, they feel they can be themselves only with kindred fringers. Members feel they are "at home" because they share a common language with which they can communicate about their views and problems to alters who share their meanings.

Communication within the group provides further confirming evidence for the belief system. For instance, several Espers will be able to "read" a given individual's psychic aura. In considering such confirmation through consensus, the reader might recall that many tests of validity in science rest directly or indirectly on intersubjective agreement. Thus, a psychiatric staff reaches agreement on the Oedipal conflict of a patient and a group of similarly trained sociologists agree that certain items measure "anomia." Often an individual's judgment is not accepted until he has been socialized into the group and has learned the processes for arriving at the "right" answer. This provides the group with a rationale for saying that those who disagree are not competent to judge. Thus the Espers explained that the ordinary layman could not read psychic auras because he had not been trained to do so and because he was not in touch with his own spiritual powers.

With regard to this communication of shared meanings, we might note an incident which occurred several times when Espers were dealing with non-Espers. Those who were tolerant toward Esper views were, in every case the writer was able to observe, judged to be psychic

[7] For a provocative discussion of this point cf. Erich Fromm, *May Man Prevail?* New York: Anchor, 1961.

[8] For a recent summary statement of the principles underlying this point cf. Daniel Glaser, "The Differential Association Theory of Crime," in Arnold Rose, editor, *Human Behavior and Social Processes,* Boston: Houghton-Mifflin, 1962, pp. 425–443.

themselves. Those who were indifferent or positively rejecting might be judged to be psychic themselves but if they were, they were judged to be evil. The Espers seemed to be unaware of this "latent criterion" for judging non-Espers.

Finally, Espers and similar fringe groups are aided in maintaining their beliefs by the ambivalence of the larger culture toward them. In our culture, a mystical worldview is a well established counter-theme to the more predominant rationalism and pragmatism. In describing Puerto Rican spiritualism Rogler and Hollingshead have noted, "if you ever talk to a Puerto Rican who says he doesn't believe in Spirits, you know what that means? It means you haven't talked to him long enough."[9] Tales of psychic happenings and of individuals gifted with extra-sensory perception are widely, although informally, told in our culture and a large number of Americans have perhaps been half-convinced that "there is something behind them" at one time or another. This ambivalence tends to soften the disbelief and verbal rejection by the non-fringe member when interacting with the mystic. The writer has questioned many non-fringe group members on their attitudes toward Espers and similar groups and the most frequent reply has been that, although they are a bit "crackpot," there may be something to their notions.

Fringe group members are usually keenly aware of the fact that the larger culture disagrees with their view of the world, however, and often adopt a defensive judgment of the layman as unenlightened. This judgment makes it easier for the fringe group member to disregard the rejection and derision of the unbeliever.

THE CHANGING OF BELIEFS

In general, there seem to be only two kinds of argument one can make against a particular belief system.

1. Grant the "postulates" of the system and argue deductively that some notions are incompatible with others, or that the chain of reasoning in going from "premise" to "consequent" is questionable. (The words in quotation marks are not used in their strict formal logic meaning, but rather in the looser sense of a suggestive analogy.) For instance, Espers embrace the belief that man's future is his own to manipulate, but also notions of foreseeing an inexorable future (precognition), and of strict causal determinism. (This inconsistency should have a familiar ring to the social scientist.)

2. Point out events in the real world which challenge the beliefs. The major difficulty here is that both parties must have some minimum of agreement about what these events of reality are. Everyone must make some concessions to reality or he will not survive as an individual or group. As Kluckhohn has pointed out,[10] no culture has norms about jumping over trees. But here again one must be very cautious lest he dub his own culturally learned views as necessary orientations toward external reality. There actually are cultures with beliefs about the possibility of physical levitation over trees and the projection of the astral body through space.

But if there is a minimum of consensus about what goes on in the real world, one can question beliefs in terms of these happenings. For instance, Espers believe

---

[9] Lloyd Rogler and August Hollingshead, "The Puerto Rican Spiritualist as a Psychiatrist," *American Journal of Sociology,* Vol. 67 (July, 1961), p. 21.

[10] Clyde Kluckhohn, *Mirror for Man,* New York: McGraw-Hill, 1949, p. 20.

in reincarnation and they also recognize that the human and animal population of the world is increasing. Juxtaposing these two beliefs, the writer asked three Espers, where do more souls for the greater number of living bodies come from? The Espers recognized the inconsistency between the empirical fact of population growth and their belief in reincarnation and admitted that they could give no answer. My informant became quite interested in the question; he bought some books on Eastern religions and also planned to ask other Espers when he returned to the headquarters. (The writer may have unwittingly introduced a chain of events which will result in innovations in the Esper belief system.)

One other point should be made about confirming evidence for beliefs. To the extent that the beliefs are untestable, either because they are tautological or because they are non-empirical, they are from the challenge of empirical events.[11] Just how much of a given belief system is untestable in principle remains to be demonstrated, but the proportion may be fairly large.

CONCLUSIONS

This paper has been concerned with the means employed by deviant groups in maintaining their beliefs in the face of a divergent and more or less disapproving larger society. The generalizations were drawn from the study of a small group of "mystics" and from observation of a number of other fringe groups.

The following processes or "mechanisms" facilitate the maintenance of divergent beliefs:

1. Selective attention to those perceptions which are congruent with one's beliefs.
2. Active structuring of social situations so that their outcomes support one's beliefs.
3. Interpretation of ambiguous evidence as confirming one's beliefs.
4. Differential association and identification with those who share one's beliefs, coupled with relative isolation from and disparagement of those whose beliefs differ.
5. Ambivalence of the divergent larger culture toward one's beliefs.

These processes increase the difficulty of challenging a given belief system. A belief system may be thrown into question by pointing out major inconsistencies within it. Also, if both parties agree on certain "facts" these facts may be shown to contradict some of the beliefs. However, to the extent that the beliefs are non-empirical or non-testable, they remain value-premises which are susceptible only to the persuasion of competing value-premises.

[11] Parsons, *op. cit.,* pp. 359–367.

subcultural variations ||12

While some deviants engage in solitary deviance, many are involved in deviance for which there is a definite subculture—what we call subcultural deviance. Even among those engaging in subcultural deviance, though, there is a great deal of variation. The deviants may differ in their backgrounds and social situations. Some may participate in the subculture more than others. And they may differ in the activities, both deviant and conventional, that they engage in. Associated with these variations are other differences—e.g., in self-concept and in the ways people perform deviant roles.

In this chapter the selections explore some of these subcultural variations. In the first reading Humphreys describes various forms of participation in one sector of the homosexual subculture and the social situations related to these different forms of participation. Rubington then shows how conformity to Skid Row "bottle gang" norms varies from city to city. Finally, Irwin indicates that prison inmates' pre-prison backgrounds give rise to different patterns of participation in the prison subculture.

A Typology of Tearoom Participants

LAUD HUMPHREYS

At shortly after five o'clock on a weekday evening, four men enter a public restroom in the city park. One wears a well-tailored business suit; another wears tennis shoes, shorts and teeshirt; the third man is still clad in the khaki uniform of his filling station; the last, a salesman, has loosened his tie and left his sports coat in the car. What has caused these men to leave the company of other homeward-bound commuters on the freeway? What common interest brings these men, with their divergent backgrounds, to this public facility?

They have come here not for the obvious reason, but in a search for "instant sex." Many men—married and unmarried, those with heterosexual identities and those whose self-image is a homosexual one—seek such impersonal sex, shunning involvement, desiring kicks without commitment. Whatever reasons —social, physiological or psychological— might be postulated for this search, the phenomenon of impersonal sex persists as a widespread but rarely studied form of human interaction.

There are several settings for this type of deviant activity—the balconies of movie theaters, automobiles, behind bushes—but few offer the advantages for these men that public restrooms provide. "Tearooms," as these facilities are called

in the language of the homosexual subculture, have several characteristics that make them attractive as locales for sexual encounters without involvement. . . .

Tearoom activity attracts a large number of participants—enough to produce the majority of arrests for homosexual offenses in the United States. Now, employing data gained from both formal and informal interviews, we shall consider what these men are like away from the scenes of impersonal sex. "For some people," says Evelyn Hooker, an authority on male homosexuality, "the seeking of sexual contacts with other males is an activity isolated from all other aspects of their lives." Such segregation is apparent with most men who engage in the homosexual activity of public restrooms; but the degree and manner in which "deviant" is isolated from "normal" behavior in their lives will be seen to vary along social dimensions.

For the man who lives next door, the tearoom participant is just another neighbor—and probably a very good one at that. He may make a little more money than the next man and work a little harder for it. It is likely that he will drive a nicer car and maintain a neater yard than do other neighbors in the block. Maybe, like some tearoom regulars, he

Reprinted from Laud Humphreys, *Tearoom Trade* (Chicago: Aldine Publishing Company, 1970), pp. 1–2, 104–105, 108–130; copyright © 1970 by R. A. Laud Humphreys. Reprinted by permission of the author, Aldine Atherton, Inc., and Gerald Duckworth & Co., Ltd.

will work with Boy Scouts in the evenings and spend much of his weekend at the church. It may be more surprising for the outsider to discover that most of these men are married.

Indeed, 54 percent of my research subjects are married and living with their wives. From the data at hand, there is no evidence that these unions are particularly unstable; nor does it appear that any of the wives are aware of their husbands' secret sexual activity. Indeed, the husbands choose public restrooms as sexual settings partly to avoid just such exposure. I see no reason to dispute the claim of a number of tearoom respondents that their preference for a form of concerted action that is fair and impersonal is largely predicated on a desire to protect their family relationships.

Superficial analysis of the data indicates that the maintenance of exemplary marriages—at least in appearance—is very important to the subjects of this study. In answering questions such as "When it comes to making decisions in your household, who generally makes them?" the participants indicate they are more apt to defer to their mates than are those in the control sample. They also indicate that they find it more important to "get along well" with their wives. In the open-ended questions regarding marital relationships, they tend to speak of them in more glowing terms. . . .

In most cases, fellatio is a service performed by an older man upon a younger. In one encounter, for example, a man appearing to be around 40 was observed as insertee with a man in his twenties as insertor. A few minutes later, the man of 40 was being sucked by one in his fifties. Analyzing the estimated ages of the principal partners in 53 observed acts of fellatio, I arrived at these conclusions: the insertee was judged to be older than the insertor in 40 cases; they were approximately the same age in three; and the insertor was the older in

ten instances. The age differences ranged from an insertee estimated to be 25 years older than his partner to an insertee thought to be ten years younger than his insertor.

Strong references to this crisis of aging are found in my interviews with cooperating respondents, one of whom had this to say:

Well, I started off as the straight young thing. Everyone wanted to suck my cock. I wouldn't have been caught dead with one of the things in my mouth! . . . So, here I am at 40—with grown kids—and the biggest cocksucker in [the city]!

Similar experiences were expressed, in more reserved language, by another man, some 15 years his senior:

I suppose I was around 35—or 36—when I started giving out blow jobs. It just got so I couldn't operate any other way in the park johns. I'd still rather have a good blow job any day, but I've gotten so I like it the way it is now.

Perhaps by now there is enough real knowledge abroad to have dispelled the idea that men who engage in homosexual acts may be typed by any consistency of performance in one or another sexual role. Undoubtedly, there are preferences: few persons are so adaptable, their conditioning so undifferentiated, that they fail to exercise choice between various sexual roles and positions. Such preferences, however, are learned, and sexual repertories tend to expand with time and experience. This study of restroom sex indicates that sexual roles within these encounters are far from stable. They are apt to change within an encounter, from one encounter to another, with age, and with the amount of exposure to influences from a sexually deviant subculture.

It is to this last factor that I should like to direct the reader's attention. The degree of contact with a network of friends who share the actor's sexual interests takes a central position in mediating not only his preferences for sex role, but his style of adaptation to—and rationalization of—the deviant activity in which he participates. There are, however, two reasons why I have not classified research subjects in terms of their participation in the homosexual subculture. It is difficult to measure accurately the degree of such involvement; and such subcultural interaction depends upon other social variables, two of which are easily measured.

Family status has a definitive effect on the deviant careers of those whose concern is with controlling information about their sexual behavior. The married man who engages in homosexual activity must be more cautious about his involvement in the subculture than his single counterpart. As a determinant of life style and sexual activity, marital status is also a determinant of the patterns of deviant adaptation and rationalization. Only those in my sample who were divorced or separated from their wives were difficult to categorize as either married or single. Those who had been married, however, showed a tendency to remain in friendship networks with married men. Three of the four were still limited in freedom by responsibilities for their children. For these reasons, I have included all men who were once married in the "married" categories.

The second determining variable is the relative autonomy of the respondent's occupation. A man is "independently" employed when his job allows him freedom of movement and security from being fired; the most obvious example is self-employment. Occupational "dependence" leaves a man little freedom for engaging in disreputable activity. The sales manager or other executive of a business firm has greater freedom than the salesman or attorney who is employed in the lower echelons of a large industry or by the federal government. The sales representative whose territory is far removed from the home office has

greater independence, in terms of information control, than the minister of a local congregation. The majority of those placed in both the married and unmarried categories with *dependent* occupations were employed by large industries or the government.

Median education levels and annual family incomes indicate that those with dependent occupations rank lower on the socioeconomic scale. Only in the case of married men, however, is this correlation between social class and occupational autonomy strongly supported by the ratings of these respondents on Warner's Index of Status Characteristics. Nearly all the married men with dependent occupations are of the upper-lower or lower-middle classes, whereas those with independent occupations are of the upper-middle or upper classes. For single men, the social class variable is neither so easily identifiable nor so clearly divided. Nearly all single men in the sample can be classified only as "vaguely middle class."

As occupational autonomy and marital status remain the most important dimensions along which participants may be ranked, we shall consider four general types of tearoom customers: (1) married men with dependent occupations, (2) married men with independent occupations, (3) unmarried men with independent occupations, and (4) unmarried men with dependent occupations. As will become evident with the discussion of each type, I have employed labels from the homosexual argot, along with pseudonyms, to designate each class of participants. This is done not only to facilitate reading but to emphasize that we are describing persons rather than merely "typical" constructs.

TYPE I: TRADE

The first classification, which includes 19 of the participants (38 percent), may be called "trade," since most would earn that appellation from the gay subculture. All of these men are, or have been, married—one was separated from his wife at the time of interviewing and another was divorced.

Most work as truck drivers, machine operators or clerical workers. There is a member of the armed forces, a carpenter, and the minister of a pentecostal church. Most of their wives work, at least part time, to help raise their median annual family income to $8,000. One in six of these men is black. All are normally masculine in appearance and mannerism. Although 14 have completed high school, there are only three college graduates among them, and five have had less than 12 years of schooling.

George is representative of this largest group of respondents. Born of second-generation German parentage in an ethnic enclave of the midwestern city where he still resides, he was raised as a Lutheran. He feels that his father (like George a truck driver) was quite warm in his relationship with him as a child. His mother he describes as a very nervous, asthmatic woman and thinks that an older sister suffered a nervous breakdown some years ago, although she was never treated for it. Another sister and a brother have evidenced no emotional problems.

At the age of 20 he married a Roman Catholic girl and has since joined her church, although he classifies himself as "lapsed." In the 14 years of their marriage, they have had seven children, one of whom is less than a year old. George doesn't think they should have more children, but his wife objects to using any type of birth control other than the rhythm method. With his wife working part time as a waitress, they have an income of about $5,000.

"How often do you have intercourse with your wife?" I asked. "Not very much the last few years," he replied. "It's up to when she feels like giving it to me—which ain't very often. I never suggest it."

George was cooking hamburgers on an outdoor grill and enjoying a beer as I interviewed him. "Me, I like to come home," he asserted. "I love to take care of the outside of the house . . . like to go places with the children—my wife, she doesn't."

With their mother at work, the children were running in and out of the door, revealing a household interior in gross disarray. George stopped to call one of the smaller youngsters out of the street in front of his modest, suburban home. When he resumed his remarks about his wife, there was more feeling in his description:

My wife doesn't have much outside interest. She doesn't like to go out or take the kids places. But she's an A-1 mother. I'll say that! I guess you'd say she's very nice to get along with—but don't cross her! She gets aggravated with me—I don't know why. . . . Well, you'd have to know my wife. We fight all the time. Anymore, it seems we just don't get along—except when we're apart. Mostly, we argue about the kids. She's afraid of having more. . . . She's afraid to have sex but doesn't believe in birth control. I'd just rather not be around her! I won't suggest having sex anyway—and she just doesn't want it anymore.

While more open than most in his acknowledgement of marital tension, George's appraisal of sexual relations in the marriage is typical of those respondents classified as Trade. In 63 percent of these marriages, the wife, husband or both are Roman Catholic. When answering questions about their sexual lives, a story much like George's emerged: at least since the birth of the last child, conjugal relations have been very rare.

These data suggest that, along with providing an excuse for diminishing intercourse with their wives, the religious teachings to which most of these families adhere may cause the husbands to search for sex in the tearooms. Whatever the causes that turn them unsatisfied from the marriage bed, however, the alternate outlet must be quick, inexpensive and impersonal. Any personal, ongoing affair—any outlet requiring money or hours away from home—would threaten a marriage that is already shaky and jeopardize the most important thing these men possess, their standing as father of their children.

Around the turn of the century, before the vice squads moved in (in their never-ending process of narrowing the behavioral options of those in the lower classes), the Georges of this study would probably have made regular visits to the two-bit bordellos. With a madam watching a clock to limit the time, these cheap whorehouses provided the same sort of fast, impersonal service as today's public restrooms. I find no indication that these men seek homosexual contact as such; rather, they want a form of orgasm-producing action that is less lonely than masturbation and less involving than a love relationship. As the forces of social control deprive them of one outlet, they provide another. The newer form, it should be noted, is more stigmatizing than the previous one—thus giving "proof" to the adage that "the sinful are drawn ever deeper into perversity."

George was quite affable when interviewed on his home territory. A year before, when I first observed him in the tearoom of a park about three miles from his home, he was a far more cautious man. Situated at the window of the restroom, I saw him leave his old station wagon and, looking up and down the street, walk to the facility at a very fast pace. Once inside, he paced nervously from door to window until satisfied that I would serve as an adequate lookout. After playing the insertor role with a man who had waited in the stall farthest from the door, he left quickly, without wiping or washing his hands, and drove away toward the nearest exit from the park. In the tearoom he was a frightened man, engaging in furtive sex. In his own back yard, talking with an observer whom he failed to recognize, he was warm, open and apparently at ease.

Weighing 200 pounds or more, George has a protruding gut and tattoos on both forearms. Although muscular and in his mid-thirties, he would not be described as a handsome person. For him, no doubt, the aging crisis is also an identity crisis. Only with reluctance—and perhaps never—will he turn to the insertee role. The threat of such a role to his masculine self-image is too great. Like others of his class with whom I have had more extensive interviews, George may have learned that sexual game as a teenage hustler, or else when serving in the army during the Korean War. In either case, his socialization into homosexual experience took place in a masculine world where it is permissible to accept money from a "queer" in return for carefully limited sexual favors. But to use one's own mouth as a substitute for the female organ, or even to express enjoyment of the action, is taboo in the Trade code.

Moreover, for men of George's occupational and marital status, there is no network of friends engaged in tearoom activity to help them adapt to the changes aging will bring. I found no evidence of friendship networks among respondents of this type, who enter and leave the restrooms alone, avoiding conversation while within. Marginal to both the heterosexual and homosexual worlds, these men shun involvement in any form of gay subculture. Type I participants report fewer friends of any sort than do those of other classes. When asked how many close friends he has, George answered: "None. I haven't got time for that."

It is difficult to interview the Trade without becoming depressed over the hopelessness of their situation. They are almost uniformly lonely and isolated:

lacking success in either marriage bed or work, unable to discuss their three best friends (because they don't have three); en route from the din of factories to the clamor of children, they slip off the freeways for a few moments of impersonal sex in a toilet stall.

Such unrewarded existence is reflected in the portrait of another marginal man. A jobless Negro, he earns only contempt and sexual rejection from his working wife in return for baby-sitting duties. The paperback books and magazines scattered about his living room supported his comment that he reads a great deal to relieve boredom. (George seldom reads even the newspaper and has no hobbies to report.) No wonder that he urged me to stay for supper when my interview schedule was finished. "I really wish you'd stay awhile," he said. "I haven't talked to anyone about myself in a hell of a long time!"

TYPE II: AMBISEXUALS

A very different picture emerges in the case of Dwight. As sales manager for a small manufacturing concern, he is in a position to hire men who share his sexual and other interests. Not only does he have a business associate or two who share his predilection for tearoom sex, he has been able to stretch chance meetings in the tearoom purlieu into long-lasting friendships. Once, after I had gained his confidence through repeated interviews, I asked him to name all the participants he knew. The names of five other Type II men in my sample were found in the list of nearly two dozen names he gave me.

Dwight, then, has social advantages in the public restrooms as well as in society at large. His annual income of $16,000 helps in the achievement of these benefits, as does his marriage into a large and distinguished family and his education at a prestigious local college.

From his restroom friends Dwight learns which tearooms in the city are popular and where the police are clamping down. He even knows which officers are looking for payoffs and how much they expect to be paid. It is of even greater importance that his attitudes toward—and perceptions of—the tearoom encounters are shaped and reinforced by the friendship network in which he participates.

It has thus been easier for Dwight to meet the changing demands of the aging crisis. He knows others who lost no self-respect when they began "going down" on their sexual partners, and they have helped him learn to enjoy the involvement of oral membranes in impersonal sex. As Tom, too, moves into this class of participants, he can be expected to learn how to rationalize the switch in sexual roles necessitated by the loss of youthful good looks. He will cease thinking of the insertee role as threatening to his masculinity. His socialization into the Ambisexuals will make the orgasm but one of a number of kicks.

Three-fourths of the married participants with independent occupations were observed, at one time or another, participating as insertees in fellatio, compared to only one-third of the Trade. Not only do the Type II participants tend to switch roles with greater facility, they seem inclined to search beyond the tearooms for more exotic forms of sexual experience. Dwight, along with others in his class, expresses a liking for anal intercourse (both as insertee and insertor), for group activity, and even for mild forms of sadomasochistic sex. A friend of his once invited me to an "orgy" he had planned in an apartment he maintains for sexual purposes. Another friend, a social and commercial leader of the community, told me that he enjoys having men urinate into his mouth between acts of fellatio.

Dwight is in his early forties and has two sons in high school. The school-bound offspring provide him with an excuse to leave his wife at home during frequent business trips across the country. Maintaining a list of gay contacts, Dwight is able to engage wholeheartedly in the life of the homosexual subculture in other cities—the sort of involvement he is careful to avoid at home. In the parks or over cocktails, he amuses his friends with lengthy accounts of these adventures.

Dwight recounts his first sexual relationship with another boy at the age of "nine or ten":

My parents always sent me off to camp in the summer, and it was there that I had my sexual initiation. This sort of thing usually took the form of rolling around in a bunk together and ended in our jacking each other off. . . . I suppose I started pretty early. God, I was almost in college before I had my first woman! I always had some other guy on the string in prep school—some real romances there! But I made up for lost time with the girls during my college years. . . . During that time, I only slipped back into my old habits a couple of times—and then it was a once-only occurrence with a roommate after we had been drinking.

Culminating an active heterosexual life at the university, Dwight married the girl he had impregnated. He reports having intercourse three or four times a week with her throughout their 18 married years but also admits to supplementing that activity on occasion: "I had the seven-year-itch and stepped out on her quite a bit then." Dwight also visits the tearooms almost daily:

I guess you might say I'm pretty highly sexed [he chuckled a little], but I really don't think that's why I go to tearooms. That's really not sex. Sex is something I have with my wife in bed. It's not as if I were committing adultery by getting my rocks off—or going down on some guy—in a tearoom. I get a kick out of it. Some of

my friends go out for handball. I'd rather cruise the park. Does that sound perverse to you?

Dwight's openness in dealing with the more sensitive areas of his biography was typical of upper-middle and upper-class respondents of both the participant and control samples. Actual refusals of interviews came almost entirely from lower-class participants; more of the co-operating respondents were of the upper socioeconomic ranks. In the same vein, working-class respondents were most cautious about answering questions pertaining to their income and their social and political views.

Other researchers have encountered a similar response differential along class lines, and I realize that my educational and social characteristics encourage rapport with Dwight more than with George. It may also be assumed that sympathy with survey research increases with education. Two-thirds of the married participants with occupational independence are college graduates.

It has been suggested, however, that another factor may be operative in this instance: although the upper-class deviants may have more to lose from exposure (in the sense that the mighty have farther to fall), they also have more means at their disposal with which to protect their moral histories. Some need only tap their spending money to pay off a member of the vice squad. In other instances, social contacts with police commissioners or newspaper publishers make it possible to squelch either record or publicity of an arrest. One respondent has made substantial contributions to a police charity fund, while another hired private detectives to track down a blackmailer. Not least in their capacity to cover for errors in judgment is the fact that their word has the backing of economic and social influence. Evidence must be strong to prosecute a man who can hire the best attorneys. Lower-class men are rightfully more suspicious, for they have fewer resources with which to defend themselves if exposed.

This does not mean that Type II participants are immune to the risks of the game but simply that they are bidding from strength. To them, the risks of arrest, exposure, blackmail or physical assault contribute to the excitement quotient. It is not unusual for them to speak of cruising as an adventure, in contrast with the Trade, who engage in a furtive search for sexual relief. On the whole, then, the action of Type II respondents is apt to be somewhat bolder and their search for "kicks" less inhibited than that of most other types of participants.

Dwight is not fleeing from an unhappy home life or sexless marriage to the encounters in the parks. He expresses great devotion to his wife and children: "They're my whole life," he exclaims. All evidence indicates that, as father, citizen, businessman and church member, Dwight's behavior patterns—as viewed by his peers—are exemplary.

Five of the 12 participants in Dwight's class are members of the Episcopal church. Dwight is one of two who were raised in that church, although he is not as active a churchman as some who became Episcopalians later in life. In spite of his infrequent attendance to worship, he feels his church is "just right" for him and needs no changing. Its tradition and ceremony are intellectually and esthetically pleasing to him. Its liberal outlook on questions of morality round out a religious orientation that he finds generally supportive.

In an interview witnessed by a friend he had brought to meet me, Dwight discussed his relationship with his parents: "Father ignored me. He just never said anything to me. I don't think he ever knew I existed." [His father was an attorney, esteemed beyond the city of Dwight's birth, who died while his only son was yet in his teens.] "I hope I'm a better father to my boys than he was to me," Dwight added.

"But his mother is a remarkable woman," the friend interjected, "really one of the most fabulous women I've met! Dwight took me back to meet her —years ago, when we were lovers of a sort. I still look forward to her visits."

"She's remarkable just to have put up with me," Dwight added:

Just to give you an idea, one vacation I brought another boy home from school with me. She walked into the bedroom one morning and caught us bare-assed in a 69 position. She just excused herself and backed out of the room. Later, when we were alone, she just looked at me—over the edge of her glasses—and said: "I'm not going to lecture you, dear, but I do hope you don't swallow that stuff!"

Although he has never had a nervous breakdown, Dwight takes "an occasional antidepressant" because of his "moodiness." "I'm really quite moody, and I go to the tearooms more often when my spirits are low." While his periods of depression may result in increased tearoom activity, his deviant behavior does not seem to produce much tension in his life:

I don't feel guilty about my little sexual games in the park. I'm not some sort of sick queer. . . . You might think I live two lives; but, if I do, I don't feel split in two by them.

Unlike the Trade, Type II participants recognize their homosexual activity as indicative of their own psychosexual orientations. They think of themselves as bisexual or ambisexual and have intellectualized their deviant tendencies in terms of the pseudopsychology of the popular press. They speak often of the great men of history, as well as of certain movie stars and others of contemporary fame, who are also "AC/DC."

Erving Goffman has remarked that stigmatized Americans "tend to live in a literarily-defined world." This is nowhere truer than of the subculturally oriented participants of this study. Not only do they read a great deal about homosexuality, they discuss it within their network of friends. For the Dwights there is subcultural support that enables them to integrate their deviance with the remainder of their lives, while maintaining control over the information that could discredit their whole being. For these reasons they look upon the gaming encounters in the parks as enjoyable experiences.

TYPE III: GAY GUYS

Like the Ambisexuals, unmarried respondents with independent occupations are locked into a strong subculture, a community that provides them with knowledge about the tearooms and reinforcement in their particular brand of deviant activity. This open participation in the gay community distinguishes these single men from the larger group of unmarrieds with dependent occupations. These men take the homosexual role of our society, and are thus the most truly "gay" of all participant types. Except for Tim, who was recruited as a decoy in the tearooms by the vice squad of a police department, Type III participants learned the strategies of the tearooms through friends already experienced in this branch of the sexual market.

Typical of this group is Ricky, a 24-year-old university student whose older male lover supports him. Ricky stands at the median age of his type, who range from 19 to 50 years. Half of them are college graduates and all but one other are at least part-time students, a characteristic that explains their low median income of $3,000. Because Ricky's lover is a good provider, he is comfortably situated in a midtown apartment, a more pleasant residence than most of his friends enjoy.

Ricky is a thin, good-looking young man with certain movements and manners of speech that might be termed effeminate. He is careful of his appearance, dresses well, and keeps an immaculate apartment, furnished with an expensive stereo and some tasteful antique pieces. Seated on a sofa in the midst of the things his lover has provided for their mutual comfort, Ricky is impressively self-assured. He is proud to say that he has found, at least for the time being, what all those participants in his category claim to seek: a "permanent" love relationship.

Having met his lover in a park, Ricky returns there only when his mate is on a business trip or their relationship is strained. Then Ricky becomes, as he puts it, "horny" and he goes to the park to study, cruise and engage in tearoom sex:

The bars are o.k.—but a little too public for a "married" man like me. . . . Tearooms are just another kind of action, and they do quite well when nothing better is available.

Like other Type III respondents, he shows little preference in sexual roles. "It depends on the other guy," Ricky says, "and whether I like his looks or not. Some men I'd crawl across the street on my knees for—others I wouldn't piss on!" His aging crisis will be shared with all others in the gay world. It will take the nightmarish form of waning attractiveness and the search for a permanent lover to fill his later years, but it will have no direct relationship with the tearoom roles. Because of his socialization in the homosexual society, taking the insertee role is neither traumatic for him nor related to aging.

Ricky's life revolves around his sexual deviance in a way that is not true of George or even of Dwight. Most of his friends and social contacts are connected with the homosexual subculture. His attitudes toward and rationalization of his sexual behavior are largely gained from this wide circle of friends. The gay men claim to have more close friends than do any other type of control or participant respondents. As frequency of orgasm is reported, this class also has more sex than any other group sampled, averaging 2.5 acts per week. They seem relatively satisfied with this aspect of their lives and regard their sexual drive as normal—although Ricky perceives his sexual needs as less than most.

One of his tearoom friends has recently married a woman, but Ricky has no intention of following his example. Another of his type, asked about marriage, said: "I prefer men, but I would make a good *wife* for the right *man*."

The vocabulary of heterosexual marriage is commonly used by those of Ricky's type. They speak of "marrying" the men they love and want to "settle down in a nice home." In a surprising number of cases, they take their lovers "home to meet mother." This act, like the exchange of "pinky rings," is intended to provide social strength to the lovers' union.

Three of the seven persons of this type were adopted—Ricky at the age of six months. Ricky told me that his adoptive father, who died three years before our interview, was "very warm and loving. He worked hard for a living, and we moved a lot." He is still close to his adoptive mother, who knows of his sexual deviance and treats his lover "like an older son."

Ricky hopes to be a writer, an occupation that would "allow me the freedom to be myself. I have a religion [Unitarian] which allows me freedom, and I want a career which will do the same." This, again, is typical: all three of the Unitarians in the sample are Type III men, although none was raised in that faith; and their jobs are uniformly of the sort to which their sexual activity, if exposed, would present little threat.

Although these men correspond most closely to society's homosexual stereotype, they are least representative of the tearoom population, constituting only 14 percent of the participant sample. More than any other type, the Rickys seem at ease with their behavior in the sexual market, and their scarcity in the tearooms is indicative of this. They want personal sex—more permanent relationships—and the public restrooms are not where this is to be found.

That any of them patronize the tearooms at all is the result of incidental factors: they fear that open cruising in the more common homosexual market places of the baths and bars might disrupt a current love affair; or they drop in at a tearoom while waiting for a friend at one of the "watering places" where homosexuals congregate in the parks. They find the anonymity of the tearooms suitable for their purposes, but not inviting enough to provide the primary setting for sexual activity.

TYPE IV: CLOSET QUEENS

Another dozen of the 50 participants interviewed may be classified as single deviants with dependent occupations, "closet queens" in homosexual slang. Again, the label may be applied to others who keep their deviance hidden, whether married or single, but the covert, unmarried men are most apt to earn this appellation. With them, we have moved full circle in our classifications, for they parallel the Trade in a number of ways:

1. They have a few friends, only a minority of whom are involved in tearoom activity.
2. They tend to play the insertor role, at least until they confront the crisis of aging.

3. Half of them are **Roman Catholic** in religion.

4. Their median annual income is $6,000; and they work as teachers, postmen, salesmen, clerks—usually for large corporations or agencies.

5. Most of them have completed only high school, although there are a few exceptionally well-educated men in this group.

6. One in six is black.

7. Not only are they afraid of becoming involved in other forms of the sexual market, they share with the Trade a relatively furtive involvement in the tearoom encounters.

Arnold will be used as the typical case. Only 22, Arnold is well below the median age of this group; but in most other respects he is quite representative, particularly in regard to the psychological problems common to Type IV.

A routine interview with Arnold stretched to nearly three hours in the suburban apartment he shares with another single man. Currently employed as a hospital attendant, he has had trouble with job stability, usually because he finds the job unsatisfactory. He frequently is unoccupied.

Arnold:
I hang around the park a lot when I don't have anything else to do. I guess I've always known about the tearooms . . . so I just started going in there to get my rocks off. But I haven't gone since I caught my lover there in September. You get in the habit of going; but I don't think I'll start in again—unless I get too desperate.

Interviewer:
Do you make the bar scene?

Arnold:
Very seldom. My roommate and I go out together once in a while, but everybody there seems to think we're lovers. So I don't really operate in the bars. I really don't like gay people. They can be so damned bitchy! I really like women better than men—except for sex. There's a lot of

the female in me, and I feel more comfortable with women than with men. I understand women and like to be with them. I'm really very close to my mother. The reason I don't live at home is because there are too many brothers and sisters living there. . . .

Interviewer:
Is she still a devout Roman Catholic?

Arnold:
Well, yes and no. She still goes to Mass some, but she and I go to seances together with a friend. I am studying astrology and talk it over with her quite a bit. I also analyze handwriting and read a lot about numerology. Mother knows I am gay and doesn't seem to mind. I don't think she really believes it though.

Arnold has a health problem: "heart attacks," which the doctor says are psychological and which take the form of "palpitations, dizziness, chest pain, shortness of breath and extreme weakness." These attacks, which began soon after his father's death from a coronary two years ago, make him feel as if he were "dying and turning cold." Tranquilizers were prescribed for him, "but I threw them out, because I don't like to become dependent on such things." He quoted a book on mental control of health that drugs are "unnecessary, if you have proper control."

He also connects these health problems with his resentment of his father, who was mentally ill:

Arnold:
I don't understand his mental illness and have always blamed him for it. You might say that I have a father complex and, along with that, a security complex. Guess that's why I always run around with older men.

Interviewer:
Were any of your brothers gay?

Arnold:
Not that I know of. I used to have sex with the brother closest to my age when we were little kids. But he's married now, and I don't think he is gay at all. It's just that most of the kids I ran around with

always jacked each other off or screwed each other in the ass. I just seemed to grow up with it. I can't remember a time when I didn't find men attractive. . . . I used to have terrible crushes on my gym teachers, but nothing sexual ever came of it. I just worshipped them, and wanted to be around them all the time. I had coitus with a woman when I was 16—she was 22. After it was over, she asked me what I thought of it. I told her I would rather masturbate. Boy, was she pissed off! I've always liked older men. If they are under 30, I just couldn't be less interested. . . . Nearly all my lovers have been between 30 and 50. The trouble is that *they* always want sex—and sex isn't really what I want. I just want to be with them—to have them for friends. I guess it's part of my father complex. I just want to be loved by an older man.

Few of the Type IV participants share Arnold's preference for older men, although they report poorer childhood relationships with their fathers than do those of any other group. As is the case with Arnold's roommate, many closet queens seem to prefer teenage boys as sexual objects. This is one of the features that distinguishes them from all other participant types. Although scarce in tearooms, teenagers make themselves available for sexual activity in other places frequented by closet queens. A number of these men regularly cruise the streets where boys thumb rides each afternoon when school is over. One closet queen from my sample has been arrested for luring boys in their early teens to his home.

Interaction between these men and the youths they seek frequently results in the sort of scandal feared by the gay community. Newspaper reports of molestations usually contain clues of the closet queen style of adaptation on the part of such offenders. Those respondents whose lives had been threatened by teenage toughs were generally of this type. One of the standard rules governing one-night-stand operations cautions against becoming involved with such "chicken." The frequent violation of this rule by closet queens may contribute to their general disrepute among the bar set of the homosexual subculture, where "closet queen" is a pejorative term.

One Type IV respondent, an alcoholic whose intense self-hatred seemed always about to overflow, told me one night over coffee of his loneliness and his endless search for someone to love:

I don't find it in the tearooms—although I go there because it's handy to my work. But I suppose the [hustler's hangout] is really my meat. I just want to love every one of those kids!

Later, this man was murdered by a teen-ager he had picked up.

Arnold, too, expressed loneliness and the need for someone to talk with. "When I can really sit down and talk to someone else," he said, "I begin to feel real again. I lose that constant fear of mine—that sensation that I'm dying."

STYLES OF DEVIANT ADAPTATION

Social isolation is characteristic of Type IV participants. Generally, it is more severe even than that encountered among the Trade, most of whom enjoy at least a vestigial family life. Although painfully aware of their homosexual orientations, these men find little solace in association with others who share their deviant interests. Fearing exposure, arrest, the stigmatization that might result from a participation in the homosexual subculture, they are driven to a desperate, lone-wolf sort of activity that may prove most dangerous to themselves and the rest of society. Although it is tempting to look for psychological explanations of their apparent preference for chicken, the sociological ones are evident. They resort to the more dangerous game because of a lack of both the normative restraints and adult markets that prevail in the more overt subculture. To them, the costs (financial and otherwise) of operating among street corner youths are more acceptable than those of active participation in the gay subculture. Only the tearooms provide a less expensive alternative for the closet queens.

I have tried to make it impossible for any close associate to recognize the real people behind the disguised composites portrayed in this article. But I have worked equally hard to enable a number of tearoom players to see themselves in the portrait of George, and others to find their own stories in those of Dwight, Ricky or Arnold. If I am accurate, the real Tom will wonder whether he is trade or ambisexual; and a few others will be able to identify only partly with Arnold or Ricky.

My one certainty is that there is no single composite with whom all may identify. It should now be evident that, like other next door neighbors, the par-

ticipants in tearoom sex are of no one type. They vary along a number of possible continua of social characteristics. They differ widely in terms of sexual career and activity, and even in terms of what that behavior means to them or what sort of needs it may fulfill. Acting in response to a variety of pressures toward deviance (some of which we may never ascertain), their adaptations follow a number of lines of least resistance.

In delineating styles of adaptation, I do not intend to imply that these men are faced with an array of styles from which they may pick one or even a combination. No man's freedom is that great. They have been able to choose only among the limited options offered them by society. These sets of alternatives, which determine the modes of adaptation to deviant pressures, are defined and allocated in accordance with major sociological variables: occupation, marital status, age, race, amount of education. That is one meaning of social probability.

Variations in Bottle-Gang Controls

EARL RUBINGTON

Those who practice deviance openly in groups face internal and external controls. Overt deviants, in addition to managing their own deviant careers, have to screen their activities from conformists and regulate both their own conduct and that of other similar deviants.

Theory states that the solution to these problems comes from a deviant subculture.[1] Such a subculture teaches skills, supplies a more favorable self-image, sets down rules for dealing with others, deviant or conformist, and justifies deviant behavior by a special ideology.

Deviant subcultures, however, supply ideas on social actions; they do not guarantee that prescribed actions will take place. It becomes necessary then to ask how well deviant beliefs, values, and norms are honored in practice, the extent to which conformity to deviant norms produces rewards, and exactly how deviants control one another.

This paper raises questions on social control in deviant groups. The group to be considered here, the "bottle gang," is relevant since it meets three conditions. Bottle gangs are public, not private in character; their members have more contacts with persons like themselves than with conformists; and their members participate in Skid Row subculture. Rules and sanctions are the major concerns here. The central question is: How well does the bottle gang regulate interaction

and activity, and screen both from outsiders?

To answer the question this paper (a) gives a description of a typical East Coast bottle gang; (b) abstracts the rules and functions of the gang; (c) discusses typical breaches and their sanctions; and (d) posits a set of conditions that may account for differences in social control in East Coast and West Coast bottle gangs.

The general argument of this paper is that control in the deviant group rests in part on the number of overt deviants who are visible and known to one another, in part on whether they have a territory and sufficient resources for engaging in deviant activities and interaction, and in part on the nature of their contact with authorities. To the extent that public deviants are more or less left to themselves to control their activities, to that extent will the amount of public deviance be within tolerable limits. But, given high visibility of deviance, frequent attempts at external control will combine with ineffective internal controls to produce a lessened tolerance of deviant behavior.

THE BOTTLE GANG

Bottle gang refers to the typical form of street drinking in which indigent, unattached men engage. The men appear

---

Somewhat revised version of a paper presented at the 62nd annual meetings of the American Sociological Association, San Francisco, California, August 31, 1967.

[1] Howard S. Becker, *Outsiders: Studies in the Sociology of Deviance* (New York: The Free Press of Glencoe, 1963), pp. 37–39; Albert K. Cohen, *Delinquent Boys: The Culture of the Gang* (Glencoe: The Free Press, 1955), 49–72.

to be heavy drinkers by conventional standards and are usually said to be "alcoholics," "bums," "drunks" or "winos." Generally they meet on the street, pool meager funds, send a member to a package store to buy an inexpensive bottle of fortified wine, share the bottle in some public place (e.g., alley, doorstep, park, or street corner, in rooming-house areas, urban slums, or Skid Row quarter), and split up once the bottle is emptied.

SETTING AND METHODS

Maple City, the setting for the present study, is an East Coast city of some 165,000, with no definable Skid Row quarter. Institutions and establishments catering to homeless men are scattered around the center of the city in various pockets. All are in walking distance, rather than being concentrated as they would be on a typical Skid Row. Lodging houses, rooming-houses, second-hand clothing stores that sell wine, restaurants and taverns catering to the homeless, missions and shelters all radiate out from the center of the city. Important public places for local and transient homeless are the King Street Mission and a grassy common in the center of the city called the Big Green. The present study relies on anthropological methods of field work. The data come from informants, direct observation, and participation, in that order.

A TYPICAL BOTTLE GANG

The setting assumed for the portrait to follow is the Big Green in Maple City during mild weather in mid-afternoon. The Green is within easy walking distance of the King Street Mission, several package stores, rooming-houses, employment agency, police station, and important street-corner hangouts. There are six stages in the bottle-gang cycle: salutation, negotiation, procurement, consumption, affirmation, and dispersal.

1. Salutation. Potential bottle-gang participants come into each other's view on the various paths that criss-cross the Green. Once in each other's presence, they acknowledge their mutual awareness. Each has worked together, drunk together at some time, or is known to a set of mutual acquaintances. They sit down on a bench, pass the time of day, and share information about "the boys." After a brief exchange of news both prepare to negotiate.

2. Negotiation. By now, each has read the signs that the other is "on the prowl" (that is, searching for a drink). Typically, one begins the negotiation by saying that he has a certain amount of money that he is willing to contribute towards the purchase of a bottle of wine. He may say, for example: "I have 18 cents; how much are you holding?" The other, if interested, reports his holdings. Generally, they will be "short" the "price of a bottle" (a half-pint of wine generally retails for fifty cents). The initiator collects the money, announces how much more they need, and leads them to others. The leader asks if they wish to "go in on a bottle." If they are still short, a brief excursion in panhandling will be necessary until the price is collected.

3. Procurement. When the little group has collected enough money ("made the price" or "scored"), they are now ready to get a bottle and drink it together. The leader picks one of the men to buy the bottle. Buying the bottle is called "making the run" and the buyer is called "the runner." The runner should be a person who is neither too shabbily dressed nor acutely intoxicated, and who is dependable; i.e., if given money, he can be trusted to return with a bottle. While the runner leaves on his errand, the remainder of the gang take seats on a bench and await his return.

4. Consumption. The runner returns with the wine (usually Muscatel), concealed on his person. The bottle, still in the brown bag the clerk wrapped it in, is inside his belt, under his jacket or in his back pocket. He gives the bag to the leader. The leader looks up and down the pathways of the Big Green, peels the plastic seal, uncaps the bottle, takes two short drinks, and then passes the bottle, still in the brown bag, to the runner. The runner takes two short drinks, then passes the bottle to one of the other men. After the bottle has made its full circle around the gang, the last one to drink from it returns it to the leader. He pockets the bottle, still in the brown bag. After the first round, the men sit back on their bench, light up cigarettes and talk. All during the phases of consumption, each looks up and down the walkways for police officers or outsiders who might jeopardize the activity. All drink surreptitiously.

5. Affirmation. The leader, as donor-host, sets style, tone, and topics of talk. There is little talk on personal troubles, much on others' troubles. All make negative comments on outsiders. All compliment the leader on how well or how fast he promoted "bottle money," praise the runner for his speed, and compare and contrast, usually favorably, the ease and sociability of the present gang with others they have been in. The phrase "you're all right," is heard frequently. In addition, all claim that when they have it, they share with others, and, when it comes to "making the run," they can always be counted on to come back.

6. Dispersal. The leader decides when the next round takes place. Again the bottle circles through the small group, traveling the same route as before. Each man takes the customary two drinks. In time, the bottle is emptied. With that, the gang is ready to disband. The man holding the empty bottle, still in its brown paper bag, gets up and disposes of it in a nearby trash container or puts it under the bench. The rest announce their plans, and then leave. Any or all are free to activate the cycle of bottle-drinking; if so, the gang remains intact. Sometimes, one member will decide to "treat" the rest to a bottle. At other times, the cycle will begin with negotiation and run on through to dispersal.

RULES AND FUNCTIONS

Tacit rules for each stage are as follows:

1. Salutation
   a. Never snub drinking "buddies."
   b. Say hello to friends and acquaintances alike.
   c. Always be ready to pass the time of day with an equal.
2. Negotiation
   a. Be as ready to offer a drink as you are to accept one.
   b. Show your money and be willing to share it.
   c. Buy or work your way into a bottle gang; don't chisel in.
3. Procurement
   a. Make the run quickly, but not obviously.
   b. Have faith in the runner; wait patiently and be discreet.
4. Consumption
   a. Let the leader split the seal and drink.
   b. Wait your turn, then match his drinks.
   c. Take two and pass the bottle.
   d. Don't show the world you're drinking.
5. Affirmation
   a. Follow the leader in talk and action.
   b. Praise him, the runner, and your partners.

c. Criticize persons known to have broken gang rules.
6. *Dispersal*
    a. Duck the empty.
    b. Say goodbye and go when the going's good.

Functions for each stage in the cycle are as follows:

1. *Salutation*
    a. Ready greetings cement past ties and open up chances of future ones.
    b. Opening ceremonies signify inclusion in an in-group, thereby reducing pains of stigma.
2. *Negotiation*
    a. Assigns one status as a suitable drinking companion, opens up a role in a face-to-face group, no matter how deviant, stigmatized, or short-lived it may be.
    b. Makes it possible to tailor a small budget and a large need for alcoholic drinks to a wider number of drinking encounters throughout the day.
3. *Procurement*
    a. Reduces the visibility of the bottle-gang's activities.
    b. Awaiting the runner's return helps to create a drinking-centered drama.
4. *Consumption*
    a. Satisfies the need for alcohol and drinking company.
    b. Reduces the tension and anxiety brought on while awaiting the runner's return.
5. *Affirmation*
    a. Ratifies one's identity as a person and one's solidarity with gang members present in the immediate situation.
    b. Signifies that each is a "good man" and a good drinking partner.
6. *Dispersal*
    a. Disposing of the empty bottle re-

moves evidence and cuts down risks of exposure.
    b. Shows respect for decency and public order and signifies the gang is about to break up.
    c. Signifies that all rights and duties are at an end. The contract has been fulfilled. All are now free of each other's company, for the time being.

Whether transitory or permanent in character, whether composed of transient or regular participants, the bottle gang seems ideally suited to the needs of indigent alcoholics. Participation in bottle gangs stretches meager funds so that men get the maximum amount of alcohol possible for their money. For instance, a two-ounce shot of whiskey in a bar costs forty cents. For one-fourth of that amount contributed towards a group bottle, a man can get almost as much absolute alcohol, now in the form of wine.

Participation in bottle gangs increases the range of acquaintance given the easy entry rules. In turn, participation in the simple ritual of the bottle gang gives one status and membership in a group. The exchange is made possible by the display of elementary social skills. Some men, indeed, simply trade presence rights for drinking rights.

Finally, as all become more deeply involved in a drinking-centered existence, statuses and roles, beliefs and norms coalesce around this axis of life. In the process, the usual urban complexities change in meaning and shrink in scope. Now obvious social failures can sustain a life which is to be understood in terms of the metaphors of deviant social drinking with all of its rewards and punishments. Obtaining and maintaining a supply of drinks in accordance with a set of rules provides a schedule, a calendar, a routine, and a morality all its own. The net effect of this life-style is to deny failure in the pursuit of drink in company.

BREACHES AND SANCTIONS

It would seem that such a well-designed social form as the bottle gang, so nicely suited to the conditions of the homeless alcoholic life as it is, should not produce many problems of social control. Given the fixity of its ritual, the limited skills required in the activity, the few and simple roles in the interaction, there ought to be few strains. In turn, the brevity of the encounter so nicely tuned to the Skid Row demand on non-involvement, seems, on its face, a guarantee of efficiency.

Yet this most elementary form of the deviant drinking life has more than its share of deviance and problems in social control. If informants are to be believed, deviance rather than conformity characterizes most stages of the bottle-gang cycle. There appear to be an abundance of breaches of the rules at all of the six stages; in addition, there seems to be either erratic, unpredictable application of sanctions on the one hand, and, on the other, actual failure to apply sanctions. In addition to failures to solve internal problems of control, there is the obvious failure of either screening activities from other drinking men as well as from the police. So that in the first instance, the internal peace and flow of interaction in the gang is upset, while in the second instance the very life of the gang is suddenly aborted.

A brief catalogue of the infraction of bottle-gang rules coupled with the ideal sanction and the frequency of its application follows.

1. Salutation breaches consist mainly of saying hello to a person as if he is known when in fact both served time in jail but were never formally introduced. The sanction here is exclusion but it is rarely applied.

2. Negotiation breaches are all instances of attempts at illicit entry into a bottle gang. Illicit entries take the form of inducing an obligaion, trying to obtain repayment for a past obligation, or partial evasion of entry rules. Some hover in the vicinity hoping to be invited to share a drink from the bottle; others simulate tremors. Some offer a drink from their own bottle, particularly when it only has a drop or two left. Others insist on repayment for drinks that one of the members of the gang owes them. Finally, a person may go in on the bottle, yet not really put up as much money as he could have afforded. The ideal sanction, of course, is to exclude all of these men from getting in on the current bottle; this is done but almost at random. All are typed by the manner in which they sought entry and these labels become a part of their reputation. The generic term for all is "chiseler" or "moocher." Those who stand at the periphery of the drinking group are called "merchants," "lap dogs," or "waiters." One who feigns tremors, the signs of acute withdrawal symptoms, is called an "actor" and a man who does not contribute as much as he might is called a "hold-out artist." Labeling is the predictable sanction, but not exclusion. This is always more or less a matter of chance. For instance, if a gang member can persuade the gang to invite in the person to whom the particular gang member is obligated to, he gains while they lose. For in the future, the person whom he paid off with the group's bottle need not feel any obligations to repay the favor. The other members of the group would lose out, should they comply with this request, since they would only be helping one of their number pay off a debt without incurring an obligation to return their favor.

3. Procurement breaches include a failure to return with the bottle, returning very slowly, or returning with a bottle from which the runner has already drunk himself or/and has offered a few

"pulls" at the bottle to people to whom he owes some drinks. Sometimes failure to return is due to accident, loss of memory, or police arrest. In this last case just as in the one of giving drinks to others not in the gang, the runner has violated cover-up rules. He became socially visible[2] with consequences for the gang. Sometimes failure to return was by intention; the runner kept the bottle for himself. In view of the difficulty of knowing what really happened the gang generally labels the man as untrustworthy; e.g., he is a "Dick Smith," he is a person who "went South with the bottle." This label is disseminated and meant to exclude him from future drinking encounters. Again, the label is much more likely to be applied than the sanction by the current as well as future gang-members.

4. A person breaches consumption rules by drinking too fast, too much, or too obviously from the bottle. Here the gang can tell the person about his failings. Later he will get a label for his troubles, but once again there is a marked reluctance to actually apply sanctions against such a person. On the other hand, if his drinking is so blatant as to call attention of the police, he is a little more apt to be excluded from subsequent gangs. But all is markedly contingent on a host of other factors.

5. Affirmation violations include incorrect talk or actions. Here some men talk out of turn, on the wrong subjects, or become argumentative or experts on uninteresting subjects. Their talk earns them appropriate labels; again whether they will be kept out of subsequent gangs by men who know their label is problematic. Exclusion in the future is a little more likely in the case of those men who "act up" either by fighting with the gang or by engaging in antics. Either calls attention of the police or disrupts the gang and sometimes does both. These men are all labeled as "performers," "wacks," "characters," "nuts," "psychos," "jail bait," etc. and they are avoided in the future whenever possible.

6. Dispersal violations include continuing to call attention to one's self or the activities of the gang or being ostentatious in hiding the empty bottle. In addition, they include illicit ways of continuing the drinking episode at the expense of one of the members. Some beg, or "con" money from the men present for their own drinking. Others sometimes try to rob, steal, or just beat up members thought to have some money. The more violent ones do get labeled and their reputations become widely known. Exclusion does take place; the sanction is much more apt to be applied against them.

DISCUSSION

The East Coast bottle gang reported in this study seems characterized by simple rules, and extreme variability in both conformity and sanctions on deviance. Some plausible hypotheses accounting for these variations in social control can be derived by contrasting these bottle gangs with those reported for the West Coast. There appear to be differences in both ecology and social organization in both areas and these differences may explain the variance. Ecology includes numbers, territory, resources, and the deviance contract with authorities. Social organization encompasses types of drinking patterns and experiences in bottle gangs. First we shall deal with ecology, next with social organization.

[2] Howard M. Bahr suggests that increased social visibility may be a general consequence of the dispersion of homeless men in his "The Gradual Disappearance of Skid Row," *Social Problems,* XV (Summer 1967), 41–45.

1. *Numbers.* West Coast Skid Rows concentrate a relatively large number of men who are in close contact with one another. Maple City bottle-gang drinkers are much fewer in number and are scattered around the city. Given the same meager resources and strong desires to drink, West Coast Skid Row men have access to a greater number of potential gangs. In turn, they need to invest less, while participating in a greater number of different gangs throughout the day. In Maple City, the smaller the number, the poorer the chances of getting in on a bottle. Needing more money to get into fewer gangs poses problems for a slender budget. This situation is more apt to encourage holding out, scheming, attempts to chisel into gangs, etc.

2. *Territory.* Having an established territory, the West Coast bottle-gang participant goes relatively unnoticed in contrast to his Maple City counterpart. The Maple City bottle-gang drinker needs to move around much more, thereby increasing his exposure to police, citizens who may lodge a complaint, and other men also searching for a drink. On a West Coast Skid Row his actions would go unnoticed, due principally to the fact that his actions would be undistinguished from many others in the vicinity. Lack of a territory increases social visibility in Maple City just as its presence decreases it on West Coast Skid Row. Increased exposure is a problem in particular in encouraging illegal entry into bottle gangs.

3. *Resources.* Again there are more resources on a Skid Row than off it for bottle-gang participants. Panhandling, a way of getting money for a bottle, is less noticed, more tolerated on rather than off Skid Row. In addition, package stores and other liquor outlets are plentiful in the neighborhood. By contrast, when a man "makes the run" in Maple City he

enters enemy territory. Again his activity becomes visible to those he would prefer did not see it.

4. *The Deviance Contract.* Police have a contract with Skid Row men. They agree to make predictable expeditions into the territory to arrest a certain number of agreed-upon violations of public order. Hence, West Coast Skid Rows are subjected to less surveillance. This permits more relaxed, leisurely, and less tense interaction in street-corner bottle gangs. In contrast, Maple City men must maintain constant vigilance on their activities; many claim to suffer from the "cop horrors." The result is surreptitious drinking, gulping drinks rapidly, and conveying this tension to all members of the gang. This concern with avoiding exposure to external controls weakens internal controls in the Maple City bottle gang.

Social organization, along with ecology, affects bottle-gang controls. A city that has a Skid Row has a way of life for homeless men.[3] A social organization, replete with statuses and roles results from the manner in which they follow Skid Row culture. A homeless alcoholic community exists in Maple City but dispersion reduces the chances of maintaining those stable patterns of interaction that sustain a subculture. As a result, drinking patterns and experience with bottle gangs are two major factors affecting the presence or absence of bottle-gang controls.

1. *Drinking patterns.* The Skid Row social system of heavy drinkers is based on sifting out and sorting types of drinking patterns. As in any status system, the attempt is always to maintain status homogeneity wherever possible. Maple City bottle drinkers do not participate in such a well-ordered social system; as a

[3] Samuel E. Wallace, *Skid Row as a Way of Life* (Totowa, New Jersey: Bedminster Press, 1965).

result, heterogeneity is more likely. The consequences for social control can be seen clearly in the case of drinking patterns. "Plateau drinkers," for instance, make ideal bottle-gang drinkers, since they seek only to maintain a certain level of alcohol in the blood stream over the course of any given day.[4] "Blitz drinkers,"[5] on the other hand, seek to drink as much as they can and as fast as they can in order to get drunk and stay drunk. These men make the poorest bottle-gang participants. Nevertheless poverty and need drives them into bottle gangs. It is only a short time before the deviant style of drinking upsets the ritual of the bottle gang. Heterogeneity happens more often in Maple City bottle gangs than on West Coast Skid Row gangs. Similarly, because of the greater need for companions, there is a greater tendency to waive admission requirements. Hence, persons who have bad reputations of one kind or another will still be accepted in the Maple City bottle gang. This is less likely on the West Coast Skid Row scene.

2. Experience in bottle gangs. The evidence suggests that the more extensive the experience in bottle gangs on the West Coast, the more conformist the gang member is. On the other hand, the Maple City material suggests that the more extensive the gang member's experience, the more deviant he is (that is, primarily, in the sense of violating gang rules). These two notions on individual gang-member experience are related to responses to deviant behavior in these gangs. For violations of gang norms and their punishments seem to be reversed for both coasts in the following ways:

a. Violations of bottle-gang norms are less likely to happen on the West Coast, but if they should occur, they are more apt to be punished. There, rules and sanctions are interdependent.

b. Violations of bottle-gang norms are more apt to happen on the East Coast, but if they do occur, they are more apt to go unpunished. Rules and sanctions are relatively independent.

More experienced bottle-gang drinkers on both the West Coast and in Maple City are aware of these relationships between breaches and sanctions, and each acts upon his knowledge to sustain the status quo. But they do so in different ways, though for perhaps the same reasons. Given the relationship between rules and sanctions in their own experience, seasoned West Coast bottle-gang drinkers take conformity for granted, thus need to state the rules on how to drink in a bottle gang less frequently. Affirmation of its rules, sentiments, and sanctions are less often required. On the other hand because of unpredictable relations between rules and sanctions in Maple City bottle gangs, seasoned participants talk about gang rules at great length, affirm them and the sentiments attaching to them, and continually point to the sanctions for failing to abide by the rules. They continually point to the failure of others to obey gang rules while simultaneously proclaiming their own loyalty and dependability.

The net effect of their talk is to provide all participants, but most particularly the newcomer, with an illusory sense of a social order replete with definite rules and sanctions. Those experienced members who wish to can gain the conformity of others while they themselves deviate in secret. In time, with increased experience in gangs, the

---

[4] Robert Straus and Raymond G. McCarthy, "Nonaddictive Pathological Drinking Patterns of Homeless Men," *Quarterly Journal of Studies on Alcohol,* XII (December 1951), 601–611.

[5] Richard J. Kingham, "Alcoholism and the Reinforcement Theory of Learning," *Quarterly Journal of Studies on Alcohol,* XIX (June 1958), 320–330.

level of suspicion and distrust rises with the knowledge that so many violators go unpunished. It becomes clear that non-conformity is frequently rewarded much more and at much less cost than conformity. As each comes to see more clearly that his own self-interest comes to lie more and more in non-conformity, he in turn comes to expect more violations of bottle-gang norms from his partners. This only triggers more talk about the rules, about loyalty to them, and about the necessity for punishing violators.

When, as happens so very frequently in this impoverished setting, the need to drink increases inversely with the resources for getting drinks, sanctions become a luxury. For to the extent that past violators may become current donor-hosts, if not men who will actually treat one to a desperately needed drink, it behooves bottle-gang drinkers to be tolerant of behavior that deviates from their own norms. Most, because of their need and their poverty, do not feel that they are in a position to apply sanctions against those who have broken any of the rules. Such control as may come about can only be of a symbolic character. The incessant talk about how others have breached the rules is, on occasion, a plea that the same thing will not happen in the immediate drinking group.

Control in East Coast bottle gangs, such as it is, rests more on talking about rules and sanctions than in taking action on either. This suggests that any deviant subculture is only as good as the organizational conditions that surround it. Because of the tenuous organizational conditions surrounding Maple City homeless men, bottle-gang drinking there is more precarious and less internally controlled than it is for participants in such gangs on the Skid Rows of the West Coast.

The Social Organization of Convicts in California Prisons

JOHN IRWIN

[In California prisons] the type of group affiliations the convict forms, the impact of this group participation, and the general impact of the prison experience upon his extended career are related to a wide range of factors, some systematic, some relatively random. Presently four of these factors seem to stand out. These are (1) his preprison identity, (2) his prison adaptive mode, (3) his race-ethnicity, and finally (4) his relationship to perspective and identity of the "convict." The following paragraphs will focus primarily on the prison-adaptive modes, but the relationship between these modes and criminal identities will be considered. Race-ethnicity and the convict perspective will be treated later. . . .

PRISON-ADAPTIVE MODES

Many studies of prison behavior have approached the task of explaining the convict social organization by posing the hypothetical question—how do convicts adapt to prison? It was felt that this was a relevant question because the prison is a situation of deprivation and degradation, and, therefore, presents extraordinary adaptive problems. Two adaptive styles were recognized: (1) an individual style—withdrawal and/or isolation, and (2) a collective style—participation in a convict social system

which, through its solidarity, regulation of activities, distribution of goods and prestige, and apparent opposition to the world of the administration, helps the individual withstand the "pains of imprisonment."

I would like to suggest that these studies have overlooked important alternate styles. First let us return to the question that theoretically every convict must ask himself: How shall I do my time? or, What shall I do in prison? First, we assume by this question that the convict is able to cope with the situation. This is not always true; some fail to cope with prison and commit suicide or sink into psychosis. Those who do cope can be divided into those who identify with and therefore adapt to a broader world than that of the prison, and those who orient themselves primarily to the prison world. This difference in orientation is often quite subtle but always important. In some instances it is the basis for forming very important choices, choices which may have important consequences for the felon's long term career. For example, Piri Thomas, a convict, was forced to make up his mind whether to participate in a riot or refrain:

I stood there watching and weighing, trying to decide whether or not I was a con first and an outsider second. I had been doing time inside yet living every mental minute

Reprinted from John Irwin, *The Felon,* © 1970, pp. 66–85. Reprinted by permission of Prentice-Hall, Inc., Englewood Cliffs, New Jersey.

I could outside; now I had to choose one or the other. I stood there in the middle of the yard. Cons passed me by, some going west to join the boppers, others going east to neutral ground. The call of rep tore within me, while the feeling of being a punk washed over me like a yellow banner. I had to make a decision. *I am a con. These damn cons are my people . . . What do you mean, your people? Your people are outside the cells, home, in the streets. No! That ain't so . . . Look at them go toward the west wall. Why in hell am I taking so long in making up my mind? Man, there goes Papo and Zu-Zu, and Mick the Boxer; even Ruben is there.*[1]

This identification also influences the criteria for assigning and earning prestige —criteria relative to things in the outside world or things which tend to exist only in the prison world, such as status in a prison social system or success with prison homosexuals. Furthermore, it will influence the long term strategies he forms and attempts to follow during his prison sentence.

It is useful to further divide those who maintain their basic orientation to the outside into (1) those who for the most part wish to maintain their life patterns and their identities—even if they intend to refrain from most law breaking activities—and (2) those who desire to make significant changes in life patterns and identities and see prison as a chance to do this.

The mode of adaptation of those convicts who tend to make a world out of prison will be called "jailing." To "jail" is to cut yourself off from the outside

world and to attempt to construct a life within prison. The adaptation of those who still keep their commitment to the outside life and see prison as a suspension of that life but who do not want to make any significant changes in their life patterns will be called "doing time." One "does time" by trying to maximize his comfort and luxuries and minimize his discomfort and conflict and to get out as soon as possible. The adaptation made by those who, looking to their future life on the outside, try to effect changes in their life patterns and identities will be called "gleaning."[2] In "gleaning," one sets out to "better himself" or "improve himself" and takes advantage of the resources that exist in prison to do this.

Not all convicts can be classified neatly by these three adaptive styles. Some vacillate from one to another, and others appear to be following two or three of them simultaneously. Still others, for instance the noncopers mentioned . . . cannot be characterized by any of the three. However, many prison careers fit very closely into one of these patterns, and the great majority can be classified roughly by one of the styles.

Doing Time. When you go in, now your trial is over, you got your time and everything and now you head for the joint. They furnish your clothing, your toothbrush, your toothpaste, they give you a package of tobacco, they put you up in the morning to get breakfast. In other words, everything is furnished. Now you stay in there two years, five years, ten years, whatever you stay in there, what difference does it make? After a year or so you've been . . . after six

---

[1] Piri Thomas, *Down These Mean Streets* (New York: Alfred A. Knopf, Inc., 1967), p. 281.

[2] "Gleaning" is one term which is not natural to the prison social world, and the category itself is not explicitly defined. Convicts have recognized and labeled subparts of it, such as "intellectuals," "programmers," and "dudes on a self-improvement kick," but not the broader category which I have labeled gleaners. However, whenever I have described this category to convicts, they immediately recognized it and the term becomes meaningful to them. I chose the term gleaning because it emphasizes one very important dimension of this style of adaptation, the tendency to pick through the prison world (which is mostly chaff) in search of the means of self-improvement.

months, you've become accustomed to the general routine. Everything is furnished. If you get a stomachache, you go to the doctor; if you can't see out of your cheaters, you go to the optician. It don't cost you nothing.[3]

As the above statement by a thief indicates, many convicts conceive of the prison experience as a temporary break in their outside career, one which they take in their stride. They come to prison and "do their time." They attempt to pass through this experience with the least amount of suffering and the greatest amount of comfort. They (1) avoid trouble, (2) find activities which occupy their time, (3) secure a few luxuries, (4) with the exception of a few complete isolates, form friendships with small groups of other convicts, and (5) do what they think is necessary to get out as soon as possible.[4]

To avoid trouble the convict adheres to the convict code—especially the maxims of "do your own time" and "don't snitch," and stays away from "lowriders" —those convicts engaged in hijacking and violent disputes. . . .

To occupy their time, "time-doers" work, read, work on hobbies, play cards, chess, and dominoes, engage in sports, go to movies, watch TV, participate in some group activities, such as drama groups, gavel clubs, and slot car clubs, and while away hours "tripping" with friends. They seek extra luxuries through their job. Certain jobs in prison, such as jobs in the kitchen, in the officers' and guards' dining room, in the boiler room, the officers' and guards' barber shop, and the fire house, offer various extra luxuries—extra things to eat, a radio, privacy, additional shows, and more freedom. Or time-doers purchase luxuries legally or illegally available in the prison market. If they have money on the books, if they have a job which pays a small salary, or if they earn money at a hobby, they can draw up to twenty dollars a month which may be spent for foodstuffs, coffee, cocoa, stationery, toiletries, tobacco, and cigarettes. Or using cigarettes as currency they may purchase food from the kitchen, drugs, books, cell furnishings, clothes, hot plates, stingers, and other contraband items. If they do not have legal access to funds, they may "scuffle"; that is, sell some commodity which they produce—such as belt buckles or other handicraft items—or some commodity which is accessible to them through their job—such as food items from the kitchen. "Scuffling," however, necessitates becoming enmeshed in the convict social system and increases the chances of "trouble," such as conflicts over unpaid debts, hijacking by others, and "beefs"—disciplinary actions for rule infractions. Getting into trouble is contrary to the basic tenets of "doing time," so time-doers usually avoid scuffling.

The friendships formed by time-doers vary from casual acquaintanceships with persons who accidentally cell nearby or work together, to close friendship groups who "go all the way" for each other— share material goods, defend each other against others, and maintain silence about each other's activities. These varying friendship patterns are related closely to their criminal identities.

Finally, time-doers try to get out as soon as possible. First they do this by staying out of trouble, "cleaning up their hands." They avoid activities and persons that would put them in danger of receiving disciplinary actions, or "beefs." And in recent years with the increasing emphasis on treatment, they "program." To program is to follow, at least tokenly,

---

[3] Maurer, *Whiz Mob* (New Haven: College and University Press, 1964), p. 196.
[4] Erving Goffman has described this mode of adaptation, which he calls "playing it cool" in *Asylums* (Garden City, N.Y.: Anchor Books, 1961), pp. 64–65.

a treatment plan which has been outlined by the treatment staff, recommended by the board, or devised by the convict himself. It is generally believed that to be released on parole as early as possible one must "get a program." A program involves attending school, vocational training, group counseling, church, Alcoholics Anonymous, or any other special program that is introduced under the treatment policy of the prison.

All convicts are more apt to choose "doing time," but some approach this style in a slightly different manner. For instance, doing time is characteristic of the thief in prison. He shapes this mode of adaptation and establishes it as a major mode of adaptation in prison. The convict code, which is fashioned from the criminal code, is the foundation for this style. The thief has learned how to do his time long before he comes to prison. Prison, he learns when he takes on the dimensions of the criminal subculture, is part of criminal life, a calculated risk, and when it comes he is ready for it. . . .

Like the majority of convicts, the dope fiend and the head usually just "do time." When they do, they don't vary greatly from the thief, except that they tend to associate with other dope fiends or heads, although they too will associate with other criminals. They tend to form very close bonds with one, two, or three other dope fiends or heads and maintain a casual friendship with a large circle of dope fiends, heads, and other criminals. Like the thief, the dope fiend and the head tend not to establish ties with squares.

The hustler in doing time differs from the other criminals in that he does not show a propensity to form very tight-knit groups. Hustling values, which emphasize manipulation and invidiousness, seem to prevent this. The hustler maintains a very large group of casual friends. Though this group does not show strong bonds of loyalty and mutual aid, they share many activities such as cards, sports, dominoes, and "jiving"—casual talk.

Square johns do their time quite differently than the criminals. The square john finds life in prison repugnant and tries to isolate himself as much as possible from the convict world. He does not believe in the convict code, but he usually learns to display a token commitment to it for his own safety. A square john indicated his forced obedience to the convict code:

Several times I saw things going on that I didn't like. One time a couple of guys were working over another guy and I wanted to step in, but I couldn't. Had to just keep moving as if I didn't see it. (Interview, Soledad Prison, June 1966)

He usually keeps busy with some job assignment, a hobby, cards, chess, or various forms of group programs, such as drama groups. He forms friendships with one or two other squares and avoids the criminals. But even with other squares there is resistance to forming *close* ties. Square johns are very often sensitive about their "problems," and they are apt to feel repugnance toward themselves and other persons with problems. Besides, the square usually wants to be accepted by conventional people and not by other "stigmatized" outcasts like himself. So, many square johns do their time isolated from other inmates. . . .

The lower-class man, though he doesn't share the square john's repugnance towards criminals or the convict code, usually does not wish to associate closely with thieves, dope fiends, heads, and disorganized criminals. In his life outside he has encountered and avoided these persons for many years and usually keeps on avoiding them inside. He usually seeks a job to occupy himself. His actual stay in prison is typically very short, since he is either released very early and/or he is classified at minimum custody and sent to a forestry camp or one of the minimum-custody institutions, where he has increased freedom and privileges.

Jailing. Some convicts who do not retain or who never acquired any commitment to outside social worlds, tend to make a world out of prison.[5] These are the men who

seek positions of power, influence and sources of information, whether these men are called "shots," "politicians," "merchants," "hoods," "toughs," "gorillas," or something else. A job as secretary to the Captain or Warden, for example, gives an aspiring prisoner information and consequent power, and enables him to influence the assignment or regulation of other inmates. In the same way, a job which allows the incumbent to participate in a racket, such as clerk in the kitchen storeroom where he can steal and sell food, is highly desirable to a man oriented to the convict subculture. With a steady income of cigarettes, ordinarily the prisoner's medium of exchange, he may assert a great deal of influence and purchase those things which are symbols of status among persons oriented to the convict subculture. Even if there is not a well-developed medium of exchange, he can barter goods acquired in his position for equally-desirable goods possessed by other convicts. These include information and such things as specially-starched, pressed, and tailored prison clothing, fancy belts, belt buckles or billfolds, special shoes, or any other type of dress which will set him apart and will indicate that he has both the influence to get the goods and the influence necessary to keep them and display them despite prison rules which outlaw doing so. In California, special items of clothing, and clothing that is neatly laundered, are called "bonaroos" (a corruption of *bonnet rouge,* by means of which French prison trustees

were once distinguished from the common run of prisoners), and to a lesser degree even the persons who wear such clothing are called "bonaroos."[6]

Just as doing time is the characteristic style of the thief, so "jailing" is the characteristic style of the state-raised youth. This identity terminates on the first or second prison term, or certainly by the time the youth reaches thirty. The state-raised youth must assume a new identity, and the one he most often chooses, the one which his experience has prepared him for, is that of the "convict." The prison world is the only world with which he is familiar. He was raised in a world where "punks" and "queens" have replaced women, "bonaroos" are the only fashionable clothing, and cigarettes are money. This is a world where disputes are settled with a pipe or a knife, and the individual must form tight cliques for protection. His senses are attuned to iron doors banging, locks turning, shakedowns, and long lines of blue-clad convicts. He knows how to survive, in fact prosper, in this world, how to get a cell change and a good work assignment, how to score for nutmeg, cough syrup, or other narcotics. More important, he knows hundreds of youths like himself who grew up in the youth prisons and are now in the adult prisons. . . .

The state-raised youth often assumes a role in the prison social system, the system of roles, values, and norms described by Schrag, Sykes, and others. This does not mean that he immediately rises to power in the prison system. Some of the convicts have occupied their positions for many years and cannot tolerate the threat of every new bunch of reform-school graduates. The state-raised youth who has just graduated to adult prison must start at the bottom; but he knows

[5] Fifteen per cent of the 116 ex-prisoners were classified as "jailers."
[6] Irwin and Cressey, "Thieves, Convicts, and the Inmate Culture," *Social Problems* (Fall, 1962), p. 149.

the routine, and in a year or so he occupies a key position himself. One reason he can readily rise is that in youth prison he very often develops skills, such as clerical and maintenance skills, that are valuable to the prison administration.

Many state-raised youths, however, do not tolerate the slow ascent in the prison social system and become "lowriders." They form small cliques and rob cells, hijack other convicts, carry on feuds with other cliques, and engage in various rackets. Though these "outlaws" are feared and hated by all other convicts, their orientation is to the convict world, and they are definitely part of the convict social system.

Dope fiends and hustlers slip into jailing more often than thieves, due mainly to the congruities between their old activities and some of the patterns of jailing. For instance, a central activity of jailing is "wheeling and dealing," the major economic activity of prison. All prison resources—dope, food, books, money, sexual favors, bonaroos, cell changes, jobs, dental and hospital care, hot plates, stingers, cell furnishings, rings, and buckles—are always available for purchase with cigarettes. It is possible to live in varying degrees of luxury, and luxury has a double reward in prison as it does in the outside society: first, there is the reward of consumption itself, and second there is the reward of increased prestige in the prison social system because of the display of opulence.

This prison life style requires more cigarettes than can be obtained legally; consequently, one wheels and deals. There are three main forms of wheeling and dealing for cigarettes: (1) gambling (cards, dice and betting on sporting events); (2) selling some commodity or service, which is usually made possible by a particular job assignment; and (3) lending cigarettes for interest—two for three. These activities have a familiar ring to both the hustler and the dope fiend, who have hustled money or dope

on the outside. They very often become intricately involved in the prison economic life and in this way necessarily involved in the prison social system. The hustler does this because he feels at home in this routine, because he wants to keep in practice, or because he must present a good front—even in prison. To present a good front one must be a success at wheeling and dealing.

The dope fiend, in addition to having an affinity for wheeling and dealing, may become involved in the prison economic life in securing drugs. There are a variety of drugs available for purchase with cigarettes or money (and money can be purchased with cigarettes). Drugs are expensive, however, and to purchase them with any regularity one either has money smuggled in from the outside or he wheels and deals. And to wheel and deal one must maintain connections for securing drugs, for earning money, and for protection. This enmeshes the individual in the system of prison roles, values, and norms. Though he maintains a basic commitment to his drug subculture which supersedes his commitment to the prison culture and though he tends to form close ties only with other dope fiends, through his wheeling and dealing for drugs he becomes an intricate part of the prison social system.

The head jails more often than the thief. One reason for this is that the head, especially the "weed head" tends to worship luxuries and comforts and is fastidious in his dress. Obtaining small luxuries, comforts, and "bonaroo" clothing usually necessitates enmeshing himself in the "convict" system. Furthermore, the head is often vulnerable to the dynamics of narrow, cliquish, and invidious social systems, such as the "convict" system, because many of the outside head social systems are of this type.

The thief, or any identity for that matter, *may* slowly lose his orientation to the outside community, take on the convict categories, and thereby fall into jailing. This occurs when the individual has spent a great deal of time in prison and/or returned to the outside community and discovered that he no longer fits in the outside world. It is difficult to maintain a real commitment to a social world without firsthand experience with it for long periods of time.

The square john and the lower-class man find the activities of the "convicts" petty, repugnant, or dangerous, and virtually never jail.

Gleaning. With the rapidly growing educational, vocational training, and treatment opportunities, and with the erosion of convict solidarity, an increasing number of convicts choose to radically change their life styles and follow a sometimes carefully devised plan to "better themselves," "improve their mind," or "find themselves" while in prison.[7] One convict describes his motives and plans for changing his life style:

I got tired of losing. I had been losing all my life. I decided that I wanted to win for a while. So I got on a different kick. I knew that I had to learn something so I went to school, got my high school diploma. I cut myself off from my old YA [Youth Authority] buddies and started hanging around with some intelligent guys who minded their own business. We read a lot, a couple of us paint. We play a little bridge and talk, a lot of time about what we are going to do when we get out. (Interview, Soledad Prison, June 1966) . . .

In trying to "improve himself," "improve his mind," or "find himself," the convict gleans from every source available in prison. The chief source is books: he reads philosophy, history, art, science, and fiction. Often after getting started he devours a sizable portion of world literature. . . .

Besides this informal education, he often pursues formal education. The convict may complete grammar school and high school in the prison educational facilities. He may enroll in college courses through University of California (which will be paid for by the Department of Corrections), or through other correspondence schools (which he must pay for himself). More recently, he may take courses in various prison college programs.

He learns trades through the vocational training programs or prison job assignments. Sometimes he augments these by studying trade books, correspondence courses, or journals. He studies painting, writing, music, acting, and other creative arts. There are some facilities for these pursuits sponsored by the prison administration, but these are limited. This type of gleaning is done mostly through correspondence, through reading, or through individual efforts in the cell.

He tries to improve himself in other ways. He works on his social skills and his physical appearance—has his tattoos removed, has surgery on physical defects, has dental work done, and builds up his body "pushing iron."

He shys away from former friends or persons with his criminal identity who are not gleaners and forms new associations with other gleaners. These are usually gleaners who have chosen a similar style of gleaning, and with whom he shares many interests and activities, but they may also be those who are generally trying to improve themselves, although they are doing so in different ways.

Gleaning is a style more characteristic of the hustler, the dope fiend, and the state-raised youth than of the thief. When the former glean, though they tend to associate less with their deviant

---

[7] In the sample of 116 ex-prisoners, the records indicated that 19 per cent had followed a gleaning course in prison.

friends who are doing time or jailing, they are not out of the influence of these groups, or free from the influence of their old subculture values. The style of gleaning they choose and the future life for which they prepare themselves must be acceptable to the old reference group and somewhat congruent with their deviant values. The life they prepare for should be prestigious in the eyes of their old associates. It must be "doing good" and cannot be "a slave's life."

The state-raised youth who gleans probably has the greatest difficulty cutting himself off from his former group because the state-raised values emphasize loyalty to one's buddies:

I don't spend much time with my old YA partners and when I do we don't get along. They want me to do something that I won't do or they start getting on my back about my plans. One time they were riding me pretty bad and I had to pull them up. (Interview, Soledad Prison, June 1966)

He also has the greatest difficulty in making any realistic plans for the future. He has limited experience with the outside, and his models of "making it" usually come from the mass media—magazines, books, movies, and TV.

The dope fiend and the head, when they glean, tend to avoid practical fields and choose styles which promise glamor, excitement, or color. Most conventional paths with which they are familiar seem especially dull and repugnant. In exploring ways of making it they must find some way to avoid the humdrum life which they rejected long ago. Many turn to legitimate deviant identities such as "intellectual outsiders," "bohemians," or "mystics." Often they study one of the creative arts, the social sciences, or philosophy with no particular career in mind.

The hustler, who values skills of articulation and maintained a good "front" in his deviant life, often prepares for a field where these skills will serve him,

such as preaching or political activism.

The square john and the lower-class man, since they seldom seek to radically change their identity, do not glean in the true sense, but they do often seek to improve themselves. The square john usually does this by attacking his problem. He is satisfied with his reference world—the conventional society—but he recognizes that to return to it successfully he must cope with that flaw in his makeup which led to his incarceration. There are three common ways he attacks this problem: (1) he joins self help groups such as Alcoholics Anonymous, (2) he seeks the help of experts (psychiatrists, psychologists or sociologists) and attends the therapy programs, or (3) he turns to religion.

The lower-class man is usually an older person who does not desire or deem it possible to carve out a radically new style of life. He may, however, see the prison experience as a chance to improve himself by increasing his education and his vocational skills.

The thief tends to be older and his commitment to his identity is usually strong, so it is not likely that he will explore other life styles or identities. This does not mean that he is committed for all time to a life of crime. Certain alternate conclusions to a criminal career are included in the definitions of a proper thief's life. For instance, a thief may retire when he becomes older, has served a great deal of time, or has made a "nice score." When he retires he may work at some well-paying trade or run a small business, and in prison he may prepare himself for either of these acceptable conclusions to a criminal career. . . .

RACE AND ETHNICITY

Another variable which is becoming increasingly important in the formation of cleavages and identity changes in the convict world is that of race and ethnicity. For quite some time in California prisons, hostility and distance between three segments of the populations—white, Negroes and Mexicans—have increased. For several years the Negroes have assumed a more militant and ethnocentric posture, and recently the Mexicans—already ethnocentric and aggressive—have followed with a more organized, militant stance. Correspondingly, there is a growing trend among these two segments to establish, reestablish or enhance racial-ethnic pride and identity. Many "Blacks" and "Chicanos" are supplanting their criminal identity with a racial-ethnic one. This movement started with the Blacks.[8] A black California convict gives his recently acquired views toward whites:

All these years, man, I been stealing and coming to the joint. I never stopped to think why I was doing it. I thought that all I wanted was money and stuff. Ya know, man, now I can see why I thought the way I did. I been getting fucked all my life and never realized it. The white man has been telling me that I should want his stuff. But he didn't give me no way to get it. Now I ain't going for his shit anymore. I'm a Black man. I'm going to get out of here and see what I can do for my people. I'm going to do what I have to do to get those white motherfuckers off my people's back. (Interview, San Quentin, March 1968).

Chicanos in prison have maintained considerable insulation from both whites and Blacks—especially Blacks—towards whom they have harbored considerable hostility. They possess a strong ethnic-racial identity which underpins their more specialized felonious one—which has usually been that of a dope fiend or lower-class man. This subcultural identity and actual group unity in prison has been based on their Mexican culture—especially two important dimensions of Mexican culture. The first is their strong commitment to the concept of "machismo"—which is roughly translated manhood. . . . The second is their use of Spanish and Calo (Spanish slang) which has separated them from other segments. Besides these two traits there are many other ethnic subcultural characteristics which promote unity among Chicanos. For instance, they tend to be stoic and intolerant of "snitches" and "snivelers" and feel that Anglos and Blacks are more often snitches and snivelers. Furthermore, they respect friendship to the extreme, in fact to the extreme of killing or dying for friendship.

Until recently this has meant that Chicanos constituted the most cohesive segment in California prisons. In prison, where they intermingle with whites and Negroes, they have felt considerable distance from these segments and have maintained their identification with Mexican culture. However, there have been and still are some divisions in this broad category. For instance, various neighborhood cliques of Chicanos often carry on violent disputes with each other which last for years. Furthermore, Los Angeles or California cliques wage disputes with El Paso or Texas cliques. Many stabbings and killings have resulted from confrontations between different Chicano groups. Nevertheless, underpinning these different group affiliations and the various criminal identities there has been a strong identification with Mexican culture.

Recently the Chicanos, following the footsteps of the Negroes in prison and the footsteps of certain militant Mexican-American Groups outside (e.g., MAPA and the Delano strikers) have started organizing cultural-activist groups in prison (such as Empleo) and shaping a new identity built upon their Mexican

---

[8] This movement was foretold by Malcolm X. See *The Autobiography of Malcolm X* (New York: The Macmillan Company, 1965), p. 183.

ancestry and their position of disadvantage in the white society. As they move in this direction they are cultivating some friendship with the Negroes, towards whom they now feel more affinity.

This racial-ethnic militance and identification will more than likely become increasingly important in the prison social world. There is already some indication that the identity of the Black National and that of the Chicano is becoming superordinate to the criminal identities of many Negroes and Mexican-Americans or at least is having an impact on their criminal identities.

A dude don't necessarily have to become a Muslim or a Black National now to get with Black Power. He may still be laying to get out there and do some pimping or shoot some dope. But he knows he's a brother and when the shit is down we can count on him. And maybe he is going to carry himself a little differently, you know, like now you see more and more dudes— oh, they're still pimps, but they got naturals now. (Interview, San Quentin, April 1968)

The reassertion or discovery of the racial-ethnic identity is sometimes related to gleaning in prison. Frequently, the leaders of Blacks or Chicanos, for example, Malcolm X and Eldridge Cleavor, have arrived at their subcultural activism and militant stance through gleaning. Often, becoming identified with this movement will precipitate a gleaning course. However, this is not necessarily the case. These two phenomena are not completely overlapping among the Negro and Chicano.

The nationalistic movement is beginning to have a general impact on the total prison world—especially at San Quentin. The Blacks and Chicanos, as they focus on the whites as their oppressors, seem to be excluding white prisoners from this category and are, in fact, developing some sympathy for them as a minority group which itself is being oppressed by the white establishment and the white police. As an indication of this recent change, one convict comments on the present food-serving practices of Muslim convicts:

It used to be that whenever a Muslim was serving something (and this was a lot of the time, man, because there's a lot of those dudes in the kitchen), well, you know, you wouldn't expect to get much of a serving. Now, the cats just pile it on to whites and blacks. Like he is giving all the state's stuff away to show his contempt. So I think it is getting better between the suedes and us. (Interview, San Quentin, April 1968)

THE CONVICT IDENTITY

Over and beyond the particular criminal identity or the racial-ethnic identity he acquires or maintains in prison and over and beyond the changes in his direction which are produced by his prison strategy, to some degree the felon acquires the perspective of the "convict."

There are several gradations and levels of this perspective and attendant identity. First is the taken-for-granted perspective, which he acquires in spite of any conscious efforts to avoid it. This perspective is acquired simply by being in prison and engaging in prison routines for months or years. Even square johns who consciously attempt to pass through the prison experience without acquiring any of the beliefs and values of the criminals, do to some extent acquire certain meanings, certain taken-for-granted interpretations and responses which will shape, influence, or distort reality for them after release. . . .

Beyond the taken-for-granted perspective which all convicts acquire, most convicts are influenced by a pervasive but rather uncohesive convict "code." To some extent most of them, especially those who identify with a criminal system, are consciously committed to the major dictum of this code—"do your own time." As was pointed out earlier, the basic meaning of this precept is the obligation to tolerate the behavior of others unless it is directly affecting your physical self or your possessions. If another's behavior surpasses these limits, then the problem must be solved by the person himself; that is, *not* by calling for help from the officials.

The convict code isn't any different than stuff we all learned as kids. You know, nobody likes a stool pigeon. Well, here in the joint you got all kinds of guys living jammed together, two to a cell. You got nuts walking the yard, you got every kind of dingbat in the world here. Well, we got to have some rules among ourselves. The rule is "do your own number." In other words, keep off your neighbors' toes. Like if a guy next to me is making brew in his cell, well this is none of my business. I got no business running to the man and telling him that Joe Blow is making brew in his cell. Unless Joe Blow is fucking over me, then I can't say nothing. And when he's fucking over me, then I got to stop him myself. If I can't then I deserve to get fucked over. (Interview, San Quentin, May 1968)

Commitment to the convict code or the identity of the convict is to a high degree a lifetime commitment to do your own time; that is, to live and let live, and when you feel that someone is not letting you live, to either take it, leave, or stop him yourself, but never call for help from official agencies of control.

At another level, the convict perspective consists of a more cohesive and sophisticated value and belief system. This is the perspective of the elite of the convict world—the "regular." A "regular" (or, as he has been variously called, "people," "folks," "solid," a "right guy," or "all right") possesses many of the traits of the thief's culture. He can be counted on when needed by other regulars. He is also not a "hoosier"; that is, he has some finesse, is capable, is level-headed, has "guts" and "timing." The following description of a simple bungled transaction exemplifies this trait:

Man, you should have seen the hoosier when the play came down. I thought that that motherfucker was all right. He surprised me. He had the stuff and was about to hand it to me when a sergeant and another bull came through the door from the outside. Well, there wasn't nothing to worry about. Is all he had to do was go on like there was nothin' unusual and hand me the stuff and they would have never suspected nothing. But he got so fucking nervous and started fumbling around. You know, he handed me the sack and then pulled it back until they got hip that some play was taking place. Well you know what happened. The play was ranked and we both ended up in the slammer. (Field notes, San Quentin, February 1968)

The final level of the perspective of the convict is that of the "old con." This is a degree of identification reached after serving a great deal of time, so much time that all outside-based identities have dissipated and the only meaningful world is that of the prison. The old con has become totally immersed in the prison world. This identification is often the result of years of jailing, but it can result from merely serving too much time. It was mentioned previously that even thieves after spending many years fall into jailing, even though time-doing is their usual pattern. After serving a very long sentence or several long sentences with no extended period between, any criminal will tend to take on the identity of the "old con."

The old con tends to carve out a narrow but orderly existence in prison. He has learned to secure many luxuries and learned to be satisfied with the prison forms of pleasure—e.g., homosexual activities, cards, dominoes, handball, hobbies, and reading. He usually obtains jobs which afford him considerable privileges and leisure time. He often knows many of the prison administrators—the warden, the associate wardens, the captain, and the lieutenants, whom he has known since they were officers and lesser officials.

Often he becomes less active in the prison social world. He retires and becomes relatively docile or apathetic. At times he grows petty and treacherous. There is some feeling that old cons can't be trusted because their "head has become soft" or they have "lost their guts," and are potential "stool pigeons."

The convict identity is very important to the future career of the felon. In the first instance, the acquiring of the taken-for-granted perspective will at least obstruct the releasee's attempts to reorient himself on the outside. More important, the other levels of the identity, if they have been acquired, will continue to influence choices for years afterward. The convict perspective, though it may become submerged after extended outside experiences, will remain operative in its latency state and will often obtrude into civilian life contexts.

The identity of the old con—the perspective, the values and beliefs, and other personality attributes which are acquired after the years of doing time, such as advanced age, adjustment to prison routines, and complete loss of skills required to carry on the normal activities of civilians—will usually make living on the outside impossible. The old con is very often suited for nothing except dereliction on the outside or death in prison.

deviant identity

When a person asks "Who am I?" there are private answers as well as public ones. The private answers—how a person views him/herself—form one's *personal* identity. The public answers— the image others have of the person—provide one's *social* identity. There is sometimes little consistency between the two. Con men, for example, may studiously present social identities that diverge widely from their true, personal identities. Thus they assume social identities that their personal identities, if known, would discredit. This is true for covert deviants generally. When in the company of heterosexuals, for example, the secret homo- sexual may ridicule or condemn homosexuality, or pretend to be interested in the opposite sex, in order to achieve a heterosexual social identity. The task of harmonizing one's personal and social identities is hard enough for conventional people. For certain kinds of deviants, particularly secret deviants, it is even more complex.

A deviant social identity may lead to a deviant personal identity when a person finds it prudent to accept a publicly attributed deviant status. This passive style of bringing personal and social identities together probably produces relatively little identity conflict. When a person identified as a deviant refuses to take on a deviant personal identity, however, greater identity problems are likely to result.

Social identities may be devised by the person or by others. Spies, for example, consciously devise and enact their own deceptive social identities. Public relations people, gossips, and agents of social control, on the other hand, often cast other people into social identities that may or may not conform to their personal identities.

In a complex, urban society where many people relate to a wide assortment of new, previously unknown people, the opportunity for taking on a new social identity comes up all the time. Similarly, the chance of being cast by someone else into a new social identity is also more likely. In addition, the possibility of having multiple social identities, with different identities for different audiences, also arises. In such a society, then, people often find it difficult to develop a single, coherent social identity; they may also find it difficult to harmonize their personal and social identities. In fact, attempts to manage this problem may produce the very deceitfulness that is presumed to be characteris- tic of so many deviants.

Part Four

Because a social identity as a conforming person is usually preferred to a deviant social identity, most deviants need to practice some duplicity. The steady practice of duplicity may enable the deviant to avert conflict between his or her various positions and roles. On the other hand, duplicity may cause such a strain that the deviant gives it up. With regard to the systematic check forger, for example, the need to assume many legitimate social roles and social identities produces a heavy strain; constant impersonations are not easy to maintain. Hence, paradoxically, discovery and arrest actually solve an identity problem for the forger. In prison the forger at least has an authentic social identity. The strains confronting the systematic check forger typify the kinds of identity problems that many deviants must come to terms with in one way or another.

In this part of the book we examine the issue of deviant identity more specifically. First we consider the importance of audiences for a person's identity. Then we look at the ways a person sustains a particular identity. Finally, we consider the conditions under which a person is most likely to change a deviant identity.

AUDIENCE AND IDENTITY

Audiences confirm a person's social identity. A group may accept a person into their midst, thus supporting a particular identity. By accepting a new pledge, for example, a prestigious sorority supports the pledge's social identity as "popular." In other cases a group may show that they want nothing to do with a person, thus supporting another social identity. By excluding a Jewish or a black coed, for example, the same sorority confirms this girl's social identity as a minority group member who cannot expect full acceptance in groups dominated by white Christians. In the case of deviants, one might expect that exclusion from the so-called conventional world would automatically gain a person a deviant social identity and admission into a deviant group. Frequently, however, as noted in Part Three, the underworld has its own system of accepting members and confirming social identity. Thus many people are marginal deviants, who do not really fit into either the conventional world or the deviant world. Child molesters, for example, are stigmatized in the conventional world and are rejected by the criminal underworld as well.

Deviants demonstrate the importance of audiences in shaping and sustaining both personal and social identity. In deviant groups novices often seek the approval of other deviants; thus the novice begins to imitate their behaviors and to define situations as veteran deviants would. Novices begin to appraise their position, behaviors, and self-image mainly through the eyes of the deviant group. To the extent that they want to belong to the group, they learn and abide by the group's rules. In time they come to judge themselves by the group's criteria even when they are not with the group. When this happens, the group has become an effective audience, or reference group, for the person.

MANAGING DEVIANT IDENTITY

In order to sustain a deviant social identity and membership in a deviant group, new members have to incorporate the group's signs and symbols into their own personal styles and to behave according to deviant norms even when they may not especially want to. The novice's deviant identity may then be confirmed by the group. A deviant who fails to learn the appropriate ways probably will not be truly accepted as a member of the group.

Sometimes deviant identities and acts are based on mistaken assumptions about one's audience. For instance, a young sailor may believe that he is expected to be tough, which includes getting drunk and tattooed on his first leave. He may be hesitant to get tattooed, but he may be even more concerned about being ridiculed by his peers. Actually, his buddies may also be hesitant, but each may keep his concern to himself and not realize that his friends feel the same way. Thus social identities can take precedence over personal ones.

Attempts at being a deviant can fail if the audience refuses to confirm the person's deviant social identity. Then there is no effective audience to reward the person's deviant actions or to confirm his/her self-typing. A jack-of-all-trades offender, for instance, may be considered too inept or "unprofessional" to be accepted into more skillful criminal circles. An audience—conformist or deviant—will not confirm the social identity desired by a person who has obviously miscast him/herself, who does not look the part.

Some deviant statuses imply more than one audience, and the various audiences may demand different, sometimes contradictory, roles on the part of the deviant. Deviants with multiple audiences will have problems of identity unless they can clearly understand which audience they are confronting and which role is required at a particular time. It is often the case, for example, that "front ward" patients in mental hospitals are expected by fellow inmates to act "normal," while they are expected by outsiders to act "sick" and in need of treatment.

It should be noted that deviants can often choose among deviant identities, and this is often one facet of managing a deviant identity. This means that there can be "imposters" who sustain deviant identities as well as "imposters" who sustain conventional identities. Some epileptics, for example, try to pass as alcoholics because they see alcoholism as less stigmatized than epilepsy. As long as these pseudo-alcoholics have only limited contact with genuine alcoholics, their secret is probably safe.

To sustain a deviant identity and membership in a deviant group, then, it is necessary to act like other members of the group. Some social conditions are more conducive to this than others. For example, becoming more involved with other deviants and avoiding contact with nondeviants facilitates developing the deviant identity and maintaining the deviant role. It also makes it easier to cast off conventional traits and loyalties. Thus a deviant identity is easier to sustain under these optimum conditions.

THE TRANSFORMATION OF DEVIANT IDENTITY

As suggested above, some deviants have trouble sustaining a deviant identity. Fitting social positions, roles, and self-concepts together is too hard or undesirable. Thus the deviant may face an identity crisis that can become the turning point in his or her deviant career. Nonetheless, it is not necessarily true that most deviants are unhappy and wish to renounce their deviance. Conventional stereotypes of deviants suggest as much, but the facts are otherwise. If people can successfully conceal their deviance, for example, they can continue to enjoy their deviance without "paying the price."

A profound identity crisis usually becomes one of the conditions for transforming a deviant identity back to a more conventional one. Discovery, or recurrent feelings of remorse, can produce the crisis, impelling the person to contemplate making some radical changes in his/her life. In such a crisis the mechanisms that successfully sustain deviant identity usually show signs of breaking down, which in turn intensifies the crisis.

As already noted, assuming and maintaining a deviant identity is not an easy matter. Renouncing one is even more difficult. Even if a deviant experiences an extreme identity crisis, that person may not succeed in transforming his/her deviant identity to a more conventional one. Three factors imperil successful transformation: lack of practice in conventional roles, continued distrust by conventional people, and pressure from fellow deviates to return to their group. Time spent in deviance is time spent away from the conventional world. Legitimate skills may fall into disuse; for example, the alcoholic toolmaker who returns to his craft after years of heavy drinking and unemployment may find that he cannot pick up where he left off. The ex-convict's difficulty in finding work may exemplify the continued suspicion and disapproval that deviants arouse in the larger society. Finally, fellow deviants may press one to continue former deviations; thus the drug addict, on release from a hospital, may be quickly surrounded by former friends who are eager to supply a free fix.

Deviants who want to return to a more conventional way of life ordinarily have the best chance of success if they join a primary group with similar intentions. The best-known example of such a primary group is Alcoholics Anonymous. The group members reward the ex-drinker for making changes toward conventionality, and they confirm his/her new social identity as a nondrinker. These conditions encourage the deviant to return to conventional life. Such social and cultural supports are not available, however, to many deviants who might want to return to conformity.

13 the deviant and his/her audience

One important factor in the development of a deviant identity is the deviant's audience. The audience may consist of other deviants, or it may consist of conventional friends or family. A deviant audience can provide role models—people with whom one can identify. It can also provide a new perspective on deviance and support for deviant ways. A conventional audience, on the other hand, may disapprove of deviance and shame the deviant. Ironically, instead of reforming the deviant, such reactions by conventional audiences may simply reinforce the person's deviance. In any case social identities lie in the eye of the beholder, and audiences play an important role in the development of a deviant identity.

In the first selection Lemert discusses the difference between primary deviance (the initial deviant act or trait) and secondary deviance (the deviant role and identity that develop as a result of people's reaction to the initial deviation). Glaser then shows how people can develop deviant identities by modeling their actions after those of a deviant group. Korn and McCorkle, discussing youthful robbers, describe the conditions under which people do things that none of them really wants to do. Finally, Cameron shows that amateur shoplifters, when they are caught, generally quit shoplifting because neither they nor the people close to them think of them as being "the thieving type."

Primary and Secondary Deviation

EDWIN M. LEMERT

There has been an embarrassingly large number of theories, often without any relationship to a general theory, advanced to account for various specific [deviations] in human behavior. For certain types of [deviance], such as alcoholism, crime, or stuttering, there are almost as many theories as there are writers on these subjects. This has been occasioned in no small way by the preoccupation with the origins of [deviant] behavior and by the fallacy of confusing *original* causes with *effective* causes. All such theories have elements of truth, and the divergent viewpoints they contain can be reconciled with the general theory here if it is granted that original causes or antecedents of deviant behaviors are many and diversified. This holds especially for the psychological processes leading to similar [deviance], but it also holds for the situational concomitants of the initial aberrant conduct. A person may come to use excessive alcohol not only for a wide variety of subjective reasons but also because of diversified situational influences, such as the death of a loved one, business failure, or participating in some sort of organized group activity calling for heavy drinking of liquor. Whatever the original reasons for violating the norms of the community, they are important only for certain research purposes, such as assessing the extent of the "social problem" at a given time or determining the requirements for a rational program of social control. From a narrower sociological viewpoint

. . . deviations are not significant until they are organized subjectively and transformed into active roles and become the social criteria for assigning status. The deviant individuals must react symbolically to their own behavior aberrations and fix them in their sociopsychological patterns. The deviations remain primary deviations or symptomatic and situational as long as they are rationalized or otherwise dealt with as functions of a socially acceptable role. Under such conditions normal and pathological behaviors remain strange and somewhat tensional bedfellows in the same person. Undeniably a vast amount of such segmental and partially integrated [deviant] behavior exists in our society and has impressed many writers in the field of [deviance].

Just how far and for how long a person may go in dissociating his [deviant] tendencies so that they are merely troublesome adjuncts of normally conceived roles is not known. Perhaps it depends upon the number of alternative definitions of the same overt behavior that he can develop. . . . However, if the deviant acts are repetitive and have a high visibility, and if there is a severe societal reaction, which, through a process of identification is incorporated as part of the "me" of the individual, the probability is greatly increased that the integration of existing roles will be disrupted and that reorganization based upon a new role or roles will occur. (The "me" in this context is simply the subjective aspect of the societal reaction.) Reorganization may be the adoption of another normal role in which the tendencies previously defined as ["deviant"] are given a more acceptable social expression. The other general possibility is the assumption of a deviant role, if such exists; or, more rarely, the person may organize an aberrant sect or group in which he creates a special role of his own. *When a person begins to employ his deviant behavior or a role based upon it as a means of defense, attack, or adjustment to the overt and covert problems created by the consequent societal reaction to him, his deviation is secondary.* Objective evidences of this change will be found in the symbolic appurtenances of the new role, in clothes, speech, posture, and mannerisms, which in some cases heighten social visibility, and which in some cases serve as symbolic cues to professionalization.

ROLE CONCEPTIONS OF THE INDIVIDUAL MUST BE REINFORCED BY REACTIONS OF OTHERS

It is seldom that one deviant act will provoke a sufficiently strong societal reaction to bring about secondary deviation, unless in the process of introjection the individual imputes or projects meanings into the social situation which are not present. In this case anticipatory fears are involved. For example, in a culture where a child is taught sharp distinctions between "good" women and "bad" women, a single act of questionable morality might conceivably have a profound meaning for the girl so indulging. However, in the absence of reactions by the person's family, neighbors, or the larger community, reinforcing the tentative "bad-girl" self-definition, it is questionable whether a transition to sec-

ondary deviation would take place. It is also doubtful whether a temporary exposure to a severe punitive reaction by the community will lead a person to identify himself with a [deviant] role, unless, as we have said, the experience is highly traumatic. Most frequently there is a progressive reciprocal relationship between the deviation of the individual and the societal reaction, with a compounding of the societal reaction out of the minute accretions in the deviant behavior, until a point is reached where ingrouping and outgrouping between society and the deviant is manifest.[1] At this point a stigmatizing of the deviant occurs in the form of name calling, labeling, or stereotyping.

The sequence of interaction leading to secondary deviation is roughly as follows: (1) primary deviation; (2) social penalties; (3) further primary deviation; (4) stronger penalties and rejections; (5) further deviation, perhaps with hostilities and resentment beginning to focus upon those doing the penalizing; (6) crisis reached in the tolerance quotient, expressed in formal action by the community stigmatizing of the deviant; (7) strengthening of the deviant conduct as a reaction to the stigmatizing and penalties; (8) ultimate acceptance of deviant social status and efforts at adjustment on the basis of the associated role.

As an illustration of this sequence the behavior of an errant schoolboy can be cited. For one reason or another, let us say excessive energy, the schoolboy engages in a classroom prank. He is penalized for it by the teacher. Later, due to clumsiness, he creates another disturbance and again he is reprimanded. Then, as sometimes happens, the boy is blamed for something he did not do. When the teacher uses the tag "bad boy" or "mischief maker" or other invidious terms, hostility and resentment are excited in

[1] Mead, G., "The Psychology of Punitive Justice," *American Journal of Sociology,* 23, March, 1918, pp. 577–602.

the boy and he may feel that he is blocked in playing the role expected of him. Thereafter, there may be a strong temptation to assume his role in the class as defined by the teacher, particularly when he discovers that there are rewards as well as penalties deriving from such a role. There is, of course, no implication here that such boys go on to become delinquents or criminals, for the mischief-maker role may later become integrated with or retrospectively rationalized as part of a role more acceptable to school authorities.[2] If such a boy continues this unacceptable role and becomes delinquent, the process must be accounted for in the light of the general theory of this volume. There must be a spreading corroboration of a [deviant] self-conception and societal reinforcement at each step in the process.

The most significant personality changes are manifest when societal definitions and their subjective counterpart become generalized. When this happens, the range of major role choices becomes narrowed to one general class.[3] This was very obvious in the case of a young girl who was the daughter of a paroled convict and who was attending a small Middle Western college. She continually argued with herself and with the author, in whom she had confided, that in reality she belonged on the "other side of the railroad tracks" and that her life could be enormously simplified by acquiescing in this verdict and living accordingly. While in her case there was a tendency to dramatize her conflicts, nevertheless there was enough societal reinforcement of her self-conception by the treatment she received in her relationship with her father and on dates with college boys to lend it a painful reality. Once these boys took her home to the shoddy dwelling in a slum area where she lived with her father, who was often in a drunken condition, they abruptly stopped seeing her again or else became sexually presumptive. . . .

---

[2] Evidence for fixed or inevitable sequences from predelinquency to crime is absent. Sutherland, E. H., *Principles of Criminology*, 1939, 4th ed., p. 202.

[3] Sutherland seems to say something of this sort in connection with the development of criminal behavior. *Ibid.*, p. 86.

Role Models and Differential Association

DANIEL GLASER

. . . Slightly paraphrased, Sutherland's last formulation of his theory[1] is as follows: Criminal behavior is learned in interaction with others, principally in intimate personal groups. That which is learned includes techniques, attitudes, and rationalizations. Whether a person's motives and drives are criminal or noncriminal is a function of whether the legal codes have been defined by those around him in a manner favorable to their observance or to their violation. Most people encounter a mixture of these two types of influence. A person will become criminal if his associations result in an excess of definitions favorable to violation of law over definitions unfavorable to violation of law. The influence of such differential association is a function of its frequency, duration, priority, and intensity, in one direction or another. Both criminal and noncriminal behavior is acquired in such association by the same learning mechanisms, and both satisfy the same general human needs and values; but differential association determines the extent to which a person's experience promotes learning and motivation by criminal rather than noncriminal influences.

Sutherland seems to have formulated this theory as a way in which the many actual and alleged correlates of crime, such as poverty, family conflicts, personality disturbance, and slum residence, could be causally related to crime. These conditions, to be factors in the criminality of an individual, must so affect his social relationships as to promote his being influenced by criminals and restrict the influence of noncriminal persons on him. Attention to the social relationships of each person studied, however, would also explain why such correlates of crime as family conflict and poverty also may, in some cases, support noncriminal ambitions. From the standpoint of Sutherland's theory, any correlate of crime must be shown to affect an individual's learning experience if it is to be thought of as having a causative function in his criminality. Sutherland's critics generally overlook this integrating function of his theory and the broad sense in which he uses the phrase "differential association." They misrepresent him when they suggest that he predicted that criminality would result with mechanical certainty in any individual whose contacts with criminals exceed contacts with noncriminals.

Essentially, Sutherland set forth a broad point of view for approaching an understanding of criminals, rather than a simple formula for predicting crime. In

Reprinted by permission of the author and publisher from "The Sociological Approach to Crime and Correction" from a symposium, Crime and Correction, in *Law and Contemporary Problems,* Vol. 23, No. 4 (Autumn, 1958), pp. 688–693, published by the Duke University School of Law, Durham, N.C. Copyright, 1959, by Duke University.

[1] First set forth in Edwin H. Sutherland, *Principles of Criminology* 5–7 (3rd ed. 1939).

modern social-psychological terms, what he seems to have had in mind might more aptly be labeled "differential identification," "differential reference," or even "differential learning." It involves a conception of crime as a subclass of the totality of all deliberate human action, as something to be explained as other so-called "voluntary" behavior is explained. It is based on a social-psychological conception of deliberate action as guided by the actors in accordance with the way in which they have learned to rationalize their actions. Such an approach to understanding behavior is convergent with many developments in psychology and sociology. It is a deterministic conception of crime, since it ascribes a person's anticipations to his learning experience; yet, it is consistent with the legal conception of crime as wilful, for it focuses on decision-making as a phenomenon to be studied. This approach contrasts sharply with explanations for crime in terms of biological drives, unconscious motivation, or pressure of external forces, since such explanations do not as completely trace the connection between the alleged causes and specific, consciously-directed criminal acts.[2]

Sutherland presented his theory in highly abstract form and apart from its illustration. His illustrative chapters on "processes in criminal behavior" and "behavior systems in crime" cogently described the ways in which professional criminals become enculturated in crime, but he did not illustrate the influence of associations opposing crime. This neglect probably reflects the fact that it has been much easier to study criminals than noncriminals, for criminals may be studied conveniently when they are in custody or under supervision. Noncriminals are more difficult to study, as a rule, and excriminals are most difficult (for they seek to hide their past); yet, studying these people may be essential for a more useful understanding of crime. Thus, the most available applications of Sutherland's theory make it appear to be merely the old enculturation explanation for crime, even though its abstract formulation suggests that it might also be a frame of reference for theoretically connecting correlated conditions with specific crimes and for the analysis of noncriminal behavior and correctional processes.

RECENT THEORETICAL EMPHASIS

No more adequate general theory of crime causation has replaced differential association. Several recent developments, however, suggest some of the ways in which such a theory would modify the heritage from Sutherland. The criminology which now seems to be emerging in sociology is one focused on change and operating with a more complex conception of the criminal than that involved in earlier theories. These developments reflect long-term trends in general sociological theory, and they are convergent with some new emphases in the other behavioral sciences. Notable among these trends are: (1) attention to all reference groups—not just membership groups—in tracing social influences on individual behavior; [and] (2) the interpretation of motivation as the way in which a person's representation of the behavioral alternatives which he perceives affects his self-conception and his anticipations. . . .

By "reference groups," we designate any persons or groups from whose standpoint an individual evaluates himself and others. These include both groups in which he is a member and groups to which he does not belong, but to which he aspires, or which, for other reasons,

[2] George M. Kelly, *The Psychology of Personal Constructs* (1955); A. R. Lindesmith and Anselm Strauss, *Social Psychology* (2d ed. 1956).

provide the standpoint from which he views his own situation. The enculturation approach to crime grew out of the study of the influence of groups on the behavior of their members. Reference-group theory helps to account for much of the behavior of individuals who deviate from the expectations of their membership groups, for this theory focuses our attention on all of the groups to which these individuals are oriented. The general conditions under which a person is most likely to evaluate his behavior from the standpoint of groups to which he does not belong include: (1) when the other groups have higher status than his own group; (2) when he is an isolate or a failure in his own group; or (3) when change in group affiliation is not strongly counter to the traditions of his society.[3]

While the term "reference group" is fairly new and the analysis of behavior by tracing the influence both of membership and nonmembership groups receives more emphasis now than formerly, such a common-sense idea is by no means completely new. Early students of the gang, while centering their attention on the influence of that group, also noted that most juvenile delinquents drifted out of gang affiliations and became law-abiding members of society in late adolescence and young adulthood if they became interested in marriage or acquired steady employment. The latter interests involve change of reference from their peers exclusively to older persons of legitimate professions and to stable family members.[4] The Tannenbaum and Sutherland enculturation analyses were significant in showing how the transition from enculturation in delinquent gangs to identification with conventional groups becomes unlikely when extensive involvement in criminal groups alienates a youth from conventional circles and increases his ties with professional criminals. Unfortunately, the effects of being caught and prosecuted may be to make criminals the only group to which a youth will aspire. But the task of corrections may be said to be the promotion of noncriminal reference groups; a prisoner is rehabilitated when this promotion is successful.

The study of the *non*delinquent in high-delinquency areas has been undertaken on an extensive basis in recent years by persons of diverse academic background. The outstanding finding, expressed in general terms, is that the youth who avoids extreme enculturation in delinquency, despite extensive contact with delinquents, generally is the youth who maintains strong bonds with a noncriminal family. Reckless sees the influence of noncriminal figures as giving such a youth a conception of himself as "good" which "insulates" him from all situations in which he may be encouraged to be delinquent.[5] This is consistent with psychoanalytic interpretation: the family gives the boy a strong conventional superego—that is, conscience. The problem for criminological theory is to handle adequately the fact that everyone in our society is exposed to multiple influences, some making for criminality and some

[3] *Cf.* Robert K. Merton, *Social Theory and Social Structure,* cc. 9 and 10 (2d ed. 1957); Turner, "Role-taking, Role-standpoint and Reference Group Behavior," 61 *Am. J. Sociology* 316 (1956), reprinted in L. A. Coser and B. Rosenberg, *Sociological Theory* 272 (1957).

[4] *Cf.* W. F. Whyte, *Street Corner Society* (1943).

[5] *Cf.* Reckless, Dinitz, and Kay, "The Self Component in Potential Delinquency and Potential Non-Delinquency," 22 *Am. Sociological Rev.* 566 (1957); S. and E. Glueck, *Unraveling Juvenile Delinquency* 281 (1950). One of the most sophisticated analyses of the extent of family influence on delinquency is Jackson Toby's statistical analysis of court and census data, "The Differential Impact of Family Disorganization," 22 *Am. Sociological Rev.* 505 (1957).

making for conventionality, some from membership groups and some from perceived groups in which one is not a fully-accepted member. An understanding of behavior change, from noncriminal to criminal and vice versa, requires a theory of behavior which accounts for human inconsistency and, therefore, permits some prediction and control of the range of this inconsistency.

Several preliminary explorations and formulations of a theory of behavior change and inconsistency have been undertaken by sociologists in terms of analysis of motivation and decision-making in individual behavior. One of Sutherland's students, Cressey, posed a crucial problem for differential association theory: How does one explain the conduct of persons who reach adulthood as highly conventional persons and, therefore, are placed in positions of financial trust, but suddenly violate such trust by embezzlement? Cressey's interviews with 133 embezzlers and his examination of life histories on over 200 other cases of embezzlement led him to an explanation which seemed to fit every case.[6] He found, first, that trusted persons committed embezzlement only when faced by a financial problem which they could not divulge to others. Nevertheless, he found that in spite of need and opportunity for the crime, the offense was never committed until the embezzler had developed a rationalization which legitimated the offense to him. When frustrated humans perceive a solution to their problems, they seem unable to grasp the solution until they can represent it to themselves in such a manner as to permit them to maintain a favorable conception of themselves. In Cressey's cases, differential association in terms of membership affiliations rarely seemed to explain this reinterpretation of criminal behavior. A shift of perspective, often by taking the standpoint of new reference groups, was needed to change the trustworthy person into an embezzler.

In view of the evidence that most delinquent youth have some acceptance of conventional values, Gresham M. Sykes and David Matza suggest that delinquents must "neutralize" their conventional ties and moral scruples before they can commit delinquency.[7] They illustrate as common "techniques of neutralization" a variety of rationalizations, such as blaming the theft on pressures from bad parents or on misfortune, defining the victim as a worthless person who deserves to be victimized, justifying the offense in terms of loyalty to a friend, or noting the faults of those who condemn the delinquency. The process of rationalization reconciles crime or delinquency with conventionality; it permits a person to maintain a favorable conception of himself, while acting in ways which others see as inconsistent with a favorable self-conception. In this analysis of motivation by the verbal representation of the world with which a person justifies his behavior, sociologists are converging with many psychologists.[8] This seems to

---

[6] Donald R. Cressey, *Other People's Money* (1953).

[7] Sykes and Matza, "Techniques of Neutralization: A Theory of Delinquency," 22 *Am. Sociological Rev.* 664 (1957). These authors, unfortunately, neglect the influence of delinquent subcultures in transmitting and reinforcing these very techniques of neutralization which permit delinquents to adhere simultaneously to delinquent and nondelinquent cultures. Thus, these authors may exaggerate the incompatibility of their views with those propounded in Albert K. Cohen, *Delinquent Boys: The Culture of the Gang* (1955).

[8] For psychological formulation, see Kelly, *op. cit. supra* note 2. Considerable convergence with the multiple-reference and rationalization analysis of sociologists also is apparent in the psychoanalytic work, Fritz Redl and David Wineman, *Children Who Hate* (1951).

be individualistic analysis of behavior, but the so-called "symbolic interactionist" viewpoint is gaining acceptance, and it sees individual human thought as essentially a social interaction process: the individual "talks to himself" in thinking and reacts to his own words and gestures in "working himself" into an emotional state in much the same manner as he does in discussion or in emotional interaction with others.[9]

---

[9] Cf. Lindesmith and Strauss, op. cit. supra note 2; Anselm Strauss, The Social Psychology of George Herbert Mead (1956); George H. Mead, Mind, Self, and Society (1934).

The Reluctant Robbers

RICHARD R. KORN
LLOYD W. McCORKLE

The significance of the interpersonal context of motivation is underscored by the next example to be cited. In his classic work, *The Gang,* Thrasher writes about a group of college students, who, one night, for reasons which none of them could explain, suddenly decided to rob a post-office. Thrasher presents the story in the form of a verbatim report by one of the participants.

We three college students—Mac, Art, and Tom—were rooming together while attending V——— University, one of the oldest colleges in the South. On the day of our crime all three of us spent over three hours in the library—really working. That was on Sunday and our crime was committed at 1:30 that night (or rather Monday morning).

The conversation began with a remark about the numerous recent bank failures in the state, probably stimulated by one of us glancing at a map of the state. It then shifted to discussion of a local bank that had closed its doors the day before. Tom, who worked at the post-office occasionally as special mail clerk, happened to mention that a sack containing a large amount of money had been received at the post-office that afternoon, consigned to a local bank that feared a run.

The conversation then turned to the careless way in which the money was handled at the office—a plain canvas sack thrown into an open safe. We discussed the ease with which a thief could get into the building and steal the money. Tom drew a plan showing the desk at which the only clerk worked and the location of the only gun in the office. At first the conversation was entirely confined to how easily criminals might manage to steal the money. Somehow it shifted to a personal basis: as to how easily we might get the money. This shift came so naturally that even the next morning we were unable to decide when and by whom the first vital remark had been made.

A possible plan was discussed as to how we might steal the package. Tom could go to the office and gain admittance on the pretense of looking for an important letter. Then Art and I, masked and armed, could rush in, tie Tom and the clerk, and make off with the package. We had lost sight of the fact that the package contained money. We were simply discussing the possibility of playing an exciting prank with no thought of actually committing it. We had played many harmless pranks and had discussed them in much the same way before; but the knowledge that there was danger in this prank made it a subject to linger over.

After about an hour and a half of talk, I started to take off my shoes. As I unlaced them, I thought of how it looked as if I were the one to kill our interesting project. I foolishly said something to the effect that if Tom was going down town, I thought I would write a letter that was already overdue. Tom was anxiously awaiting a letter that should be in that night. He suggested that I go down also as it was a very decent night. I consented and Art

Reprinted from Chapter 14, "Toward the Clarification of Criminological Theory," from *Criminology and Penology* by Richard R. Korn and Lloyd W. McCorkle. Copyright © 1959 by Holt, Rinehart and Winston, Inc., pp. 336–339. Reprinted by permission of Holt, Rinehart and Winston, Inc.

decided to join us. I sat down and wrote the letter—meanwhile we continued our talk about the money package.

My letter finished, something seemed to change. We found further inaction impossible: we had either to rob the post-office or go to bed. Tom brought out his two guns; I hunted up a couple of regular plain handkerchiefs, and Art added some rope to the assortment. At the time we were still individually and collectively playing a game with ourselves. Each of us expected one of the other two to give the thing the horse laugh and suggest going to bed and letting the letters wait till morning. But it seemed that we forgot everything—our position in school, our families and friends, the danger to us and to our folks. Our only thought was to carry out that prank. We all made our preparations more or less mechanically. Our minds were in a daze.

Putting on our regular overcoats and caps, we left the rooms quietly. On the way down town we passed the night patrolman without any really serious qualms. Tom entered the post-office as was his usual custom, being a sub-clerk, and Art and I crept up to the rear door. Tom appeared at a window with his hat, a signal that there were no reasons why our plan would not be effective. At the door, in full illumination of a light, we arranged our handkerchiefs over our faces and took our guns out of our pockets. We were ready.

"Have you enough guts to go through with this thing?" I asked, turning to Art, who was behind me.

"If you have," he answered.

Frankly I felt that I had gone far enough, but for some unknown reason I did not throw out a remark that would have ended it all then and there. And Art didn't. He later said that he was just too scared to suggest anything. We were both, it seems, in a sort of daze.

Tom opened the door and we followed our plan out to the end. There was no active resistance by the regular night man.

Then after we left the office with thousands of dollars in our hands we did not realize all that it meant. Our first words were not about getting the money. They were about the fact that our prank (and it was still that to us) had been successful. When we reached our rooms, having hidden the money in an abandoned dredger, the seriousness of the thing began to penetrate our minds. For an hour or so we lay quietly and finally settled on a plan that seemed safe in returning the money without making our identity known. Then I went to sleep.[1]

This incident, reported by one of the participants, described a cooperative group activity directed toward a criminal object. What is interesting about the incident is that none of the participants was a criminal, that each was secretly opposed to the undertaking, and that all were personally disinterested in the goal. Why, then, did they do it?

The narrative suggests several clues. In the first place, each was reluctant to occupy the humiliating role of the one who "backs out." Apparently, then, though each was afraid, the prospect of humiliation was more threatening. Moreover, in order to avoid the appearance of reluctance, each found it necessary to keep up the pretense of his own willingness—at the same time nourishing the secret hope that *somebody else* would realize that things were going too far and back out. At this point it is probable that each still felt that the others were merely testing him, and that nobody really intended to go through with it. Then, as preparations advanced, the security of this belief began to wane and each boy began to believe that the others might not be fooling after all. This served to isolate each in the intolerable position of the only one who would be chicken-hearted. When the illusion of group daring reaches this level of mutual deception, there could be no turning back. In this manner, with the need to conceal their mounting anxiety forcing them to shows

[1] Frederic M. Thrasher, *The Gang* (Chicago: The University of Chicago Press, 1936), pp. 300–303.

of increased bravado, the boys literally pushed each other over the threshold of fantasy into the criminal act.

Thus there arose a situation of group motivation, based on an illusion and contrary to the actual wishes of each participant. A condition of group motivation exists *when each member is behaving in accordance with the same interpretation of what is expected of him*—whether or not this is in accord with his own wishes and regardless of the correctness of the interpretation. Each of the unwilling bandits was behaving *as if* the others were expecting him to participate. (Actually, they were hoping he would back out.) The illusion went further: though each personally dreaded participating, each was eventually convinced that the others were willing. The curious thing was that none of the group, at any point, put any direct pressure on the others to go along. Each was coerced by a similar image of what the others expected and each dreaded an imagined group reaction.

What was it that committed each to conform to this imaginary expectation in violation of his own wishes? A tentative answer might be that conformity involved certain psychological rewards; nonconformity, certain penalties. Apparently, in the mutual roles in which they found themselves *the way each boy felt about himself was dependent on how he imagined the others were feeling about him.*

Here again, the group authority was exercised by each member over himself. The strength of this authority was related to the extent to which each one's self-evaluation was open to influence by the real or imagined attitudes of the others. Each was intent on fulfilling the expectations of his role, on conforming to its conceived requirements. The behavioral requirements of the role were, as it turned out, secondary, since none of the boys actually desired to engage in the activity itself. Thus the commitment was not to the *act* or to the *goal* of the act (the money), but rather to the *group expectations*—which, in the given situation, ordained that each take the role of a fearless, daring character. In another situation the usages of this group might have cast the members in different roles, ordaining different responses.

Identity and the Shoplifter

MARY OWEN CAMERON

It seems probable that most adult pilferers start their careers as children or adolescents in groups where the techniques of successful pilfering are learned from other more experienced children. Later as group activity is abandoned some of the group members continue the practices they learned as adolescents. The lavish displays of merchandise which department stores exhibit to encourage "impulse buying" are, for the experienced pilferer, there for the taking.

Adult women pilferers, generally belonging to families of rather modest income, enter department stores with a strong sense of the limitations of their household budgets. They do not steal merchandise which they can rationalize purchasing: household supplies, husband's clothes, children's wear. But beautiful and luxury goods for their personal use can be purchased legitimately only if some other member of the family is deprived. Although pilferers often have guilt feelings about their thefts, it still seems to them less wrong to steal from a rich store than to take from the family budget. Pilferers seem to be, thus, narcissistic individuals in that they steal for their own personal use, but, on the other hand, they do not use the limited family income for their own luxury goods.

Pilferers differ in one outstanding respect, at least, from other thieves: They generally do not think of themselves as thieves. In fact, even when arrested, they resist strongly being pushed to admit their behavior is theft. This became very clear as I observed a number of interrogations of shoplifters by the store detective staff, and it was supported in conversations with the detectives who drew on their own wider experience. It is quite often difficult for the store staff to convince the arrested person that he has actually been arrested, even when the detectives show their licenses and badges. Again and again store police explain to pilferers that they are under arrest as thieves, that they will, in the normal course of events, be taken in a police van to jail, held in jail until bond is raised, and tried in a court before a judge and sentenced. Much of the interview time of store detectives is devoted to establishing this point; in making the pilferer understand that what happens to him from the time of his arrest is a legal question, but it is still a question for decision, first of all, by the store staff.

Store detectives use the naivete of pilferers as an assistance in arrest procedures while the pilferer is in the presence of legitimate customers on the floor of the store. The most tactful approach possible is used. The store detective will say, for example, "I represent the store office, and I'm afraid the office will have to see what's in your shopping bag. Would you care to come with me, please?" If the pilferer protests, the detective adds, "You wouldn't want to be embarrassed in front of all these people, would you? In the office we can talk things over in private."

Edwards states that the method of making an arrest is important in preventing excitement and even disorder.

A gentle approach will usually disarm any shoplifter, amateur or professional, while a rough seizure or loud accusation may immediately put him on the defensive. At other times it may result in a nervous or hysterical condition accompanied by an involuntary discharge which may be embarrassing to both the arrestor and the arrested.[1]

Inbau adds the thought that the gentle approach is helpful too in forestalling suits for false arrest.

The finesse with which defendant accosts plaintiff is a definite factor also affecting the temper with which the court approaches a case. The defendant acting in good faith with probable cause, whose attitude is quiet, non-threatening, and deferential to the plaintiff's feelings can weather an honest mistake much more cheaply than otherwise. At the most it may induce a court to find there was no imprisonment at all. At the least, it will relieve defendant of punitive damages and reduce the amount of actual damages.[2]

The "deference" of the arresting detective combined with the already existing rationalizations of the pilferer sustain in him the belief that whereas his behavior might be reprehensible, the objects taken were, after all, not of great value, he would be glad to pay for them and be on his way. "Yes, I took the dress," one woman sobbed as she was being closely interrogated, "but that doesn't mean I'm a thief."

Arrest forces the pilferer to think of himself as a thief. The interrogation procedure of the store is specifically and consciously aimed at breaking down any illusions the shoplifter may have that his behavior is regarded as merely "naughty" or "bad." The breakdown of illusions is, to the store detective staff, both a goal in itself and a means of establishing the fact that each innocent-appearing pilferer, is not in fact, a professional thief "putting on an act." In the interrogation the shoplifter is searched for other stolen merchandise and for identification papers. Pockets and pocketbooks are thoroughly examined. All papers, letters, tickets, bills, etc., are read in detail in spite of considerable protest from the arrested person. Each person is made to explain everything he has with him. If suspect items such as public locker keys, pawn tickets, etc., are found, he will have to explain very thoroughly indeed and agree to have the locker examined and the pawned merchandise seen to avoid formal charge. In any event, once name, address, and occupation have been established (and for women, the maiden name and names in other marriages), the file of names and identifying material of all persons who have, in the past years, been arrested in any of the State Street department stores is consulted. The shoplifter is questioned at length if similarities of names or other identifying data are encountered.

While identification and prior record are being checked, store detectives, persons in charge of refunds, and even experienced sales clerks may be summoned to look at the arrested person to determine if he has been previously suspected of stealing merchandise or has been noted as behaving suspiciously.

In the course of all this investigation, it becomes increasingly clear to the pil-

[1] Loren Edwards, *Shoplifting and Shrinkage Protection for Stores* (Springfield, Ill.: Charles C Thomas, 1958), p. 134.

[2] Inbau, Fred E., "Protection and Recapture of Merchandise from Shoplifters," *Illinois Law Review*. Vol. 46, No. 6, 1952.

ferer that he is considered a thief and is in imminent danger of being hauled into court and publicly exhibited as such. This realization is often accompanied by a dramatic change in attitudes and by severe emotional disturbance. Occasionally even hysterical semi-attempts at suicide result.

The professional shoplifter who has been arrested and knows he is recognized, on the other hand, behaves quite differently. He does, of course, make every effort possible to talk his way out of the situation. But once he finds that this is impossible, he accepts jail and its inconveniences as a normal hazard of his trade.

"This is a nightmare," said one woman pilferer who had been formally charged with stealing an expensive handbag. "It can't be happening to me! Why, oh why can't I wake up and find that it isn't so," she cried later as she waited at a store exit, accompanied by a city and a store policeman, for the city police van to arrive. "Whatever will I do? Please make it go away," she pleaded with the officer. "I'll be disgraced forever. I can never look anyone in the face again."

Pilferers expect no "in-group" support for their behavior. As they become aware of the possible serious consequences of their arrest (trial, jail, etc.), pilferers obviously feel isolated from all supporting relationships. Store detectives report that the most frequent question women ask is, "Will my husband have to know about this?" Men, they say, express immediate fear that their employers will be informed of their arrest when questions about employment are raised. Children are apprehensive of parental reaction. Edwards says,

The composure of juveniles being detained has never ceased to amaze me, that is, until notified that they must tell a parent of their misdemeanor. Then the tears flow and pleadings begin. The interviewer must be firm in his denial that notification will "kill" the parent, and he must sell the child on the idea that any deviation from accepted practice must be discussed with the person most interested in his welfare.[3]

Pilferers feel that if their family or friends learn about their arrest they will be thoroughly disgraced. The fear, shame, and remorse expressed by arrested pilferers could not be other than genuine and a reflection of their appraisal of the attitudes they believe others will take toward them. One woman was observed who, thoroughly shaken as the realization of her predicament began to appear to her, interrupted her protestations of innocence from time to time, overwhelmed at the thought of how some particular person in her "in-group" would react to her arrest. Her conversation with the interrogator ran somewhat as follows: "I didn't intend to take the dress. I just wanted to see it in daylight. [She had stuffed it into a shopping bag and carried it out of the store.] Oh, what will my husband do? I *did* intend to pay for it. It's all a mistake. Oh, my God, what will my mother say! I'll be glad to pay for it. See, I've got the money with me. Oh, my children! They can't find out I've been *arrested*! I'd never be able to face them again."

Pilferers not only expect no in-group support, but they feel that they have literally *no* one to turn to. The problem of being embroiled in a wholly unfamiliar legal situation is obviously not only frightening but unexpected. Apparently they had anticipated being reprimanded; they had not anticipated being searched by a licensed detective, identified, etc., and on the whole, placed in a position in which the burden of argument for keeping out of jail is theirs.

The contrast in behavior between the pilferer and the recognized and self-

[3] Edwards, *op. cit.*, pp. 135–136.

admitted thief is striking. The experienced thief either already knows what to do or knows precisely where and how to find out. His emotional reactions may involve anger directed at himself or at features in the situation around him, but he is not at a loss for reactions. He follows the prescribed modes of behavior, and knows, either because of prior experience or through the vicarious experiences of acquaintances, what arrest involves by way of obligations and rights. He has some familiarity with bonding practice and either already has or knows how to find a lawyer who will act for him.

Because the adult pilferer does not think of himself, prior to his arrest, as a thief and can conceive of no in-group support for himself in that role, his arrest forces him to reject the role (at least insofar as department store shoplifting is concerned). The arrest procedure, even though not followed by prosecution, is in itself sufficient to cause him to redefine his situation. He is, of course, informed that subsequent arrest by any store will be followed by immediate prosecution and probably by a considerable jail sentence. But since this does not act as a deterrent to the self-admitted thief nor

could this kind of admonition deter the compulsive neurotic, neither the fear of punishment nor the objective severity of the punishment in itself is the crucial point in relation to the change from criminal to law-abiding behavior. Rather the threat to the person's system of values and prestige relationships is involved. Social scientists who have investigated criminal activities which have subcultural support are unanimous in pointing out the persistence of criminal activity, the high rate of recidivism and the resistance to reform shown by law violators. Pilfering seems to be the other side of the coin. Not having the support of a criminal subculture, pilferers are very "reformable" individuals. If the findings of this study are substantiated by studies of other offenses in which the offenders are similarly without support of a criminal subculture, there would be a strong argument in favor of keeping pilferers out of jail lest they receive there the kinds of knowledge and emotional support they need to become "successful" commercial thieves. Crime prevention would seem best achieved by helping the law violators retain their self-image of respectability while making it clear to them that a second offense will really mean disgrace.

14 | *managing deviant identity*

Once a deviant identity has been acquired, problems can arise in managing it. Deviants must decide how much to integrate their social identities with their personal identities in various social situations. With other deviants it is often wise to be open about one's deviance; with nondeviants it is seldom so. How deviants manage their deviant identities affects how they fare in their deviant careers—how long their careers last, how successful they are, and whether and how they can ever terminate these careers.

In the first reading Goffman shows how deviants may hide their deviance by managing the information people have about them. Sykes and Matza then discuss how juvenile delinquents justify their actions. Reiss describes how teenage youths can engage in homosexual activity without developing a homosexual identity. Erikson then describes how mental patients manage the problem of contradictory role expectations. Finally, Lemert shows how check forgers are required to assume multiple roles, with resulting strain on their personal identities.

The Management of Spoiled Identity

ERVING GOFFMAN

THE DISCREDITED AND THE DISCREDITABLE

When there is a discrepancy between an individual's actual social identity and his virtual one, it is possible for this fact to be known to us before we normals contact him, or to be quite evident when he presents himself before us. He is a discredited person. . . . We are likely to give no open recognition to what is discrediting of him, and while this work of careful disattention is being done, the situation can become tense, uncertain, and ambiguous for all participants, especially the stigmatized one.

The cooperation of a stigmatized person with normals in acting as if his known differentness were irrelevant and not attended to is one main possibility in the life of such a person. However, when his differentness is not immediately apparent, and is not known beforehand (or at least known by him to be known to the others), when in fact his is a discreditable, not a discredited, person, then the second main possibility in his life is to be found. The issue is not that of managing tension generated during social contacts, but rather that of managing information about his failing. To display or not to display; to tell or not to tell; to let on or not to let on; to lie or not to lie; and in each case, to whom, how, when, and where. For example, while the mental patient is in the hospital, and when he is with adult members of his own family, he is faced with being treated tactfully as if he were sane when there is known to be some doubt, even though he may not have any; or he is treated as insane, when he knows this is not just. But for the ex-mental patient the problem can be quite different; it is not that he must face prejudice against himself, but rather that he must face unwitting acceptance of himself by individuals who are prejudiced against persons of the kind he can be revealed to be. Wherever he goes his behavior will falsely confirm for the other that they are in the company of what in effect they demand but may discover they haven't obtained, namely, a mentally untainted person like themselves. By intention or in effect the ex-mental patient conceals information about his real social identity, receiving and accepting treatment based on false suppositions concerning himself. It is this second general issue, the management of undisclosed discrediting information about self, that I am focusing on in these

Reprinted from Erving Goffman, *Stigma: Notes on the Management of Spoiled Identity,* pp. 41–48, © 1963. Reprinted by permission of Prentice-Hall, Inc., Englewood Cliffs, New Jersey.

notes, in brief, "passing." The concealment of creditable facts—reverse passing—of course occurs, but is not relevant here.[1]

SOCIAL INFORMATION

The information of most relevance in the study of stigma has certain properties. It is information about an individual. It is about his more or less abiding characteristics, as opposed to the moods, feelings, or intents that he might have at a particular moment. The information, as well as the sign through which it is conveyed, is reflexive and embodied; that is, it is conveyed by the very person it is about, and conveyed through bodily expression in the immediate presence of those who receive the expression. Information possessing all of these properties I will here call "social." Some signs that convey social information may be frequently and steadily available, and routinely sought and received; these signs may be called "symbols."[2]

The social information conveyed by any particular symbol may merely confirm what other signs tell us about the individual, filling out our image of him in a redundant and unproblematic way. Some lapel buttons, attesting the social club membership, are examples, as are male wedding rings in some contexts.

However, the social information conveyed by a symbol can establish a special claim to prestige, honor, or desirable class position—a claim that might not otherwise be presented or, if otherwise presented, then not automatically granted. Such a sign is popularly called a "status symbol," although the term "prestige symbol" might be more accurate, the former term being more suitably employed when a well-organized social position of some kind is the referent. Prestige symbols can be contrasted to *stigma symbols,* namely, signs which are especially effective in drawing attention to a debasing identity discrepancy, breaking up what would otherwise be a coherent overall picture, with a consequent reduction in our valuation of the individual. The shaved head of female collaborators in World War II is an example, as is an habitual solecism through which someone affecting middle class manner and dress repeatedly employs a word incorrectly or repeatedly mispronounces it.

In addition to prestige symbols and stigma symbols, one further possibility is to be found, namely, a sign that tends—in fact or hope—to break up an otherwise coherent picture but in this case in a positive direction desired by the actor, not so much establishing a new claim as throwing severe doubt on the validity of the virtual one. I shall refer here to *disidentifiers.* One example is the "good

[1] For one instance of reverse passing, see "H. E. R. Cules," "Ghost-Writer and Failure," in P. Toynbee, ed., *Underdogs* (London: Weidenfeld and Nicolson, 1961), Chap. 2, pp. 30–39. There are many other examples. I knew a physician who was careful to refrain from using external symbols of her status, such as car-license tags, her only evidence of profession being an identification carried in her wallet. When faced with a public accident in which medical service was already being rendered the victim, or in which the victim was past helping, she would, upon examining the victim at a distance from the circle around him, quietly go her way without announcing her competence. In these situations she was what might be called a female impersonator.

[2] The difference between mood information and other kinds of information is treated in G. Stone, "Appearance and the Self," in A. Rose, *Human Behavior and Social Processes* (Boston: Houghton Mifflin, 1962), pp. 86–118. See also E. Goffman, *The Presentation of Self in Everyday Life* (New York: Doubleday & Co., Anchor Books, 1959), pp. 24–25.

English" of an educated northern Negro visiting the South[3]; another is the turban and mustache affected by some urban lower class Negroes.[4] A study of illiterates provides another illustration:

Therefore, when goal orientation is pronounced or imperative and there exists a high probability that definition as illiterate is a bar to the achievement of the goal, the illiterate is likely to try to "pass" as literate. . . . The popularity in the group studied of windowpane lenses with heavy horn frames ("bop glasses") may be viewed as an attempt to emulate the stereotype of the businessman-teacher-young intellectual and especially the high status jazz musician.[5]

A New York specialist in the arts of vagrancy provides still another illustration:

After seven-thirty in the evening, in order to read a book in Grand Central or Penn Station, a person either has to wear horn-rimmed glasses or look exceptionally prosperous. Anyone else is apt to come under surveillance. On the other hand, newspaper readers never seem to attract attention and even the seediest vagrant can sit in Grand Central all night without being molested if he continues to read a paper.[6]

Note that in this discussion of prestige symbols, stigma symbols, and disidentifiers, signs have been considered which routinely convey social information. These symbols must be distinguished from fugitive signs that have not been institutionalized as information carriers. When such signs make claims to prestige, one can call them points; when they discredit tacit claims, one can call them slips.

Some signs carrying social information, being present, first of all, for other reasons, have only an overlay of informational function. There are stigma symbols that provide examples: the wrist markings which disclose that an individual has attempted suicide; the arm pock marks of drug addicts; the handcuffed wrists of convicts in transit[7]; or black eyes when worn in public by females, as a writer on prostitution suggests:

"Outside [the prison where she now is] I'd be in the soup with it. Well, you know how it is: the law sees a chick with a shiner figures she's up to something. Bull figures maybe in the life. Next thing trails her around. Then maybe bang! busted."[8]

Other signs are designed by man solely for the purpose of conveying social information, as in the case of insignia of military rank. It should be added that the significance of the underlay of a sign can become reduced over time, becoming, at the extreme, merely vestigial, even while the informational function of the activity remains constant or increases in importance. Further, a sign that appears to be present for non-informational reasons may sometimes be manufactured with malice aforethought solely because of its informing function, as when dueling scars were carefully planned and inflicted.

Signs conveying social information vary according to whether or not they are congenital, and, if not, whether, once employed, they become a permanent part

---

[3] G. J. Fleming, "My Most Humiliating Jim Crow Experience," *Negro Digest* (June, 1954), pp. 67–68.

[4] B. Wolfe, "Ecstatic in Blackface," *Modern Review*, III (1950), p. 204.

[5] H. Freeman and G. Kassebaum, "The Illiterate in America," *Social Forces*, XXXIV (1956), p. 372.

[6] E. Love, *Subways Are for Sleeping* (New York: Harcourt, Brace & World, 1957), p. 28.

[7] A. Heckstall-Smith, *Eighteen Months* (London: Allan Wingate, 1954), p. 43.

[8] T. Rubin, *In the Life* (New York: The Macmillan Company, 1961), p. 69.

of the person. (Skin color is congenital; a brand mark or maiming is permanent but not congenital; a convict's head-shave is neither congenital nor permanent.) More important, impermanent signs solely employed to convey social information may or may not be employed against the will of the informant; when they are, they tend to be stigma symbols.[9] Later it will be necessary to consider stigma symbols that are voluntarily employed.

It is possible for signs which mean one thing to one group to mean something else to another group, the same category being designated but differently characterized. For example, the shoulder patches that prison officials require escape-prone prisoners to wear[10] can come to mean one thing to guards, in general negative, while being a mark of pride for the wearer relative to his fellow prisoners. The uniform of an officer may be a matter of pride to some, to be worn on every possible occasion; for other officers, weekends may represent a time when they can exercise their choice and wear mufti, passing as civilians. Similarly, while the obligation to wear the school cap in town may be seen as a privilege by some boys, as will the obligation to wear a uniform on leave by "other ranks," still there will be wearers who feel that the social information conveyed thereby is a means of ensuring control and discipline over them when they are off duty and off the premises.[11] So, too, during the eighteen hundreds in California, the absence of a pigtail (queue) on a Chinese man signified for Occidentals a degree of acculturation, but to fellow-Chinese a question would be raised as to respectability—specifically, whether or not the individual had served a term in prison where cutting off of the queue was obligatory; loss of queue was for a time, then, very strongly resisted.[12]

---

[9] In his *American Notes,* written on the basis of his 1842 trip, Dickens records in his chapter on slavery some pages of quotations from local newspapers regarding lost and found slaves. The identifications contained in these advertisements provide a full range of identifying signs. First, there are relatively stable features of the body that in context can incidentally provide partial or full positive identification: age, sex, and scarrings (these resulting from shot and knife wounds, from accidents, and from lashings). Self-admitted name is also provided, though usually, of course, only the first name. Finally, stigma symbols are often cited, notably branded initials and cropped ears. These symbols communicate the social identity of slave but, unlike iron bands around the neck or leg, also communicate something more narrow than that, namely, ownership by a particular master. Authorities then had two concerns about an apprehended Negro: whether or not he was a runaway slave, and, if he was, to whom did he belong.

[10] See G. Dendrickson and F. Thomas, *The Truth About Dartmoor* (London: Victor Gollancz, 1954), p. 55, and F. Norman, *Bang to Rights* (London: Secker and Warburg, 1958), p. 125. The use of this type of symbol is well presented in E. Kogon, *The Theory and Practice of Hell* (New York: Berkley Publishing Corp., n.d.), pp. 41–42, where he specifies the markings used in concentration camps to identify differentially political prisoners, second offenders, criminals, Jehovah's Witnesses, "shiftless elements," Gypsies, Jews, "race defilers," foreign nationals (according to nation), feeble-minded, and so forth. Slaves on the Roman slave market also were often labeled as to nationality; see M. Gordon, "The Nationality of Slaves Under the Early Roman Empire," in M. I. Finley, ed., *Slavery in Classical Antiquity* (Cambridge: Heffer, 1960), p. 171.

[11] T. H. Pear, *Personality, Appearance and Speech* (London: George Allen and Unwin, 1957), p. 58.

[12] A. McLeod, *Pigtails and Gold Dust* (Caldwell, Idaho: Caxton Printers, 1947), p. 28. At times religious-historical significance was also attached to wearing the queue; see *ibid.*, p. 204.

Signs carrying social information vary of course as to reliability. Distended capillaries on the cheek and nose, sometimes called "venous stigmata" with more aptness than meant, can be and are taken as indicating alcoholic excess. However, teetotalers can exhibit the same symbol for other psychological reasons, thereby giving rise to suspicions about themselves which aren't justified, but with which they must deal nonetheless.

A final point about social information must be raised; it has to do with the informing character of the "with" relationship in our society. To be "with" someone is to arrive at a social occasion in his company, walk with him down a street, be a member of his party in a restaurant, and so forth. The issue is that in certain circumstances the social identity of those an individual is with can be used as a source of information concerning his own social identity, the assumption being that he is what the others are. The extreme, perhaps, is the situation in criminal circles: a person wanted for arrest can legally contaminate anyone he is seen with, subjecting them to arrest on suspicion. (A person for whom there is a warrant is therefore said "to have smallpox," and his criminal disease is said to be "catching.")[13] In any case, an analysis of how people manage the information they convey about themselves will have to consider how they deal with the contingencies of being seen "with" particular others.

[13] See D. Maurer, *The Big Con* (New York: Pocket Books, 1949), p. 298.

On Neutralizing Delinquent Self-images

GRESHAM M. SYKES
DAVID MATZA

THE DENIAL OF RESPONSIBILITY

In so far as the delinquent can define himself as lacking responsibility for his deviant actions, the disapproval of self or others is sharply reduced in effectiveness as a restraining influence. As Justice Holmes has said, even a dog distinguishes between being stumbled over and being kicked, and modern society is no less careful to draw a line between injuries that are unintentional, i.e., where responsibility is lacking, and those that are intentional. As a technique of neutralization, however, the denial of responsibility extends much further than the claim that deviant acts are an "accident" or some similar negation of personal accountability. It may also be asserted that delinquent acts are due to forces outside of the individual and beyond his control such as unloving parents, bad companions, or a slum neighborhood. In effect, the delinquent approaches a "billiard ball" conception of himself in which he sees himself as helplessly propelled into new situations. From a psychodynamic viewpoint, this orientation toward one's own actions may represent a profound alienation from self, but it is important to stress the fact that interpretations of responsibility are cultural constructs and not merely idiosyncratic beliefs. The similarity between this mode of justifying illegal behavior assumed by the delinquent and the implications of a "sociological" frame of reference or a "humane" jurisprudence is readily apparent.[1] It is not the validity of this orientation that concerns us here, but its function of deflecting blame attached to violations of social norms and its relative independence of a particular personality structure.[2] By learning to view himself as more acted upon than acting, the delinquent prepares the way for deviance from the dominant normative system without the necessity of a frontal assault on the norms themselves.

THE DENIAL OF INJURY

A second major technique of neutralization centers on the injury or harm involved in the delinquent act. The criminal law has long made a distinction between crimes which are *mala in se* and

Reprinted from "Techniques of Neutralization: A Theory of Delinquency" in *American Sociological Review*, Vol. 22 (December, 1957), pp. 667–670, by permission of the authors and publisher.

[1] A number of observers have wryly noted that many delinquents seem to show a surprising awareness of sociological and psychological explanations for their behavior and are quick to point out the causal role of their poor environment.

[2] It is possible, of course, that certain personality structures can accept some techniques of neutralization more readily than others, but this question remains largely unexplored.

mala prohibita—that is between acts that are wrong in themselves and acts that are illegal but not immoral—and the delinquent can make the same kind of distinction in evaluating the wrongfulness of his behavior. For the delinquent, however, wrongfulness may turn on the question of whether or not anyone has clearly been hurt by his deviance, and this matter is open to a variety of interpretations. Vandalism, for example, may be defined by the delinquent simply as "mischief"—after all, it may be claimed, the persons whose property has been destroyed can well afford it. Similarly, auto theft may be viewed as "borrowing," and gang fighting may be seen as a private quarrel, an agreed upon duel between two willing parties, and thus of no concern to the community at large. We are not suggesting that this technique of neutralization, labelled the denial of injury, involves an explicit dialetic. Rather, we are arguing that the delinquent frequently, and in a hazy fashion, feels that his behavior does not really cause any great harm despite the fact that it runs counter to law. Just as the link between the individual and his acts may be broken by the denial of responsibility, so may the link between acts and their consequences be broken by the denial of injury. Since society sometimes agrees with the delinquent, e.g., in matters such as truancy, "pranks," and so on, it merely reaffirms the idea that the delinquent's neutralization of social controls by means of qualifying the norms is an extension of common practice rather than a gesture of complete opposition.

THE DENIAL OF THE VICTIM

Even if the delinquent accepts the responsibility for his deviant actions and is willing to admit that his deviant actions involve an injury or hurt, the moral indignation of self and others may be neutralized by an insistence that the injury is not wrong in light of the circumstances. The injury, it may be claimed, is not really an injury; rather, it is a form of rightful retaliation or punishment. By a subtle alchemy the delinquent moves himself into the position of an avenger and the victim is transformed into a wrong-doer. Assaults on homosexuals or suspected homosexuals, attacks on members of minority groups who are said to have gotten "out of place," vandalism as revenge on an unfair teacher or school official, thefts from a "crooked" store owner—all may be hurts inflicted on a transgressor, in the eyes of the delinquent. As Orwell has pointed out, the type of criminal admired by the general public has probably changed over the course of years and Raffles no longer serves as a hero[3]; but Robin Hood, and his latter day derivatives such as the tough detective seeking justice outside the law, still capture the popular imagination, and the delinquent may view his acts as part of a similar role.

To deny the existence of the victim, then, by transforming him into a person deserving injury is an extreme form of a phenomenon we have mentioned before, namely, the delinquent's recognition of appropriate and inappropriate targets for his delinquent acts. In addition, however, the existence of the victim may be denied for the delinquent, in a somewhat different sense, by the circumstances of the delinquent act itself. Insofar as the victim is physically absent, unknown, or a vague abstraction (as is often the case in delinquent acts committed against property), the awareness of the victim's existence is weakened. Internalized norms and anticipations of the reactions of others must somehow be activated, if they are to serve as guides for behavior; and it is

[3] George Orwell, *Dickens, Dali, and Others,* New York: Reynal, 1946.

possible that a diminished awareness of the victim plays an important part in determining whether or not this process is set in motion.

THE CONDEMNATION OF THE CONDEMNERS

A fourth technique of neutralization would appear to involve a condemnation of the condemners or, as McCorkle and Korn have phrased it, a rejection of the rejectors.[4] The delinquent shifts the focus of attention from his own deviant acts to the motives and behavior of those who disapprove of his violations. His condemners, he may claim, are hypocrites, deviants in disguise, or impelled by personal spite. This orientation toward the conforming world may be of particular importance when it hardens into a bitter cynicism directed against those assigned the task of enforcing or expressing the norms of the dominant society. Police, it may be said, are corrupt, stupid, and brutal. Teachers always show favoritism and parents always "take it out" on their children. By a slight extension, the rewards of conformity—such as material success—become a matter of pull or luck, thus decreasing still further the stature of those who stand on the side of the law-abiding. The validity of this jaundiced viewpoint is not so important as its function in turning back or deflecting the negative sanctions attached to violations of the norms. The delinquent, in effect, has changed the subject of the conversation in the dialogue between his own deviant impulses and the reactions of others; and by attacking others, the wrongfulness of his own behavior is more easily repressed or lost to view.

THE APPEAL TO HIGHER LOYALTIES

Fifth, and last, internal and external social controls may be neutralized by sacrificing the demands of the larger society for the demands of the small social groups to which the delinquent belongs such as the sibling pair, the gang, or the friendship clique. It is important to note that the delinquent does not necessarily repudiate the imperatives of the dominant normative system, despite his failure to follow them. Rather, the delinquent may see himself as caught up in a dilemma that must be resolved, unfortunately, at the cost of violating the law. One aspect of this situation has been studied by Stouffer and Toby in their research on the conflict between particularistic and universalistic demands, between the claims of friendship and general social obligations, and their results suggest that "it is possible to classify people according to a predisposition to select one or the other horn of a dilemma in role conflict."[5] For our purposes, however, the most important point is that deviation from certain norms may occur not because the norms are rejected but because other norms, held to be more pressing or involving a higher loyalty, are accorded precedence. Indeed, it is the fact that both sets of norms are believed in that gives meaning to our concepts of dilemma and role conflict.

The conflict between the claims of friendship and the claims of law, or a similar dilemma, has of course long been recognized by the social scientist (and the novelist) as a common human problem. If the juvenile delinquent frequently resolves his dilemma by insisting that he must "always help a buddy" or "never squeal on a friend," even when it throws

[4] Lloyd W. McCorkle and Richard Korn, "Resocialization Within Walls," *The Annals of the American Academy of Political and Social Science,* 293 (May, 1954), pp. 88–98.

[5] See Samuel A. Stouffer and Jackson Toby, "Role Conflict and Personality," in *Toward a General Theory of Action,* edited by Talcott Parsons and Edward A. Shils, Cambridge: Harvard University Press, 1951, p. 494.

him into serious difficulties with the dominant social order, his choice remains familiar to the supposedly law-abiding. The delinquent is unusual, perhaps, in the extent to which he is able to see the fact that he acts on behalf of the smaller social groups to which he belongs as a justification for violations of society's norms, but it is a matter of degree rather than of kind.

"I didn't mean it." "I didn't really hurt anybody." "They had it coming to them." "Everybody's picking on me." "I didn't do it for myself." These slogans or their variants, we hypothesize, prepare the juvenile for delinquent acts. These "definitions of the situation" represent tangential or glancing blows at the dominant normative system rather than the creation of an opposing ideology; and they are extensions of patterns of thought prevalent in society rather than something created *de novo*.

Techniques of neutralization may not be powerful enough to fully shield the individual from the force of his own internalized values and the reactions of conforming others, for as we have pointed out, juvenile delinquents often appear to suffer from feelings of guilt and shame when called into account for their deviant behavior. And some delinquents may be so isolated from the world of conformity that techniques of neutralization need not be called into play. Nonetheless, we would argue that techniques of neutralization are critical in lessening the effectiveness of social controls and that they lie behind a large share of delinquent behavior. Empirical research in this area is scattered and fragmentary at the present time, but the work of Redl,[6] Cressey,[7] and others has supplied a body of significant data that

has done much to clarify the theoretical issues and enlarge the fund of supporting evidence. Two lines of investigation seem to be critical at this stage. First, there is need for more knowledge concerning the differential distribution of techniques of neutralization, as operative patterns of thought, by age, sex, social class, ethnic group, etc. On *a priori* grounds it might be assumed that these justifications for deviance will be more readily seized by segments of society for whom a discrepancy between common social ideals and social practice is most apparent. It is also possible however, that the habit of "bending" the dominant normative system—if not "breaking" it—cuts across our cruder social categories and is to be traced primarily to patterns of social interaction within the familial circle. Second, there is need for a greater understanding of the internal structure of techniques of neutralization, as a system of beliefs and attitudes, and its relationship to various types of delinquent behavior. Certain techniques of neutralization would appear to be better adapted to particular deviant acts than to others, as we have suggested, for example, in the case of offenses against property and the denial of the victim. But the issue remains far from clear and stands in need of more information.

In any case, techniques of neutralization appear to offer a promising line of research in enlarging and systematizing the theoretical grasp of juvenile delinquency. As more information is uncovered concerning techniques of neutralization, their origins, and their consequences, both juvenile delinquency in particular, and deviation from normative systems in general may be illuminated.

[6] See Fritz Redl and David Wineman, *Children Who Hate,* New York: The Free Press, 1956.

[7] See D. R. Cressey, *Other People's Money,* New York: The Free Press, 1953.

The Social Integration of Queers and Peers

ALBERT J. REISS, JR.

. . . An attempt is made in this paper to describe the sexual relation between "delinquent peers" and "adult queers" and to account for its social organization. This transaction is one form of homosexual prostitution between a young male and an adult male fellator. The adult male client pays a delinquent boy prostitute a sum of money in order to be allowed to act as a fellator. The transaction is limited to fellation and is one in which the boy develops no self-conception as a homosexual person or sexual deviator, although he perceives adult male clients as sexual deviators, "queers" or "gay boys." . . .

THE DATA

Information on the sexual transaction and its social organization was gathered mostly by interviews, partly by social observation of their meeting places. Though there are limitations to inferring social organization from interview data (particularly when the organization arises through behavior that is negatively sanctioned in the larger society), they provide a convenient basis for exploration.

Sex histories were gathered from 18.6 per cent of the 1008 boys between the ages of 12 and 17 who were interviewed in the Nashville, Tennessee, SMA for an investigation of adolescent conforming and deviating behavior. These represent all of the interviews of one of the interviewers during a two-month period, together with interviews with all Nashville boys incarcerated at the Tennessee State Training School for Boys. . . .

HOW PEERS AND QUEERS MEET

Meetings between adult male fellators and delinquent boys are easily made, because both know how and where to meet within the community space. Those within the common culture know that contact can be established within a relatively short period of time, if it is wished. The fact that meetings between peers and queers can be made easily is mute evidence of the organized understandings which prevail between the two populations.

There are a large number of places where the boys meet their clients, the fellators. Many of these points are known to all boys regardless of where they reside in the metropolitan area. This is particularly true of the central city locations where the largest number of contact points are found within a small territorial area. Each community area of

Reprinted from *Social Problems,* Vol. 9, No. 2 (Fall, 1961), pp. 102, 104, 106–109, 112–119, by permission of the author and *Social Problems.*

the city, and certain fringe areas, inhabited by substantial numbers of lower-class persons, also have their meeting places, generally known only to the boys residing in the area.

Queers and peers typically establish contact in public or quasi-public places. Major points of contact include street corners, public parks, men's toilets in public or quasi-public places such as those in transportation depots, parks or hotels, and "second" and "third-run" movie houses (open around the clock and permitting sitting through shows). Bars are seldom points of contact, perhaps largely because they are plied by older male hustlers who lie outside the peer culture and groups, and because bar proprietors will not risk the presence of under-age boys.

There are a number of prescribed modes for establishing contact in these situations. They permit the boys and fellators to communicate intent to one another privately despite the public character of the situation. The major form of establishing contact is the "cruise," with the fellator passing "queer-corners" or locations until his effort is recognized by one of the boys. A boy can then signal—usually by nodding his head, a hand gesticulation signifying OK, following, or responding to commonly understood introductions such as "You got the time?"—that he is prepared to undertake the transaction. Entrepreneur and client then move to a place where the sexual activity is consummated, usually a place affording privacy, protection and hasty exit. "Dolly," a three-time loser at the State Training School, describes one of these prescribed forms for making contact:

Well, like at the bus station, you go to the bathroom and stand there pretendin' like . . . and they're standin' there pretendin' like . . . and then they motions their head and walks out and you follow them, and you go some place. Either they's got a car,

or you go to one of them hotels near the depot or some place like that . . . most any place.

Frequently contact between boys and fellators is established when the boy is hitchhiking. This is particularly true for boys' first contacts of this nature. Since lower-class boys are more likely than middle-class ones to hitch rides within a city, particularly at night when such contacts are most frequently made, they perhaps are most often solicited in this manner.

The experienced boy who knows a "lot of queers," may phone known fellators directly from a public phone, and some fellators try to establish continued contact with boys by giving them their phone numbers. However, the boys seldom use this means of contact for reasons inherent in their orientation toward the transaction, as we shall see below.

We shall now examine how the transaction is facilitated by these types of situations and the prescribed modes of contact and communication. One of the characteristics of all these contact situations is that they provide a *rationale* for the presence of *both* peers and queers in the *same* situation or place. This rationale is necessary for both parties, for were there high visibility to the presence of either and no ready explanation for it, contact and communication would be far more difficult. Public and quasi-public facilities provide situations which account for the presence of most persons since there is relatively little social control over the establishment of contacts. There is, of course, some risk to the boys and the fellators in making contact in these situations since they are generally known to the police. The Morals Squad may have "stake-outs," but this is one of the calculated risks and the communication network carries information about their tactics.

A most important element in furnishing a rationale is that these meeting places must account for the presence of delinquent boys of essentially lower-class dress and appearance who make contact with fellators of almost any class level. This is true despite the fact that the social settings which fellators ordinarily choose to establish contact generally vary according to the class level of the fellators. Fellators of high social class generally make contact by "cruising" past streetcorners, in parks, or the men's rooms in "better" hotels, while those from the lower class are likely to select the public bath or transportation depot. There apparently is some general equation of the class position of boys and fellators in the peer-queer transaction. The large majority of fellators in the delinquent peer-queer transaction probably are from the lower class ("apes"). But it is difficult to be certain about the class position of the fellator clients since no study was made of this population.

The absence of data from the fellator population poses difficulties in interpreting the contact relationship. Many fellators involved with delinquent boys do not appear to participate in any overt or covert homosexual groups, such as the organized homosexual community of the "gay world."[1] The "gay world" is the most visible form of organized homosexuality since it is an organized community, but it probably encompasses only a small proportion of all homosexual contact. Even among those in the organized homosexual community, evidence suggests that the homosexual members seek sexual gratification outside their group with persons who are essentially anonymous to them. Excluding homosexual married couples, Leznoff and Westley maintain that there is ". . . a prohibition against sexual relationships within the group. . . ."[2] Ross indicates that young male prostitutes are chosen, among other reasons, for the fact that they protect the identity of the client.[3] Both of these factors tend to coerce many male fellators to choose an anonymous contact situation.

It is clear that these contact situations not only provide a rationale for the presence of the parties to the transaction but a guarantee of anonymity. The guarantee does not necessarily restrict social visibility as both the boys and the fellators may recognize cues (including, but not necessarily, those of gesture and dress) which lead to mutual role identification.[4] But anonymity is guaranteed in at least two senses; anonymity of presence is assured in the situation and their personal identity in the community is protected unless disclosed by choice.

There presumably are a variety of reasons for the requirement of anonymity. For many, a homosexual relationship must remain a secret since their other relationships in the community—families, business relationships, etc.—must be protected. Leznoff and Westley refer to these men as the "secret" as contrasted with the "overt" homosexuals,[5] and in the organized "gay world," they are known as "closet fags."

---

[1] See, for example, Maurice Leznoff and William A. Westley, "The Homosexual Community," *Social Problems,* 4 (April, 1956), pp. 257–263.

[2] *Ibid.,* p. 258.

[3] H. Laurence Ross, "The 'Hustler' in Chicago," *The Journal of Student Research,* 1 (September, 1959), p. 15.

[4] The cues which lead to the queer-peer transaction can be subtle ones. The literature on adult male homosexuality makes it clear that adult males who participate in homosexual behavior are not generally socially visible to the public by manner and dress. Cf., Jess Stearn, *The Sixth Man,* New York: Macfadden Publications, 1962, Chapters 1 and 3.

[5] *Op. cit.,* pp. 260–261.

For some, there is also a necessity for protecting identity to avoid blackmail.[6] Although none of the peer hustlers reported resorting to blackmail, the adult male fellator may nonetheless hold such an expectation, particularly if he is older or of high social class. Lower-class ones, by contrast, are more likely to face the threat of violence from adolescent boys since they more often frequent situations where they are likely to contact "rough trade."[7] The kind of situation in which the delinquent peer-queer contact is made and the sexual relationship consummated tends to minimize the possibility of violence.

Not all male fellators protect their anonymity; some will let a boy have their phone number and a few "keep a boy." Still, most fellators want to meet boys where they are least likely to be victimized, although boys sometimes roll queers by selecting a meeting place where by prearrangement, their friends can meet them and help roll the queer, steal his car, or commit other acts of violence. Boys generally know that fellators are vulnerable in that they can't report their victimization. Parenthetically, it might be mentioned that these boys are not usually aware of their own institutional invulnerability to arrest. An adolescent boy is peculiarly invulnerable to arrest even when found with a fellator since the mores define the boy as exploited.[8]

Situations of personal contact between adolescent boys and adult male fellators also provide important ways to *communicate intent* or to carry out the transaction *without* making the contact particularly visible to others. The wall writings in many of these places are not without their primitive communication value, e.g., "show it hard," and places such as a public restroom provide a modus operandi. The entrepreneur and his customer in fact can meet with little more than an exchange of non-verbal gestures, transact their business with a minimum of verbal communication and part without a knowledge of one another's identity. In most cases, boys report "almost nothing" was said. The sexual transaction may occur with the only formal transaction being payment to the boy. . . .

NORMS GOVERNING THE TRANSACTION

Does the peer society have any norms about personal relations with fellators? Or, does it simply induct a boy into a relationship by teaching him how to effect the transaction? The answer is that there appear to be several clear-cut norms about the relations between peers and queers, even though there is some deviation from them.

The first major norm is that *a boy must undertake the relationship with a queer solely as a way of making money; sexual gratification cannot be actively sought as a goal in the relationship.* This norm does not preclude a boy from sexual gratification by the act; he simply must not seek this as a goal. Put another way, a boy cannot admit that he failed to get money from the transaction unless he used violence toward the fellator and he

---

[6] Ross notes that, failing in the con-man role, some hustlers resort to extortion and blackmail since they provide higher income. See Ross, *op. cit.,* p. 16. Sutherland discusses extortion and blackmail of homosexuals as part of the practice of professional thieves. The "muzzle" or "mouse" is part of the role of the professional thief. See Edwin Sutherland, *The Professional Thief,* Chicago: University of Chicago Press, 1937, pp. 78–81. See also the chapter on "Blackmail" in Jess Stearn, *op. cit.,* Chapter 16.

[7] Jess Stearn, *op. cit.,* p. 47.

[8] Albert J. Reiss, Jr., "Sex Offenses: The Marginal Status of the Adolescent," *Law and Contemporary Problems,* 25 (Spring, 1960), pp. 322–324 and 326–327.

cannot admit that he sought it as a means of sexual gratification.

The importance of making money in motivating a boy to the peer-queer transaction is succinctly stated by Dewey H.:

This guy in the Rex Theatre came over and sat down next to me when I was 11 or 12, and he started to fool with me. I got over and sat down another place and he came over and asked me, didn't I want to and he'd pay me five bucks. I figured it was *easy money* so I went with him . . . I didn't do it before that. That wasn't too long after I'd moved to South Nashville. I was a pretty good boy before that . . . not real good, but I never ran with a crowd that got into trouble before that. But, I met a lot of 'em there. (Why do you run with queers?) It's *easy money* . . . like I could go out and break into a place when I'm broke and get money that way . . . but that's harder and *you take a bigger risk* . . . with a queer it's *easy money*.

Dewey's comments reveal two important motivating factors in getting money from queers, both suggested by the expression, "easy money." First, the money is easy in that it can be made quickly. Some boys reported that when they needed money for a date or a night out, they obtained it within an hour through the sexual transaction with a queer. All the boy has to do is go to a place where he will be contacted, wait around, get picked up, carried to a place where the sexual transaction occurs, and in a relatively short period of time he obtains the money for his service.

It is easy money in another and more important sense for many of these boys. Boys who undertake the peer-queer transaction are generally members of career-oriented delinquent groups. Rejecting the limited opportunities for making money by legitimate means or finding them inaccessible, their opportunities to make money by illegitimate means may also be limited or the risk may be great. Theft is an available

means, but it is more difficult and involves greater risk than the peer-queer transaction. Delinquent boys are not unaware of the risks they take. Under most circumstances, delinquents may calculate an act of stealing as "worth the risk." There are occasions, however, when the risk is calculated as too great. These occasions occur when the "heat" is on the boy or when he can least afford to run the risk of being picked up by the police, as is the case following a pickup by the police, being put on probation or parole, or being warned that incarceration will follow the next violation. At such times, boys particularly calculate whether they can afford to take the risk. Gerald L., describing a continuing relationship with a fellator who gave him his phone number, reflects Dewey's attitude toward minimizing risk in the peer-queer transaction: "So twic'd after that when I was gettin' real low and couldn't risk stealin' and gettin' caught, I called him and he took me out and blowed me." Here is profit with no investment of capital and a minimum of risk in social, if not in psychological, terms.

The element of risk coupled with the wish for "easy money" enters into our understanding of the peer-queer relationship in another way. From a sociological point of view, the peer-queer sexual transaction occurs between two major types of deviators—"delinquents" and "queers." Both types of deviators risk negative sanctions for their deviant acts. The more often one has been arrested or incarcerated, the more punitive the sanctions from the larger social system for both types of deviators. At some point, therefore, both calculate risks and seek to minimize them, at least in the very short-run. Each then becomes a means for the other to minimize risk.

When the delinquent boy is confronted with a situation in which he wants money and risks little in getting it, how is he to get it without working? Illegitimate activities frequently provide the "best" opportunity for easy money. These activities often are restricted in kind and number for adolescents and the risk of negative sanctions is high. Under such circumstances, the service offered a queer is a chance to make easy money with a minimum of risk.

Opportunities for sexual gratification are limited for the adult male fellator, particularly if he wishes to minimize the risk of detection in locating patrons, to avoid personal involvement and to get his gratification when he wishes it. The choice of a lower-class male, precisely because of his class position somewhat reduces the risk. If the lower-class male also is a delinquent, the risk is minimized to an even greater degree.

This is not to say that the parties take equal risks in the situation. Of the two, the fellator perhaps is less able to minimize his risk since he still risks violence from his patron, but much less so if a set of expectations arise which control the use of violence as well. The boy is most able to minimize his risk since he is likely to be defined as "exploited" in the situation if caught.

Under special circumstances, boys may substitute other gratifications for the goal of money, provided that these gratifications do not include sexual gratification as a major goal. These special circumstances are the case where an entire gang will "make a night (or time) of it" with one or more adult male fellators. Under these circumstances, everyone is expected from the subcultural expectations about making money from the fellator because everyone participates and there is no reason for everyone (or anyone) to make money. For the group to substitute being given a "good time" by a "queer" for the prescribed financial

transaction is, of course, the exception which proves the rule.

Several examples of group exemption from the prescribed norm of a financial gain were discovered. Danny S., leader of the Black Aces, tells of his gang's group experiences with queers: "There's this one guy takes us to the Colonial Motel out on Dickerson Pike . . . usually it's a bunch of us boys and we all get drunk and get blowed by this queer . . . we don't get any money then . . . it's more a drinking party." The Black Aces are a fighting gang and place great stress on physical prowess, particularly boxing. All of its members have done time more than once at the State Training School. During one of these periods, the school employed a boxing instructor whom the boys identified as "a queer," but the boys had great respect for him since he taught them how to box and was a game fighter. Danny refers to him in accepting terms: "He's a real good guy. He's fought with us once or twice and we drink with him when we run into him. . . . He's taken us up to Miter Dam a coupla times, he's got a cabin up there on the creek and he blows us. . . . But mostly we just drink and have a real good time." These examples illustrate the instrumental orientation of the gang members. If the expense of the gang members getting drunk and having a good time are borne by a "queer," each member is released from the obligation to receive cash. The relationship in this case represents an exchange of services rather than that of money for a service.

The second major norm operating in the relationship is that *the sexual transaction must be limited to mouth-genital fellation. No other sexual acts are generally tolerated.*[9] The adult male fellator

---

[9] It is not altogether clear why mouth-genital fellation is the only sexual act which is tolerated in the peer-queer transaction. The act seems to conform to the more "masculine" aspects of the role than do most, but not all possible alternatives. Ross has suggested to me that it also involves less bodily contact and therefore may be less threatening to

(Continued)

must deport himself in such a way as to re-enforce the instrumental aspects of the role relationship and to insure affective neutrality.[10] For the adult male fellator to violate the boy's expectation of "getting blowed," as the boys refer to the act, is to risk violence and loss of service. Whether or not the boys actually use violent means as often as they say they do when expectations are violated, there is no way of knowing with precision. Nevertheless, whenever boys reported they used violent means, they always reported some violation of the subcultural expectations. Likewise, they never reported a violation of the subcultural expectations which was not followed by the use of violent means, unless it was clearly held up as an exception. Bobby A. expresses the boys' point of view on the use of violent means in the following exchange: "How much did you usually get?" "Around five dollars; if they didn't give that much, I'd beat their head in." "Did they ever want you to do anything besides blow you?" "Yeh, sometimes . . . like they want me to blow them, but I'd tell them to go to hell and maybe beat them up."

Boys are very averse to being thought of in a queer role or engaging in acts of fellation. The act of fellation is defined as a "queer" act. Most boys were asked whether they would engage in such behavior. All but those who had the status of "punks" denied they had engaged in behavior associated with the queer role. Asking a boy whether he is a fellator meets with strong denial and often with open hostility. This could be interpreted as defensive behavior against latent homosexuality. Whether or not this is the case, strong denial could be expected because the question goes counter to the subcultural definitions of the peer role in the transaction.

A few boys on occasion apparently permit the fellator to perform other sexual acts. These boys, it is guessed, are quite infrequent in a delinquent peer population. Were their acts known to the members of the group, they would soon be defined as outside the delinquent peer society. Despite the limitation of the peer-queer sexual transaction to mouth-genital fellation, there are other sexual transactions which the peer group permits members to perform under special circumstances. They are, for example, permitted to perform the *male* roles in "crimes against nature," such as in pederasty ("cornholing" to the boys), bestiality (sometimes referred to as buggery) and carnal copulation with a man involving no orifice (referred to as "slick-legging" among the boys) provided that the partner is roughly of the same age and not a member of the group and provided also that the boys are confined to the single-sex society of incarcerated delinquent boys. Under no circumstances, however, is the female role in carnal copulation acceptable in any form. It is taboo. Boys who accept the female role in sexual transactions occupy the lowest status position among delinquents. They are "punks."

The third major norm operating on the relationship is that *both peers and queers, as participants, should remain affectively neutral during the transaction.* Boys within the peer society define the ideal form of the role with the fellator as one in which the boy is the entrepreneur

the peers' self-definitions. One possible explanation therefore for the exclusiveness of the relationship to this act is that it is the most masculine alternative involving the least threat to peers' self-definition as nonhustler and nonhomosexual.

[10] Talcott Parsons in *The Social System* (New York: The Free Press, 1951, Chapter III) discusses this kind of role as ". . . the segregation of specific instrumental performances, both from expressive orientations other than the specifically appropriate rewards and from other components of the instrumental complex." (p. 87).

and the queer is viewed as purchasing a service. The service is a business deal where a sexual transaction is purchased for an agreed upon amount of money. In the typical case, the boy is neither expected to enjoy or be repulsed by the sexual transaction; mouth-genital fellation is accepted as a service offered in exchange for a fee. It should be kept in mind that self-gratification is permitted in the sexual act. Only the motivation to sexual gratification in the transaction is tabooed. But self-gratification must occur without displaying either positive or negative affect toward the queer. In the prescribed form of the role relationship, the boy sells a service for profit and the queer is to accept it without show of emotion.

The case of Thurman L., one of three brothers who are usually in trouble with the law, illustrates some aspects of the expected pattern of affective neutrality. Thurman has had a continuing relationship with a queer, a type of relationship in which it would be anticipated that affective neutrality would be difficult to maintain. This relationship continued, in fact, with a 21 year old "gay" until the man was "sent to the pen." When queried about his relationship with this man and why he went with him, Thurman replied:

Don't know . . . money and stuff like that I guess. (What do you mean? . . . stuff like that?) Oh, clothes. . . . (He ever bought you any clothes?) Sure, by this one gay. . . . (You mind being blowed?) No. (You like it?) Don't care one way or the other. I don't like, and I don't not like it. (You like this one gay?) Nope, can't say that I liked anythin' about him. (How come you do it then?) Well, the money for one thing. . . . I need that. (You enjoy it some?) Can't say I do or don't.

More typical than Thurman's expression of affective neutrality is the boy who accepts it as "OK" or, "It's all right; I don't mind it." Most frequent of all is some variant of the statement: "It's OK, but I like the money best of all." The definition of affective neutrality fundamentally requires only that there be no positive emotional commitment to the queer *as a person*. The relationship must be essentially an impersonal one, even though the pure form of the business relationship may seldom be attained. Thus, it is possible for a boy to admit self-gratification without admitting any emotional commitment to the homosexual partner.

Although the peer group prescribes affective neutrality toward the queer in the peer-queer transaction, queers must be regarded as low prestige persons, held in low esteem, and the queer role is taboo. The queer is most commonly regarded as "crazy, I guess." Some boys take a more rationalistic view "They're just like that, I guess" or, "They're just born that way." While there are circumstances under which one is permitted to like a particular fellator, as in the case of all prejudices attached to devalued status, the person who is liked must be the exception which states the rule. Though in many cases both the boy and the fellator are of very low class origins, and in many cases both are altogether repulsive in appearance, cleanliness and dress by middle-class standards, these are not the standards of comparison used by the boys. The deviation of the queers from the boy's norms of masculine behavior places the fellator in the lowest possible status, even "beneath contempt." If the fellator violates the expected affective relationship in the transaction, he may be treated not only with violence but with contempt as well. The seller of the service ultimately reserves the right to set the conditions for his patrons.

Some boys find it difficult to be emotionally neutral toward the queer role and its occupants; they are either personally offended or affronted by the behavior of queers. JDC is an instance of a boy who is personally offended by their behavior; yet he is unable to use violence even when expectations governing the transaction are violated. He does not rely very much on the peer-queer relationship as a source of income. JDC expresses his view: "I don't really go for that like some guys; I just do it when I go along with the crowd. . . . You know. . . . That, and when I do it for money. . . . And I go along. . . . But . . . I hate queers. They embarrass me." "How?" "Well, like you'll be in the lobby at the theatre, and they'll come up and pat your ass or your prick right in front of everybody. I just can't go for that— not me." Most of the boys wouldn't either, but they would have resorted to violent means in this situation.

Two principal types of boys maintain a continuing relationship with a known queer. A few boys develop such relationships to insure a steady income. While this is permitted within peer society for a short period of time, boys who undertake it for extended periods of time do so with some risk, since in the words of the boys, "queers can be got too easy." The boy who is affectively involved with a queer or his role is downgraded in status to a position, "Ain't no better'n a queer." There are also a few boys affectively committed to a continuing relationship with an adult male homosexual. Such boys usually form a strong dependency relationship with him and are kept much as the cabin boys of old. This type of boy is clearly outside the peer society of delinquents and is isolated from participation in gang activity. The sociometric pattern for such boys is one of choice into more than one gang, none of which is reciprocated.

Street-hustlers are also downgraded within the peer society, generally having reputations as "punk kids." The street-hustler pretty much "goes it alone." Only a few street-hustlers were interviewed for this study. None of them was a member of an organized delinquent group. The sociometric pattern for each, together with his history of delinquent activity, placed them in the classification of non-conforming isolates.

A fourth major norm operating on the peer-queer relationship serves as a primary factor in stabilizing the system. This norm holds that *violence must not be used so long as the relationship conforms to the shared set of expectations between queers and peers*. So long as the fellator conforms to the norms governing the transaction in the peer-queer society, he runs little risk of violence from the boys.

The main reason, perhaps, for this norm is that uncontrolled violence is potentially disruptive of any organized system. All organized social systems must control violence. If the fellator clients were repeatedly the objects of violence, the system as it has been described could not exist. Most boys who share the common expectations of the peer-queer relationship do not use violent means unless the expectations are violated. To use violence, of course, is to become affectively involved and therefore another prescription of the relation is violated.

It is not known whether adult male fellators who are the clients of delinquent entrepreneurs share the boys' definition of the norm regarding the use of violence. They may, therefore, violate expectations of the peer society through ignorance of the system rather than from any attempt to go beyond the set of shared expectations.

There are several ways the fellator can violate the expectations of boys. The first concerns money: refusal to pay or paying too little may bring violence from most boys. Fellators may also violate peer expectations by attempting to go beyond the mouth-genital sexual act. If such an attempt is made, he is usually made an object of aggression as in the following excerpt from Dolly's sex history:

(You like it?) It's OK. I don't mind it. It feels OK. (They ever try anything else on you?) They usually just blow and that's all. (Any ever try anything else on you?) Oh sure, but we really fix 'em. I just hit 'em on the head or roll 'em . . . throw 'em out of the car. . . . Once a guy tried that and we rolled him and threw him out of the car. Then we took the car and stripped it (laughs with glee).

Another way the fellator violates a boy's expectations is to introduce considerable affect into the relationship. It appears that affect is least acceptable in two forms, both of which could be seen as "attacks on his masculinity." In one form, the queer violates the affective neutrality requirement by treating the adolescent boy as if he were a girl or in a girl's role during the sexual transaction, as for example, by speaking to him in affectionate terms such as "sweetie." There are many reasons why the feminine sex role is unacceptable to these lower-class boys, including the fact that such boys place considerable emphasis on being "tough" and masculine. Walter Miller, for example, observes that:

. . . The almost compulsive lower class concern with "masculinity" derives from a type of compulsive reaction-formation. A concern over homosexuality runs like a persistent thread through lower class culture— manifested by the institutionalized practice of "baiting queers," often accompanied by violent physical attacks, an expressed contempt for "softness" or frills, and the use of the local term for "homosexual" as a general pejorative epithet (e.g., higher class individuals or upwardly mobile peers are frequently characterized as "fags" or "queers").[11]

Miller sees violence as part of a reaction-formation against the matriarchal lower-class household where the father often is absent. For this reason, he suggests, many lower-class boys find it difficult to identify with a male role, and the "collective" reaction-formation is a cultural emphasis on masculinity. Violence toward queers is seen as a consequence of this conflict. Data from our interviews suggest that among career-oriented delinquents, violation of the affective-neutrality requirement in the peer-queer relationship is at least as important in precipitating violence toward "queers." There are, of course, gangs which were not studied in this investigation which "queer-bait" for the express purposes of "rolling the queer."

The other form in which the fellator may violate the affective neutrality requirement is to approach the boy and make suggestive advances to him when he is with his age-mates, either with girls or with his peer group when he is not located for "business." In either case, the sexual advances suggest that the boy is not engaged in a business relationship within the normative expectations of the system, but that he has sexual motivation as well. The delinquent boy is expected to control the relationship with his customers. He is the entrepreneur "looking" for easy money or at the very least he must appear as being merely receptive to business; this means that he is receptive only in certain situations and under certain circumstances. He is not in business when he is with girls and he is not a businessman when he is cast in a female role. To be cast in a female role before peers is highly unacceptable, as the following account suggests:

This gay comes up to me in the lobby of the Empress when we was standin' around

[11] Walter Miller, "Lower-Class Culture as a Generating Milieu of Gang Delinquency," The Journal of Social Issues, 14, No. 3, (1958), p. 9.

and starts feelin' me up and callin' me Sweetie and like that . . . and, I just couldn't take none of that there . . . what was he makin' out like I was a queer or somethin' . . . so I jumps him right then and there and we like to of knocked his teeth out.

The sexual advance is even less acceptable when a girl is involved:

I was walkin' down the street with my steady girl when this gay drives by that I'd been with once before and he whistles at me and calls, "hi Sweetie." . . . And, was I mad . . . so I went down to where the boys was and we laid for him and beat on him 'til he like to a never come to . . . ain't gonna take nothin' like that off'n a queer.

In both of these instances, not only is the boys' masculinity under attack, but the affective neutrality requirement of the business transaction is violated. The queer's behavior is particularly unacceptable, however, because it occurs in a peer setting where the crucial condition is the maintenance of the boy's status within the group. A lower-class boy cannot afford to be cast in less than a highly masculine role before lower-class girls nor risk definition as a queer before peers. His role within his peer group is under threat even if he suffers *no* anxiety about masculinity. Not only the boy himself but his peers perceive such behavior as violating role expectations and join him in violent acts toward the fellator to protect the group's integrity and status.

If violence generally occurs only when one of the major peer norms has been violated, it would also seem to follow that *violence is a means of enforcing the peer entrepreneurial norms of the system*. Violence or the threat of violence is thus used to keep adut male fellators in line with the boys' expectations in his customer role. It represents social control, a punishment meted out to a fellator who violates the cultural expectation. Only so long as the fellator seeks gratification from lower-class boys in a casual pick-up or continuing relationship where he pays money for a "blow-job" is he reasonably free from acts of violence.

There is another, and perhaps more important reason for the use of violence when the peer defined norms of the peer-queer relationship are violated. The formally prescribed roles for peers and queers are basically the roles involved in all institutionalized forms of prostitution, the prostitute and the client. But in most forms of prostitution, whether male or female, the hustlers perceive of themselves in hustler roles, and furthermore the male hustlers also develop a conception of themselves as homosexual whereas *the peer hustler in the peer-queer relationship develops no conception of himself either as prostitute or as homosexual.*

The fellator risks violence, therefore, if he threatens the boy's self-conception by suggesting that the boy may be homosexual and treats him as if he were.

Violence seems to function, then, in two basic ways for the peers. On the one hand, it integrates their norms and expectations in controlling and combatting behavior which violates them. On the other hand, it protects the boy's self-identity as nonhomosexual and reinforces his self-conception as "masculine."

The other norms of the peer society governing the peer-queer transaction also function to prevent boys in the peer-queer society from defining themselves as homosexual. The prescriptions that the goal is money, that sexual gratification is not to be sought as an end in the relationship, that affective neutrality be maintained toward the fellator and that only mouth-genital fellation is permitted, all tend to insulate the boy from a homosexual self-definition. So long as he conforms to these expectations, *his "significant others" will not define him as homosexual;* and this is perhaps the most crucial factor in his own self-definition.

The peers define one as homosexual not on the basis of homosexual *behavior* as such, but on the basis of participation in the homosexual *role,* the "queer" role. The reactions of the larger society, in defining the *behavior* as homosexual is unimportant in their own self-definition. What is important to them is the reactions of their peers to violation of peer group norms which define roles in the peer-queer transaction.

Patient Role and Social Uncertainty

KAI T. ERIKSON

The concept of role has become widely used in the field of mental health to relate the behavior of mental patients to the social setting of their illness. The literature in which this concept has appeared, however, has been largely concerned with the specialized culture of the mental hospital—the formal and informal structures of ward life—almost as if the universe to which a patient relates when he enacts a "patient role" is neatly contained within hospital walls.[1] To the sociologist, who generally uses the concept of role in a broader social context, this tends to place a one-sided emphasis on the institution itself as the essential focus of the patient's social life.

When a person enters a mental hospital for treatment, to be sure, he abandons many of the social ties which anchored him to a definite place in society. However, the act of becoming a mental patient effects a fundamental *change* in the person's relationship to the ongoing processes of society, not a complete withdrawal from them; and while the forms of his participation are altered, he remains acutely sensitive to outer influences. Even in the relative isolation of the hospital ward, then, the patient's behavior to some extent articulates his relationship to the larger society and reflects the social position which he feels is reserved for him in its organizational structure. It is this aspect of the role of the patient which the present paper will consider.

DEFINITIONS

Role usually is used to designate a set of behaviors or values about behavior which is commonly considered appropriate for persons occupying given statuses or positions in society. For the purposes of this paper, it will be useful to consider that the acquisition of roles by a person involves two basic processes: *role-validation* and *role-commitment*.

Reprinted by special permission of The William Alanson White Psychiatric Foundation, Inc., from *Psychiatry: Journal for the Study of Interpersonal Processes,* Vol. 20 (August 1957), pp. 263–268, by permission of the author and The William Alanson White Psychiatric Foundation, Inc. The writer would like to thank Nelson N. Foote, formerly director of the Family Study Center, for the opportunity to do this study and for many helpful criticisms.

[1] See, for example, the following: J. F. Bateman and H. W. Dunham, "The State Hospital as a Specialized Community Experience," *Amer. J. Psychiatry* (1948) 105:445–448; William Caudill, Fredrick C. Redlich, Helen R. Gilmore, and Eugene B. Brody, "Social Structure and Interaction Processes on a Psychiatric Ward," *Amer. J. Orthopsychiatry* (1952) 22:314–334; George Devereux, "The Social Structure of the Hospital as a Factor in Total Therapy," *Amer. J. Orthopsychiatry* (1949) 19:493–500; Howard Rowland, "Interaction Processes in a State Mental Hospital," *Psychiatry* (1938) 1:323–327; Alfred Stanton and Morris S. Schwartz, "Medical Opinion and the Social Context in the Mental Hospital," *Psychiatry* (1949) 12:243–249; Stanton and Schwartz, *The Mental Hospital;* New York, Basic Books, 1954.

Role-validation takes place when a community "gives" a person certain expectations to live up to, providing him with distinct notions as to the conduct it considers appropriate or valid for him in his position.[2] Role-commitment is the complementary process whereby a person adopts certain styles of behavior as his own, committing himself to role themes that best represent the kind of person he assumes himself to be, and best reflect the social position he considers himself to occupy.

Normally, of course, these processes take place simultaneously and are seldom overtly distinguished in the relationship between the person and his community. The person learns to accept the image that the group holds up to him as a more-or-less accurate reflection of himself, is able to accept as his own the position which the group provides for him, and thus becomes more or less committed to the behavior values which the group poses as valid for him. The merit of making a distinction between these two processes, then, is solely to visualize what happens in marginal situations in which conflict does occur—in which the person develops behavior patterns which the community regards as invalid for him, or the community entertains expectations which the person feels unable to realize. Sociologists, traditional specialists in this aspect of deviance, have generally been more concerned with the process of validation than that of commitment, concentrating on the mechanisms which groups employ to persuade individuals that roles validated for them deserve their personal commitment.

In so doing, sociologists have largely overlooked the extent to which a person can *engineer* a change in the role expectations held in his behalf, rather than passively waiting for others to "allocate" or "assign" roles to him. This he does by being so persistent in his commitment to certain modes of behavior, and so convincing in his portrayal of them, that the community is persuaded to accept these modes as the basis for a new set of expectations on its part.

Thus the process by which persons acquire a recognized role may, at times, involve long and delicate negotiations between the individual and his community. The individual presents himself in behavior styles that express his personal sense of identity and continuity;[3] the group validates role models for him that fit its own functional needs.[4] The negotiation is concluded when a mutually satisfactory definition of the individual is reached and a position established for him in the group structure—or when the issue becomes stalemated and suppressive sanctions against deviance are called into play.

The argument to be presented here is that such a negotiation is likely to follow a mental patient's admission to a mental hospital, particularly if he does not qualify as a "certified" patient with a circumscribed disease. In accepting hospitalization, the patient is often caught in the pull of divergent sets of expectations: on the one hand, he is exposed to psychiatry's demand that he make a wholehearted commitment to the process of treatment, and, on the other, he is confronted by a larger society which is

[2] Validation, it might be pointed out, is meant to be more than a community's attempt to impose its moral preferences upon members. The community may validate certain behavior as appropriate for certain individuals even while remaining completely outraged by it. By naming a criminal "habitual" or "confirmed," for instance, people declare their intention of punishing him, not because his conduct violates their expectations or is "unlike" him, but precisely because it *is* like him and is thus the valid way for him to act.

[3] See, in this connection, Erik H. Erikson, "The Problem of Ego Identity," *J. Amer. Psychoanal. Assn.* (1956) 4:56–121.

[4] See Talcott Parsons, *The Social System;* New York, The Free Press, 1951.

often unwilling to validate these commitments. He is left, then, with no consistent and durable social role, with no clear-cut social models upon which to fashion his behavior. The patient is thus often persuaded by the logic of psychiatric institutions to attempt to engineer validation in the role this society provides for the *medical* patient—in which, to be sure, distinctly psychotic patients are presumed to belong. To establish his eligibility for this conventional role, the mental patient must negotiate, using his illness as an instrumentality. He must present his illness to others in a form which they recognize as legitimate, perhaps even exaggerating his portrayal of those behaviors which qualify medical patients for their role. In having to do so, the argument continues, he is often left with little choice but to become sicker or more chronically sick.

THE PATIENT

This section is based primarily on data collected in a small, "open" psychiatric hospital which offered analytically oriented psychotherapy for a fairly selective group of patients. Diagnoses in his population ranged, for the most part, from the severe psychoneuroses to borderline psychoses. The institutional setting lacked the scheduled rigidity of closed hospital routines and allowed for an unusual degree of personal initiative. Since the patients received almost daily individual therapy and were, in a certain respect, volunteers for treatment who recognized the implications of their patienthood, they could hardly be considered representative of the average ward population. But the experienced clinician will be able to determine to what extent generalizations made from observation of this group apply to patients in custodial institutions, whose contacts with the outside world are more limited. No doubt many of the same

social forces act upon patients in any hospital situation, even where behavior is more strictly routinized and confined within the limiting boundaries of a closed ward so that it may seem to reflect the common setting in which it took place rather than the common motivations which produced it. Thus it is possible that the uniqueness of the therapeutic setting in which these observations took place simply affords a more spontaneous picture of social forces operating in any psychiatric hospital.

While doing some sociological work in this setting, the writer took a brief inventory of behavior themes which seemed characteristic of the patient group and which appeared to be among the central motifs of the patients' role behavior.

One may begin by noting certain contradictions implicit in the very act of becoming a mental patient. By accepting hospitalization, the patient makes a contractual agreement to cooperate in a therapeutic partnership: he agrees to want and to appreciate treatment, to be realistic about his need for help, to volunteer relevant information, and to act as reliably as possible upon the recommendations of his therapist. Yet it is widely considered a condition of his illness that he is unable to make meaningful contact with any reality, therapeutic or otherwise. In the grip of these discrepant expectations, his behavior is likely to be a curious mixture of the active and the passive, a mosaic of acts which tend to confirm his competence and acts which tend to dramatize his helplessness. He must test the limits of his own uncertain controls and look for consistent expectations to guide him, as the following fragment from a case history illustrates:

One of the outstanding characteristics of this patient is his absolute uncertainty about his illness and what is expected of him in the institution and in therapy. He is uncertain whether he actively produces his hysterical states or whether they come upon him without his being able to do anything about them. He does not know whether he is supposed to show his symptoms or suppress them, to "let go" of his impulses and act out or to exert active self-control and "put the lid on." He is afraid that if he does the former, he is psychotic and will be considered too sick for the open institutional setting here; if he does the latter, he will be a pretending psychopath and considered too well to continue treatment here at all. He does not know what he should expect from himself, from other patients, from his sickness, from other people he knows, or even from his therapist. Perhaps his most crucial problem at the moment is to define for himself what are the conditions of his stay here as a patient.

This fragment sums up the bewildering social situation in which the patient must act, and it is not difficult to understand how the final assumption of a consistent social role might represent to him a clarification and partial adjustment. To demonstrate this, I shall try to isolate a few strands of behavior from this complicated fabric.

All children are taught in this culture that it is impolite to stare at or make reference to the infirmities of cripples. So it is interesting to note that the generous impulse of outsiders to overlook a patient's less visible infirmities is likely to put the patient in an instant state of alarm, and to bring urgent assurances on his part that he is severely sick and in serious need of treatment. Patients often bring this topic into conversation on scant provocation and continue to talk about it even when fairly vigorous attempts are made by visitors to change the subject. The patient is likely to describe this as "accepting the realities of his illness," by which he means that he frankly admits the seriousness of his sickness and refuses to take refuge in some convenient defense that might deny it. Yet to the observer it often appears that

this is an attempt to convince *others* of these realities as well as to remind himself, as if he were afraid they would be overlooked entirely. The patient seems to feel it crucial that his illness be accepted as a fundamental fact about himself, the premise on which he enters into relations with others.

Side by side with this severe "honesty," the patient can develop a considerable degree of responsibility in carrying out the therapeutic recommendations of his therapist. And if the hospital tries to foster the patient's social initiative, he may respond with resources that even the therapist did not know were at his disposal. Such initiative is usually in evidence only during certain hospital activities and sometimes appears to belie the very weaknesses which the patient, at other times, displays so insistently. Patients at the hospital in question, for instance, have organized and produced dramatic plays before outside audiences, performing with a skill that surprised professional dramatic observers, and succeeding even when the therapists themselves had severe reservations about the outcome. At a prize-winning performance in a neighboring city, some of the audience were and remained under the impression that the players were members of the medical staff rather than patients of the institution.

Yet as one records this accomplishment, it must be noted that such positive efforts can sometimes be as deceptive as they are surprising, and that, at times, they can produce negative undercurrents that threaten to cancel out the accomplishment altogether. In reporting on the plays performed at the hospital, one journalist noted this. He said that the patients produce and act in plays before paying audiences with a competence which, according to Clifford Odets, who saw one of his plays so performed, is equal to that of any good amateur group. At the same time, the reporter said, one of the doctors had remarked ruefully, "I was very upset when one of my patients, after doing a fine job in the play, went back to the patients' dormitory and tried to set fire to it."

The example is extreme, but it illustrates the conflict a patient encounters in committing himself to positive and constructive activity. Like Penelope, who wove a cloak by day only to unravel it at night, the mental patient often portrays the insecurity of his position by staging, after every advance of this kind, a dramatic retreat into impulsivity and destruction.

Thus at once the patient accepts responsibility for a type of performance rarely asked of the average person, yet is unable to control actions which, in the light of the earlier accomplishment, would seem to be well within his realm of mastery. This seeming paradox is a recurring motif that runs through the whole complex of the patient's role behavior. As has been shown in the case abstract that introduced this section, the patient has potentialities for activity and passivity, for resourcefulness and helplessness, in any given area of action. To organize these into a coherent role pattern, it seems, the patient partitions his hospital world into areas where he considers one or the other of these potential responses specifically appropriate.

In some decisive situations, as has been described, the patient faces his hospital life with remarkable initiative. Yet in others, an overwhelming theme of helplessness seems to dominate his behavior. He is likely to insist, in terms far stronger than the situation would appear to necessitate, that he is unable to control his behavior and must be given a wide license for conduct that is certainly unconventional according to the values prevalent outside the hospital. A patient was asked, "Why did you do that?" His answer, "How should I know? If I knew these things, I wouldn't be here," reflects the values thus emerging in the patient

role pattern. Patients have been heard comforting one another by saying, "Of course you can't do it." This process of "giving up defenses" is, of course, presumed to be essential for successful treatment, particularly in intensive analytic therapy, and a certain license for impulsivity and acting out seems to be part of much of psychotherapy in general. But the patient often seems to reserve his right for such license with what appear to be unnecessary claims that he "can't help it."

One might add that whereas clinical evidence indicates that patients often feel a strong guilt at "having let others down," the values of the patient group seldom allow its overt expression—and even supply convenient channels for its projection elsewhere. It is not uncommon for patients to bitterly indict their parents, often for the same weakness they themselves "can't help," sometimes talking as if a kind of deliberate conspiracy was involved in the events that led to their own illness. The weakness of this logic seems evident even to those who use it most persistently, which again indicates that the social usages which allow its expression must have an important social function to the patient group. If a little harsh, it may be one way to deny one's responsibility for being sick, while nevertheless accounting for one's illness in terms that are current outside the hospital walls.

The point is that most of the persons a patient encounters in the hospital, certainly the other patients, are perfectly willing to acknowledge that ego deficiencies are not his "fault" and that he is often compelled to act without the benefit of sufficient controls. To what audience, then, does he address his continual protest that he has the *right* to some license and can't help the fact that he is sick? Largely, one begins to think, these assertions are broadcast not to the audience assembled in the confined orbit of the hospital at all—but to the omnipresent public which, as shall be seen, fails to validate his commitment to therapy. To assume that hospital walls or the implicit ideology of psychiatric institutions protect the patient from this audience would be an unfortunate oversight. The image of the public audience is firmly incorporated within the patient himself, and this image is constantly reinforced by newspapers, movies, radio, and television. The specialized values which psychiatry introduces into the hospital setting cannot entirely overcome the fact that the patient remains sensitive to current public notions about mental illness, and, on certain levels of awareness, even shares them in substance.

What does the outside audience ask of the patient—and its internalized image make him ask of himself? Essentially, he is asked to justify his voluntary retirement to a hospital by demonstrating that he *needs* it, by displaying a distinct illness requiring highly specialized help. The reason for a person's therapy in a residential setting is obviously the wish on everybody's part that he develop adjustive initiative. Yet if large parts of society doubt his claim to illness when he appears to have a certain competence —when, for instance, he rehearses healthy modes of behavior on or off the stage—he is left in the exposed position of one who has to *look* incompetent even while learning to become the exact opposite. A few minutes before going on the stage, a patient-actor announced, "It is a tradition here that the show *never* goes on!" This tradition is of particular interest because it has no basis in fact whatever. The show in question did go on, as had all of its predecessors. Yet even in the act of positive accomplishment the patient feels it important to repeat that failure is the norm among mental patients, for he always anticipates the question, "Look here, if you can do these things so well, why are you here?"

This prominent theme of helplessness which runs through the patient's verbal and behavioral repertoire again reasserts the basic paradox. For while much of the time he may display a passivity that almost suggests disability, he shows a certain ingenuity in organizing his passive behavior strategically; he can put considerable energy into maneuvers which show him to be helpless; in short, he can go to ample expense to give the impression of one who has nothing to expend. This does not imply, of course, that the patient is deliberately staging a deceptive performance. On the contrary, it suggests that the psychological needs which motivate such behavior are as compelling, in a certain way, as those considered to be anchored somewhere in the dynamics and genetics of his illness, and, in fact, tend to reinforce them.

In the absence of clear-cut organic symptoms, a "real" illness which "can't be helped" is the most precious commodity such patients have in their bargaining with society for a stable patient role. It is the most substantial credential available in their application for equal rights with the medical patient, and as such, may come to have an important social value to them. The fatal logic of this may be that the patient will find his social situation better structured for him if he gives in to his illness and helps others to create an unofficial hospital structure which supports the perpetuation of patienthood. . . .

The Check Forger and His Identity

EDWIN M. LEMERT

. . . Check forgery, in contrast to crimes such as assault, robbery, or burglary, is distinguished by its low social visibility. At the time the bogus check is passed there is nothing in the act which reveals that it is deviant or criminal. No special tools or equipment are needed for the crime, as with burglary, nor is any special setting required for the action, as is true with the "store" or the front of a bank, where the confidence man activates his fraudulent enterprises. Furthermore, there are few or no cues in interaction which give feedback to the forger from the victim nor from his own overt responses to indicate that he is behaving contrary to expectations; only later does the act become so defined and then never in direct interaction between the forger and his victim. Here is deviant behavior whose manifest or "existential" qualities do not differentiate or identify the person as a deviant.

Studies of the characteristics of check forgers based upon samples of those in jails, prisons, or on probation show considerable heterogeneity. However, it can be said that in general they more nearly resemble the general middle-class population than they do the populations of jails and prisons. They tend to be native white in origin, male, and much older than other criminals when they commit their first crimes—somewhere in their late 20's or early 30's. Their intelligence averages much higher than that of other criminals and they equal or surpass the general population in years of education completed. Skilled, clerical, professional, and managerial occupations are at least as fully represented among forgers as in the general population, perhaps more so. An impressive small minority have come from prestigeful, wealthy families, or those in which siblings have achieved social eminence, although considerable discounting of forgers' claims on this point is necessary. A high percentage of forgers have been long-time residents in the communities in which they committed their first offenses, but relatively few have lived in so-called "delinquency areas." Forgers are less likely than other criminals to have had a record of delinquency in their youth.

Prior socialization as delinquents or criminals is insufficient to explain the crimes of a large per cent, or even the majority, of persons who pass bad checks. Many have acquired and lived a considerable part of their early adult lives according to conventional middle-class morality. Typically they tend to express aversion to the idea of using violence in interpersonal dealings for whatever purpose. At the same time it must be said that an occasional person comes into forgery via the criminal route—the "short" con man turned forger, or the "old pro" burglar fallen on hard times, who has turned to passing bad checks for a livelihood. . . .

Reprinted from Edwin M. Lemert, *Human Deviance, Social Problems, and Social Control,* pp. 119–20, 121–24, 124–26, 131–32. © 1967. Reprinted by permission of Prentice-Hall, Inc., Englewood Cliffs, N.J.

PSEUDONYMITY

Once a check forger passes a series of worthless checks, the central fact of his existence becomes the threat of arrest. The business community through the police is strongly organized against the check forger, and when his checks appear, a number of procedures are activated. The more checks he has outstanding the more intensified and widespread are the efforts to apprehend him. Nearly all of these procedures have to do with identification, for once the check forger is identified as working in an area, apprehension and arrest quickly follow. Consequently if he is to survive as a forger he must develop and use techniques which prevent his identification.

Other criminals anticipate and adapt to the threat of arrest through anonymity, e.g., the burglar who works as night, or the bank robbers who work swiftly, sometimes wearing masks, which will confuse witnesses and make subsequent identification difficult or impossible. The confidence man manipulates his victims so that they often remain unaware they have been duped, or so that they fear to go to the police. The check forger cannot use these alternatives a defense against arrest because he must work during daylight hours and face large numbers of victims who require identification before they will cash his checks. While the forger might "cool out" a few victims in the manner of the con man, he can't psychologically disarm them all, nor can he employ the "fix" with any great degree of success. The district attorney usually has stacks of checks in evidence and numerous complainants ready to testify against him when he is arrested. The check forger by necessity relies upon pseudonyms as the preferred solution to his technical problem.

In a very literal sense the check forger becomes a real life actor, deliberately assuming a variety of roles and identities which both facilitate the cashing of checks and conceal his former or, if preferred, his "real" identity. Thus he may become a spurious customer in a supermarket, a guilty husband purportedly buying his wife a gift, an out-of-town real estate buyer, a corporation executive seeking to set up a branch office, an army officer on leave, or even an investigator for the Department of Internal Revenue.

The systematic forger's problem is the selection or fabrication of roles rather than the learning of new roles. His role models are occupational or leisure time roles or conventional society. Their distinctive quality is their high degree of superficiality.[1] While they require some acting ability, it is of a low order and easily learned. Such roles, as Goffman[2] suggests, are easily put together in response to situational cues from "bits and pieces of performances" which are already in the repertoire of most people.

Some negative learning is done by forgers in jail or prison, in the sense of things not to do, through listening to the stories of other check criminals. This is reflected in an adage followed by some, of "never try another man's stunt." While check forgers are responding to what they expect of others and what others expect of them, they do so in order to maintain deception and avoid arrest. Their behavior is fundamentally more in the nature of strategy or a swiftly moving game than it is a formal

---

[1] One forger reported using 285 names during his career. He also argued that the less documentary identification used the less suspicion aroused in the victim. Leonard Hart, "You're a Sucker If You Cash My Check," *Colliers,* February 7, 1953.

[2] Erving Goffman, *The Presentation of the Self in Everyday Life* (New York: Doubleday Anchor, 1959), pp. 72 ff.

or constituted pattern. In this sense it is generically similar to that of the confidence man, representing, however, a lower order of creativity and strategy.

MOBILITY

While the check man employs pseudonyms to avoid exposure when passing his worthless checks, he cannot simply don a different or innocuous identity afterward; he must move on, out of the vicinity of his crime or crimes. This, of course, can be said for other kinds of crimes, but mobility is more or less "built in" the check forger's situation largely because he preys upon resident businessmen, rather than on transients, as do pickpockets or con men.[3] His mobility is shaped by continual awareness of the time required to deposit checks, clear them, and communicate notification of non-payment to law enforcement and business protective agencies. In large part his daily activities are geared to the tempo and rhythms of banking and business, which demarcate the length of time he can pass checks and remain in a given area, ending in a critical interval during which danger of arrest is ubiquitous.[4] Experienced check forgers develop an almost intuitive sense of these points in time which punctuate their periodic movements.

The movements of the systematic check passer take on a circularity of action and motivation in the sense that their mobility begets more mobility. When queried as to why they stay on the move, check forgers usually explain that it is expensive to travel, and also that if they are to impress their businessmen-victims they must appear to have a bank account appropriate to the checks they cash.[5]

When you're moving around like that you've got to put up a front and look the part. You can't cash checks if you look seedy. How can I impress a clerk that I'm a businessman with a fat bank account if I don't have good quality clothes and stay in better hotels and drive an expensive make of car (rented).

The result of their high levels of expenditure is that forgers usually cash numerous checks in order to defray costs of constant travel and to maintain their prosperous style of life. The local "spreads" of checks stir strong indignation in the business community and quickly mobilize law enforcement people, sensing of which becomes the forger's motivation to move frequently. This suggests one of the main reasons why some check forgers speak of being caught up in something they can't stop.

SECLUSIVENESS

The vulnerability of the forger to recognition and identification impels him away from unnecessary contacts with other persons. Furthermore he must, if he is to remain free from arrest, keep himself from progressive involvement in social relationships, for with intimate in-

[3] Sheldon Messinger thoughtfully suggests that this factor prevents the forger from setting up accommodative relationships with police which are the basis of the fix, by which professional thieves protect themselves—personal communication.

[4] In one case, a forger traced his itinerary for the author. It uncovered a nine-months period, during which he worked in 25 cities between Oakland, California, and Atlanta, Georgia, never remaining longer than two weeks in each.

[5] This is only partially revealing of the motivation of the forger; it will become apparent that he also needs large amounts of money to underwrite the kinds of recreation or activities he pursues to relieve his tensions and sense of loneliness.

terchange of experiences there comes the danger of inadvertent as well as deliberate exposure by others. Free and unguarded interaction, even with persons whom he likes and trusts, becomes an indulgence.

The forger's seclusiveness, in large part a learned response of wariness, is reinforced by his high mobility, which necessarily makes his contacts and interactions of short-lived variety; he simply does not have the time to build up close relationships with the people he meets. His relationships or social activities tend to be those which he can enter and leave quickly, with a minimum of commitment; the roles he enacts apart from the passing of his checks are for the most part casual in nature. In addition to this role selectivity he learns to avoid specific forms of behavior likely to lead beyond casual interaction.

The forger often meets people in settings where drinking is expected behavior, yet he must take care not to drink to the point of intoxication for fear of letting slip revealing or inconsistent facts about himself. If he gets drunk he is likely to do it alone, but this is risky, too, for he might be picked up on a drunk charge and be exposed by a routine fingerprint check. If the forger gambles it is likely to be at a crowded race track or casino, not at a friendly poker game.

The preference for seclusiveness puts its stamp upon the sexual participation of the forger. He is more limited than other criminals in seeking erotic pleasures; for he seldom has a common law wife or a regular traveling companion. Prostitutes are not in keeping with his pseudonyms of respectability, and association with them may lead to unwanted brushes with the police. When he picks up a girl he is apt to be discriminating in his choice, and typically he will treat her lavishly, but seldom will he give her his true name. In this role, as in others, he remains an actor, although at times the temptation to be otherwise is great. . . .

THE GROWTH OF ANXIETY

An unavoidable conclusion seems to be that the more successfully the forger plays his roles the greater becomes the anxiety. The more checks he has outstanding the greater is his perception of the danger of arrest, and hence the greater his necessity to move on and devise new identities which conceal his previous behavior. The mounting sense of strain is made real to the forger by occasional "close calls" in which he barely escapes identification and arrest. As the anxiety magnifies it is reflected in jumpiness, stomach upsets, and other physical disturbances. A few check forgers develop acute symptoms, such as stomach ulcers.

My routine ran like this: I usually picked my city, then after I arrived I opened a savings account with cash. That's on Monday. On Tuesday I deposited some checks to my account, no good, of course. Wednesday I deposited another check and then drew out part of the account in cash. Then I left town. I worked this all over California, depositing maybe $50,000 altogether in I don't know how many banks. I suppose I got about $10,000 in cash. By this time the ulcers kicked up and I laid off in a resort.

Anxiety serves to amplify the suspiciousness of the forger; in some instances it is aggravated into a paranoidlike state, called the "bull horrors" by professional criminals. This is what is implies—abnormal fear of the police. In this state any unusual behavior of a victim, or a chance knock on a hotel room door, may be taken by the forger to mean that he has been discovered or that detectives have arrived to arrest him. At this point it is clear that the symbolic process has been affected; anxiety has begun to distort or interfere with the forger's ability to take over or realistically appraise the responses of others to his actions.

Cooler or highly experienced forgers

may be able to objectify the sources of their anxiety and symbolize it in the jargon of the professional criminal as "heat." As one forger put it, "The checks get hot, not me." As a solution to their psychic problems some forgers take a vacation, or "lay off at a resort." In this setting they continue to use a pseudonym but refrain from passing checks during the interim. This has the merit of reducing anxiety attributable to the fear of being recognized by victims or police, but it does not solve what by now has usually become an identity problem. In any event, contingencies or the need for more money are apt to cut short these palliative respites.

PERSONAL CRISIS

Detectives, police, and the check forgers themselves all agree that arrest is inevitable for the person who persists in passing bad checks for any length of time. A few check men manage to evade detection for several years, and one is known to have foiled the FBI for ten years, but these are the rare exceptions which prove the rule. Efficiently organized police work and fortuitous events undeniably have much to do with the forger's ultimate downfall, but from the point of view adopted here, these are constant factors with which he contends. That with which he is unable to cope is a kind of massive personal crisis which inheres in the prolonged enactment of his spurious roles.

That the forger reaches a dead end in his motivation can be inferred from the circumstances and attendant behavior at the time of the arrest. While a number of systematic forgers are apprehended entirely by chance or by police efforts, an impressive number of others engineer their own downfalls. For example, some phone the police or a parole officer and tell them where they can be found. Closely akin are those who foreclose their current criminal careers rather simply by remaining where they are, knowing full well that police or detectives will soon catch up with them, to find them in a resigned mood awaiting their arrival.[6] Still other forgers, like fabled animals wending back to their mythical graveyard to die, return to their home community, there either to court arrest or to arrange for the inevitable in familiar surroundings. In more complex cases an otherwise accomplished check man makes a mistake, knowing at the time that it is a mistake which probably will land him in jail or prison.

After a weekend of drinking and sleeping with this girl I had known before, I woke up in my room at the Mark Hopkins with a hangover and no money left. I had one check left from those I had been passing in the city. It was over two weeks since I had started passing this series and knew I shouldn't try to cash this one. But I did anyway—and now here I am at Folsom.

When queried as to reasons for their sometimes open, sometimes oblique surrenders to detectives or other law enforcement agents, check forgers frequently refer to a cumulative state of apathy or sense of psychic exhaustion,[7]

---

[6] One check man, who spent much of his free time in bars, sensed that bartenders had been alerted to his presence in the area. He brought about his arrest in a bar simply by talking a little louder than was his custom. The owner overheard him and phoned the police.

[7] An appropriate descriptive term for this state is not easily found. It resembles the indifference to the threat of death which appeared among some inmates of Nazi concentration camps, as a response to "provisional detention without a time limit." See Bruno Bettelheim, "Individual and Mass Behavior in Extreme Situations," *Journal of Abnormal and Social Psychology,* 38 (1948), p. 434; Elie Cohen, *Human Behavior in the Concen-*

expressed in such statements as the following:

After that I began to appreciate what a heck of a job it is to pass checks.

In Seattle I got just plain tired of cashing checks.

The thrill I got from passing checks was gone.

I reached a point where I didn't care whether I stayed in Balboa or went to jail.

It's the same thing over and over again; you get tired of running.

It gets to be more and more of an effort.

You have a sense of being caught in something you can't stop.

One meaning that can be readily assigned to such statements is that, assuming satisfactions or rewards of the forger's activities remain unchanged or constant, their costs of acquisition in terms of effort and expenditure of psychic energy (anxiety) increase to a prohibitive point. What started out as "easy" check passing becomes more and more work or sheer labor, until that game is no longer worth the effort.

A second, less apparent implication of the sense of apathy which finally overwhelms the highly mobile check forger was suggested by a thoughtful older inmate of San Quentin prison, who had in his lifetime been both con man and a notorious utterer of very large checks. His interpretation was simply that during the course of a check passing spree, "You come to realize that kind of life has a false structure to it." This in sociological terms speaks of the inherent difficulty of establishing and maintaining identity by reference to purely extrinsic rewards. To admit this is for the forger in effect to admit that the roles he plays, or his way of life, make impossible a stable identity or the validation of a self ideal. An excerpt from an older published autobiography of a forger states the problem clearly.[8]

I could not rid myself of the crying need for the sense of security which social recognition and contact with one's fellows, and their approval furnishes. I was lonely and frightened and wanted to be where there was someone who knew me as I had been before.

IDENTITY CRISES AND NEGATIVE IDENTITY

The foregoing argues strongly that the personal crisis of the systematic forger stems less from a moral dilemma than it does from the erosion of identity. So conceived, his problem resides in a neutral component or dimension of the self, namely the sense of separateness and relationship to others, which is assumed to have its own consequences for behavior apart from substantive social value, "good or bad," assigned to it.[9] In a sense the forger fails because he suc-

tration Camp (New York: W. W. Norton & Company, Inc., 1953), p. 129. The reaction also suggests the idea of a "breaking point" or limits of effective response under stress. See Eli Ginzberg, et al., The Ineffective Soldier (New York: Columbia University Press, 1959). Something of "acute depersonalization" also seems involved. See Paul Schilder, The Image and Appearance of the Human Body (London: Kegan Paul, Trench, Trubner and Co., 1935).

[8] Roger Benton, Where Do I Go From Here (New York: L. Furman, 1936), p. 80.

[9] A conception approximating this distinction can be found in D. L. Burnham, "Identity Definition and Role Demand in Hospital Careers of Schizophrenic Patients," Psychiatry, 24 (1961), pp. 96–122.

ceeds; he is able to fend off or evade self-degradative consequences of his actions but in so doing he rejects forms of interaction necessary to convert his rewards in positive, status-specific self-evaluations. In time he reaches a point at which he can no longer define himself in relation to others on any basis. The self becomes amorphous, without boundaries; the identity substructure is lost. Apathy replaces motivation, and in phenomenological terms, "life" or "this way of life" is no longer worth living. This is the common prelude to the forger's arrest.

There is, of course, an adaptive aspect to the psychic surrender which precedes or attends the forger's almost casual entry into legal custody, which can be seen quite clearly in the sense of relief which is experienced at the time and also later in jail. From a moral perspective, the forger is "being brought to justice"; he "pays his debt to society." However, from the perspective of this chaper, his apathy or carelessness and subsequent arrest function to end his anxiety which is the subjective aspect of the organized "hue and cry" of modern crime detection. More importantly, they solve his identity problem; arrest immediately assigns the forger an identity, undesirable though it may be, as a jail or prison inmate. In effect, he receives or chooses a *negative identity*,[10] which despite its invidious qualities, is nearest and most real to him. At this juncture he is much like the actor who prefers bad publicity to none at all, or the youth who is willing to be a scapegoat for the group rather than not be part of the group at all.

[10] Erik H. Erikson, "The Problems of Ego Identity," in *Identity and Anxiety,* ed. M. R. Stein, *et al.* (New York: Free Press of Glencoe, Inc., 1960), pp. 60–62.

transforming deviant identity

Over the course of time deviance sometimes proves to be more punishing than rewarding. People whose deviance is self-destructive (e.g., alcoholics, drug addicts) are especially apt to try to relinquish their deviant ways and identity. But terminating a deviant career is no easy matter. The conditions for successfully transforming a deviant identity are narrow and exacting. They include the development of a conventional life style and identity, support from deviants and nondeviants alike, and opportunities to adopt conventional ways. Without these conditions, a transformation of social identity is unlikely.

In the first reading Wiseman shows how the hospital personnel who treat Skid Row alcoholics encourage them to occupy legitimate statuses that are simply not available to them outside a hospital setting; the result is that, after discharge from the hospital, many of these people return to Skid Row life. Trice and Roman then analyze the factors involved in the success of Alcoholics Anonymous. In the next reading Ray describes the problems drug addicts encounter in casting off their deviant identities—problems that often lead to relapse. In the final reading Johnson and Cressey show how Synanon provides the group conditions for successfully changing addict identity.

The Alcoholic's Return to Society

JACQUELINE P. WISEMAN

In the atmosphere of the institution, with the clear, friendly, logical counsel of the average middle-class professional worker, exhortations to re-enter society seem to make a great deal of sense. True, much hard work is demanded; but the plans suggested also appear to offer progress and the goal seems worthwhile. Middle-class non-drinkers seem like the world's happiest people from this vantage point.

When asked what he is going to do upon release from an institution, the Skid Row alcoholic typically says:

I'm hoping to "make it" in the outside world this time. I'm really going to try and not drink and to get back on the track. . . .

I'm going to try to get back into society. I know that I've been leading an aimless, useless life. It's really no kind of life for anyone, there on Skid Row. . . .

I'm going to work on my problem. I'm going to try to get back on my feet and live with the respectable world again. . . .

The Skid Row drunk is encouraged in this stance while in the institution by the professional posture of friendship offered by his therapist and other patients. Psychologists and social workers attempt to "gain rapport" with the patient. The alcoholic is also a part of the pseudo-mutual interaction that is a sought characteristic of group therapy sessions. These institutionally-created social success experiences often make the Skid Row man feel quite capable of inserting himself into any desirable primary group in the "outside world."

It is easy to forget that the environment of friendship at the institution is *contrived*[1] for the express purpose of offering the alcoholic a warm, supportive (therapeutic) community, and that the professionals who do this are actually trained to ultilize empathetic techniques as part of their jobs.[2] Mainstream society does not concern itself with being therapeutic, however, and the reaction of the man-on-the-street or the boss-on-the-job to the ex-alcoholic is often a cold wind

Reprinted from Jacqueline P. Wiseman, *Stations of the Lost: The Treatment of Skid Row Alcoholics,* pp. 227–38, © 1970. Reprinted by permission of Prentice-Hall, Inc., Englewood Cliffs, New Jersey.

[1] This is not to say that professional rehabilitation workers are not sincere in their feelings of friendship toward their patients or clients. It is rather that these friendships are not of the type to carry past quitting time, when the off-duty professional usually prefers the company of persons of his own educational and social background.

Alcoholics are not the only persons to mistake professional friendliness for the genuine thing. The following was overheard at County Jail between ex-state prison inmates who were discussing parole officers:

At least those guys who go by the book, you know what they are going to do. You don't overestimate their show of friendliness and get out of line and get slapped down. (Overheard while observing in the Jail.)

[2] See, for instance, William Schofield, *Psychotherapy, the Purchase of Friendship* (Englewood Cliffs, N.J.: Prentice-Hall, 1964).

TABLE [1]   Social Characteristics of Skid Row Men

Occupation (in month preceding interview)	Percent of Skid Row Men in Pacific City ($N = 2,582$)
(as indicated by current occupation)	
General laborers and construction workers	12
Culinary workers	6
Sales and clerical	5
Hotel managers and clerks	2
Teamsters	4
Longshoremen and warehousemen	3
Seamen and stewards	3
Domestics	1
Other	15
Not reported	6
No employment in preceding month	43

Source: *Pacific City Urban Redevelopment Association Report* (1963).

that clears away the haze of such pretensions to easy acceptance. Thus there is minimum transfer of personal adjustment training from the institution to the outside world.[3] Often this is a reality shock of no mean proportions, one sufficient to send the recipient back to the warm unreality of alcohol.

Furthermore, the fact is that the Skid Row alcoholic is really not *returning* to any niche being held for him in society in the same sense that it often is for the middle-class alcoholic.[4] Rather, the Skid Row man is trying to break into mainstream society *for the first time* and he usually must do this without the support of friends or relatives as "starters."[5]

Using current occupation as an indicator, Table [1] is quite suggestive of just how much social distance there is be-

[3] See Robert Rapaport, *Community as Doctor: New Perspectives on a Therapeutic Community* (London: Tavistock Publications, 1959; and Springfield, Illinois: Charles C Thomas, 1960), for a discussion of the deliberate creation of a permissive, security-oriented atmosphere that is no doubt helpful in reducing anxieties in patients but bears little resemblance to the less well-planned outside world.

[4] For the middle-class returnee, the problem is one of breaking down the counterrole relationships that were built up during the heavy drinking period when they were "irresponsible," according to middle-class standards. The middle-class ex-alcoholic's problems in overcoming the dependency relationships he helped to create have been well-chronicled. See Joan K. Jackson, "Family Structure and Alcoholism," *Mental Hygiene* (July 1959), 403–7. Jackson points out that "if the husband does stop drinking, he is usually permitted to exercise his family roles *only on probation*." (Emphasis mine.)

[5] At least, there usually are no relatives to whom he is willing or able to return. Sometimes this is by choice. As one man put it:

I got to straighten myself out *before* I go to see my family. I can't let them see me this way. . . .

Another said:

Most of us would starve rather than call our relatives. That relationship is *over*. . . .

tween middle-class society, in general, and the average Skid Row alcoholic's position upon release. (Note the absence of professional, semi-professional, managerial, and technical occupations, as well as skilled workers—the backbone of the middle class. Additionally, almost half of the Row men [43 percent] had *no* employment in the preceding month.)

Furthermore, . . . the Skid Row man is much more often a man of inadequate skills and education than a man who has "skidded," in the social mobility sense of the term, from a relatively high position down to the bottom of the barrel. A number of studies previously cited indicate many Skid Row alcoholics were never in any stratum of society but were "wanderers" or working or living in institution-like settings from early youth.[6] Others relinquished their social niche so long ago and so completely that they have no one waiting for them to "return." (The possible exception is among those men who still have parents living. But here the choice is not too attractive— living with [and possibly caring for] an aged parent.)[7]

[6] This is not intended to suggest that the Skid Row alcoholic was not of some higher status before coming to Skid Row. By the very term "bottom of the barrel" Skid Row residents suggest they were higher at *some* time, at least in their own eyes. However, both Donald J. Bogue, in *Skid Row in American Cities* (Chicago: University of Chicago Press, 1963), pp. 320–22, and Howard M. Bahr, *Homelessness and Disaffiliation* (New York: Columbia University Bureau of Applied Social Research, 1968), pp. 220–30, indicate that these men started out in the lower portion of the status continuum and rose only slightly before losing status. As previously mentioned, skidding from high status to Skid Row happens in only a few well-publicized cases.

Pittman and Gordon's study of the chronic police case inebriate produced the following socio-economic characteristics, scarcely indicative of middle-class status:

Approximately . . .
90 percent are skilled and unskilled workers (as compared with 59 percent of the general population)
75 percent had only a grade school education (as compared with 41 percent of the general population)
85 percent had no permanent residence, lived at a mission or shelter, a hotel or shelter, a hotel or rooming house (as compared with 21 percent of the general population).

See David J. Pittman and C. Wayne Gordon, *Revolving Door* (Glencoe, Ill.: The Free Press, 1958), Chap. 2, "The Sociocultural Profile," pp. 16–58.

Bogue, *Skid Row in American Cities,* pp. 13–14, reports that, "in comparison with the adult population of the city of Chicago as a whole, the . . . Skid Row men are:

a. Foreign born white or "other nonwhite" race (American Indian).
b. Single, widowed, or divorced: half have never married.
c. Middle-aged or older men, concentrated in the ages of 45–74.
d. Very poorly educated, with more than one-fifth being "functionally illiterate" (having completed fewer than five years of elementary school).
e. Unemployed. The unemployment rate among the Skid Row men was more than eight times that of the general population.
f. Not in the labor force, with "unable to work" as the primary reason.
g. Employed as wage or salary workers.
h. Of extremely low income, with almost one-half living on less than $90 per month. Almost one-fourth of the men had received less than $500 in cash during the preceding year.

[7] Agents of social control report a large proportion of Skid Row alcoholics keep in contact (usually through correspondence) with their mothers. (Maintenance of this mother-son tie is often cited by those Freudianly inclined group therapy leaders as

DETAILS OF EXECUTING "THE PLAN"

The plan the Skid Row alcoholic is presented for his "return" to middle-class society is not only demanding, in the face of his social class and occupational limitations, but somewhat skimpy as to details. The plan emphasizes only a few of the needs that he must meet and problems he must overcome to lead any sort of satisfactory existence.

Getting a job, a room, and maintaining sobriety (partially through avoidance of drinking friends) is the gist of the plan, but these maxims do not offer a guide to fulfilling other needs and solving other problems without resorting to Skid Row tactics. What is he to do for social contact, contact with the opposite sex? How is he to get the job, the room, and avoid old friends? How can he change from a today-oriented, no-social-stake person to a future-oriented, middle-class person with margin? How is he to feel a *part* of this middle-class society?

Once the Skid Row alcoholic is "on the streets," the plan is not at all so logical or easy to follow as it seemed to be when presented to him in the institution. His framework for constructing meaning must shift from the professional formulas of the return to a society, which is substantially middle-class in concept, to that of the homeless man coping with day-to-day needs in a world that is alien and unfriendly.

This disjunction in viewpoint inside and outside the institution could easily account for the paucity of reasons offered by the Skid Row alcoholic for drinking excessively again, as well as his apparent insincerity about trying to stay dry. The Row men stop drinking while imbued with the rehabilitator's framework; they start drinking when they *see things differently* on the outside; they are at a loss to explain their lapse when they *return to the rehabilitation framework again,* for the decision to drink was not made within this framework.[8]

If these men were to give a detailed account of the framework that makes taking a drink seem like the most feasible thing to do at the time it is done, they would have to recount their life as experienced while trying to follow the re-entry plan. In such a description, the following items are pertinent:

SOCIAL STRUCTURE AND EMPLOYMENT OPPORTUNITIES

Even in times of high employment, it is difficult for a Skid Row alcoholic who has made the loop to get a job. In part, this is because (as has been mentioned) his union membership has lapsed during drinking bouts, or he cannot get a job in

---

evidence many alcoholics have not passed the oedipus crisis successfully, are latently homosexual as a result, and thus drink to forget the guilt attached to this perversion. Of course, there are no comparative figures on the proportion of nonalcoholic males who maintain contact with their mothers.)

[8] The fact there are an infinite number of mental frameworks, and a given individual may use more than one on the same phenomena, was discussed in chapter 1 to explain how Skid Row may be seen as both a disgusting and exciting place in which to live.

The point is that motivation to act is not, as seen by conventional psychological theory, the result of either inner personality characteristics or external cues alone but is rather the result of the way in which the situation is defined by the actor. The "wisdom" of a given plan of action is dependent upon the ground rules for such wisdom —that is, the theoretical framework by which the ingredients of the situation are "understood." When presumably intelligent individuals do things and later admit they "should have known better," they are referring to the fact they are now viewing the action from another, less sympathetic framework.

his trade as an electrician, metal worker, or one of the other crafts because so much of this work is tied in with contracts demanding security clearance for all workers.

To be unbondable means that the Skid Row man cannot work on many jobs connected with the handling of money or expensive equipment. His status as an alcoholic (or ex-alcoholic) means he cannot work around heavy machinery because of high-risk insurance provisions. Add to this his age, his loss of current experience in his field, and the suspiciously long gaps in his job record (which are hard to explain in any case), and the picture of a virtually unemployable man emerges.

Here is what these men say about the agony of job hunting:

I know what is going to happen. Everything will be going along all right until they find I didn't work for nine months. When they ask why, and I tell them I was in a mental institution for a drinking problem—that's all brother. They say, "Don't call us, we'll call you." . . .

I wish that someone would go in ahead of me and say, "Look, this guy is an ex-alcoholic, but he's okay now. He hasn't had a drink for some time and he's really trying to make it." That would clear the air, and then I could go in and talk about my abilities. . . .

If I get the job by lying about the past, sure as shootin' they find out.[9] I've been told nine months later that my security clearance didn't work out and I would have to leave even though my work was okay. Now, I'm afraid to accept something for fear I'll just lose it. . . .

My references are so old that there is no use using them. I don't have any recent ones because all the work I've been doing is in institutions. I was an orderly in the mental hospital and I'd like to work as an orderly now, but I don't dare tell where I got my experience. . . .

A final blow to his job-getting ability is his address and lack of telephone:

Skid Row is a bad address to have to put down on job applications. Right away they suspect you. And you don't have a telephone either so they can get in touch with you. I sometimes offer to check back from time to time, but you can see they aren't impressed. . . .

What kind of employment can these men get?

The range is limited to menial jobs with low pay. Such jobs often do not involve the man's former skill, or if they do, they are combined with other, low-status tasks. Gardening and "landscaping" the grounds of the numerous colleges and universities that dot the Pacific City area is a major resource for placement of ex-alcoholics by rehabilitation agents. Custodial work or cafeteria jobs are also available at such institutions. Other nonprofit institutions such as hospitals and rest homes hire these men as attendants or orderlies.

In Pacific City itself, the Row men must be willing to work as dishwashers, busboys and on other general clean-up jobs. If they are lucky, they may find employment as an elevator operator or night clerk in a cheap hotel. The Row men who were merchant seamen can try to get their papers reinstated and go back to sea.

If he gets a job, the Skid Row alco-

---

[9] Joan Emerson has suggested the Skid Row alcoholic (often accused of being a con-artist) apparently does not know how to lie sensibly in an employment interview situation. He either lacks the middle-class job-seeker's training in fictionalizing his job experience and covering up embarrassing spots with plausible excuses, or he has become out of practice in such activity.

holic finds himself torn between fear of failure and anger at what he conceives to be exploitation.

First of all, as his work experience recedes into dim memory, the Row man loses confidence in his abilities to hold a job. Mistakes and problems that cause a secure jobholder some uneasiness cause the ex-alcoholic trying to "make it" to endure true agony. As one man put it:

You aren't "current" on your job anymore. You forget how to do it. You are certain that people are watching you and saying, "He can't handle it." . . .

Another Row man related the following as what he conceived to be *his failure,* and as the reason he ultimately resumed drinking:

I had a good job in the filing department, it was arranged for me by the Welfare Home, and I was doing well when they put me in charge of six young high school drop-outs on a government project to train them for jobs. I couldn't get them to do anything! I worked and worked with them, but they weren't interested in learning. I felt like I was a failure as a supervisor. It made me so nervous I started taking tranquilizers, but they didn't really help, so one day I just walked out and went back to drinking. I couldn't handle that job. It was too much for me. . . .

Furthermore, the Skid Row man trying to stay dry usually feels he is treated differently than the rest of the employees. He is constantly reminded that he is lucky to have a job. He is often paid less than usually offered for the work.[10] He is asked to do things he does not think should be part of the job (such as mopping floors, when he was hired to do gardening). And he is expected to perform these extra tasks in good spirit. His experience is that if society wants him back at all . . . it is to exploit him. Often he does as he is told for a while, but the moment comes when anger at what he feels to be an injustice gets the better of him. Years of unemployment have not taught him the discipline of patience on the job, nor does he yet have enough social margin to make the cultivation of such forbearance seem worthwhile, being still "now" oriented. He quits, usually telling the boss off in the bargain (which means no recommendation for future job hunting), and the unemployment part of the cycle starts again.

PROBLEMS OF LIVING QUARTERS

The problems of living quarters, once the Row man is "outside" again, come up almost immediately. Based on the type of job he can get, the Row man can usually afford only a single room, perhaps with cooking privileges, and probably near or in Skid Row. As previously

[10] . . . Skid Row men are often exploited by employers who pay them below-standard or state-minimum wages, taking advantage of their desperate need for work and money. Bogue, in *Skid Row in American Cities,* p. 492, also noted this in his study of the Chicago Skid Row and incorporated the following into his recommendations for eliminating the area:

The minimum-wage laws are openly broken, both in spirit and in deed, along Skid Row. Some industries . . . manage to get their work done at rates as low as fifty cents an hour, by declaring the men . . . are independent operators. Skid Row hotels and restaurants also pay very low wages to night watchmen, janitors, and dishwashers. By making a tie-in arrangement between salary and room or board, the man gets paid less than the minimum wage, even when his pay check and benefits are given their combined cash value. . . . A careful review of minimum-wage compliance should be made of every hotel, restaurant, mission, employment agency, and firm known to employ numbers of Skid Row men.

mentioned, a single man who is not well dressed has difficulty renting a room, even in parts of the city that cater to laboring-class families or to single professional men. This is why the reformed alcoholic usually is resigned to living in Skid Row or the Tenderloin, where he blends in better. However, he is living in a drinking culture again.

Skid Row men who are given welfare vouchers through arrangements with jail welfare workers, the Christian Missionaries, the Welfare Home, or on direct appeal to the Welfare office, are sent to Skid Row hotels, inasmuch as the budget for such aid is limited and cannot support numerous men in any but the cheapest of rooms.[11] Skid Row cafes are the only eating establishments that take Welfare food tickets. Thus with the aid of Welfare, the Skid Row man finds himself sent to Skid Row, a drinking culture, and told not to start drinking again.

An alternative housing arrangement is the halfway house. There are quite a few such establishments in Pacific City, but they are not popular with the Skid Row man. Halfway houses are, from his point of view, too much like an institution in their scheduling of meals, lights out, and required attendance at AA meetings. Furthermore, these facilities are used by the state parole board to place prison parolees because this solves some surveillance problems. These ex-convicts are avoided by the Skid Row alcoholic unless he has also done some "hard time." Finally, those Skid Row men who have jobs complain they are constantly "hit up" for money by those without jobs.[12] This combination of association with ex-cons and penniless peers makes the halfway house an atmosphere charged with suspicion, uneasiness, and coolness. As one Skid Row man explained it:

There isn't much friendliness in a halfway house. You have to be careful who you speak to. Either they are broke and want to put the touch on you, or they are ex-cons and will take advantage of you. As a result, every man sort of keeps to himself. It's a cold and suspicious place. . . .[13]

SOBRIETY AND SOCIABILITY

The resolution not to drink and to avoid old drinking companions means spending most free time alone. As many of these men said:

---

[11] It seems strange that Pacific City Welfare officials do not see any contradiction in returning an alcoholic to live in a Skid Row hotel after he has been dried out and his health rebuilt at their Welfare Home for Homeless Men. When I was first granted permission to interview men at the Welfare Home for Homeless Men, the director said, as he bemoaned the high rate of recidivism among alcoholics:

If you can tell us why, after all we try to do for these men, that they go right back to Skid Row and drinking, you will be doing a great service with your research project. . . .

[12] Earl Rubington has done some of the few analyses of the problem of operating or living in a halfway house. (The tone of most literature on halfway houses reads like annual reports—glowingly successful.) Rubington outlines the problems faced by ex-alcoholic administrators in "Organizational Strains and Key Roles," *Administrative Science Quarterly*, 9, No. 4 (March 1965), 350–69, and the panhandling problems Skid Row alcoholics face within the halfway house itself. See "Panhandling and the Skid Row Subculture," paper read at 53rd Annual Meeting of the American Sociological Society (Seattle, Washington, August 28, 1958).

[13] My limited visits to halfway houses seem to confirm this. They are *very* quiet and the atmosphere is "cold." At one co-educational house, men and women could not eat meals at the same table. There was little talking in either the lounge or the coffee room. The alcoholism units at State Mental Hospital were swinging places by comparison.

I ate all my meals alone. Most of the time, I had to cook them in my room on my hot plate. About once a month, I could afford dinner out, but it's really no fun to eat out alone.

Sometimes, I'd go to an early movie, then home, read in bed a while, and go to sleep. Those four walls really close in on you after a while. . . .

I was trying to live on Valoda Street in Gadsen District of Pacific City [working class]. It was very lonesome. I finally went to Skid Row where you know everyone. I hadn't even had anything to drink, but was picked up for drunk. . . .

As previously mentioned, most Skid Row alcoholics do not seek support for their abstinence from liquor by attending local Alcoholics Anonymous meetings or by socializing at AA clubs. AA has never had much appeal for the lower-class alcoholic. It is primarily a middle-class organization, focused on helping ex-alcoholics regain their lost status. Skid Row alcoholics dislike what they refer to as "drunkalogs," in which members tell with relish just how low they had sunk while drinking. They dislike what they call the "snottiness" and "holier-than-thou" attitude of the reformed alcoholic (or "AA virgins" as they call them). The only reason Skid Row men go to AA is to convince another person (someone who would be impressed by such attendance) that they are really trying to lick the alcohol problem. As one put it:

I plan to join AA. Then people will believe I'm not drinking. As it is now, if I get drunk for three days, they don't count it if I'm sober for three weeks. . . .

Other Skid Row men tell of going to AA meetings out of desperation for *any* companionship and for the refreshments served. After the meeting, they feel a very strong urge to drink so that life becomes a round of early evening AA sessions followed by late evening drinking, and morning hangovers:

It got so that I just went to AA meetings and from there would get a bottle and go to my room and drink—usually Vodka, and then sober up in time for the next AA meeting. . . .

One might ask why the Skid Row alcoholic does not make friends with co-workers on his new job—if he has found one. The answer given by many of the men is that they have nothing in common with the average worker. Experiences on the loop seem to socialize the Row man so that he is unable to enjoy the company of those who do not share such experiences as living in institutions on the circle, fooling the authorities, panhandling, and general Skid Row adventures.[14] This is especially true if the Skid Row alcoholic has been placed in a gardening or groundskeeper job. His co-workers are seldom urban men, and the Skid Row man keenly misses the presence of the "city" and the men who have knowledge of its many-faceted underlife.[15]

[14] . . . these subjects constitute a substantial proportion of small talk among Skid Row men.

[15] Howard M. Bahr has been engaged in some well-constructed tests of generally-accepted hypotheses concerning life on Skid Row with special emphasis on the area of socialization. His findings seem to indicate Skid Row men develop a rather strong attachment to Skid Row drinking companions, which aid in their identification with the Row and their feelings of alienation off the Row. See Howard M. Bahr and Stephen J. Langfur, "Social Attachment and Drinking in Skid Row Life Histories," *Social Problems*, 14, No. 4 (Spring 1967), 464–72. Also, see Howard M. Bahr, "Drinking, Interaction, and Identification: Notes on Socialization into Skid Row," *Journal of Health and Social Behavior*, 8, No. 4 (December 1967), 272–85.

Of new on-the-job acquaintances, the Skid Row drinker says:

They don't speak my language. They are square-Johns.

I got so lonesome for someone who talked my language. You can't talk to some jerks. . . .

I want to talk with someone who knows what I'm talking about. Some guys have never done nothing. . . .[16]

THE PROBLEM WITH WOMEN

A Skid Row man trying to "make it" back into society has a particularly complicated problem so far as women are concerned.

As previously mentioned, the average Skid Row man is usually quite charming and has no trouble attracting female companions on the Row or partners at the State Mental Hospital. However, neither of these types of women is seen by the alcoholic as a good influence for a man who is attempting to stop drinking. What he wants, in his own words, is "a decent woman."

The problem is, though, that he is shy and awkward about pursuing a woman of this type. As one Skid Row man put it:

It's been so long since I been around a decent woman, I don't know how to act. . . .

Furthermore, if the Skid Row man has recently been in jail, at the Christian Missionaries, in a non-coeducational half-way house, or spending his time in all-male company on the Row, he has lost practice in communicating with women. Wallace quotes one such man's insecurity about women:

Now, how shall I ask one of these girls for a dance? No need of introductions, that much I knew. Which would be best, "C'mon kid, let's prance this out?" Or, "May I have this dance?" How I wished these girls were men. I could talk to men.[17]

Another worry is the lack of acceptable credentials.[18]

What can I offer a decent woman? I have no job and no prospects. If I go with a drinking woman, sure as shootin' I'll wind up drinking again. . . .

As noted, the Skid Row alcoholic does have some access to professional women who would like to mother him, but here he must relinquish any hope of being head of the house, and must settle instead for being sort of a house pet.

---

[16] The experience of being "on the other side" apparently does not leave a man unmarked psychologically and, paradoxically, although it is degrading, it is simultaneously a source of pride to have survived it. As a survivor, a man actually feels superior to those who have not had this experience, and this creates a chasm between deviants and nondeviants that may never be closed again. John Irwin, in his study, *The Felon* (Englewood Cliffs, N.J.: Prentice-Hall, 1970), speaks of "the enduring affinity" ex-convicts have for each other—others with the same experience. It is also said that drug addicts at Synanon still consider themselves "hipper" than the nonuser.

[17] Samuel E. Wallace, *Skid Row as a Way of Life* (Tottowa, N.J.: The Bedminister Press, 1965), p. 174.

[18] George Orwell, in *Down and Out in Paris and London* (New York: Harcourt, Brace & World Company, 1933), p. 148, speaks of "the degration worked in a man who knows that he is not even considered fit for marriage. . . . Cut off from the whole race of women, a tramp feels himself degraded to the rank of a cripple or a lunatic. No humiliation could do more damage to a man's self-respect."

THE DAILY ROUTINE

What is the daily round like for this man who is trying to gain some social margin so as to get in and stay in the society depicted by the middle-class professional? The mundane experiences of this project form the framework within which the Skid Row man gives up and takes a drink.

A composite description might go something like this: rise early in a lonely room; breakfast fixed on a hot plate, eaten alone in the room, or eaten alone in a cheap restaurant; ride the bus to work (often quite a distance), because an alcoholic usually has lost his driver's license or cannot afford a car and cannot afford to live near work; work all day at a boring, menial, poorly paid job with dull, unsympathetic (to the alcoholic) co-workers and an unsympathetic (to the alcoholic) boss; return at night to eat dinner alone and watch television in the hotel lobby, or read, attempt to freshen his limited wardrobe, or go to bed, knowing a similar day awaits him tomorrow.

Although he may be seeing a welfare worker or a therapist on a regular basis, the dried-out chronic drunk trying to "make it" discovers his relationship with these professionals is not the same as it was in institutions, and he has no claim on their outside social time for informal friendship.

The solitary status of the Skid Row man also affects his opportunities for *experiencing* success. Success, like margin, is an attribute ascribed by others. The Skid Row man has no friends or relatives to reinforce his determination to

"make it" or congratulate him on progress. No one (except for an occasional professional therapist) seems even aware of his efforts to prove worthiness. Respectable society is not an entity, and it neither hands out keys to the city nor certificates of social integration. It seems almost impossible for a Skid Row man to know when he has, indeed, "made it." Certainly, merely going through the motions of being respectable will not necessarily elicit immediate recognizable rewards.[19]

The agents of social control counsel "patience" and that "better things will eventually come." But patience means future-orientation, a psychological state of mind that is foreign to a man who has been operating for many years on here-and-now satisfactions.

The story that follows is typical. The man was first interviewed at the Welfare Home for Homeless Men and then seen about a month later, quite by chance, at County Jail. He explained his lapse this way:

I got a job at the Green Pine Hotel in the suburbs as janitor. I was terribly lonesome. I had no friends, I was on the job there two weeks and then came down to the city. There's quite a few fellows I know around. I want to be with somebody I know once in a while. I liked the job, but I got lonesome. There's nothing to do and no one to talk to. If I had had companionship, it wouldn't have happened. You get lonesome in one room. . . .

Also revealing is the answer to the question, "How were things out there?", asked of a Skid Row alcoholic who had just returned to jail after two weeks of freedom. He replied:

[19] Additionally, trying and failing to gain acceptance is much more ego-debilitating than not trying at all. Like going through college rush week and not getting a bid from a sorority or fraternity, there is no longer any doubt about your social acceptance with a group deemed desirable. The Skid Row alcoholic, in his efforts to get back into society may also encounter a "reality shock" not intended by his rehabilitators—that of finding that he is socially undesirable to the society he seeks, regardless of his efforts to the contrary.

Pretty rough! Everything moves so fast. No one knows or cares if you are alive. You just don't fit in anywhere. . . .

GOING FULL CIRCLE: "AND THEN I DECIDED TO HELL WITH IT"

In contrast to a return to the society and reality suggested as a goal by professional rehabilitators, there exists also the Skid Row society with its instant warmth, friendliness, and general conviviality. Here, many of the friends of the job-holding Skid Row alcoholic are living on welfare and spending their time drinking, partying, and making out. The dole in Pacific City provides a standard of living probably only slightly lower than the pay of the first menial job available to the alcoholic just discharged from an institution. The room of the "unreformed drunk" may compare favorably with the room in which the struggling "ex-alcoholic" is living. The amount and quality of food each is able to obtain varies but little, even though the unreformed man may be getting part of his daily bread from missions and other charitable organizations.

Furthermore, having once made the loop and learned its machinations, the Skid Row alcoholic trying to "make it" knows that these institutions are always available to him. Compared to the way he is living while trying to make a comeback, some of the stations that he despised and feared at first seem pleasant in retrospect.[20] Old friends are certain to be in any institutions he should choose (or be sent to). Although "admission to society" is so nebulous as to defy definition or provide any feeling of belonging, admission to an institution is just the opposite. While progress toward the goal of reintegration into society is difficult to apprehend, progress in an institution is well marked. On the inside the alcoholic is often told if he has done well on a task, and may be given a higher status job; in therapy, he is praised for "being honest and not holding back"; at the Christian Missionaries he may be promoted to a better room or a larger gratuity; he may even have "institutional margin" on the basis of past performance.[21] Outside the loop station, in Skid Row society, there are the small triumphs of making out and sharing one's

---

[20] Before it happens, the thought of being sent to jail for drunkenness, or going to a mental hospital for "the cure," seems like one of the worst experiences that a man can have. However, when he finds he *can* survive it, going through the same thing again holds fewer terrors. At times he even feels strengthened by the experience. Jack Black, a confessed thief of all trades, explains this phenomenon in terms of his reactions to the whipping post (*You Can't Win* [New York: The Macmillan Co., 1927], p. 278):

> As a punishment, it's a success; as a deterrent it's a failure; if it's half and half, one offsets the other and there's nothing gained. The truth is I wouldn't have quit no matter how I was treated. The flogging just hardened me more, that's all. I found myself somewhat more determined. . . . I had taken everything they had in the way of violence and could take it again. Instead of going away in fear, I found my fears removed. *The whipping post is a strange place to gather fresh confidence and courage, yet that's what it gave me. . . .*

. . . Furthermore, while the quest for society is fraught with uncertainty, life in an institution offers security of rules and regulations plus provisions for all the exigencies of living which are a problematic struggle on "the outside."

[21] Howard Bahr's analysis of the relationship of drinking and social disaffiliation to presumed "institutionalization" indicates that it is not the simple one-to-one relationship some persons have thought. Rather, it is a complicated, interactive process. Howard M. Bahr, "Institutional Life, Drinking, and Disaffiliation," a paper read at the 1968 annual meeting of the Society for the Study of Social Problems in Boston.

cleverness with friends over a bottle.

Thus where the road into respectable society is cold and lonely, Skid Row and the stations of the loop offer conviviality, feeling of accomplishment, as well as an opportunity to forget the struggle.[22] The Row man can stop seeking an idealized society at the end of the rainbow, stop leading a treadmill existence, and return to being seen by his most significant others as a real person again.[23]

An important character in the "Return of the Prodigal Son" story is the respectable brother who stayed at home and out of trouble. In a very true sense, he epitomizes the general attitude of the average citizen toward anyone who strays from the fold too long or too completely and then expects to be granted amnesty merely by some suffering and an apology.

When asked to come to the party given in honor of the returning prodigal son, the self-righteous brother was angry and said to his father:

Lo, these many years do I serve thee, neither transgress I at any time thy commandment; and yet thou never gavest me a kid, that I might make merry with my friends; but as soon as this thy son was come, which hath devoured thy living with harlots, thou hast killed for him the fatted calf.

Luke 15:29–30

To which the Skid Row alcoholic might reply, as he gives up the fight for acceptance in the rehabilitator's society and returns to Skid Row living and inevitably a loop institution:

And then I decided to hell with it, and I started drinking again.

CYCLING OUT

Is there any way off the loop? Besides the few who stick it out long enough to get back sufficient social margin to reclaim a lost existence, what other ways are there for Skid Row men to escape?

There appear to be three major ways off Skid Row:

1. Become a live-in servant for an institution (or, once in a while, for a professional woman).
2. Go into alcoholic rehabilitation as a profession.
3. Die.

The first has been amply discussed. Ex-alcoholics may be found at many nonprofit institutions, especially hospitals and rest homes, for some small wages plus board and room. This becomes, then, their new way of life.

The second escape route has possibly been traveled successfully by more alcoholics than is generally known. During the course of this study, the number of ex-alcoholics in positions of agents of social control on the loop was astounding. Ex-alcoholics can be found in ad-

---

[22] It could be the grinding monotony of regular but boring and often physically demanding work, the lack of desirable or interesting companions, and the bleakness of his living quarters contribute to a certain "flatness" of experience quite unlike the little adventures the Skid Row alcoholic has enjoyed both in institutions and on the Row. Just as soldiers returning from the war find civilian life flat at first so may the Skid Row man find the square life dull.

[23] It is indeed a paradox that the Skid Row man must return to an *ad hoc* existence (where neither his past nor his future is seriously affected by present adventures) to feel he is accepted as a real person. Only on Skid Row, where times of pleasure are momentarily "sealed off" from their consequences, can he enjoy himself. When he is working at his low-status job and living his ascetic "attempting-to-make-it" life, he has all the burdens of responsibility to the past and cognizance of the future without any of the rewards.

ministrative positions in the Courts, County Jail, the City Hospital, the State Mental Hospital, Welfare Home for Homeless Men, and the Christian Missionaries.

Other ex-alcoholics are to be found making a career of operating Alcoholics Anonymous clubs, halfway houses, and therapy groups. The newest halfway house for me to be started under the sponsorship of the Pacific City Department of Public Health will be manned by ex-alcoholics.

The factors underlying the success of this maneuver to get off the loop may well center about the fact that "going into rehab work" converts what is a vice in the outside world (i.e., excessive drinking, institutionalization, familiarity with other alcoholics, and absence of recent job experience) into an employable virtue. Indeed, this idea has been formally accepted by many agencies concerned with reform and rehabilitation of deviants.[24] "It takes one to know and understand one" philosophy prevails. Paradoxically, however, the assumption an ex-alcoholic will be more understanding in working with alcoholics has not generally held true if we are to accept the testimony of the men they work with. Alcoholics complain that, "There's nothing colder than an ex-alcoholic," which

suggests that once a man makes it to "the right side" he no longer empathizes with former buddies but rather identifies with the associates of his newly-established status—other agents of social control.[25]

Death is the third way off the loop. Six Row men died in Pacific City during the course of this study of such causes as acute alcoholism, cirrhosis of the liver, brutal beatings in an alley, a seizure, and an internal hemorrhage. Men who get off the loop permanently in this way, have long ago given up the fight for reentrance into society. After a few such attempts they unhesitatingly take a drink the moment they leave an institution. Such men can be roughly divided into two types—both of whom accept the consequences of the bridges they have burned and the lonely life that will be their future.

They are:

1. The so-called institutionalized man, the perennial and resigned loop maker. This includes the chronic drunkenness offender who uses the jail as an emergency hotel in bad weather, the self-admitted State Hospital man who uses that institution for drying out and building up both physically and financially, and the mission rounder who,

[24] See, for instance, National Institute of Mental Health, *Experiments in Culture Expansion,* Report of proceedings of a conference on "The Use of Products of a Social Problem in Coping with the Problem" (Norco, California, July 1963), and *Offenders as a Correctional Manpower Resource,* Report of a seminar convened by the Joint Commission on Correctional Manpower and Training (Washington, D.C., March 1968). Erving Goffman has called the phenomenon of the deviant using his stigma to advantage as "going into business for himself." "Twelfth-step work" in Alcoholics Anonymous and Synanon (for drug users) are other examples of this phenomenon.

[25] An excellent description of the way in which the ex-alcoholic seeks to identify with agents of social control to the extent that he is actually rude to ex-drinking partners is to be found in Earl Rubington's "Grady 'Breaks Out': A Case Study of an Alcoholic's Relapse," *Social Problems,* 11, No. 4 (Spring 1964), 372–80. This phenomenon of upwardly mobile low-caste persons turning with vehemence upon those who were formerly "their own kind" has been noted by many sociologists and psychologists, and has been given many labels including "identification with the aggressor," and "self-hatred of one's membership in a despised group.". . .

cursing the hand who feeds him, still goes back when forced by hunger and illness.

2. *The Welfare Skid Row man* who "graduates" to vouchers and settles down to living on what his check provides, plus what he can earn on pick-up jobs. He drinks heavily except on the days he has an appointment with his social worker. Intermittent institutionalizations keep him alive.

Both these types of Row men are trapped on the loop. Death is their only avenue of escape.

Delabeling, Relabeling, and Alcoholics Anonymous

HARRISON M. TRICE
PAUL MICHAEL ROMAN

An increasing amount of research emphasis in social psychiatry in recent years has been placed upon the rehabilitation and return of former mental patients to "normal" community roles (Sussman, 1966). The concomitant rapid growth of community psychiatry as a psychiatric paradigm parallels this interest, with community psychiatry having as a primary concern the maintenance of the patient's statuses within the family and community throughout the treatment process so as to minimize problems of rehabilitation and "return" (Pasamanick *et al.,* 1967; Susser, 1968). Despite these emphases, successful "delabeling" or destigmatization of mental patients subsequent to treatment appears rare (Miller, 1965; Freeman and Simmons, 1963). It is the purpose of this paper to explore an apparent negative instance of this phenomenon, namely a type of social processing which results in *successful* delabeling, wherein the stigmatized label is replaced with one that is socially acceptable.

The so-called labeling paradigm which has assumed prominence within the sociology of deviant behavior offers a valuable conceptualization of the development of deviant careers, many of which are apparently permanent (Scheff, 1966). In essence, labeling theory focuses upon the processes whereby a "primary deviant" becomes a "secondary deviant" (Lemert, 1951:75–76). Primary deviance may arise from myriad sources. The extent and nature of the social reaction to this behavior is a function of the deviant's reaction to his own behavior (Roman and Trice, 1969), the behavior's visibility, the power vested in the statuses of the deviant actor, and the normative parameters of tolerance for deviance that exist within the community. Primary deviance that is visible and exceeds the tolerance level of the community may bring the actor to the attention of mandated labelers such as psychiatrists, clinical psychologists, and social workers.

If these labelers see fit "officially" to classify the actor as a type of deviant, a labeling process occurs which eventuates in (1) self concept changes on the part of the actor and (2) changes in the definitions of him held by his immediate significant others, as well as the larger community. Behavior which occurs as a consequence of these new definitions is called secondary deviance. This behavior is substantively similar to the original primary deviance but has as its source the actor's revised self concept, as well as the revised social definition of him held in the community.

Previous research and theoretical literature appear to indicate that this proc-

Reprinted from *Social Problems,* Vol. 17, No. 4 (Spring 1970), pp. 538–546, pp. 536–548, by permission of the Society for the Study of Social Problems and the authors.

ess is irreversible, particularly in the cases of mental illness or so-called residual deviance (Miller, 1965; Myers and Bean, 1968). No systematic effort has been made to specify the social mechanisms which might operate to "return" the stigmatized secondary deviant to a "normal" and acceptable role in the community. In other words, delabeling and relabeling have received little attention as a consequence of the assumption that deviant careers are typically permanent.

Conceptually, there appear to be at least three ways whereby delabeling could successfully occur. First, organizations of deviants may develop which have the primary goal of changing the norms of the community or society, such that their originally offending behavior becomes acceptable (Sagarin, 1967). For example, organized groups of homosexuals have strongly urged that children be educated in the dual existence of homosexuality and heterosexuality as equally acceptable forms of behavior.

Secondly, it is possible that the mandated professionals and organizations who initially label deviant behavior and process the deviant through "treatment" may create highly visible and explicit "delabeling" or "status-return" ceremonies which constitute legitimized public pronouncements that the offending deviance has ceased and the actor is eligible for re-entry into the community. Such ceremonies could presumably be the reverse of "status degradation" rituals (Garfinkel, 1957).

A third possible means is through the development of mutual aid organizations which encourage a return to strict conformity to the norms of the community as well as creating a stereotype which is socially acceptable. Exemplary of this strategy is Alcoholics Anonymous. Comprised of 14,150 local groups in the United States in 1967, this organization provides opportunities for alcoholics to join together in an effort to cease disruptive and deviant drinking behavior

in order to set the stage for the resumption of normal occupational, marital, and community roles (Gellman, 1964).

The focus of this paper is the apparent success in delabeling that has occurred through the social processing of alcoholics through Alcoholics Anonymous and through alcoholics' participation in the A.A. subculture. The formulation is based chiefly on participant observation over the past 15 years in Alcoholics Anonymous and data from various of our studies of the social aspects of alcoholism and deviant drinking. These observations are supplemented by considerable contact with other "self-help" organizations. These experiences are recognized as inadequate substitutes for "hard" data; and the following points are best considered as exploratory hypotheses for further research.

THE "ALLERGY" CONCEPT

The chronic problem affecting the reacceptance into the community of former mental patients and other types of deviants is the attribution of such persons with taints of permanent "strangeness," immorality, or "evil." A logical method for neutralizing such stigma is the promulgation of ideas or evidence that the undesirable behavior of these deviants stems from factors beyond their span of control and responsibility. In accord with Parsons' (1951) cogent analysis of the socially neutralizing effects of the "sick role," it appears that permanent stigmatization may be avoided if stereotypes of behavior disorders as forms of "illness" can be successfully diffused in the community.

Alcoholics Anonymous has since its inception attempted to serve as such a catalyst for the "delabeling" of its members through promulgating the "allergy concept" of alcohol addiction. Although not part of official A.A. literature, the allergy concept plays a prominent part in

A.A. presentations to non-alcoholics as well as in the A.A. "line" that is used in "carrying the message" to non-member deviant drinkers. The substance of the allergy concept is that those who become alcoholics possess a physiological allergy to alcohol such that their addiction is predetermined even before they take their first drink. Stemming from the allergy concept is the label of "arrested alcoholic" which A.A. members place on themselves.

The significance of this concept is that it serves to diminish, both in the perceptions of the A.A. members and their immediate significant others, the alcoholic's responsibility for developing the behavior disorder. Furthermore, it serves to diminish the impression that a form of mental illness underlies alcohol abuse. In this vein, A.A. members are noted for their explicit denial of any association between alcoholism and psychopathology. As a basis for a "sick role" for alcoholics, the allergy concept effectively reduces blame upon one's *self* for the development of alcoholism.

Associated with this is a very visible attempt on the part of A.A. to associate itself with the medical profession. Numerous publications of the organization have dealt with physicians and A.A. and with physicians who are members of A.A. (*Grapevine,* 1968). Part of this may be related to the fact that one of the co-founders was a physician; and a current long time leader is also a physician. In any event, the strong attempts to associate A.A. with the medical profession stand in contrast to the lack of such efforts to become associated with such professions as law, education, or the clergy.

Despite A.A.'s emphasis upon the allergy concept, it appears clear that a significant portion of the American public does not fully accept the notion that alcoholism and disruptive deviant drinking are the result of an "allergy" or other organic aberration. Many agencies associated with the treatment of alcohol-related problems have attempted to make "alcoholism is an illness" a major theme of mass educational efforts (Plaut, 1967). Yet in a study of 1,213 respondents, Mulford and Miller (1964) found that only 24 percent of the sample "accepted the illness concept without qualification." Sixty-five percent of the respondents regarded the alcoholic as "sick," but most qualified this judgment by adding that he was also "morally weak" or "weak-willed."

The motivation behind public agencies' efforts at promulgating the "illness" concept of behavior disorders to reduce the probability of temporary or permanent stigmatization was essentially upstaged by A. A. Nonetheless, the data indicate that acceptance of the "illness" notion by the general public is relatively low in the case of alcoholism and probably lower in the cases of other behavior disorders (cf. Nunnally, 1961). But the effort has not been totally without success. Thus it appears that A.A.'s allergy concept does set the stage for reacceptance of the alcoholic by part of the population. A more basic function may involve the operation of the A.A. program itself; acceptance of the allergy concept by A.A. members reduces the felt need for "personality change" and may serve to raise diminished self-esteem.

Other than outright acceptance of the allergy or illness notion, there appear to be several characteristics of deviant drinking behavior which reduce the ambiguity of the decision to re-accept the deviant into the community after his deviance has ceased.

Unlike the ambiguous public definitions of the causes of other behavior disorders (Nunnally, 1961), the behaviors associated with alcohol addiction are viewed by the community as a direct consequence of the inappropriate use of alcohol. With the cessation of drinking behavior, the accompanying deviance is assumed to disappear. Thus, what is basically wrong with an alcoholic is that he drinks. In the case of other psychiatric disorders the issue of "what is wrong" is much less clear. This lack of clarity underlies Scheff's (1966) notion of psychiatric disorders as comprising "residual" or relatively unclassifiable forms of deviance. Thus the mentally ill, once labeled, acquire such vague but threatening stereotypes as "strange," "different," and "dangerous" (Nunnally, 1961). Since the signs of the disorder are vague in terms of cultural stereotypes, it is most difficult for the "recovered" mental patient to convince others that he is "cured."

It appears that one of the popular stereotypes of former psychiatric patients is that their apparent normality is a "coverup" for their continuing underlying symptoms. Thus, where the alcoholic is able to remove the cause of his deviance by ceasing drinking, such a convincing removal may be impossible in the case of the other addictions and "mental" disorders. Narcotic addiction represents an interesting middle ground between these two extremes, for the cultural stereotype of a person under the influence of drugs is relatively unclear, such that it may be relatively difficult for the former addict to convince others that he has truly removed the cause of his deviance. This points up the fact that deviant drinking and alcoholism are continuous with behavior engaged in by the majority of the adult population, namely "normal" drinking (Mulford, 1964). The fact that the deviant drinker and alcohol addict are simply carrying out a common and normative behavior to excess reduces the "mystery" of the alcoholic experience and creates relative confidence in the average citizen regarding his abilities to identify a truly "dry" alcoholic. Thus the relative clarity of the cultural stereotype regarding the causes of deviance accompanying alcohol abuse provides much better means

for the alcoholic to claim he is no longer a deviant.

To summarize, A.A. promulgates the allergy concept both publicly and privately, but data clearly indicate that this factor alone does not account for the observed success at "re-entry" achieved by A.A. members. Despite ambiguity in public definitions of the etiology of alcoholism, its continuity with "normal" drinking behavior results in greater public confidence in the ability to judge the results of a therapeutic program. An understanding of A.A.'s success becomes clearer when this phenomenon is coupled with the availability of the "repentant" role.

THE REPENTANT ROLE

A relatively well-structured status of the "repentant" is clearly extant in American cultural tradition. Upward mobility from poverty and the "log cabin" comprises a social type where the individual "makes good" for his background and the apparent lack of confomity to economic norms of his ancestors. Redemptive religion, emergent largely in American society, emphasizes that one can correct a moral lapse even of long duration by public admission of guilt and repentance (cf. Lang and Lang, 1960).

The A.A. member can assume this repentant role; and it may become a social vehicle whereby, through contrite and remorseful public expressions, substantiated by visibly reformed behavior in conformity to the norms of the community, a former deviant can enter a new role which is quite acceptable to society. The re-acceptance may not be entirely complete, however, since the label of alcoholic is replaced with that of "arrested alcoholic;" as Gusfield (1967) has stated, the role comprises a social type of a "repentant deviant." The acceptance of the allergy concept by his significant others may well hasten his re-acceptance, but the more important factor seems to be the relative clarity by which significant others can judge the deviant's claim to "normality." Ideally the repentant role is also available to the former mental patient; but as mentioned above, his inability to indicate clearly the removal of the symptoms of his former deviance typically blocks such an entry.

If alcohol is viewed in its historical context in American society, the repentant role has not been uniquely available to A.A. members. As an object of deep moral concern no single category of behavior (with the possible exception of sexual behavior) has been laden with such emotional intensity in American society. Organized social movements previous to A.A. institutionalized means by which repentants could control their use of alcohol. These were the Washingtonians, Catch-My-Pal, and Father Matthews movements in the late 1800's and early 1900's, which failed to gain widespread social acceptance. Thus not only is the repentant role uniquely available to the alcoholic at the present time, but Alcoholics Anonymous has been built on a previous tradition.

SKID ROW IMAGE AND SOCIAL MOBILITY

The major facet of Alcoholics Anonymous' construction of a repentant role is found in the "Skid Row image" and its basis for upward social mobility. A central theme in the "stories" of many A.A. members is that of downward mobility into Skid Row or near Skid Row situations. Research evidence suggests that members tend to come from the middle and lower middle classes (Trice, 1962; Straus and Bacon, 1951). Consequently a "story" of downward mobility illustrates the extent to which present members had drastically fallen from esteem on account of their drinking. A.A. stories about "hitting bottom" and the many degradation ceremonies that they experienced in entering this fallen state act to legitimize their claims to downward mobility. Observation and limited evidence suggests that many of these stories are exaggerated to some degree and that a large proportion of A.A. members maintained at least partially stable status-sets throughout the addiction process. However, by the emphasis on downward mobility due to drinking, the social mobility "distance" traveled by the A.A. member is maximixed in the stories. This clearly sets the stage for impressive "comeback accomplishments."

Moral values also play a role in this process. The stories latently emphasize the "hedonistic underworld" to which the A.A. member "traveled." His current status illustrates to others that he has rejected this hedonism and has clearly resubmitted himself to the normative controls and values of the dominant society, exemplified by his A.A. membership. The attempt to promulgate the "length of the mobility trip" is particularly marked in the numerous anonymous appearances that A.A. members make to tell their stories before school groups, college classes, church groups, and service clubs. The importance of these emphases may be indirectly supported by the finding that lower-class persons typically fail in their attempts to successfully affiliate with A.A., i.e., their social circumstances minimize the distance of the downward mobility trip (Trice and Roman, 1970; Trice, 1959).

A.A. AND AMERICAN VALUES

The "return" of the A.A. member to normal role performance through the culturally provided role of the repentant and through the implied social mobility which develops out of an emphasis upon the length of the mobility trip is given its meaning through tapping directly into certain major American value orientations.

Most importantly, members of Alcoholics Anonymous have regained self control and have employed that self control in bringing about their rehabilitation. Self control, particularly that which involves the avoidance of pleasure, is a valued mode of behavior deeply embedded in the American ethos (Williams, 1960). A.A. members have, in a sense, achieved success in their battle with alcohol and may be thought of in that way as being "self-made" in a society permeated by "a systematic moral orientation by which conduct is judged" (Williams, 1960:424). This illustration of self control lends itself to positive sanction by the community.

A.A. also exemplifies three other value orientations as they have been delineated by Williams: humanitarianism, emphases upon practicality, and suspicion of established authority (Williams, 1960:397–470). A definite tendency exists in this society to identify with the helpless, particularly those who are not responsible for their own afflictions.

A.A. taps into the value of efficiency and practicality through its pragmatism and forthright determination to "take action" about a problem. The organization pays little heed to theories about alcoholism and casts all of its literature in extremely practical language. Much emphasis is placed upon the simplicity of its tenets and the straightforward manner in which its processes proceed.

Its organizational pattern is highly congruous with the value, suspicion of vested authority. There is no national or international hierarchy of officers, and local groups maintain maximum autonomy. Within the local group, there are no established patterns of leadership, such that the organization proceeds on a basis which sometimes approaches anarchy. In any event, the informality and equal-itarianism are marked features of the organization, which also tend to underline the self control possessed by individual members.

A.A.'s mode of delabeling and relabeling thus appears in a small degree to depend upon promulgation of an allergy concept of alcoholism which is accepted by some members of the general population. Of greater importance in this process is the effective contrivance of a repentant role. Emphasis upon the degradation and downward mobility experienced during the development of alcoholism provides for the ascription of considerable self control to middle-class members, which in turn may enhance their prestige and "shore up" their return to "normality." The repentance process is grounded in and reinforced by the manner in which the A.A. program taps into several basic American value orientations.

A.A.'S LIMITATIONS

As mentioned above, A.A. affiliation by members of the lower social classes is frequently unsuccessful. This seems to stem from the middle-class orientation of most of the A.A. programs, from the fact that it requires certain forms of public confessions and intense interpersonal interaction which may run contrary to the images of masculinity held in the lower classes, as well as interpersonal competence.

Perhaps an equally significant limitation is a psychological selectivity in the affiliation process. A recent followup study of 378 hospitalized alcoholics, all of whom had been intensely exposed to A.A. during their treatment, revealed that those who successfully affiliated with A.A. upon their re-entry into the community had personality features significantly different from those who did not affiliate (Trice and Roman, 1970). The successful affiliates were more guilt prone, sensitive to responsibility, more serious, and introspective. This appears to indicate a definite "readiness" for the adoption of the repentant role among successful affiliates. To a somewhat lesser extent, the affiliates possessed a greater degree of measured ego strength, affiliative needs, and group dependency, indicating a "fit" between the peculiar demands for intense interaction required for successful affiliation and the personalities of the successful affiliates. Earlier research also revealed a relatively high need for affiliation among A.A. affiliates as compared to those who were unsuccessful in the affiliation process (Trice, 1959).

These social class and personality factors definitely indicate the A.A. program is not effective for all alcoholics. Convincing entry into the repentant role, as well as successful interactional participation in the program, appear to require middle-class background and certain personality predispositions.

SUMMARY

In summary, we shall contrast the success of A.A. in its delabeling with that experienced by other self help groups designed for former drug addicts and mental patients (Wechsler, 1960; Landy and Singer, 1961). As pointed out above, the statuses of mental patients and narcotic addicts lack the causal clarity accompanying the role of alcoholic. It is most difficult for narcotic addicts and former mental patients to remove the stigma since there is little social clarity about the cessation of the primary deviant behavior. Just as there is no parallel in this respect, there is no parallel in other self-help organizations with the Skid Row image and the status-enhancing "mobility trip" that is afforded by this image. The primary deviant behaviors which lead to the label of drug addict or

which eventuate in mental hospitalization are too far removed from ordinary social experience for easy acceptance of the former deviant to occur. These behaviors are a part of an underworld from which return is most difficult. On the other hand, Alcoholics Anonymous possesses, as a consequence of the nature of the disorder of alcoholism, its uniqueness as an organization, and the existence of certain value orientations within American society, a pattern of social processing whereby a labeled deviant can become "delabeled" as a stigmatized deviant and relabeled as a former and repentant deviant.

REFERENCES

Anonymous (1968). "Doctors, alcohol and A.A." *Alcoholics Anonymous Grapevine,* October, 1968, entire number.

Freeman, H., and O. Simmons (1963). *The Mental Patient Comes Home.* New York: Wiley.

Garfinkel, H. (1957). "Conditions of successful degradation ceremonies." *American Journal of Sociology* 61 (November): 420–425.

Gellman, I. (1964). *The Sober Alcoholic.* New Haven: College and University Press.

Gusfield, J. (1967). "Moral passage: The symbolic process in public designations of deviance." *Social Problems* 15 (Winter): 175–188.

Landy, D., and S. Singer (1961). "The social organization and culture of a club for former mental patients." *Human Relations* 14 (January): 31–40.

Lang, K., and G. Lang (1960). "Decisions for Christ: Billy Graham in New York City." Pp. 415–427 in M. Stein *et al.* (eds.), *Identity and Anxiety.* New York: The Free Press.

Lemert, E. (1951). *Social Pathology.* New York: McGraw-Hill.

Miller, D. (1965). *Worlds That Fail.* Sacramento, California: California Department of Mental Hygiene.

Mulford, H. (1964). "Drinking and deviant drinking, U.S.A., 1963." *Quarterly*

Journal of Studies on Alcohol, 25 (December): 634–650.

Mulford, H., and D. Miller (1964). "Measuring public acceptance of the alcoholic as a sick person." *Quarterly Journal of Studies on Alcohol,* 25 (June): 314–323.

Myers, J., and L. Bean (1968). *A Decade Later.* New York: Wiley.

Nunnally, J. (1961). *Popular Conceptions of Mental Health.* New York: Holt, Rinehart and Winston.

Parsons, T. (1951). *The Social System.* Glencoe, Ill.: The Free Press.

Pasamanick, B. *et al.* (1967). *Schizophrenics in the Community.* New York: Appleton, Century, Crofts.

Plaut, T. (1967). *Alcohol Problems: A Report to the Nation,* New York: Oxford University Press.

Roman, P., and H. Trice (1969). "The self reaction: A neglected dimension of labeling theory." Presented at American Sociological Association Meetings, San Francisco.

Sagarin, E. (1967). "Voluntary associations among social deviants." *Criminologica* 5 (January): 8–22.

Scheff, T. (1966). *Being Mentally Ill.* Chicago: Aldine.

Susser, M. (1968). *Community Psychiatry.* New York: Random House.

Sussman, M. (ed.) (1966). *Sociology and Rehabilitation.* Washington: American Sociological Association.

Straus, R., and S. Bacon (1951). "Alcoholism and social stability." *Quarterly Journal of Studies on Alcohol* 12 (June): 231–260.

Trice, H. (1959). "The affiliation motive and readiness to join Alcoholics Anonymous." *Quarterly Journal of Studies on Alcohol* 20 (September): 313–320.

——— (1962). "The job behavior of problem drinkers." Pp. 493–510 in D. Pittman and C. Snyder (eds.), *Society, Culture and Drinking Patterns.* New York: Wiley.

Trice, H., and P. Roman (1970). "Sociopsychological predictors of successful affiliation with Alcoholics Anonymous." *Social Psychiatry* 5 (Winter): 51–59.

Wechsler, H. (1960). "The self-help organization in the mental health field: Recovery, Inc." *Journal of Nervous and Mental Disease* 130 (April): 297–314.

Williams, R. (1960). *American Society.* New York: A. A. Knopf.

Abstinence Cycles and Heroin Addicts

MARSH B. RAY

Those who study persons addicted to opium and its derivatives are confronted by the following paradox: A cure from physiological dependence on opiates may be secured within a relatively short period, and carefully controlled studies indicate that use of these drugs does not cause psychosis, organic intellectual deterioration, or any permanent impairment of intellectual function.[1] But, despite these facts, addicts display a high rate of recidivism. On the other hand, while the rate of recidivism is high, addicts continually and repeatedly seek cure. It is difficult to obtain definitive data concerning the number of cures the addict

takes, but various studies of institutional admissions indicate that it is relatively high,[2] and there are many attempts at home cure that go unrecorded.

This paper reports on a study[3] of abstinence and relapse in which attention is focused on the way the addict or abstainer orders and makes meaningful the objects of his experience, including himself as an object,[4] during the critical periods of cure and of relapse and the related sense of identity or of social isolation the addict feels as he interacts with significant others. It is especially concerned with describing and analyzing the characteristic ways the addict or

Reprinted from *Social Problems,* Vol. 9, No. 2 (Fall 1961), pp. 132–140.

[1] See as examples: C. Knight Aldrich, "The Relationship of the Concept Formation Test to Drug Addiction and Intelligence," *Journal of Nervous and Mental Diseases,* 100 (July, 1944), pp. 30–34; Margaret E. Hall, "Mental and Physical Efficiency of Women Drug Addicts," *Journal of Abnormal and Social Psychology,* 33 (July, 1938), pp. 332–345; A. Z. Pfeffer and Dorothy Cleck, "Chronic Psychoses and Addiction to Morphine," *Archives of Neurology and Psychiatry,* 56 (December, 1946), pp. 665–672.

[2] Michael J. Pescor, *A Statistical Analysis of the Clinical Records of Hospitalized Drug Addicts,* Supplement No. 143 to the Public Health Reports, United States Public Health Service (Washington: Government Printing Office, 1943), p. 24; Victor H. Vogel, "Treatment of the Narcotic Addict by the U.S. Public Health Service," *Federal Probation,* 12 (June, 1948), pp. 45–50.

[3] The basic data consisted of case histories collected in repeated depth interviews with 17 addicts and abstainers over a two year period. During this time several of the active addicts became abstainers and vice-versa. Additional material was gathered while the author worked for a year as a social worker in a rehabilitation program for addicts.

[4] "Object" is employed here in the sense intended by George Herbert Mead in his development of the concept in *Mind, Self and Society* (Chicago: University of Chicago Press, 1934), Part III, pp. 135–226. Two earlier studies have applied this kind of thinking in studying the behavior of addicts, see: L. Guy Brown, "The Sociological Implications of Drug Addiction," *Journal of Educational Sociology,* 4 (February, 1931), pp. 358–369, and Alfred R. Lindesmith, *Opiate Addiction* (Bloomington, Indiana: Principia Press, 1947).

abstainer defines the social situations he encounters during these periods and responds to the status dilemmas he experiences in them.

SECONDARY STATUS CHARACTERISTICS OF ADDICTS

The social world of addiction contains a loose system of organizational and cultural elements, including a special language or argot, certain artifacts, a commodity market and pricing system, a system of stratification, and ethical codes. The addict's commitment to these values gives him a status and an identity.[5] In addition to these direct links to the world of addiction, becoming an addict means that one assumes a number of secondary status characteristics in accordance with the definitions the society has of this activity.[6] Some of these are set forth in federal and local laws and statutes, others are defined by the stereotypic thinking of members of the larger society about the causes and consequences of drug use.

The addict's incarceration in correctional institutions has specific meanings which he finds reflected in the attitudes adopted toward him by members of non-addict society and by his fellow addicts. Additionally, as his habit grows and the demands for drugs get beyond any legitimate means of supply, his own activities in satisfying his increased craving give him direct experiential evidence of the criminal aspects of self. These meanings of self as a criminal become internalized as he begins to apply criminal argot to his activities and institutional experiences. Thus shop-lifting becomes "boosting," the correctional settings become "joints," and the guards in such institutions become "screws."

The popular notion that the addict is somehow psychologically inadequate is supported by many authorities in the field. In addition, support and definition is supplied by the very nature of the institution in which drug addicts are usually treated and have a large part of their experience since even the names of these institutions fix this definition of addiction. For example, one of the outpatient clinics for the treatment of addicts in Chicago was located at Illinois Neuropsychiatric Institute, and the connotations of Bellevue Hospital in New York City, another treatment center for addicts, are socially well established. Then, too, the composition of the staff in treatment centers contributes substantially to the image of the addict as mentally ill, for the personnel are primarily psychiatrists, psychologists, and psychiatric social workers. How such a definition of self was brought forcefully home to one addict is illustrated in the following quotation:

When I got down to the hospital, I was interviewed by different doctors and one of them told me, "you now have one mark against you as crazy for having been down here." I hadn't known it was a crazy house. You know regular people [non-addicts] think this too.

Finally, as the addict's habit grows and almost all of his thoughts and efforts are directed toward supplying himself with drugs, he becomes careless about his personal appearance and cleanliness. Consequently non-addicts think of him as a "bum" and, because he persists in his use of drugs, conclude that he lacks

[5] Marsh B. Ray, "Cure and Relapse Among Heroin Addicts" (unpublished M.A. thesis, Department of Sociology, University of Chicago, 1958).

[6] For a general discussion of the important role that auxiliary status characteristics play in social situations, see Everett C. Hughes, "Dilemmas and Contradictions in Status," *American Journal of Sociology,* 50 (March, 1945), pp. 253–259.

"will power," is perhaps "degenerate," and is likely to contaminate others.

The addict is aware that he is judged in terms of these various secondary social definitions, and while he may attempt to reject them, it is difficult if not impossible to do so when much of his interpersonal and institutional experience serves to ratify these definitions. They assume importance because they are the medium of exchange in social transactions with the addict and non-addict world in which the addict identifies himself as an object and judges himself in relation to addict and non-addict values. Such experiences are socially disjunctive and become the basis for motivated acts.

THE INCEPTION OF CURE

An episode of cure begins in the private thoughts of the addict rather than in his overt behavior. These deliberations develop as a result of experience in specific situations of interaction with important others that cause the addict to experience social stress, to develop some feeling of alienation from or dissatisfaction with his present identity, and to call it into question and examine it in all of its implications and ramifications. In these situations the addict engages in private self-debate in which he juxtaposes the values and social relationships which have become immediate and concrete through his addiction with those that are sometimes only half remembered or only imperfectly perceived.

I think that my mother knew that I was addicted because she had heard rumors around the neighborhood. Around that time [when he first began to think about cure] she had been telling me that I looked like a "bum," and that my hair was down the back of my neck and that I was dirty. I had known this too but had shoved it down into the back of my mind somewhere. She used to tell me that to look like this wasn't at all like me. I always wanted to look present-able and her saying this really hurt. At that time I was going to [college] and I wanted to look my best. I always looked at myself as the clever one—the "mystery man"—outwitting the "dolts." I always thought that no one knew, that when I was in my room they thought I was studying my books when actually I wasn't studying at all.

After mother said those things I did a lot of thinking. I often used to sit around my room and think about it and even look at myself in the mirror and I could see that it was true. What is it called . . . ? When you take yourself out of a situation and look at yourself . . . ? "Self appraisal" . . . I guess that's it. Well I did this about my appearance and about the deterioration of my character. I didn't like it because I didn't want anything to be master over me because this was contrary to my character. I used to sit and look at that infinitesimal bit of powder. I felt it changed my personality somehow.

I used to try staying in but I would get sick. But because I had money I couldn't maintain it [withstand the demands of the withdrawal sickness] and when the pain got unbearable, at least to me it was unbearable, I would go out again. I wanted to be independent of it. I knew then that if I continued I would have to resort to stealing to maintain my habit and this I couldn't tolerate because it was contrary to my character. The others were robbing and stealing but I couldn't be a part of that. I first talked with my uncle about it because my mother was alive then and I thought she would crack up and maybe not understand the problem. I didn't want to be reprimanded, I knew I'd done wrong. I had been through a lot and felt I wanted to be rid of the thing. He was very understanding about it and didn't criticize me. He just talked with me about going to the hospital and said he thought this would be the best way to do it.

In the above example, the meanings of the complex of secondary status characteristics of the addict identity when used as self referents in bringing this identity into question is shown in dramatic fashion.

But the social psychological prerequisites to the inception of an episode of abstinence need not precede physical withdrawal of the drug. It is frequently the case that following the enforced withdrawal that begins a period of confinement in a correctional institution or hospital, the addict engages in self debate in which the self in all of its ramifications emerges as an object and is brought under scrutiny. Such institutional situations constrain the addict's perspectives about himself and have a dual character. On the one hand, they serve to ratify a secondary status characteristic, while on the other, as addicts interact with older inmates of jails and hospitals, they provide daily concrete models of what life may be like in later years as a consequence of continued use of drugs.

On occasion, however, the addict group itself, rather than non-addict society, provides the socially disjunctive experience that motivates the addict to abstain, although the non-addict world and its values are still the reference point. An addict who had been addicted for several years and had had several involuntary cures in correctional institutions describes such an experience as follows:

When I first started using we were all buddies, but later we started "burning" each other. One guy would say, "Well, I'll go 'cop' " [buy drugs]. Then he'd take the "bread" [money] and he'd never come back. I kicked one time because of that. I didn't have no more money and I got disgusted. First I started to swear him up and down but then my inner conscience got started and I said maybe he got "busted" [arrested]. Then I said, "Aw, to hell with him and to hell with all junkies—they're all the same." So I went home and I tried to read a couple of comic books to keep my mind off it. I was very sick but after a couple of days I kicked.

While the above situation may not be typical, it illustrates the same process to be observed in the other examples—a disruption of the social ordering of experience that has become familiar, a calling into question of the addict identity, and the rejection of this identity and the values associated with it. The more typical situations that evoke such conduct would appear to involve a non-addict or some concrete aspect of the non-addict world as the catalytic agent.

THE ADDICT SELF IN TRANSITION

The addict who has successfully completed withdrawal is no longer faced with the need to take drugs in order to avert the disaster of withdrawal sickness, and now enters a period which might best be characterized as a "running struggle" with his problems of social identity. He could not have taken such a drastic step had he not developed some series of expectations concerning the nature of his future relationships with social others. His anticipations concerning these situations may or may not be realistic; what matters is that he has them and that the imagery he holds regarding himself and his potentialities is a strong motivating force in his continued abstinence. Above all, he appears to desire ratification by significant others of his newly developing identity, and in his interactions during an episode of abstinence he expects to secure it.

In the early phases of an episode of cure, the abstainer manifests considerable ambivalence about where he stands in addict and non-addict groups, and in discussions of addiction and addicts, he may indicate his ambivalence through his alternate use of the pronouns "we" and "they" and thus his alternate membership in addict and non-addict society. He may also indicate his ambivalence through other nuances of language and choice of words. Later, during a successful episode of abstinence, the ex-addict indicates his non-membership in the addict group through categorizations that place addicts clearly in the third person, and he places his own addiction and matters pertaining to it in the past tense. For example, he is likely to preface a remark with the phrase "When I was an addict. . . ." But of equal or greater importance is the fact that the ex-addict who is successful in remaining abstinent relates to new groups of people, participates in their experience, and to some extent begins to evaluate the conduct of his former associates (and perhaps his own when he was an addict) in terms of the values of the new group.

I see the guys around now quite often and sometimes we talk for a while but I don't feel that I am anything like them anymore and I always leave before they "make up" [take drugs]. I tell them, "You know what you are doing but if you keep on you'll just go to jail like I did." I don't feel that they are wrong to be using but just that I'm luckier than they are because I have goals. It's funny, I used to call them "squares" for not using and now they call me "square" for not using. They think that they are "hip" and they are always talking about the old days. That makes me realize how far I've come. But it makes me want to keep away from them, too, because they always use the same old vocabulary—talking about "squares" and being "hip."

Thus, while some abstainers do not deny the right of others to use drugs if they choose, they clearly indicate that addiction is no longer a personally meaningful area of social experience for them. In the above illustration the abstainer is using this experience as something of a "sounding board" for his newly developed identity. Of particular note is the considerable loss of meaning in the old symbols through which he previously ordered his experience and his concern with one of the inevitable consequences of drug use. This is a common experience for those who have maintained abstinence for any length of time.

During the later stages of the forma-

tion of an abstainer identity, the ex-addict begins to perceive a difference in his relations with significant others, particularly with members of his family. Undoubtedly their attitudes, in turn, undergo modification and change as a result of his apparent continued abstinence, and they arrive at this judgment by observing his cleanliness and attention to personal neatness, his steady employment, and his re-subscription to other values of non-addict society. The ex-addict is very much aware of these attitudinal differences and uses them further to bolster his conception of himself as an abstainer.

Lots of time I don't even feel like I ever took dope. I feel released not to be dependent on it. I think how nice it is to be natural without having to rely on dope to make me feel good. See, when I was a "junkie" I lost a lot of respect. My father wouldn't talk to me and I was filthy. I have to build up that respect again. I do a lot of things with my family now and my father talks to me again. It's like at parties that my relatives give, now they are always running up to me and giving me a drink and showing me a lot of attention. Before they wouldn't even talk to me. See, I used to feel lonely because my life was dependent on stuff and I felt different from regular people. See, "junkies" and regular people are two different things. I used to feel that I was out of place with my relatives when I was on junk. I didn't want to walk with them on the street and do things with them. Now I do things with them all the time like go to the show and joke with them and I go to church with my uncle. I just kept saying to myself that "junkies" are not my people. My relatives don't say things behind my back now and I am gaining their respect slow but sure.

In this illustration there may be observed a budding sense of social insight characteristic of abstainers in this period of their development. Another characteristic feature is the recognition that subscription to non-addict values must be grounded in action—in playing the role of non-addict in participation with non-addicts and thus sharing in their values and perspectives.

THE PROCESS OF RELAPSE

The tendency toward relapse develops out of the meanings of the abstainer's experience in social situations when he develops an image of himself as socially different from non-addicts, and relapse occurs when he redefines himself as an addict. When his social expectations and the expectations of others with whom he interacts are not met, social stress develops and he is required to re-examine the meaningfulness of his experience in non-addict society and in so doing question his identity as an abstainer. This type of experience promotes a mental realignment with addict values and standards and may be observed in the abstainer's thoughts about himself in covert social situations, in his direct interpersonal relations with active addicts, and in his experience with representatives of non-addict society. It is in these various settings that his developing sense of self as an abstainer is put to the test.

Experiences with Other Addicts That Promote Relapse. Re-addiction most frequently occurs during the period immediately following the physical withdrawal of the drug—the period described earlier as a time of "running struggle" with identity problems for the ex-addict. It is at this point, when the old values and old meanings he experienced as an addict are still immediate and the new ordering of his experience without narcotics is not well established, that the ex-addict seems most vulnerable to relapse. Sometimes the experiences that provoke the questioning of identity that precedes relapse occur within the confines of the very institution where the addict has gone to seek cure. The social expectations of other addicts in the hospital are of vital

importance in creating an atmosphere in which identification with the values of non-addict society is difficult to maintain.

[The last time we talked you said that you would like to tell me about your experiences in the hospital. What were they like?]

Well, during the first time I was at the hospital most of the fellows seemed to hate [to give] the "square" impression, not to hate it exactly but refuse to admit [to] it. My own feelings were that everyone should have been a little different in expressing themselves that I would like to accept the extreme opposite. But I felt that I would have disagreements about this with the fellow inmates. They thought I was a very queer or peculiar person that constantly showed disagreement about the problem as they saw it. I never did reach an understanding with them about the problem.

But addicts do not always relapse on first contact with members of the old group. In fact, there is nothing to indicate that addicts relapse only as a result of association. Instead, contacts may go on for some time during which the ex-addict carries on much private self debate, feeling at one point that he is socially closer to addicts and at another that his real interest lies in future new identities on which he has decided. Typically he may also call to mind the reason he undertook cure in the first place and question the rationality of relapsing. An interesting example of the dilemma and ambivalence experienced under these circumstances and the partial acceding to social pressures from the addict group by applying the definitions of that group to one's own conduct are the experiences of another addict.

[He had entered the hospital "with the key" and after completing withdrawal he stayed at the hospital for three weeks before voluntarily signing out, although the required period of treatment for a medical discharge at the time was four and one-half months.]

This one kid who was a friend of mine came to me one night and said, "Let's get out of here." So I went and checked out too. Then I got to thinking, "I don't want to go home yet—I'm still sick—and what did I come down here for anyway." So I went up and got my papers back from the officer and tore them up. Then I found this kid and told him that I was staying and he said, "Oh we knew you weren't going to do it—we knew you'd chicken out." Then I went back and put my papers through again. I felt they were trying to "put me down."

When we got out I could have had a shot right away because one of these guys when we got to town said he knew a croaker who would fix us up, but I didn't go with them. I didn't care what they thought because I got to figuring that I had went this far and I might as well stay off.

When I got home I stayed off for two months but my mother was hollering at me all the time and there was this one family in the neighborhood that was always "chopping me up." I wanted to tell this woman off because she talked all right to my face but behind my back she said things like she was afraid I would turn her son on because I was hanging around with him. She would tell these things to my mother. I never turned anybody on! She didn't know that but I wanted to tell her. Finally I just got disgusted because nobody wanted to believe me and I went back on.

The experiences of this addict provide an interesting denial of the notion that addicts relapse because of association *per se* and support the thesis that relapse is a function of the kind of object ex-addicts make of themselves in the situations they face.

Relations with Non-addicts As a Prelude to Relapse. While the ex-addict's interaction with addict groups is often a source of experiences which cause him to question the value to him of an abstainer

identity, experiences with non-addict groups also play a vital role. In most instances the addict has established a status for himself in the eyes of non-addicts who may be acquainted with his case—members of his family, social workers, law enforcement officers, physicians and so forth. Through gestures, vocal and otherwise, these non-addicts make indications to the ex-addict concerning his membership and right to participation in their group, for example, the right to be believed when he attempts to indicate to the non-addict world that he believes in and subscribes to its values. In his contacts with non-addicts, the former addict is particularly sensitive to their cues.

During the early phases of an episode of abstinence the abstainer enters various situations with quite definite expectations concerning how he should be defined and treated. He indicates his desire for ratification of his new status in many ways, and finds it socially difficult when he sees in the conduct of others toward him a reference to his old identity as an addict. He is not unaware of these doubts about his identity.

My relatives were always saying things to me like "Have you really quit using that drug now?" and things like that. And I knew that they were doing a lot of talking behind my back because when I came around they would stop talking but I overheard them. It used to burn my ass.

On the other hand, the non-addicts with whom he has experience during this period have their own expectations concerning the abstainer's probable conduct. Based in part on the stereotypic thinking of non-addict society concerning addiction, in part on unfortunate previous experiences, they may exhibit some skepticism concerning the "cure" and express doubt about the abstainer's prognosis.[7]

[7] Family members may have been subjected to thefts by the addict, or other kinds of trickery, and they tend to be on their guard lest the experience be repeated. Interest-

THE SOCIAL PSYCHOLOGICAL MEANING OF RELAPSE

On an immediate concrete level, relapse requires that the individual reorient himself to the market conditions surrounding the sale of illicit drugs. He must reestablish his sources of supply and, if he has been abstinent for very long, he may have to learn about new fads and fashions in drug use. He may learn, for example, that dolophin is more readily available than heroin at the moment of his return to drug use, that it requires less in the way of preparation, that it calls for such and such amount to safely secure a certain effect, what the effects will be, and so on.

But the ex-addict's re-entrance into the social world of addiction has much deeper meanings. It places demands and restraints upon his interactions and the meaningfulness of his experience. It requires a recommitment to the norms of addiction and limits the degree to which he may relate to non-addict groups in terms of the latter's values and standards. It demands participation in the old ways of organizing conduct and experience and, as a consequence, the readoption of the secondary status characteristics of addiction. He again shows a lack of concern about his personal appearance and grooming. Illicit activities are again engaged in to get money for drugs, and as a result the possibility of more firmly establishing the criminal aspect of his identity becomes a reality.

The social consequences of these experiences and activities is the re-establishment of the sense of social isolation from the non-addict group and a recaptured sense of the meaningfulness of experience in the social world of addiction. It is through these familiar meanings and the reapplication of the symbolic meanings of the addict world to his own conduct that identity and status as an addict are reaffirmed. The ex-addict who relapses is thus likely to comment, "I feel like one of the guys again," or as Street has put it, "It was like coming home."[8]

While repeated relapse on the addict's part may more firmly convince him that "once a junkie, always a junkie" is no myth but instead a valid comment on his way of life, every relapse has within it the genesis of another attempt at cure. From his however brief or lengthy excursions into the world of non-addiction, the relapsed addict carries back with him an image of himself as one who has done the impossible—one who has actually experienced a period when it was unnecessary to take drugs to avoid the dreaded withdrawal sickness. But these are not his only recollections. He recalls, too, his identification of himself as an abstainer, no matter how tentatively or imperfectly this may have been accomplished. He thinks over his experiences in situations while he occupied the status of abstainer and speculates about the possible other outcomes of these situations had he acted differently.

[Originally from Chicago, he experienced the only voluntary period of abstinence in a long career of addiction while living with his wife in Kansas City, Missouri. After an argument with his wife, during which she reminded him of his previous addiction and its consequences for her, he left her and returned to Chicago, where he immediately relapsed. After three weeks he was using about $12 worth of morphine daily.] He reports on his thoughts at the time as follows:

ingly, the matter of thefts of either money or small household objects (a radio or a clock) is often used by family members as an index as to whether "he's back on that stuff again" or not. His physical appearance is another gauge.

[8] Leroy Street (pseudonym) and D. Loth, *I Was a Drug Addict,* Pyramid Books (New York: Random House, 1953), p. 71.

Now and then I'm given to rational thinking or reasoning and somehow I had a premonition that should I remain in Chicago much longer, shoplifting and doing the various criminal acts I did to get money for drugs, plus the criminal act of just using the drug, I would soon be in jail or perhaps something worse, for in truth one's life is at stake each day when he uses drugs. I reflected on the life I had known in Kansas City with Rose in contrast to the one I had returned to. I didn't know what Rose thought had become of me. I thought that more than likely she was angry and thoroughly disgusted and glad that I was gone. However, I wanted to return but first thought it best to call and see what her feelings were.

[At his wife's urging he returned to Kansas City and undertook a "cold turkey" cure in their home. He remained abstinent for a considerable period but subsequently relapsed again when he returned to Chicago.]

Reflections of the above kind provide the relapsed addict with a rich body of material for self-recrimination and he again evaluates his own conduct in terms of what he believes are the larger society's attitudes toward addicts and addiction. It is then that he may again speculate about his own potential for meaningful experiences and relationships in a non-addict world and thus set into motion a new attempt at cure.

SUMMARY

Addiction to narcotic drugs in our society commits the participant in this activity to a status and identity that has complex secondary characteristics. These develop through shared roles and common interpersonal and institutional experience, and as a consequence addicts develop perspectives about themselves and about non-addict values. They evaluate social situations, and in turn are evaluated by the other participants in these situations, in these terms, often with the result that the value of the addict's identity relative to the social world of addiction is brought into question. When this happens the identification of oneself as an addict, committed to the values and statuses of the addict group, is contrasted with new or remembered identities and relationships, resulting in a commitment to cure with its implications of intense physical suffering. In the period following physical withdrawal from heroin, the addict attempts to enact a new social reality which coincides with his desired self-image as an abstainer, and he seeks ratification of his new identity from others in the situations he faces.

But the abstainer's social expectations during a period when he is off drugs are frequently not gratified. Here again, socially disjunctive experiences bring about a questioning of the value of an abstainer identity and promote reflections in which addict and non-addict identities and relationships are compared. The abstainer's realignment of his values with those of the world of addiction results in the redefinition of self as an addict and has as a consequence the actions necessary to relapse. But it should be noted that the seeds of a new attempt at abstinence are sown, once addiction has been reestablished, in the self-recriminations engaged in upon remembrance of a successful period of abstinence.

Differential Association and the Rehabilitation of Drug Addicts

RITA VOLKMAN JOHNSON

DONALD R. CRESSEY

In 1955 Cressey listed five principles for applying Edwin Sutherland's theory of differential association to the rehabilitation of criminals.[1] While this article is now frequently cited in the sociological literature dealing with group therapy, "therapeutic communities," and "total institutions," we know of no program of rehabilitation that has been explicitly based on the principles. The major point of Cressey's article, which referred to criminals, not addicts, is similar to the following recommendation by the Chief of the United States Narcotics Division: "The community should restore the former addict to his proper place in society and help him avoid associations that would influence him to return to the use of drugs."[2]

Cressey gives five rules (to be reviewed below) for implementing this directive to "restore," "help," and "influence" the addict. These rules, derived from the sociological and social-psychological literature on social movements, crime prevention, group therapy, communications, personality change, and social change, were designed to show that sociology has distinctive, non-psychiatric, theory that can be used effectively by practitioners seeking to prevent crime and change criminals. Sutherland also had this as a principal objective when he formulated his theory of differential association.[3]

Assuming, as we do, that Cressey's principles are consistent with Sutherland's theory and that his theory, in turn, is consistent with more general sociological theory, a test of the principles would be a test of the more general formulations. Ideally, such a test would involve careful study of the results of a program rationally designed to utilize the principles to change criminals. To our knowledge, such a test has not been made.[4] As a "next best" test, we may study rehabilitation programs that use the

Reprinted from *The American Journal of Sociology,* Vol. 69, No. 2 (September, 1963), pp. 129–42, by permission of the authors and The University of Chicago Press. Copyright 1963 by The University of Chicago.

[1] Donald R. Cressey, "Changing Criminals: The Application of the Theory of Differential Association," *The American Journal of Sociology,* LXI (September, 1955), 116–20 (see also Cressey, "Contradictory Theories in Correctional Group Therapy Programs," *Federal Probation,* XVIII [June 1954], 20–26).

[2] Harry J. Anslinger, "Drug Addiction," *Encyclopaedia Britannica,* VII (1960), 677–79.

[3] Edwin H. Sutherland and Donald R. Cressey, *Principles of Criminology* (6th ed.; Philadelphia: J. B. Lippincott Co., 1960), pp. 74–80.

[4] See, however, Joseph A. Cook and Gilbert Geis, "Forum Anonymous: The Techniques of Alcoholics Anonymous Applied to Prison Therapy," *Journal of Social Therapy,* III (First Quarter, 1957), 9–13.

principles, however unwittingly. Such a program has been in operation since 1958. Insofar as it is remarkably similar to any program that could have been designed to implement the principles, the results over the years can be viewed as at least a crude test of the principles. Since the principles are interrelated, the parts of any program implementing them must necessarily overlap.

"Synanon," an organization of former drug addicts, was founded in May, 1958, by a member of Alcoholics Anonymous with the assistance of an alcoholic and a drug addict. In December, 1958, Volkman (a non-addict) heard about the two dozen ex-addicts living together in an abandoned store, and she obtained permission of the Synanon Board of Directors[5] to visit the group daily and to live in during the weekends. In July, 1959, she moved into the girls' dormitory of the group's new, larger quarters and continued to reside at Synanon House until June, 1960. Cressey (also a non-addict) visited the House at Volkman's invitation in the spring of 1960; for one year, beginning in July, 1960, he visited the organization on the average of at least once a week. He deliberately refrained from trying to influence policy or program, and his theory about the effects of group relationships on rehabilitation were unknown to the group. Most of the interview material and statistical data reported below were collected by Volkman during the 1959–60 period of residence and were used in the thesis for her Master's degree, prepared under the direction of C. Wayne Gordon.[6] As both a full-fledged member of Synanon and as a participant observer, Volkman attended about three hundred group sessions, a few of which were recorded. She was accorded the same work responsibilities, rights, and privileges as any other member, and she was considered one of Synanon's first "graduates."

THE SUBJECTS

Background data were available on only the first fifty-two persons entering Synanon after July, 1958. These records were prepared by a resident who in July, 1959, took it upon himself to interview and compile the information. We have no way of determining whether these fifty-two persons are representative of all addicts. However, we believe they are similar to the 215 persons who have resided at Synanon for at least one month.

Age and sex distributions are shown in Table 1: 44 per cent of the fifty-two were Protestant, 35 per cent Catholic, 8 per cent Jewish.[7] Racially, 27 per cent were Negro, and there were no Orientals; 19 per cent of the Caucasians were of Mexican origin and 13 per cent were of Italian origin. Educational attainment is shown in Table 2. Although the data on early family life are poor because the resident simply asked "What was your family like?" it may be noted that only five of the fifty-two indicated satisfaction with the home. Words and phrases such as "tension," "arguing," "bickering," "violence," "lack of warmth," "went

---

[5] The Board at first was composed of the three original members. It is now made up of the founder (an ex-alcoholic but a non-addict) and seven long-term residents who have remained off drugs and who have demonstrated their strict loyalty to the group and its principles.

[6] Rita Volkman, "A Descriptive Case Study of Synanon as a Primary Group Organization" (unpublished Master's thesis, Department of Education, University of California, Los Angeles, 1961).

[7] In May, 1961, 20 per cent of the residents were Jewish.

TABLE 1 Age and Sex*

Age (In Years)	Males No.	Males Per Cent	Females No.	Females Per Cent	Total No.	Total Per Cent
18–20	0	0	1	7	1	2
21–30	17	44	11	79	28	54
31–40	18	48	2	14	20	38
41–50	1	3	0	0	1	2
51–60	2	5	0	0	2	4
Total	38	100	14	100	52	100

* Median ages: males, 31.0; females, 27.5.

back and forth," and "nagged" were common.[8]

The sporadic and tenuous occupational ties held by the group are indicated in Table 3. This table supports the notion that addicts cannot maintain steady jobs because their addiction interferes with the work routine; it suggests also that these members had few lasting peer group contacts or ties, at least so far as work associations go. In view of their poor employment records, it might be asked how the addicts supported their addictions, which cost from $30 to $50 a day and sometimes ran to $100 a day.

Only four of the men reported that they obtained their incomes by legitimate work alone; thirty (79 per cent) were engaged in illegitimate activities, with theft, burglary, armed robbery, shoplifting, and pimping leading the list. One man and seven women were supplied with either drugs or money by their mates or families, and five of these females supplemented this source by prostitution or other illegitimate work. Five of the fourteen women had no income

TABLE 2 Educational Attainment

	No.	Per Cent
Part grade school	1	2
Completed grade school	3	6
Part high school	24	46
Completed high school	11	21
Part college	13	25
Completed college	0	0
Total	52	100

TABLE 3 Length and Continuity of Employment

No. of Years on One Job	Unsteady (Discontinuous or Sporadic)	Steady (Continuous)	Total
Under 1	36*	4	40
2–3	3	2	5
4–5	1	3	4
6 or over	2	1	3
Total	42	10	52

* Of this category 67 per cent defined their work as "for short periods only."

[8] Cf. Research Center for Human Relations, New York University, *Family Background as an Etiological Factor in Personality Predisposition to Heroin Addiction* (New York: the Author, 1956).

except that from illegitimate activities, and none of the women supported themselves by legitimate work only.

Institutional histories and military service histories are consistent with the work and educational histories, indicating that the fifty-two members were not somehow inadvertently selected as "easy" rehabilitation cases. The fifty-two had been in and out of prisons, jails, and hospitals all over the United States. Table 4 shows that ten men and one woman

TABLE 4 Confinements in Institutions

No. of Confinements	Male	Female	Total*
1– 3	6	6	15
4– 6	12	7	19
7– 9	8	0	8
10–12	0	1	1
13–15	2	0	0
Total confinements	166	59	225

* Three males indicated "numerous arrests," and four supplied no information. These seven were not included in the tally.

had been confined seven or more times; the mean number of confinements for males was 5.5 and for females 3.9. The table seems to indicate that whatever value confinement in institutions might have had for this group, it clearly did not prevent further confinements.

In sum, the pre-Synanon experiences of the fifty-two residents seem to indicate non-identification with pro-legal activities and norms. Neither the home, the armed services, the occupational world, schools, prisons, nor hospitals served as links with the larger and more socially acceptable community. This, then, is the kind of "raw material" with which Synanon has been working.[9]

THE PROGRAM

Admission

Not every addict who knocks on the door of Synanon is given admission. Nevertheless, the only admission criterion we have been able to find is *expressed willingness* to submit one's self to a group that hates drug addiction. Use of this criterion has unwittingly implemented one of Cressey's principles:

If criminals are to be changed, they must be assimilated into groups which emphasize values conducive to law-abiding behavior and, concurrently, alienated from groups emphasizing values conducive to criminality. Since our experience has been that the majority of criminals experience great difficulty in securing intimate contacts in ordinary groups, special groups whose major common goal is the reformation of criminals must be created.

This process of assimilation and alienation begins the moment an addict arrives at Synanon, and it continues throughout his stay. The following are two leaders' comments on admission interviews; they are consistent with our own observations of about twenty such interviews.

1. When a new guy comes in we want to find out whether a person has one inkling of seriousness. Everybody who comes here is what we call a psychopathic liar. We don't take them all, either. We work off the top spontaneously, in terms of feeling. We use a sort of intuitive faculty. You know he's lying, but you figure, "Well,

---

[9] Of the fifty-two members 60 per cent first heard about Synanon from addicts on the street or in jails, prisons, or hospitals; about a fourth heard about it on television or read about it in a magazine; and the remainder were told of it by members or past members.

maybe if you get a halfway positive feeling that he'll stay. . . ." We ask him things like "What do you want from us?" "Don't you think you're an idiot or insane?" "Doesn't it sound insane for you to be running around the alleys stealing money from others so's you can go and stick something up your arm?" "Does this sound sane to you?" "Have you got family and friends outside?" We might tell him to go do his business now and come back when he's ready to do business with us. We tell him, "We don't need you." "You need *us*." And if we figure he's only halfway with us, we'll chop off his hair.

It's all in the *attitude*. It's got to be positive. We don't want their money. But we may just tell him to bring back some dough next week. If he pleads and begs— the money's not important. If he shows he really cares. If this attitude is good. It's all in the attitude.

2. Mostly, if people don't have a family outside, with no business to take care of, they're ready to stay. They ain't going to have much time to think about themselves otherwise. . . . Now, when he's got problems, when he's got things outside, if he's got mickey mouse objections, like when you ask him "How do you feel about staying here for a year?" and he's got to bargain with you, like he needs to stay with his wife or sick mother—then we tell him to get lost. If he can't listen to a few harsh words thrown at him, he's not ready. Sometimes we yell at him, "You're a goddamned liar!" If he's serious he'll take it. He'll do anything if he's serious.

But each guy's different. If he sounds sincere, we're not so hard. If he's sick of running the rat race out there, or afraid of going to the penitentiary, he's ready to do anything. Then we let him right in. . . .

This admission process seems to have two principal functions. First, it forces the newcomer to admit, at least on a verbal level, that he is willing to try to conform to the norms of the group, whose members will not tolerate any liking for drugs or drug addicts. From the minute he enters the door, his expressed desire to join the group is tested by giving him difficult orders—to have his hair cut off, to give up all his money, to sever all family ties, to come back in ten days or even thirty days. He is given expert help and explicit but simple criteria for separating the "good guys" from the "bad guys"—the latter shoot dope. Second, the admission process weeds out men and women who simply want to lie down for a few days to rest, to obtain free room and board, or to stay out of the hands of the police. In the terms used by Lindesmith, and also in the terms used at Synanon, the person must want to give up drug *addiction,* not just the drug *habit.*[10] This means that he must at least *say* that he wants to quit using drugs once and for all, in order to realize his potentials as an adult; he must not indicate that he merely wants a convenient place in which to go through withdrawal distress so that he can be rid of his habit for a short time because he has lost his connection, or for some other reason. He must be willing to give up all ambitions, desires, and social interactions that might prevent the group from assimilating him completely.

If he says he just wants to kick, he's no good. Out with him. Now we know nine out of ten lie, but we don't care. We'd rather have him make an attempt and *lie* and then get him in here for thirty days or so—then he might stick. It takes months to decide to stay.

Most fish [newcomers] don't take us seriously. We know what they want, out in front. A dope fiend wants dope, nothing else. All the rest is garbage. We've even taken that ugly thing called money. This shows that they're serious. Now this guy today was sincere. We told him we didn't want money. We could see he would at least give the place a try. We have to find out

[10] Alfred R. Lindesmith, *Opiate Addiction* (Bloomington: Principia Press, 1947), pp. 44–66.

if he's sincere. Is he willing to have us cut off his curly locks? Imagine cutting his hair off makes him take us seriously. . . .

Although it is impossible to say whether Synanon's selective admission process inadvertently admits those addicts who are most amenable to change, no addict has been refused admission on the ground that his case is "hopeless" or "difficult" or that he is "unreachable." On the contrary, before coming to Synanon, twenty-nine of the fifty-two addicts had been on drugs for at least ten years. Two of these were addicted for over forty years, and had been in and out of institutions during that period. The average length of time on drugs for the fifty-two was eleven years, and 56 per cent reported less than one month as the longest period of time voluntarily free of drugs after addiction and prior to Synanon.

Indoctrination. In the admission process, and throughout his residence, the addict discovers over and over again that the group to which he is submitting is antidrug, anticrime, and antialcohol. At least a dozen times a day he hears someone tell him that he can remain at Synanon only as long as he "stays clean," that is, stays away from crime, alcohol, and drugs. This emphasis is an unwitting implementation of Cressey's second principle:

The more relevant the common purpose of the group to the reformation of criminals, the greater will be its influence on the criminal members' attitudes and values. Just as a labor union exerts strong influence over its members' attitudes toward management but less influence on their attitudes toward say, Negroes, so a group organized for recreation or welfare purposes will have less success in influencing criminalistic attitudes and values than will one whose explicit purpose is to change criminals.

Indoctrination makes clear the notion that Synanon exists in order to keep addicts off drugs, not for purposes of recreation, vocational education, etc. Within a week after admission, each newcomer participates in an indoctrination session by a spontaneous group made up of four or five older members. Ordinarily, at least one member of the Board of Directors is present, and he acts as leader. The following are excerpts from one such session with a woman addict. The rules indicate the extreme extent to which it is necessary for the individual to subvert his personal desires and ambitions to the antidrug, anticrime group.

Remember, we told you not to go outside by yourself. Whenever anybody leaves this building they have to check in and out at the desk. For a while, stay in the living room. Don't take showers alone or even go to the bathroom alone, see. While you're kicking, somebody will be with you all the time. And stay away from newcomers. You got nothing to talk to them about, except street talk, and before you know it you'll be splitting [leaving] to take a fix together. Stay out of the streets, mentally and physically, or get lost now.

No phone calls or letters for a while—if you get one, you'll read it in front of us. We'll be monitoring all your phone calls for a while. You see, you got no ties, no business out there any more. You don't need them. You never could handle them before, so don't start thinking you can do it now. All you knew how to do was shoot dope and go to prison.

You could never take care of your daughter before. You didn't know how to be a mother. It's garbage. All a dope fiend knows how to do is shoot dope. Forget it.

There are two obvious illustrations of the antidrug and anticrime nature of the group's subculture. First, there is a strong taboo against what is called "street talk." Discussion of how it feels to take a fix, who one's connection was, where one took his shot, the crimes one has committed, or who one associated with is severely censured. One's best friend and confidant at Synanon might well be the person that administers a tongue lashing for street talk, and the person who calls your undesirable behavior to the attention of the entire group during a general meeting.

Second, a member must never, in any circumstances, identify with the "code of the streets," which says that a criminal is supposed to keep quiet about the criminal activities of his peers. Even calling an ordinary citizen "square" is likely to stimulate a spontaneous lecture, in heated and colorful terms, on the notion that the people who are *really* square are those that go around as bums sticking needles in their arms. A person who, as a criminal, learned to hate stool pigeons and finks with a passion must now turn even his closest friend over to the authorities, the older members of Synanon, if the friend shows any signs of nonconformity. If he should find that a member is considering "sneaking off to a fix somewhere," has kept pills, drugs, or an "outfit" with him when he joined the organization, or even has violated rules such as that prohibiting walking alone on the beach, he must by Synanon's code relinquish his emotional ties with the violator and expose the matter to another member or even to the total membership at a general meeting. If he does not do so, more pressure is put upon him than upon the violator, for he is expected to have "known better." Thus, for perhaps the first time in his life he will be censured for *not* "squealing" rather than for "squealing."[11] He must identify with the law and not with the criminal intent or act.

The sanctions enforcing this norm are severe, for its violation threatens the very existence of the group. "Guilt by association" is the rule. In several instances,

during a general meeting the entire group spontaneously voted to "throw out" both a member who had used drugs and a member who had known of this use but had not informed the group. Banishment from the group is considered the worst possible punishment, for it is stressed over and over again that life in the streets "in your condition" can only mean imprisonment or death.

That the group's purpose is keeping addicts off drugs is given emphasis in formal and informal sessions—called "haircuts" or "pull ups"—as well as in spontaneous denunciations, and in denunciations at general meetings. The "synanon," discussed below, also serves this purpose. A "haircut" is a deliberately contrived device for minimizing the importance of the individual and maximizing the importance of the group, and for defining the group's basic purpose—keeping addicts off drugs and crime. The following is the response of a leader to the questions, "What's a haircut? What's its purpose?"

When you are pointing out what a guy is doing. We do this through mechanisms of exaggeration. We blow up an incident so he can really get a look at it. The Coordinators [a coordinator resembles an officer of the day] and the Board members and sometimes an old timer may sit in on it. We do this when we see a person's attitude becoming negative in some area.

For a *real* haircut, I'll give you myself. I was in a tender trap. My girl split. She called me on the job three days in a row. I made a date with her. We kept the date and I stayed out all night with her. Now, she was loaded [using drugs]. I neglected —or I refused—to call the house. By doing this I ranked everybody. You know doing something like that was no good. They were all concerned. They sent three or four autos looking for me because I didn't come

[11] See Lewis Yablonsky, "The Anti-Criminal Society: Synanon," *Federal Probation*, XXVI (September, 1962), 50–57; and Lewis Yablonsky, *The Violent Gang* (New York: Macmillan Co., 1962), pp. 252–63.

back from work. You see, I was in Stage II.

X found me and he made me feel real lousy, because I knew he worked and was concerned. Here he was out looking for me and he had to get up in the morning.

Well, I called the house the next morning and came back. I got called in for a haircut.

I sat down with three Board members in the office. They stopped everything to give the haircut. That impressed me. Both Y and Z, they pointed out my absurd and ridiculous behavior by saying things like this—though I did not get loaded, I associated with a broad I was emotionally involved with who was using junk. I jeopardized my *own* existence by doing this. So they told me, "Well, you fool, you might as well have shot dope by associating with a using addict." I was given an ultimatum. If I called her again or got in touch with her I would be thrown out.

("Why?")

Because continued correspondence with a using dope fiend is a crime against *me*—it hurts *me*. It was also pointed out how rank I was to people who are concerned with me. I didn't seem to care about people who were trying to help me. I'm inconsiderate to folks who've wiped my nose, fed me, clothed me. I'm like a child, I guess. I bite the hand that feeds me.

To top that off, I had to call a general meeting and I told everybody in the building what a jerk I was and I was sorry for acting like a little punk. I just sort of tore myself down. Told everyone what a phony I had been. And then the ridiculing questions began. Everybody started in. Like, "Where do you get off doing that to us?" That kind of stuff. When I was getting the treatment they asked me what I'd do—whether I would continue the relationship, whether I'd cut it off, or if I really wanted to stay at Synanon and do something about myself and my problem. But I made the decision before I even went in that I'd stay and cut the broad loose. I had enough time under my belt to know enough to make that decision before I even came back to the house. . . .

Group Cohesion. The daily program at Synanon is consistent with Cressey's third principle, and appears to be an unwitting attempt to implement that principle:

The more cohesive the group, the greater the members' readiness to influence others and the more relevant the problem of conformity to group norms. The criminals who are to be reformed and the persons expected to effect the change must, then, have a strong sense of belonging to one group: between them there must be a genuine "we" feeling. The reformers, consequently, should not be identifiable as correctional workers, probation or parole officers, or social workers.

Cohesion is maximized by a "family" analogy and by the fact that all but some "third-stage" members live and work together. The daily program has been deliberately designed to throw members into continuous mutual activity. In addition to the free, unrestricted interaction in small groups called "synanons," the members meet as a group at least twice each day. After breakfast, someone is called upon to read the "Synanon Philosophy," which is a kind of declaration of principles, the day's work schedule is discussed, bits of gossip are publicly shared, the group or individual members are spontaneously praised or scolded by older members. Following a morning of work activities, members meet in the dining room after lunch to discuss some concept or quotation that has been written on a blackboard. Stress is on participation and expression: quotations are selected by Board members to provoke controversy and examination of the meaning, or lack of meaning, of words. Discussion sometimes continues informally during the afternoon work period and in "synanons," which are held after dinner. In addition, lectures and classes, conducted by any member or outside speaker who will take on the responsibility, are held several times a week for all members who feel a need for them. Topics have included "semantics," "group dynamics," "meaning of truth," and "Oedipus complex."

There are weekend recreational activities, and holidays, wedding anniversaries, and birthdays are celebrated. Each member is urged: "Be yourself," "Speak the truth," "Be honest," and this kind of action in an atmosphere that is informal and open quickly gives participants a strong sense of "belonging." Since many of the members have been homeless drifters, it is not surprising to hear frequent repetition of some comment to the effect that "This is the first home I ever had."

Also of direct relevance to the third principle is the *voluntary* character of Synanon. Any member can walk out at any time; at night the doors are locked against persons who might want to enter, but not against persons who might want to leave. Many do leave.

Holding addicts in the house once they have been allowed to enter is a strong appeal to ideas such as "We have all been in the shape you are now in," or "Mike was on heroin for twenty years and *he's* off." It is significant, in this connection, that addicts who "kick" (go through withdrawal distress) at Synanon universally report that the sickness is not as severe as it is in involuntary organizations, such as jails and mental hospitals. One important variable here, we believe, is the practice of not giving "kicking dope fiends" special quarters. A newcomer kicks on a davenport in the center of the large living room, not in a special isolation room or quarantine room. Life goes on around him. Although a member will be assigned to watch him, he soon learns that his sickness is not important to men and women who have themselves kicked the habit. In the living room, one or two couples might be dancing, five or six people may be arguing, a man may be practicing the guitar, and a girl may be ironing. The kicking addict learns his lesson: These others have made it. This subtle device is supplemented by explicit

comments from various members as they walk by or as they drop in to chat with him. We have heard the following comments, and many similar ones, made to new addicts lying sick from withdrawal. It should be noted that none of the comments could reasonably have been made by a rehabilitation official or a professional therapist.

"It's OK boy. We've all been through it before."

"For once you're with people like us. You've got everything to gain here and nothing to lose."

"You think you're tough. Listen, we've got guys in here who could run circles around you, so quit your bull_____."

"You're one of us now, so keep your eyes open, your mouth shut and try to listen for a while. Maybe you'll learn a few things."

"Hang tough, baby. We won't let you die."

Status Ascription. Cressey's fourth principle is:

Both reformers and those to be reformed must achieve status within the group by exhibition of "pro-reform" or anti-criminal values and behavior patterns. As a novitiate . . . he is a therapeutic parasite and not actually a member until he accepts the group's own system for assigning status.

This is the crucial point in Cressey's formula, and it is on this point that Synanon seems most effective. The house has an explicit program for distributing status symbols to members in return for staying off the drug and, later, for actually displaying antidrug attitudes. The resident, no longer restricted to the status of "inmate" or "patient" as in a prison or hospital, can achieve any staff position in the status hierarchy.

The Synanon experience is organized into a career of roles that represent stages of graded competence, at whose end are roles that might later be used in the broader community. Figure 1 shows the status system in terms of occupational roles, each box signifying a stratum. Such cliques as exist at Synanon tend to be among persons of the same stratum. Significantly, obtaining jobs of increased responsibility and status is almost completely dependent upon one's attitudes toward crime and the use of drugs. To obtain a job such as Senior Coordinator, for example, the member must have demonstrated that he can remain free of drugs, crime, and alcohol for at least three to six months. Equally important, he must show that he can function without drugs in situations where he might have used drugs before he came to Synanon. Since he is believed to have avoided positions of responsibility by taking drugs, he must gradually take on positions of responsibility without the use of drugs. Thus, he cannot go up the status ladder unless his "attitudes" are right, no matter what degree of skill he might have as a workman. Evaluation is rather casual, but it is evaluation nevertheless—he will not be given a decent job in the organization unless he relinquishes the role of the "con artist" and answers questions honestly, expresses emotions freely, co-operates in group activities, and demonstrates leadership. In a letter to a public official in May, 1960, the founder explained the system as follows:

Continued residence [at Synanon], which we feel to be necessary to work out the problem of interpersonal relationships which underlie the addiction symptom is based on adherence by the individual to standards of behavior, thinking, and feeling acceptable to our culture. There is much work to be done here, as we have no paid help, and each person must assume his share of the burden. Increased levels of responsibility are sought and the experience of self-satisfaction comes with seeking and assuming these higher levels and seems to

be an extremely important part of emotional growth.[12]

An analogy with a family and the development of a child also is used. Officially, every member is expected to go through three "stages of growth," indicated by Roman numerals in Figure 1. Stage I has two phases, "infancy" and "adolescence." In the "infancy" phase (I-A) the member behaves like an infant and is treated as one; as he kicks the habit "cold turkey" (without the aid of drugs) in the living room, he is dependent on the others, and he is supervised and watched at all times. When he is physically and mentally able, he performs menial tasks such as dishwashing and sweeping in a kind of "preadolescent" stage (I-AB) and then takes on more responsible positions (I-B). In this "adolescence" phase he takes on responsibility for maintenance work, participates actively in group meetings, demonstrates a concern for "emotional growth," mingles with newcomers and visitors, and accepts responsibilities for dealing with them. In work activities, for example, he might drive the group's delivery truck alone, watch over a sick addict, supervise the dishwashing or cleanup crews, or meet strangers at the door.

Stage II is called the "young adult stage." Here, the member is in a position to choose between making Synanon a "career," attending school, or going to work at least part time. If he works for Synanon, his position is complex and involves enforcing policy over a wide range of members. In Stage III, "adult," he moves up to a policy-making position in the Board of Directors or moves out of Synanon but returns with his friends and family for occasional visits. He can apparently· resist the urge to resort to drugs in times of crisis without the direct help of Synanon members. One man

[12] See Volkman, *op. cit.*, pp. 90–96.

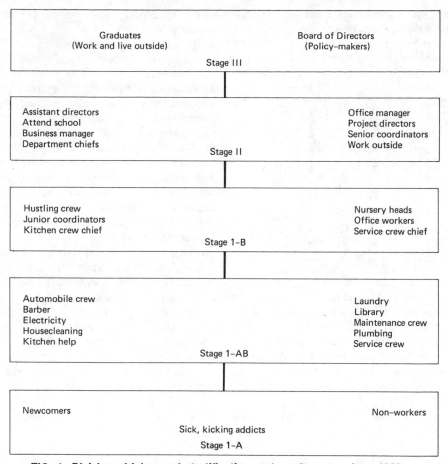

FIG. 1. Division of labor and stratification system, Synanon, June 1962.

described this stage by saying, "They go out, get jobs, lose jobs, get married, get divorced, get married again, just like everyone else." However, the group does maintain a degree of control. Graduates are never supposed to cut off their ties with their Synanon "family," and they are expected to return frequently to display themselves as a "dope fiend made good."

From Table 5 it is apparent that seniority in the form of length of residence (equivalent to the number of "clean" days) is an important determinant of status. As time of residence

increases, responsibilities to the group, in the forms of work and leadership, tend to increase. In June, 1962, twenty-seven of the 105 members of Synanon were in Stage III. It should be noted that while stage is associated with length of residence, advancement through the stages is not automatic. The longer one lives at Synanon, the "cleaner" he is, the more diffuse the roles he performs, and the higher his status.

It is also important to note that high status does not depend entirely upon one's conduct within the house. Before he graduates to Stage III a member must

TABLE 5 Length of Residence and "Stage" of Members, June, 1962

Length of Residence (In Months)	Stages			No.	Per Cent
	I	II	III		
1–3	20	0	0	20	19
4–6	15	0	0	15	14
7–9	7	3	0	10	9
10–12	2	0	0	2	2
13–15	3	4	0	7	7
16–18	3	0	2	5	5
19–21	4	1	0	5	5
22–24	0	4	1	5	5
25 and over	0	12	24	36	34
Total	54	24	27	105	100

retary, photographer), and executive (purchasing agent) posts.

Further, the legitimate status of the *group* has increasingly risen during the last two years. Since the summer of 1960, an average of 100–150 guests have attended open-house meetings, and the guests have included distinguished persons from all walks of legitimate life. Well-known psychiatrists, correctional workers, businessmen, newspapermen, and politicians have publicly praised the work of the group. There have been requests for Synanon houses and for Synanon groups from several communities, and Synanon projects are now being conducted at Terminal Island Federal Prison and the Nevada State Prison. Recently, the group has been featured in films, on television and radio shows, and in national magazines. At least two books and a movie are being written about it. Over five hundred citizens have formed an organization called "Sponsors of Synanon." Even strong attacks from some members of the local community and complicated legal battles about zoning ordinances have served principally to unite the group and maximize the *esprit de corps*.

The "Synanon." Synanon got its name from an addict who was trying to say "seminar." The term "Synanon" is used to refer to the entire organization, but when it is spelled with a lower-case *s* it refers only to the meetings occurring in the evenings among small groups of six to ten members. Each evening, all members are assigned to such groups, and membership in the groups is rotated so that one does not regularly interact with the same six or ten persons. The announced aim of these meetings is to "trigger feelings" and to allow what some members refer to as "a catharsis." The sessions are not "group therapy" in the usual sense, for no trained therapist is present. Moreover, the emphasis is on enforcing anticriminal and antidrug

in some way be accorded an increase in status by the legitimate outside community. This is further insurance that status will be conferred for activities that are antidrug in character. In early 1960, the members began to take an active part in legitimate community activities, mostly in the form of lectures and discussion groups. Since Synanon's inception, more than 350 service groups, church groups, political groups, school and college classes, etc., have been addressed by speakers from Synanon. Such speeches and discussions gain community support for the organization, but they further function to give members a feeling of being important enough to be honored by an invitation to speak before community groups. Similarly, members are proud of those individuals who have "made good" in the outside community by becoming board members of the P.T.A., Sunday-school teachers, college students, and members of civic and service organizations. Over thirty-five Synanon members are now working full or part time in the community, holding a wide range of unskilled (janitor, parking attendant), skilled (truck driver, carpenter, electrician), white-collar (sec-

norms, as well as upon emotional adjustment.[13] These sessions, like the entire program, constitute a system for implementing Cressey's fifth principle, although they were not designed to do so.

The most effective mechanism for exerting group pressure on members will be found in groups so organized that criminals are induced to join with noncriminals for the purpose of changing other criminals. A group in which criminal A joins with some noncriminals to change criminal B is probably most effective in changing criminal A, not B; in order to change criminal B, criminal A must necessarily share the values of the anticriminal members.

In the house, the behavior of all members is visible to all others. What a member is seen to do at the breakfast table, for example, might well be scrutinized and discussed at his synanon that evening. The synanon sessions differ from everyday honesty by virtue of the fact that in these discussions one is expected to *insist on* the truth as well as to tell the truth. Any weapon, such as ridicule, cross-examination, or hostile attack, is both permissible and expected. The sessions seem to provide an atmosphere of truth-seeking that is reflected in the rest of the social life within the household so that a simple question like "How are you?" is likely to be answered by a five-minute discourse in which the respondent searches for the truth. The following discussion is from a tape recording of a synanon session held in June, 1961. It should be noted that an "innocent" question about appearance, asked by an older member who has become a non-criminal and a non-addict, led to an opportunity to emphasize the importance of loyalty to the antidrug, anticrime group.

"What are you doing about losing weight?"

"Why? Is that your business?"

"I asked you a question."

"I don't intend to answer it. It's not your business."

"Why do you want to lose weight?"

"I don't intend to answer it."

"Why?"

"Because it's an irrelevant and meaningless question. You know I had a baby only three weeks ago, and you've been attacking me about my weight. It's none of your business."

"Why did you call your doctor?"

"Why? Because I'm on a diet."

"What did he prescribe for you?"

"I don't know. I didn't ask him."

"What did you ask for?"

"I didn't. I don't know what he gave me."

"Come on now. What kind of pills are they?"

"I don't know. I'm not a chemist. Look the doctor knows I'm an addict. He knows I live at Synanon. He knows a whole lot about me."

"Yeah, well, I heard you also talking to him on the phone, and you sounded just like any other addict trying to cop a doctor out of pills."

"You're a goddamned liar!"

"Yeah, well X was sitting right there. Look, does the doctor know and does the Board know?"

"I spoke to Y [Board member]. It's all been verified."

"What did Y say?"

"I was talking to . . ."

"What did Y say?"

"Well, will you wait just a minute?"

"What did Y say?"

"Well, let her talk."

"I don't want to hear no stories."

"I'm not telling stories."

"What did Y say?"

"That it was harmless. The doctor said he'd give me nothing that would affect me. There's nothing in it. He knows it all. I told Y."

[13] See Cressey, "Contradictory Theories in Correctional Group Therapy Programs," *op. cit.*

"Oh, you're all like a pack of wolves. You don't need to yell and scream at her."

"Look, I heard her on the phone and the way she talked she was trying to manipulate the doctor."

"Do you resent the fact that she's still acting like a dope fiend and she still sounds like she's conning the doctor out of something? She's a dope fiend. Maybe she can't talk to a doctor any differently."

"Look, I called the doctor today. He said I should call him if I need him. He gave me vitamins and lots of other things."

"Now wait a minute. You called to find out if you could get some more pills."

"Besides, it's the attitude they heard over the phone. That's the main thing."

"Yeah, well they probably projected it onto me."

"Then how come you don't like anyone listening to your phone calls?"

"Are you feeling guilty?"

"Who said?"

"Me. That's who. You even got sore when you found out X and me heard you on the phone, didn't you? You didn't like that at all, did you?"

"Is that so?"

(Silence.)

"I don't think her old man wants her back."

"Well, who would? An old fat slob like that."

"Sure, that's probably why she's thinking of leaving all the time and ordering pills."

"Sure."

(Silence.)

"My appearance is none of your business."

"Everything here is our business."

"Look, when a woman has a baby you can't understand she can't go back to normal weight in a day."

"Now you look. We're really not interested in your weight problem now. Not really. We just want to know why you've got to have pills to solve the problem. We're going to talk about that if we want to. That's what we're here for."

"Look, something's bugging you. We all know that. I even noticed it in your attitude toward me."

"Yeah, I don't care about those pills. I want to know how you're feeling. What's behind all this? Something's wrong. What is it?"

(Silence.)

"Have you asked your old man if you could come home yet?"

(Softly.) "Yes."

"What did he say?"

(Softly.) "He asked me how I felt. Wanted to know why I felt I was ready to come home. . . ."

(Softly.) "I did it out of anger. I wasn't very happy. (Pause.) A day before I tried [telephoning him] and he wasn't there. (Pause.) Just this funny feeling about my husband being there and me here. My other kid's there and this one's here. (Pause.) A mixed-up family."

"Why do you want to stay then? Do you want to be here?"

"No. I don't want to be here. That's exactly why I'm staying. I need to stay till I'm ready."

"Look, you've got to cut them loose for a while. You may not be ready for the rest of your life. You may not ever be able to be with those people."

(Tears.)

"I know. . . ."

After the synanon sessions, the house is always noisy and lively. We have seen members sulk, cry, shout, and threaten to leave the group as a result of conversation in the synanon. The following comments, every one of which represents the expression of a pro-reform attitude by the speaker, were heard after one session. It is our hypothesis that such expressions are the important ones, for they indicate that the speaker has become a reformer and, thus, is reinforcing his own pro-reform attitudes every time he tries to comfort or reform another.

"Were they hard on you?"

"I really let him have it tonight."

"I couldn't get to her. She's so damned blocked she couldn't even hear what I was trying to tell her."

"Hang tough, man; it gets easier."

"One of these days he'll drop those defenses of his and start getting honest."

"Don't leave. We all love you and want you to get well."

At Synanon, disassociating with former friends, avoiding street talk, and becoming disloyal to criminals are emphasized at the same time that loyalty to non-criminals, telling the truth to authority figures, and legitimate work are stressed. We have no direct evidence that haircuts, synanons, and both formal and spontaneous denunciations of street talk and the code of the streets have important rehabilitative effects on the actor, as well as (or, perhaps even "rather than") on the victim. It seems rather apparent, however, that an individual's own behavior must be dramatically influenced when he acts in the role of a moral policeman and "takes apart" another member. It is significant that older members of Synanon like to point out that the "real Synanon" began on "the night of the big cop out" (confession). In its earliest days, Synanon had neither the group cohesiveness nor the degree of control it now has. Some participants remained as addicts while proclaiming their loyalty to the principle of anti-addiction, and other participants knew of this condition. One evening in a general meeting a man spontaneously stood up and confessed ("copped out") that he had sneaked out for a shot. One by one, with no prompting, the others present rose to confess either their own violations or their knowledge of the violations of their friends. From that moment, the Board of Directors believe, the organization became a truly antidrug group; there has been no problem of drug use since.

THE RESULTS

Of the fifty-two residents described earlier, four are "graduates" of Synanon, are living in the community, and are not using alcohol or drugs. Twenty-three (44.2 per cent) are still in residence and are not using alcohol or drugs. Two of these are on the Board of Directors and eleven are working part or full time. The remaining twenty-five left Synanon against the advice of the Board and the older members.

Information regarding the longest period of voluntary abstinence from drugs after the onset of addiction but prior to entering Synanon was obtained on forty-eight of the fifty-two persons. Eleven reported that they were "never" clean, six said they were continuously clean for less than one week, ten were continuously clean for less than one month. Thirty-nine (81 per cent) said they had been continuously clean for less than six months, and only two had been clean for as long as a one-year period. Twenty-seven (52 per cent) of the fifty-two residents have not abstained for at least six months; twelve of these have been clean for at least two years and two have been off drugs continually for over three years.

Between May, 1958 (when Synanon started), and May, 1961, 263 persons were admitted or readmitted to Synanon. Of these, 190 (72 per cent) left Synanon against the advice of the Board of Directors and the older members. Significantly, 59 per cent of all dropouts occurred within the first month of residence, 90 per cent within the first three months. Synanon is not averse to giving a person a second chance, or even a third or fourth chance: of the 190 persons dropping out, eighty-three (44 per cent) were persons who had been readmitted. The dropout behavior of persons who were readmitted was, in general, similar to first admissions; 64 per cent of their dropouts occurred within the first month, 93 per cent within the first three months after readmission.

Of all the Synanon enrolees up to August, 1962, 108 out of 372 (29 per cent) are known to be off drugs. More significantly, of the 215 persons who have remained at Synanon for at least one month, 103 (48 per cent) are still off drugs; of the 143 who have remained for at least three months, 95 (66 per cent) are still non-users; of the 87 who have remained at least seven months, 75 (86 per cent) are non-users. These statistics seem to us to be most relevant, for they indicate that once an addict actually becomes a member of the antidrug community (as indicated by three to six months of participation), the probability that he will leave and revert to the use of drugs is low.

CONCLUSIONS

Synanon's leaders do not claim to "cure" drug addicts. They are prone to measure success by pointing to the fact that the organization now includes the membership of forty-five persons who were heroin addicts for at least ten years. Two of these were addicted for more than thirty years and spent those thirty years going in and out of prisons, jails, the U.S. Public Service Hospital, and similar institutions. The leaders have rather inadvertently used a theory of rehabilitation that implies that it is as ridiculous to try to "cure" a man of drug addiction as it is to try to "cure" him of sexual intercourse. A man can be helped to stay away from drugs, however, and this seems to be the contribution Synanon is making. In this regard, its "suc-cess" rate is higher than that of those institutions officially designated by society as places for the confinement and "reform" of drug addicts. Such a comparison is not fair, however, both because it is not known whether the subjects in Synanon are comparable to those confined in institutions, and because many official institutions do not concentrate on trying to keep addicts off drugs, being content to withdraw the drug, build up the addicts physically, strengthen vocational skills, and eliminate gaps in educational backgrounds.[14]

We cannot be certain that it is the group relationships at Synanon, rather than something else, that is keeping addicts away from crime and drugs. However, both the times at which dropouts occur and the increasing antidrug attitudes displayed with increasing length of residence tend to substantiate Sutherland's theory of differential association and Cressey's notion that modifying social relationships is an effective supplement to the clinical handling of convicted criminals. Drug addiction is, in fact, a severe test of Sutherland's sociological theory and Cressey's sociological principles, for addicts have the double problem of criminality and the drug habit. The statistics of dropouts suggest that the group relations method of rehabilitation does not begin to have its effects until newcomers are truly integrated into the antidrug, anticrime group that is Synanon.

[14] Cf. Harrison M. Trice, "Alcoholism: Group Factors in Etiology and Therapy," *Human Organization*, XV (Summer, 1956), 33–40 (see also Donald R. Cressey, "The Nature and Effectiveness of Correctional Techniques," *Law and Contemporary Problems*, XXIII [Fall, 1958], 754–71).